Volume 2   Fourth Edition

PATTERNS IN
Western Civilization

Sarah Chappell Trulove • James Woelfel • Stephen Auerbach • Rachel Epp Buller

D1472956

PEARSON

Custom
Publishing

Printed in the United States of America

10 9 8 7 6 5 4 3 2 1

ISBN 0-536-91225-4

2006300117

RS/EW

Please visit our web site at *www.pearsoncustom.com*

PEARSON CUSTOM PUBLISHING
75 Arlington Street, Suite 300, Boston, MA 02116
A Pearson Education Company

CONTENTS

MAPS

Hello

Hola

Bonjour

ПРИВЕТ

你好

مرحبا بالعالم...

안녕하세요

こんにちは

buon giorno

Guten Tag

สวัสดี

INTRODUCTION TO THE FOURTH EDITION, VOLUME TWO

Patterns in Western Civilization was first published in 1991 as a large single volume with a miscellany of chapters contributed by twenty-five scholars, most of them faculty of the University of Kansas. A second edition appeared in 1998, incorporating a number of revisions in response to criticisms and suggestions and to changes in the primary sources, but retaining the essential structure of the first edition. With the third edition, published in 2002, we substantially altered the format and content, dividing *Patterns* into two volumes corresponding to the two semesters of the Western Civilization curriculum, with fourteen "streamlined" chapters in each volume correlated to the fourteen weeks of assigned primary source readings. The third edition proved popular with both students and instructors because of the shorter chapters, each dedicated to providing background to and guidance in reading the primary text for the week.

In the fourth edition we wanted to maintain the format of the previous edition, but thought there was unevenness in the handling of the historical material in the third edition. Thus we decided to create separate sections providing historical background of the periods appropriate to the chapters that follow them. Volume I has six such sections and Volume II has five.

Historical background sections. The first historical background section introduces the seventeenth century, a century that was still searching for stability following the disruption of the Reformation. The successful challenge to the hegemony of the Catholic Church was in many ways a paradigm shift in the West. Following close behind as further challenge to the stable worldview of the Middle Ages were the new ideas and discoveries of the Scientific Revolution. Chapters One and Two,

respectively, feature René Descartes and John Locke, who explored philosophical, scientific, and political frontiers.

The second historical section announces the Birth of the Modern Era and the period we know as the Enlightenment. Jean-Jacques Rousseau, a major figure in both the Enlightenment and the Romantic movement, is the featured figure in Chapter Three. Chapter Four leaps across the Atlantic to tell the story of the founding of the United States of America and to review the founding documents. Historical section three provides background for the next seven chapters, each featuring nineteenth-century figures. Chapter Five discusses Romanticism through Mary Shelley's novel, *Frankenstein*. Chapter Six explains liberal democracy and political liberalism and the contributions of John Stuart Mill. Chapter Seven introduces Darwin's and Wallace's theory of the evolution of species by natural selection and concludes with explanation of the pseudo-theory of Social Darwinism and the response by T. H. Huxley.

The Enlightenment, with its promise of progress and its individualism, had its negative side. The Industrial Revolution it produced resulted in the impoverishment of large numbers of workers. Karl Marx and Friedrich Engels propose a revolutionary solution in Chapter Eight. In Chapter Nine, Fyodor Dostoevsky challenges Western ways and optimism, suggesting that human beings will assert their freedom even when it is irrational and contrary to self-interest. Friedrich Nietzsche attacks Western philosophy and religion, proposing that the only answer is a complete "revaluation of all values." The nineteenth-century section closes with a return to the U.S. and the telling of the unhappy history of slavery.

Section Four covers little more than two decades, but these decades ended Enlightenment hopes and set history on a course of war and slaughter that lasted most of the twentieth century. Chapter Twelve introduces us to Sigmund Freud and his theory of psychoanalysis, which would transform dramatically how we understand human beings. In Chapter Thirteen we are introduced to three major voices for women's equality. Reaching back to the late eighteenth century the chapter introduces Mary Wollstonecraft, who argued for women's equality on the basis of natural rights theory. In the mid-twentieth century Simone de Beauvoir interprets the fate of women in terms of the existentialist emphasis on the individual's freedom to change. Central to the chapter is Virginia Woolf, one of the great representatives of literary modernism, who explains why there are not more women writers and what women must have in order to write. Our final historical section concludes on a somber note with a narrative of the Second World War and its aftermath. This is followed by the concluding chapter on the Holocaust and a Holocaust memoir.

Art and music.   Two additions to the textbook are separate sections on art and on music. We are delighted to have color plates for the first time and an increased number of images throughout the text. The essays that follow each section explain the various artistic periods and important artists in each and add significantly to the history of each period. There is also a CD with selections of music from each historical period, and there are commentaries on the musical periods and the musical selections.

Changes in the primary sources assigned to accompany the text.   There was only one change in the reading selections. Jean-Jacques Rousseau's *Discourse on the Origin of Inequality* has replaced Voltiare's *Candide*. What this means is that in the relevant chapter (Three) the material on Voltaire has been somewhat reduced and additional material on Rousseau added. For those who are familiar with the third edition we want to report that several chapters remain very much the same. Others have undergone significant changes. This has involved rearrangement, removal, or addition of material. Those that have undergone changes are: Chapters One, Three, Six (beginning section), Eight, Eleven

(beginning sections) and Thirteen. Small additions or omissions can be found in chapters that are otherwise familiar. We have added two documents to the Appendix: material on the Suffrage Movement and Second Wave feminism (formerly in Chapter Thirteen) and the Universal Declaration of Human Rights.

Finally we want to thank the many people who were involved in this project. Steve Auerbach, our historian, did a masterful job of condensing centuries of history into coherent and helpful summaries. This is not an easy thing to do. Rachel Epp Buller's selection of images was nothing short of brilliant. Many of the selections are more or less "traditional," but others perhaps not. Note particularly Bety Saar, "The Liberation of Aunt Jemima," Marcel Duchamp, *Fountain*, and Adrian Piper, *My Calling (Card)*#1, which we found very creative choices. The mother of three small children, Rachel works from her home in Newton, Kansas. Before he began his work on Volume II, Jim Woelfel announced that his problem with this volume, in contrast to Volume I, would be too many choices, rather than too few. But he finally narrowed it down and in the end he produced an exciting "menu" of music. Tuck this disc into your computer or add it to your iPod and listen to musical hits from the last four centuries. Carrie McDonald was on board from the beginning, but it is the fate of a copy editor that her job begins at the end. She sacrificed many an evening and weekend to complete the project and was an invaluable help. Her gentle laugh and cheerful "we'll get it done" attitude always brought reassurance. In the end, however, it all comes back to me as managing editor. So as tradition demands, I assume full editorial responsibility: all the errors are my own, or the result of my own decisions.

As readers of previous editions of this text know, since its inception several people have contributed material to it. We are grateful for their knowledge and expertise. Those who have been resources for *Patterns*, Volume II, are listed after the editorial staff biographies

Finally we want to say thank you to the Pearson staff. Debbie Schwartz has been with us since the first edition and has seen through its development from a sort of a rough draft to the present polished, professional, and attractive book. Jennifer Sczerbinski worked closely with Rachel Epp Buller in finding the best images possible. We are pleased with the results. This was Rachel Snyder's first project with us. Our interaction on Volume I took place during the final stages of publication, several of them from Boston to the Starbuck's on Old Brompton Road in London. Tony Bolfeta, our acquisitions editor, who has worked with us through two editions, has been endlessly patient and always helpful. In the last weeks of our work he even offered to send me lunch. He is a good friend to all the staff at the Humanities and Western Civilization Program. Thanks everyone!

Sarah Chappell Trulove

THE STUDY OF WESTERN CIVILIZATION

What is Western civilization, and why study it? Western civilization, like all human civilizations, is not a single thread or even a weave of many strands, but something more like the varied patterns in a quilt of complex design. There are diverse basic colors and designs, continuities and discontinuities, harmonies and disharmonies, dominant and subordinate themes. "Western civilization" is a very broad term intended to designate the common features of the human cultures that have dominated Europe and been transplanted to the Americas and other parts of the world. Those common features have their roots in ancient Mesopotamia and Egypt, Israel, Greece, and Rome—all very different cultures whose heritages came to be woven together and transmitted by the Christian European civilization of the Middle Ages. That original diversity was further enriched by native European populations such as the Franks, Goths, Saxons, Lombards, and Celts, and later by races and peoples from other parts of the world.

Furthermore, from their origins to the present day the cultures that have contributed to the shaping of Western civilization, like almost all human cultures, have not existed in isolation but in the context of and in interaction with other cultures. This pattern of mutual influence and conflict has been a continuous one. The ancient Hebrews were influenced by and struggled with surrounding Middle Eastern and North African cultures such as Mesopotamia (Iraq), Syria, Persia (Iran), Egypt, and Ethiopia, and for long the Jews were subject to the Romans. In the fourth century BCE Alexander the Great conquered and brought Greek culture to lands as far away as India, and today one can see ancient Indian statues of the Buddha showing Greek influence. The Roman Empire included an enormous variety of peoples, religions, and cultural traditions stretching from Spain and Britain in the west to Syria in the east. Throughout the Middle Ages Christian Europe and the empire of Islam engaged in centuries of struggle with each other for control over parts of Europe and the Middle East, a contact which at the same time opened up trade for Europe and bequeathed to Europe a rich legacy of learning that included the ideas of Muslim philosophers, theolo-gians, physicians, and scientists and the works of Aristotle they had preserved. Because of this intimate, albeit contested, history between Christian and Islamic civilizations, one that has continued to the present day, it is vitally important for students of Western civilization to gain a basic knowledge of the Qur'an and the formative history of Islam. Intercultural conflict and exchange between the West and the non-Western world generally have momentously shaped the modern world, on the one hand through the global dominance of Western imperialism, colonialism, capitalism, warfare, science, technology, and communications; and on the other hand by immigration to Western countries and the reaffirmation by other cultures of their distinctive heritage and contributions.

The culturally diverse richness of Western civilization, and its ongoing interaction with other cultures are facts the student of Western Civilization needs always to keep in mind. A number of our chapters provide reminders of these facts within the context of a focus on the distinctive development and character of that heritage we call Western. At the same time, in a course emphasizing Western thought we are centrally concerned with those distinctive ideas, values, and institutions that have become the common property of the Western world. That common property is itself a plurality of different and often conflicting responses to the fundamental and perennial human questions. Every human civilization asks these questions and comes up with answers that show both great variety and also overlap and similarity. In Western Civilization courses we learn about and critically examine the answers that have taken shape over millennia in one complex world civilization, while recognizing that these Western answers take their place within a larger human conversation on the great questions and have their counterparts and alternatives in other civilizations.

But it has also become essential to recognize that the characteristically Western responses to the great human questions are even more richly pluralistic than we used to think. Through a wealth of research in areas such as African and African-American and other ethnic and world area studies,

Judaic studies, and women's studies over the past thirty years, we are now acutely aware of voices in the Western conversation that have not been heard because historically they have been marginalized and suppressed. We have tried to incorporate some of that research into this textbook, offering glimpses, explanations, and sometimes sustained treatments of the historic situation and the achievements of women in various Western societies, the modern phenomenon of Western racism and the response to it of Africans and African-Americans, and the story of the Jewish people and of anti-Semitism in the Western world.

We now realize, for example, that because of their historic subordination—which has often meant exclusion from educational opportunity and public life as well as legal disabilities—women's experience and outlooks have been seriously under-represented in the influential writings of the Western world. Those women who have managed to contribute publicly, as political and religious leaders, writers, artists, scientists, and philosophers, have often had their contributions neglected, denigrated, and denied—not because of the quality of their work but because of their sex. This recognition makes the study of the influential writings of Western civilization more complex and also more stimulating and rewarding.

People used to read the "great books of the Western world"—written almost entirely by Caucasian European men—as definitive statements on various aspects of the human condition. Now we recognize the need to balance a continuing recognition of their greatness and enduring insights with what some scholars call a "hermeneutics of suspicion." What this means, first, is that we must examine closely their assumptions about the roles of women and men and about sexuality generally. Secondly, we must consider their assumptions about human groups other than their own—other social classes, races, and cultures. Thirdly, we must ask how these assumptions affect their ideas about humans and the world and their claims to universality. At the same time, we must become aware of how women and other marginalized and oppressed groups in Western civilization have based their struggles for dignity and equality precisely on ideas and values that are enshrined in the "great works" of Western religion, philosophy, and art, seeing in

those ideas and values universal implications that their authors often did not see. In addition, we have the task, in today's Western Civilization courses, of including some of these hitherto suppressed voices in the Western heritage alongside the "classic texts," to enrich and make more fully "whole" the Western world's discussion of the great human issues.

And what are those great human issues? There are various ways we might formulate the basic questions that all human cultures ask, but they include the following: What can we know about the world and ourselves, and what is true and false? What is the meaning of our brief existence in the world, and is it to be found in nature and ourselves or in higher powers? What is the good life for the individual, and what are our responsibilities toward one another? Do humans choose freely, or are we determined by fate, divine will, or heredity and environment? What is the good society, and how is justice to be defined? What is the meaning of being male and female and in other ways diverse as humans? What are the roles of love and work in our lives? What is beauty, and why do we enjoy it and create it? Is the realm of human events a history with a meaning and a goal, or repeating cycles? Why do we suffer and inflict suffering? What is the significance of death for human life? Is there a destiny beyond death, and if so what is it? At the bottom of all these questions is the most fundamental question of all: What are we human beings, these strange creatures who ask so many questions of life?

Now of course cultures and individuals have asked and answered these questions implicitly and explicitly, inchoately and articulately, simply and sophisticatedly. They have also typically asked and answered them quite concretely and not in the general way indicated above. Humans have lived in families and tribes, democracies and monarchies; they have worshipped gods and goddesses; they have created songs and pictures and stories; they have toiled in fields and towns; they have struggled to get along with one another; they have observed the movement of the planets and stars. That is to say that humans raise the great issues of human life and grapple with them largely through the realities of human community, religious faith and tradition, politics and law, artistic expression, intellectual curiosity, the customs and mores of society, work and family.

Out of this concrete matrix emerge some individuals who quite consciously and single-mindedly ponder the foundational questions and try to give expression to the best answers they can. Among these men and women are prophets and mystics, poets and artists, philosophers and theologians, scientists and historians. They are the main sources of the oral traditions, writings, and works of art that have shaped and interpreted the common ideas and values of civilizations. In this book and in a course on the civilization of the West our interest is in those who have played such a role in the Western world, looking at them and their achievements against the background of the social, economic, political, religious, and cultural life of their time and place.

But *why* study Western civilization, and particularly its ideas, values, and institutions? The most obvious answer is that most of us who learn and teach in colleges and universities in the United States are children of and participants in that civilization, and one of the marks of a well-educated human being is knowledge of the roots and development of her or his own cultural heritage. Those students who also claim another cultural legacy—Native Americans, African-Americans, Latin Americans and Latinos, Asian-Americans, Arab-Americans—have been profoundly shaped by Western civilization even as it has often tried to reject or suppress their other cultural traditions. Similarly, in a world that has come to be heavily influenced by so many things European and American, it is important for students from non-Western nations and cultures to learn of the history, ideas, and values of this civilization that has had such an impact—in both positive and negative ways—on their own lives and the lives of their people.

But the study of Western civilization alone is not nearly enough. It is equally important for American and European students to learn of civilizations other than their own. Indeed, in our ever-shrinking "global village" knowledge of other human cultures has become imperative for informed persons, and in international relations we continue to make serious mistakes even at the highest levels of diplomacy out of ignorance of other countries and peoples. Courses in the language, geography, politics, history, religion, philosophy, and arts of other civilizations should be an integral part of one's education together with courses in Western civilization.

To be human is to have a personal story and to be part of a larger story, and the past—history—is everything about me and the larger world in which I live up to the moment I am telling the story. When I "open up" to another person about who I am, I inevitably begin to tell a story—to be a historian in miniature. I talk about the place or places I came from, where I went to school, something about my parents and siblings. If I really ponder in depth who I am, I realize that my story includes not only my immediate family but also a wider family (aunts, uncles, and cousins) and earlier generations of family (grandparents and great-grandparents). I become aware that I am a link in a chain of human generations stretching back through time and forward through the children and grandchildren I may have.

Probing still further, I come to recognize that my personal identity is inseparable from the fact that I am, say, black rather than white, female rather than male, middle-class rather than working-class, and what it means to be one or the other in the society in which I grew up. Then I come to all the things that I simply take for granted in my self-definition because they are part of the very fabric of my society: democratic ideas and institutions, religious freedom together with the dominance of Christianity, characteristically American customs and prejudices, capitalism and consumerism, science and advanced technology, colleges and universities, certain traditions and tastes in music and literature. I begin to grasp that the story of who I am is part of a much larger story going back generations without number and encompassing a whole civilization. I may begin to wonder how all these things that I have always taken for granted started, how they came to be in the form in which I know them, and how they compare to other alternatives. That kind of curiosity is what the study of Western civilization tries to help stimulate and satisfy.

A Western Civilization program is part of a liberal education. A basic assumption of liberal education is that people can be liberated from the tyranny of attitudes controlled entirely by custom and convention and can make informed and independent choices concerning those questions of fundamental human concern about which we spoke earlier. The root of the word "liberal" is the Latin word meaning "free," and we may think of a liberal education as one designed to enlarge human freedom. Free choices can only be informed choices, made in the context of the knowledge of alternative possible answers to the questions and in view of a careful study of the arguments and evidence that are relevant to evaluating the worth of those answers.

The role of a Western Civilization program within a liberal education is to acquaint us with the history, variety, and content of the responses that some of the influential and representative authors of the Western world have given to those perennial human questions. We in the present enter thereby into a dialogue with them in a great conversation through the ages—learning from them, questioning them, weighing the strengths and weaknesses of the alternatives they present, discovering their impact on issues of our day and how we think about those issues. The perspectives we develop personally from our dialogue with the past may be other than those which the ancient, medieval, and modern shapers of Western civilization have forged. But in the process of our study we discover that we cannot develop our own views in an informed manner without their aid. We find that our views— whether unconscious, half-formed, or really thought out—are inescapably indebted to traditions of thought those men and women have created, carried forward, built on, revised, and criticized.

The ancient Greek philosopher Socrates is famous for his exhortation, "Know yourself." For the liberally educated person an important part of acquiring self-knowledge is learning and coming seriously to grips with the sources and history of the ideas and institutions that have molded the modern Western world and all who grow up in it or are affected by it.

James Woelfel

BIOGRAPHIES

MANAGING EDITOR

Sarah Chappell Trulove has an M.A. in Religious Studies from the University of Kansas. She has been involved in the Humanities and Western Civilization Program for more than twenty years. She co-authored a 1984 NEH grant that inaugurated significant changes in the Western Civilization Program. She helped develop the program's Semester Abroad in Florence and Paris in 1995 and has been a Lecturer in the Program since 1997. She co-directed the Semester Abroad in 2001. In addition to her work in developing the 4th edition of *Patterns* she is the instructor for the Western Civilization Independent Study course.

SENIOR EDITOR

James Woelfel has a Ph.D. from the University of St. Andrews, Scotland, and is Professor of Philosophy and Professor and Director of the Humanities and Western Civilization Program at the University of Kansas. He has done extensive teaching and research in modern European philosophical and religious thought. He recently published the *Legacy of Existentialism and Other Essays on Philosophy and Religion* (University Press of America, 2006).

EDITOR

Stephen Auerbach received his Ph.D. in 2001 from Louisiana State University and is currently an Assistant Professor of History at Georgia College and State University. He specializes in intellectual and cultural history and his primary area of research examines the origins of the French Revolution. He is currently working on a book entitled *Bordeaux and the End of the Old Regime in France, 1750–1789*.

ART HISTORY EDITOR

Rachel Epp Buller has a Ph.D. in art history from the University of Kansas. She works in the area of twentieth century art history and has specific interests in German art, feminist art, and photomontage/collage. She was Visiting Assistant Professor of Art History at Bethel College and currently works as a freelance writer, editor, and curator.

LIST OF CONTRIBUTORS

Robert Anderson	Katherine P. Clark
Richard T. De George	Jonathan Earle
Diane R. Fourny	James Leiker
Rex Martin	Lewis McKinney
Norman Saul	Emily Wicktor

SECTION ONE

THE SEVENTEENTH CENTURY
AND THE SEARCH FOR STABILITY

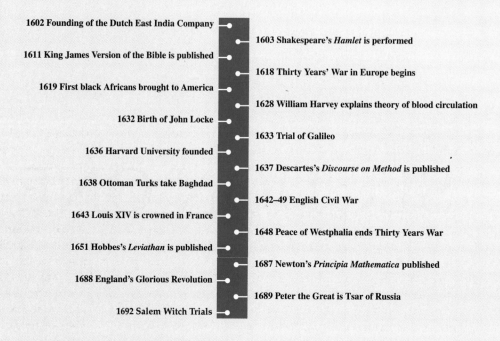

1602 Founding of the Dutch East India Company

1603 Shakespeare's *Hamlet* is performed

1611 King James Version of the Bible is published

1618 Thirty Years' War in Europe begins

1619 First black Africans brought to America

1628 William Harvey explains theory of blood circulation

1632 Birth of John Locke

1633 Trial of Galileo

1636 Harvard University founded

1637 Descartes's *Discourse on Method* is published

1638 Ottoman Turks take Baghdad

1642–49 English Civil War

1643 Louis XIV is crowned in France

1648 Peace of Westphalia ends Thirty Years War

1651 Hobbes's *Leviathan* is published

1687 Newton's *Principia Mathematica* published

1688 England's Glorious Revolution

1689 Peter the Great is Tsar of Russia

1692 Salem Witch Trials

THE SEVENTEENTH CENTURY AND THE SEARCH FOR STABILITY

The reforming movements of Martin Luther and John Calvin in the sixteenth century challenged the hegemony of the Catholic Church and resulted in near-constant warfare extending well into the middle of the seventeenth century. Following the Council of Trent (1545–63) the Church launched its Counter-Reformation, committed to quell the Protestant heresies. The Pope, in partnership with the Habsburg Holy Roman Emperor, declared war on Lutherans and Calvinists alike. The Germanic states became the central site of conflict and were devastated as a consequence. France too was torn apart by religious wars and Protestants in the Spanish-ruled Netherlands[1] rose up against their Habsburg rulers.[2] While religion was certainly at the forefront of these wars, never far behind were the political ambitions of the leaders. For example, many Germanic princes embraced the new Protestant faith as a way to declare their independence from Rome and the Habsburgs in order to govern their own small states autonomously.

The seventeenth century brought little cessation to the violence gripping Europe. In 1618 what ostensibly began as a local revolt in Bohemia (Czechoslovakia) degenerated into a European-wide conflict referred to as The Thirty Years' War. This struggle grew to involve every major power in Europe. As C.V. Wedgwood noted, the war was "morally subversive, economically destructive, socially degrading, confused in its causes, devious in its course, futile in its result, . . . the outstanding example in European history of meaningless conflict."[3]

The war can be divided into four separate phases: Bohemian phase, 1618–20; Danish intervention, 1625–29; Swedish intervention, 1630–32; and French intervention, 1635–48). It ended with

---

[1]The territory referred to as the Netherlands consisted of a loosely linked federation of seventeen provinces. The Peace of Westphalia in 1648 recognized seven of these provinces as the United Provinces. This region is what we consider the Netherlands or Dutch Republic today, sometimes referred to incorrectly as Holland (named after the largest province), and the people are called the Dutch. What is now northern Belgium was called Flanders and its people referred to as Flemish. The remaining provinces became Belgium and Luxembourg.

[2]The Habsburg dynasty that originated in Austria in the eleventh century had held the imperial title since the 15th century. The power of the family had grown over the centuries in large part through diplomacy and marriages. When Charles V was emperor (1516–1556) he ruled Austria, parts of Germany and of Italy, the Netherlands and Spain and the Spanish overseas empire. With his abdication in 1556 the HRE was divided between his son Philip II, who acquired Spain, the Italian territories, the Netherlands and the overseas colonies, and his brother Ferdinand I, who ruled Austria, Hungary, and Bohemia and held the imperial title. Habsburg rule of Spain passed to a Bourbon king in 1700. The Austrian Habsburgs held power until 1918.

[3]C.V. Wedgwood, *The Thirty Years' War*, New York: Metheun and Co., 1981, 526.

Europe in 1648. Reprinted from *Longman Atlas of World History* (2003), by permission of maps.com.

the Peace of Westphalia in 1648 but the results were long term. First, the Holy Roman Empire was significantly weakened, which prevented the unification of Germany until the nineteenth century. France no longer faced a unified military threat on its eastern border and thus was assured its ascension as the continent's leading military power. Therefore, the Thirty Years' War represents a critical turning point in the history of the seventeenth century.

The seventeenth century was also a period of frequent poor harvests and food shortages due to colder climatic conditions, fueling frequent waves of famine, disease, and consequently, peasant revolts. Plague returned in the 1650s and spread across the continent and into England. Revolutions (or uprisings) would affect virtually every capital in every state of Europe during the 1640s to the 1660s.[4]

Reaction to this period of tremendous upheaval took two directions. Some thinkers concluded that

---

[4]The one bright spot in this otherwise bleak picture of the seventeenth century was the expulsion of the Ottoman Turks from "Western" territories. At various periods in a 300-year-long border struggle, the Turks had occupied parts of eastern Europe (Hungary and Croatia). In the seventeenth century the Holy League, composed of Austria and Poland, repulsed the Turks at Vienna (1683) and went on to reconquer Hungary. The Treaty of Karlowitz (1699) ended the war against the Ottomans, and the Turkish threat to the West.

what was needed to guarantee stability and order was a monarchy with absolute and undivided power. Others argued that only a government that divided its power between the crown and some intermediary or representative body could bring a cessation to the violence and disorder. That is to say, in response to the worst crisis the West had faced since the fourteenth century there emerged two of the great political systems of world history: **absolutism** and **constitutionalism**.

ABSOLUTISM

According to the theory of absolutism all power resides in the king alone, who does not share power with any representative institutions of the realm. Under absolutism, politics are the private concern of the monarch and are regularly referred to as the "secret of the king." Sovereignty, that is, the right to rule, comes from God, not from the people. Hence, absolute monarchs rule by Divine Right. The king is God's representative on earth. While he can delegate authority, ultimately authority resides solely in him. The support underpinning absolute monarchy was in ceremony, ritual, art, architecture, symbolism, a powerful military, and an omnipresent bureaucracy that reached all parts of the country. While other rulers adopted the absolutist model in the seventeenth century, French King Louis XIV (r. 1643–1715), called the Sun King, personified the absolute monarch.

In the medieval and early modern period France had grown by incorporating more and more territories, but the local rights and privileges of these areas were usually respected. For instance, the province of Brittany, which was fully integrated into the monarchy only in the sixteenth century, continued to be governed by its own laws, customs, and political institutions. The kingdom of France as a whole was simply all those privileged entities— of provinces, of social orders such as the nobility, as well as of corporations, including the incorporated towns—that owed allegiance to the king of France. The single unifying factor was the Catholic Church, which the king was required to protect, and which took on a decidedly French identity, separating it in subtle ways from Rome. The king even took precedence over the pope in that he had the right to appoint bishops, cardinals and the rest of the church hierarchy in France.

The rise of absolutism marked that stage of the monarchy when it attempted to reduce the independence of the special groups. It is important to note that while French kings in the seventeenth and eighteenth century were absolute monarchs, this did not mean they ruled arbitrarily. In theory an enormous amount of power was vested in the hands of one man. In practice, however, French kings were limited by law and tradition. That is, they could not act arbitrarily without fear of destroying the traditional fabric of society.

For the purposes of strengthening France against its external enemies, the king and his ministers began in the course of the seventeenth century to shift power away from these semi-autonomous bodies and toward the central government by sending out into the provinces new royal agents. The *intendents*, as they were called, were directly responsible to the king. The monarchy created the first effective centralized bureaucracy in European history. This new bureaucracy made it clear to the French that their allegiance belonged to the king and not with their local governors. Louis XIV also established a huge army to quell any uprisings and challenge all foreign powers.

Yet, in order to achieve absolutism in France, French monarchs faced two obstacles. The first of these came from the French nobility. The most privileged class was divided into two groups. The old nobility, or "nobles of the sword," was composed of those who had held fiefs for centuries and by right and tradition had high degrees of political authority and control of the cities and countryside. But in the previous century Henry IV (d. 1610) had created and sold offices that conferred noble status. This was a new type of noble, the "nobility of the robe" (so called because these new offices were typically magisterial positions requiring the wearing of robes). The "nobles of the sword" saw this as a ploy to dilute the power of the nobility, rightly understanding that this new class would owe its existence and therefore allegiance to the kings of France. Naturally tension was created between the new and old forms of nobility. When Anne of Austria, mother of Louis XIV and regent, together with her closest advisor Cardinal Mazarin, decided to raise revenues in order to pay for France's role in the Thirty Years' War by creating more ennobling offices, many of France's traditional nobility declared themselves in open rebellion against the crown. The conflict, called the Fronde,[5] which began in 1643 and lasted until 1652 was essentially a power struggle between some of the nobility and the crown over rights and prerogatives. But the nobility lacked unity and leadership and in the end Louis XIV effectively and decisively put down the Fronde rebellion and brought the agitated nobility under his dominion.

Louis XIV's second obstacle was the presence of Protestants on French soil. The Reformation had gained many converts in France and incurred the wrath of the Catholic majority and the royalty. The second half of the sixteenth century was marred by bloody wars of religion. These ended when in 1598 Henry IV promulgated The Edict of Nantes, which granted limited religious freedom to Protestants. But nearly a century later, in 1685, Louis XIV signed the revocation of this edict, putting an end to religious tolerance. To Louis, the head of the Catholic Church in France and God's representative on earth, the presence of French Protestants or Huguenots represented an explicit challenge to his absolute authority.

After 1685, Protestants in France were forced to conceal their true religious beliefs. The only legal marriage was a Catholic marriage; Protestant education was forbidden; persecution of known Protestants was rampant. French Protestants had a choice between going underground or into exile. Large communities of Protestants moved to The Netherlands/United Provinces, England, and Prussia. They maintained their French identity and developed centers of French civilization outside of France, at a cost to the nation. The role of these communities (in Amsterdam, London, and Berlin) proved to be crucial in the dissemination of new philosophical and scientific knowledge. The French community in The Netherlands went so far as to establish a number of French-language publishing houses whose books and pamphlets were circulated throughout all of Europe.

By 1685 Louis XIV was the most powerful of the absolute monarchs of the Western world. As self-proclaimed Sun King, he established his palace at Versailles as the symbolic center of the world and used architecture, art, music, and ritual to enhance the power of the monarchy. Architects Mansart and Le Brun transformed the palace of Versailles into the largest and most extravagant royal court ever seen.

The last decades of the seventeenth century and the beginning of the eighteenth century are marked by the aggression of France under Louis XIV. The King's main goal in the foreign arena was to extend French power as far as possible. The problem he faced was France's geographic encirclement by the Habsburgs (in Spain and Austria). In 1667 France invaded the Spanish Netherlands and defeated the Spanish army there but was halted a year later by the combined forces of England, Sweden and the Dutch Republic. The Treaty of Aix-la-Chapelle in 1668 recognized French control of a few towns along the border between France and the Spanish Netherlands.

Not satisfied with his limited territorial acquisitions, Louis XIV once again sent his forces across the border, this time into the Dutch Republic in 1672. A year later he declared war on Spain, which brought the Dutch Republic into an alliance with Spain, its former colonial master. The King of France also attacked the Holy Roman Empire, which served to bring many German states into the anti-French alliance with Spain and the Dutch Republic. Despite the enemies arrayed against him, Louis XIV and the French army more than held their own on the battlefield. The Treaty of Nijmegen (1678-1679) temporarily ended hostilities on terms favorable to the French. The most notable gain for France was the acquisition of Alsace, which would become the subject of heated disputes between the French and Germans for the next two centuries. Although Louis XIV emerged from the Dutch War victorious, it was not without cost. French debts were mounting and the tax burden on France's subjects was growing.

Undeterred by peace treaty or soaring debt, the Sun King sent his armies further eastward. In 1681 the French seized important territory in Alsace; in 1684 they took the province of Lorraine; and in 1688 French forces engaged the Holy Roman Empire. The years 1689 to 1697 were marked by near-

---

[5]*Fronde* is the French word for "sling." Parisian mobs put rocks in slings and hurled them at the windows of government officials. Later *frondeur* became a word for anyone who opposed absolutism.

The immense Palace of Versailles symbolized the absolute power of Louis XIV. Not simply a home for the king, Versailles proclaimed the ruler's power through construction on a gigantic scale, including an entire satellite city for government officials and military personnel. Versailles further illustrated the rationalistic thought of the period. The palace complex incorporates an entire forest that has been transformed into an enormous park, and the massive buildings are imposed onto the natural landscape. The design of Versailles affirmed the dominance of human intelligence over nature.

Figure I-1   Versailles (aerial view). 1668–85. Courtesy of Réunion des Musées Nationaux/ Art Resource, NY.

continual warfare between the French and an alliance of military powers brought together with the sole aim of defeating France. This alliance, called the League of Augsburg, was made up of England, Spain, Sweden, the Dutch Republic, and the Holy Roman Empire. The Peace of Rijswijk of 1697 ended hostilities in a stalemate. Louis XIV was forced to cede some of the territory he gained through war but kept important holdings including the city of Strasbourg.

This was not to be the end of France's foreign military adventures under the rule of Louis XIV. In 1701, the king of Spain, Charles II, a Habsburg, died. The crown passed not to a Habsburg but to Philip V, the grandson of Louis XIV. Instantly Spain was transformed from an enemy to an ally of France, and an emboldened Louis sent his troops east where he attempted a land grab in the territories of the Holy Roman Empire and Austria. The coalition leaders recognized that if Louis succeeded, he would represent a fundamental threat across Europe and to England.

After a decade of war, France's push to the east was halted. The Treaty of Utrecht (1713) and the

Treaty of Rastatt (1714) allowed Austria to expand its territory in central Europe, establishing the eastern border of France. It also prevented Philip V of Spain from becoming King of France upon the death of Louis XIV. The lesson learned by the leaders of Europe was that a "Balance of Power" had to be maintained among the nations in order to prevent other European-wide conflicts.

Louis XIV died in 1715 leaving behind him a nation bankrupt by his extravagance and pursuit of territorial gain. Thus while absolutism reached its apex in France during the seventeenth century, it would prove to be short-lived. In 1789, the French would overthrow the monarchy and replace it with a republican form of government.

CONSTITUTIONALISM

England. Another form of government developed in the seventeenth century primarily in England and The Netherlands—constitutionalism. More than any other country in Europe, England had a strong *parliamentary* tradition with deep roots in the Middle Ages. It began as an "advisory" group of powerful nobles and clergy whom the king consulted on various matters. By the fourteenth century it had become a permanent institution of English government and was known as a "Parliament." Although the medieval Parliament served only as an advisory body, it established the right to question royal decisions, and Parliament and king were seen as interdependent. Membership came to be based on property, not church titles or titles of nobility, so that not only the aristocracy and the upper clergy but also prosperous landowners (called gentry) and merchants could serve.

There also emerged during the Middle Ages what the English came to call (and still call) their *constitution*. In its broader meaning, the word "constitution" simply refers to the organized system of relationships governing the state and the citizen. Constitutions may be unwritten or written, embodied in a single document or in a whole system of laws and institutions, articulating types of government from monarchy through oligarchy to democracy. (In ancient Greece, Aristotle discussed many different kinds of constitutions of various Greek city-states in his *Politics*.) What developed into the English constitution was not a single written document as the U.S. Constitution is, but a whole body

of written and unwritten precedents and laws (such as the *Magna Carta* of 1215 and the "common law" judicial tradition). These came to define the basic principles of English government.

The English Reformation under King Henry VIII (ruled 1509–47) strengthened royal power, especially with regard to the Church and its extensive property. However, it also strengthened Parliament because Henry needed the support of the nobility and the wealthy property owners in pushing through his reforms. But religion proved to be a very divisive issue politically and socially. For a long time after the Reformation many families remained loyal to Catholicism, even in the face of persecution. Within the reformed Church of England, a split arose between those who preferred the conservative reforms under Henry VIII, which had preserved much of the Catholic tradition, and those who believed the church required further "purification" of its liturgy, doctrine, and practices. The latter group was the *Puritans*, who represented the Calvinist approach to reformation in England. These religious divisions were to some degree reflected in class divisions, with the old aristocracy inclined to be either conservatively Anglican or Catholic and the newer landowning and merchant classes favoring Puritanism. This religious and social fracturing was in turn reflected in divisions within Parliament and between Parliament and king.

These religious struggles intensified during the reigns of Henry VIII's children, but under the long and effective rule of Elizabeth I (1558–1603), Henry's daughter by Anne Boleyn, the distinctive English Reformation became solidified in the established Church of England or Anglican Church. *The Book of Common Prayer* provided an official liturgy and its Protestant doctrines were defined in *The Thirty-Nine Articles of Religion*. Catholics and Protestant dissenters were subject to legal restrictions, while Puritans within the Church of England continued to agitate for more radical reformation.

Elizabeth I died without issue and the monarchy passed to James I, son of her cousin Mary Queen of Scots, and then to his son Charles I. Like the French kings of that time, James and Charles were both firmly committed to royal absolutism and believed in the divine right of kings. James conducted foreign policy without consulting Parliament, and centralized and consolidated the power of the royal government. Charles, a "high" Anglican with Catholic sympathies, went a step further and in 1629 suspended Parliament and tried to rule through his advisers. His goal was to rid the nation of Puritans and to eliminate the pro-parliamentary forces, many of which were Puritans. This set the king on a collision course with the Parliament and a substantial portion of the English population.

What precipitated the English Civil War was Charles's need for money in 1640 to defend England against a Scottish invasion. He needed the support of the powerful people who made up Parliament, so he called it back into session after having suspended it for eleven years. Parliament refused to cooperate unless Charles granted it basic rights, such as consultation in all matters of taxation, trial by jury, and a truly Protestant Church of England. Charles refused what he considered an attack on royal authority.

Civil war began in 1642, with the Parliamentary forces financed by taxes and wealthy merchants. Parliament's "New Model Army" was commanded by Oliver Cromwell (1599–1658), a Puritan landowner and long-time member of Parliament. This citizen army defeated the Royalist forces representing the king, the aristocracy, and the hierarchy of the church. In 1649 Charles I was publicly executed by order of Parliament. For the next eleven years England was a republican commonwealth led by Cromwell, Parliament, and the army. But the triumph of this anti-monarchical citizens' revolt raised the expectations and heightened the grievances of the rural and urban poor, who made up most of the rank and file of the army. A radical group who called themselves the *Levellers* emerged who rejected moderate republicanism in favor of egalitarian democracy and the redistribution of wealth. Religiously, the Levellers also rejected not only established Anglicanism but also moderate Puritanism. This popular discontent, exacerbated by inefficient government administration throughout the country, brought about the end of the commonwealth two years after Cromwell's death in 1658. No strong leadership emerged and the populace preferred a restored monarchy over the austere and disordered rule of the commonwealth. Charles I's son, Charles II, long exiled in France, was invited back in 1660 on the condition that he would cooperate with Parliament and agree to a Protestant Church of England. Although he chafed at any limitations to his power and tried to reduce the power of Parliament, Charles avoided the confrontations that had destroyed his father. Having no legitimate male heirs, Charles was succeeded by his brother James II (ruled 1685–88).

James II was both a royal absolutist and an outspoken Catholic, and it was his Catholicism that brought about his downfall. Married to a Catholic queen, surrounding himself with Catholic advisers at court, James alienated even the established Anglican Church. Like his unfortunate father Charles I, James dealt highhandedly with Parliament, issuing and enforcing decrees granting religious toleration to Catholics without any consultation with Parliament. In 1688 the queen gave birth to a long-awaited son who would by law be the heir to the throne, and he was baptized a Catholic. James had two daughters by his first marriage, but a son took precedence.

Fears of both a revived royal absolutism and a Catholic monarchy led some members of Parliament to engineer a royal *coup d'état*. This time the resistance was led by Anglican aristocrats and gentry who wanted to preserve the established church and assure a monarchy limited by Parliament. Fearing a repeat of the religious and social extremisms that had characterized the Civil War and Commonwealth, they kept the Puritans and their supporters out of it. Late in 1688 they invited the Dutch prince William of Orange, husband of Mary, the Protestant daughter of James II, to invade England. James II fled to France, and Parliament ratified his "abdication." Parliament declared the throne vacant, and on its own authority proclaimed William and Mary the new monarchs.

The condition imposed upon King William and Queen Mary II was the *Parliamentary Declaration of Rights*, a "bill of rights" that guaranteed the civil liberties of the English privileged classes, subjected England's monarchs to the rule of law and the consent of Parliament, and perpetually guaranteed that the succession to the throne would be Protestant. Partisans of this new constitutional arrangement called what had happened a "Glorious Revolution"; it was, unlike most other revolutions, bloodless. With the establishment of the *Parliamentary Declaration of Rights* in 1689, England became the first *constitutional monarchy*. In constitutional, as opposed to absolute, monarchies, the power of the king or queen is limited by an elected parliamentary or representative body having independent power. In twentieth-century constitutional monarchies such as Britain, Sweden, and Holland, political power resides for all practical purposes entirely with parliaments and their leaders, and the monarch plays a largely formal and ceremonial role as symbolizing personally the unity and continuity of the nation.

The Netherlands. In the sixteenth century Calvinist Protestants had made inroads in parts of the Spanish Netherlands. In 1566 a rebellion began against the Spanish Habsburgs in Antwerp (and elsewhere) when Calvinists attacked Catholic churches, smashing stained glass windows and statues of the Virgin Mary. Spain responded with force of arms that had the result of uniting both Catholic Dutch and Calvinist Dutch against the Spanish. War ended effectively in 1609 when Spain granted independence to seven provinces who joined as the United Provinces or Dutch Republic under the leadership of William of Orange. The remaining ten Catholic provinces remained under the rule of Spain.

The Dutch Republic was organized as a federation of provinces with a strong tradition of local rights and autonomy. Each province had a leader called a "stadholder" and there was a stadholder as head of all the provinces. The first stadholder was William I of Orange, and it was his great-grandson William III who was called to the English throne with his wife Mary. The central government under William I lacked any real authority over the provinces. Unlike France, wealthy merchants and their families dominated political life on both the local and national levels.

In the seventeenth century, the Dutch economy was by far the most vital in all of Europe. Amsterdam and Rotterdam became two of the largest and most important ports in the world. The Dutch were able to claim this position by importing goods from every corner of the globe into the European market while at the same time exporting Europe's products around the world. By 1670 the Dutch commercial fleet was larger than the fleets of all the European powers put together. Amsterdam was not only a leading port city but also became the center for European banking.

One of the distinctive characteristics of the Dutch Republic was its religious tolerance, but this must be seen in seventeenth century terms. Orthodox Calvinists ran the government and only they could hold public office. However, other Protestant groups were allowed to worship freely. The country's Catholic minority (about thirty percent of the population) was tolerated, although they had to meet for worship in private. Perhaps most strikingly, Jews who had been driven out of Spain and Portugal in 1492 had for a hundred years found refuge in the Netherlands. They were allowed to worship openly, and Amsterdam was home to a large synagogue.

The Netherlands' vibrant economy also gave birth to a "middle class" of wealthy merchants that not only controlled the political life of the nation but also the intellectual and cultural life as well. With prosperity came a rising level of education and literacy and an energetic press attracted distinguished thinkers and teachers. It was not by accident that Descartes, the French philosopher and mathematician, chose to settle in the Netherlands. Indeed, it was in the Netherlands that he wrote *Discourse on Method* as well as his other seminal works. Another well-known philosopher, Baruch Spinoza (1633–1677), a Dutch Jew, made important contributions to the reconciliation of biblical teachings with science and mathematics.

Finally, the seventeenth century was also the Golden Age of Dutch art. Dutch merchants sought to display their wealth and good taste by commissioning works of art from famed Dutch painters such as Rembrandt van Rijn (1606–1669), Frans Hals (1580–1666) and Jan Vermeer (1632–1675).

SLAVERY IN THE SEVENTEENTH CENTURY

In the sixteenth century, Spain and Portugal took the lead in conquering and colonizing much of the new world. By the end of that century Spain controlled nearly all of present-day South America, Central America and the west coast of the United States. Portugal was in control of Brazil and islands in the "west Indies" or what we today call Caribbean islands. In the seventeenth century, England and France entered the race for colonies in the new world and quickly came to possess most of North America and gained important holdings in the Caribbean such as Saint Domingue (today called Haiti), Guadalupe, and Barbados.

Once in firm control of their colonies, the European powers developed plantation economies: large parcels of land were established to grow staple crops such as sugar, coffee, tobacco, and cotton. White European settlers owned the land and black African slaves were brought in to work the land. The result was phenomenal wealth for the white landowners and their home countries and misery and death for millions of African slaves.

European merchants and overseas traders took advantage of this demand for slave labor and established the "triangular trade" originating from port cities such as Bordeaux and Liverpool. Ships left European port cities and sailed to the west coast of Africa where slaves were purchased. The human cargo was sold to plantation owners and slave dealers. Then European merchants purchased local colonial products such as coffee and sugar. The final leg of the triangle came when the ships returned to the ports of Europe to sell the "exotic" products to an eager public. By the eighteenth century coffee sweetened with sugar was in high demand as coffee houses and cafes became all the rage among European elites. From the beginning of the seventeenth century until the middle of the nineteenth century about eleven million slaves were brought to new world colonies to work the plantations.

Racism was also introduced in European colonies in the Americas, fueled by the alarming growth of indentured and slave labor exploited as commercial and agricultural investments in the new colonies. Time-worn racial stereotypes gleaned from Christian and Muslim theological speculation and the copious collections of three centuries of travel literature often portrayed "peoples of color" (black Africans, Amerindians) as amoral heathens, cannibals, barbarians, and sexually lubricious individuals, good for doing the work of animals, "owing to their low degree of humanity and their proximity to the animal stage." The use and abuse of slaves was so prolific and horrifying in the French colonies of the seventeenth century that Louis XIV's administration finally passed into law the infamous *Black Code* (1685), which legislated the "rights of slaves" to be uniformly (and forcibly) converted to the true faith (Catholicism) and uniformly treated (disciplined) in the area of punishable crimes. Owners could not arbitrarily whip, maim, torture or kill slaves. Every offense would carry a specific penalty, perhaps "softening" the inhumane treatment of slaves to a small degree, yet legalizing their status as human chattel to be corporally punished and stripped of any political rights.

INTELLECTUAL TRENDS

The seventeenth century saw the publication of some of the most important and controversial works of science and political thought ever written. The dissemination of printed materials together with a rise in literacy challenged individuals to think for themselves, a suggestion that some found liberating and others threatening. Revolutionary scientific theories brought with them an entirely new worldview to replace the Christian cosmology of the Middle Ages. The Protestant reformers had successfully called into question a single interpretation of the Christian faith. Political philosophers continued to ponder the interrelationship between humans and their government, reviving the idea of natural law and deriving from it a theory of natural rights due every human being by virtue of birth.

ART IN THE SEVENTEENTH CENTURY

The term "baroque," which is generally applied to art of the seventeenth century, characterizes works of dynamic composition and dramatic lighting effects. The rational, static figures of the Renaissance yielded in the Baroque era to emotionally charged scenes filled with diagonal movement. Diagonal compositions conveyed emotion and excitement to the viewer, which were compounded by the intensity of the subject matter, showcasing the climactic moment of a tale. Not all Baroque art exhibited these qualities in the same way, however. European artistic production was heavily influenced by Italy, with artists traveling to Rome to study classical antiquity as well as art of the Renaissance, but many returned home to develop their own interpretations. This resulted in a diverse body of "baroque" art from country to country, with the dynamic classicism of Italian Baroque giving way to, for example, a more restrained classicism in French Baroque painting.

Furthering the diversity of styles was the widely ranging subject matter, something defined largely by the artist's patron. In predominantly Catholic countries such as Italy or Flanders (now northern Belgium), art was most often commissioned by or for the church. Under the Counter-Reformation, art of religious subject matter became a tool with which the church hoped to inspire the viewer to religious devotion. In a predominantly Protestant country such as the Netherlands, on the other hand, art was commissioned not by the church but by the prosperous middle class. Dutch Baroque art favored portraiture, still lifes, and scenes of everyday life, subjects more appropriate to hanging in the patron's home. Artworks commissioned by a political ruler, as in England, often functioned as a form of propaganda to glorify the reigning monarch.

ITALIAN BAROQUE ART

Building on their strong foundation of academic training, Italian artists became expert at realistic representation of the human body, particularly from unusual perspectives. The single artist most associated with the Baroque era, because of his highly complex compositions, dramatic angles, and theatrical lighting, was Michelangelo Merisi, known as Caravaggio. Caravaggio favored intense emotional scenes in his paintings and became most known for his dramatic use of light. Demonstrating an effect called *tenebrism*, Caravaggio's forms emerged from a dark background into a strong light. Often the source of light appeared to come from outside the painting but angled across the entire composition in what is called a "raking light," dramatically illuminating the scene and highlighting the focal point. Caravaggio's tenebrist style so influenced other artists that similar paintings were sometimes described as *Caravaggesque*, and a group of Dutch artists favoring a tenebrist style became known as the *Utrecht Caravaggisti*.

Given their emotional power and dramatic religious subjects, Caravaggio's paintings lent themselves readily to the Counter-Reformation movement. Frequent commissions from churches reflected Caravaggio's ability to engage his viewer with the subject at hand. In *Entombment* of ca.1603 (Plate 1), painted for the Vittrice Chapel in Rome, the viewer is nearly overpowered by the sheer physical force of the painting. The large-scale, over-life-size figures tower above the viewer, whose perspective is from the burial pit. So dwarfed, the viewer is then primed to be bowled over emotionally, as well, by the dramatic subject matter. Saint John, to the right, and a laborer, to the left, lower the lifeless body of Jesus into the tomb. Behind them are the female mourners, including the Virgin Mary and Mary Magdalen. Emerging from darkness, the figures form a diagonal trajectory across the canvas and the main light falls on Jesus's body, the clear focal point. His outstretched arm and the hanging drapery direct the viewer's attention again to the final resting place.

One of Caravaggio's most successful Italian followers, Artemisia Gentileschi, adapted his tenebrist style to illuminate scenes in which women were often the protagonists. Artemisia, one of only a few well-known female artists of the time, depicted such biblical figures as Mary Magdalen, Susanna and the Elders, and Judith and Holofernes, a pairing that she painted repeatedly. As told in the Jewish Apocrypha, a set of biblical texts not considered canonical by all Christians, Judith was a beautiful widow who saved her people from Assyrian domination by plying the enemy's general with liquor, then decapitating him. In *Judith Beheading Holofernes* of 1620 (Plate 2), Artemisia depicts the climactic moment in which Judith, a Jewish heroine, severs the Assyrian general's head from his body, thus saving the Israelites. The painting testifies to Artemisia's artistic virtuosity, not only through her expert use of Caravaggesque lighting but also through her skillful depiction of unusual angles, as in the foreshortened body of the general. Departing from the timid depictions often seen in earlier portrayals of Judith, Artemisia emphasized the physicality of the act: Judith's maidservant, at center, holds down Holofernes with all of her might while Judith vigorously works the blade. The strong diagonals and the criss-crossing of arms within the composition, together with the large-scale format, strong lighting and spurting blood, all rivet the viewer's attention to the murder in progress.

The Counter-Reformation employed not only art but also magnificent architecture as a way to encourage religious devotion. Baroque church architecture featured opulent embellishments meant to heighten the spiritual involvement of the congregation. In Italy, Gianlorenzo Bernini spent decades renovating Saint Peter's Basilica and Square. The focus of the church's interior is a bronze canopied altar that marks the burial site of Saint Peter. Bernini's enormous *baldacchino* exemplifies the Baroque and Counter-Reformation aim of fully engaging the viewer in a spectacular, theatrical display of swirling color and light. Four spiraling, gigantic columns, over one hundred feet in height, draw the viewer's eye up to the heavens. Ornately decorated with sculpted leaves and vines and topped by four massive angels, the *baldacchino* visually and physically overpowers the viewer with its awesome beauty and size.

BAROQUE ART IN FLANDERS AND FRANCE

Like Italy, France and Flanders were under Catholic rule and so witnessed a flourishing of Counter-Reformation religious artwork. Peter Paul Rubens, a Flemish artist, studied and worked for years in Italy. Employed by the Duke of Mantua, Rubens traveled and made copies of many famous paintings for the royal collection, a job that exposed him to Counter-Reformation masterpieces and heavily influenced his own artistic production. Upon his return to Antwerp, his first major commission was a triptych (or three-paneled painting) for the main altarpiece of the Church of Saint Walpurga. The resulting painting, *The Raising of the Cross*, 1609–10 (Plate 3), clearly exhibits an Italian Baroque influence. The emotional intensity of the scene, conveyed by the agony on Jesus's face and by the weeping of the mourners, parallels the physical drama, visible in the Herculean efforts of the laborers to raise the cross. The dynamic composition, seen most clearly in the strong diagonal of Jesus's body, is reminiscent of Caravaggio's manner in its level of drama and its physical overpowering of the viewer. Commissioned by the Church, Rubens's painting was clearly intended to inspire the congregants to piety.

Contrasting markedly to the overwrought emotions of Rubens's altarpiece, Nicolas Poussin's *Landscape with Saint John on Patmos*, of 1640 (Plate 4), depicts a calm and orderly scene. Poussin's painting shows the disciple in his isolated retreat to the

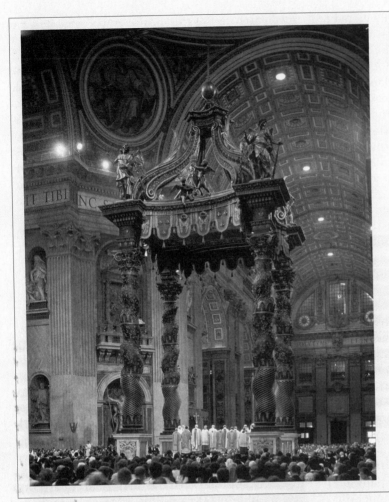

Figure I-2   Gianlorenzo Bernini,
Baldacchino. Saint Peter's Basilica,
Rome. 1624–1633. Gilded bronze,
100' high (30.48m). Courtesy of Saskia
Ltd./Art Resource, NY.

island of Patmos following Jesus's death and resurrection, where he is thought to have written the book of Revelation.[1] Rather than focusing on the religious figure, however, Poussin's John is nearly incidental to the scene. The subject, instead, appears to be the classically inspired landscape. John and his symbol, the eagle, sit among classical ruins in the foreground, while in the background we see an obelisk, ruins of a temple, and even the rounded outline of Hadrian's tomb. Poussin's carefully ordered composition, in which he balanced even the placement of the trees and ruins, demonstrates how Baroque art could vary in style and subject from country to country.

DUTCH BAROQUE

While the Catholic-ruled countries of Italy and Flanders inspired a host of Counter-Reformation artwork, the largely Protestant Netherlands witnessed an expanding diversity of both subject matter and patronage. Commissions came not from the Church but from civic entities and from a prosperous middle class. As such, Dutch artists favored small-scale paintings of subjects appropriate to

---

[1]Modern biblical scholarship concurs that the John of the Book of Revelation is not the author of the Gospel of John.

hanging in the patron's household, such as portraits, still lifes, and *genre* scenes, or scenes of everyday life.

The most famous Dutch painter, Rembrandt van Rijn, amassed a prodigious body of work ranging from history paintings to portraits to genre scenes. In 1632, Rembrandt accepted a commission from the wealthy Guild of Surgeons, resulting in *The Anatomy Lesson of Dr. Nicolaes Tulp* (Plate 5). The surgeons held anatomy lessons twice weekly, but only a few times a year with a corpse. Rembrandt's painting functions as a group portrait of the surgeons and was intended to commemorate their profession, and originally was displayed in the anatomy theater. Although far from the emotional intensity of Counter-Reformation paintings, Rembrandt's painting possesses an unlikely dynamism, given its subject. The figures are placed in a pyramidal formation so as to guide the viewer's eye around the composition, while the doctor animatedly demonstrates with his own hand the function of a particular grouping of muscles and tendons. Not simply a celebration of their discipline, however, Rembrandt's painting of the doctors speaks to the larger Enlightenment interest in science and nature.

While Rembrandt and others such as Frans Hals produced numerous large-scale civic and military portraits, the majority of Dutch painters catered to a middle-class audience and often sold works in an open market context rather than necessarily on commission. Dutch painters and patrons particularly favored scenarios based on moralizing proverbs. Jan Steen became the best-known purveyor of moralizing genre scenes, in which characters display a raucous indulgence along with a knowing look at the viewer. In *As the Old Sing, So Pipe the Young*, of 1663–65 (Plate 6), Steen illustrated a popular proverb, depicting a busy interior that simultaneously celebrates and warns against overindulgent behavior. According to the work's title, the children imitate the intemperance of their elders. Drinking and smoking mark the depravity of the scene. The slouching woman at left is the epitome of indulgence, glass raised and blouse scandalously untied. While viewers of Counter-Reformation paintings were called to spiritual devotion, viewers of Steen's genre scenes were expected to have a twofold reaction—recognizing the moral lesson, but also enjoying the hedonistic behavior of the scene at hand.

ENGLISH BAROQUE

As demonstrated by the Dutch and Italian works discussed above, the subject and style of Baroque art depended largely upon its audience. In England, the Baroque paintings of Anthony van Dyck duly reflected their commission by King Charles I. A Flemish painter and contemporary of Rubens, Van Dyck moved to England in 1632 to become court painter to Charles I. Van Dyck's many royal portraits testify to his skillful manipulations of scenes in order to show the king in the best possible light. In *Charles I of England*, ca.1635 (Plate 7), Van Dyck subtly altered the traditional equestrian portrait in order to flatter his sitter. An extremely short man, Charles I would have appeared childlike if pictured atop a large horse. By picturing the monarch standing next to a horse with a bowed head, Van Dyck allowed the king to appear taller than he actually was.

THE BAROQUE ERA IN MUSIC

The term *baroque* is used to characterize European art, architecture, and music of the period roughly from 1600–1750. Although the word came to have other meanings, it originally referred to an irregularly shaped pearl, an appropriate designation because such pearls were prized in the ornate jewelry of the period. The music of the Baroque period, like the art and architecture, was richly elaborate, exuberant, freely embellished, and designed to be emotionally appealing. (Later critics of the Baroque style would consider its ornateness excessive—"too much.")

The great patrons of the music of the Baroque era were the church and the state. Both Catholic and Protestant churches vied with one another in promoting themselves through architectural, artistic, and musical splendor. The royal courts of national monarchs, such as George I in England and Louis XIV in France, and many of the smaller European principalities also competed with one another in their patronage of high culture. Cities would also hire composers and musical directors to enrich their cultural life and add luster to their reputation. The two greatest composers of the Baroque era, George Frideric Handel (1685–1759) and Johann Sebastian Bach (1685–1750), nicely illustrate the varied forms of patronage. Handel's patron as a composer and music director was the Elector of Hanover in Germany, whom Handel followed to England when he became King George I, while Bach spent most of his career as a composer, director, and organist at St. Thomas Church in Leipzig, Germany.

Baroque composers continued the Renaissance tradition of *polyphony* (music with two or more independent melodies played together) and *counterpoint* (polyphonic music in which the melodies harmonize while remaining independent), but introduced innovations that would fully exploit the possibilities of polyphonic music. Baroque music is characterized by sharp contrasts, such as alternating movements of a concerto between slow and fast and musical "opposition" between the solo and the orchestral parts. This contributed to a greater emotional intensity in Baroque compositions, which typically express a single particular emotion such as joy or grief. Another innovation was the *basso continuo* (continuing bass) line, a steady "bottom line" in the music that provided a foundation on which strikingly varied and intricately constructed higher melody lines could be built. The Baroque era introduced music written for virtuoso singers and instrumentalists, complex and often demanding to perform, and encouraging a great deal of improvisation by the performer.

Musical instruments underwent continuing development during the Baroque period. The organ came fully into its own, with much music written specifically for the organ or including the organ in instrumental ensembles. Improvements in the tuning of the harpsichord, a keyboard instrument with a mechanism that plucked the strings to make the sound, made it the other major keyboard instrument, although by late in the Baroque period it was being supplanted by the much more versatile piano. The violin became the supreme bowed stringed instrument, and the greatest violin-maker of the time, Antonio Stradivari (1644-1737), created violins that are still unsurpassed for their quality, continue to be prized by professional violinists, and fetch huge prices.

New forms of instrumental music that characterized the age of Baroque included the *fugue*, a polyphonic composition in which a melody or musical theme is repeated by the other musical lines, which come in with the theme at different times from the original line but in such a way that the music harmonizes contrapuntally (i.e., as counterpoint). Fugues are excellent examples of how intricate and complex Baroque music can be. Bach was the master composer of fugues. Another new form was the *concerto*, a composition for a solo instrument and an instrumental group (the *solo concerto*) or for two instrumental groups (typically a smaller contrasted with a larger, as in the *concerto grosso* or "big" concerto).

The solo concerto became one of the most widely represented of modern musical forms. Most of the great composers, from Antonio Vivaldi to George Gershwin and down to the present day, have written solo concertos, with concertos for piano or violin and orchestra being the most common. Another Baroque innovation was the *sonata* (from the Italian *sonare*, to sound), which during the Baroque era could refer to any piece played on instruments rather than sung. The most popular was the *trio sonata*, featuring two high parts for violin, flute, or oboe, and a bass part for cello or bassoon.

In vocal music the Baroque era introduced the *cantata* (the Italian word meaning "sung"). Cantatas are compositions for voices accompanied by instruments, the words being either a religious text (e.g., something from the Bible) or a secular text. Most cantatas were written for solo soprano voice, although composers used various combinations of solo and ensemble voices. Perhaps the greatest of the composers of cantatas was the Italian Alessandro Scarlatti (1660–1725), who wrote six hundred of them. In Germany cantatas were almost always composed for religious texts. As choirmaster of St. Thomas Church, Bach had to compose a cantata a week, and became the other great figure associated with the cantata.

The other great development in vocal music that took place during the Baroque era was *opera*, short for *opera in musica*, which in Italian means "a musical work." An opera is a drama set to music. Opera wonderfully exemplifies the elaborate and "spectacular" character of the Baroque arts: it involves music, drama, dance, visual art (scenery and costumes), and architecture (the opera house). Opera began in Italy actually during the later Renaissance period, among a group of poets and musicians who wanted to create a new kind of music that would emulate ancient Greek tragedy, the stories of which were told through choral music and dance together with actors (soloists) who apparently delivered their lines in a half-sung, half-spoken way—what the creators of opera would call *recitative* ("recited"). The first operas grew out of Renaissance madrigals, and the first surviving opera, *Eurydice* (based on the ancient Greek tragedy of Orpheus and Eurydice), was by an Italian named Jacopo Peri (1561–1633). But it was Claudio Monteverdi (1567–1643), the brilliant pioneer of the transition from Renaissance to Baroque music, who really created the first full-blown opera, *Orfeo* (1607), another telling of the myth of Orpheus and Eurydice that is still performed to this day. His English contemporary Henry Purcell (1658–1695), produced another memorable opera of the period, *Dido and Aeneas*, retelling the tragic love story from the *Aeneid*. Opera became one of the major musical forms of the modern era, and later composers such as Bizet, Verdi, Wagner, and Puccini would be chiefly known for their operas.

Closely related to opera as a creation of the Baroque period is the *oratorio*, a large-scale work for soloists, chorus, and orchestra on a broad religious theme and using biblical or other religious texts. Like operas, oratorios are dramatic, with the soloists playing specific characters, but unlike operas they are performed as a concert, without dramatic action, costumes, and sets. The supreme master of the oratorio in the Baroque era was Handel.

The Baroque era produced a dazzling number of fine composers, of whom we are highlighting only a few. Among the others we will just mention, in Germany, Heinrich Schütz, Dietrich Buxtehude, Johann Pachelbel, and Georg Philipp Telemann; in France, Jean-Baptiste Lully, François Couperin, and Jean-Philippe Rameau; and in Italy, Arcangelo Corelli, Tomaso Albinoni, Domenico Scarlatti, and Giovanni Pergolesi.

CD SELECTIONS

The first seven tracks of the accompanying CD feature music of the Baroque era, beginning with Monteverdi and Purcell early in the period and ending with Handel and Bach, who brought Baroque music to its fullest expression. Track 1 is the introductory music to Monteverdi's *Vespers* of 1610, published and first performed the same year that Galileo published *The Starry Messenger*. The *Vespers* is a musical setting of an evening liturgy of the Catholic Church, consisting mainly of some of the Psalms from the Bible. The title of this opening part, "Deus in adjutorium/Domine ad adjuvandum" means "O God, make speed to save me/O Lord, make haste to help me," and is sung by a solo voice and the chorus. This is a good example of Monteverdi's mixing of sacred and secular styles of music: the introduction is based on the opening of his opera *Orfeo*. The brightness of the voices and instruments (especially the brass) is a fitting introduction to the "age of splendor" that the Baroque era was in the history of Western music.

Track 2 is Dido's dramatic aria "When I am laid in earth," from Purcell's opera *Dido and Aeneas*. It tells the "love story" part of the *Aeneid*. In Purcell's version, a sorceress assisted by witches causes Dido, Queen of Carthage, to fall passionately in love with Aeneas, a Trojan prince and survivor of the Trojan War. Reminded by the god Mercury of his larger destiny to voyage on to Italy to be the founder of the Italian people, Aeneas leaves Dido. Devastated, Dido kills herself after pouring out her grief to her servant Belinda: "When I am laid, am laid in earth, may my wrongs create /No trouble, no trouble in thy breast. . . . Remember me, remember me, but ah! forget my fate." Purcell composed the opera when he was twenty-two, in 1680. The libretto (the words) was written by Nahum Tate. It was first performed at "Mr. Josias Priest's Boarding-School at Chelsey by Young Gentlewomen."

"Spring," from *The Four Seasons*, on Track 3, is probably Antonio Vivaldi's most familiar violin concerto, written in 1725. *The Four Seasons* is an early example of "program music," designed to portray musically specific aspects of the natural or human world—in this case, spring, summer, fall, and winter. Vivaldi alternates an opening theme with depictions of the singing of birds, a flowing stream, a storm, and the return of the birds. The concerto consists of three movements: *Allegro* (fast, lively), *Largo e Pianissimo Sempre* (slow and always very soft), and back to *Allegro*.

Tracks 4 and 5 include two familiar pieces by George Frideric Handel (1685–1759), one sacred and one secular. Track 4 is "And the glory of the Lord," the first chorus from Handel's oratorio *Messiah*, one of the best-known and beloved of all works of classical music. Using texts from the Old and New Testaments as they appear in the King James version of the Bible, it tells the story of Jesus' birth, death, and resurrection, and closes with the theme of the redemption of all humankind. Handel composed *Messiah* in twenty-four days in 1741. Track 5 contains the "Hornpipe" from Handel's *Water Music: Suite in D Major*. King George I commissioned Handel to write music to be played as the king and members of his court traveled on the royal barge on the River Thames. The Water Music is divided into three suites or groups of pieces: in F major, G major, and D major. Each suite consists of a wide variety of different musical types, including various dances such as minuets, jigs, gavottes, country dances, and the hornpipe traditionally danced by sailors.

Johann Sebastian Bach (1785–1750) is likewise represented by two works, one sacred and the other secular, on Tracks 6 and 7. On Track 6 is a very small portion of his monumental *Mass in B Minor*, which stands with his *St. John Passion*, *St. Matthew Passion*, and *Christmas Oratorio* as one of his greatest choral works. He wrote parts of it in 1733 but did not decide to expand it into a full-scale musical setting of the whole mass until 1747, just a few years before his death. It was probably not actually performed in full until 1835. Bach was a Lutheran, but his prince was Friedrich August II, Elector of Saxony, a Catholic. Unhappy with his position in Leipzig, Bach wrote the first parts of the *Mass in B Minor* as part of his "credentials" in offering his services as music director for the royal court. (He got the job, but it was a mere formality and he had to continue in Leipzig.) Track 6 is the final part of the Mass in B Minor, the *Dona nobis pacem* ("Grant us peace").

Bach's six *Brandenburg Concertos* are among his most brilliant and popular compositions, offering the listener splendid melodic lines and structurally varied counterpoint. As a long-delayed response to the request of Christian Ludwig, the Margrave of Brandenburg, for more of his compositions, in 1721 Bach presented him with these six concertos. They come from one of the happiest and most productive periods of Bach's life. Track 7 features the Third Movement (*Allegro assai*, "fast enough") from *Brandenburg Concerto No. 2*. Years ago this was used as the theme song for a long-running "current events and ideas" discussion show, *Firing Line*, hosted by William Buckley on national public television.

CHAPTER ONE

INTELLECTUAL CURRENTS
IN THE SEVENTEENTH CENTURY: RENÉ DESCARTES

The Scientific Revolution dominated the intellectual currents that shaped the work of seventeenth-century scientists and philosophers. It also separated earlier forms of science and disrupted the fabric of the culture that had fostered them. The period from about 1550 to 1650 laid the foundations for fundamental changes in the worldview of the Western world. Prior to the Scientific Revolution, the great majority of Europeans saw the world, and their place in it, through a Christian cosmology. The earth was God's creation and was at the center of the universe, with the sun and the stars revolving around it. Copernicus's heliocentric theory challenged this picture by calling into question the traditional Christian cosmology resting on the authority of the Bible, Christian doctrine, and Aristotelian science. These new ideas met with resistance by both Catholics and Protestants.

Basic to the new model of understanding the world of nature was what we have come to call the scientific method: a method of inquiry in which experiment and observation play a central role. This method of studying nature is considerably different from the methods employed in classical antiquity and the late Middle Ages. Medieval methods of investigating natural phenomena resulted in elaborate, sometimes convoluted answers to questions, the answers to which were already known. That may appear paradoxical, but there were two recognized sources of authority in the late Middle Ages: principally Aristotle's writings, including his immensely influential *Physics*, and Christian theology. Thomas Aquinas's synthesis of Aristotelian philosophy and Christian theology in the thirteenth century is a well-known and influential example of this approach, which we refer to as scholasticism. Inquiry was often little more than confirmation of received opinion or new modes of explaining the essential compatibility between the Aristotelian worldview and Scripture. In the process, empirical data were rarely examined and almost never subjected to experiments. Instead the terms that denoted natural objects were defined and redefined and the arguments in their support searchingly examined for logical consistency and scriptural harmony. Even the simpler quantitative techniques such as counting, weighing, and measuring were ignored on the grounds that the nature or properties of discrete natural objects could not contravene theories supported by the Christianized Aristotelianism. And it was the later medieval forms of scholasticism against which many of these new scientists were reacting when they insisted upon methods that directly investigated nature. In neither of the earlier cases, moreover, was there a belief that nature was to be understood in order to be used for human benefit. These characteristics of modern science have become so ingrained in our culture that it requires considerable effort to visualize a culture in which the experimental method is not a model for all inquiry.

One group that made significant contributions to the Scientific Revolution were the artisans and craftspeople—metal workers, tool makers, dyers, painters, tanners, and the like. They had long recognized, and taken advantage of, the physical and behavioral properties of natural objects. Eventually these craftspeople committed the techniques and results of their professional expertise to writing in, of course, the vernacular. The invention of the printing press in 1450 made it possible for them to publish and disseminate this information much more widely than had previously been possible in Western culture. The technical manuals that they wrote, while unprepossessing and of little literary pretense, were valued by some contemporary scholars in their attempt to provide a more generalized explanation and understanding of nature that was consistent with nature itself, if not necessarily consistent with the prevailing intellectual authorities.

The readers of such technical manuals were mainly urban, like-minded members of the middle class: merchants, burghers, and, of course, other craftspeople. They were eager to exploit a new understanding of nature but were unable to read scholarly books written in Latin. In time this body of technical manuals, usually written in the vernacular and conveniently known today as *Fachliteratur* (technical literature), reached an even more important audience. By a process known today as "technology transfer," members of three other groups studied, and, in turn, wrote similar texts: physicians, apothecaries (pharmacists), and "gentleman and lady" scholars—members of the aristocracy who pursued learning of various sorts. These *literati*, many of whom had only a tenuous connection with the universities, often established informal societies or associations where topics of mutual interest were debated and sometimes even experimentally tested, without much concern for scholastic or ecclesiastical authority.

Despite an indifference to things scientific, the intellectuals of the Renaissance made an important contribution to the Scientific Revolution. They energetically made new translations of rediscovered ancient texts. Some of these texts were technical treatises on such subjects as mathematics, astronomy, zoology, botany, medicine, agriculture, and architecture. In many cases these texts had been so coated over with scholastic exegetical commentary that important data was obscured. In the new translations, new data and new ways of looking at nature were revealed. Thus the humanism of the Renaissance joined forces with the artisans' less polished attempts to understand and to explain a physical world that had been obscured and whose details had been regarded as unworthy of study.

Skepticism was another approach that characterized the scientists and philosophers of the Scientific Revolution. There can be no one absolute definition of skepticism, but generally, a skeptic is someone who doubts all assertions or conclusions regarding truth and knowledge, pointing out the counter-evidence and opposing arguments to any claim. Developed by the ancient Greeks, skepticism (especially in areas of religious certainty), which had been widely used in the writings of the humanists of the Renaissance, also fed the rise of science, along with a renewed interest in the ethical dimension of human society. A skeptic in the seventeenth century, as exemplified by René Descartes (1596–1650), questioned received ideas and employed

Frans Hals is remembered primarily as a talented portraitist, second only in his time to Rembrandt. Hals produced a variety of group portraits, from militias to religious factions, in addition to individual portrayals. While Hals earned an impressive reputation, Descartes was by far his most famous sitter. In this portrait, as in others of his late career, Hals deftly captures a psychological intensity and exhibits a loose brushwork that apparently later influenced Edouard Manet and the Impressionists.

Figure I-3   Frans Hals, *Descartes*, ca.1649. Oil on canvas. (77.5 x 68.5 cm). Musée du Louvre, Paris. Courtesy of Erich Lessing/Art Resource, NY.

logical argument to arrive at what he believed were indisputable truths. Descartes was able to affirm the existence of God but many skeptics could not—or were uncertain—so to be a skeptic was a dangerous enterprise, as Galileo and others would learn.

SCIENTISTS AND PHILOSOPHERS

The image of the lone scholar, isolated from the mundane world and acquiring arcane knowledge by questionable means, is in many ways not an unfaithful picture of the early scientific pioneers. That image was to undergo a radical transformation with the development and gradual acceptance of the potential of science to answer questions by means of controlling nature. To do that, however, required the patience and dedication of many investigators working toward the same end.

An early seventeenth-century philosopher, Englishman Francis Bacon (1561–1626), proposed that science should be a collective enterprise. In his influential book, *Novum Organum* (*A New Instrument or Method* [of knowledge]) (1620), Bacon expounded the view that humans should be the masters of nature, but as a collective venture. He called for a restoration (*instauratio*) of the sciences by a new method, the inductive or experimental method, to replace the deductive analysis of scholastic Aristotelianism. He envisioned that this new science would be conducted by teams of investigators who worked together—a scientific community.

That Bacon's dream was not an idle one is indicated by the chartering in April 1663 of the Royal Society of London for Improving Natural Knowledge. Such was its success that four years later, Thomas Sprat (1635–1773), future Bishop of Rochester, published his *History of the Royal Society*. Praising the Royal Society's accomplishments, and at the same time defending the role of science against its detractors, Sprat left no doubt that science had become a part of a new society. In 1660 a scientific center for new experimental science based on work by Galileo, the Accademia del Cimento, was founded in Florence, Italy. In 1666, the Académie des Sciences was established in Paris. Although some time would elapse before courses in science were routinely available to university students, all the necessary constituents of the scientific enterprise were available by the beginning of the eighteenth century: scientific instruments, a scientific press, governmental recognition and patronage, and, of course, a growing number of professional scientists. As a result, science became institutionalized.

The richness of the intellectual accomplishments of scientists or "natural philosophers" of the seventeenth century can be seen in this brief summary:

1543: Nicolas Copernicus asserts heliocentrism. 1572: Tycho Brahe establishes accurate data on planetary/lunar orbits and first modern star catalog. 1600: William Gilbert writes on the magnetic properties of bodies (earth). 1609: Johannes Kepler writes on the laws of planetary motion. 1610: Galileo Galilei makes his first telescopic observations of celestial phenomena which convinces him of the truth of the Copernican theory. 1628: William Harvey demonstrates the circulation of blood. 1637: Descartes publishes *Discourse on Method* and the mathematical treatise setting forth analytic geometry. 1642: Blaise Pascal constructs the first adding machine. 1644: Descartes publishes *Principles of Philosophy* giving mechanistic explanations for matter and motion and for physical, chemical, and biological phenomena. 1654: Pascal and Pierre de Fermat begin to work on probability theory. 1657: Robert Boyle works on pressure/volume and designs a pneumatic pump. 1664: posthumous publication of Descartes's *L'Homme* (Man) expounding a mechanistic interpretation of the animal body. 1665: the first scientific journal in the English-speaking world, *Philosophical Transactions* (Royal Society of London), is published. 1666: Louis XIV establishes the Académie Royale des Sciences and its journal (*Journal des Savants*). 1669: Isaac Newton develops calculus and the reflecting telescope (1672). 1684: Gottfried Wilhelm Leibniz publishes his work on differential calculus. 1687: Newton's *Principia Mathematica*, formulating the laws of motion and of universal gravitation, is published. 1688: Francesco Redi challenges the ancient belief in spontaneous generation, beginning a two-century debate on the subject.

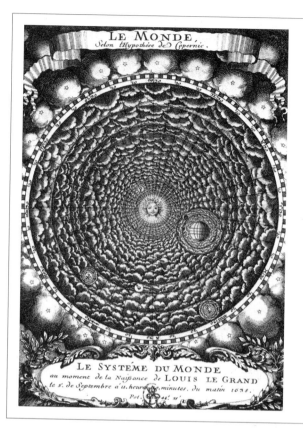

In Part Six of his *Discourse on Method*, Descartes relates how in 1633 he had completed a book entitled *Traité du Monde (Treatise on the World)*, a comprehensive scientific account of the physical universe, and describes the principles and the method he had used. In *The World* he affirmed the Copernican theory of the universe, but just as the book was about to go to press he heard through a close friend that Galileo had been tried and silenced by the Inquisition for advocating Copernicanism. Fearful of suffering the same fate, Descartes immediately had the publication of *The World* suppressed. The book was not published until 1673, long after Descartes' death, during the reign of Louis XIV. This illustration from the book portrays, as the text at the top says, "the world according to the hypothesis of Copernicus." The words at the bottom are political flattery: "The system of the world at the moment of the birth of Louis the Great [Louis XIV] on September 5, 1638. As Louis was the "Sun King," around whom the politics of Europe revolved, so the universe revolves around the sun.

Figure I-4 *System of the World.* Engraving. Cabinet des Estampes, Bibliothèque National, Paris. Courtesy of Cabinet des Estampes, Bibliothèque National, Paris.

POLITICAL THEORISTS

New political thinkers also had an important impact on the intellectual ferment of the seventeenth century. Hugo Grotius (Dutch, 1583–1645) wrote several tracts dealing with the subject of international relations. He proposed laws pertaining to the freedom of the seas for trade. The universally accepted three-mile limit extending from the shores of a country evolved from his proposals. He wrote on the idea of natural law—a concept that would become central in the eighteenth century during the American and French revolutions. Grotius argued that natural law was a universal, unchanging law that neither church nor state had the ability to modify. Indeed, for Grotius, natural law was the only legitimate source for both secular and religious authority. Baron Samuel von Pufendorf (1632–1694) a German statesman and historian, also adopted the ancient idea of natural law as a system of universal law. He had read Thomas Hobbes and adopted his idea of the state of nature, but disagreed with Hobbes that it was a state of war. He

concluded that the state was defined by the will of a collection of individuals.

The best-known political theorists of the seventeenth century are Englishmen, Thomas Hobbes (1588–1679) and John Locke (1632–1704). Both worked from the hypothesis of a state of nature that was ruled by natural law and in which humans had natural rights. From that starting point they reached radically differing conclusions regarding the best government. Thomas Hobbes, in *Leviathan*, (1661) wrote in support of absolute monarchy. John Locke, in *Two Treatises On Government*, (1688) argued against absolutism and supported constitutional monarchy.

ACADEMIES AND SALONS

The seventeenth century was also characterized by the growth of academies and salons. Academies had formed in the sixteenth century as an occasion for intellectual discourse. Academies were generally organized by a member of the aristocracy or sometimes a member of the royal family. One reason for their growth in the seventeenth century was that they served as an outlet for nobles who had little political power in the increasingly absolutist government in France and England. Academies that surrounded the court often concerned themselves with art and music, but other academies explored the new trends in the sciences. The degree of seriousness in these meetings varied. The term "salon" came into use in the middle of the century. Some salons served only for the exchange of gossip and assignations while others engaged in serious discussions. Cafés became meeting places, mostly for men, who debated political issues. By the middle of the century the number of academies declined as they came under the "observation" of the government. Upper-class women became increasingly influential in shaping taste and ideas, fostering the early development of feminist circles of thinkers and writers intent on crediting women for their part in having "civilized" the modern nation-state in areas of manners, language, style, and domestic life. The well-known playwright Molière (1622–1673) satirized both the vulgar manners of the aspiring merchant class and the exaggerated gentility of these women, known as *précieuses*, in such comedies as *The Bourgeois Gentleman* and *The Learned Ladies*.

SCIENTIFIC "LADIES"

The excitement generated by the new scientific methods and discoveries in the seventeenth and later in the eighteenth centuries stimulated numbers of upper- and middle-class European men and women to take up the study of science. The fact that the women were women, and often wives or sisters of male scientific investigators, caused them to be stereotyped as "scientific ladies": strictly amateurs, useful assistants to men, who could fill their time satisfyingly in such pursuits but lacked both the education and the intellectual capacity to do creative theoretical science. But behind the stereotype was the reality that a number of women in the upper strata of society became scientifically knowledgeable, and some made noteworthy contributions to the new science.

The Scientific Revolution produced a large number of women astronomers. The contribution of most was in the realm of observation and calculation rather than of new discovery, but by no means entirely. Sofie Brahe (ca. 1556–1643), the sister of the influential Danish astronomer Tycho Brahe (1546–1601), was a self-taught astronomer and alchemist who worked with her brother at his observatory and helped him in making the observations that led to Kepler's determination of the elliptical orbits of the planets. Maria Winckelmann Kirch (1670–1720), a German astronomer, discovered the comet of 1702 but did not receive recognition as its discoverer. She also made observations on the aurora borealis in 1707 and wrote on the conjunction of the sun with Saturn and Venus in 1709.

The one woman astronomer who achieved wide fame and respect—and during her lifetime—was Caroline Herschel (1750–1848), a German who for fifty years conducted scientific study in England. In 1782, Herschel began her career as an independent observer and became an expert on comets. In 1786 she became the first woman to be recognized for discovering a comet; she discovered seven in all. By the end of the eighteenth century Caroline Herschel was known and respected as an astronomer throughout Europe. Women likewise played a role in furthering the mechanistic model in science and popularizing the work of scientific pioneers such as Newton. One of the most notable European women of the eighteenth century was Gabrielle-Emilie Le Tonnelier de Breteuil, the Marquise du Châtelet-Lomont (1706–1749). Highly regarded among the scientists and mathematicians of her day, it may have been Emilie du Châtelet who more than anyone else brought about the end of the dominance of French science by Descartes and its replacement by Newtonian science.

Du Châtelet is also a classic example of the denigration and even theft of women's achievements. History remembers her best as the lover of the famous French Enlightenment writer and thinker Voltaire (1694–1778), and an associate named Samuel Koenig falsely claimed that he had dictated to her the book *Institutions de physique*, which she first published anonymously in 1740. When she and Voltaire remodeled a family estate at Cirey, they installed one of the finest collections of books in France and a large laboratory where the marquise carried out experiments in Newtonian optics. They collaborated in writing the book that played an important role in introducing Newtonian science to the French, stimulating debate on it among intellectuals, and displacing the influence of Descartes. *Eléments de la philosophie de Newton*, first published in 1738, appeared under Voltaire's name and has always been officially attributed to him, despite his repeatedly stating that "Lady Newton," as he called her, knew more about Newtonian science than he, and he clearly implied in the Dedication that hers was the larger contribution to the book. We know for a fact that the chapters on Newton's optics were largely her work. Emilie du Châtelet's last influential project was her two-volume translation of Newton's *Principia Mathematica*, including her mathematical commentaries together with a greatly improved revision of the *Eléments*. With its posthumous publication in 1759, Newtonian science became firmly established as the approach to knowledge that would dominate the French Enlightenment, and hers remains the only French translation of Newton's great work.

"Scientific ladies" were also active in other branches of the new methods of scientific investigation, including chemistry, medicine, and biological classification. For instance, throughout their marriage the Frenchwoman Marie Lavoisier (1758–1836) collaborated closely with her husband Antoine (1743–1794), the founder of modern chemistry, such that her contributions became inseparable from his. Lady Mary Wortley Montagu (1689–1762), a scientific researcher and outspoken early feminist, introduced smallpox vaccination to Britain and Western Europe after carefully studying its successful practice in Turkey, despite strong opposition from the medical profession and the Church. Her work on variolation (inoculation with a small amount of smallpox virus) was an early contribution to the eventual development of the germ theory of disease. Maria Sybille Merian (1647–1717), of Dutch-Swiss parentage, was a pioneering entomologist and botanist and an excellent scientific artist who, assisted by her daughter Dorothea, illustrated her books with her own engravings. She wrote a three-volume work on insects of Europe and a book on insects of Surinam (Dutch Guiana, in South America), where she and her daughter studied insects and plants for two years (1698–1700). Merian's books on insects became standard works in entomology.

What feminist historians of science have uncovered in recent years is the considerable role that patriarchal or sexist bias has played in scientific investigation—predominantly, and for obvious reasons, in the fields of biology, human anatomy and physiology, psychology, and medicine—and the negative impact this has had on women. This has been true in terms both of perpetuating ancient prejudices in new forms, with their restriction of women's rights and opportunities, and of directly affecting women's physical and mental health and reproductive life. One out of many examples is the widely held medical opinion, which appeared in standard medical textbooks until the early years of the twentieth century, that too much education was harmful to women because it drained away vital energy needed for their reproductive role. Because most of us think of the methods and conclusions of the natural sciences as objective, neutral, impersonal, and unbiased, it is important to be reminded that science too is a human activity that grows out of and is shaped and sometimes distorted by the values and limitations that always characterize human cultures. The considerable value of science as a reliable way of gaining knowledge of the world is not only that its methods have proven enormously fruitful in terms of their explanatory and predictive power, but also that it is an essentially self-correcting enterprise—testing, improving, and discarding its hypotheses in the light of new data or better interpretations of existing data. This self-critical attitude that is so vital to scientists in their inquiries must and at its best does include the disclosure of bias in their previous investigations.

THE OCCULT

The new approaches to scientific discovery and philosophy were not the only ways employed to find answers. Exploration into the occult was an accepted mode of inquiry for many. Prior to the Scientific Revolution people had viewed the world as an organism, a nurturing "mother," and it was not incompatible with Christian belief to believe in spirits who could affect observable realities. There were those who functioned in ordinary society who had a knowledge of the healing properties of herbs, were the dispensers of potions, and called upon the spirit world to aid in their supplications. These explorations sometimes led to a suspicion of witchcraft.

The backdrop to the witchcraft persecutions is the uncertainty, conflict, and confusion created by the religious, social, and political turmoil of the six-teenth and early seventeenth centuries. In the mid-dle of the sixteenth century there was a sudden, dramatic increase in arrests and trials for witchcraft, which just as suddenly and dramatically decreased in the middle of the seventeenth century. All over Europe, pre-Christian religious and folklore tradi-tions had continued throughout the Middle Ages and would continue into the twentieth century. These traditions centered on figures whom people called the "cunning folk": usually wise women and midwives who with their magic, spells, and cures were perceived as seers and healers. "Witch" was not originally a negative term; it is from "wicca," which means simply a wizard or wise person. The cunning folk practiced mostly "white magic" (good), but their power was believed to be capable of "black magic" (evil) as well. Women who practiced these arts usually lived alone and were single, which made them suspect in an age when marriage or the con-vent were the only conventionally acceptable roles for women. A standard charge against women accused of witchcraft was that their lust was insa-tiable and they copulated with Satan. Witchcraft per-secutions were carried on by both Catholics and Protestants and were directed overwhelmingly against women. By the early seventeenth century witch-hunting was completely out of control, and church and civil authorities attempted to restrain the persecutors. It continued here and there until the eighteenth century. The famous Salem witch trials occurred in the American colonies in the late seven-teenth century. After the witchcraft furor died down, many country people returned to their old ways. They saw no problem in being a Catholic or a Protes-tant and at the same time consulting the cunning folk and practicing the old pre-Christian magic.

Feminist historians have called the persecutions the "holocaust of women" and "the most hideous example of misogyny in European history." Estimates of the total number who were tortured and killed vary widely because of the difficulty of compiling enough evidence from that period. Anywhere from 100,000 to a million individuals were persecuted and killed, about 80 per cent of whom were women.

The Scientific Revolution brought about a "par-adigm shift" in Western attitudes toward nature. Nature came to be imaged and thought about as a vastly complex *machine*. Through the power of the rational mind humans were set apart from and over nature, and the human role became the dominat-ing one of wresting its secrets from it, conquering and exploiting it for human benefit. The advantages of the new attitude were obvious in terms of the widespread human benefits of the rapid expansion of scientific knowledge and the dramatic techno-logical revolution that began in the eighteenth cen-tury and is still going on. The liabilities we have only recently begun to acknowledge and deal with: the serious depletion of earth's resources; the human encroachment on more and more of the nat-ural environment; the destruction of thousands of animal species; global air and water pollution, including well-known phenomena such as acid rain, global warming and ozone depletion; the dan-gers of nuclear weapons, nuclear accident, and nuclear waste; overpopulation.

THE PHILOSOPHER OF THE SCIENTIFIC REVOLUTION

René Descartes was born on March 31, 1596 in the small French town of La Haye, France, situated in the rich province of Touraine, widely visited today for its magnificent châteaux and gardens. As an adolescent, he spent several years studying at the best Jesuit institution, the Royal College in La Flèche. Descartes writes about the education he received there in Part 1 of the *Discourse on Method*. By 1616, Descartes was enrolled at the University of Poitiers where he received his law degree two years later. In 1618, he embarked on a two-year career as a "gentleman soldier" that eventually took him north to Holland and then to Germany. The opening pages of Part 2 of the *Discourse* recount Descartes's thoughts while staying in his military camp in Ulm, Germany during the month of November, 1619. Descartes's first trip to Holland marked a turning point in his intellectual life. It was then that he met the mathematician and logician, Isaac Beeckman, whose work was to stimulate and redirect Descartes's interests toward mathematics and the new science. After dropping his short mil-itary career, Descartes returned to France, spend-ing most of his time in Paris with intermittent trips to other regions (Brittany) and to Italy and again Holland. The environment in Holland was much more intellectually tolerant than France, and Descartes moved there permanently in 1629.

Although Descartes never married, he conceived a child with a serving maid who bore a daughter, Francine, born in 1635. He seems to have provided support for mother and daughter, though his having fathered a child was never made public. Very little else is known about Descartes's relationship with them; however, he expressed feelings of apparent distress in a letter to a friend upon the death of his daughter at the age of five, saying that it had left him "with the greatest sorrow that he had ever experienced in his life." Other than this one affair, Descartes was never known to have maintained any other intimate relationships with women. By contrast, Descartes's intellectual relations with fellow thinkers across Europe were numerous and sometimes contentious. He remained very much a solitary individual, preferring written exchanges to face-to-face conversation. He guarded his ideas jealously and was known to accuse others of frequently misunderstanding and sometimes plagiarizing his theories. Despite the very cold, impersonal, and exacting style of most of his writing, Descartes revealed himself a man of strong emotions and convictions as his times dictated. Later in life, starting in 1643, Descartes kept up an active correspondence with a royal princess, Elizabeth of Bohemia, who herself was a gifted and well-read twenty-five-year-old woman with a keen interest in mathematics, physics, theology, and philosophy. Their letters reveal a mutually felt, deep friendship, if not altogether a platonic love for each other. While Descartes apparently went to great pains to avoid meeting with Elizabeth in person (for fear of exacerbating his affections for a woman well above his own station?), he dedicated his last work to her, *The Passions of the Soul* (published 1650), a treatise on the general relation between the mind and the body from moral and psychological as well as physiological perspectives. Having gained an international reputation for his work in mathematics and philosophy, in 1649 Descartes was invited by Queen Christina of Sweden to join her at court in Stockholm. He had been in Sweden less than a year when he succumbed to the harsh winters of Scandinavia and fell ill with pneumonia, dying in 1650 at the age of 54.

Descartes was deeply and creatively involved in the Scientific Revolution. The inventor of analytic geometry, he was also an experimental scientist who studied physiology (see the *Discourse*, Part 5) and wrote scientific treatises on meteorology and a theory of vision. As he promises in the title, *Discourse on the Method for Rightly Conducting One's Reason and for Seeking Truth in the Sciences*, in Parts 5 and 6 Descartes describes and illustrates his understanding of scientific method, which had considerable influence but was displaced by Newton's inductive understanding of science. In the *Discourse* Descartes sounds like Francis Bacon in his enthusiasm for science as giving humans the power to be "masters and possessors of nature."

The Scientific Revolution raised three philosophical issues in new ways. The first was the problem of appearance and reality. The new science challenged the common-sense realism of Aristotle and demonstrated—as in the case of Copernican astronomy—that we cannot rely uncritically on the evidence of our senses. This contributed to the centrality of skepticism in modern philosophy: How do we know when we have accurate knowledge of the world? How do we bridge the gap between the knowing mind (subject) and the external world (object)? The second issue was the status of the human soul (self, mind) and free will. The new science explained all natural phenomena in terms of causal laws and physical activity. Could not the mind and human choice also be explained as properties of matter? Another hallmark of modern philosophy has been this preoccupation with the nature of the human self. A third problem was the relationship between reason and revelation. The success of the new science seemed to show that reason was capable of understanding everything. The bitter conflict within Christianity and a general decline of its influence, along with the new science, raised questions about the authority of the Bible and the Church. Critical questioning of claims to revelation became central to eighteenth-century Enlightenment thought and has continued as an important theme of modern thought generally.

The *Discourse on Method*, which Descartes published in 1637, was—together with his other philosophical writings—an attempt to find solutions to these problems. (We call Descartes's ideas, and ideas based on them, *"Cartesian."* Thus people speak, for example, of the Cartesian theory of the relation between mind and body.) Descartes cast this writing in the form of an intellectual autobiography, describing how philosophical problems arose for him and how he tried to solve them. He also wrote the *Discourse* in French, to reach a wider audience (including women) than professional scholars.

Descartes's project involved rethinking the foundations of human knowledge. In Part 1 of the *Discourse* Descartes describes his education and the doubts he had about what he had learned. He believes that most people are roughly equal in their capacity to reason, and his approach is to rely on ordinary reason and direct experience. The belief that every normal person has the ability and the obligation to think for him- or herself became a central theme of Enlightenment thought.

In Part 2 Descartes describes his day in the "stove-heated room" in 1619, during the Thirty Years' War. Here, as a young man, he formulated his project for rethinking the foundations of knowledge. Although he does not indicate it in this account, this was a visionary experience in which the ideas came to him with the force of revelation. The following night he had dreams that seemed to convey the divine seal of approval to his project. Note Descartes's statement of the fourfold method he would use to guide his thinking, and see how he carries it out in succeeding chapters.

In Part 3 Descartes describes how he formulated a "provisional moral code" to guide his practical life while he was working on his project. Look carefully at the four principles or maxims in the moral code. Notice in the first maxim that Descartes does not intend to apply his method of radical doubt to the government and religion of his country. Later thinkers, influenced by Descartes's method, did not stop, as he did, with questioning theoretical knowledge, but also questioned the politics and religion of their day. Despite being accused of atheism for his philosophical writings, Descartes always considered himself a faithful Catholic, doing for the faith in the seventeenth century what Thomas Aquinas had done in the thirteenth. Descartes was also a man of circumspection and caution, as can be seen in his decision not to publish a book defending Copernican astronomy when he heard of the trial of Galileo. In examining the four maxims we can see the influence of Aristotle and of Stoicism.

Part 4 is the pivotal chapter of the *Discourse*. With his new method Descartes questioned whether there is anything that cannot possibly be doubted, anything that is not merely possible or probable but certain. He uses the method of *formal or methodological doubt*: using radical skepticism in order to overcome skepticism and attain certainty. (Using a skeptical method and arriving at skeptical conclusions are not the same thing. Descartes uses a skeptical method but comes to certain conclusions. By contrast, the eighteenth-century British philosopher David Hume uses a skeptical method and also comes to skeptical conclusions. Hence we consider him a skeptic.) Descartes provides a much more detailed account of his reasonings in his book *Meditations on First Philosophy*, which he published in 1641.

Having doubted everything he can conceivably doubt—even the truths of mathematics—Descartes hits bedrock: The one thing he cannot doubt is that he is doubting, which is a form of thinking. The proposition "I think, therefore I am" is his foundational truth, the certainty from which he will proceed to build up the edifice of knowledge. This is one of the most famous statements in philosophy, and it is called the *Cogito* after its Latin formulation: *Cogito ergo sum* (in the original French, *Je pense, donc je suis*). The "I" whose existence Descartes cannot doubt is the mind—purely a "being that thinks," not the body. When Descartes thinks about his basic proposition, he derives from it two criteria for determining whether something is true: absolute clarity and absolute distinctness.

From his own existence Descartes then proceeds to demonstrate the existence of God—twice. Remember that at this point the objective reality of the external world is still a matter of doubt.

1. If I can conceive of a perfect being, one attribute of a perfect being must be existence, because it is more perfect to exist than not to exist. So God must exist. Just as three angles are essential to a triangle so existence is essential to God.
2. I have an idea of perfection, but I know I am not perfect because I doubt. The cause of my idea of perfection can only be a perfect being. That perfect being, of course, is God. Therefore God exists. Since a perfect being is not a deceiver, I can trust in the reality of the physical world that I perceive with my senses.

In Parts 5 and 6 Descartes applies his method to gaining knowledge in the sciences. Examine carefully how he understands scientific knowledge. His understanding of how science works is *deductive*, and his model is mathematics. The deduction process involves deriving from general premises specific conclusions that are contained in the premises. From the nature of God and general natural laws we can deduce the nature of the universe, according to Descartes, but we need observation and experiment to determine the actual effects among the possible effects of various causes. Descartes illustrates his understanding of scientific method from the anatomy and physiology of the heart. This concept of scientific reasoning was challenged by Newton's *inductive* understanding of science as beginning with observation of or experiment on particular things and inferring generalized conclusions on that basis.

How are Descartes's methods and conclusions a response to the three issues posed by the Scientific Revolution? (1) Regarding the problem of appearance and reality, Descartes uses skepticism to overcome skepticism by uncovering "clear and distinct ideas" (his own existence as a thinking being and the existence of God) which he believes cannot be doubted and are therefore the foundations of all thought. (2) Descartes's answer to the problem of the human soul or self is what is called *Cartesian dualism*. Two absolutely different substances make up the universe: *res cogitans* or "thinking things"—minds—which are non-material, independent, free, and immortal; and *res extensa* or "extended things," physical objects (including the human body) which are material, composite, changing, perishable, and causally determined. Descartes uses the model of the machine to characterize the physical universe, a model that was to dominate all thinking about nature in the Enlightenment. Descartes speculated that the point at which mind and body interacted—where the physical and non-physical universes were synchronized—was the pineal gland (a cone-shaped structure in the brain whose precise function is still unknown). (3) Regarding the relation between revelation and reason, Descartes confidently believed that he had only confirmed and strengthened Catholic doctrine by his independent demonstrations of the independence, freedom, and immortality of the soul and of the existence of a supremely perfect Being.

Descartes became the source of what is called *Continental Rationalism*. Its exponents were all from the Continent of Europe: Descartes from France, Baruch Spinoza from Portugal and Holland, and Gottfried Leibniz from Germany. Central to Rationalism was Descartes's belief that the human mind contains *innate ideas* or "certain seeds of truth that are in our souls." All clear and distinct ideas are innate: the *Cogito*, God, the laws of thought such as the principle of identity ("A thing is what it is and not something else"), the idea of causality, mathematical and geometrical principles such as "the whole is equal to the sum of its parts," and the universal laws of nature. Our sense experience provides the occasions for the mind to call on its innate ideas to organize and understand experience. The theory of innate ideas has its ancient roots in Plato's theory that learning is recollection, but the Continental Rationalists reformulated it. They argued that the human mind or reason (hence "rationalism") is richly "furnished" and powerful in its ability to know itself, God, and nature. This means that for the Rationalist the ideal of knowledge is certainty.

Responding critically to the Continental Rationalists were the *British Empiricists*—John Locke in the seventeenth century and Bishop George Berkeley and David Hume in the eighteenth. (Newton was also an empiricist in his scientific writings.) They argued that there are no innate ideas. All knowledge is derived from experience ("empiricism" is from the Greek word meaning "experience"): from sense impressions, mental intuitions, and feeling states. The human mind is limited in the scope of its knowledge, and the ideal of knowledge is probability and not certainty.

Descartes is commonly called the "father of modern philosophy," because of his creative effort to rethink the problems of philosophy in a completely fresh way and "from the ground up," not assuming the truth of anything that had gone before. His philosophical legacy can be seen in the fact that much modern philosophy begins with individual human consciousness as the source of all experience and knowledge, and focuses on the problem of what humans can know of the world and how claims to knowledge can be justified. But Descartes's legacy is also important in the history of modern science, and he must be seen as an influential figure in the Scientific Revolution. He invented analytic geometry and made contributions to physics, optics, meteorology, and physiology.

A striking, and by no means incidental, aspect of Descartes's influence in his own time was the appeal of his philosophy to educated lay people (non-specialists in science and philosophy), and especially to women. He wrote certain of his major works, such as the *Discourse on Method*, in French, and translated or approved the translation of others from Latin into French, so that they would have a wider audience than simply the academic community. He insisted, as in the *Discourse*, that every normal person is capable of thinking things through as he did, because all human beings, regardless of sex or education, possess reason. Combined with his sharp distinction between the mind and the body and his identification of the essential person with the mind, this meant that women could think of themselves as in some sense equal despite the general belief in their physical inferiority to men. Descartes attracted a large following among educated women such as Princess Elizabeth and the "scientific ladies." They came to be called *Cartésiennes*—Cartesian women—and their motto was "The mind has no sex."

It is not hard to criticize Descartes's philosophical ideas and arguments, and criticisms began with his contemporaries. Locke and the other British Empiricists rejected the whole Cartesian model of the mind and how it knows, completely rejecting the concept of innate ideas. Descartes's belief that the *Cogito* reveals the mind as a thinking substance or entity has been standardly criticized as reflecting the scholastic heritage that he thought he was rejecting, with its description of the world in terms of substances: entities that endure through time and manifest themselves in various properties. (Strictly speaking, all one can legitimately conclude from the *Cogito* is that there is a "thinking" or mental process going on, not that it is an activity of a certain kind of underlying thing.) Related to this criticism is the near-universal rejection among philosophers today of any sort of mind-body dualism. Many in the seventeenth century and later rejected Descartes's arguments for the existence of God—not as illogical, but as having questionable or mistaken premises. Many of Descartes's scientific hypotheses have also been shown to be mistaken, such as his account of the functioning of the heart. And, as we have seen, his deductive model for understanding how scientific inquiry works, in which empirical observation and experiment play a subordinate role to innate ideas, was nevertheless displaced by Newton's inductive model, in which scientific investigation is entirely seen as a process of generalization on the basis of empirical investigations that results in hypotheses and theories.

Yet Descartes stands as one of the great pioneering thinkers of the modern era. The boldness and originality of his work stimulated and continues to stimulate the thought of many others working on the problems to which he addressed himself. We should remember, of course, that Descartes was among the earliest among seventeenth-century scientists after Galileo to discuss and argue for the Copernican theory of the universe. Important figures in modern philosophy, such as Immanuel Kant, Edmund Husserl, and Jean-Paul Sartre, all went back to Descartes's *Cogito* as the starting-point for their own investigations, and philosophers of language and of mind today continue to be indebted to the tradition of analysis he began.

QUESTIONS FOR STUDY AND DISCUSSION

1. What was Descartes's project, and what method did he adopt in pursuing it? Be specific about the stages and progression of the method. What was the connection between his project and the Scientific Revolution? Why is Descartes called the founder of modern philosophy?

2. Compare and contrast Descartes's philosophical method and conclusions with those of Plato and Aristotle. With which of the two ancient philosophers does Descartes seem to have the closer affinities, and why? Do you see any relationship between the answer to this question and Descartes's involvement in the Scientific Revolution?

3. Descartes "set the agenda" for subsequent philosophers, even those who disagreed with him. Describe the differences between *rationalism* and *empiricism* as the two dominant philosophical approaches Descartes influenced. Which approach did Descartes initiate, and which did Locke initiate? Which one came to prevail among French Enlightenment thinkers?

4. How did transformations of the political landscape of seventeenth-century Europe encourage

new ways of thinking? In what ways did the Scientific Revolution not contribute to the social and political progress of the age?

5. In what ways were women involved in the Scientific Revolution?

SUGGESTIONS FOR FURTHER READING

Alic, Margaret. *Hypatia's Heritage: A History of Women in Science from Antiquity through the Nineteenth Century*. Boston: Beacon Press, 1986.

Briggs, Robin. *The Scientific Revolution of the Seventeenth Century*. New York: Harper and Row, 1969.

Clarke, Desmond M. *Descartes: A Biography*. Cambridge University Press, 2006

Cohn, I. Bernard. *Revolution in Science*. Cambridge, MA and London, England: the Belknap Press of Harvard University, 1985.

Dekosky, Robert K. *Knowledge and Cosmos: Development and Decline of the Medieval Perspective*. Washington, D.C.: University Press of America, 1979.

Gaukroger, Stephen. Descartes: An *Intellectual Biography*. Oxford: Clarendon Press, 1995.

Hall, A.R. *The Scientific Revolution 1500-1800: The Formation of the Modern Scientific Attitude*. Boston: Beacon Press, 1956.

Kearney, Hugh. *Science and Change, 1500-1700*. New York: McGraw-Hill, 1971.

Merchant, Carolyn. *The Death of Nature: Women, Ecology, and the Scientific Revolution*. San Francisco: Harper & Row, 1980.

Robinson, Dave and Chris Garratt. *Introducing Descartes*. United Kingdom: Icon Books, 1998. This is an illustrated book and fun for beginners.

Rossi, Paolo. *Philosophy, Technology, and the Arts in the Early Modern Era*. Translated by Salvator Attanasio. New York: Harper and Row, 1970.

Sorell, Tom. *Descartes: A Very Short Introduction*. Oxford: Oxford University Press, 2000.

Spencer, Samia, ed. *French Women and the Age of Enlightenment*. Bloomington: Indiana University Press, 1985.

Westfall, Richard. *The Construction of Modern Science: Mechanisms and Mechanics*. New York: John Wiley & Sons, Inc., 1971.

Wightman, W. P. D. *Science and the Renaissance*. 2 vols. New York: Hafner, 1962.

CHAPTER TWO

JOHN LOCKE AND MODERN POLITICAL THOUGHT

Seventeenth-century ideas of natural rights and of government by consent are often held to have fueled the two great revolutionary movements of the eighteenth century, the American and the French Revolutions, which inaugurated the modern era in political and social thought and institutions. The belief that individual civil rights and representative, multi-branched government, can form part of a program for re-creating political authority were undoubtedly part of the background to what happened in Philadelphia in 1787 to 1791, when the framers of the U. S. Constitution embodied in that document the separation of powers, the federal system, and the Bill of Rights. These ideas flowed into the language of other documents following the establishment of the Constitution and are alive and active in the twenty-first century. The expression "human rights," however, has largely replaced "natural rights." A few examples of many in the past one hundred and fifty years are the *Declaration of Rights and Sentiments* of the first women's rights convention in 1848, the United Nations' *Universal Declaration of Human Rights* of 1948, and the many appeals to the language of human rights in the Eastern European revolutions of 1989. It matters greatly, therefore, exactly what the origins of these modern ideas are and that we can trace them back to their seventeenth-century roots. With an historical perspective, we can often appreciate the meanings of writers of the past in two ways: the meanings of what they wrote at the time, and the meanings that later ages read into them.

We will begin this enquiry, therefore, with the historic meaning of the ideas of John Locke (1632–1704) which address the situation in England during his lifetime. It was after his death that his seventeenth-century English ideas were used as if he had spoken to and for people at all times and everywhere.

Many modern constitutional historians have interpreted seventeenth-century English political history in terms of a stark contrast between monarchical absolutism and constitutionalism: that is, between the idea that the king was arbitrary and could do whatever he chose, and the idea that the king could only rule in conformity with fundamental law. More recent scholars have shown that this is a false antithesis. Most people at the time wanted a strong monarchy and a strong parliament together (they saw kings as absolute in their jurisdiction but not thereby arbitrary in their power), and England's "ancient constitution" had for centuries included both a monarchy and a parliament.

From the 1640s, however, some extremists did indeed side with one or the other alternative. Extreme royalists like Sir Robert Filmer (d. 1653) argued that kings were both absolute and arbitrary, and that this was good. Extreme parliamentarians agreed that "absolute" and "arbitrary" were the same, but repudiated monarchy in an attempt to establish a republic. Most people in the middle, who held that kings were absolute but not arbitrary, thought that monarchs were obliged to rule in accord with natural, that is, divine, law.

The English monarchy, as restored in 1660, healed this rift: it abandoned its earlier attempts to raise certain taxes without parliamentary approval. Another major source of conflict now arose, however: the question of religious toleration. Few people in the first century after the Reformation

Born in Germany, Godfrey Kneller moved to the Netherlands to study under Rembrandt before settling in England, where he became the leading portraitist of his day. Kneller served as court painter to four British monarchs, from Charles II to George I. This painting is one of several portraits of John Locke executed by Kneller. The celebrity of both the sitter and the artist were underscored by the popularity of the painting, which generated over a dozen different engraved versions. Sometimes printed by the hundreds, commercial engravings ensured widespread dissemination of a painting's original image.

Figure I-5   Godfrey Kneller, *John Locke, English Philosopher*, ca.1680–1704. Oil on canvas, 10 $^1/_4$" × 6 $^2/_3$" (26 × 17 cm). Oxford Science Archive, Oxford, Great Britain. Courtesy of Oxford Science Archive/HIP/Art Resource, NY.

thought religious toleration was a virtue: most claimed to have the correct answers in matters of religion, and thought they had a right and even a duty to impose those right answers on others. After his restoration to the throne in 1660, Charles II displayed a novel and worrying tendency: he preferred to settle the religious disputes of the age by the concession—as an act of royal prerogative—of religious toleration—even toleration of the feared Roman Catholics. The most virulent political slogan of the age was now to be "Popery and arbitrary power." Some feared, or said they feared, that Charles II (r. 1660–85) and James II (r. 1685–88) intended not toleration but an attempt to institute arbitrary rule through an alliance with international Roman Catholicism.

DIFFERING SOLUTIONS

How did seventeenth-century English thinkers respond to what was increasingly spoken of as "absolutism"? They reacted in very different ways. Thomas Hobbes (1588–1670) came to support absolutism on essentially secular and pragmatic grounds. He posited as the starting point of his analysis the "state of nature," existing before government, in order to deduce conclusions from what he claimed were the essential attributes of human nature. Hobbes held that people were unchangingly egoistic, and ruthlessly sought their individual advantage; a "state of nature" in which every one was free and equal because there was no government and law would be a state of war. Only a strong state could preserve civil peace among such individuals. Hobbes believed that his gloomy picture of human life without government was solidly based on what we can observe of human behavior generally, but he also had the England of his own day vividly in mind, wracked as it was by political and religious conflict and then torn apart by civil war.

We have witnessed civil wars in many places in the world in our own time—for example, in former Yugoslavia, Rwanda and Burundi, Afghanistan, the Sudan, and now Iraq. In such situations people do things they would never normally do, even savage and violent things. If one were to imagine order gradually breaking down completely, so that eventually anarchy occurred, and there was no place to escape from it, then it is possible to see how Hobbes reached his very pessimistic conclusion that a state of nature (that is, life without government) is like a war, a "war of all against all." For Hobbes, civil society, even under conditions that would seem to us oppressive or restrictive, was infinitely preferable to life in the state of nature, and the preservation of human life and the securing of peace were the two highest values.[1]

Other thinkers came to support the monarchy on religious grounds. The most authoritative political text in seventeenth-century England was the Bible, and many argued that it showed that God had instituted monarchy rather than any other form of government. In 1680 one such book, Sir Robert Filmer's *Patriarcha*, was published posthumously. It was untypically extreme in one way: it argued that subjects must obey even the unjust commands of their monarch and did not have the right, as taught by the Church of England, of "passive obedience" (our term for this is "civil disobedience"). But Filmer was useful for royalists, most of whom were members of the Church of England ("Anglicans"), because he was a firm monarchist as well as an ardent anti-Catholic. His book was published during the "Exclusion Crisis," a parliamentary crisis of 1679–83 caused by the attempt of the opposition in Parliament to bar James, Duke of York, from the succession to the throne on the grounds of his open Catholicism. The opposition failed, and James succeeded his brother Charles II as James II in 1685. Locke and his friends were terrified.

John Locke, at least in his early writings around 1660, also supported a strong monarchy as the only antidote to chaos, but he moved to the opposite end of the spectrum by the 1670s. We now know that his book *Two Treatises of Government* (although not published until 1690) was drafted during the Exclusion Crisis. It therefore focused on dynastic questions and said little about many of the other political questions that generally concern people and would

be raised in the Revolution of 1688. Locke's immediate aim was to find arguments to justify resistance to monarchs, and it has been suggested that he was involved in conspiracies to assassinate Charles and James (the failed "Rye House plot" of 1683). Although Charles survived attempted assassination, and James survived two failed rebellions soon after his accession in 1685, his opponents were unremitting in their hostility. James swiftly alienated his natural supporters, the Anglican royalists, by favoring his co-religionists the Catholics, and when a son was born to the Queen in 1688, thereby possibly providing a Catholic succession and a permanent alliance with France, his enemies had to act. William of Orange, Stadtholder of the United Provinces and a sworn enemy of Louis XIV, transported an army to England. The English did little to support James, whose power therefore collapsed; he fled to France, and William and his wife, Mary, eldest daughter of James II, became King and Queen. This coup of 1688–9 was soon known, by its admirers, as the "Glorious Revolution."

In the wake of the Revolution, the political landscape was transformed. Locke quickly adapted his *Two Treatises of Government* and published the book, with a preface praising William III. Read in the light of the Glorious Revolution, it could be interpreted not as the call for armed resistance (and even radical revolution) that it had been in 1683 but as a rationale for the moderate, constitutional monarchy that William claimed to have safeguarded. Indeed, William III's supporters, called the Whigs, argued that England's ancient constitution of mixed and limited monarchy had been restored (a debatable claim) and that the Stuarts had all along stood for arbitrary government, popery and tyranny (also debatable); but since the Whigs had won, so did their interpretation of events. Because Locke was now thought to be on the winning side, his book was interpreted in the light of

---

[1] It is important to know that the great majority of people in this time period were subsistence farmers whose only concern was to have enough food to eat, shelter, to see their children live to maturity, and hopefully get to heaven. Whether the ruler was an absolute monarch by inheritance or a constitutional monarch by election did not matter to them. They only wanted to live in peace. The "people" who debated the best form of government were an educated minority coming from the aristocracy or the middle class. They wanted the freedom to criticize the government and to change it if it were to their advantage.

the values that the new regime was claimed by its supporters to embody. Gradually, over decades, those values changed, and Locke was eventually held to be the champion or even the founding father of democracy, of mixed government, of liberalism, and of capitalism. We need to examine his text carefully if we are to see just how his ideas fed into later ones, or how later ages misread him for their own purposes.

FROM SCHOLAR TO REVOLUTIONARY

John Locke (1632–1704) came from the west of England, born in Wrington, Somerset, the son of a minor landowner. Locke's family were Puritans rather than Royalists, and his father served as a captain in the Parliamentary army during the Civil War. After graduating from Oxford University Locke became a Student (i.e., a Fellow) of Christ Church, Oxford's largest college. There he taught Greek and moral philosophy, turned to the study of medicine in order to avoid taking Holy Orders, and was eventually licensed as a physician. He was early exposed to the philosophy of Descartes and influenced by the new developments in science. Critical of Descartes's rationalism, in which the mind contains a number of "innate ideas" independently of experience, Locke developed what he considered to be a "common sense" empiricist approach in which all knowledge depends on sense experience. Thus he is often considered as the "father" of British empiricism, which in the seventeenth and eighteenth centuries was the main rival and alternative to the Continental rationalism associated with Descartes.

In 1665 Locke became physician and adviser to a member of the aristocracy, Lord Ashley, the first Earl of Shaftesbury. Shaftesbury was politically active as a prominent member of the Parliamentary opposition to the throne. In 1668 he became seriously ill from a liver ailment that had troubled him for twelve years. An excellent physician, Locke devised a silver and later a gold shunt to drain Shaftesbury's abscess. Shaftesbury's health completely recovered, and he wore the shunt the rest of his life. In 1672 Shaftesbury was appointed Lord Chancellor of England by Charles II, the highest office in the land under the king. From 1676–79 Locke was in France for reasons of health. He returned to the service of Lord Shaftesbury in 1679,

and wrote his *Two Treatises on Government* during the period 1679–83. (While there is some scholarly disagreement about exactly when Locke wrote the two treatises, one widely accepted view is that he wrote the *Second Treatise* first, between 1679 and 1681, and the *First Treatise* in 1683. He did not publish them until 1690, after the Glorious Revolution.) Locke followed Shaftesbury into exile in Holland following an unsuccessful plot to keep James, Duke of York, from succeeding to the throne as James II. Shaftesbury died in Amsterdam early in 1683, and Locke arrived there later in the year.

It was during his six years in Holland, a republic with a tradition of religious toleration, that Locke wrote his most important philosophical work, which was not published until after his return to England: his *Essay Concerning Human Understanding*, the book that established him as the founder of the British empiricist tradition in philosophy. While in Holland he also wrote *A Letter Concerning Toleration* (published in 1689), a pioneering essay on behalf of religious toleration, and *Some Thoughts Concerning Education* (published 1695), which revealed Locke's ideas on childhood and education.

Locke returned to England in the wake of the Glorious Revolution, and after the accession of William and Mary he published, although anonymously, his *Two Treatises of Government* in 1690. Some have seen in this book a call, too late, for a more radical revolution; others have seen it as an endorsement of William's rule. After his return Locke served with distinction as a commissioner of trade until 1700, and continued to write and publish philosophical works, including *The Reasonableness of Christianity* (1695). Locke never married, although his writings on fatherly power and the education of children are sometimes today treated as practical rather than academic texts. Locke died one of the most honored philosophers in Europe; yet only at his death did he acknowledge authorship of what is now his most famous work, *Two Treatises of Government*. Scholarly opinion differs on the influence of Locke in the first two centuries after his death, but in the twentieth century he acquired the reputation of being a chief founder of our modern ideas of human rights and a philosopher who provided the foundations of political and economic liberalism.

KEY THEMES IN THE *TWO TREATISES* OF GOVERNMENT

Locke's *Two Treatises of Government* was his most important book on politics. Its immediate purpose was to destroy the late Stuart monarchy in England. However, while addressing the political situation in late seventeenth-century England, Locke subtitled the *Second Treatise* "an essay concerning the true original, extent, and end of civil government," and many have interpreted it as a general theory of government. That is the way many enduring ideas arise: although a response to a particular situation of the author's time and place, they transcend that situation and achieve universality (or are considered as doing so).

Locke wrote both treatises as a reply to Robert Filmer, whose posthumously published book *Patriarcha* was an extreme and provocative defense of royal absolutism. The *First Treatise* is a detailed refutation of Filmer's arguments. Locke polemically misstated the essence of Filmer's views: "[Filmer's] system . . . is no more but this: *That all government is absolute monarchy*. And the ground he builds on is this: *That no man is born free*." In the *Second Treatise* Locke developed his own theory of government, arguing for just the opposite: that all humans are born free in the state of nature, and that therefore all legitimate government is limited in power. The *First Treatise* is difficult and detailed, but the shorter and more generalized *Second Treatise* is often thought to lay the theoretical foundations of modern ideas of human rights and representative democracy.

One basis of Locke's arguments in the *Second Treatise* is often taken to be his theory of human nature, which he set forth in his *Essay Concerning Human Understanding*. According to Locke, our behavior is propelled by our natural desires ("appetites") and aversions—generally speaking, by the desire for happiness and the avoidance of pain. Locke recognized the dominance of self-regarding or egoistic motives, which manifest themselves prominently in the desire for recognition, status, and possessions. But Locke also emphasized the inherent rationality of human beings: our natural ability to direct and control our behavior through knowledge and choice, and particularly to acknowledge and put into practice standards of morality. Others have argued that Locke's two books were inconsistent, for the *Essay Concerning Human Understanding* ignored the idea of natural law so important in the *Two Treatises*.

The state of nature. This famous phrase refers to *human existence without government*—that is, without any common political authority over people. This concept had roots in the late Middle Ages, but Locke developed the idea in what would become a powerfully influential way. He formulated a hypothesis about what human life would look like if stripped of all political institutions—what he called *civil society*—and imagined how people would behave and relate to one another without civil society, that is, in a *state of nature*. In this way, he believed, we can gain some understanding of the rationale for civil society, grounded as it is in human needs, relations, and reflections. While Locke often used the idea of the state of nature to help in understanding government in the abstract, he wrote in other passages as if there was originally a time when humans actually lived in that state. He also believed that there were isolated groups of people in his own time that lived in a state of nature (for example—and incorrectly—some Indian tribes in North America). In addition, he used the term to describe the relations that always exist between *different* civil societies, such as England and France, since different societies do not recognize any common political authority over them. Locke argued that in the state of nature humans are *free* (independent) and *equal*. What Locke meant by that is that in the state of nature there is no subordination or supremacy among individuals (equality), and no human authority over them (freedom). (In Locke's thinking all human beings, even those living in the state of nature, were under the authority of God, but here he was speaking only of *political* authority or government.) When Thomas Jefferson in the Declaration of Independence stated that "all men are created equal," he had in mind the Lockeian idea of equality in the state of nature.

The law of nature. According to Locke, the state of nature, even without society and government, is not the sheer anarchy it was for Hobbes. Whereas Hobbes characterized the state of nature *psychologically*, in terms of the individual's entirely

Constable gained renown for his revival of naturalistic landscape painting in the nineteenth century. Influenced by the agricultural vistas of his youth in southern England, Constable became known for his pastoral scenes of farming life, such as *The Hay Wain*, in which nature, buildings, and people at work blend harmoniously. By repeatedly picturing the land around his boyhood home, much of which he owned or was to inherit, Constable gained intimate knowledge of the property and demonstrated his understanding of the importance of stewardship. Somewhat fancifully, we might see in it a visualization of Locke's state of nature, in which people live in harmony with nature while transforming a portion of it into their own property by cultivating the land and producing what they need.

Figure I-6   John Constable, *The Hay Wain*, 1821. Oil on canvas, 4'3" × 6'2". National Gallery, London. Courtesy of Art Resource, NY.

egoistic powers and desires, Locke told his version of the "story" in terms of the inherently *moral* character of life in the state of nature. Even in this state, wrote Locke, there was a moral law governing human conduct: the *law of nature*. Here Locke departed dramatically from Hobbes. When Hobbes wrote of the "law of nature," he meant a purely prudential or practical rule that individuals adopt: not to do anything that will harm their own self-preservation. By contrast, when Locke wrote of the "law of nature," he stood in the tradition of natural law developed by Christian thinkers such

as Thomas Aquinas. Locke affirmed a universal moral law, with its source in God, of which all humans inherently have some knowledge as reasoning beings. In his interpretation of natural law Locke was influenced by the sixteenth-century Anglican theologian Richard Hooker, and Locke often quotes from Hooker in the *Second Treatise*. According to Locke, even in the state of nature individuals did not simply do anything they could to preserve their lives and possessions, as Hobbes would have it. Individuals are constrained in their behavior toward one another by natural moral principles. It is those principles—the law of nature—that in fact reveal what natural rights are.

Natural rights. Natural rights are *the rights that individual human beings would have in the state of nature.* These are rights a person has simply by being a member of the human race and therefore a rational and moral agent, *independently* of government. The idea of natural rights has an even older history than the idea of the state of nature. It grew out of the ancient theory of *natural law*, the view that there is a universal, objective moral law that all humans know through their natural capacity to reason. This idea was developed by the Stoic philosophers, incorporated by early Catholic Christianity, and through Thomas Aquinas in the Middle Ages became an influential way of thinking about ethics and politics down to our own day. The idea of natural law affirmed that all human beings, just by virtue of being rational animals, and quite apart from the particular laws, customs, and morals of the societies they happen to live in, know universal moral principles such as not harming or murdering others, and recognize (even if they often do not follow) their obligation to follow those principles.

But the idea of natural *rights* of individuals was only implicit in natural law theory until Locke made it the very center of his theory of government. In the medieval world, rights were typically seen as connected with the "estate" to which an individual belonged, whether clergy, aristocracy, or commoners. Each estate had its own set of rights and its own set of obligations. But Locke, and later natural rights thinkers such as Jean-Jacques Rousseau, derived from their hypotheses of the state of nature ideas about what inherent or natural rights all individuals, equally and without exception, would have in the state of nature. The theory of natural rights, as famously expressed in the American Declaration of Independence in terms of "life, liberty, and the pursuit of happiness," is one of the most powerful political ideas of the modern world.

Having described the state of nature as regulated by the law of nature, Locke then enumerated the main moral principles that comprise the law of nature: *not harming, robbing, subjecting, enslaving, or killing other human beings.* Such violations of others are, said Locke, violations of people's *natural rights*

of *life*, *liberty*, and *possessions*. It's important to note that in writing the *Declaration of Independence*, Jefferson saw his phrase "life, liberty, and the pursuit of happiness" as simply reiterating Locke's original triad of rights. Not only in Locke's writings and the eighteenth-century Enlightenment thought that influenced Jefferson, but also in the New England Puritan tradition that influenced many of those who signed the *Declaration*, "happiness" was equated with "property." That was because these traditions did not understand a person's labor and possessions in a purely economic way. The individual's right to "pursue happiness" had as its essential core the right to his or her own labor and possessions, but Jefferson's usage embraced all the many and varied ways—not only economic but also social, aesthetic, intellectual, and spiritual—in which individuals pursue happiness.

Locke regarded rights as *moral claims* each person has on other persons, which entail *moral obligations* on the part of other persons. Locke's interpretation of rights as claims on others involving obligations on their part became one source of the dominant understanding of rights in modern political thought. As I naturally want to preserve my life, liberty, and possessions, so I recognize that I am obligated not to kill or harm you, enslave you to my will, or deprive you of your possessions. I know these things—which are the law of nature—because I have the capacity to reason. In fact, at one point Locke simply refers to the law of nature as "reason."

Locke understood the law of nature as both a rationally discoverable fact about human beings and the expression of the will of God. Throughout the *Second Treatise* he appealed to both reason and revelation. As a philosopher Locke believed that his arguments stood on their own on the basis of observation and sound reasoning. As a reflective Christian, like Thomas Aquinas, he believed that the Bible contained divine confirmation of many things we know independently through reason.

The state of war. Locke's characterization of the state of war was directly related to his portrayal of the state of nature as governed by the law of nature. Hobbes defined war not only as actual conflict but also as the predisposition to conflict. Given his picture of the state of nature as egoistic individuals aggressively doing whatever they can to preserve and enhance their lives, Hobbes simply identified the state of nature with a state of war, the "war of all against all." By contrast, Locke defined war as actual "enmity and destruction," in which one person tries to rob another person of his or her liberty, to dominate and enslave him or her. Since the state of nature was characterized not simply by egoistic self-aggrandizement but by rational recognition of the law of nature, which morally constrained individuals to recognize both rights and duties, it followed that the state of nature was not simply a state of war but also of peace and cooperation. The problem with the state of nature, said Locke, is that in cases of war—of aggression by one or more persons against others—every individual, whether aggressor or victim, was his own judge, jury, and punisher. Since humans were apt to be self-regarding, this meant that each person's natural rights were inadequately protected in the state of nature.

The meanings of property. "Property" is a key term in Locke's political philosophy. In reading Locke it is crucial to understand that he used the term in two senses, a broad and a narrow one, and the reader has to figure out which meaning from the context. The word "property" is from the Latin word *proprium*, which means "what is one's own." In the *broad* sense "property" includes anything that is one's own, including one's life and liberty, and Locke usually used the word that way. In this broad sense all natural rights—life, liberty, and possessions—are property rights. In the *Second Treatise* Locke argued that the preservation of property is the main reason humans leave the state of nature and form organized societies with governments. He explicitly stated that under "property" he includes people's "lives, liberties, and estates [possessions]."

In a long chapter of the *Second Treatise* entitled "Of Property," (V) however, Locke used the term "property" in the *narrow* sense in which we usually use it: to refer only to one of the natural rights, the right of "possessions" or "estates"—what we call "private property." Locke said that God originally gave the goods of the earth to humans in common; in other words, there were no private possessions. But in the state of nature individuals changed the original situation by appropriating land by their labor—by cultivating it and making it productive. Since it is essential to the preservation and maintenance of an individuals' life and liberty, this appropriation of possessions through one's own work (e.g., farming a piece of land) was a natural right.

Initially the right to property in the narrow sense was strictly *limited*: the individual had a right only to what he or she could use before it spoiled, not to unlimited acquisition. Historically the introduction of *money* then changed everything. Money is a non-perishable medium of exchange that replaced direct bartering of goods and resolved the problem of spoilage. The introduction of money, Locke argued, meant that the right to private property through "mixing" one's own labor (or, he added, the labor of others one hires) with what occurs in nature now became an *unlimited* right of acquisition. This produced the great inequalities of wealth with which we are familiar. But because human ingenuity and labor have greatly improved human life for everyone from what it was originally in the state of nature, even the poor are better off than people generally were before the introduction of money, and those who acquire wealth through farming or manufacturing are society's benefactors.

The social compact and the nature of government. The idea that government is based on a social contract goes back to the argument of some medieval political thinkers that governments, including monarchies, ultimately rest upon the consent of the governed. Locke preferred the term "compact," which signified the creation of a legal trust, rather than "contract," which implied that both parties (and so perhaps a monarch) would receive benefits from it. Although Locke is today often seen as a "contract theorist," his term "compact" did not imply short-term, easily revocable agreements; once civil society was formed, Locke's rationales for its social institutions were more often drawn from natural law than from the device of contract.

In the thought of Locke, the *social compact* is *an agreement by a group of people to leave the state of nature and live together in civil society for greater security and peace.* That compact is based upon the mutual *consent* of persons living independently in the state of nature to submit themselves to a common political authority. As we have seen, Locke argued that the main reason people leave the state of nature and create "civil society" is to preserve their property, that is, their life, liberty, and possessions. In the state of nature people were without established law and without judges to adjudicate disputes on the basis of law, and therefore lacked the power to enforce judicial decisions. That meant, given human tendencies to selfishness and injustice, that individuals' rights—their *proprium*—were never secure. The formation of civil society was designed to correct these deficiencies.

In the state of nature every individual had (1) the right to do whatever one thought was necessary for one's own preservation and that of others, within the constraints of the law of nature; and (2) the right to punish crimes committed against the law of nature—that is, against one's own or other people's natural rights. In making a social compact a group of people agreed to transfer these powers from individuals to the community, thus creating *civil society*. But they relinquished the individual right to judge in their own cause precisely for the sake of preserving their natural rights: as Locke wrote, "for their comfortable, safe, and peaceable living amongst one another, in a *secure enjoyment of their properties*, and a greater security against any that are not of it." Or as Locke famously stated it, the "chief end" or purpose of government was the *preservation of property* in the broad sense, that is, the preservation of the natural rights to life, liberty, and estate of its citizens.

Each person must voluntarily consent to the compact, but Locke assumed that consent may be implicit as well as explicit. Sovereignty or authority ultimately lies with those consenting. (This is the idea, enshrined in the Declaration of Independence, that governments rest upon "the consent of the governed.") They agree to be governed and bound by the will of the majority, since for practical reasons unanimous agreement on all the decisions necessary to a civil society is impossible. The government created in this way, consisting of a *legislative* and an *executive* body, is the agent of the people's sovereignty, and looked to as the preserver of their rights.

Thus Locke argued that legitimate government was *limited in its powers* and *functions on behalf of* the members of the community. It may be that he defined things in this way in order to argue that absolute monarchy was not a legitimate form of government at all. Locke formally conceded that his analysis of political authority as ultimately lying with the people was compatible with any of the traditional three types of government—monarchy, oligarchy, or democracy. Yet he believed that absolute monarchy, in which all political power is placed in one person's hands, inevitably produced tyranny and argued instead for a constitution in which the "executive" was checked by the "legislative."

Locke considered the supreme power in the state to be the legislative power, since the making of laws directed to the public good was the fundamental task of government. The executive power carried out and enforced the laws, a role which included the prerogative of making decisions that mitigate or modify the application of the laws in specific circumstances. If either the legislative or the executive power violated the limited authority they possessed in trust to the people, it forfeited the people's obligations to be bound by his decisions and might be resisted and replaced. Yet Locke said little about when or how a *legitimate* government might forfeit that trust.

The right of resistance. The primary purpose of the *Second Treatise* was to define the "right of resistance," which Locke himself called the right of "rebellion." Jefferson and others who contributed to the Declaration of Independence appealed to this right (which they found not only in Locke but also in other sources) in presenting their reasons for breaking their allegiance to the British crown. Locke believed that the events of his own time had dramatically demonstrated that tyranny was the worst thing that could befall civil societies. When a monarch claimed absolute power, he violated everything a legitimate government exists to do: to exercise limited power on behalf of the people and in preservation of their rights under natural law. Locke viewed absolute monarchy, as for example the rule of Louis XIV in France or Charles II in England, as an illegitimate form of government. Contrary to Hobbes, who argued that any state (even a tyranny) was legitimate and was preferable to the state of nature, and to Filmer, who argued that monarchy was the form of government preferred by God, Locke thought all absolute monarchies illegitimate. In a clear case of tyranny, the people have the right of rebellion.

Locke claimed that people generally would put up with a great deal before they resorted to revolt. For him, the fact of rebellion showed that the people had suffered the most extreme provocation. The people were the only judges of when resistance was justified. In writing of legitimate governments, he recognized that the executive power needed strong authority and must be allowed latitude in governing, and that the legislative body must be granted the right, after due discussion, to formulate laws in accordance with the majority of its members' perceptions of the public good. Only the most extreme circumstances, and the failure of all other means available within the social compact, justified rebellion. Yet this he envisaged in his writing, and may have tried himself to bring about in the reign of Charles II.

Grounds for rebellion, argued Locke, are constituted by any acts by which the monarch puts himself into a state of war against the people he is supposed to defend. He would thereby violate the trust reposed in him to preserve people's rights and to be limited by natural law. Rebellion would be justified when a monarch put his arbitrary will above the law or prevented the legislative body from performing its legitimate functions, as Charles II had done with Parliament. Other circumstances justifying rebellion included the monarch's allowing the people to be made subject to a foreign power, or neglecting or abandoning his responsibilities. All these generalized points were coded references to what Charles II, according to Locke's patron Shaftesbury, had actually done.

For Locke the right of rebellion was the canceling of all obligation on the part of the citizens. Locke placed the exercise of the right of rebellion in the hands of the people (though whether this meant individuals, a majority, or "the people" collectively is still debated). Since in rebellion the parties at odds are in a state of war with each other, the question arises as to who can adjudicate between them. Here Locke used the notion of an "appeal to Heaven." By this he meant that only God can ultimately judge between an aggrieved citizenry and a sovereign perceived as unjust: there is no higher earthly authority to which either side can appeal in pleading its cause. Living in an age of civil wars, he must have meant such an appeal to be decided by armed conflict, with God determining the victor.

When rebellion occurred, civil society was dissolved; though scholarly opinion differs on whether, in Locke's theory, people then returned to the state of nature or to some intermediate stage of community. In either case, when sovereignty reverted to the people, the people had the right to create new forms of government. Some commentators have seen in Locke at this point a radical individualism that revealed anarchist elements in his thought; others have seen him as the architect of stable, limited government and the separation of powers.

According to some interpreters, from Locke and his contemporaries came three ideas that have had a major influence on modern political thought and action: the *state of nature*, the *natural rights* of individuals, and the *social contract*. These ideas are now familiar to us from political thought since Locke's day. We should consider them carefully, however. Are our terms identical with Locke's? How were they employed by Locke? Were there any inconsistencies between them? To what extent are they still really accepted in today's world?

QUESTIONS FOR STUDY AND DISCUSSION

1. Describe the difference between absolute and constitutional monarchy. What were the circumstances that led to the establishment of constitutional monarchy in England?

2. What is the idea of the state of nature, and how was it useful to Locke in analyzing the nature of government? Is the state-of-nature hypothesis useful today?

3. What, according to Locke, were natural rights? Cite some historic examples of the practical political implementation of the idea of natural rights, and suggest why it has been a powerful idea.

4. What were the broader and the narrower meanings of "property" in Locke's *Second Treatise*? How did he characterize the rise and development of property in the narrower sense?

5. How did Locke understand the nature and function of government, in the light of natural rights and the social compact?

6. What was the "right of resistance," and how did Locke explain and justify it? Do we enjoy such a right today?

7. The American Declaration of Independence of 1776 is often said to be a "Lockeian" document. How did the American colonists differ from Locke in their interpretation of the best kind of government?

8. What evidence would you use to argue that the U.S. Constitution, including the Bill of Rights, was inspired by Lockeian values?

SUGGESTIONS FOR FURTHER READING

Locke's key text is *Two Treatises of Government* (1690). The essential modern edition is edited by Peter Laslett (Cambridge University Press, 1960, 1988). It has a valuable introduction, and Laslett's editorial work is the starting point for modern Locke scholarship.

Important but advanced monographs on Locke include:

Ashcraft, Richard. *Revolutionary Politics and Locke's 'Two Treatises of Government.'* Princeton University Press, 1986.

Dunn, John, *The Political Thought of John Locke.* Cambridge University Press, 1969.

Marshall, John. *John Locke: Resistance, Revolution and Responsibility.* Cambridge University Press, 1994.

Useful short summaries include:

Chappell, V. ed. *The Cambridge Companion to Locke.* Cambridge University Press, 1994.

Dunn, John. *Locke.* Oxford University Press, 1984.

Spellman, W. M. *John Locke.* Palgrave Macmillan, 1997.

For background on seventeenth-century political thought, see:

Burgess, Glenn. *Absolute Monarchy and the Stuart Constitution.* Yale University Press, 1996.

Burns, J. H. ed. *The Cambridge History of Political Thought, 1450–1700.* Cambridge University Press, 1991.

Schochet, Gordon. *Patriarchalism in Political Thought.* Oxford University Press, 1975.

For introductions to seventeenth-century England, see:

Coward, Barry. *The Stuart Age: England, 1603–1714.* Longman, 1980.

Kenyon, J. P. *Stuart England.* Penguin, 1978.

Morrill, John, ed. *The Oxford Illustrated History of Tudor and Stuart Britain.* Oxford University Press, 1996.

SECTION TWO

THE EIGHTEENTH CENTURY
AND THE BIRTH OF THE MODERN ERA

1703 Founding of St. Petersburg

       1713 Treaty of Utrecht

1739 Wesley founds Methodist Church

       1753 Linnaeus publishes system of plant classification

1755 Jean-Jacques Rousseau publishes *Discourse on Inequality*

       1756 Seven Years' War begins

1759 Voltaire writes *Candide*

       1762 Mozart performs (age six)
            Catherine the Great ascends the Russian throne

1769 Invention of the steam engine

       1773 Boston Tea Party

1775 American War of Independence begins

       1783 First hot-air balloon flight

1789 French Revolution begins
George Washington is elected President of United States

       1790 Metric system is devised

1792 Louis XVI goes to the guillotine

       1798 Napoleon invades Egypt

THE EIGHTEENTH CENTURY AND THE BIRTH OF THE MODERN ERA

In many ways the eighteenth century was a time of recovery and renewal. After the expensive and devastating wars of the seventeenth century, the eighteenth century was relatively peaceful. The religious hatreds that so dominated the previous one hundred and fifty years of European history were held in check in the eighteenth century and the "balance of power" achieved at the end of Louis XIV's reign helped to prevent domination by any one state. Conflicts that did occur between the great European powers (France, Britain, Austria, and Prussia) would take place on the geographic fringes of the West: in the New World colonies and on the eastern periphery.

The population decline of the previous century was also reversed thanks in large measure to the restoration of law and order. Improved agricultural methods allowed for greater food yields which in turn led to a decrease in famine and disease, particularly plague. As a result, by the first half of the eighteenth century, the population of the West had increased twenty percent. Cities grew at an even more rapid pace. From 1600 to 1750 the population of London tripled while Paris doubled.

The eighteenth century was also a time of general economic prosperity based on agricultural growth, a growing maritime economy tied to colonial trade, and the birth of new industry. Leading the way was overseas trade and commerce as a web of trading routes fanned out from Europe and expanded over the globe. Exotic and luxury products like sugar, tobacco, coffee, chocolate, oranges, indigo, and spices became commonplace in Europe over the course of the century due to ever-expanding networks of trade.

The century also witnessed remarkable cultural and intellectual transformations. The eighteenth-century movement known as the Enlightenment provided a growing literate public with new ideas based on individual rights, religious toleration, and the essential goodness of human nature. The Enlightenment also provided the public with a new vocabulary with which to express those new ideas. By 1750 this new "enlightened" public, based in nontraditional institutions such as coffee houses and salons, became key players in the political culture of the West.

The eighteenth century was brought to a close with two major revolutions that would bring constitutional republics to the West. Britain's North American colonies declared independence in 1776, while in 1789 the French people dissolved their thousand-year-old monarchy. The two revolutions represented a coming to power of the principles of Enlightenment and signaled the birth of the modern era.

ENLIGHTENMENT

The Enlightenment was the dominant intellectual and cultural movement of the eighteenth century. It constituted a period in which Western humanity, through a newly found faith in the powers of human reason, dared to question and shake off the authorities—philosophical, political, and religious—that had governed its development since the Middle Ages. Like the Renaissance of the fifteenth and sixteenth centuries, the Enlightenment was a period of renewed humanism, a concentrated striving on the part of men and women to analyze, understand, and improve both the world about them and their potential as human beings living on this earth. In

The salon played a vital role in the dissemination of Enlightenment thought. The term salon, a French word meaning "living room," came to denote a regularly convened gathering of people who discussed, debated, and listened to lectures on ideas of philosophy, science, literature, and art. In art, the term "salon-style hanging" is used to describe the exhibition format seen here, with paintings stacked from floor to ceiling. The hostess of the evening, Madame Geoffrin, is on the right, facing the viewer. The gathering's focus on Enlightenment philosophy is underscored by the bust of Voltaire, at center, as well the presence of Rousseau, fifth person on the left from the bust, and behind him, Raynal.

Figure II-1   Anicet-Charles Lemonnier, *In the Salon of Madame Geoffrin in 1755,* 1812. Oil on canvas. (62.5 × 96 cm). Musée des Beaux-Arts, Rouen, France. Courtesy of Erich Lessing/Art Resource, NY.

contrast to the Renaissance thinkers and movers, however, the major figures of the Enlightenment enjoyed a certainty in their approach to changing the world. They were convinced that the methods for understanding nature developed by the Scientific Revolution of the seventeenth century would permit them to arrive at a total comprehension of the physical universe and the workings of the human mind. Never before or afterwards in the history of Western civilization has there been so intense a faith in the power of reason to lead to the betterment of human life, both individual and social.

By the last third of the eighteenth century, the Enlightenment had become international in scope: a general Western phenomenon. In many ways we can see the Enlightenment as a reaction against monarchical absolutism. Therefore, just as absolutism was most pronounced in France, so too was France (and more specifically Paris) the center of the enlightened world in the eighteenth century.

The subject of Wright's painting epitomizes the Age of Reason: a philosopher-scholar uses a special model (called an orrery) to demonstrate a scientific theory of the universe. The awed children and attentive adults are captivated by the wonders of scientific knowledge. The lamp, which represents the sun, provides dramatic lighting, heightening the anticipation and excitement of the event.

Figure II-2 Joseph Wright, *A Philosopher Giving a Lecture at the Orrery (in which a lamp is put in place of the sun),* 1763–65. Oil on canvas, 58 × 80". Derby Museums and Art Gallery, Derby, England. Courtesy of Giraudon/Art Resource, NY.

The leading thinkers of the Enlightenment were called Men of Letters (though women did participate in the Enlightenment) or *philosophes*. *Philosophe* is a French word meaning "philosopher," though eighteenth-century French *philosophes* differed from traditional philosophers in important ways. The *philosophes* of the Enlightenment were not interested in abstract ideas. They did not contemplate the nature of virtue or justice. Rather, ideas interested the *philosophes* only in their transformative powers: the power of ideas to change society, politics, and culture.

The *philosophes'* primary weapon was criticism. For them, everything in eighteenth-century society ought to be subjected to criticism: all institutions, traditions, laws. Denis Diderot, one of the leading French *philosophes*, wrote, "we will criticize senseless laws until they are reformed." Immanuel Kant, a German *philosophe,* echoed that sentiment when he wrote in 1781, "our age is an age of criticism and to criticism everything must submit." This spirit of criticism was utterly new. Under monarchical absolutism there was no right to criticize and no freedom of speech. The newspaper press was heavily censored and there was no freedom of association. The king, not just his person but his policies, was supposed to be beyond criticism. Therefore, the *philosophes* were engaged in a new and dangerous project.

Today, the Enlightenment is significant because it has helped to shape and define the modern world. The Enlightenment not only helped influence the American and French revolutions, but those two nations are often considered to be experiments in Enlightenment. Further, the ideas of the Enlightenment are generally regarded as necessary for the formation of capitalism and democracy in the west.

France. Louis XIV was succeeded by his five-year-old great-grandson Louis XV (r. 1715–74). The young king's uncle ruled as regent until Louis reached the age of majority. During the regency we see a reemergence of the nobility and their traditional institutions like the *parlements* that Louis XIV had so successfully managed to stifle. The Regent gave back power to nobles as a way to end their resentment that had been building at least since the Fronde and more likely since the end of the Wars of Religion. Newly empowered nobility became a fact of political life in France during the eighteenth century. While the French monarchy was still absolutist and still reigned by "divine right," neither Louis XV nor Louis XVI were as skillful and adept practitioners of absolutism as was the Sun King.

Still, there was relative peace in France until the mid-century. That was when Louis XV's most important and influential minister, as well as his tutor, the Cardinal Fleury, died. In an attempt to emulate the reign of his great-grandfather, Louis XV decided that he could rule without a primary minister. This turned out to be a major mistake. Louis XV was not as competent as the Sun King nor was he as interested in the daily minutiae of governing. Louis XV was more interested in hunting, court frivolity, and his mistresses. As a result, the long period of peace and stability that marked the first decades of the eighteenth century gave way to a series of ill-fated foreign adventures. First was the War of Austrian Succession (1740–1748) in which the French fought a costly but inconclusive war against Britain and Austria. Then came the Seven Years' War (1756–63), which resulted in a decisive military and economic defeat for the French at the hands of their arch-nemesis, the British.

Louis XV also attempted to rule as his predecessor did by reclaiming authority from the nobility. This too proved to be an ill-fated move. The king rightly recognized that the parlements, particularly the Parlement of Paris, were a barrier to monarchical power. Therefore, in 1771, the king had his minister Maupeou disband them. Magistrates of the parlements labeled the king's actions as despotic and appealed to the tribunal of public opinion—that is, France's growing literate, elite public. Louis XV died during the crisis but one the first acts of the new king—the twenty-nine year old Louis XVI (r. 1774–93)—was to restore the parlements and dismiss Maupeou. Thus, Louis XVI tacitly acknowledged the growing power of public opinion in French political life.

In addition to resurgent nobility, both Louis XV and his successor were plagued by massive financial difficulties throughout the eighteenth century. The cost of France's wars, combined with the high price of maintaining the sumptuous lifestyles of the kings at Versailles, brought the nation to the brink of bankruptcy. Ordinarily, the monarchy would simply raise taxes in order to increase governmental revenues. Indeed, both monarchs attempted just that. However, by right and tradition neither the clergy nor the nobility paid much in the way of taxes. Therefore, the tax burden fell nearly exclusively on the Third Estate.[1] Various attempts to reform the tax system—that is, to get the church and nobility to pay more in taxes—failed. So too did attempts to modernize the French economy. In 1776, for example, Louis XVI's minister Turgot attempted to abolish the guild system and liberalize the grain trade within France. Both efforts failed. That same year, France supported the American colonies in their revolt against England. While the colonists, and by extension the French, were ultimately successful, this "victory" only served to further cripple French finances. In the years leading up to the French Revolution of 1789 Louis XVI was left weak and bankrupt.

---

[1]The Third Estate comprised about ninety-five percent of the French population. In the countryside it included farmers. In the cities it included merchants, doctors, lawyers, shopkeepers and artisans.

Britain. In the eighteenth century England built upon its tradition of constitutional rule. Throughout the course of the century, the role of Parliament, particularly the House of Commons, expanded and political parties emerged. In 1707 the Act of Union united the English and Scottish parliaments into one, creating the United Kingdom of Great Britain.

In 1714 the Elector of Hanover—a Germanic territory—succeeded Queen Anne as ruler of the United Kingdom. This led to a minor uprising by the supporters of the Catholic Stuart dynasty. These supporters saw the Stuart James III as the legitimate heir to the throne. The uprising, beginning in Scotland and spreading no further, was quickly put down. Hunger for Stuart rule among some would not be quenched so easily, however. Another Stuart power grab came in 1745 when Charles Edward Stuart, or "bonnie Prince Charlie," arrived in Scotland from France, raised a small army composed of supporters and Scotsmen, marched into England where he found little support and returned to Scotland and was finally defeated a year later. This ensured that the House of Hanover would reign throughout the eighteenth century. Indeed, the Hanover dynasty, renamed the House of Windsor during World War I to distance themselves from their German ancestry, still reigns in Britain to this day. The first two Hanoverian monarchs, George I (r. 1714–27) and George II (r. 1727–60), were unremarkable, spoke little English, and spent long periods of time in Germany.

The best known and most important leader during the first half of the eighteenth century was neither of the Hanoverian kings but Robert Walpole, the first prime minister of the nation (though the official title was not created until later). Walpole, who led the government in Parliament from 1721 to 1742, was a consummate politician, able to effectively deal with both King and Parliament, while keeping the landed gentry and merchants happy. During his tenure the country experienced political stability and established the important tradition that the leader of the ruling party in Parliament guides legislation. He also played a significant role in defusing religious conflicts, allowing Catholics to serve in government (despite a law requiring all office holders to be members of the Anglican Church). Thus by the middle of the eighteenth-century Britain had become a relatively free and open society with a vibrant civil society and some degree of political representation.

In the second half of the eighteenth century Britain became a major military might, thanks in large part to its great navy. During the Seven Years' War England defeated France and was able to greatly extend its territorial holdings in North America and the Caribbean. This expansion in the New World was largely snuffed out, however, by the colonists' War of American Independence in 1776. Despite that significant set-back, the British Empire was the world's largest until well into the twentieth century.

Russia and Prussia. Both of these countries became dominant European powers in the eighteenth century. Both were ruled by a form of government historians call "Enlightened Despotism." The enlightened despots were monarchs who embraced seemingly contradictory impulses: unlimited authority to govern combined with the reforming zeal of the Enlightenment. The two monarchs most commonly referred to as enlightened despots were Catherine the Great of Russia and Frederick the Great of Prussia.

The first Russian tsar of the eighteenth century was Peter I (r. 1689–1725). Peter, called the Great by his people, helped to modernize and Westernize Russia. That is, in short, he believed Russia ought to become more like Europe. While in power, Peter not only emulated the political system of Western absolutists but built the navy and improved the quality of Russian education, particularly in the area of technical knowledge. He ordered the translation of classical Western novels and plays into Russian and founded the nation's first newspaper. He also encouraged the Russian nobility to adopt European manners, wear Western clothing, and speak French (the language of European diplomacy).

While Enlightened despots did embrace some of the modernizing impulses of the *philosophes*, we ought not discount their brutality. Peter raised a massive army and forcibly conscripted Russians to serve, often using torture and execution to achieve his ends. Ultimately, his actions, whether enlightened or not, led Russia to becoming one of the great powers in the eighteenth century, beginning with its defeat of Sweden in the Great Northern War in 1709, which made Russia the dominant power in the Baltic.

Catherine II of Russia (r. 1762–96) was also called the Great and was perhaps the best known enlightened absolutist. Born the daughter of a minor German prince, Catherine married the future tsar Peter III in 1745. In 1762 she helped to lead a palace coup against her husband and when he was killed she became Empress of Russia.

Once in power, Catherine seemed to have a genuine desire to improve the lives of the Russian people. She was open to the new ideas of the Enlightenment, and corresponded with Voltaire and Diderot, the leading French *philosophes*. In practice this meant abolishing some of the nastier practices of the Russian crown, such as torture of recalcitrant nobles, but in the end she refused to liberate the serfs.

Like Peter the Great, Catherine presided over a remarkable growth of Russian power on the world stage. She continued her predecessor's drive eastward by aligning with Prussia in 1772 against Poland. Between Russia and Prussia the two nations partitioned Poland so that the country disappeared from European maps.

In Prussia, Frederick the Great (r. 1740–86) was also considered to be an enlightened despot. Like Catherine in Russia, Frederick was an admirer of the *philosophes*, engaged in a long correspondence with, and played host to, Voltaire. During his reign Frederick imposed some reforms on the Prussian social and educational systems. He opened some careers to men of talent rather than solely to the Prussian nobility. He also streamlined the economy while undertaking educational and judicial reforms. Perhaps even more so than Catherine, Frederick saw his position as absolute ruler as an opportunity to make Prussia a more rational and therefore a more moral state.

Very much like Catherine, and Peter as well, Frederick took his first job to be strengthening his army and acquiring more territory. "The fundamental rule of governments," Frederick wrote, "is the principle of extending their territories." The War of Austrian Succession and the Seven Years' War offered him just that opportunity.

WAR OF AUSTRIAN SUCCESSION (1740–48)

In 1740 the Holy Roman Emperor and leader of Austria, Charles VI, died without a male heir. His twenty-three year old daughter Maria Theresa (r. 1740–80) assumed the leadership of the Habsburg family, becoming Archduchess of Austria and Queen of Hungary. As a woman, however, she could not assume the throne of the Holy Roman Empire. This lack of succession, plus the fact that she was a woman, created the appearance of weakness and only whetted the appetites of Frederick the Great of Prussia and Louis XV of France. Frederick saw an opportunity for expansion while Louis could not pass up a chance to humiliate the Habsburgs. The war began when Frederick invaded Silesia—a wealthy part of the Habsburg's territory. England, hoping to preserve a balance of power by preventing France's expansion, entered the war on the side of the Austrians.

The majority of the war was fought over possession of Silesia with battles also occurring in Italy and southwest Germany between Austrian and France. The Treaty of Aix-la-Chapelle ended the war and restored the status quo. Britain and France essentially fought to a standoff. Frederick the Great and Prussia were allowed to keep possession of Silesia. This represented a humiliating defeat for Austria—a situation the Austrians would rectify in the Seven Years' War.

SEVEN YEARS' WAR (1756–1763)

The Seven Years' War represented a shift in alliances among the great powers of Europe. By mid-century France was in heated competition with the British for dominance of North America and the Caribbean. The Habsburgs—no friends of Bourbons in France—were eager to seek revenge against Frederick the Great of Prussia. Therefore, during the Seven Years' War France aligned with Austria (and Russia, which saw an opportunity to gain land at Prussia's expense) against Britain and Prussia. Historians often call the Seven Years' War the Great War for Empire because it was, in a very real sense, a world war involving not just European powers but the colonies in North America, the West Indies, and India. Europe's pursuit of empire brought the great powers into conflict over far-away but incredibly valuable territory.

On the continent, the war between Prussia, Austria, and Russia was fought largely to a stalemate. The colonial conflicts known as the French and Indian War between France and Britain were far different, however. The thirteen British colonies in North America

Europe in 1763. Redrawn from *Historical Atlas of the World*, Newly Revised Edition, (1997), Hammond Incorporated.

were experiencing a remarkable population growth by mid-century. Many factors—inexpensive land, religious freedom, and economic opportunities—fed the population boom and as more settlers came the growth spread westward. In contrast, the French population—largely in Louisiana and Quebec—was sparse and thinly spread. To defend their commercial interests against the British, the French established military forts in Nova Scotia, along the Gulf of St. Lawrence, and near the Great Lakes. France began the hostilities by attacking British forts along the Great Lakes as well as on British-controlled Majorca, in the Caribbean, and Calcutta in India. Unfortunately for the French, they could not sustain their early victories. Seeking to reverse a series of setbacks in North America, France planned to invade the British Isles in 1759 and bring a decisive end to the war. The British were ready for such a tactic and all but destroyed France's navy. While France still had a superior army, they had no way to deploy or reinforce their troops in North America. England stood unopposed on the seas. French colonial holdings in the New World, Africa, and India fell one after the other to the British—a terrible humiliation for the French. At the Paris Peace Conference of 1763 the French were able to recoup some of their losses although they ceded Canada, India and some lucrative islands in the West Indies to the British.

THE FRENCH REVOLUTION

The French Revolution looms large in the Western imagination. Absolute monarchy was abolished and replaced with a republican and democratic form of government. Rigid social divisions based on the prerogatives of birth and inheritance were supplanted by notions of equality and merit. In the words of the most famous slogan of the period, the revolutionaries of 1789 created a new nation based upon the principles of "liberty, equality, and fraternity." The French Revolution is considered to be one of the founding events of the modern era.

The Pre-Revolutionary Crisis.

The immediate cause of the French Revolution was the nation's mounting fiscal crisis. By the 1780s, France was on the brink of bankruptcy. Government spending far outpaced its income from tax revenues and other sources. While the monarchy had always spent lavishly, it was King Louis XVI's decision to support the Americans against the British in the American War of Independence that drove France to the brink of financial ruin. The French government was forced to borrow enormous sums to aid the colonists. In the years immediately following the war, France devoted nearly fifty percent of its budget to paying interest on this debt.

To help solve this problem Louis XVI and his finance minister proposed raising taxes. The king and his ministers knew that in order to raise revenue, they would have to target the wealthy. In 1787, Louis XVI asked the nobility and the clergy to voluntarily begin shouldering some of the tax burden. Sensing weakness and desperation on the part of the king, the nobility and clergy insisted that only the Estates General—a meeting of representatives from all three estates—could authorize new taxes. The Estates General had not met in 175 years. To call it would have been an open acknowledgement of weakness on the part of Louis XVI. Yet, the situation was grave and drastic measures were necessary. The king ultimately gave in to the demands, calling for a meeting of the Estates General to begin on May 4, 1789.

While the nation was occupied with electing representatives to the Estates General, poor weather was plaguing the country. The fall harvest of 1787 was a disaster. Thunderstorms and hail produced widespread crop damage. Throughout France bread prices rose and peasants faced starvation. As representatives gathered in Versailles for the meeting of the Estates General, riots spread throughout the countryside. Over the next several months the fiscal problems gripping the nation mutated into political and social crises, making the revolution all but inevitable.

The Moderate Phase, 1789–1791.

As an historical event, the French Revolution is best understood as occurring in two phases: the moderate phase, 1789–1791, during which France went from being ruled by an absolute monarchy to a constitutional monarchy; and the radical phase, 1792–1794, characterized by war abroad and unprecedented violence at home.

The Estates General immediately bogged down on disagreements over format and procedure. The nobility insisted that the three estates each meet separately and vote as individual bodies. Since the nobility and clergy often were natural allies, this format would have made the Third Estate a permanent minority. Representatives of the Third Estate adamantly opposed this arrangement. In a nation comprised of one hundred thousand clergy, four hundred thousand nobles, and twenty five million peasants, urban workers, artisans, doctors, lawyers, and merchants, the representatives of the Third Estate demanded equality with the other two estates. Abbé Emmanuel-Joseph Sieyès summed up the position of the Third Estate with three questions: "What is the Third Estate?— *everything*. What has it been until now in the political order?—*nothing*. What does it seek?—To be *something*."

On June 7, 1789, the representatives of the Third Estate took a revolutionary step. Locked out of their meeting hall (either by accident or design), deputies reconvened at a nearby tennis court and declared themselves the National Assembly, the legitimate representative ruling body of the nation. Members of the Third Estate invited representatives from the nobility and clergy to join them and vowed not to disband until a constitution for the nation had been written. This event became known as the Tennis Court Oath.

The king responded in two ways. He ordered the first and second estates to join the new National Assembly. Yet, at the same time he massed troops around Paris and fired his reform-minded finance minister. To many in Paris it looked as if the King would call a halt to the activity of the National Assembly.

The reaction in Paris to this aggressive move was predictable. Already agitated by high bread prices—by July 1789 a working-class Parisian spent eighty percent of his income on bread—the common people of Paris began to arm themselves and

黄酉

to attack places where either weapons or food were stored. On July 14, 1789 an armed mob marched on the Bastille, a fortress turned into a royal prison located in the heart of working-class Paris. The crowd stormed the Bastille, hacked its commander to death, and displayed his head on a pike to a cheering populace. The fall of the Bastille was of minor military or strategic significance, but was an important symbolic victory. In the minds of many, the Bastille represented the worst excesses of absolute monarchy. With its fall, the Old Regime came to a symbolic end and the French Revolution began.

That summer, spurred by high bread prices, food shortages, and the fear of starvation, the violent revolt that started in Paris spread to the rural areas. Peasants blamed their tenuous situation on the nobility. The result was widespread rioting, looting, and destruction of nobles' property. In Versailles, the National Assembly focused on a way to quell the violence. Its solution was to end all legal distinctions between nobles and commoners. On the night of August 4, 1789 representatives of the nobility renounced all claims to special rights and privileges.

Three weeks later, on August 26, the Assembly ratified the Declaration of the Rights of Man and of the Citizen. The "Declaration" offered a clear and bold statement of Enlightenment principles: "Men are born free and remain free and equal in rights." In its seventeen articles, the "Declaration" articulated a vision of the nation that valued equality, individual rights, and a government that can exist only with the consent of the governed.

Louis XVI, however, was reluctant to approve the "Declaration." On October 5, 1789, six thousand Parisian men and women marched to Versailles in protest of high bread prices. Shortly after, the crowd was joined by twenty thousand armed militia sympathetic to their cause. The crowd forced the King and his queen, Marie Antoinette, to return to Paris. Once there the king was required to accept the reforms.

With the king and queen virtual prisoners in the Tuileries Palace in Paris, deputies to the Assembly—now called the Constituent Assembly—set about to write a constitution for the nation. Two years later, on September 1791, the Assembly completed its work. The new constitution remade the face of France. First, and perhaps most importantly,

absolute monarchy was abolished, transforming Louis XVI into a constitutional monarch. The Assembly created a legislature as an equal branch of government with the monarchy. Landowning men were granted suffrage. All officials were elected; no offices could be bought, sold, or inherited. Second, the Catholic Church became legally subordinate to the state. The Church's vast tracts of land were seized and sold off to the highest bidders. For the first time, Catholics, Protestants, non-Christians, and non-believers stood equal before the law.

By the end of 1791, the revolutionaries were satisfied with their accomplishments. France had a constitution, the power of the monarchy was severely curtailed, and all citizens were equal in the eyes of the law. Yet revolutions can take on a dynamic and a logic all their own. The years 1792 to 1794 would see the French Revolution move in unanticipated and often undesirable ways.

The Radical Phase, 1792–1794. By 1792, sentiment for the Revolution was divided into two opposing camps. On one side were those who wanted to press on with revolutionary reforms. On the other side were the counterrevolutionary forces. This second group included French aristocrats who had fled the country shortly after the fall of the Bastille, and disgruntled clergy and peasants who were disturbed by the revolutionary actions taken against the Church. Louis XVI was also secretly among this group.

On June 20, 1791, the royal family, in disguise, escaped the Tuileries Palace in Paris. Their plan was to flee the city, raise a counterrevolutionary force, and overturn the Revolution. They were thwarted, however, when the king was arrested in the city of Varennes and forcibly returned to Paris. The "flight to Varennes," as the episode came to be known, exposed a schism among the revolutionaries: the moderate elements still believed the king had a role to play in the government, while the radicals viewed him as a traitor and an enemy of the state.

As war approached, the moderate position became untenable. An alliance between France and Austria had been sealed years earlier by the marriage of Marie Antoinette, daughter of the Austrian Archduchess, Maria Theresa, to the Dauphin of France, later to become King Louis XVI. Now the

Declaration of the R_____ and of the Citizen

French queen's brother, Emperor Joseph II of Austria, together with Prussia sent troops to free the French royal family and end the revolution. By the summer of 1792, Austrian-Prussian armies penetrated deep into French territory. The commander of the approaching forces warned the French that if the king and queen were harmed, Paris would be destroyed. Under the threat of foreign invasion, the National Convention (the new parliament) suspended the constitution, outlawed the monarchy and declared France a republic. New elections were held based on universal manhood suffrage. A governing body was created to write a new constitution. However, the Revolution was about to enter a new and more violent phase.

By September, with Austrians and Prussians on the outskirts of the city, Parisians resorted to mob violence. Crowds indiscriminately attacked anyone suspected of being in league with the enemy forces. Over one thousand people were killed, their bodies mutilated and displayed in public. In December, 1792, Louis XVI was placed on trial, and the following month he was beheaded as an enemy of the French people. Marie Antoinette was guillotined in October, 1793.

While the French successfully counterattacked and drove the enemy steadily towards the border, the political life of France fell increasingly under the authority of the most radical elements of the National Convention. In June, 1793, twenty-nine moderate members of the Convention were arrested without warning. Dissent became intolerable. Under the leadership of Maximilian Robespierre (1758–1794), a provincial lawyer, the twelve-member Committee of Public Safety was established to guide the war effort and run the nation. He instituted what was known as The Reign of Terror throughout France.

The Terror began as a military dictatorship with intent to preserve the new republic during a time of war. By 1793 the majority of European nations favored putting down the Revolution. Robespierre and the Committee believed that the new republic must be saved at all costs. The Reign of Terror was instituted to punish the enemies of the republic, both foreign and domestic. However, it quickly degenerated into a brutal and frenzied search for dissenters of any kind. Around the nation, thousands were hauled before revolutionary tribunals: the verdicts were either acquittal or death. The Committee also turned on its own allies. Groups such as the radical Parisian *sans-culottes*[2], who had supported revolutionary activity from the outset, faced the guillotine. Unsure of whom the Committee might turn on next, the National Convention finally moved against Robespierre. He and other members of the Committee were arrested. On July 28, 1794, having sentenced nearly forty thousand of his fellow-Frenchmen to death, Robespierre himself was guillotined.

With the death of Robespierre and the dismantling of the Committee of Public Safety, revolutionary leadership fell once again into the hands of more moderate elements. Yet the nation still faced many problems. The war against united Europe still raged, the nation had yet to recover from the Terror, and the initial problem that triggered the revolution—the failing economy—had not been solved. These were the problems Napoleon Bonaparte would face in his rise to power.

---

[2]Literally "without breeches." The *sans-culottes* aligned themselves with the working people who wore long trousers in contrast to the educated classes who wore knee-breeches.

EIGHTEENTH CENTURY ART: FROM ROCOCO TO NEOCLASSICISM

European art of the eighteenth century spanned a range of styles, many of them specific to their countries of origin. Early in the century, French artists and designers favored a delicate, graceful form known as Rococo. Originally a manner of interior decoration, Rococo decorative arts featured complicated curvilinear ornamentation. Designers strictly avoided straight lines, opting instead for curlicues, flowers, leaves, and shells. The Rococo style was embraced by the French aristocracy and quickly spread across Europe, reflecting the gilded lifestyle of its patrons. The frivolous, pleasure-seeking nobility identified with the Rococo style, from overwrought interior decoration to paintings in pastel colors of fanciful, light-hearted subjects.

In England, the visual arts matured significantly during the eighteenth century. In the Renaissance and Baroque eras, the most famous English painters were imported, foreign-born artists such as Anthony van Dyck, who worked for English royalty. The subject matter of English art was also quite limited: given that Puritan churches banned religious art and few English patrons favored mythological subjects, portraiture became the nearly exclusive subject of choice. In the eighteenth century, artists such as Thomas Gainsborough brought renown to a distinctive English portraiture, while William Hogarth popularized satirical prints and paintings in a type of artistic social commentary.

The late eighteenth century witnessed a revival of Classicism in France, England, and the United States. Artists and architects, reacting in part against the frivolity of the Rococo style, returned to elements of Greek and Roman art as a way to convey seriousness and grandeur. Ancient historical subjects replaced scenes of leisure, imparting moral messages of patriotism and civic virtue. Stylistically, too, Neoclassicism departed from the delicate brushwork of busy Rococo paintings, favoring instead a simplicity with clear scenes and precise lines.

ROCOCO: THE FRENCH STYLE

The short-lived Rococo style, sometimes called Louis XV-style, characterized an informality that, in part, turned away from the courtly formality of life in the seventeenth century. The paintings of Jean-Antoine Watteau, a Flemish artist living in Paris, exemplified the Rococo manner in their mood, subject, and artistic style. Watteau's *The Departure from Cythera*, 1717 (Plate 8), exhibits loose, delicate brushwork, pastel tones, and a whimsical mood in this scene of partygoers. Sometimes translated as *Pilgrimage to Cythera*, it is unclear whether Watteau's scene represents the beginning or the end of the journey to the isle of Venus. This detail, however, appears unimportant, for Watteau focused his attention on evoking poignant feelings in the viewer. Well-dressed couples stand amidst an imaginary landscape on the mythical island of love, transporting the viewer on an armchair journey.

Reflecting the penchant of Rococo artists for pastel colors, pastel chalks became a popular medium at this time. Chalks allowed artists to render quick sketches in color, capturing momentary impressions. While pastels previously had been used for preparatory sketches, Rosalba Carriera, a Venetian artist, is believed to have introduced French artists to using pastel chalks for serious portraiture. A highly successful portraitist, Carriera spent most of her career traveling across

Europe to work for courtly patrons. During a year in Paris, Carriera made the acquaintance of many Rococo artists and produced pastel portraits of numerous prominent individuals, including Watteau. Her pastel portrait of *Louis XV of France as Dauphin*, 1720 (Plate 9), is a delicate rendering of the young king in all his finery. Carriera's works in pastel were so well received that she was invited to become a member of the French Royal Academy, an unprecedented honor for a foreign woman.

The Rococo style fell out of fashion in France in the second half of the century, but painters such as Jean-Honoré Fragonard continued to find an audience for the style among aristocratic clientele. In 1771, Madame du Barry, a mistress of Louis XV, commissioned Fragonard to paint fourteen canvases for her chateau. Fragonard executed the series on the theme of *The Loves of the Shepherds*. *The Meeting* (Plate 10), in which the young lovers meet secretly in a garden, is Rococo in both subject and style. Everything from the facial expressions to the pastel colors and free brushwork marks the painting as lighthearted and carefree. To Fragonard's dismay, however, Madame du Barry rejected the paintings and commissioned a series in the newly fashionable style of the day, Neoclassicism.

AN ENGLISH ART

During the eighteenth century, England produced several great artists. Perhaps because of England's geographical separation from the European mainland, artistic styles in England had evolved at a somewhat slower pace than elsewhere. Due also to religious restrictions in subject matter and the general unpopularity of mythological subjects, English painting had not witnessed the same breadth of genres as seen in other European countries.

William Hogarth developed a reputation as an important social critic through his series of satirical paintings and prints. Hogarth's series were antecedents to the modern-day comic strip, with sequential panels and prints poking fun at the social ills of the day. Building in part upon the Dutch Baroque tradition of genre painting, Hogarth invented a type of moral genre painting,

through which he aimed to improve society. Unlike the Dutch works, which combined moral lessons with an invitation to enjoy the debauchery pictured, as seen in the paintings of Jan Steen (Plate 6), Hogarth's works were much more didactic and left little room for ambiguity. In *Marriage á la Mode*, a series of paintings from 1743–45, Hogarth addressed the issue of arranged marriage versus a marriage based on love. Hogarth's series sharply criticized the apparent marital exchange of money for social status, with the loveless union becoming ever more disastrous as the series progresses. In *The Breakfast Scene*, the second of six works, the couple is already losing interest in each other. Their evident exhaustion, as well as the playing cards and the overturned chair, refer to their respective overindulgences of the previous night. Their accountant, disgusted, leaves with his stack of unpaid bills. Other works of the series point to drinking, gambling, and adultery, and by the end, the man has been murdered by his wife's lover and the poverty-stricken widow then takes her own life. Hogarth could not have been clearer in his critique of the upper class. While the series was not initially popular, the many engravings printed after the paintings point to their eventual commercial popularity.

Portraiture continued to be a favored subject by English painters and patrons. In the eighteenth century, some artists, notably Sir Joshua Reynolds, initiated a vogue for historiated portraiture, or portraiture couched in an historical, religious, classical, or mythological setting. Thomas Gainsborough, however, found a large clientele among the aristocracy for his more naturalistic style. Adapting the portrait style set forth by Van Dyck, Gainsborough placed his figures in informal poses and in pastoral settings. In *Portrait of Mrs. Richard Brinsley Sheridan*, 1785–87 (Plate 11), Gainsborough positioned his sitter on a rock, flanked by a large tree and an angled landscape. Sheridan, a professional singer and the wife of a playwright, appears casual and relaxed, her windswept hair echoing the swirl of foliage around her. The rustic settings in Gainsborough's portraits echoed the contemporaneous Enlightenment embrace of nature as the source of beauty and goodness.

Figure II-3   William Hogarth, Plate II: *The Tète à Tète*, [sometimes called *The Breakfast Scene*] from *Marriage à la Mode*, ca.1743–45. Engraved by Bernard Baron. Etching and engraving, (46 × 58.2 cm). The Whitworth Art Gallery, The University of Manchester, United Kingdom. Copyright © Whitworth Art Gallery, The University of Manchester, UK/The Bridgeman Art Library International.

THE REBIRTH OF CLASSICISM

In the United States and parts of Europe, the end of the eighteenth century heralded a return to elements of the Classic style in painting, sculpture, and architecture. Thomas Jefferson was perhaps the biggest American proponent of Neoclassicism (meaning a "return to Classicism"), designing his own home in Monticello in a Neoclassical style and envisioning Classical elements for an official state architecture. While the advent of a spartan Neo-classicism may be understood in part as a reaction against the ornate Rococo style, it also may be understood in a broader context. Enlightenment philosophy espoused reason and logic; aesthetically and stylistically, Neoclassicism was more suited to imparting these Enlightenment ideals than were fanciful Rococo paintings of party scenes.

The French artist, Jacques-Louis David, a prominent Neoclassical artist, adopted a Classical revival style after a trip to Rome, where he was

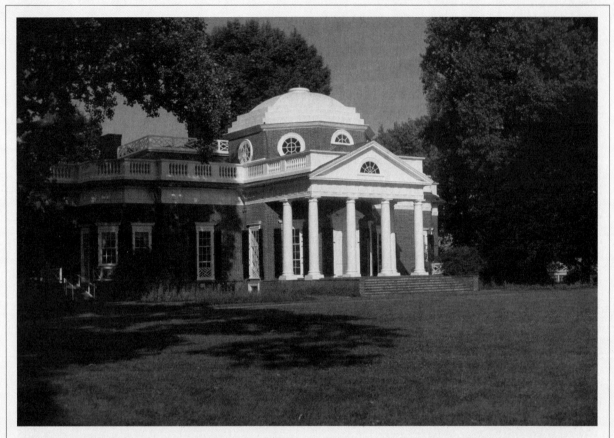

Jefferson, a self-taught architect, dreamt of an official United States architecture in a Classical style as a way to impart ideas of stability and order. For his home in Virginia, Jefferson combined a temple front with a dome, much in the manner of the Pantheon in Rome. More modest than ostentatious, however, Jefferson favored local wood and brick for the building materials of Monticello, and through his design sought to unite the house, gardens, and countryside as a metaphorical link between people and nature.

Figure II-4   Thomas Jefferson, *Monticello*, Charlottesville, Virginia. 1770–84, 1796–1806. Courtesy of Art Resource, NY.

greatly impressed by ancient sculpture. One of his most famous paintings, *Oath of the Horatii*, 1784–85 (Plate 12), exhibits this Neoclassicism in both style and subject. A shallow space set against columns and arches provides the backdrop for a dramatic story from Roman Republican history. Rome and Alba, neighboring city-states, decided to settle their war by waging a battle between the three best soldiers from each side. David's painting shows the three sons of Horace (the Horatii) with their father, pledging allegiance to the Roman state. While the men take their oaths, the women of the family weep in the background. They mourn for the potential

deaths of both the Horatii and the opposing Albans, who are related to them by marriage.

David believed that Neoclassical art could impart ideals of nationalism and self-sacrifice, principles that contrasted sharply with the self-indulgent mood of the Rococo style. His divergent representations of male and female characters in *Oath of the Horatii*, however, underscore his discriminatory belief that men would sacrifice themselves willingly for a greater good while women would forever cling to their loved ones, unable to rise above a focus on the individual. David depicted the men as upright and muscular, appendages

Vigée-Lebrun's portrait of the queen conforms to Rousseau's writings on the good mother who educates her children and nurtures their inherent goodness. In the painting, Marie-Antoinette appears as a kind and gentle presence, surrounded by her affectionate children. Vigée-Lebrun did not simply paint what she saw, however; the painting functioned as propaganda, meant to counteract the queen's public image of immorality and selfishness. Vigée-Lebrun not only portrayed Marie-Antoinette as a good mother but also attempted to elicit the viewer's sympathy through the dauphin's gesture to the empty cradle, alluding to a recently deceased child.

Figure II-5   Marie-Louise-Élisabeth Vigée-Lebrun, *Portrait of Marie-Antoinette with her Children,* 1787. Oil on canvas, 9' ¹/₄" × 7' ⁵/₈" (2.75 × 2.15m). Musée National du Château de Versailles. Courtesy of Réunion des Musées Nationaux/Art Resource, NY.

thrust at strong angles, whereas the women are shown limp, their bodies falling upon one another as they weep.

Not all Neoclassical art, however, conveyed such stereotypical representations of gender. Angelica Kauffman, a Swiss-born artist who eventually settled in England, used the Neoclassical style to embody the civic virtues of women as well. In *Cornelia Pointing to Her Children as Her Treasures,* 1785 (Plate 13), Kauffman illustrated an anecdote from Roman Republican history and, like David, employed a shallow space with Classical columns as a backdrop for her storyline. In the narrative, an apparently wealthy female visitor, seated at the right, shows off a necklace. In response, Cornelia points to her children, displaying them as her "jewels." Kauffman's painting is a didactic message for the viewer, holding up the example of a female role model who treasures her children above all else and devotes her life to raising them well. Cornelia exemplified the role of the good mother in part because her two sons, Tiberius and Gaius Gracchus, became political reformers who served the state. This convention of the "good mother" painting is seen also in Elisabeth Vigée-Lebrun's depiction of Marie-Antoinette.

MUSIC OF THE CLASSICAL ERA

Eighteenth-century Enlightenment ideals of reason and equality influenced change and development in music as they did in other aspects of thought and culture. In the second half of the century the emphasis on reason manifested itself in the arts in a revival of the classical (i.e., Greco-Roman) ideal, embodying qualities of clarity, "naturalness," simplicity, balance, and proportion. Baroque art, architecture, and music came to be looked upon as excessive in its complexity and elaborateness. The new affirmation of "natural" human equality and rights combined with the growth and increasing influence of the middle class to widen the audience and hence the range of themes and styles for artists, composers, and musicians. Unlike the visual arts, music had no actual surviving models from ancient Greece and Rome, but composers and musicians affirmed the classical ideal. Hence while we call the visual arts of the latter eighteenth century "Neoclassical," we call the music simply "Classical." This can be confusing, since we commonly use the term "classical" to refer to *all* music associated with "high culture," from the Renaissance to the present day—whether Baroque, Classical, Romantic, or Modern. In this chapter, we are using the term "Classical" with a capital "C" and speaking of the Classical era or period to refer to the music of the latter half of the eighteenth and the beginning of the nineteenth centuries.

By the time of his death in 1750 Bach, the greatest of the Baroque composers, was already considered "old-fashioned," and while his music was appreciated and built upon by Classical composers it was not widely performed until the nineteenth century. Interestingly, his most famous composer son, Carl Philipp Emmanuel Bach (1714–88), is considered by some music historians to be a main figure in making the transition from Baroque to Classical. His "expressive style" of composition simplified the harmonic complexities of polyphonic music and emphasized the expression of multiple emotions in a single musical work. Although composers of the Classical era continued to use polyphony, they generally simplified it and emphasized dominant melody lines. Musical works of the Classical era are often marked by "memorable tunes" that became popular and appealed to the listener's emotions. They express a wide range of often contrasting emotions, expressed through varying melodies, harmonies, and rhythms, and changing dynamics (faster/slower, louder/softer). It was these characteristics that enabled the piano to supplant the harpsichord as the standard keyboard instrument, because the piano allows for a great deal more subtlety and range in performing classical works.

In instrumental music the sonata underwent further development. While "sonata" continued to refer broadly to musical compositions involving several movements and usually a limited variety of instruments, the *sonata form* became the dominant musical structure of the Classical period, used in sonatas and in symphonies, typically in the first movement. The structure of the sonata form is threefold: an opening exposition, announcing the musical theme or theme; development, in which the theme is presented in different ways; and recapitulation, where the music returns to the main theme.

The Classical era decisively shaped the development of the *symphony* (from the Latin *symphonia*, a "sounding together"). Symphonies are large musical works, typically with four movements and lasting anywhere from half an hour to an hour, and performed by a large orchestra. The orchestra of the Classical period was composed largely of stringed instruments—mainly violins, but with violas, cellos, and double basses—and with perhaps two each of other instruments including flutes, oboes, bassoons, trumpets, French horns, clarinets (a new instrument), and kettledrums. The first great symphony composer was the Austrian Franz Josef Haydn (1732–1809), who composed 104 symphonies beginning in 1757. His fellow Austrian, Wolfgang Amadeus Mozart (1756–91), wrote forty-one symphonies, the last six his best known and most fully developed. Although Ludwig van Beethoven (1770–1827) wrote only nine symphonies, he pushed the range and possibilities of the symphony to the limit and also expanded the size and composition of the symphony orchestra.

Vocal music saw the development and expansion of the themes and the dramatic possibilities of opera. Mozart is undoubtedly the greatest operatic comoser of the Classical era, and his operas exemplify the newer appeal to middle-class audiences. His best-known and –loved operas, such as *The Marriage of Figaro, Cosí Fan Tutte, Don Giovanni*, and *The Magic Flute*, leave ancient classical themes behind and instead tell or retell popular stories and legends in which ordinary people are among the main characters.

Patronage of composers in the Classical era essentially continued as it had during the Baroque period: the church, various municipalities, and royal courts. However, the growth of the increasingly prosperous middle-class audience for music meant the growth of financial support in the form of ticket sales for concerts and operas, fees for music students, and commissions to compose specific works. While Haydn always enjoyed excellent patronage, Mozart was singularly unfortunate and as a result experienced financial difficulties. Virtually all composers, including Haydn and Mozart, made a part of their income from giving music lessons.

CD SELECTIONS

Tracks 8–11 consist of music of the Classical era, featuring the most eminent and enduring composers: Haydn, Mozart, and Beethoven. We begin this part of the CD, on Track 8, with the Third Movement (*Allegro*) from Haydn's *Concerto for Cello and Orchestra*, Op. 101. "Papa" Haydn was the most celebrated and beloved composer of his day in Europe, enjoying prestige and covered with honors during much of his long life. This is an example of a solo concerto, here with the cello as the solo instrument playing with an orchestra. Composed probably around 1783, the *Cello Concerto* has been for over two hundred years a standard in the orchestral repertoire. Like most concertos, it has three movements, and it follows the pattern laid down in the Baroque era: an initial fast or lively movement (here *Allegro moderato*, or "moderately fast"), followed by a slow second movement (*Adagio*), and returning to a brisk and lively tone and tempo in the third movement (*Allegro*), which is the one you are listening to. Notice the main theme at the beginning, a very listenable and learnable melody, to which the cellist and the orchestra return repeatedly and with variations; for example, at one point they switch the main theme from the major to a minor key.

Haydn was Mozart's older contemporary, and each admired and learned from the other's music. Mozart is represented by two selections, the short Third Movement of his *Symphony No. 41* ("Jupiter") and an aria from his wonderful comic opera *The Marriage of Figaro*. Some consider Mozart the greatest genius in the history of Western music; all certainly consider him a universal musical genius, and 250 years after his birth he is unquestionably one of the most beloved and performed composers in the world. One aspect of Mozart's genius is that he excelled in composing just about every type of music—concertos, symphonies, operas, sonatas, masses, string quartets, and many others. A child prodigy as both a composer and a pianist, writing his first music and performing all over Europe by the age of six, in his short life he wrote more than 600 musical compositions, including some twenty operas (the first at age eleven) and forty-one symphonies (the first at age eight).

Track 9 is the Third Movement of the *Symphony No. 41*, called the "Jupiter" Symphony, composed in 1788. Mozart's largest and most complex symphony, it was nicknamed "Jupiter" by a London concert hall director who thought it had a kind of "Olympian" grandeur like the highest god of the Romans. Characteristically, this symphony has four movements moving through the familiar contrasts between fast and slow: *Allegro vivace* (brightly fast), *Andante cantabile* (slow and songlike), *Menuetto: Allegro* (fast minuet-style music), and *Molto allegro* (very fast). The minuet was a stately popular dance introduced in the seventeenth century. Minuet music is always in

3/4 time (three quarter-note beats to a measure), as we hear in the Third Movement. The violins dominate, and as with the Haydn selection the main theme is melodious and memorable. Notice the ways in which Mozart returns to the main theme, and also the structure of building to a crescendo by repeating the same bar in progressively higher registers.

Track 10 is an aria from *The Marriage of Figaro* sung by Figaro himself, a role for a baritone singer. The plot of *The Marriage of Figaro* is both delightfully funny and complicated. Mozart wrote some of his operas with German texts and others, like *Figaro*, with Italian. Mozart and his librettist Lorenzo Da Ponte based it on a highly popular play by the same name written by the French playwright Pierre Augustin Caron de Beaumarchais (1732–99). Beaumarchais's play contains explicitly revolutionary ideas—the main character is a servant who outwits his master, a member of the nobility—and is credited with having contributed to the ferment that resulted in the French Revolution. Although the play was written in 1782, King Louis XVI refused to allow it to be performed for two years precisely because it mocked and undermined the pretensions of the aristocracy. While Mozart's and Da Ponte's opera has a lighter and more comedic touch, the revolutionary element is still there. Figaro and Susanna, both servants of the Count and Countess Almaviva, are engaged to be married. The Count, a philanderer, has his eye on Susanna as his next conquest. He invokes the traditional *droit du seigneur* (right of the lord), the right of the lord of the estate to sleep with a bride from among his staff on her wedding night. Count Almaviva appears to bless and encourage the couple's wedding but is actually scheming to get Susanna for himself. Figaro is furious when he finds out, and immediately devises a plan to foil the Count. As in Beaumarchais, the servant outwits the master. His aria on Track 10 is "Se vuol ballare" ("If he wants to dance"). Some of the words are as follows:

> If Signor the Count wants to dance,
> I'll play the guitar.
> If he wants to come to my school,
> I'll teach him the tricks, yes,
> I'll teach him. . . .
> I'll scope out his secret plan. . . .
> I'll overthrow all his machinations. . . .

Beethoven is represented on Track 11. The Fourth Movement of the *Symphony No. 9 in D Minor*, the choral movement featuring Schiller's poem "Ode to Joy," is one of the most exalted and exuberant moments in Western music. Beethoven must certainly rank with Bach and Mozart among the all-time geniuses among composers, and like them he is one of the most performed in the world. Beethoven was "pushing the envelope" musically in new and daring ways, and it is not only for a great deal of beautiful music but also as a kind of meteoric innovator that he ranks among the musical immortals. Indeed, Beethoven is typically seen as a transitional figure between the Classical and the Romantic eras in music, straining to push beyond the restrictions of the Classical forms and striving for more intense emotional depth and wider emotional range in his compositions. So the Beethoven selection fittingly leads on to compositions from the Romantic era.

If Mozart, for all his financial problems and career frustrations, is forever to us the irrepressible and playful "child," dedicated to pleasure and gaiety (an image that was irretrievably reinforced by Milos Forman's sumptuous and mostly fictional 1984 film *Amadeus*), Beethoven lives on as the lonely, volcanically angry, brooding , unhappy man—a stereotype that places him more with the Romantics than with the age of Haydn and Mozart. Beethoven wanted to study with Mozart, who died before he was able to, but he did study with Haydn. Beethoven was a brilliant pianist and enjoyed success as a concert performer. The greatest disappointment of Beethoven's life was his unfulfilled desire to be married. The greatest tragedy of his life was his deafness, which began probably around 1796 and ended in total deafness by 1814. We can only be filled with wonder and astonishment when we realize that the man who composed the Ninth Symphony could not hear a note of what he had written except inside his head.

Beethoven's *Symphony No. 9 in D Minor, Op. 125*, is quite simply one of the great works in the history of modern Western music, and the Fourth (choral) Movement contains some of the most familiar and often played music in the Western world. The Fourth Movement marks the first time a major composer uses the human voice as an important element in symphonic music. The choral music is a version of the poet Friedrich Schiller's exuberant "Ode to Joy." It is used as the official anthem of the European Union, and is part of UNESCO's Memory of the World Register. American churchgoers are familiar with part of the melody, which is the tune to the hymn "Joyful, joyful we adore thee." Track 11 is an excerpted version of the Fourth Movement. It features, besides the orchestra, soprano, alto, tenor, and bass soloists and a chorus. The main theme is joyous and stirring, affirming the universal fellowship of all humankind. The opening and closing stanzas are as follows:

(Opening)   Joy, beautiful spark of the gods,
Daughter of Elysium,
We approach fire-drunk,

Heavenly One, your shrine.
Your magic reunites
What custom sternly divides;
All people become brothers
Where your gentle wing alights. . . .

(Finale)   Be embraced, ye millions!
This kiss for the whole world!
Brothers, beyond the star-canopy
Must a loving Father dwell.
Be embraced,
This kiss for the whole world!
Joy, beautiful spark of the gods,
Daughter of Elysium,
Joy, beautiful spark of the gods.

CHAPTER THREE

THE ENLIGHTENMENT: JEAN-JACQUES ROUSSEAU

The Enlightenment was the dominant intellectual and cultural movement of the eighteenth century. Also called the Age of Reason, it was a period in which educated people in the Western world, through a newly found faith in the powers of human reason, dared to question and change the traditional authorities—philosophical, religious, and political—that had dominated European life since the Middle Ages. Like the Renaissance of the fifteenth and sixteenth centuries, the Enlightenment was a time of renewed humanism: of concentrated effort by men and women to analyze, understand, and improve both the world around them and human life. The Enlightenment's advance beyond the humanistic thinking of the Renaissance was the result of the Scientific Revolution in the seventeenth century. Advocates of Enlightenment believed that the methods for understanding nature developed by scientific pioneers such as Galileo and Newton made possible for the first time in history a complete and accurate understanding of the physical universe and human nature and behavior. The knowledge gained through science would in turn make possible, for the first time in history, the betterment of human life and institutions. It was the Enlightenment that gave birth to the modern belief in progress. The centers of the Enlightenment were France and Britain, but its influence spread throughout Europe and also to Russia and North America.

NEW CURRENTS IN THE EIGHTEENTH CENTURY

During the first twenty years of the eighteenth century, London and Paris were centers of intellectual and social ferment. Rationalist and empiricist philosophies were compared and debated. Enthusiasm and optimism abounded about the role science might play in the betterment of human affairs, chiefly as a result of Sir Isaac Newton's brilliant synthesis of the achievements of the Scientific Revolution. Accounts of exploratory voyages to Turkey, India, and China became popular reading and kindled hopes of far-reaching and financially profitable trade circuits for European countries. Occurring as a by-product of broadened commercial horizons, a new relativism developed in the areas of moral and religious thought. Could it be possible that people who lived on this earth in total ignorance of Western philosophy and Christianity led moral, happy, productive lives?

Four North American Indian chiefs visited England in 1710 and were received in intellectual circles with great curiosity, furthering European interest in the concept of the "noble savage," that is, in a thinking, sensitive, and morally upright being who had become what he was without the benefits of "civilization." In France, the publication of travel diaries and a translation into French in 1704 of the Persian *Thousand and One Nights* focused attention on the "Orient," its people, customs, religion, and political systems. An image of the "good sultan" emerged in both literature and philosophy, replacing that of the "barbarous" Muslim whom Europeans had fought so ferociously during the Crusades of the Middle Ages. As a result of this new interest in "foreign" countries and civilizations, prevailing adherence to national ethnocentrism and religious prejudice was called into question.

The year 1715 marked the death of Louis XIV, the king whose absolute political power, elegant court, and magnificent royal palace at Versailles had become the envy of monarchs throughout Europe. Inside France itself, however, the last years of the old king's all-too-long reign (1643–1715) were marred by a conservatism that stifled intellectual and social activities. Following his death, the period of the Regency (1715-1723) under Louis XIV's nephew Philippe d'Orléans witnessed a return of the court from Versailles to Paris and a loosening of political and religious constraints, engendering a new optimism toward recent developments in science, philosophy, and the arts. The rising upper middle class, or *haute bourgeoisie*, that was as prosperous and well-educated as most of the nobility, began to assert itself as an intellectual and political power whose concerns about the betterment of society could no longer be ignored. The stage was set, especially in Paris and London, for major social and political changes, to be made in the name of progress and the perfectibility of men and women as social beings.

Two influential intellectual institutions, products for the most part of the preceding century, began to assume pivotal roles in the development, discussion, and articulation of new ideas in politics, science, and the righting of social wrongs. There were, in both France and England, the several *academies* of learned people founded by royal edict: the British Royal Society for Improving Natural Knowledge, and the French Academy of Sciences and Academy of Inscriptions. On an informal level there was the *salon*, regular gatherings of intellectuals at the regal houses of socially prominent and influential women. The *salon* was a French phenomenon, while its British equivalent was the "club," groups of philosophers and writers meeting regularly to discuss modern trends in thought and literature.

Another feature of the Enlightenment in France was the writing, copying, and clandestine circulation of a group of manuscripts, by authors named and unnamed, aimed at the dissemination of controversial ideas in philosophy. Because of the increasing government hostility to unorthodox or potentially inflammatory books, the liberal thinkers and writers of these decades resorted to the use of scribes and copyists for their works, convinced that this was less dangerous than having them printed. Permeating this body of clandestine manuscripts

was the new critical spirit of the age—a reaffirmation of the potential of human reason. Influenced at first by Descartes's method, the authors' inspiration gradually changed to Locke and Newton, tending towards the idea that the experimental or empirical method alone was of value in philosophy. All ideas stem from the senses; revealed religion should be questioned; government must proceed from the principles of reason—these were the themes developed in these manuscripts.

The circulation of the clandestine manuscripts led to a unification, not just of the period's great thinkers, but of all readers who were sufficiently open-minded to realize that significant improvement of human life could be brought about through a change in philosophical, religious, and political outlook. An intellectual kinship arose from this commonality of purpose, as many people throughout France and the French-speaking Protestant settlements in Europe realized that they, too, could use their reason to better society, and not leave important decision-making up to established authority.

During the first half of the eighteenth century the word *philosophe* (originally meaning "philosopher" in French) began to take on a new meaning for the French, and ultimately for most of Western Europe. To that generation a *philosophe* was any intelligent person who had the courage to reject the influence of traditional philosophy and religion, accept the validity of inductive reasoning, and recognize his or her responsibilities as a social being. Voltaire, whose life and work we examine below, is often regarded as the epitome of the *philosophe*, his life spanning the major portion of the century, and given over to the critique of society and the service of humanity. No *philosophe* in the old sense, that is, creator of metaphysical systems or analytical methods, Voltaire combated with fervor, irony, and dedication the social ills of his age: religious intolerance and fanaticism, political inequalities and injustices, social prejudice, war, and every other social aberration resulting from misuse of human reason.

Beginning in the mid 1740s, the *philosophes* and their supporters took center stage in the dramatic confrontation between the new ideas and the old. Two figures, Denis Diderot and Jean-Jacques Rousseau, assumed the important roles they would play during the next thirty years in reshaping philosophy and society. Like Voltaire, with whom they

The French artist Houdon sculpted several busts and statues of Voltaire, including this seated version begun shortly before the philosopher's death in 1778. Voltaire's niece, Madame Denis, commissioned the portrait and donated a marble version to the Comédie Française. The likeness of Voltaire in his old age exhibits a sarcastic smirk, perhaps a reference to his tireless critical activism and struggle with established authority.

Figure II-6   Jean-Antoine Houdon, *Voltaire*, 1778. Terracotta, 47" high. Institut et Musée Voltaire, Geneva, Switzerland. Courtesy of Erich Lessing/Art Resource, NY.

alternately agreed and disagreed on specific points, they understood the dangers implicit in simply replacing one metaphysical system with another. In the years to follow, Diderot was to become France's principal champion of empirical philosophy, while Rousseau developed an increasing distaste for both rationalism and empiricism. Each was intent upon aiding humanity to better itself, but they differed

radically in explaining how this could be done. We will discuss their lives and works in the next section.

MAJOR FIGURES OF THE ENLIGHTENMENT

Baron de Montesquieu.   The first published work to reflect the intellectual and philosophical ferment of the early eighteenth century appeared in 1721. *Les Lettres persanes (Persian Letters)* was written by Charles Louis de Secondat, Baron de Montesquieu (1689–1755), best known for his much later book *L'Esprit des lois (The Spirit of the Laws)*. In this work, published in 1748, Montesquieu advocated a government composed of different branches that would "check and balance" each other. This idea would significantly influence the framers of the United States Constitution.

Les Lettres persanes takes the form of a novel, an imaginary voyage made by two Persian noblemen into Western Europe for the purpose of acquiring knowledge about foreign political institutions, customs, and morals. As they travel, the Persians write letters to family and friends at home, expressing amazement at the "strange" people and customs they have encountered in Europe.

Montesquieu's purpose in *Les Lettres persanes* was to shake the French out of their provincialism and complacency, forcing them to confront simple, clear, and logical commentaries made by the Persians on the "bizarre" nature of French politics, religion, and social life, aspects of their existence which the French had always taken for granted as absolute models of civilization to be imitated, not questioned. The novel's philosophical bases are very clear: the desirability of a representative form of government and political liberty; examination and discussion of the emerging doctrine of materialism (the whole universe, including the human soul, is composed exclusively of matter); and skepticism concerning revealed religion.

Tempering the shock of such direct criticism of "sacred" institutions is the literary device employed by Montesquieu in the work. He is a ventriloquist, speaking through the mouths of his admirably learned Persians, who quickly win the reader's sympathy. Such a device is transparent, of course, but quite useful in permitting expression of outspoken sentiment. Humor, too, serves Montesquieu well as he seeks to convince his compatriots that

France is perhaps not the center of the universe, absolute monarchy not the ideal form of government, and austere Catholicism not the only true religion. His Muslim travelers must return to Persia for fear of being "soiled" and perverted by contact with inhabitants of the Western world. The Italians and the French are as "barbaric" to the Persians in their politics, religion, and social customs as Orientals had seemed to the Westerners who had published accounts of their travels in the East. Usbek, the older of the two travelers, declares at one point that he was so angry at his treatment by the French that he was on the verge of "swearing like a Christian," echoing in a delightful manner the French phrase of "swearing like an infidel."

Montesquieu's book met with immediate success and was translated, copied, and imitated throughout Europe. Though published anonymously by one of the French Huguenot communities in Holland, with Cologne (Germany) listed as place of printing on the title page, the identity of its author was widely known, and Montesquieu, in part because of his status as a noble, and also because of the liberal political climate of the period, never suffered politically or socially as a result of *Les Lettres persanes*.

Alexander Pope. In 1734, across the English Channel, another seminal philosophical work was published, this time from the pen of Alexander Pope (1688–1744), poet and member of the Scriblerus Club. Pope's purpose in his elegant verse essay, *Essay on Man*, was to proclaim that the universe, as it exists, follows the divine plan of an omniscient creator ("One truth is clear. WHATEVER IS, IS RIGHT," Epistle I, line 294) and that humankind's seeming dissatisfaction with the world stems from limited vision, an inability to see the whole of God's plan. The focus of human philosophical endeavors has been wrong, Pope contends: "Know then thyself, presume not God to scan; / The proper study of Mankind is Man." (Epistle II, lines 1–2). (The idea that "whatever is, is right" found expression also in the German philosopher Leibniz's argument that this is the "best of all possible worlds"—an argument mercilessly satirized by Voltaire in *Candide*.)

The *Essay on Man* is a humanistic work concerned principally with the human being's role as both individual and social being, and not so much with his or her relationship to a God and Creator whom he or she will never come to understand completely. It represents a deistic "distancing" of God from humanity, conflicting with contemporary Christian dogma, which stressed the immediate and continuous involvement of God in all earthly and human affairs. Pope's work quickly met with success in his native England, but it enjoyed even more fame in France, where it was translated into French six times and went through seventy separate editions before 1800.

Voltaire. A writer of poetry, fiction, drama, history, popular science, political philosophy, and much more, François-Marie Arouet, who took the pen name "Voltaire" (1694–1778), was celebrated as much for his radical critique of the society of his time as for his literary brilliance. Voltaire was born in Paris to an upper-middle-class family: his father was a lawyer and his mother a member of the minor aristocracy. Educated in a prestigious Jesuit school from ages ten to seventeen, he was a precocious student with a love of poetry and theater and a burning ambition. Rebelling against his father's desire that he become a lawyer, Voltaire became part of a pleasure-loving crowd. He wrote poetry offensive to those in power, resulting in his imprisonment in the Bastille[1] in 1717. But in 1718 his first play, *Oedipe* (Oedipus), was produced and was a smash hit. He wrote France's first epic poem, the *Henriade*, in 1722, his effort to rival Virgil's *Aeneid* and would come to be regarded as the greatest French poet of the eighteenth century. By 1720, Voltaire's anti-establishment attitudes sent him for another stay in the Bastille. During his imprisonment he made a serious commitment to a literary career that was to last through the greater part of the century. Known and admired for his wit and talent, he was soon welcomed into the best of Parisian society, producing a number of poems and tragedies dealing with socio-political issues, which made him famous.

---

[1]The famous political prison that would be attacked in 1789 by an unruly mob in Paris, marking the beginning of the French Revolution.

In 1726 an altercation with an aristocrat caused Voltaire to be beaten and expelled from France. He spent the years 1726–29 in exile in England, where he was "royally" welcomed and met all the leading English writers and intellectuals. Voltaire admired Britain's constitutional monarchy, individual liberty, religious toleration, and comparative lack of strict censorship of speech and published writings—all things he desired for France. He came under the influence of Locke's and Newton's ideas, and became an important transmitter of their ideas to France. He was drawn to the English Quakers for their pacifism and simplicity of life. Voltaire learned English well and wrote the first edition of his book *Letters Concerning the English Nation* in English. He later expanded it, put it into French, and published it as his *Lettres Philosophique (Philosophical Letters)*. Voltaire, it must be added, also made a lot of money in England and became interested in accumulating wealth—which he did for the rest of his life.

Returning to France in 1729, Voltaire was in trouble again within five years. He published his *Philosophical Letters* in France in 1734, which of course advocated such things as greater political freedom, religious toleration, and the ideas of Locke and Newton. The book has the distinction of being the first Enlightenment book to be banned! Copies were seized and Voltaire was threatened with arrest. He fled to the province of Lorraine and was not permitted to return to Paris. By this point, and until 1748, Voltaire had a refuge in Cirey, in a chateau owned by Madame Emilie du Châtelet, one of the great women of the Enlightenment. They were both lovers and intellectual co-workers. Her chateau contained a laboratory where they conducted scientific experiments, and they frequently discussed Newtonian physics. Her translation of Newton's *Principia Mathematica* remains the standard French version. It was through du Châtelet's influence that Voltaire became more welcome at the royal court at Versailles. Tragically Madame du Châtelet died in 1749. By that time they were no longer lovers, but they had remained dear friends and Voltaire was devastated by her death.

During the Cirey years Voltaire also became a friend and frequent correspondent of King Frederick the Great of Prussia, perhaps the greatest of the eighteenth-century "enlightened despots" of Europe. For three years Voltaire was Frederick's guest at the royal palace of *Sans Souci* in Potsdam, but the friendship soured and Voltaire left in anger. Despite being named the official (royal) historiographer to the French king, Louis XV, in 1745 and elected to the prestigious Académie Francaise for life in 1746, Voltaire nevertheless remained extremely wary of kings and clergy and of the arbitrary manner in which authorities chose to censor writings and imprison authors.

Still forbidden to return to Paris, Voltaire lived in Geneva, Switzerland, Rousseau's hometown, for awhile, but he was too controversial for the Genevans. By this time he was quite wealthy, and in 1753 he bought an estate at Ferney, where he lived out his days as a "kingly patriarch" and the "Sage of Ferney." Ferney was in France, but just over the border from Switzerland so he could slip across the border if the authorities were after him. The estate at Ferney became an intellectual and cultural center, where Voltaire housed many guests.

Voltaire was one of the famous contributors to *L'Encyclopédie*, a great monument of the French Enlightenment which we will discuss later in the chapter, and knew and frequently corresponded with other leading *philosophes* including Diderot and D'Alembert. He also debated—with some exasperation—important issues with Rousseau, who criticized the exaltation of reason by the *philosophes* and emphasized the importance of feelings. Voltaire continued to write a great deal—novels (such as *Candide*), short stories, and essays that called attention to and satirized social injustices. He also wrote histories, including *The Century of Louis XIV* (1751). Widely regarded as the greatest French playwright of the eighteenth century, his popularity as a dramatist was beginning to decline with the rise of popularity of Shakespeare's plays (which Voltaire had introduced to France). But he became known as the "conscience of Europe" because he put the full weight of his reputation and influence into the cause of social justice. He was actively involved throughout the rest of his life in fighting for justice for victims of persecution, and he was successful in advocating for many innocent people accused of crimes.

Voltaire's immensely popular and still widely-read novel *Candide*, published in 1759, exemplifies both his social criticism and his literary style. *Can-*

dide is a *satire*. Satire is an entertaining and dramatic form of social criticism using irony, derision, and caustic wit to expose human folly and stupidity. As we have seen, the hallmark of Enlightenment Thought, rooted in its commitment to reason and thinking for oneself, was criticism of existing ideas and institutions on the grounds of their irrationality and inhumanity.

There are many targets of Voltaire's satire in *Candide*. The satirical thread running throughout the book is a many-sided attack on the rationalism of the seventeenth-century German philosopher Gottfried Leibniz, embodied in the character of Dr. Pangloss. Leibniz believed in the power of reason to understand not only the physical universe but also metaphysical realities such as God and the soul. Like the other Continental rationalists, Leibniz thought that the highest and surest form of reasoning was deductive reasoning, starting with first principles and logically deducing everything else from them.

An excellent example is Leibniz's proof that the universe as it exists is "the best of all possible worlds" in which all that happens is "for the best"—phrases that appear frequently in *Candide* on the lips of Dr. Pangloss or Candide. Beginning with the classical Christian idea of God, Leibniz argued this way: God the Creator is omnipotent, omniscient, and perfectly good. When the omniscient God decided to create a universe God could envision an infinite number of possible universes (worlds) from which to choose. But since God is perfectly good, God could choose only the best from among all the possible universes. Since God is omnipotent, God had the power to bring into being and maintain in being and goodness the best possible universe. Therefore this universe as we have it is the best of all possible universes. It follows from this that it must be the case that a universe containing evil is better than one without evil. In *Candide* Voltaire is lampooning this abstract deductive argument by piling up example after example of the human suffering and horror that are part of actual experience in the world.

Voltaire also levels his satirical wit at the horror and folly of war—the Seven Years' War in particular, which was going on when he was writing the book, but war in general. Famous for his anti-Catholic slogan "Ecrasez l'infame!" ("Crush the infamous thing!") and his lifelong criticism of the church, Voltaire in *Candide* continues his assault on organized religion. Satirizing their authoritarianism, superstitions, and moral corruption, he reminds the reader that much suffering and death has been perpetrated by religious institutions believing they were acting in the name and with the authority of God. His harsh portrayals of the Jesuits in South America and of the Muslims in Turkey are good examples of his religious satire. Significantly, the good people in *Candide* are religious heretics in the eyes of both Catholicism and Protestantism: James the Anabaptist and Martin the Manichaean. Other objects of satire in *Candide* include social prejudice and injustice, human pride, selfishness, and stupidity, feeling sorry for oneself, romantic love, physicians, merchants, publishers, and French and German attitudes toward each other.

In his later years as one of the most famous people in Europe, Voltaire triumphantly returned to Paris in 1778. This description by a historian, based on contemporary accounts, shows all too clearly the juxtaposition of acclaim and harassment that Voltaire had experienced throughout his life:

> At the age of 83 he returned to his native Paris for a triumph such as few authors have ever enjoyed. Delegations from the Académie Française and the Comédie Française, personages as diverse as Mme du Barry and Mme Necker [wife of Louis XVI's Minister of Finance], Diderot and [Benjamin] Franklin, Glück [the composer] and the English ambassador, came to pay him their respects. Crowds cheered him in the streets. At the sixth performance of his tragedy *Irene*, he in his box and later his bust on the stage were crowned with wreaths amid wild acclaim. Yet he had come to Paris with no clear authorization after 24 years of exile. When he died there ten weeks later (May 30, 1778) the religious authorities denied him burial, and his body was removed secretly at night to be interred in the abbey of Scellieres in Champagne.

Several years later, during the tumultuous years of the French Revolution, Voltaire's remains were transferred to the Panthéon, a national shrine in Paris that holds the remains of several great French intellectuals and statesmen.

Denis Diderot.   Born in 1713 into a fairly wealthy middle-class provincial family, Diderot received the classical Jesuit education in language, literature, and religion that was standard for a young man of his social standing. Continuing his education on his own in Paris, he taught himself Latin and English, and concentrated on work in the natural sciences, which were to become of great importance as the foundation of his philosophical views. In Paris, Diderot supported himself by translating English works into French, frequented literary *salons*, and soon won the attention of prominent *philosophes*, including Voltaire.

Diderot's first "enlightened" work, *Pensées philosophiques (Philosophical Thoughts),* was published anonymously in 1746 and quickly denounced by the French *Parlement* and condemned to be burned. A very short book expressing daring ideas of an anti-religious character, the *Philosophical Thoughts* reflected a deistic orientation more radical than that of Pope's *Essay on Man*, distancing God from man to the point of questioning the philosophical necessity of God's existence. Three years later, Diderot published an even stronger attack on religion, the *Lettre sur les aveugles à l'usage de ceux qui voient (Letter Concerning the Blind, for the Use of Those Who See).* This was a short study developing the Lockean theory that all ideas come to us through the senses, and stating that blind people, unable to see the wonders of nature, were unlikely to be convinced by religious theories that proved the existence of God through an examination of the natural perfection surrounding them. Attacked for the materialistic and atheistic implications of this work, in 1749 Diderot was imprisoned for three months in the Chateau de Vincennes, a political prison on the eastern edge of Paris.

Diderot's most influential achievement was his leading role in the most ambitious intellectual project of the century, *L'Encyclopédie, ou dictionnaire raisonné des sciences, des arts, et des métier (Encyclopedia, or "Reasoned" Dictionary of Sciences, Arts, and Crafts).* Begun by a group of Parisian printers as simply the translation of a popular British work (Ephraim Chambers' *Cyclopedia,* 2 volumes, 1728), *L'Encyclopédie* soon took on larger proportions, and Diderot was hired as its editor-in-chief. Between 1751 and 1772, there appeared seventeen volumes of text and eleven volumes of engraved illustrations (all published with Diderot as editor), and these were followed by four supplementary volumes of text, a twelfth of illustrations, and two of index (1776–1780). In the hands of Diderot and his collaborators, the *Encyclopédie* became the first comprehensive "anatomy" of humankind and the world, a work based on Enlightenment faith in the powers of human reason, whose creators were determined to set down, in a clear and organized fashion, all the achievements of humanity, from the achievements of thought such as philosophy and science to the arts and crafts, such as glass-blowing and wine-making.

A complete list of contributors to the *Encyclopédie* will probably never be established, but it is clear that they numbered more than 200, including the great *philosophes* of the period—Montesquieu, Voltaire, Rousseau, and Diderot, himself author of many articles. Seeking the editorial collaboration of someone better known in philosophical and scientific circles than he himself was at the time, Diderot called upon the services of Jean le Rond D'Alembert (1717–1783), distinguished mathematician and member of the Academy of Science, who wrote the *Encyclopédie's Preliminary Discourse,* or introduction to the public, one of the great documents of the Enlightenment.

The boldest aspect of D'Alembert's *Preliminary Discourse* was its wholehearted endorsement of the Lockean doctrine that all human knowledge comes to us through the senses, asserting the supremacy of the empiricists (Bacon, Newton, Locke) over the rationalists (Descartes, Malebranche, Leibnitz). Such a philosophical position was generally regarded as indicative of the eighteenth century's "modernity" in the history of human thought, and the *Encyclopédie* was viewed as a concrete symbol of the age's dedication to progress in human affairs.

In reality, the *Encyclopédie* was all this and more, as became clear with publication of Volumes I (1751) and II (1752). Major articles dealing with philosophy and religion reflected a materialist—if not completely atheistic—orientation, while those treating politics were characterized by the liberal and anti-monarchical trends of the century. This was accomplished not by direct statement of controversial ideas, but rather through inference, innuendo, and a creative use of the cross-reference system, encouraging readers of the more conservative articles to move on to others that applied methodological doubt to existing philosophical, religious, and political beliefs.

On February 7, 1752, King Louis XV issued a decree officially condemning the first two volumes of the *Encyclopédie* for containing "several maxims tending to destroy royal authority, establishing a spirit of independence and revolt, and, in obscure and equivocal terms, supporting the bases of error, the corruption of morals, anti-religious thought, and unbelief [in God]" (from the *Decree of the King's State Council*). Following censure of their work by public authority, the Encyclopedists went underground, while continuing to maintain the support of many influential people, especially Guillaume Chrétien de Lamoignon de Malesherbes (1721–1794), royally-appointed director of the printing trade and the official censorship of books. With Malesherbes' protection, five additional volumes appeared by 1757, despite the *Encyclopédie's* condemnation.

In the same year, however, an attempt was made to assassinate Louis XV, and almost every political, religious, and philosophical faction was implicated, including the Encyclopedists. Louis XV retorted with an edict stating that the author of any subversive work would be put to death. To make matters even worse, the following year, 1758, saw the publication of *De L'Esprit (On The Mind)* by Claude-Adrien Helvétius (1715–1771), a wealthy *philosophe* who had only recently allied himself with the Encyclopedists. Thoroughly empirical in his methodology, Helvétius develops in this work the bases of *Utilitarian* philosophy that the Englishman Jeremy Bentham was to popularize a number of years later. Religion, absolute monarchy, the nobility of the human mind and reason—all were questioned by Helvétius in *De L'Esprit*, which was quickly condemned by the *Parlement*. This condemnation heavily damaged the Encyclopedists' reputation, though they really had nothing to do with the publication of *De L'Esprit*.

Throughout his long editorship of *L'Encyclopédie*, Diderot continued to write "scandalous" novels and plays, among them *La Réligieuse (The Nun)* (1760) and *Le neveu de Rameau (Rameau's Nephew)* (1761). Because of his radicalism, several of his later works were not published until after his death. The best-known of these is his *Supplement au Voyage de Bougainville (Supplement to Bougainville's*

Voyage) (1796), a powerful indictment of slavery and colonialism. Another was his humorous novel *Jacques le fataliste et son maitre (Jacques the Fatalist and his Master)* (1796), a kind of takeoff on *Candide*. But like Voltaire, Diderot had "friends" in unusually high and unexpected places. Empress Catherine II (the Great) of Russia was a devoted reader and correspondent of Diderot, and in 1765 he sold his library to her. In 1773–74 he made a long and difficult journey to the imperial palace in St. Petersburg to thank her personally and to plan the creation of a Russian university. The hardships of the journey and the Russian weather weakened his already somewhat delicate health. However, he lived on until 1784, dying of emphysema and dropsy in Paris.

Jean-Jacques Rousseau. Rousseau was born in Geneva, Switzerland, in 1712. His mother died nine days after his birth, and his father, a feckless and itinerant watchmaker, walked out of his life in 1722, leaving Rousseau to be raised by aunts and other relatives. His schooling was haphazard, and he always felt both self-educated and under-educated. After working as an apprentice to a notary and then an engraver, Rousseau left Geneva in 1728, working at various jobs, including teaching and tutoring in music, in Switzerland and France. He was converted to Catholicism during this time, renouncing the Calvinist Protestantism in which he had been raised but without much real conviction. The agent of his conversion was also the "older" woman who would initiate him sexually, Madame de Warens, at whose country house he lived for ten years (1731–41).

In 1741 Rousseau set off for Paris to present a system of numbered musical notation he had invented for learning music to the Académie des Sciences, which rejected the idea. From 1741–44 he was secretary to the French ambassador in Venice. Returning to Paris, he entered into a long-lasting relationship with a servant, Thérèse Levasseur, with whom he would eventually have five children, all of whom they gave to an orphanage. (Harshly criticized for this when he became well-known, Rousseau pleaded that he would have been a poor father and the children would actually have a better life.) Engaged in musical composition and copying, he was active in Parisian musical circles and came to know (and to disagree with) the preeminent French composer, Jean-Philippe Rameau. More importantly in terms of his legacy to the world, Rousseau became friends with some of the leading *philosophes*, notably Voltaire and Diderot, and attended the salons of leading hostesses such as Madame d'Epinay. Through his acquaintance with Diderot Rousseau contributed several articles to *L'Encyclopédie*, beginning with articles on music.

While imprisoned in the Chateau de Vincennes in 1749, Diderot received a visit from Rousseau. The visit was a turning-point in Rousseau's career. Reading a newspaper as he walked to Vincennes from Paris, he learned that the Academy of Dijon (an important intellectual group in Dijon, a city southeast of Paris) had announced an essay competition on the following subject: "Has the modern advancement of the sciences and the arts served to purify or to corrupt manners and morals?" Diderot is said to have advised Rousseau to attack the arts and sciences as morally corrupting forces, which Rousseau did, winning the competition. His essay was published as *Discourse on Sciences and the Arts* in 1750, and made him both famous and controversial.

Rousseau's essay was a spirited attack on the Enlightenment assumption that the growth of knowledge and the flourishing of the arts represented overall progress for humankind. He attacked civilization itself for all the ways in which it had corrupted natural human goodness and simplicity. In the first discourse, and in his *Discours sur l'origine et les fondements de l'inégalité parmi les hommes* (*Discourse on the Origin and Bases of Inequality among Men*, 1755), which we will discuss in detail below, Rousseau laid out the tenets of his philosophy: the theory that humans were born free, naturally good, and happy, but have been enslaved, corrupted, and rendered unhappy through the process of civilization. Directly opposing the contemporary Enlightenment belief that humankind and society were perfectible through the proper use of reason, Rousseau proposes a "return to nature," a renunciation of the social, scientific, and artistic "progress" which has served only to distance humanity from its natural simplicity and goodness. Rousseau's theory did not, however, constitute a naive demand for his fellow humans to repudiate "civilization," and he fully realized that we cannot return to the state of nature. Rather, he was arguing that the key to human happiness lay not in social and technological advancement, but in the reconciliation of human beings with their own original nature and with the natural world around them. In his later writings he envisioned and sought to describe forms of education and political society that would enable human beings to achieve a measure of such naturalness, harmony, and simplicity without renouncing civilization.

Rousseau's wide-ranging interests and abilities can be seen in the fact that during the late 1740s and early 1750s he was composing an opera, *Le devin du village* (*The Village Soothsayer*), which was performed for the court of King Louis XV in 1752. As in his philosophy generally, in his musical composition he tried to achieve a naturalness and simplicity of words and music. At this time he also played a leading role in an ongoing dispute between advocates of the French style in contemporary music, notably Rameau, and enthusiasts for the Italian style. Rousseau was a strong supporter of the Italian style, and contributed his *Letter on French Music* to the debate.

In 1754 Rousseau returned to Geneva, where he reconverted to Calvinist Protestantism and gained back his Genevan citizenship. In 1755 he again submitted an essay to the Dijon Academy competition, the *Discourse on the Origin and Foundations of Inequality Among Men*. This time the question was, "What is the origin of inequality among humans, and is this inequality authorized by natural law?" The second discourse did not win the prize, but it became one of his most important and influential works on human society. Rousseau had always been a difficult person to deal with and it was at this time that his relationships with various friends and benefactors began to be strained, and he had fallings out with Diderot, Voltaire, and Madame d'Epinay among others.

The period from 1755–1762 was also, however, perhaps the most creative period in his life for Rousseau the philosopher and writer. In 1761 he published what was to become the most popular novel of his century, *Julie, ou la nouvelle Hèloïse* (*Julie, or the New Eloise*), one of the foundations of the Romantic movement. In 1762 he published two major works, both of which were to become widely influential: a controversial novel-philosophical tract, *Emile, ou de l'éducation* (*Emile, or On Education*); and a book on political theory, *Du Contrat social* (*On the Social Contract*).

In *Emile*, Rousseau totally rejects educational theory and practice since the Middle Ages. Recognizing that children are not simply adults in miniature, he constructs an educational program for his imaginary pupil, Emile, derived from study of the child's nature, his physical and emotional needs, and his capacity for learning at different stages of his childhood and adolescence. Emile's intellectual development (that is, his use of his rational faculties) is seen as only a part of his overall growth into a physically robust, economically productive, thinking and feeling citizen with an acute religious and political consciousness.

The first educational philosopher to explore at length the relationship between student and teacher, Rousseau emphasizes the necessity of a bond, or "contract," between the two, a mutual understanding and cooperation which will enable Emile to apply what he has learned to living his adult life. Such an approach to the teaching and learning processes contrasted dramatically with the training of young men at the time, a rigid and impractical holdover from the scholastic tradition. *Emile* has been an important influence on educational philosophy and innovation well into the twentieth century.

Having created and educated his ideal citizen in *Emile*, Rousseau proceeded to design, in *The Social Contract*, the nature of the political entity or state best suited for his pupil, one that would enable people living in civil society to come as close as is possible to restoring the naturalness and harmony humans enjoyed in the state of nature. The ideal government for him stems from a social contract made willingly by all citizens of a society among themselves, that is, not forced upon them by a more powerful person or group. The people themselves are sovereign, and all law results from self-imposed limits freely agreed upon by this sovereign body. The form of government (whether democracy, monarchy, or oligarchy) is chosen and empowered by the people. Should this government at any time devolve into an entity no longer corresponding to the people's wishes, it may be modified or revoked. *The Social Contract* was a powerful influence on the ideas of some of the leading figures of the French Revolution.

Both *Emile* and *The Social Contract* criticized the organized religion of the time, and were banned in both France and Geneva. Rousseau had to flee Geneva in order to avoid arrest, temporarily enjoying the protection of King Frederick the Great of Prussia but mostly "on the run." In 1765 he was offered safe haven in England by his friend the philosopher David Hume, and a pension from King George III. Rousseau met distinguished Britons such as Samuel Johnson and Edmund Burke in London, and wrote the first six books of his autobiography, the *Confessions*, in a town in Staffordshire. However, he felt isolated and miserable there, and his always somewhat suspicious mind descended into paranoia. He imagined that Hume and others were plotting against him. He returned to France under an assumed name in 1767, completed the *Confessions*, and in 1770, the official end of his banishment, he went back to Paris on condition that he could no longer publish any more books. Thus his *Confessions* was published posthumously, in 1782. It is the first "modern" autobiography, in which Rousseau seeks to explain his life as frankly and fully as possible, including his sexual feelings and experiences.

Rousseau continued writing despite the fact that he was not allowed to publish. Having previously been asked to be a consultant on drafting a constitution for Corsica, he was invited in 1772 to make recommendations for a constitution for Poland, which resulted in his *Considerations on the Government of Poland*. In 1776 he completed another autobiographical work, *Dialogues: Rousseau Judge of Jean-Jacques*, and began work on still further autobiographical reflections, *Reveries of a Solitary Walker*. Both were published after his death. Rousseau spent his last years in solitude. While taking a morning walk on a patron's estate in Ermenonville, twenty-eight miles northeast of Paris, he suffered a stroke and died on July 2, 1778. In 1794, as an act of recognition and honor by the revolutionary French Republic, his remains were moved with great ceremony to the Panthéon and interred directly across from those of Voltaire.

Rousseau was a transitional figure between the Enlightenment and the Romantic movement. On the one hand, Rousseau was a child of the Enlightenment who was thoroughly involved in the issues of the Age of Reason and made important contributions to the thought of the period. In his political thought he is clearly a successor of Hobbes and Locke, basing

This popular engraving records Rousseau's funeral procession to the Panthéon in Paris. The mass of people marks Rousseau's popularity among the revolutionaries, as does the subtitle of the print, which describes the procession as his "apotheosis," indicating god-like status. The Panthéon demonstrates the renewed popularity of Classical architecture, both through its temple façade and through its titular reference to the Roman Pantheon. The crypt houses not only the remains of Rousseau but also those of Voltaire, Victor Hugo, and Marie Curie, the only woman to be interred there.

Figure II-7   Jules Girardet, *Apothéose de J.J. Rousseau, sa translation au Panthéon [Apotheosis and Funeral Procession of Jean-Jacques Rousseau to the Pantheon].* Collection of Jean-Jacques Monney, Geneva, Switzerland. Courtesy of the Granger Collection, NY.

his ideas on the state of nature, natural rights, and the social contract and developing a theory of the origin and rationale of government. Although converting successively from Protestant to Catholic and back to Protestant, in his religious beliefs Rousseau was clearly a deist who believed in a vaguely benevolent Creator and emphasized the importance to a good society of a broad "civil religion" as providing its moral foundations and cohesion. As we have seen, Rousseau was one of the noted contributors to the great French Enlightenment project, the *Encyclopedia*, knew Diderot, Voltaire, and the other leading *philosophes*, and was a friend of the British skeptical philosopher David Hume.

On the other hand, Rousseau was a founding figure of the Romantic movement that was to flourish at the end of the eighteenth and during the first half of the nineteenth centuries throughout Europe—in the visual arts, music, literature, philosophy, theology, and political thought. He was skeptical about the Enlightenment's exaltation of reason, he emphasized the dominance of feeling, intuition, and imagination in human life, and he affirmed humans' unity with nature and was critical of the artificialities of society. These would become themes of the Romantic Movement, which will be examined in more detail in the chapter on Mary Shelley.

The Discourse on Inequality. Two themes in Rousseau's life and thought help in a concrete way to illuminate the reading of the *Discourse on Inequality.* The first is the importance to Rousseau's political thought of his hometown, Geneva, Switzerland; the second is the importance of personal feelings in his life. Geneva was always a key symbol or model in Rousseau's political thought, even though he spent most of his life living in other places. By Rousseau's time, Geneva had been a city-state and a republic for two centuries. John Calvin had made the city a center of the Reformation, and it had a long tradition as the "capital" of Calvinist or Reformed Protestantism. The Protestant faith played a key role in unifying its citizens, functioning as the "civil religion" that bound them together in a common life. Calvinist Protestantism also provided a strict moral code for Geneva's citizens, and Geneva was a somewhat austere city in sharp contrast to Paris. Although he participated fully in Parisian intellectual and artistic life, Rousseau despised much about Paris, which was to him one of the best examples of all that was wrong with civilization. He always admired the higher moral tone of Geneva and its citzens' long tradition of public responsibility, believing that it made for a healthier and more vigorous citizenry.

Rousseau's concept of a state was always a city-state and a republic something like an idealized version of Geneva. In *The Social Contract* this can be seen in his theory of the general will of the people as the fundamental law, of the *polis* as the molder of virtue in its citizens, and of religion as the civil "glue" binding people together. Similarly, Rousseau admired ancient Sparta, with its strong community discipline, and criticized ancient Athens, with its more free and easy-going ways. Rousseau's description of the ideal state is not really applicable to a large nation-state like France, but his ideas became an important contributor to the ideology of the French Revolution especially in its second "radical" or "republican" phase.

For these reasons, the reader of the *Discourse on Inequality* should not overlook Rousseau's "Letter to the Republic of Geneva" which is its dedicatory preface. Although we must acknowledge an element of flattery in it as he seeks to be recognized by his home town, there is no reason to doubt the sincerity of the things he says about Geneva and the revealing things they show about his views on government, the ideal republic, and the role of religion—not to mention his painfully conventional and condescending views on women.

The reader should also note the importance of feelings, of passions, in Rousseau's life and personality. He was a sentimental, excessively emotional person, hyper-sensitive to real or imagined criticisms. Never an easy person to get along with, we have seen that later in his life his suspiciousness deepened into paranoia, as Hume was to learn to his discomfort. Yet for all his problems, Rousseau's immensely creative mind transposed the importance of feelings in his own life into perceptive insights into the powerful and foundational role that passions or emotions play in human life, morality, and knowledge generally. His understanding of the role emotions play is a central part in *Discourse on Inequality* and place him as a leading harbinger of the Romantic Movement. Like the rest of us, and perhaps more so than most, Rousseau's reach exceeded his grasp. His imagination could envision human ideals that he was in some ways pathetically incapable of realizing in his own life.

The *Discourse on the Origins of Inequality* was Rousseau's second indictment of human civilization for alienating humans from themselves, turning them into beings who love appearances and not realities, and creating the monstrous inequalities and other injustices among humans that cause such misery to most of the human race. Among his fellow *philosophes*, Voltaire was scandalized. In a letter to Rousseau he said, "I have received, Monsieur, your new book against the human race. No one has employed so much intelligence to turn us men into beasts. One starts wanting to walk on all fours after reading your book." For all his justly admired iconoclasm, Voltaire had become a wealthy member of the middle class, and Rousseau's attack on private property may have contributed to his dissatisfaction with the book. By contrast, Diderot, who was poor, liked the book very much. It stands as one of the most important, influential, and controversial of modern studies of the origins of human society and government.

Part One.   The theme of Part One of the *Discourse on Inequality* is human life in the state of nature. Keep in mind Hobbes's and Locke's interpretations of the state of nature, both of which Rousseau criticizes, and compare and contrast them. Rousseau asks: If humans have been corrupted by civilization, what must we have been like in the state of nature, before there was any civilization? He seems clearly to have understood "state of nature" historically, and not simply as a working hypothesis. He really sought to understand what the human race was like in its beginnings and early development. There was no theory of evolution in Rousseau's time, but he envisions a very long and very gradual process by which humans emerged from the state of nature into civil and then political societies—that is, into civilization. Rousseau recognized that in his day there was no empirical knowledge of the human race before the advent of civil and political society. Two hundred years later, evolutionary biology and anthropology have given us a considerable amount of empirical knowledge of early humans, but whether this data enables us to identify a "state of nature" in Rousseau's sense, in distinction from "civilized society," is dubious since the data suggests that *homo sapiens sapiens* has lived in family and tribal groups throughout its 100,000-year history. So even though Rousseau was trying to describe the remote human past, he had to resort to a purely hypothetical account of the state of nature, just as Hobbes and Locke had to, by taking human beings as we know them and abstracting from all those characteristics that humans have acquired only through centuries of living together in societies. This is what he means by "putting aside the facts."

Rousseau imagines humans in the state of nature as being physically robust and healthy, with very keen senses of sight, hearing, and smell—although not of taste and touch, which are senses that are refined by civilization. In this state there are natural inequalities among people of mind and body, which are negligible, and no moral or political inequalities—thus far a view similar to those of Hobbes and Locke. The individual's main concern is self-preservation, and each individual lives a solitary life. Rousseau pictures early humans "wandering in the forests, without industry, without speech, without dwelling, without war [contra Hobbes], without relationships, with no need for his fellow men, and correspondingly with no desire to do them harm. . . ."

In the state of nature humans have many things in common with other animals, and Rousseau emphasizes this more than do Hobbes and Locke. Like other animals, humans are governed by instincts, feelings (particularly pain and pleasure), perceptions, and primitive conceptions, and are "programmed" for physical survival. But humans differ from other animals in two important ways: they have (1) freedom and (2) the capacity for self-improvement. Like other eighteenth-century thinkers, he sees animals and humans physically, as "machines." This sounds like Descartes, who sharply distinguished the body-machine and *mind*, which humans alone possess. But Rousseau argues, against Descartes, that human power of thought differs from that of animals only in degree, not in kind. Human freedom lies instead in the human power of choice, in will, which is simply beyond the mechanistic explanations of science. Like Descartes, but with this important difference, Rousseau vigorously rejects any purely materialistic account of human nature and behavior.

The other crucial difference between humans and other animals is the human capacity for what Rousseau calls "self-perfection," or self-improvement, both as individuals and as a species. Generation after generation, the lives of other animal species never change; the fox or the frog today lives just as its remote ancestors did. But clearly the life of the human species has changed dramatically and continually through time.

Rousseau recognizes that freedom and the capacity for self-perfection are precisely the sources of the problems for which he blames civilization. But he attributes the emergence of organized society to contingent circumstances which might have been otherwise. In Rousseau's analysis, even the human transition to civil society did not necessarily lead to political society. Had humans remained in their local societies of family and kin, they would have had a better life than they have since the development of political power. Nevertheless, Rousseau cannot finally get around the fact that the ultimate source of human problems is human nature itself. Furthermore, since perfectibility or self-improvement is essential to being human, it must be possible to reform society and government and to improve civilized life, and later in *The Social Contract* he presents a blueprint of what such a society would look like.

Strictly speaking, according to Rousseau, humans do not have moral qualities in the state of nature; but that does not mean that humans in that condition are bad. At this point Rousseau takes on Hobbes's account of the state of nature as a state of "war of everyone with everyone" and rejects it. Hobbes was correct, says Rousseau, in saying that the basic human instinct is self-love. But self-love, which manifests itself initially as the instinct for self-preservation, is not inherently egoistic, aggressive, or violent. Hobbes's mistake was to apply self-love *as we know it in civilization*—as selfishness, vanity, ambition, and aggression—to the state of nature.

Here it will be helpful to introduce Rousseau's famous distinction between two kinds of self-love, which he discusses in a footnote to the *Discourse*: *amour de soi* and *amour-propre*. *Amour de soi* (love of oneself) in itself is good and in accordance with the nature of things. It is the foundation of all other human passions, and the source of moral values. In *Emile* Rousseau writes that "the origin of our passions, the root and spring of all the rest, the only which is born with man, which never leaves him as long as he lives, is self-love; this passion is primitive, instinctive, it precedes all the rest, which are in a sense only modifications of it." What has happened is that civilization has changed this natural and good impulse into *amour-propre* or egocentrism: an artificial reaction in which the individual anxiously compares herself to others and asserts her superiority in a variety of ways. It is a thoroughly illusory form of self-love.

Recall that according to Rousseau, humans in the state of nature live on their own, not together. They ignore one another and come together only for sex or some common physical task or to help another who is in distress. It is this individual liberty in the state of nature that Rousseau terms *natural right*. When individuals in the state of nature come into contact with other individuals who are hurt or otherwise in need, the instinct of pity or compassion comes into play. Pity is really a derivative of self-love: the individual feels compassion for those who are less fortunate than herself; she identifies with the sufferer.

In Rousseau's moral analysis, humans in the state of nature, although without morality in the sense of consciously formulated rules or laws, are genuinely good. In a letter to the Archbishop of Paris in 1763, Rousseau wrote that the basic moral principle is that humans are naturally good. There is no original sin, as Christianity teaches, nor is there an original competitive egoism as in Hobbes's interpretation. The later principles of morality, developed in human societies and when reason had come to play a role in human life, are all rooted in the natural instinct of self-love and its equally important derivative, pity.

Even sex in the state of nature was not a source of the problems we associate with it—jealousy, possessiveness, aggression and dominance, conflict among males. The sexual desire of one gender for the other is another natural human instinct. Rousseau distinguishes between the *physical* and the *moral* aspects of sex. The physical aspect of sex is simply the general desire of one gender for the other. The moral aspect is someone's sexual desire for one object of desire or one preferred object of desire. Rousseau believes that the moral aspect is purely a product of society, and says that its biggest supporters are women, who he believes are the chief promoters of sexual exclusivity.

Rousseau's views on women provide yet another example of the many men who have been powerfully revolutionary and innovative on all sorts of issues but conventional in their attitudes toward the other half of the human race. Ironically, it is perhaps in *Emile*, a book on education with far-reaching influence because of its innovative proposals for the reform of the education of boys, that we see Rousseau at his worst on women. While he calls for important changes in the education of girls (such as emphasizing physical exercise), its final aim is to train women for their essential role in life: pleasing men. Women's role is to obey, although Rousseau never tires of saying that they secretly rule. He proclaims the equality of the sexes, but it is the "equality" of complementarity, not of equal rights. Like almost all his predecessors (and successors) among the influential thinkers of the Western world, Rousseau simply assumes that he is talking to and chiefly about men, and women function as the human "Other." But interestingly, in the *Discourse on Inequality* Rousseau attributes the differences in the social roles of the sexes entirely to the formation of civil societies, centered in the family unit, and asserts that in the state of nature women and men had the same lifestyle.

It is worth calling attention to Rousseau's account of the development of speech, of language, among early humans. His speculations here are really quite interesting. Have you ever thought about just how humans developed language? Rousseau frankly says that he cannot explain how language in its full human complexity, as expressing general ideas or abstractions (such as "red," "tree," "human"), developed from its primitive form. Nor can he explain what the relationship is between the development of speech and the development of organized society (a chicken-and-egg problem). But he does suggest what has become standard thinking: that the development of human thought would have been impossible without language; that thinking is a linguistic activity, whether inside one's head or expressed to others.

Part Two.   In Part Two Rousseau deals with the emergence of human social existence (civil society) and then of government (the political organization of society). His analysis here is interesting to compare to Aristotle's *Politics*. What Rousseau calls the "first revolution" was the gradual formation of civil societies, a very long transitional period between the state of nature and fully formed political societies. Humans came together, first in families, and then in small groups of families or tribes. During this long period humans developed language, "a kind of property," and moral distinctions. Competition, vanity, and envy arose, as did arts and crafts. The new state of things required the development of qualities humans did not have

in the state of nature, and in Rousseau's view most of the human qualities are social creations, not innate. Although evils begin to appear and develop during this transitional period, Rousseau calls it "the happiest and most durable epoch" of human social existence, and waxes quite eloquently on this state of things. He sees modern "savages" (so-called "primitive" peoples) of his own day as living at this stage of existence, and worth recalling here is the eighteenth-century European myth of the "noble savage," used to describe, for example, Native Americans.

But the "serpent in the garden" of this long transitional period was the institution of private property, which Rousseau introduces with a famous statement: "The first person who, having enclosed a plot of land, took it into his head to say *this is mine* and found people simple enough to believe him, was the true founder of civil society." It is this "mine" versus "thine" which, more than anything else, eventually undermines the relative stability of early civil societies and requires the establishment of political systems. It is interesting to contrast Rousseau's interpretation of property with that of Locke. For Rousseau private property is *not* a natural right; only individual liberty is. In the state of nature, there is neither need nor desire for defining what is mine against others, because there is little social contact. Private property, then, says Rousseau, is "merely the result of convention." It was agriculture (land) and metallurgy (technology) that mainly produced this revolution. The division of land produced the right of property, not natural law. Property became the chief opportunity for human competition, ambition, greed, pride, power, and inequality to develop. Rousseau here clearly anticipates Karl Marx's argument that the institution of private property was the source of class conflict, inequality, exploitation, and the state itself.

The "second revolution" was the beginnings of political society—of government and laws. There is an interesting foreshadowing here of Marx's view of the state as inherently exploitative, since it exists to promote and protect the interests of the ruling class. According to Rousseau, the rich and powerful in societies introduced law and government to protect their interests and security. The reasons those with power gave to the other members of their society were rationalizations, such as protection of the weak from the strong and guarantees of fairness. Believing in the promised advantages, but not seeing the dangers, "[t]hey all ran to chain themselves," Rousseau writes, and later he will famously begin the first chapter of *The Social Contract* with the sentence, "Man is born free, and everywhere he is in chains."

Different societies developed different forms of government. While these early political systems reflected the desires of the rich and powerful, they did not represent *arbitrary* power as many later forms of government did. They were formed by a *social contract*, in which both the people and their leaders obligated themselves to observe the fundamental laws to which they had agreed. Rousseau states that in the contract "the populace has united all its wills into a single one." This is an early statement of the important idea of the "general will" which he elaborates in *The Social Contract*. The general will is the foundation of the laws, and the laws, not the governing body, constitute the very essence of the state or political society.

Rousseau goes on to discuss the various types of government, and it is worth comparing his analysis here with those of Aristotle, Thomas Aquinas, and Machiavelli. Once human societies began to develop laws and government, human history, says Rousseau, became a "progress of inequality." The *first* stage saw the establishment of law and the right of property, which legitimated the distinction between rich and poor. This seems to be part of the transitional stage leading up to the institution of governmental authority. The *second* stage was characterized by the institution of "magistracy" (government), which legitimated the distinction between the strong and the weak. The *third* stage, which has characterized most governments during recorded history, has seen the transformation of legitimate political authority into arbitrary, tyrannical power (despotism). Now the operative distinction is between masters and slaves. According to Rousseau, in this final stage everything has come full circle. Everyone becomes equal again, as in the state of nature, but now as slaves rather than as free. The principles of justice (law) and goodness vanish and the social contract is dissolved, thus creating a "new state of nature" that is far worse than the first.

Rousseau's later political thought was the articulation of his quest to define and describe a political society that would restore to humans what they have lost, but in a form appropriate to life in civilization. As we have seen, his model was based on his idealized picture of Geneva, a small state with face-to-face encounter among citizens, a republican or representative government, moral discipline, and religious unity. Central to his political theory was the idea of the *general will*. He defined the state or political society as "a moral being, possessed of a will." This general will expresses the real will of all its members; it is a sort of secular rendering of the old idea of a natural law of morality in every human heart. The general will constitutes the rule of what is just and unjust and is the source of the laws; it always tends to the preservation and welfare of the society, both corporately and individually. Virtue on the part of the individual citizen consists of conformity to the general will. Governments and particular laws may or may not adequately express the general will, and may be criticized on that basis. Rousseau ingeniously resolves the problem of restoring freedom to humans enslaved by tyrannical governments by arguing that, in obeying the laws of society which express the general will, a person is really obeying his or her own reason and following his or her own will—and to follow one's own will is to be free. Thus the obedient citizen of a just state is the truly free human being.

Conclusion.   Though none of the major *philosophes* lived to witness the French Revolution, it was clear that they had set the stage for the radical changes that would take place in 1789 and the decade that followed. Though strikingly different in their thought and methodology, intellectual leaders like Voltaire, Montesquieu, Diderot, and Rousseau, convinced of the need to bring about change for the benefit of society and the individual, helped set in motion forces that would alter forever the face of Europe and eventually of the world.

QUESTIONS FOR STUDY AND DISCUSSION

1. What were Locke's and Newton's important influences in shaping Enlightenment thought? How did they influence Voltaire's thinking?

2. Montesquieu's *Persian Letters* are said to have exemplified a new sense of "cultural relativism" among some educated Europeans of the eighteenth century. What does that mean, and how did he present it in the *Letters*?

3. List some of the targets of Voltaire's criticism in *Candide*. How do they express Enlightenment values?

4. What was *L'Encyclopédie*, who were its editor and some of its most famous contributors, and what role did it play as an expression of Enlightenment thinking? Why was its publication repeatedly stopped by the government?

5. What are the two characteristics that, according to Rousseau, humans uniquely and naturally possess? What reasons does he give for selecting them?

6. What is Rousseau's ideal of a good society with a good government? Why does he take this view?

7. Compare and contrast Hobbes's and Rousseau's descriptions of the state of nature. What, according to Rousseau, was wrong with Hobbes's view?

8. Why is Rousseau considered a transitional figure between the Enlightenment and Romanticism? Give specific examples of both sides of Rousseau from the *Discourse on Inequality*.

9. What are two principles that Rousseau believes all people naturally possess?

10. How does Rousseau describe the beginnings of civil society and government? Why is his characterization of civilization largely negative?

11. What is the difference, according to Rousseau, between self-love *(amour de soi)* and egocentrism *(amour-propre)?* Which dominates nature and which dominates civilization?

SUGGESTIONS FOR FURTHER READING

Baker, Keith Michael. *What's Left of Enlightenment: A Postmodern Question*. Stanford University Press, 2001.

Blum, Carol. *Rousseau and the Republic of Virtue: the Language of Politics in the French Revolution*. Cornell University Press, 1986.

Damrosch, Leo. *Jean-Jacques Roussseau: Restless Genius*. Boston: Houghton Mifflin, 2006.

Gay, Peter. *The Enlightenment: An Interpretation*, 2 vols. New York: Knopf, 1966. (Norton Paperback, 1977).

———. *The Party of Humanity: Essays in the French Enlightenment*. New York: Columbia University Press, 1970.

Goodman, Dena. *The Republic of Letters: A Cultural History of the French Enlightenment*. Cornell University Press, 1994

Hampson, Norman. *A Social History of the French Revolution*. London: Routledge, Chapman and Hall, 1987.

Outram, Dorinda. *The Enlightenment*. Cambridge University Press, 1995.

Spencer, Samia, ed. *French Women and the Age of Enlightenment*. Bloomington: Indiana University Press, 1985.

Wokler, Robert. *Rousseau, A Very Short Introduction*. Oxford University Press, 2001.

CHAPTER FOUR

BUILDING AN AMERICAN REPUBLIC: 1765–1788

In the midst of a bloody war for independence from Great Britain (1775–83), the members of the Second Continental Congress faced a gauntlet of formidable challenges. Militarily, Congress had to raise, train, and feed a Continental Army to defeat the world's strongest military power. Congress also had to find a way to pay for a war that was growing more expensive by the hour. And as royal authority collapsed during the Revolution, members of Congress had to come up with legal and, more importantly, popular ways to govern the citizens of states, counties, and towns who had until recently been subjects of King George. With an eye to each of these problems, Congress in May 1776 called on each colony to form a state government and draw up written state constitutions based on "the authority of the people."

This idea that "the people"—not kings—were sovereign reflected a political philosophy called republicanism, a complex and fluid body of ideas with origins in classical antiquity, Renaissance Italy, and early modern England. Essentially, republicanism suggested that "self-government" by the people themselves (or by their elected representatives) better insured individual freedom and happiness than rule by kings or aristocrats. One central tenet of republicanism was that governments should operate only with the consent of the governed. Another involved a suspicion of any strong, centralized authority, a suspicion that arose out of the opposition between rural British politicians and the London supporters of the king. Finally, republicanism required a virtuous, public-minded and, above all, *independent* citizenry—without one, republics were doomed to failure. As Plato and

Aristotle wrote, once citizens abandoned self-sacrifice for individual gain, republics crumbled into monarchies, oligarchies (rule by a powerful few) or, worse still, anarchy (rule by the mob).

Any reasonably educated eighteenth century person knew that republics were fragile and prone to spectacular failure. In the ancient world, Athenian democracy was short-lived, while Rome's once-stable republic had collapsed into empire. Europe's three surviving republics (Switzerland, the Netherlands, and Venice) were on the whole anti-democratic and corrupt societies that did little to inspire republican thinkers. What made eighteenth century Americans believe that they could be different—that they could "fix" the problems inherent in history's failed republics? And what did it mean to say, as the ex-colonists did time and again, that "the people" are sovereign? Finally, who were "the people?"

Between 1765 and 1789, British colonists in America fought a War for Independence against the world's most powerful nation, adopted governments built on popular rule, joined together in a confederation based on the absolute sovereignty of each new state, then threw aside this union in favor of our current "federal" system. They also debated questions of power, sovereignty, citizenship, republicanism, and happiness at great length. These debates will form the backdrop for this chapter's discussion of Jefferson's Declaration of Independence, the U.S. Constitution, essays written by James Madison, Alexander Hamilton, and John Jay to defend it, and George Mason's essay critiquing it. Yet to understand these arguments, it will be necessary to return, briefly, to the political, economic, and social conditions that preceded them: the imperial crisis with Great Britain (1765–1775), the War for Independence (1775–1783) and the Confederation (or "first republic" 1783–1789). This prelude will help explain the competing—and contrasting—visions Americans held for a truly revolutionary democratic and republican society.

The Imperial Crisis. A dramatic series of crises destroyed Great Britain's empire in North America between 1765 and 1775. In the process, Englishmen in the colonies conducted a spirited debate among themselves over the legitimacy of the king's and Parliament's authority over them.

When twenty-two-year-old George III inherited the British throne from his grandfather in 1760, the country was in the midst of a war in Europe. Although it had important European components, the Seven Years' War (in America the French and Indian War) could justifiably be called "the war for North America." When the French accepted defeat, they ceded to the British all of North America east of the Mississippi except the port of New Orleans. Great Britain's North American subjects were ecstatic: for generations the French and their Indian allies had raided British settlements on the frontier. With the Peace of Paris in 1763, most colonists foresaw a long period of prosperity. They took pride in their new king and status as Englishmen. Most colonists believed the English system of government—a "balance" of monarchy (represented by the king), aristocracy (represented by the House of Lords), and democracy (represented by the House of Commons)—was the most perfect ever put into practice. Certainly it was the most stable. The year 1763 was without a doubt the high water mark of Britain's empire in the Americas.

From a financial perspective, however, things were not so rosy for Britain. During the war the national debt had nearly doubled, and more than half of the empire's annual revenues went to pay the interest on the debt. Added to this was the financial necessity of garrisoning all of Britain's New World conquests. Advisors recommended leaving at least twenty battalions (10,000 men) behind in North America, concentrating in Canada, Florida, and Indian country. This would surely add to Britain's tax burden, even though Englishmen were already among the most heavily taxed people on

earth. Who should pay for the defense of the Atlantic colonies? The answer was simple to members of Parliament: the settlers themselves, since they were the people who benefited most directly from the soldiers' presence.

The British government thus began a series of policies aimed at forcing the colonists to pay for their own defense, as well as giving the government in London more direct control over its North American possessions. Each of these policies was viewed by growing numbers of recalcitrant colonists as an illegitimate abuse of royal power that subjugated an underrepresented population. The most important of these policies was the Stamp Act, passed by Parliament in February 1765. The Stamp Act imposed a tax on colonial documents like deeds, wills, licenses, newspapers, pamphlets, and ships' bills of lading—and required that a special "stamp" be embossed on the documents proving that the tax had been paid. But unlike previous taxes that regulated trade, the Stamp Tax's sole purpose was raising money for the British government (making it a "direct" tax). When they first heard of the plans for the tax, all thirteen colonial assemblies petitioned Parliament to reject the Stamp Act as "taxation without representation." The British Prime Minister replied that the colonists were already "virtually" represented in Parliament, since members of the House of Commons represented all Englishmen, wherever they happened to be. The Maryland lawyer Daniel Dulany ridiculed this concept in a popular pamphlet, arguing that no member of Parliament paid the duties they imposed on the colonies. Others joined in this questioning of the sovereignty of royal authority.

Organized colonial resistance to the Stamp Act began as soon as ships arrived in April 1765 with news of its passage. Leading the charge was a twenty-nine-year-old lawyer and member of the Virginia House of Burgesses named Patrick Henry. Henry introduced a series of resolutions in May 1765 that argued that the popularly elected Virginia assembly alone possessed the right to tax Virginians. Even though his more radical resolutions never passed, newspapers in other colonies printed each of Henry's resolves, implying that Virginia's assembly had endorsed all seven measures. Nine colonies sent delegates to a special Stamp Act Congress in New York to protest the law, although the body was careful to underscore its loyalty to the king.

government was one that abandoned the "balanced" government of England in favor of one based on "separation of powers": a legislature, an executive armed with veto power, and a judiciary independent of both. This system, Adams believed, would avoid the problems inherent in legislative bodies such as making "arbitrary laws for their own interest, [executing] all laws arbitrarily for their own interest, and [adjudging] all controversies in their own favor." Yet some critics of Adams' theories worried about a legislature that could then *create* its own constitution. These concerns led to a truly innovative idea: the constitutional convention. Constitutional conventions would be called into existence for one purpose only (drafting a constitution), and then disband, embodying "popular sovereignty" in pristine form.

For Virginia's constitution, a respected planter named George Mason drafted a declaration (or "bill") of rights that was adopted before the constitution itself. It affirmed the right to life, liberty, property, and the pursuit of happiness, while condemning all forms of hereditary privilege, guaranteeing trial by jury, extolling religious toleration, and calling for frequent turnover in office. Massachusetts' influential constitution, following Mason, also began with a bill of rights. But Massachusetts' delegates added a strong, popularly elected governor with a qualified veto and submitted the document to the citizens themselves for approval. In 1780, they did. Other states followed Massachusetts' example.

The Challenges of Independence.

Following a military strategy that kept the small Continental Army intact while escalating the costs of a British victory, General George Washington was able to sustain the war effort through nearly constant struggles in Congress and on the battlefield. After a difficult campaign near Yorktown in Virginia, the British general Cornwallis surrendered an army of 8,000 men. News of the surrender brought down the British government in March 1782, yielding a new ministry willing to grant America's independence in exchange for peace. John Adams and the New Yorker John Jay opened secret negotiations with the British soon thereafter that produced the Treaty of Paris in February 1783. The war was over, but the new nation's economy was in shambles. Each state was left with considerable war debts and soldiers had not been paid. Serious weaknesses in the Articles of Confederation could no longer be ignored.

First and foremost, Congress had no authority to impose taxes. And since states had their own debts, most declined to fund the government. The economic recession and high state taxes pressed especially hard on debtors who sought relief by desperate means. In Massachusetts, the absence of any legislation to protect debtors' farms and property from seizure led to a serious armed rebellion in 1786–87. Under the leadership of Daniel Shays, a debtor and former Revolutionary War captain, an organized "army" closed courts by force to stop the government from foreclosing on farms and auctioning property for back taxes owed. The governor, supported by merchants from the eastern part of the state, put down Shays's rebellion with state militia and a call to Congress for additional troops. But the Shaysites proved how unequally the fruits of revolutionary victory (and the costs of war) were being shared. Leaders in most colonies were deeply shaken by the rebellion, noting that the nearly bankrupt Congress was impotent to put down future outbreaks. Nationalist politicians—a growing faction concerned about the republic as a whole more than its individual states—were convinced that the only way to save the new nation was to strengthen the central government, and soon.

Who were the "nationalists"? Mostly officials, diplomats and military officers who had served in or with the Continental Congress, and had shed overarching loyalties to their home states. They included men like George Washington, Benjamin Franklin, John Adams, and John Jay. They were joined by younger, energetic leaders like James Madison, Jefferson's neighbor from Virginia, and Alexander Hamilton, a New York lawyer. By 1786 the nationalists were worried that rebellions like Shays's would extinguish the republican experiment. "What a triumph for the advocates of despotism," wrote Washington, "to find that we are incapable of governing ourselves." Washington's view held sway in Congress, which called for a convention in May 1787 to revise the Articles of Confederation "adequate to the exigencies of government and the preservation of the Union."

The Philadelphia Convention.   The fifty-five delegates who arrived in Philadelphia to amend the confederation were hardly a cross-section of American society. As slaveholders, merchants, lawyers and financiers—none of the delegates were artisans, tenants, or backcountry settlers and only one was a yeoman farmer—they favored a stronger central government and supported creditors' property rights. Some delegates were well-known patriots from the Revolutionary era, including George Washington (elected president of the convention) and Benjamin Franklin. Thomas Paine was in Europe, as were Thomas Jefferson and John Adams who were there as American ministers. Samuel Adams was not chosen as a delegate by the state legislature, while Patrick Henry was—but Henry refused to attend, saying he favored limited government and "smelt a rat." James Madison was sent by Virginia, and Alexander Hamilton by New York.

After selecting Washington as presiding officer, the delegates voted to close off the proceedings and deliberate only in secret. They decided each state would have one vote (identical to the rules of the Confederation) and that a majority of states would decide any single issue. Lastly, they decided to take up the so-called "Virginia Plan," conveniently compiled in advance by Madison.

James Madison and the Virginia Plan.   James Madison was born in Orange County, Virginia in 1751. Slight and bookish, he left home to attend Princeton (then called the College of New Jersey), where he excelled in languages, history, and political theory. He had served in the Continental Congress, participated in framing the Virginia

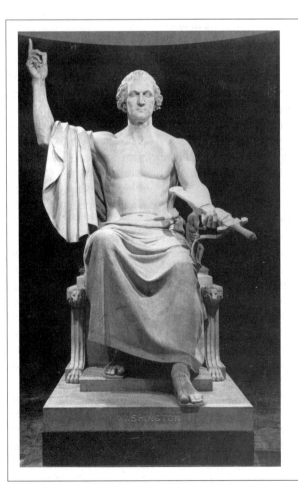

The Classical style so favored by Thomas Jefferson in architecture made an appearance in American art of the time as well. Horatio Greenough modeled his sculpture of George Washington on a famous statue of the Greek god Zeus. He aimed to represent "Washington the peacemaker" by showing him with a sheathed sword, hilt extended forward. The revival of Classicism, however, was perhaps better suited to architecture than art, for the American public rejected this half-nude representation of the country's first president and the sculpture was deemed a failure.

Figure II-8   Horatio Greenough, *George Washington.* 1832–1841. Marble, approx. 11'4" high. National Museum of American Art, Smithsonian Institution, Washington, D.C. Courtesy of the Smithsonian American Art Museum, Washington, DC/Art Resource, NY.

Constitution of 1776, and was a leader in the Virginia assembly, where he developed a low regard for state political leaders, who he accused of "narrow ambition" and a dangerous lack of republican virtue. Madison spent the winter months of 1786–87 studying the defects of Greek and European confederacies and drafting his Virginia Plan, a scheme for a truly national government and strong national union. The overriding goals of Madison's plan were an attempt to ensure government by men of high republican character while controlling factional disputes, which he called "vices of the political system." To achieve this, he eclipsed state sovereignty in favor of the "supremacy of national authority": a new central government that had the power to overturn state laws. Madison outlined a government with three "layers": a lower house elected by voters, an upper house elected by members of the lower house, and an executive and judiciary chosen by both upper and lower houses. Delegates from the larger states loved the Virginia Plan. Since the lower house was based on population, it guaranteed the power of states like Virginia and Massachusetts; conversely, low-population states that had equal representation under the Articles of Confederation would be dominated. They offered their own alternative, known as the New Jersey Plan. Under this outline, Congress would be given the power to tax and make binding requisitions on the states—but each state would keep just one vote in the unicameral legislature. It looked a lot like the model proposed by Thomas Paine in *Common Sense*. Perhaps the only thing keeping the delegates going as the summer turned sultry was the knowledge that whatever plan they adopted would have to be approved by the voters.

In the last week of July, Connecticut delegates suggested a compromise between the Virginia and New Jersey plans. One house of a bicameral Congress would have "state equality" while the other was based on "proportional representation." Terms for representatives were laid out: two years for members of the lower house, six for senators, and four for a new executive chosen indirectly by an "electoral college." Each state was left to itself as to how it would choose electors, with the number totaling a state's total representatives in the House and Senate. This was just one of the methods the framers hit upon for giving states a prominent role in the new constitutional structure while removing much power to the new, central government.

The "Great Compromise" over representation left just one issue to fight over: slavery. Slavery was never a prominent issue in the convention, but it revealed that important differences between regions existed at the end of the eighteenth century. Pennsylvania delegate Gouverneur Morris spoke for many northern delegates when he attacked the institution as nefarious, and George Mason (himself a wealthy slaveholder) bitterly attacked the international slave trade. Representatives from South Carolina and Georgia, which still depended on the flow of imported slave labor, threatened to walk out of the convention if Mason's measure was passed. The Constitution thus prohibited Congress from legislating against the slave trade until 1808. Delegates also agreed to a fugitive slave clause that would help slaveholders reclaim "servants" (the word slavery does not appear in the Constitution) who escaped to other states. Finally, southern states were given a boost in Congressional representation—and their share of the tax burden—when the convention agreed to count each slave as three-fifths of a free person. While this opened up slaveholders to higher taxes, it turned into a political windfall, as the "three-fifths rule" allowed Southerners a larger share of federal power than their northern counterparts.

The final issue to hammer out was the scope of national power. Each delegate had arrived in Philadelphia prepared to add to Congress' power, but the final draft of the Constitution went farther than that. The result was a central government that had broad powers to tax, regulate commerce, and provide for military defense, as well as the authority to make any law "necessary and proper" to implement the other powers—an elastic clause indeed. The Constitution also guaranteed that federal laws and treaties would be the "supreme" law of the land and that the United States would honor the Confederation's existing debt. This amounted to a huge giveaway to the nation's creditors and a huge disappointment to debtors like the ones who followed Daniel Shays. Finally, over the eloquent objection of delegate George Mason, delegates voted not to include a bill of rights. Still, thirty-nine of the remaining forty-two delegates signed the document and sent it to "the people" for ratification—or defeat.

But there would be no direct, popular referendum on the Constitution; instead, each state would elect a special convention to vote up or down on the new system of government. Unlike a legislature, the special conventions would disband after the vote.

Ratification.   With surprisingly little debate, the convention specified that the Constitution would go into effect as soon as it was ratified by special conventions in nine of the thirteen states. This clause was especially revolutionary considering that any amendment of the Articles of Confederation clearly required unanimous approval of all thirteen states. Rhode Island, and perhaps two or three other state legislatures, would likely have voted the new covenant down. Each of the delegates was thus fully cognizant of what he hoped to accomplish: a peaceful, but illegal, overthrow of the Confederation's legal and political order. If all the states approved, of course, the legal issues would die away, and the government would rest squarely on the republican foundation of popular (not state) sovereignty. But first, the Constitution had to be ratified; its defenders would need to martial all their powers of persuasion to make it happen.

Those in favor of the Constitution began the debate over ratification with some advantages. First, they seized the initiative by calling themselves Federalists, a moniker that masked their pursuit of a strong central government with a name that instead suggested a decentralized system. The name stuck, as did their term for their opponents: Antifederalists. There was little doubt who had the better name. Second, they began a brilliant, coordinated campaign of lectures, pamphlets, and newspaper articles to justify the new Constitution. The opposition, made up mostly of localists who had little or no reputation beyond their home states, was caught completely off guard.

Federalists and their Congressional allies also took charge of the calendar. Congress submitted the Constitution to the states on September 28, 1787, and the first ratifying conventions were called for December. By New Year's Day 1788 Delaware, Pennsylvania, and New Jersey had ratified the document. Connecticut followed on January 2. Excepting Pennsylvania, three of the first four states to ratify were small states, which surprised some commentators. But once the issue of representation in Congress was settled, small states stood to gain much from a stronger central government, including an end to the system of paying import duties to other states like New York and Pennsylvania. Small states also realized early on that they could not survive on their own as independent states, as a big state like Virginia or Massachusetts likely could have.

In Massachusetts the convention delegates debated furiously before the Federalists won 187–168. Antifederalists had demanded a host of conditional amendments, as well as taking up George Mason's stand for a bill of rights. To achieve their narrow victory, Massachusetts Federalists promised to support a bill of rights by amendment after the Constitution went into effect. Ratification came easily in Maryland and South Carolina in the spring of 1788, but there was increasing evidence that the Federalists had peaked. The Rhode Island legislature voted overwhelmingly against summoning a ratifying convention at all. And in the next group of states to call conventions—North Carolina, Virginia, New Hampshire, and New York—initial majorities opposed the Constitution.

The Antifederalist Critique.   Caught off guard in the fall of 1787, Antifederalists soon pulled together and became better at stating their case. By the summer of 1788, their arguments began to take hold. Eloquent voices took up the Antifederalist cause, including Virginians George Mason, Richard Henry Lee, and Patrick Henry; New Yorkers George Clinton and Melancton Smith; and Mercy Otis Warren and James Winthrop of Massachusetts. Despite the patrician tinge of these leaders, Antifederalists came from more diverse backgrounds than the Federalists, who tended to be well educated, wealthy, and lawyers. As a result, many Antifederalists believed the new Constitutional order was a giant power grab by society's elite: "these lawyers and men of learning and monied men expect to be managers of the Constitution," wrote a Massachusetts farmer. "[They intend to] get all the power and all the money into their own hands and then they will swallow up all us little folks . . . just like the whale swallowed up Jonah." Others argued that, in order to survive, republics had to remain small—more like city-states than a 1,500 mile-wide swath of a continent. James Winthrop declared that "no extensive empire can be governed on republican principles." Moreover, Antifederalists worried that the new government outlined in the Constitution would be too far away from most people to be trusted with its new, broad powers. With the House of Representatives divided up into 30,000-person districts, few citizens would know their elected officials, most of whom would undoubtedly come from the wealthiest families. Antifederalists preferred a nation of closely knit but independent states tied together only for defense and trade purposes. Finally, Antifederalists saw in the Constitution the outlines of a new type of aristocracy, one that could legally impose heavy taxes and other burdens on distant, subjugated citizens. In sum, Antifederalists' version of republicanism was slightly different than their Federalist opponents'. While the Federalists stressed the need for society's elite—educated men, creditors, the wealthy—to lead the new government, the Antifederalists were far more concerned with centralized power and the potential for the creation of a new aristocracy. Both sides claimed to be the true spokesmen for true republican values.

***Hamilton and* The Federalist.** New York Antifederalists like Governor George Clinton and Melancton Smith adopted Mason's rhetoric and arguments for opposing the federal compact, adding more of their own. Smith was especially eloquent in calling for a government run by "a representative body, composed principally of respectable yeomanry . . . the best possible security to liberty" as opposed to a Congress composed of wealthy men from giant districts. Eight states had already ratified the Constitution when New York's convention got underway, but a clear vote *against* the compact in any one of four key states—New York and Virginia chief among them—could derail the entire enterprise. New York was especially vital for several reasons. New York City was rapidly becoming the commercial and cultural center of the new nation, set to eclipse Philadelphia and Boston in the early years of the coming century. It was the seat of Congress under the Articles of Confederation, located strategically on the eastern seaboard, and associated neither

with New England nor with Virginia. Finally, it was the home of Governor Clinton, whose outspokenness against the Constitution made the Federalists' job there even more pivotal.

It was clearly with these facts in mind that Alexander Hamilton, the leader of the ratification forces in the state, turned his formidable intellect to the task of securing the document's passage. His plan centered on a series of thorough, persuasive, and thoughtful essays, published in the popular press, that would explain and justify the proposed Constitution. Hamilton knew he was speaking to a rather small audience—those influential men who made up New York's Constitutional Convention or held sway over them. Still, he hoped the essays would reach those key figures, and serve as an up-to-the-minute debate primer for speakers in the conventions in Virginia and New York. Even with his unrivaled skills in debate and rhetoric Hamilton would not be able to complete this task on his own, and he was extremely fortunate to find two extremely able allies in John Jay and James Madison. Jay (1745–1829) was far more influential than the thirty-three-year-old Hamilton, having distinguished himself as a lawyer, the author of New York's Constitution of 1777 (an important source for the delegates in Philadelphia), a member of the team to negotiate peace with Britain in 1783, and the Secretary of Foreign Affairs under the Articles of Confederation. Madison, already talked about as the "father" of the Constitution, was in New York City as a member of Congress and agreed to take on a large share of the essays. "Publius," the pseudonymous author of the *Federalist* whose name in Latin translates as "the public voice," was born.

Although he had worthy allies, Hamilton was Publius' prime mover. He wrote fifty-one of the eighty-five public letters, and kept the project going long after Jay became ill and Madison returned to Virginia when Congress recessed. Hamilton's biography was perhaps the most colorful of all the founders. He was born in 1757 on the island of Nevis, in the British West Indies, the illegitimate son of an itinerant Scottish merchant and a planter's daughter. The boy was clearly bright, and a Presbyterian clergyman provided Hamilton with a basic education and cast about for other proprietors to support the young man's higher education. He arrived in New York City in 1772 bearing letters of introduction from some of the Caribbean's most influential merchants and eventually attended King's College (later Columbia University). He rose quickly through the ranks in the Revolution, eventually becoming a lieutenant-colonel and General Washington's trusted aide-de-camp. When he married into one of New York's most wealthy and prominent families, Hamilton's rise from obscurity was complete: he was elected to Congress, established a successful law practice, and became a delegate to the Constitutional Convention in Philadelphia.

The Federalist was the most comprehensive body of political thought produced by the founding generation. Day after day essays by Publius appeared in the New York papers (reprinted nationwide) defending the need for a strong government to conduct foreign affairs but pointing out that centralized authority did not necessarily mean domestic tyranny. Why? Because the Constitution rested on "mixed government" (a President, bicameral legislature, and independent judiciary) that "checked" as well as "balanced" each branch.

"Publius" took Antifederalist arguments against the Constitution quite seriously, and attempted to rebut them point-by-point. But he also took great pains to pick apart the failings of the Articles of Confederation, devoting seven entire essays to the subject. At the heart of the Federalist critique was the notion that, in Hamilton's words, because "men are ambitious, vindictive, and rapacious," the trick was to suppress these tendencies by never allowing any one group or faction to dominate all the others. In *Federalist No. 6* ("Concerning Dangers from War Between the States"), Hamilton deals at length on the weakness and wickedness of human nature, and foresees "frequent and violent contests" among the confederated states unless a strong union is created. He points to festering and competing revolts in North Carolina, Pennsylvania, and Massachusetts (Shays's Rebellion) as potentially fatal to a young republic, unless "a FIRM Union" is established as a barrier against domestic faction and insurrection. According to Hamilton, although both state and central governments necessarily exercise direct authority over their citizens, the latter must be supreme.

Madison took up similar points in *Federalist No. 10*, his most influential installment of the series and one of the most significant American contributions to the theory of representative government. In this letter Madison challenges two thousand years of accepted wisdom about republics, namely that only small ones could remain stable and survive to avoid the twin pitfalls of anarchy and monarchy. Turning conventional thought on its head, Madison suggested that the immense size of the United States would make it far more stable than a smaller one, since "factions" could not easily gain power, overwhelm the public good, and trample on the rights of minorities. Since factions were, unfortunately, the product and price of liberty and thus inevitable, it was the goal of good government to control them, not suppress them outright. Madison's solution was to "extend the sphere . . . and you take in a greater variety of parties and interests; you make it less probable that a majority of the whole will have a common motive to invade the rights of other citizens." Finally, Madison suggested that in a large republic, each representative would be chosen by enough citizens that elections would be "more likely to center on men who possess the most attractive merit and the most diffusive and established characters." In other words, the new government would draw on the talents of the best-educated, wisest and most virtuous citizens—a hallmark of classical republicanism. Other essays, most notably *Federalist No. 51*, carried on Madison's brilliant argument.

Supreme Court Justices still cite Publius as an authority in their opinions about constitutional questions, and many members of Congress toted dog-eared copies of *The Federalist* along during the impeachment proceedings that rocked Washington in 1998. But it was political hard-ball that won the day for the Federalists in New York's ratifying convention, including the threat that New York City would secede from the state and ratify the Constitution on its own. New York's delegates approved the Constitution by a vote of 30–27 in July 1788, and Madison himself guided the Federalists to victory in Virginia (despite the eloquence of Patrick Henry) in June. With the addition of New Hampshire, eleven states entered the new federal compact. North Carolina rejected the Constitution in 1788 but ratified in November 1789 after the first U.S. Congress drafted a Masonian Bill of Rights; Rhode Island voted seven times against even calling a constitutional convention, but finally ratified the document in May 1790.

It was official *and* legal: sovereignty had been removed from the king, then from government in general, and bestowed squarely on the shoulders of "the people," who then empowered different branches and levels of government through separate constitutions. There was now a strong central government, reversing the autonomy won by the individual states during the Revolution. Creditors and merchants also tended to reclaim power temporarily gained by debtors, yeomen, artisans, and ordinary citizens. Finally, a single political system—enshrined in a concise, written document—bound the concerns and interests of groups as diverse as Philadelphia blacksmiths, Virginia planters, Providence merchants, and Nantucket fishermen.

THE DOCUMENTS

The Declaration of Independence. The Declaration of Independence is one of those important documents that are so familiar they are unfamiliar: apart from a few well-worn phrases, few people have actually read carefully what it says. It is a bold statement, combining a list of specific grievances against the mother country with an undergirding rationale and a rhetoric based on Enlightenment political philosophy. Notice, first, that the opening paragraph addresses itself to the entire "civilized world": ". . . a decent respect to the opinions of mankind requires that they should declare the causes which impel them to the separation." The truth was, however, that the purpose of the Declaration was much more to explain and justify separation from Britain to the colonists themselves. Up to that point the war had been largely a New England affair and probably most people in the thirteen colonies were not yet inclined to separate from Britain. A sizeable number, the "Tories," remained loyal to the mother country and were often persecuted and sometimes forced into exile. To declare formally that the thirteen colonies were independent of Britain at such an early stage in the conflict was an extremely daring act engineered by a handful of men chosen by a handful of men in the various colonies. For the Declaration to be titled "The unanimous declaration of the thirteen United States of America" much more expressed a kind of wild hope or supreme presumption than a reality.

The political philosophy enshrined in the first two paragraphs bears the clear influence of John Locke and Locke-inspired ideas. We read in the first paragraph of "the laws of nature and of nature's God." The famous lines that open the second paragraph are very Lockean. The "self-evident" truths are truths about the state of nature and natural rights, which Jefferson claims are intuitively obvious to anyone rightly using his or her reason. "Unalienable rights" are simply natural rights: those universal rights humans possess in the state of nature or just by virtue of being human, and which therefore cannot legitimately be "alienated" or taken away by governments.

When Jefferson then turns from the state of nature to civil society he again follows the tradition initiated by Locke. Humans leave the state of nature and form governments in order "to secure these [natural] rights," and all legitimate governments rest on the social contract, "deriving their just powers from the consent of the governed." Jefferson also follows Locke's doctrine of the "right of revolution": the right to "alter or abolish" any government that no longer protects rights or expresses consent. Like Locke, Jefferson is at least formally cautionary about the right of revolution, saying that "governments long established should not be changed for light and transient causes." He goes on, however, to argue that the British government has offended so egregiously against its colonial subjects that "it is their right, it is their duty, to throw off such government." Then follows the list of specific grievances.

The specific grievances listed in the Declaration refer to the various impositions upon the colonists by the British government, some of which we mentioned in the introductory paragraphs such as the quartering of troops, monopolizing trade, and above all many violations of the colonists' rights and privileges as British subjects. Notice, in the last of the "He" grievances, the reference to "the merciless Indian savages" and their barbarous methods of warfare. We are abruptly confronted here with the prevailing attitudes of Euro-Americans in 1776 and for at least another hundred years toward the native peoples of the continent. This stands in sharp and revealing juxtaposition with the noble sentiments enshrined in Jefferson's Lockean language of universal human rights.

The Declaration concludes by rehearsing all the ways in which the thirteen colonies have properly and peacefully sought redress of their grievances, to no avail. In the final paragraph Jefferson calls the signers "the representatives of the United States of America." At that stage, for the members of the Second Continental Congress to call themselves "representatives" acting "in the name and by the authority" of thirteen "united" colonies or states, was more wishful thinking than fact. Observe, finally, that the Declaration declares that "these united colonies are, and of right ought to be, free and independent states." Historically the word "state" has referred to a sovereign political and geographical entity in its own right, not to a subordinate region or unit. While the thirteen states were declared "united," they were each regarded as a "free and independent" state. This loosely defined unity among sovereign states was not only a problem throughout the war, but after the war threatened the very existence of the new republic.

The U.S. Constitution.   As with the Declaration of Independence, people often have a vague idea of some part of the Constitution but little real knowledge of what it says. This chapter is your opportunity to familiarize or re-familiarize yourself with its specific contents. The *Preamble* sets forth the purposes for which the Constitution is written. What are they? How do you think the convention delegates would have justified their presumptuous-sounding beginning, "We the people of the United States. . . ."?

As you read through the Constitution, notice how the government as structured by the framers is for the most part not directly responsive to the will of the electorate at large. Except for election to the House of Representatives, offices are filled by election from various much smaller representative bodies or by appointment. For example, the two Senators from each state were originally elected by their state legislatures (Article I, Section 3). The President is still elected, not directly by the people, but by electors appointed by state legislatures, their number the total of the Senators and Representatives from that state (Art. II, Sec. 1). And of course justices of the Supreme Court and all other federal judges are appointed (for life) by the President, "with the advice and consent of the Senate" (Art. II, Sec. 2; Art. III, Sec. 1).

The main structure of the Constitution embodies the three branches of the national government created by the Constitutional Convention: Article I describes the legislative, Article II the executive, and Article III the judicial. Notice how this threefold separation of powers has the effect of "checking and balancing" the others. As you read through the Constitution it is important to get a clear idea of what the specific duties and powers of each branch of government are, and how each provides a check on the other two. Where, for example, do all tax bills have to originate? Who has the power to declare war? What constitutes treason, and what is the punishment?

Article I, Section 10 and Article IV spell out the relative powers of the states in relation to the national government. Article V describes the process for amending the Constitution. Article VI enshrines the Constitution as "the supreme law of the land." Article VII stipulates that the Constitution will be ratified by the conventions of nine of the thirteen states, and states that at the time of signing it has been unanimously approved by the delegates of the (twelve) states present on September 17.

The Bill of Rights is the first ten amendments to the Constitution. These amendments were somewhat neglected until after the Civil War, when the Fourteenth Amendment (1868) made former slaves citizens and prohibited states from improperly depriving any citizen of "life, liberty, or property" or denying that person equal protection of the laws. Since then the Bill of Rights has played a fundamental role as a charter document of American rights and liberties. Familiarize yourself with the first ten amendments, noting for example the various freedoms catalogued in the First Amendment, the wording of the right to bear arms in the Second, and the various legal protections afforded citizens in Amendments Four to Eight. In recent years the Ninth and Tenth Amendments, which stipulate that "the people" have other rights than those specified in the Constitution, have been frequently invoked in Supreme Court cases and by politicians and state governors. These first ten amendments continue to play a vital role in U.S. law, from lower courts to the Supreme Court, and the intent of the framers continues to be passionately debated.

Since the Bill of Rights was ratified there have been only seventeen amendments to the Constitution. The framers made the amendment process a difficult one in order to make sure that changing the Constitution would not be taken lightly and would have to have substantial support in the states and the Congress. Some of the later amendments are milestones in American history: the Thirteenth, Fourteenth, outlined above, and the Fifteenth Amendments (1865–1870) abolishing slavery and establishing the full rights of citizenship for African-Americans (rights which it took another hundred years to begin fully to realize); the Sixteenth Amendment (1913), which authorized a federal income tax; Amendment 18 (1919), the short-lived attempt to prohibit alcoholic beverages throughout the nation that reflected the end of an era of evangelical Protestant hegemony and temperance crusades (it was repealed by Amendment 21 in 1933); the Nineteenth Amendment (1920), granting women the right to vote after seventy-two years of struggle; Amendment 24 (1964), the "voting rights" amendment, which struck down the poll taxes that had been used in the South for decades to prevent African-Americans from voting; and the Twenty-Sixth Amendment (1971), lowering the voting age from 21 to 18.

The *Federalist Papers.*   Now let us briefly highlight some main points of the three papers you are reading. In No. 6 Hamilton argues that the Articles of Confederation will not work and that a stronger central government is required. The weakness of the Articles is that every state is a sovereign republic, neighboring states are the most likely enemies, and therefore there will continue to be nothing but strife and disunity. Appealing to history, he argues against the assumption that republics, unlike monarchies, will not war against one another, showing that republics have behaved as badly as monarchies.

Papers No. 10 and 51, both by Madison, are two of the key *Federalist* papers. The theme is factions: what they are, how they arise, and how their influence can best be reduced by the political arrangements laid down in the Constitution. You need to be clear about how Madison defines factions. Factions, he says, are endemic to human society, rooted in human nature and especially in private property. (Think of them as "special interest groups.") The challenge is how to secure the public good and protect individual rights against factions, while preserving "popular government" and the liberty that allows factions to flourish. Notice that Madison rejects removing the cause, private property itself, because that would infringe upon a fundamental

liberty, nor does he envision the possibility of distributing property more equitably. Instead he argues that the solution is to put checks on the worst consequences of private property and the factions to which it gives rise. Of particular interest is Madison's discussion of minority and majority factions, where he argues that the chief threat comes from majority factions. This is his approach to what the French commentator on American democracy, Alexis de Tocqueville, later called the "tyranny of the majority." Direct democracy is unsatisfactory as a solution. Republican government, and especially a large federal republic such as is created by the Constitution, is the best solution because by its system of representation, its checks and balances, and its division of power between the central government and the states it will tend to diffuse and neutralize factions. In the light of Madison's discussion, did the federal structure set up by the Constitution manage to deal effectively with the glaring anomaly of slavery in a nation that defined itself in terms of human rights and liberties?

In Paper No. 51 Madison really explains the Constitution itself, focusing on the division of the branches of the national government and the checks and balances on power it provides. The "federal principle" he presents as the key to creating and preserving a viable republic was a new idea in the eighteenth century, which Madison discusses in terms of the difference between "simple" and "compound" republics. The famous lines beginning "If men were angels, no government would be necessary" deal with the crucial need of government, not only to control the governed, but also to control itself.

"Objections to the Constitution of Government Formed by the Convention."   Perhaps the most eloquent Antifederalist was the Virginian George Mason. A judge and a statesman, Mason was born in 1725 and became an early and vocal opponent of Britain's colonial tax policies. In 1774 he wrote the "Fairfax Resolves," which outlined the legal grounds for the colonists' opposition to the Boston Port Act. More important, he authored Virginia's Declaration of Rights in 1776, which became a model for the bills of rights in most state constitutions and inspired Jefferson's draft of the Declaration of Independence. The Virginia Legislature selected Mason as one of the delegates

to the Philadelphia Convention in 1787, and according to Madison's meticulous notes, he was one of the five most frequent speakers there. He was easily one of the most influential delegates in a body full of early American luminaries. Yet Mason decided in the last two weeks of the convention not to sign the document, and became the Constitution's most active and eloquent critic.

He explained his reasons for opposing the Constitution in writing and in great detail, allowing his critique to be published in November 1787. First and foremost, he wrote, the document lacked a written declaration of rights including liberty of conscience in religious matters, freedom of the press, and the right to trial by jury. This conspicuous absence, he suggested, nullified the declarations in various state constitutions, since one could conceivably possess the right of assembly in one state and not in another. He attacked the Constitution's provisions one by one. The House of Representatives was a "Shadow only of Representation . . . the Laws will therefore be generally made by Men little concern'd in, and unacquainted with their Effects and Consequences." The power of the federal judiciary would eclipse and therefore destroy the state judiciaries, rendering justice unattainable, "enabling the Rich to oppress and Ruin the Poor." Lacking a constitutional "council," Mason warned that the President—too powerful already—would be swayed by "Minions and Favorites or . . . become a tool of the Senate."

Many of Mason's objections were on the basis of republicanism: he thought the document "built in" measures to corrupt even virtuous men. He feared that the new, powerful central government could easily fall into the hands of an oppressive aristocracy or even become a monarchy if a tyrannical chief executive, legally in control of the military, decided to remain in office. Yet he also pointed to problems of constitutionalism, including a mixing between the separate branches of government. For example, the Vice President was also President of the Senate, "dangerously blending the executive and legislative powers." Finally, Mason pointed out a real flaw in the Constitution: that it could not serve as a permanent compromise between "sections": by requiring a bare majority to make commercial laws, "the five Southern states (whose produce and Circumstances are totally different from that of the eight Northern and Eastern states) will be ruined." During the nineteenth century, dis-

agreements over the Constitution and whether slavery would spread into new, western territory would tear the country apart.

QUESTIONS FOR STUDY AND DISCUSSION

1 What were the main issues and events that led to the American Revolution?

2. What parallels are there between Locke's political ideas and those of the Declaration of Independence? What arguments does Jefferson use in the Declaration to show the necessity of declaring independence from Britain?

3. Why was the Constitutional Convention called, what sort of people participated, and how did they deviate from their original purpose?

4. What is republicanism? Do present-day Americans still adhere to this ideology?

5. How representative were the men who drafted the U.S. Constitution?

6. What was Madison's role in the Constitutional Convention?

7. What sort of government did the Constitution create? What did it say about slaves and Native Americans?

8. What is the Bill of Rights, and why was it written? Discuss its importance in U.S. history.

9. What does Madison mean by "factions" in *Federalist* No. 10? What do they show about human nature, and what is the remedy for factions?

10. What were some of the differences between Federalists and Antifederalists? Describe their visions of America's future.

SUGGESTIONS FOR FURTHER READING

Amar, Akhil Reed. *The Bill of Rights: Creation and Reconstruction.* New Haven: Yale University Press, 1998.

Beeman, Richard R., Stephen Botein, Edward C. Carter II, eds. *Beyond Confederation: Origins of the Constitution and American National Identity.* Chapel Hill: University of North Carolina Press, 1987.

Cornell, Saul. *The Other Founders: Antifederalism and the Dissenting Tradition in America.* Omohundro Institute of Early American History and Culture: North Carolina, 1999.

Countryman, Edward, ed. *What did the Constitution Mean to Early Americans?* Boston: Bedford/St. Martin's Press, 1999.

Kammen, Michael G. *A Machine that Would Go By Itself: The Constitution in American Culture.* New York: A. A. Knopf, 1986.

McDonald, Forrest. *Novus Ordo Seclorum: The Intellectual Origins of the Constitution.* Lawrence, Kansas: University of Kansas Press, 1985.

Moran, Edmund S. *Inventing the People: The Rise of Popular Sovereignty in England and America.* New York: Norton Press, 1988.

Storing, Herbert. *What the Anti-Federalists Were For.* Chicago: University of Chicago Press, 1981.

Wood, Gordon S. *The Creation of the American Republic.* New York: Norton Press, 1972.

———. *The Radicalism of the American Revolution.* New York: A. A. Knopf, 1991.

BIOGRAPHIES

Bailyn, Bernard. *To Begin the World Anew: The Genius and Ambiguities of the American Founders.* New York: Alfred A. Knopf, 2003

Cunningham, Nobel E. *Thomas Jefferson versus Alexander Hamilton: Confrontations that Shaped a Nation.* Boston, MA: Bedford/St. Martin's, 2000.

Ellis, Joseph J. *Passionate Sage: The Character and Legacy of John Adams.* New York: W.W. Norton & Co., 2001.

———. *His Excellency: George Washington.* New York: Vintage Press, 2001.

Foner, Eric. *Tom Paine.* New York: Oxford University Press, 1976.

Keane, John. *Tom Paine, A Political Life.* London: Bloomsbury, 1995.

Main, Jackson Turner. *The Antifederalists: Critics of the Constitution.* Chapel Hill, Institute of Early American History & Culture: University of North Carolina Press, 1961.

McCoy, Drew. *Last of the Fathers: James Madison and the Republican Legacy.* New York: Cambridge University Press, 1989.

McCullough, David. *John Adams.* New York: Simon and Schuster, 2001.

McDonald, Forrest. *Alexander Hamilton: A Biography.* New York: Norton, 1979.

Wills, Gary. *James Madison* (The American Presidents Series). New York: Henry Holt & Co., 2003.

THE DECLARATION OF INDEPENDENCE

When, in the course of human events, it becomes necessary for one people to dissolve the political bands which have connected them with another, and to assume, among the powers of the earth, the separate and equal station to which the laws of nature and of nature's God entitle them, a decent respect to the opinions of mankind requires that they should declare the causes which impel them to the separation.

We hold these truths to be self-evident:—That all men are created equal; that they are endowed by their Creator with certain unalienable rights, that among these are life, liberty and the pursuit of happiness. That, to secure these rights, governments are instituted among men, deriving their just powers from the consent of the governed, that whenever any form of government becomes destructive of these ends, it is the right of the people to alter or to abolish it, and to institute new governments, laying its foundation on such principles and organizing its powers in such form, as to them shall seem most likely to effect their safety and happiness. Prudence, indeed, will dictate, that governments long established should not be changed for light and transient causes; and accordingly all experience hath shown that mankind are more disposed to suffer, while evils are sufferable, than to right themselves by abolishing the forms to which they are accustomed. But when a long train of abuses and usurpations, pursuing invariably the same object, evinces a design to reduce them under absolute despotism, it is their right, it is their duty, to throw off such government, and to provide new guards for their future security. Such has been the patient sufferance of these colonies; and such is now the necessity which constrains them to alter their former systems of government. The history of the present King of Great Britain is a history of repeated injuries and usurpations, all having in direct object the establishment of an absolute tyranny over these states. To prove this, let facts be submitted to a candid world.

He has refused his assent to laws, the most wholesome and necessary for the public good.

He has forbidden his governors to pass laws of immediate and pressing importance, unless suspended in their operation till his assent should be obtained; and when so suspended, he has utterly neglected to attend to them.

He has refused to pass other laws for the accommodation of large districts of people, unless those people would relinquish the right of representation in the legislature, a right inestimable to them and formidable to tyrants only.

He has called together legislative bodies at places unusual, uncomfortable, and distant from the depository of their public records, for the sole purpose of fatiguing them into compliance with his measures.

He has dissolved representative houses repeatedly, for opposing with manly firmness his invasions on the rights of the people.

He has refused for a long time, after such dissolutions, to cause others to be elected, whereby the legislative powers, incapable of annihilation, have returned to the people at large for their exercise; the State remaining in the meantime, exposed to all the dangers of invasion from without, and convulsions within.

He has endeavored to prevent the population of these States; for that purpose obstructing the laws for the naturalization of foreigners; refusing to pass others to encourage their migration hither, and raising the conditions of new appropriations of lands.

He has obstructed the administration of justice, by refusing his assent to laws for establishing judiciary powers.

He has made judges dependent on his will alone for the tenure of their offices, and the amount and payment of their salaries.

He has erected a multitude of new offices, and sent hither swarms of officers to harass our people and eat out their substance.

He has kept among us, in times of peace, standing armies, without the consent of our legislature.

He has affected to render the military independent of, and superior to, the civil power.

He has combined with others to subject us to a jurisdiction foreign to our constitutions, and unacknowledged by our laws; giving his assent to their acts of pretended legislation:

For quartering large bodies of armed troops among us;

For protecting them, by a mock trial, from punishment for any murders which they should commit on the inhabitants of these States;

For cutting off our trade with all parts of the world;

For imposing taxes on us without our consent;

For depriving us, in many cases, of the benefits of trial by jury;

For transporting us beyond seas, to be tried for pretended offenses;

For abolishing the free system of English laws on a neighboring province, establishing therein an arbitrary government, and enlarging its boundaries so as to render it at once an example and fit instrument for introducing the same absolute rule into these colonies;

For taking away our charters, abolishing our most valuable laws, and altering, fundamentally, the forms of our governments;

For suspending our own legislatures, and declaring themselves invested with power to legislate for us in all cases whatsoever.

He has abdicated government here, by declaring us out of his protection, and waging war against us.

He has plundered our seas, ravaged our coasts, burned our towns, and destroyed the lives of our people.

He is at this time transporting large armies of foreign mercenaries to complete the works of death, desolation and tyranny, already begun with circumstances of cruelty and perfidy scarcely paralleled in the most barbarous ages, and totally unworthy the head of a civilized nation.

He has constrained our fellow citizens taken captive on the high seas, to bear arms against their country, to become the executioners of their friends and brethren, or to fall themselves by their hands.

He has excited domestic insurrections among us, and has endeavored to bring on the inhabitants of our frontiers, the merciless Indian savages, whose known rule of warfare, is an undistinguished destruction of all ages, sexes and conditions.

In every stage of these oppressions we have petitioned for redress in the most humble terms; our repeated petitions have been answered only by repeated injury. A prince, whose character is thus marked by every act which may define a tyrant, is unfit to be the ruler of a free people.

Nor have we been wanting in attention to our British brethren. We have warned them from time to time of attempts by their legislature to extend an unwarrantable jurisdiction over us. We have reminded them of the circumstances of our emigration and settlement here. We have appealed to their native justice and magnanimity; and we have conjured them, by the ties of our common kindred, to disavow these usurpations, which, would inevitably interrupt our connections and correspondence. They, too, have been deaf to the voice of justice and of consanguinity. We must, therefore, acquiesce in the necessity, which denounces our separation, and hold them, as we hold the rest of mankind, enemies in war, in peace friends.

We, therefore, the representatives of the United States of America, in General Congress assembled, appealing to the Supreme Judge of the world for the rectitude of our intentions, do, in the name and by the authority of the good people of these colonies, solemnly publish and declare, that these united colonies are, and of right ought to be, free and independent states, that they are absolved from all allegiance to the British Crown, and that all political connection between them and the state of Great Britain, is and ought to be totally dissolved; and that as free and independent states, they have full power to levy war, conclude peace, contract alliances, establish commerce, and to do all other acts and things which independent states may of right do. And for the support of this declaration, with a firm reliance on the protection of Divine Providence, we mutually pledge to each other our lives, our fortunes and our sacred honor.

adams

THE CONSTITUTION OF THE UNITED STATES

We the people of the United States, in order to form a more perfect union, establish justice, insure domestic tranquillity, provide for the common defense, promote the general welfare, and secure the blessings of liberty to ourselves and our posterity, do ordain and establish this Constitution for the United States of America.

ARTICLE I

Section 1

All legislative powers herein granted shall be vested in a Congress of the United States, which shall consist of a Senate and House of Representatives.

Section 2

The House of Representatives shall be composed of members chosen every second year by the people of the several states, and the electors in each state shall have the qualifications requisite for electors of the most numerous branch of the state legislature.

No person shall be a Representative who shall not have attained to the age of twenty-five years, and been seven years a citizen of the United States, and who shall not, when elected, be an inhabitant of that state in which he shall be chosen.

Representatives and direct taxes shall be apportioned among the several states which may be included within this union, according to their respective numbers, which shall be determined by adding to the whole number of free persons, including those bound to service for a term of years, and excluding Indians not taxed, three-fifths of all other persons. The actual enumeration shall be made within three years after the first meeting of the Congress of the United States, and within every subsequent term of ten years, in such manner as they shall by law direct. The number of Representatives shall not exceed one for every thirty thousand, but each state shall have at least one Representative; and until such enumeration shall be made, the State of New Hampshire shall be entitled to choose three; Massachusetts, eight; Rhode Island and Providence Plantation one; Connecticut, five; New York, six; New Jersey, four; Pennsylvania, eight; Delaware, one; Maryland, six; Virginia, ten; North Carolina, five; South Carolina, five; and Georgia, three.

When vacancies happen in the representation from any state, the executive authority thereof shall issue writs of election to fill such vacancies.

The House of Representatives shall choose their Speaker and other officers; and shall have the sole power of impeachment.

Section 3

The Senate of the United States shall be composed of two Senators from each state, chosen by the legislature thereof, for six years; and each Senator shall have one vote.

Immediately after they shall be assembled in consequence of the first election, they shall be divided as equally as may be into three classes. The seats of the Senators of the first class shall be vacated at the expiration of the second year, of the second class at the expiration of the fourth year; and of the third class at the expiration of the sixth year, so that one-third may be chosen every second year; and if vacancies happen by resignation, or otherwise, during the recess of the legislature of any state, the executive thereof may make temporary appointments until the next meeting of the legislature, which shall then fill such vacancies.

No person shall be a Senator who shall not have attained to the age of thirty years, and been nine years a citizen of the United States, and who shall not, when elected, be an inhabitant of that state for which he shall be chosen.

The Vice President of the United States shall be President of the Senate, but shall have no vote, unless they be equally divided.

The Senate shall choose their other officers, and also a President pro Tempore, in the absence of the Vice President, or when he shall exercise the office of President of the United States.

The Senate shall have the sole power to try all impeachments. When sitting for that purpose, they shall be on oath or affirmation. When the President of the United States is tried, the Chief Justice shall preside: and no person shall be convicted without the concurrence of two-thirds of the members present.

Judgment in cases of impeachment shall not extend further than to removal from office, and disqualification to hold and enjoy any office of honor, trust or profit under the United States; but the party convicted shall nevertheless be liable and subject to indictment, trial, judgment and punishment, according to law.

Section 4

The times, places and manner of holding elections for Senators and Representatives, shall be prescribed in each state by the legislature thereof; but the Congress may at any time by law make or alter such regulations, except as to the places of choosing Senators.

The Congress shall assemble at least once in every year, and such meeting shall be on the first Monday in December, unless they shall by law appoint a different day.

Section 5

Each house shall be the judge of the elections, returns and qualifications of its own members, and a majority of each shall constitute a quorum to do business; but a smaller number may adjourn from day to day, and may be authorized to compel the attendance of absent members, in such manner, and under such penalties as each house may provide.

Each house may determine the rules of its proceedings, punish its members for disorderly behavior, and, with the concurrence of two-thirds, expel a member.

Each house shall keep a journal of its proceedings, and from time to time publish the same, excepting such parts as may in their judgment require secrecy; and the yeas and nays of the members of either house on any question shall, at the desire of one-fifth of those present, be entered on the journal.

Neither house, during the session of Congress, shall, without the consent of the other, adjourn for more than three days, nor to any other place than that in which the two houses shall be sitting.

Section 6

The Senators and Representatives shall receive a compensation for their services, to be ascertained by law, and paid out of the Treasury of the United States. They shall in all cases, except treason, felony and breach of the peace, be privileged from arrest during their attendance at the session of their respective houses, and in going to and returning from the same; and for any speech or debate in either house, they shall not be questioned in any other place.

No Senator or Representative shall, during the time for which he was elected, be appointed to any civil office under the authority of the United States, which shall have been created, or the emoluments whereof shall have been increased during such time; and no person holding any office under the United States, shall be a member of either house during his continuance in office.

Section 7

All bills for raising revenue shall originate in the House of Representatives; but the Senate may propose or concur with amendments as on other bills.

Every bill which shall have passed the House of Representatives and the Senate, shall, before it become a law, be presented to the President of the United States; if he approve he shall sign it, but if not, he shall return it, with his objections to that house in which it shall have originated, who shall enter the objections at large on their journal, and proceed to reconsider it. If after such reconsideration two-thirds of that house shall agree to pass the bill, it shall be sent, together with the objections, to the other house, by which it shall likewise be reconsidered, and if approved by two-thirds of that house, it shall become a law. But in all such cases the votes of both houses shall be determined by yeas and nays, and the names of the persons voting for and against the bill shall be entered on the journal of each house respectively. If any bill shall not be returned by the President within ten days (Sundays excepted) after it shall have been presented to him, the same shall be a law, in like manner if he had signed it, unless the Congress by their adjournment prevent its return, in which case it shall not be a law.

Every order, resolution, or vote to which the concurrence of the Senate and House of Representatives may be necessary (except on a question of adjournment) shall be presented to the President of the United States; and before the same shall take effect, shall be approved by him, or being disapproved by him, shall be repassed by two-thirds of the Senate and House of Representatives, according to the rules and limitations prescribed in the case of a bill.

Section 8

The Congress shall have power:

To lay and collect taxes, duties, imposts and excises, to pay the debts and provide for the common defense and general welfare of the United States; but all duties, imposts and excises shall be uniform throughout the United States;

To borrow money on the credit of the United States;

To regulate commerce with foreign nations, and among the several states, and with the Indian tribes;

To establish an uniform rule of naturalization, and uniform laws on the subject of bankruptcies throughout the United States;

To coin money, regulate the value thereof, and of foreign coin, and fix the standard of weights and measures;

To provide for the punishment of counterfeiting the securities and current coin of the United States;

To establish post offices and post roads;

To promote the progress of science and useful arts, by securing for limited times to authors and inventors the exclusive right to their respective writings and discoveries;

To constitute tribunals inferior to the Supreme Court;

To define and punish piracies and felonies committed on the high seas, and offenses against the law of nations;

To declare war, grant letters of marque and reprisal, and make rules concerning captures on land and water;

To raise and support armies, but no appropriation of money to that use shall be for a longer term than two years;

To provide and maintain a navy;

To make rules for the government and regulation of the land and naval forces;

To provide for calling forth the militia to execute the laws of the union, suppress insurrections and repel invasions;

To provide for organizing, arming, and disciplining the militia, and for governing such part of them as may be employed in the service of the United States, reserving to the states respectively, the appointment of the officers, and the authority of training the militia according to the discipline prescribed by Congress;

To exercise exclusive legislation in all cases whatsoever, over such district (not exceeding ten miles square) as may, by cession of particular states, and the acceptance of Congress, become the seat of the government of the United States, and to exercise like authority over all places purchased by the consent of the legislature of the state in which the same shall be, for the erection of forts, magazines, arsenals, dockyards and other needful buildings; And

To make all laws which shall be necessary and proper for carrying into execution the foregoing powers, and all other powers vested by this Constitution in the government of the United States, or in any department or officer thereof.

Section 9

The migration or importation of such persons as any of the states now existing shall think proper to admit, shall not be prohibited by the Congress prior to the year one thousand eight hundred and eight, but a tax or duty may be imposed on such importation, not exceeding ten dollars for each person.

The privilege of the writ of habeas corpus shall not be suspended unless when in cases of rebellion or invasion the public safety may require it.

No bill of attainder or ex post facto law shall be passed.

No capitation, or other direct, tax shall be laid, unless in proportion to the census or enumeration hereinbefore directed to be taken.

No tax or duty shall be laid on articles exported from any state.

No preference shall be given by any regulation of commerce or revenue to the ports of one state over those of another: nor shall vessels bound to, or from, one state, be obliged to enter, clear, or pay duties in another.

No money shall be drawn from the Treasury, but in consequence of appropriations made by law; and a regular statement and account of the receipts and expenditures of all public money shall be published from time to time.

No title of nobility shall be granted by the United States; and no person holding any office of profit or trust under them, shall, without the consent of the Congress, accept of any present, emolument, office, or title, of any kind whatever, from any King, Prince, or foreign state.

Section 10
No state shall enter into any treaty, alliance, or confederation; grant letters of marque and reprisal; coin money; emit bills of credit; make any thing but gold and silver coin a tender in payment of debts; pass any bill of attainder, ex post facto law, or law impairing the obligation of contracts, or grant any title of nobility.

No state shall, without the consent of the Congress, lay any imposts or duties on imports or exports, except what may be absolutely necessary for executing its inspection laws: and the net produce of all duties and imposts, laid by any state on imports or exports, shall be for the use of the Treasury of the United States; and all such laws shall be subject to the revision and control of the Congress.

No state shall, without the consent of Congress, lay any duty of tonnage, keep troops, or ships of war in time of peace, enter into any agreement or compact with another state, or with a foreign power, or engage in war, unless actually invaded, or in such imminent danger as will not admit of delay.

ARTICLE II

Section 1
The executive power shall be vested in a President of the United States of America. He shall hold his office during the term of four years, and, together with the Vice President, chosen for the same term, be elected, as follows:

Each state shall appoint, in such manner, as the legislature thereof may direct, a number of electors, equal to the whole number of Senators and Representatives to which the state may be entitled in the Congress: but no Senator or Representative, or person holding an office of trust or profit under the United States, shall be appointed an elector.

The electors shall meet in their respective states and vote by ballot for two persons, of whom one at least shall not be an inhabitant of the same state with themselves. And they shall make a list of all the persons voted for, and of the number of votes for each; which list they shall sign and certify, and transmit sealed to the seat of the government of the United States, directed to the President

of the Senate. The President of the Senate shall, in the presence of the Senate and House of Representatives, open all the certificates, and the votes shall then be counted. The person having the greatest number of votes shall be the President, if such number be a majority of the whole number of electors appointed; and if there be more than one who have such majority, and have an equal number of votes, then the House shall immediately choose by ballot one of them for President; and if no person have a majority, then from the five highest on the list the said house shall in like manner choose the President. But in choosing the President, the vote shall be taken by states, the representation from each state having one vote; a quorum for this purpose shall consist of a member or members from two-thirds of the states, and a majority of all the states shall be necessary to a choice. In every case, after the choice of the President, the person having the greatest number of votes of the electors shall be the Vice President. But if there should remain two or more who have equal votes, the Senate shall choose from them by ballot the Vice President.

The Congress may determine the time of choosing the electors, and the day on which they shall give their votes; which day shall be the same throughout the United States.

No person except a natural born citizen, or a citizen of the United States, at the time of the adoption of this Constitution, shall be eligible to the office of President; neither shall any person be eligible to that office who shall not have attained to the age of thirty-five years, and been fourteen years a resident within the United States.

In case of the removal of the President from office, or of his death, resignation, or inability to discharge the powers and duties of the said Office, the same shall devolve on the Vice President, and the Congress may by law provide for the case of removal, death, resignation or inability, both of the President and Vice President, declaring what officer shall then act as President; and such officer shall act accordingly until the disability be removed, or a President shall be elected.

The President shall, at stated times, receive for his services a compensation which shall neither be increased nor diminished during the period for which he shall have been elected and he shall not receive within that period any other emolument from the United States, or any of them.

Before he enter on the execution of his office, he shall take the following oath or affirmation.— "I do solemnly swear (or affirm) that I will faithfully execute the office of President of the United States, and will, to the best of my ability, preserve, protect and defend the Constitution of the United States."

Section 2

The President shall be commander in chief of the Army and Navy of the United States, and of the militia of the several states, when called into the actual service of the United States; he may require the opinion, in writing, of the principal officer in each of the executive departments, upon any subject relating to the duties of their respective offices, and he shall have power to grant reprieves and pardons for offenses against the United States, except in cases of impeachment.

He shall have power, by and with the advice and consent of the Senate, to make treaties, provided two-thirds of the Senators present concur; and he shall nominate, and by and with the advice and consent of the Senate, shall appoint ambassadors, other public ministers and consuls, judges of the Supreme Court, and all other officers of the United States, whose appointments are not herein otherwise provided for, and which shall be established by law: but the Congress may by law vest the appointment of such inferior officers, as they think proper, in the President alone, in the courts of law, or in the heads of departments.

The President shall have power to fill up all vacancies that may happen during the recess of the Senate, by granting commissions which shall expire at the end of their next session.

Section 3

He shall from time to time give to the Congress information of the state of the union, and recommend to their consideration such measures as he shall judge necessary and expedient; he may, on extraordinary occasions, convene both houses, or either of them, and in case of disagreement between them, with respect to the time of adjournment, he may adjourn them to such time as he shall think proper; he shall receive ambassadors and other public ministers; he shall take care that the laws be

faithfully executed, and shall commission all the officers of the United States.

Section 4

The President, Vice President and all civil officers of the United States, shall be removed from office on impeachment for, and conviction of, treason, bribery, or other high crimes and misdemeanors.

ARTICLE III

Section 1

The judicial power of the United States shall be vested in one supreme court, and in such inferior courts as the Congress may from time to time ordain and establish. The judges, both of the Supreme and inferior courts, shall hold their offices during good behavior, and shall, at stated times, receive for their services, a compensation, which shall not be diminished during their continuance in office.

Section 2

The judicial power shall extend to all cases, in law and equity, arising under this Constitution, the laws of the United States, and treaties made, or which shall be made, under their authority; to all cases affecting ambassadors, other public ministers and consuls; to all cases of admiralty and maritime jurisdiction; to controversies to which the United States shall be a party; to controversies between two or more states, between a state and citizens of another state, between citizens of different states, between citizens of the same state claiming lands under grants of different states, and between a state, or the citizens thereof, and foreign states, citizens or subjects.

In all cases affecting ambassadors, other public ministers and consuls, and those in which a state shall be party, the Supreme Court shall have original jurisdiction. In all the other cases before mentioned, the Supreme Court shall have appellate jurisdiction, both as to law and fact, with such exceptions, and under such regulations as the Congress shall make.

The trial of all crimes, except in cases of impeachment, shall be by jury; and such trial shall be held in the state where the said crimes shall have been committed; but when not committed within any state, the trial shall be at such place or places as the Congress may by law have directed.

Section 3

Treason against the United States, shall consist only in levying war against them, or in adhering to their enemies, giving them aid and comfort. No person shall be convicted of treason unless on the testimony of two witnesses to the same overt act, or on confession in open court.

The Congress shall have power to declare the punishment of treason, but no attainder of treason shall work corruption of blood, or forfeiture except during the life of the person attainted.

ARTICLE IV

Section 1

Full faith and credit shall be given in each state to the public acts, records, and judicial proceedings of every other state. And the Congress may by general laws prescribe the manner in which such acts, records and proceedings shall be proved, and the effect thereof.

Section 2

The citizens of each state shall be entitled to all privileges and immunities of citizens in the several states.

A person charged in any state with treason, felony, or other crime, who shall flee from justice, and be found in another state, shall, on demand of the executive authority of the state from which he fled, be delivered up, to be removed to the state having jurisdiction of the crime.

No person held to service or labor in one state, under the laws thereof, escaping into another, shall, in consequence of any law or regulation therein, be discharged from such service or labor, but shall be delivered up on claim of the party to whom such service or labor may be due.

Section 3

New states may be admitted by the Congress into this union; but no new state shall be formed or erected within the jurisdiction of any other state; nor any state be formed by the junction of two or more states, or parts of states, without the consent of the legislatures of the states concerned as well as of the Congress.

The Congress shall have power to dispose of and make all needful rules and regulations respecting the territory or other property belonging to the United States; and nothing in this Constitution shall be so construed as to prejudice any claims of the United States, or of any particular state.

Section 4

The United States shall guarantee to every state in this union a republican form of government, and shall protect each of them against invasion; and on application of the legislature, or of the executive (when the legislature cannot be convened) against domestic violence.

ARTICLE V

The Congress, whenever two-thirds of both houses shall deem it necessary, shall propose amendments to this Constitution, or, on the application of the legislatures of two-thirds of the several states, shall call a convention for proposing amendments, which, in either case, shall be valid to all intents and purposes, as part of this Constitution, when ratified by the legislatures of three-fourths of the several states, or by conventions in three-fourths thereof, as the one or the other mode of ratification may be proposed by the Congress; provided that no amendment which may be made prior to the year one thousand eight hundred and eight shall in any manner affect the first and fourth clauses in the ninth section of the first article; and that no state, without its consent, shall be deprived of its equal suffrage in the Senate.

ARTICLE VI

All debts contracted and engagements entered into, before the adoption of this Constitution, shall be as valid against the United States under this Constitution, as under the Confederation.

This Constitution, and the laws of the United States which shall be made in pursuance thereof; and all treaties made, or which shall be made, under the authority of the United States, shall be the supreme law of the land; and the judges in every state shall be bound thereby, any thing in the Constitution or laws of any state to the contrary notwithstanding.

The Senators and Representatives before mentioned, and the members of the several state legislatures, and all executive and judicial officers, both of the United States and of the several states, shall be bound by oath or affirmation, to support this Constitution; but no religious test shall ever be required as a qualification to any office or public trust under the United States.

ARTICLE VII

The ratification of the conventions of nine states, shall be sufficient for the establishment of this Constitution between the states so ratifying the same.

Done in convention by the unanimous consent of the states present the seventeenth day of September in the year of our Lord one thousand seven hundred and eighty-seven and of the Independence of the United States of America the twelfth. In witness whereof we have hereunto subscribed our names.

(Here follow the signatures of thirty-nine persons representing twelve states, headed by the name of George Washington, president of the convention.)

AMENDMENTS TO THE CONSTITUTION

ARTICLE I (1791)

Congress shall make no law respecting an establishment of religion, or prohibiting the free exercise thereof; or abridging the freedom of speech, or of the press; or the right of the people peaceably to assemble, and to petition the government for a redress of grievances.

ARTICLE II (1791)

A well regulated militia, being necessary to the security of a free state, the right of the people to keep and bear arms, shall not be infringed.

ARTICLE III (1791)

No soldier shall, in time of peace be quartered in any house, without the consent of the owner, nor in time of war, but in manner to be prescribed by law.

ARTICLE IV (1791)

The right of the people to be secure in their persons, houses, papers and effects, against unreasonable searches and seizures, shall not be violated, and no warrants shall issue, but upon probable cause, supported by oath or affirmation, and particularly describing the place to be searched, and the persons or things to be seized.

ARTICLE V (1791)

No person shall be held to answer for a capital, or otherwise infamous crime, unless on a presentment or indictment of a grand jury, except in cases arising in the land or naval forces, or in the militia, when in actual service in time of war or public danger; nor shall any person be subject for the same offense to be twice put in jeopardy of life or limb; nor shall be compelled in any criminal case to be a witness against himself, nor be deprived of life, liberty, or property, without due process of law; nor shall private property be taken for public use without just compensation.

ARTICLE VI (1791)

In all criminal prosecutions, the accused shall enjoy the right to a speedy and public trial, by an impartial jury of the state and district wherein the crime shall have been committed, which district shall have been previously ascertained by law, and to be informed of the nature and cause of the accusation; to be confronted with the witnesses against him; to have compulsory process for obtaining witnesses in his favor, and to have the assistance of counsel for his defense.

ARTICLE VII (1791)

In suits at common law, where the value in controversy shall exceed twenty dollars, the right of trial by jury shall be preserved, and no act tried by a jury shall be otherwise reexamined in any court of the United States, than according to the rules of the common law.

ARTICLE VIII (1791)

Excessive bail shall not be required, nor excessive fines imposed, nor cruel and unusual punishments inflicted.

ARTICLE IX (1791)

The enumeration in the Constitution of certain rights shall not be construed to deny or disparage others retained by the people.

ARTICLE X (1791)

The powers not delegated to the United States by the Constitution, nor prohibited by it to the states, are reserved to the states respectively, or to the people.

ARTICLE XI (1798)

The judicial power of the United States shall not be construed to extend to any suit in law or equity, commenced or prosecuted against one of the United States by citizens of another state, or by citizens or subjects of any foreign state.

ARTICLE XII (1804)

The electors shall meet in their respective states and vote by ballot for President and Vice President, one of whom, at least shall not be an inhabitant of the same state with themselves; they shall name in their ballots the person voted for as President, and in distinct ballots, the person voted for as Vice President, and they shall make distinct lists of all persons voted for as President, and of all persons voted for as Vice President, and of the number of votes for each, which lists they shall sign and certify, and transmit sealed to the seat of the government of the United States, directed to the President of the Senate,—The President of the Senate shall, in the presence of the Senate and House of Representatives, open all the certificates and the votes shall then be counted;— The person having the greatest number of votes for President, shall be the President, if such number be a majority of the whole number of electors appointed; and if no person have such majority then from the persons having the highest numbers not exceeding three on the list of those voted for as President, the House of Representatives shall choose immediately, by ballot, the President. But in choosing the President, the votes shall be taken by states, the representation from each state having one vote; a quorum for this purpose shall consist of a member or members from two-thirds of the states, and a majority of all the states shall be necessary to a choice. And if the House of Representatives shall not choose a President whenever the right of choice shall devolve upon them, before the fourth day of March next following, then the Vice President shall act as President, as in the case of the death or other constitutional disability of the President.

The person having the greatest number of votes as Vice President, shall be the Vice President, if such number be a majority of the whole number of electors appointed, and if no person have a majority, then from the two highest numbers on the list, the Senate shall choose the Vice President; a quorum for the purpose shall consist of two-thirds of the whole number of Senators, and a majority of the whole number shall be necessary to a choice. But no person constitutionally ineligible to the office of President shall be eligible to that of Vice President of the United States.

ARTICLE XIII (1865)

Section 1

Neither slavery nor involuntary servitude, except as a punishment for crime whereof the party shall have been duly convicted, shall exist within the United States, or any place subject to their jurisdiction.

Section 2

Congress shall have power to enforce this article by appropriate legislation.

ARTICLE XIV (1868)

Section 1

All persons born or naturalized in the United States and subject to the jurisdiction thereof, are citizens of the United States and of the state wherein they reside. No state shall make or enforce any law which shall abridge the privileges or immunities of citizens of the United States; nor shall any state deprive any person of life, liberty, or property, without due process of law; nor deny to any person within its jurisdiction the equal protection of the laws.

Section 2

Representatives shall be apportioned among the several states according to their respective numbers, counting the whole number of persons in each state, excluding Indians not taxed. But when the right to vote at any election for the choice of electors for President and Vice President of the United States, Representatives in Congress, the executive and judicial officers of a state, or the members of the legislature thereof, is denied to any of the male inhabitants of such state, being twenty-one years of age, and citizens of the United States, or in any way abridged, except for participation in rebellion or other crime, the basis of representation therein shall be reduced in the proportion which the number of such male citizens shall bear to the whole number of male citizens twenty-one years of age in such state.

Section 3
No person shall be a Senator or Representative in Congress, or elector of President and Vice President, or hold any office, civil or military, under the United States, or under any state, who, having previously taken an oath, as a member of Congress, or as an officer of the United States, or as a member of any state legislature, or as an executive or judicial officer of any state, to support the Constitution of the United States, shall have engaged in insurrection or rebellion against the same, or given aid or comfort to the enemies thereof. But Congress may by a vote of two-thirds of each house, remove such disability.

Section 4
The validity of the public debt of the United States, authorized by law, including debts incurred for payment of pensions and bounties for services in suppressing insurrection or rebellion, shall not be questioned. But neither the United States nor any state shall assume or pay any debt or obligation incurred in aid of insurrection or rebellion against the United States, or any claim for the loss or emancipation of any slave; but all such debts, obligations and claims shall be held illegal and void.

Section 5
The Congress shall have power to enforce, by appropriate legislation, the provisions of this article.

ARTICLE XV (1870)

Section 1
The right of citizens of the United States to vote shall not be denied or abridged by the United States or by any state on account of race, color, or previous condition of servitude.

Section 2
The Congress shall have power to enforce this article by appropriate legislation.

ARTICLE XVI (1913)
The Congress shall have power to lay and collect taxes on incomes, from whatever source derived, without apportionment among the several states, and without regard to any census or enumeration.

ARTICLE XVII (1913)

Section 1
The Senate of the United States shall be composed of two Senators from each state, elected by the people thereof, for six years; and each Senator shall have one vote. The electors in each state shall have the qualifications requisite for electors of the most numerous branch of the state legislatures.

Section 2
When vacancies happen in the representation of any state in the Senate, the executive authority of such state shall issue writs of election to fill such vacancies: *Provided,* That the legislature of any state may empower the executive thereof to make temporary appointments until the people fill the vacancies by election as the legislature may direct.

Section 3
This amendment shall not be so construed as to affect the election or term of any Senator chosen before it becomes valid as part of the Constitution.

ARTICLE XVIII (1919)

Section 1
After one year from the ratification of this article the manufacture, sale, or transportation of intoxicating liquors within, the importation thereof into, or the exportation thereof from the United States and all territory subject to the jurisdiction thereof for beverage purposes is hereby prohibited.

Section 2
The Congress and the several states shall have concurrent power to enforce this article by appropriate legislation.

Section 3
This article shall be inoperative unless it shall have been ratified as an amendment to the Constitution by the legislatures of the several states, as provided in the Constitution, within seven years from the date of the submission hereof to the states by the Congress.

ARTICLE XIX (1920)

Section 1
The right of citizens of the United States to vote shall not be denied or abridged by the United States or by any state on account of sex.

Section 2

Congress shall have power to enforce this article by appropriate legislation.

ARTICLE XX (1933)

Section 1

The terms of the President and Vice President shall end at noon on the 20th day of January, and the terms of Senators and Representatives at noon on the 3d day of January, of the years in which such terms would have ended if this article had not been ratified; and the terms of their successors shall then begin.

Section 2

The Congress shall assemble at least once in every year and such meeting shall begin at noon on the 3d day of January, unless they shall by law appoint a different day.

Section 3

If, at the time fixed for the beginning of the term of the president, the President-elect shall have died, the Vice President-elect shall become President. If a President shall not have been chosen before the time fixed for the beginning of his term, or if the President-elect shall have failed to qualify, then the Vice President-elect shall act as President until a President shall have qualified; and the Congress may by law provide for the case wherein neither a President-elect nor Vice President-elect shall have qualified, declaring who shall then act as President, or the manner in which one who is to act shall be selected, and such person shall act accordingly until a President or Vice President shall have qualified.

Section 4

The Congress may by law provide for the case of the death of any of the persons from whom the House of Representatives may choose a President whenever the right of choice shall have devolved upon them, and for the case of the death of any of the persons from whom the Senate may choose a Vice President whenever the right of choice shall have devolved upon them.

Section 5

Sections 1 and 2 shall take effect on the 15th day of October following the ratification of this article.

Section 6

This article shall be inoperative unless it shall have been ratified as an amendment to the Constitution by the legislatures of three-fourths of the several states within seven years from the date of its submission.

ARTICLE XXI (1933)

Section 1

The eighteenth article of amendment to the Constitution of the United States is hereby repealed.

Section 2

The transportation or importation into any state, territory, or possession of the United States for delivery or use therein of intoxicating liquors, in violation of the laws thereof, is hereby prohibited.

Section 3

This article shall be inoperative unless it shall have been ratified as an amendment to the Constitution by conventions in the several states, as provided in the Constitution, within seven years from the date of the submission hereof to the states by the Congress.

ARTICLE XXII (1951)

Section 1

No person shall be elected to the office of the President more than twice, and no person who has held the office of President, or acted as President, for more than two years of a term to which some other person was elected President shall be elected to the office of the President more than once.

But this article shall not apply to any person holding the office of President when this article was proposed by the Congress, and shall not prevent any person who may be holding the office of President, or acting as President, during the term within which this article becomes operative from holding the office of President or acting as President during the remainder of such term.

Section 2

This article shall be inoperative unless it shall have been ratified as an amendment to the Constitution by the legislatures of three-fourths of the several states within seven years from the date of its submission to the states by the Congress.

ARTICLE XXIII (1961)

Section 1

The district constituting the seat of government of the United States shall appoint in such manner as the Congress may direct:

A number of electors of President and Vice President equal to the whole number of Senators and Representatives in Congress to which the district would be entitled if it were a state, but in no event more than the least populous state; they shall be in addition to those appointed by the states, but they shall be considered, for the purposes of the election of President and Vice President, to be electors appointed by a state; and they shall meet in the district and perform such duties as provided by the twelfth article of amendment.

Section 2

The Congress shall have power to enforce this article by appropriate legislation.

ARTICLE XXIV (1964)

Section 1

The right of citizens of the United States to vote in any primary or other election for President or Vice President, for electors for President or Vice President, or for Senator or Representative in Congress, shall not be denied or abridged by the United States or any state by reason of failure to pay any poll tax or other tax.

Section 2

The Congress shall have power to enforce this article by appropriate legislation.

ARTICLE XXV (1967)

Section 1

In case of the removal of the President from office or of his death or resignation, the Vice President shall become President.

Section 2

Whenever there is a vacancy in the office of the Vice President, the President shall nominate a Vice President who shall take office upon confirmation by a majority vote of both houses of Congress.

Section 3

Whenever the President transmit to the President pro Tempore of the Senate and the Speaker of the House of Representatives his written declaration that he is unable to discharge the powers and duties of his office, and until he transmits to them a written declaration to the contrary, such powers and duties shall be discharged by the Vice President as Acting President.

Section 4

Whenever the Vice President and a majority of either the principal officers of the executive departments or of such other body as Congress may by law provide, transmit to the President pro Tempore of the Senate and the Speaker of the House of Representatives their written declaration that the President is unable to discharge the powers and duties of his office, the Vice President shall immediately assume the powers and duties of the office as Acting President.

Thereafter, when the President transmits to the President pro Tempore of the Senate and the Speaker of the House of Representatives his written declaration that no inability exists, he shall resume the powers and duties of his office unless the Vice President and a majority of either the principal officers of the executive department or of such other body as Congress may by law provide, transmit within four days to the President pro Tempore of the Senate and the Speaker of the House of Representatives their written declaration that the President is unable to discharge the powers and duties of his office. Thereupon Congress shall decide the issue, assembling within forty-eight hours for that purpose if not in session. If the Congress, within twenty-one days after receipt of the latter written declaration, or, if Congress is not in session within twenty-one days after Congress is required to assemble, determines by two-thirds vote of both houses that the President is unable to discharge the powers and duties of his office, the Vice President shall continue to discharge the same as Acting President; otherwise, the President shall resume the powers and duties of his office.

ARTICLE XXVI (1971)

Section 1
The right of citizens of the United States, who are eighteen years of age or older, to vote shall not be denied or abridged by the United States or by any state on account of age.

Section 2
The Congress shall have power to enforce this article by appropriate legislation.

ARTICLE XXVII
[Proposed 1789; Ratified 1992; Second of twelve Articles comprising the Bill of Rights]

No law, varying the compensation for the services of the Senators and Representatives, shall take effect, until an election of Representatives shall have intervened.

FOR THE INDEPENDENT JOURNAL
THE FEDERALIST NO. 6 (HAMILTON)

To the People of the State of New York:

The three last numbers of this paper have been dedicated to an enumeration of the dangers to which we should be exposed, in a state of disunion, from the arms and arts of foreign nations. I shall now proceed to delineate dangers of a different and, perhaps, still more alarming kind—those which will in all probability flow from dissensions between the States themselves, and from domestic factions and convulsions. These have been already in some instances slightly anticipated; but they deserve a more particular and more full investigation.

A man must be far gone in Utopian speculations who can seriously doubt that, if these States should either be wholly disunited, or only united in partial confederacies, the subdivisions into which they might be thrown would have frequent and violent contests with each other. To presume a want of motives for such contests as an argument against their existence, would be to forget that men are ambitious, vindictive, and rapacious. To look for a continuation of harmony between a number of independent, unconnected sovereignities in the same neighborhood, would be to disregard the uniform course of human events, and to set at defiance the accumulated experience of ages.

The causes of hostility among nations are innumerable. There are some which have a general and almost constant operation upon the collective bodies of society. Of this description are the love of power or the desire of pre-eminence and dominion—the jealousy of power, or the desire of equality and safety. There are others which have a more circumscribed though an equally operative influence within their spheres. Such are the rivalships and competitions of commerce between commercial nations. And there are others, not less numerous than either of the former, which take their origin entirely in private passions; in the attachments, enmities, interests, hopes, and fears of leading individuals in the communities of which they are members. Men of this class, whether the favorites of a king or of a people, have in too many instances abused the confidence they possessed; and assuming the pretext of some public motive, have not scrupled to sacrifice the national tranquility to personal advantage or personal gratification.

The celebrated Pericles, in compliance with the resentment of a prostitute, at the expense of much of the blood and treasure of his countrymen, attacked, vanquished, and destroyed the city of the *Samnians.* The same man, stimulated by private pique against the *Megarensians,* another nation of Greece, or to avoid a prosecution with which he was threatened as an accomplice in a supposed theft of the statuary of Phidias, or to get rid of the accusations prepared to be brought against him for dissipating the funds of the state in the purchase of popularity, or from a combination of all these causes, was the primitive author of that famous and fatal war, distinguished in the Grecian annals by the name of the *Peloponnesian* war; which, after various vicissitudes, intermissions, and renewals, terminated in the ruin of the Athenian commonwealth.

The ambitious cardinal, who was prime minister to Henry VIII, permitting his vanity to aspire to the triple crown, entertained hopes of succeeding in the acquisition of that splendid prize by the influence of the Emperor Charles V. To secure the favor and interest of this enterprising and powerful monarch, he precipitated England into a war with France, contrary to the plainest dictates of policy, and at the hazard of the safety and independence, as well of the kingdom over which he presided by his counsels, as of Europe in general. For if there ever was a sovereign who bid fair to realize the project of universal monarchy, it was the Emperor Charles V, of whose intrigues Wolsey was at once the instrument and the dupe.

The influence which the bigotry of one female, the petulance of another, and the cabals of a third, had in the contemporary policy, ferments, and pactfications, of a considerable part of Europe, are topics that have been too often descanted upon not to be generally known.

To multiply examples of the agency of personal considerations in the production of great national events, either foreign or domestic, according to their direction, would be an unnecessary waste of time. Those who have but a superficial acquaintance with the sources from which they are to be drawn, will themselves recollect a variety of instances; and those who have a tolerable knowledge of human nature will not stand in need of such lights, to form their opinion either of the reality or extent of that agency. Perhaps, however, a reference, tending to illustrate the general principle, may with propriety be made to a case which has lately happened among ourselves. If Shays had not been a *desperate debtor*, it is much to be doubted whether Massachusetts would have been plunged into a civil war.

But notwithstanding the concurring testimony of experience, in this particular, there are still to be found visionary or designing men, who stand ready to advocate the paradox of perpetual peace between the States, though dismembered and alienated from each other. The genius of republics (say they) is pacific; the spirit of commerce has a tendency to soften the manners of men, and to extinguish those inflammable humors which have so often kindled into wars. Commercial republics, like ours, will never be disposed to waste themselves in ruinous contentions with each other. They will be governed by mutual interest, and will cultivate a spirit of mutual amity and concord.

Is it not (we may ask these projectors in politics) the true interest of all nations to cultivate the same benevolent and philosophic spirit? If this be their true interest, have they in fact pursued it? Has it not, on the contrary, invariably been found that momentary passions, and immediate interests, have a more active and imperious control over human conduct than general or remote considerations of policy, utility, or justice? Have republics in practice been less addicted to war than monarchies? Are not the former administered by *men* as well as the latter? Are there not aversions, predilections, rivalships, and desires of unjust acquisitions, that affect nations as well as kings? Are not popular assemblies frequently subject to the impulses of rage, resentment, jealousy, avarice, and of other irregular and violent propensities? Is it not well known that their determinations are often governed by a few individuals in whom they place confidence, and are, of course, liable to be tinctured by the passions and views of those individuals? Has commerce hitherto done any thing

more than change the objects of war? Is not the love of wealth as domineering and enterprising a passion as that of power or glory? Have there not been as many wars founded upon commercial motives since that has become the prevailing system of nations, as were before occasioned by the cupidity of territory or dominion? Has not the spirit of commerce, in many instances, administered new incentives to the appetite, both for the one and for the other? Let experience, the least fallible guide of human opinions, be appealed to for an answer to these inquiries.

Sparta, Athens, Rome, and Carthage were all republics; two of them, Athens and Carthage, of the commercial kind. Yet were they as often engaged in wars, offensive and defensive, as the neighboring monarchies of the same times. Sparta was little better than a well-regulated camp; and Rome was never sated of carnage and conquest.

Carthage, though a commercial republic, was the aggressor in the very war that ended in her destruction. Hannibal had carried her arms into the heart of Italy and to the gates of Rome, before Scipio, in turn, gave him an overthrow in the territories of Carthage, and made a conquest of the commonwealth.

Venice, in later times, figured more than once in wars of ambition, till, becoming an object to the other Italian states, Pope Julius II found means to accomplish that formidable league, which gave deadly blow to the power and pride of this haughty republic.

The provinces of Holland, till they were overwhelmed in debts and taxes, took a leading and conspicuous part in the wars of Europe. They had furious contests with England for the dominion of the sea, and were among the most persevering and most implacable of the opponents of Louis XIV.

In the government of Britain the representatives of the people compose one branch of the national legislature. Commerce has been for ages the predominant pursuit of that country. Few nations, nevertheless, have been more frequently engaged in war; and the wars in which that kingdom has been engaged have, in numerous instances, proceeded from the people.

There have been, if I may so express it, almost as many popular as royal wars. The cries of the nation and the importunities of their representatives have, upon various occasions, dragged their monarchs into war, or continued them in it, contrary to their inclinations, and sometimes contrary to the real interests of the state. In that memorable struggle for superiority between the rival houses of Austria and Bourbon, which so long kept Europe in a flame, it is well known that the antipathies of the English against the French, seconding the ambition, or rather the avarice, of a favorite leader, protracted the war beyond the limits marked out by sound policy, and for a considerable time in opposition to the views of the court.

The wars of these two last mentioned nations have in a great measure grown out of commercial considerations—the desire of supplanting and the fear of being supplanted, either in particular branches of traffic or in the general advantages of trade and navigation.

From this summary of what has taken place in other countries, whose situations have borne the nearest resemblance to our own, what reason can we have to confide in those reveries which would seduce us into an expectation of peace and cordiality between the members of the recent confederacy, in a state of separation? Have we not already seen enough of the fallacy and extravagance of those idle theories which have amused us with promises of an exemption from the imperfections, weaknesses, and evils incident to society in every shape? Is it not time to awake from the deceitful dream of a golden age, and to adopt as a practical maxim for the direction of our political conduct that we, as well as the other inhabitants of the globe, are yet remote from the happy empire of perfect wisdom and perfect virtue?

Let the point of extreme depression to which our national dignity and credit have sunk, let the inconveniences felt everywhere from a lax and ill administration of government, let the revolt of a part of the State of North Carolina, the late menacing disturbances in Pennsylvania, and the actual insurrections and rebellions in Massachusetts, declare—!

So far is the general sense of mankind from corresponding with the tenets of those who endeavor to lull asleep our apprehensions of discord and hostility between the States, in the event of disunion, that it has from long observation of the progress of society become a sort of axiom in politics, that vicinity, or nearness of situation, constitutes nations' natural enemies. An intelligent writer expresses himself on this subject to this effect: "NEIGHBORING NATIONS [says he] are naturally enemies of each other, unless their common weakness forces them to league in CONFEDERATIVE REPUBLIC, and their constitution prevents the differences that neighborhood occasions, extinguishing that secret jealousy which disposes all states to aggrandize themselves at the expense of their neighbors." This passage, at the same time, points out the EVIL and suggests the REMEDY.

THE FEDERALIST NO. 10 (MADISON)

Among the numerous advantages promised by a well-constructed Union, none deserves to be more accurately developed than its tendency to break and control the violence of faction. The friend of popular governments never finds himself so much alarmed for their character and fate as when he contemplates their propensity to this dangerous vice. He will not fail, therefore, to set a due value on any plan which, without violating the principles to which he is attached, provides a proper cure for it. The instability, injustice, and confusion introduced into the public councils have, in truth, been the mortal diseases under which popular governments have everywhere perished, as they continue to be the favorite and fruitful topics from which the adversaries to liberty derive their most specious declamations. The valuable improvements made by the American constitutions on the popular models, both ancient and modern, cannot certainly be too much admired; but it would be an unwarrantable partiality, to contend that they have as effectually obviated the danger on this side, as was wished and expected. Complaints are everywhere heard from our most considerate and virtuous citizens, equally the friends of public and private faith and of public and personal liberty, that our governments are too unstable, that the public good is disregarded in the conflicts of rival parties, and that measures are

Evolution.
Adaptation
Survival of the fittes.
Natural selection.
Theory of Evolution

too often decided, not according to the rules of justice and the rights of the minor party, but by the superior force of an interested and overbearing majority. However anxiously we may wish that these complaints had no foundation, the evidence of known facts will not permit us to deny that they are in some degree true. It will be found, indeed, on a candid review of our situation, that some of the distresses under which we labor have been erroneously charged on the operation of our governments; but it will be found, at the same time, that other causes will not alone account for many of our heaviest misfortunes; and, particularly, for that prevailing and increasing distrust of public engagements and alarm for private rights, which are echoed from one end of the continent to the other. These must be chiefly, if not wholly, effects of the unsteadiness and injustice with which a factious spirit has tainted our public administration.

By a faction, I understand a number of citizens, whether amounting to a majority or minority of the whole, who are united and actuated by some common impulse of passion, or of interest, adverse to the rights of other citizens, or to the permanent and aggregate interests of the community.

There are two methods of curing the mischiefs of faction: the one, by removing its causes; the other, by controlling its effects.

There are again two methods of removing the causes of faction: the one, by destroying the liberty which is essential to its existence; the other, by giving to every citizen the same opinions, the same passions, and the same interests.

It could never be more truly said than of the first remedy that it was worse than the disease. Liberty is to faction what air is to fire, an aliment without which it instantly expires. But it could not be a less folly to abolish liberty, which is essential to political life, because it nourishes faction, than it would be to wish the annihilation of air, which is essential to animal life, because it imparts to fire its destructive agency.

The second expedient is as impracticable as the first would be unwise. As long as the reason of man continues fallible, and he is at liberty to exercise it, different opinions will be formed. As long as the connection subsists between his reason and his self-love, his opinions and his passions will have a reciprocal influence on each other, and the former

will be objects to which the latter will attach themselves. The diversity in the faculties of men, from which the rights of property originate, is not less an insuperable obstacle to a uniformity of interests. The protection of these faculties is the first object of government. From the protection of different and unequal faculties of acquiring property, the possession of different degrees and kinds of property immediately results; and from the influence of these on the sentiments and views of the respective proprietors, ensues a division of the society into different interests and parties.

The latent causes of faction are thus sown in the nature of man; and we see them everywhere brought into different degrees of activity, according to the different circumstances of civil society. A zeal for different opinions concerning religion, concerning government, and many other points, as well of speculation as of practice; an attachment to different leaders ambitiously contending for preeminence and power; or to persons of other descriptions whose fortunes have been interesting to the human passions, have, in turn, divided mankind into parties, inflamed them with mutual animosity, and rendered them much more disposed to vex and oppress each other than to cooperate for their common good. So strong is this propensity of mankind to fall into mutual animosities, that where no substantial occasion presents itself, the most frivolous and fanciful distinctions have been sufficient to kindle their unfriendly passions and excite their most violent conflicts. But the most common and durable source of factions has been the various and unequal distribution of property. Those who hold and those who are without property have ever formed distinct interests in society. Those who are creditors, and those who are debtors, fall under a like discrimination. A landed interest, a manufacturing interest, a mercantile interest, a moneyed interest, with many lesser interests, grow up of necessity in civilized nations, and divide them into different classes, actuated by different sentiments and views. The regulation of these various and interfering interests forms the principal task of modern legislation, and involves the spirit of party and faction in the necessary and ordinary operations of the government.

No man is allowed to be a judge in his own cause, because his interest would certainly bias his judgment, and, not improbably, corrupt his integrity.

With equal, nay with greater reason, a body of men are unfit to be both judges and parties at the same time; yet what are many of the most important acts of legislation, but so many judicial determinations, not indeed concerning the rights of single persons, but concerning the rights of large bodies of citizens? And what are the different classes of legislators but advocates and parties to the causes which they determine? Is a law proposed concerning private debts? It is a question to which the creditors are parties on one side and the debtors on the other. Justice ought to hold the balance between them. Yet the parties are, and must be, themselves the judges; and the most numerous party, or, in other words, the most powerful faction must be expected to prevail. Shall domestic manufacturers be encouraged, and in what degree, by restrictions on foreign manufacturers? these questions which would be differently decided by the landed and the manufacturing classes, and probably by neither with a sole regard to justice and the public good. The apportionment of taxes on the various descriptions of property is an act which seems to require the most exact impartiality; yet there is, perhaps, no legislative act in which greater opportunity and temptation are given to a predominant party to trample on the rules of justice. Every shilling with which they overburden the inferior number is a shilling saved to their own pockets.

It is in vain to say that enlightened statesmen will be able to adjust these clashing interests and render them all subservient to the public good. Enlightened statesmen will not always be at the helm. Nor, in many cases, can such an adjustment be made at all without taking into view indirect and remote considerations, which will rarely prevail over the immediate interest which one party may find in disregarding the rights of another or the good of the whole.

The inference to which we are brought is, that the *causes* of faction cannot be removed, and that relief is only to be sought in the means of controlling its *effects*.

If a faction consists of less than a majority, relief is supplied by the republican principle, which enables the majority to defeat its sinister views by regular vote. It may clog the administration, it may convulse the society; but it will be unable to execute and mask its violence under the forms of the *Constitution*. When a majority is included in a faction, the form of popular government, on the other hand, enables it to sacrifice to its ruling passion or interest both the public good and the rights of other citizens. To secure the public good and private rights against the danger of such a faction, and at the same time to preserve the spirit and the form of popular government, is then the great object to which our inquiries are directed. Let me add that it is the great desideratum by which alone this form of government can be rescued from the opprobrium under which it has so long labored, and be recommended to the esteem and adoption of mankind.

By what means is this object attainable? Evidently by one of two only. Either the existence of the same passion or interest in a majority at the same time must be prevented, or the majority, having such coexistent passion or interest, must be rendered, by their number and local situation, unable to concert and carry into effect schemes of oppression. If the impulse and the opportunity be suffered to coincide, we well know that neither moral nor religious motives can be relied on as an adequate control. They are not found to be such on the injustice and violence of individuals, and lose their efficacy in proportion to the number combined together, that is, in proportion as their efficacy becomes needful.

From this view of the subject it may be concluded that a pure democracy, by which I mean a society consisting of a small number of citizens, who assemble and administer the government in person, can admit of no cure for the mischiefs of faction. A common passion or interest will, in almost every case, be felt by a majority of the whole; a communication and concert results from the form of government itself; and there is nothing to check the inducements to sacrifice the weaker party or an obnoxious individual. Hence it is that such democracies have ever been spectacles of turbulence and contention; have ever been found incompatible with personal security or the rights of property; and have in general been as short in their lives as they have been violent in their deaths. Theoretic politicians, who have patronized this species of government, have erroneously supposed that by reducing mankind to a perfect equality in their political rights, they would, at the same time be perfectly equalized and assimilated in their possessions, their opinions, and their passions.

A republic, by which I mean a government in which the scheme of representation takes place, opens a different prospect and promises the cure for which we are seeking. Let us examine the points in which it varies from pure democracy, and we shall comprehend both the nature of the cure and the efficacy which it must derive from the Union.

The two great points of difference between a democracy and a republic are: first, the delegation of the government, in the latter, to a small number of citizens elected by the rest; secondly, the greater number of citizens, and greater sphere of country over which the latter may be extended.

The effect of the first difference is, on the one hand, to refine and enlarge the public views, by passing them through the medium of a chosen body of citizens, whose wisdom may best discern the true interest of their country, and whose patriotism and love of justice will be least likely to sacrifice it to temporary or partial considerations. Under such a regulation, it may well happen that the public voice, pronounced by the representatives of the people, will be more consonant to the public good than if pronounced by the people themselves, convened for the purpose. On the other hand, the effect may be inverted. Men of factious tempers, of local prejudices, or of sinister designs, may, by intrigue, by corruption, or by other means, first obtain the suffrages, and then betray the interests of the people. The question resulting is, whether small or extensive republics are more favorable to the election of proper guardians of the public weal; and it is clearly decided in favor of the latter by two obvious considerations:

In the first place, it is to be remarked that however small the republic may be, the representatives must be raised to a certain number, in order to guard against the cabals of a few; and that, however large it may be, they must be limited to a certain number, in order to guard against the confusion of a multitude. Hence, the number of representatives in the two cases not being in proportion to that of the two constituents, and being proportionally greater in the small republic, it follows that, if the proportion of fit characters be not less in the large than in the small republic, the former will present a greater option, and consequently a greater probability of a fit choice.

In the next place, as each representative will be chosen by a greater number of citizens in the large than in the small republic, it will be more difficult for unworthy candidates to practise with success the vicious arts by which elections are too often carried; and the suffrages of the people being more free, will be more likely to center on men who possess the most attractive merit and the most diffusive and established characters.

It must be confessed that in this, as in most other cases, there is a mean, on both sides of which inconveniences will be found to lie. By enlarging too much the number of electors, you render the representative too little acquainted with all their local circumstances and lesser interests; as by reducing it too much, you render him unduly attached to these, and too little fit to comprehend and pursue great and national objects. The federal Constitution forms a happy combination in this respect; the great and aggregate interests being referred to the national, the local and particular to the State legislatures.

The other point of difference is the greater number of citizens and extent of territory which may be brought within the compass of republican than of democratic government; and it is this circumstance principally which renders factious combinations less to be dreaded in the former than in the latter. The smaller the society, the fewer probably will be the distinct parties and interests composing it; the fewer the distinct parties and interests, the more frequently will a majority be found of the same party; and the smaller the number of individuals composing a majority, and the smaller the compass within which they are placed, the more easily will they concert and execute their plans of oppression. Extend the sphere, and you take in a greater variety of parties and interests; you make it less probable that a majority of the whole will have a common motive to invade the rights of other citizens; or if such a common motive exists, it will be more difficult for all who feel it to discover their own strength and to act in unison with each other. Besides other impediments, it may be remarked that, where there is a consciousness of unjust or dishonorable purposes, communication is always checked by distrust in proportion to the number whose concurrence is necessary.

Hence, it clearly appears, that the same advantage which a republic has over a democracy, in controlling the effects of faction, is enjoyed by a large over a small republic—is enjoyed by the Union over the States composing it. Does this advantage consist in the substitution of representatives whose enlightened views and virtuous sentiments render them superior to local prejudices and to schemes of injustice? It will not be denied that the representation of the Union will be most likely to possess these requisite endowments. Does it consist in the greater security afforded by a greater variety of parties, against the event of any one party being able to outnumber and oppress the rest? In an equal degree does the increased variety of parties comprised within the Union, increase this security. Does it, in fine, consist in the greater obstacles opposed to the concert and accomplishment of the secret wishes of an unjust and interested majority? Here again, the extent of the Union gives it the most palpable advantage.

The influence of factious leaders may kindle a flame within their particular States, but will be unable to spread a general conflagration through the other States. A religious sect may degenerate into a political faction in a part of the Confederacy; but the variety of sects dispersed over the entire face of it must secure the national councils against any danger from that source. A rage for paper money, for an abolition of debts, for an equal division of property, or for any other improper or wicked project, will be less apt to pervade the whole body of the Union than a particular member of it; in the same proportion as such a malady is more likely to taint a particular county or district than an entire State.

In the extent and proper structure of the Union, therefore, we behold a republican remedy for the diseases most incident to republican government. And according to the degree of pleasure and pride we feel in being republicans ought to be our zeal in cherishing the spirit and supporting the character of Federalists.

PUBLIUS

THE FEDERALIST NO. 51 (MADISON)

To the People of the State of New York:

To what expedient, then, shall we finally resort, for maintaining in practice the necessary partition of power among the several departments, as laid down in the *Constitution?* The only answer that can be given is, that as all these exterior provisions are found to be inadequate, the defect must be supplied, by so contriving the interior structure of the government as that its several constituent parts may, by their mutual relations, be the means of keeping each other in their proper places. Without presuming to undertake a full development of this important idea, I will hazard a few general observations, which may perhaps place it in a clearer light, and enable us to form a more correct judgment of the principles and structure of the government planned by the convention.

In order to lay a due foundation for that separate and distinct exercise of the different powers of government, which to a certain extent is admitted on all hands to be essential to the preservation of liberty, it is evident that each department should have a will of its own; and consequently should be so constituted that the members of each should have as little agency as possible in the appointment of the members. Were this principle rigorously adhered to, it would require that all the appointments for the supreme executive, legislative, and judiciary magistracies should be drawn from the same fountain of authority, the people, through channels having no communication whatever with one another. Perhaps such a plan of constructing the several departments would be less difficult in practice than it may in contemplation appear. Some difficulties, however, and some additional expense would attend the execution of it. Some deviations, therefore, from the principle must be admitted. In the constitution of the judiciary department in particular, it might be inexpedient to insist rigorously on the principle: first, because peculiar qualifications being essential in the members, the primary consideration ought to be to select that mode of choice which best secures these qualifications; secondly, because the permanent tenure by which the appointments are held in that department, must soon destroy all sense of dependence on the authority confering them.

It is equally evident, that the members of each department should be as little dependent as possible on those of the others, for the emoluments annexed to their offices. Were the executive magistrate, or the judges, not independent of the legislature in this particular, their independence in every other would be merely nominal.

But the great security against a gradual concentration of the several powers in the same department, consists in giving to those who administer each department the necessary constitutional means and personal motives to resist encroachments of the others. The provision for defense must in this, as in all other cases, be made commensurate to the danger of attack. Ambition must be made to counteract ambition. The interest of the man must be connected with the constitutional rights of the place. It may be a reflection on human nature, that such devices should be necessary to control the abuses of government. But what is government itself, but the greatest of all reflections on human nature? If men were angels, no government would be necessary. If angels were to govern men, neither external nor internal controls on government would be necessary. In framing a government which is to be administered by men over men, the great difficulty lies in this: you must first enable the government to control the governed; and in the next place oblige it to control itself. A dependence on the people is, no doubt, the primary control on the government; but experience has taught mankind the necessity of auxiliary precautions.

This policy of supplying, by opposite and rival interests, the defect of better motives, might be traced through the whole system of human affairs, private as well as public. We see it particularly displayed in all the subordinate distributions of power, where the constant aim is to divide and arrange the several offices in such a manner as that each may be a check on the other—that the private interest of every individual may be a sentinel over the public rights. These inventions of prudence cannot be less requisite in the distribution of the supreme powers of the State.

But it is not possible to give to each department an equal power of self-defense. In republican government, the Legislative authority necessarily predominates. The remedy for this inconveniency is to divide the legislature into different branches; and to render them, by different modes of election and different principles of action, as little connected with each other as the nature of their common functions and their common dependence on the society will admit. It may even be necessary to guard against dangerous encroachments by still further precau-

tions. As the weight of the legislative authority requires that it should be thus divided, the weakness of the executive may require, on the other hand, that it should be fortified. An absolute negative on the legislature appears, at first view, to be the natural defense with which the executive magistrate should be armed. But perhaps it would be neither altogether safe nor alone sufficient. On ordinary occasions it might not be exerted with the requisite firmness, and on extraordinary occasions it might be perfidiously abused. May not this defect of an absolute negative be supplied by some qualified connection between this weaker department and the weaker branch of the stronger department, by which the latter may be led to support the constitutional rights of the former, without being too much detached from the rights of its own department?

If the principles on which these observations are founded be just, as I persuade myself they are, and they be applied as a criterion to the several State constitutions, and to the federal Constitution, it will be found that if the latter does not perfectly correspond with them, the former are infinitely less able to bear such a test.

There are, moreover, two considerations particularly applicable to the federal system of America, which place that system in a very interesting point of view.

First. In a single republic, all the power surrendered by the people is submitted to the administration of a single government; and the usurpations are guarded against by a division of the government into distinct and separate departments. In the compound republic of America, the power surrendered by the people is first divided between two distinct governments, and then the portion allotted to each subdivided among distinct and separate departments. Hence a double security arises to the rights of the people. The different governments will control each other, at the same time that each will be controlled by itself.

Second. It is of great importance in a republic not only to guard the society against the oppression of its rulers, but to guard one part of the society against the injustice of the other part. Different interests necessarily exist in different classes of citizens. If a majority be united by a common interest, the rights of the minority will be insecure. There are but two methods of providing against this evil: the one by creating a will in the community independent of the majority—that is, of the society itself; the other, by comprehending in the society so many separate descriptions of citizens as will render an unjust combination of a majority of the whole very improbable, if not impracticable. The first method prevails in all governments possessing an hereditary or self- appointed authority. This, at best, is but a precarious security; because a power independent of the society may as well espouse the unjust views of the major, as the rightful interests of the minor party, and may possibly be turned against both parties. The second method will be exemplified in the federal republic of the United States. Whilst all authority in it will be derived from and dependent on the society, the society itself will be broken into so many parts, interests and classes of citizens, that the rights of individuals, or of the minority, will be in little danger from interested combinations of the majority. In a free government the security for civil rights must be the same as that for religious rights. It consists in the one case in the multiplicity of interests, and in the other in the multiplicity of sects. The degree of security in both cases will depend on the number of interests and sects; and this may be presumed to depend on the extent of country and number of people comprehended under the same government. This view of the subject must particularly recommend a proper federal system to all the sincere and considerate friends of republican government, since it shows that in exact proportion as the territory of the Union may be formed into more circumscribed Confederacies, or States, oppressive combinations of a majority will be facilitated; the best security, under the republican forms, for the rights of every class of citizens, will be diminished; and consequently the stability and independence of some member of the government, the only other security, must be proportionally increased. Justice is the end of government. It is the end of civil society. It ever has been and ever will be pursued until it be obtained, or until liberty be lost in the pursuit. In a society under the forms of which the stronger faction can readily unite and oppress the weaker, anarchy may as truly be said to reign as in a state of nature, where the weaker individual is not secured against the violence of the stronger; and as, in the latter state, even the stronger individuals are prompted, by the uncertainty of their condition, to submit to a government which may protect the weak as well as themselves; so, in the former state, will the more powerful factions or parties be gradually induced, by a like motive, to wish for a government which will protect all parties, the weaker as well as the more powerful. It can be little doubted that if the State of Rhode Island was separated from the Confederacy and left to itself, the insecurity of rights under the popular form of government within such narrow limits would be displayed by such reiterated oppressions of factious majorities that some power altogether independent of the people would soon be called for by the voice of the very factions whose misrule had proved the necessity of it. In the extended republic of the United States, and among the great variety of interests, parties, and sects which it embraces, a coalition of a majority of the whole society could seldom take place on any other prinicples than those of justice and the general good; whilst there being thus less danger to a minor from the will of a major party, there must be less pretext, also, to provide for the security of the former, by introducing into the government a will not dependent on the latter, or in other words, a will independent of the society itself. It is no less certain than it is important, notwithstanding the contrary opinions which have been entertained, that the larger the society, provided it lie within a practical sphere, the more duly capable it will be of self-government. And happily for the *republican cause*, the practicable sphere may be carried to a very great extent, by a judicious modification and mixture of the *federal principle*.

PUBLIUS

GEORGE MASON:
"OBJECTIONS TO THE CONSTITUTION OF GOVERNMENT FORMED BY THE CONVENTION," NOVEMBER 1787

There is no Declaration of Rights; and the Laws of the general Government being paramount to the Laws and Constitutions of the several States, the Declaration of Rights in the separate States are no Security. Nor are the people secured even in the Enjoyment of the Benefits of the common-Law: which stands here upon no other Foundation than its having been adopted by the respective Acts forming the Constitutions of the several States.

In the House of Representatives there is not the Substance, but the Shadow only of Representation; which can never produce proper Information in the Legislature, or inspire Confidence in the People: the Laws will therefore be generally made by Men little concern'd in, and unacquainted with their Effects and Consequences.*

The Senate have the Power of altering all Money-Bills, and of originating Appropriations of Money and the Sallerys of the Officers of their own Appointment in Conjunction with the President of the United States; altho' they are not the Representatives of the People, or amenable to them.

These with their other great Powers (vizt. their Power in the Appointment of Ambassadors and all public Officers, in making Treaties, and in trying all Impeachments) their Influence upon and Connection with the supreme Executive from these Causes, their Duration of Office, and their being a constant existing Body almost continually sitting, joined with their being one compleat Branch of the Legislature, will destroy any Balance in the Government, and enable them to accomplish what Usurpations they please upon the Rights and Libertys of the People.

The Judiciary of the United States is so constructed and extended, as to absorb and destroy the Judiciarys of the several States; thereby rendering Law as tedious[,] intricate and expensive, and Justice as unattainable, by a great part of the Community, as in England, and enabling the Rich to oppress and ruin the Poor.

The President of the United States has no constitutional Council (a thing unknown in any safe and regular Government); he will therefore be unsupported by proper Information and Advice; and will generally be directed by Minions and Favourites—or He will become a Tool to the Senate—or a Council of State will grow out of the principal Officers of the great Departments; the worst and most dangerous of all Ingredients for such a Council, in a free Country; for they may be induced to join in any dangerous or oppressive Measures, to shelter themselves, and prevent an Inquiry into their own Misconduct in Office; whereas had a constitutional Council been formed (as was proposed) of six Members; vizt. two from the Eastern, two from the Middle, and two from the Southern States, to be appointed by Vote of the States in the House of Representatives, with the same Duration and Rotation of Office as the Senate, the Executive wou'd always have had safe and proper Information and Advice, the President of such a Council might have acted as Vice President of the United States, pro tempore, upon any Vacancy or Disability of the chief Magistrate; and long continued Sessions of the Senate wou'd in a great Measure have been prevented.

From this fatal Defect of a constitutional Council has arisen the improper Power of the Senate, in the Appointment of public Officers, and the alarming Dependence and Connection between that Branch of the Legislature, and the supreme Executive.

Hence also sprung that unnecessary and dangerous Officer, the Vice President; who for want of other Employment, is made President of the

---

*This Objection has been in some Degree lessened by an Amendment, often before refused, and at last made by an Erasure, after the Engrossment upon Parchment, of the word *forty*, and inserting *thirty*, in the 3d Clause of the 2d Section of the 1st Article.

Senate; thereby dangerously blending the executive and legislative Powers; besides always giving to some one of the States an unnecessary and unjust Pre-eminence over the others.

The President of the United States has the unrestrained Power of granting Pardon for Treason; which may be sometimes exercised to screen from Punishment those whom he had secretly instigated to commit the Crime, and thereby prevent a Discovery of his own Guilt.

By declaring all Treaties supreme Laws of the Land, the Executive and the Senate have in many Cases, an exclusive Power of Legislation; which might have been avoided by proper Distinctions with Respect to Treaties, and requiring the Assent of the House of Representatives, where it cou'd be done with Safety.

By requiring only a Majority to make all commercial and navigation Laws, the five Southern States (whose Produce and Circumstances are totally different from that of the eight Northern and Eastern States) will be ruined; for such rigid and premature Regulations may be made, as will enable the Merchants of the Northern and Eastern States not only to demand an exorbitant Freight, but to monopolize the Purchase of the Commodities at their own Price, for many years: to the great Injury of the landed Interest, and Impoverishment of the People: and the Danger is the greater, as the Gain on one Side will be in Proportion to the Loss on the other. Whereas requiring two thirds of the members present in both Houses wou'd have produced mutual moderation, promoted the general Interest, and removed an insuperable Objection to the Adoption of the Government.

Under their own Construction of the general Clause at the End of the enumerated powers the Congress may grant Monopolies in Trade and Commerce, constitute new Crimes, inflict unusual and severe Punishments, and extend their Power as far as they shall think proper; so that the State Legislatures have no Security for the Powers now presumed to remain to them; or the People for their Rights.

There is no Declaration of any kind for preserving the Liberty of the Press, the Tryal by Jury in civil Causes; nor against the Danger of standing Armys in time of Peace.

The State Legislatures are restrained from laying Export Duties on their own Produce.

The general Legislature is restrained from prohibiting the further Importation of Slaves for twenty odd Years; tho' such Importations render the United States weaker, more vulnerable, and less capable of Defence.

Both the general Legislature and the State Legislatures are expressly prohibited making ex post facto Laws; tho' there never was, or can be a Legislature but must and will make such Laws, when necessity and the public Safety require them; which will hereafter be a Breach of all the Constitutions in the Union, and afford precedents for other Innovations.

This Government will commence in a moderate Aristocracy; it is at present impossible to foresee whether it will, in its Operation, produce a Monarchy, or a corrupt oppressive Aristocracy; it will most probably vibrate some Years between the two, and then terminate in the one or the other.

Plate 2 Artemisia Gentileschi, *Juditb Bebeading Holofernes,* **1620.** Oil on canvas. 78³/₈ × 64" (199 × 162.5 cm). Uffizi, Florence. Courtesy of Alinari/Art Resource, NY.

Plate 1 Caravaggio, *Entombment,* **painted for the Vittrice Chapel,** Church of Santa Maria in Vallicella, Rome, c.1603. Oil on canvas. 9'10¹/₈" × 6'7¹⁵/₁₆" (3 × 2.03 m). Musei Vaticani, Pinocateca, Rome. Courtesy of Scala/Art Resource, NY.

Plate 3 Peter Paul Rubens, *The Raising of the Cross,* painted for the Church of Saint Walpurga, Antwerp, Belgium. 1609–10. Oil on canvas, center panel 15'1⅞" × 11'1½" (4.62 × 3.39 m); each wing 15'1⅞" × 4'11" (4.62 × 1.52 m). Cathedral of Our Lady, Antwerp. Courtesy of Peter Willi/Superstock.

Plate 4 Nicolas Poussin, *Landscape with Saint John on Patmos,* 1640. Oil on canvas, 40 × 53½" (101.8 × 136.3 cm). The Art Institute of Chicago. Copyright © 2007, The Art Institute of Chicago. All rights reserved.

Plate 7 Anthony van Dyck, *Equestrian Portrait of Charles I, King of England,* ca.1635. Oil on canvas, 266 × 207 cm. Musée du Louvre, Paris. Courtesy of Erich Lessing/Art Resource, NY.

Plate 8 Jean-Antoine Watteau, *The Departure from [Pilgrimage to] Cythera,* 1717. Oil on canvas, 4'3" × 6'4¹/₂" (1.3 × 1.9 m). Musée du Louvre, Paris. Courtesy of the Art Archive/Corbis.

Plate 9 Rosalba Carriera, *Louis XV as a Boy*, 1720. Pastel on paper. 19 × 14". Museum of Fine Arts, Boston. Courtesy of Erich Lessing/Art Resource, NY.

Plate 10 Jean-Honoré Fragonard, *The Meeting*, from *The Loves of the Shepherds*, 1771–73. Oil on canvas, 10'5¼" × 7'5⅞" (3.18 × 2.15 m). The Frick Collection, New York. Courtesy of the Frick Art Reference Library.

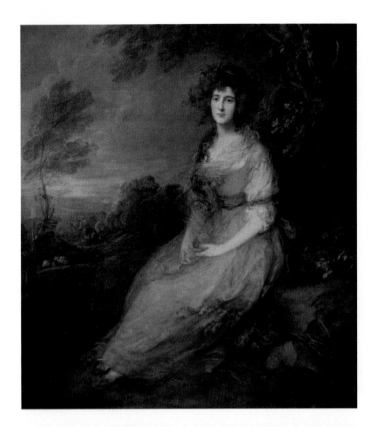

Plate 11 Thomas Gainsborough, *Portrait of Mrs. Richard Brinsley Sheridan,* 1785–87. Oil on canvas, 7'2¹/₂" × 5'1¹/₂" (2.2 × 1.54 m). National Gallery of Art, Washington, D.C. Courtesy of Mellon College, National Gallery of Art, Washington DC, USA/The Bridgeman Art Library International.

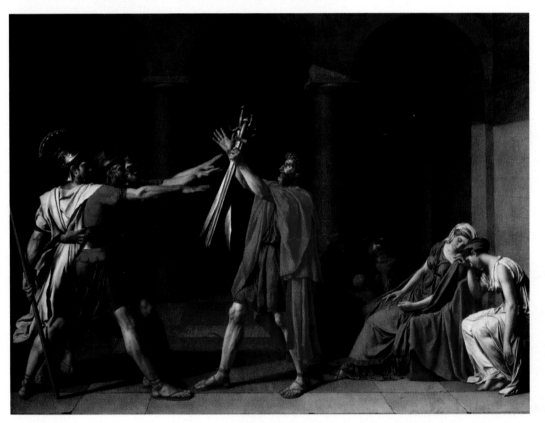

Plate 12 Jacques-Louis David, *Oath of the Horatii,* 1784–85. Oil on canvas, 10'8¹/₄" × 14' (3.26 × 4.27 m). Musée du Louvre, Paris. Courtesy of Réunion des Musées Nationaux/Art Resource, NY.

Plate 13 Angelica Kauffman, *Cornelia Pointing to Her Children as Her Treasures,* 1785. Oil on canvas, 40 × 50" (101.6 × 127 cm). Virginia Museum of Fine Arts, Richmond, Virginia. The Adolph D. and Wilkins C. Williams Fund. Photo: Katherine Wetzel. Copyright © Virginia Museum of Fine Arts.

Plate 14 Théodore Géricault. *Raft of the* Méduse, 1818–19. Oil on canvas. 16'1" × 23'6" (4.9 × 7.16 m). Musée du Louvre, Paris. Courtesy of Réunion des Musées Nationaux/Art Resource, NY.

Plate 15 Eugène Delacroix,
Liberty Leading the People,
1830. Oil on canvas, 8'6" × 10'8".
Musée du Louvre, Paris.
Courtesy of Réunion des
Musées Nationaux/Art
Resource, NY.

**Plate 16 Joseph
Mallord William
Turner,** *Slavers
Throwing
Overboard the
Dead and Dying—
Typhoon Coming On
(The Slave Ship),*
1840. Oil on canvas.
$35^3/_4 × 48^1/_4$"
(90.8 × 121.9 cm).
Museum of Fine Arts,
Boston. Courtesy of
the Burstein
Collection/Corbis.

SECTION THREE

NINETEENTH CENTURY: THE WEST TRANSFORMED

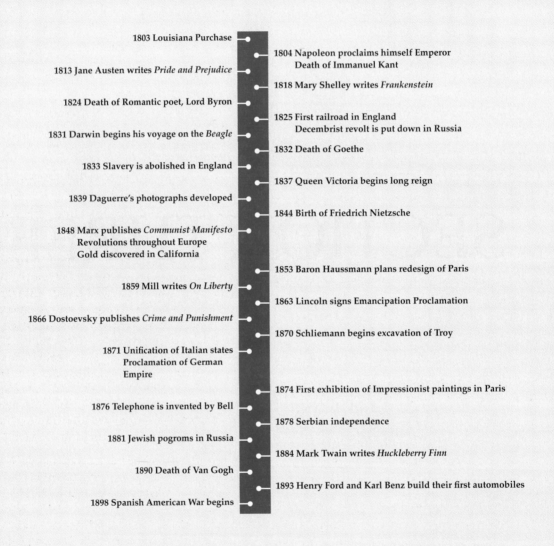

1803 Louisiana Purchase

1804 Napoleon proclaims himself Emperor
Death of Immanuel Kant

1813 Jane Austen writes *Pride and Prejudice*

1818 Mary Shelley writes *Frankenstein*

1824 Death of Romantic poet, Lord Byron

1825 First railroad in England
Decembrist revolt is put down in Russia

1831 Darwin begins his voyage on the *Beagle*

1832 Death of Goethe

1833 Slavery is abolished in England

1837 Queen Victoria begins long reign

1839 Daguerre's photographs developed

1844 Birth of Friedrich Nietzsche

1848 Marx publishes *Communist Manifesto*
Revolutions throughout Europe
Gold discovered in California

1853 Baron Haussmann plans redesign of Paris

1859 Mill writes *On Liberty*

1863 Lincoln signs Emancipation Proclamation

1866 Dostoevsky publishes *Crime and Punishment*

1870 Schliemann begins excavation of Troy

1871 Unification of Italian states
Proclamation of German
Empire

1874 First exhibition of Impressionist paintings in Paris

1876 Telephone is invented by Bell

1878 Serbian independence

1881 Jewish pogroms in Russia

1884 Mark Twain writes *Huckleberry Finn*

1890 Death of Van Gogh

1893 Henry Ford and Karl Benz build their first automobiles

1898 Spanish American War begins

NINETEENTH CENTURY: THE WEST TRANSFORMED

NAPOLEON BONAPARTE

Rise to Power. Napoleon Bonaparte's rise to power is one of the most remarkable stories in the history of the Western world. He was born in 1769 to a poor family on the island of Corsica, spoke French with an Italian accent, and was imprisoned for a time during the French Revolution. Yet, by 1800, Napoleon was the ruler of France and considered to be one of the greatest military leaders of all time.

Napoleon owed his meteoric rise to power to the French Revolution. In the pre-revolutionary French army of the Old Regime, Napoleon's background would have prevented him from rising in the ranks of the officer corps. The Revolution did away with that system, however, opening career advancement to talent and merit. Under the system created during the Revolution, Napoleon was able to begin his military career as an artillery officer.

While the Revolution gave Napoleon his start in the French army, the French Revolutionary wars provided him the chance to demonstrate his tremendous skill as a military leader. In 1792, the majority of European nations joined forces to crush the Revolution. Napoleon promptly distinguished himself on the battlefield, and in 1796, at the age of twenty-six, he was given command of French forces in Italy. Two months after taking command, Napoleon had successfully beaten back Austrian forces and conquered the Kingdom of Piedmont.

Following his victories in Italy, Napoleon gained command of French forces in Egypt. His goal was to extend French hegemony throughout the Middle East. After a year of fierce campaigns against the combined forces of the Egyptians, Turks, and British, Napoleon, seeing an opportunity to seize power in France, abandoned his troops and secretly made his way back to France.

Upon his return to Paris in 1799, Napoleon led a *coup d'état* against the revolutionary leadership of the Directory. The moderate Directory, in power since 1795, was weak, and faced stiff opposition from both radical and conservative elements in the government. The Directory was no match against the popular general. On November 10, 1799, Napoleon assumed the newly created title of "First Consul." He quickly consolidated power, strengthening his grip on France. In 1802, he proclaimed himself "First Consul for life," and on December 2, 1804, in the Cathedral of Notre Dame, Napoleon crowned himself "Emperor of the French."

Imperial Rule. Once in power, would Napoleon advance or betray the principles of the French Revolution? Ultimately, he did both. His primary task was to restore order and stability to a country shaken by a decade of revolutionary upheaval and violence. To do so, he curtailed many of the political liberties the French had enjoyed since 1789. Under Napoleon's rule it was illegal to criticize the government. Freedom of the press was severely restricted. The number of newspapers in Paris fell from seventy-four to four. The remaining few were simply mouthpieces of the government. Napoleon also censored artistic and theatrical productions, and closed political clubs around the nation.

Yet Napoleon also institutionalized many of the Revolution's central tenets. He eliminated distinctions between nobles and commoners, and kept

Europe in 1815. Reprinted from *Longman Atlas of World History* (2003), by permission of maps.com.

professions open to talent and merit. His greatest domestic achievement was the creation of a civil code of law called the *Code Napoléon*. The Code created a uniform system of justice that applied to all French citizens regardless of social or regional differences. These legal reforms protected property rights, equalized the tax burden, kept the Church subordinate to the state, guaranteed religious freedom, and granted civil rights to Jews. The civil law code also destroyed the last vestiges of feudalism by outlawing seignorial courts and abolishing serfdom.

In addition to the Code, Napoleon helped transform France into a modern, centralized, bureaucratic state. In order to facilitate trade, commerce, and communication, Napoleon ordered the construction and repairing of canals, bridges, and roadways, the standardization of a system of weights and measures, and the creation of the Bank of France. He also created France's *lycées*, a centralized school system that is the model for the educational program in France today.

The Napoleonic Empire. With his dominance secure at home, Napoleon turned his sights abroad. Between the years 1803 and 1810, no one could match Napoleon's brilliance on the battlefield or the sheer might of his *Grande Armée*. After seven years of continual warfare, France controlled the majority of continental Europe. Only Britain and Russia escaped Napoleon's grasp.

Once in control of a foreign territory, Napoleon imposed France's legal and social system on the nation. The *Code Napoléon* became the law of the land, nobility and all vestiges of feudalism were abolished, the church lost its authority in matters of state and education, people were granted the freedom to choose their religion and professions, and internal trading tariffs were removed. Napoleon's policy of reorganizing conquered lands transformed European states into modern, secularized, bureaucratic nations.

Despite being the ruler of a vast empire, Napoleon remained unsatisfied. His goal was nothing short of complete domination of Europe. Napoleon believed the way to bring Britain to its knees was to conquer its sole remaining ally and trading partner: Russia. On June 22, 1812, Napoleon led an army of 614,000 men and 250,000 horses across the Neman River onto Russian soil. Napoleon described the invasion as "the most difficult enterprise I have ever attempted." It would ultimately lead to his demise.

Russian forces retreated eastward in the face of Napoleon's army. After a brutal battle at Borodino, where seventy-five thousand men were killed, Napoleon finally entered the city of Moscow only to find it abandoned and in flames. Within a week virtually the entire city had been burned to the ground by retreating Russian forces. For lack of adequate food supplies, Napoleon and his troops were forced to retreat in the dead of winter. By the time he recrossed the Neman River, Napoleon had only 10,000 soldiers remaining.

Napoleon's empire could not survive the destruction of the *Grande Armée*. In October, 1813, Prussian, Swedish, Russian, and Austrian forces met France's army outside the city of Leipzig. European coalition forces pushed Napoleon and his troops back to Paris. He abdicated the throne and went into exile on the island of Elba, off the Italian coast.

Louis XVIII, younger brother of the executed Louis XVI, was granted the throne of France. However, Napoleon was not finished. In March, 1815, he escaped from exile and returned to Paris where he was welcomed as a hero. Louis XVIII fled the country, and the period known as the Hundred Days began. Raising a new army, Napoleon moved against a multinational European force located in Belgium. In June, 1815, Napoleon was finally defeated at the Battle of Waterloo. This time, allied forces sent Napoleon to the remote St. Helena island

in the South Atlantic where he spent the last six years of his life.

After Napoleon's final exile, European rulers met in Vienna to draw up a peace settlement, and to undo the consequences of Napoleonic rule. The leaders at the Congress of Vienna (1814–1815) sought to restore a balance of power among European nations, and to stamp out the ideas of the French Revolution. European monarchs viewed the principles of "liberty, equality, and fraternity" as a direct threat to their positions. The Congress was only a moderate success. The leaders did manage to prevent another full-scale European war until 1914. However, they were much less successful in containing the ideals of the French Revolution. Indeed, revolutions would become a regular feature of European life in the nineteenth century, erupting around the continent in 1830, 1848, and 1870.

The Industrial Revolution and Capitalism.   While the eighteenth century witnessed the outbreak of political revolutions in France and the United States, it also gave rise to a different type of revolution: the Industrial Revolution, which began in the second half of the eighteenth century and would continue to transform the material and social circumstances of human life well into the nineteenth century. So complete was this transformation that we sometimes speak of the entire history of civilization prior to this revolution as the "pre-industrial" age. Rapid technological innovation dramatically increased both agricultural and industrial productivity, factories began to replace the traditional cottage industries, new cities devoted to manufacturing arose, and people began to move in large numbers from farms to cities to work in the new factories. These structural changes in economic and social life created unprecedented challenges and problems which national and local governments had to address.

The nineteenth century also saw the emergence of *capitalism* as the dominant economic system of the Western world. While the concept of capitalism developed in the Middle Ages, it was in the nineteenth century that it "came into its own" as an economic theory put into practice. The middle class contributed significantly to the social and economic transformation of the modern West. The conjoining of natural rights theory—political ideas of individual

Honoré Daumier, best known for his political satirizations and commentaries on societal injustice, here gives a face to the plight of the urban poor. Unlike the Impressionists and other painters of modern life, who portrayed the leisure activities of a burgeoning middle class, Daumier rendered distinctions of class within a new technology of modern life, that of public transportation. *The Third-Class Carriage* portrays the interior of a horse-drawn bus, an early form of mass transit along Parisian boulevards widened under Hausmannization. Daumier here focuses on the underprivileged sector, in which a mother, grandmother, and two small children huddle together. While they appear physically and emotionally intimate with each other, they are clearly separated from the middle- and upper-class passengers seated behind them.

Figure III-1   Honoré Daumier, *The Third-Class Carriage,* c.1862. Oil on canvas, 25³/₄ × 35¹/₂" (65.4 × 90.2 cm). The National Gallery of Canada, Ottawa. Courtesy of the Granger Collection, NY.

rights, representative government, and equality before law—and the economic ideas of the free market and the inviolability of private property, produced the belief that capitalism is the rational economic system, just as representative government is the rational political system, and that basic to both is the limiting of government interference.

Beginning in the mid-eighteenth century in Britain, the Industrial Revolution saw the replacement of hand tools by machines and power tools, and the development of large-scale industrial production embodied in the factory system. By the early decades of the nineteenth century the Industrial Revolution was bringing massive changes to Britain, and in the decades that followed it produced foundational changes in the social and economic organization of other European countries, the United States, and eventually much of the world. The Industrial Revolution created the form of capitalism we know as *industrial capitalism*, which raised serious issues about the compatibility of capitalism with human rights and representative government.

Capitalist entrepreneurs organized the new technologies into new industries that could produce goods more cheaply and on a large scale. The first half of the nineteenth century witnessed the spectacular growth of what Karl Marx (1818–1883), using the French term, called the *bourgeoisie*, the propertied middle class, epitomized by the capitalist owners of the means of production and distribution of goods. They produced the *factory system*, which was characterized by what Marx called individual ownership and social production—that is, the actual producing of goods was done by a large force of workers with only their labor to sell.

Industrialization greatly accelerated the process of *urbanization* that had begun in the late Middle Ages. European societies in the late eighteenth and early nineteenth centuries were mainly agricultural, in terms of production of wealth and population location. With industrialization, farm workers began to leave the land to work in the new factories located in cities.

The long-term effects of the combination of capitalism and industrialization were a dramatic improvement in living standards for the great majority of people in Europe and the United States. But in the short run industrial capitalism created serious problems. The new industrial towns and cities spawned slums, crime, and public health problems. Working conditions in the mines and factories were appalling. Men, women, and children—whole families—had to work long hours for subsistence wages at back-breaking labor just to survive. There was typically no concern on the part of factory and mine owners about the health and safety of their workers, who often worked in dark, dangerous, disease-ridden environments. Companies provided no benefits and assumed no liability for injury or death. Workers were expendable commodities.

Decades of Revolution: 1820–1848. In the years after the defeat of Napleon and the Congress of Vienna (1815), conservatives in France, Austria, Prussia, Great Britain, and Russia sought to foster political stability by opposing liberal and reformist forces throughout the West and by reinstituting autocratic rule. In practice this meant instituting censorship of the press and imprisoning opposition forces. The goal was to kill the very dangerous ideas of the French Revolution.

Conservatives viewed notions of individual rights, democracy, and freedom of thought and speech as viruses that needed to be eradicated from the body politic of the West. Unfortunately for the conservatives, the French revolution had unleashed forces that could be contained for a time but not completely stamped out.

In 1820, Spanish revolutionaries, who opposed a restored Spanish monarchy, sought to bring some reform to the Spanish crown. The uprising was met by a quick and brutal French response. In 1823 one hundred thousand French troops, acting at the behest of the participants at the Congress of Vienna (most notably Prussia and Austria), put an end to the Spanish rebellion. A small uprising in Italy led by the Carbonari, a group dedicated to unifying Italy, triggered a disproportionate response from the combined forces of Prussia, Russia, and Austria. That uprising too was put down. As we will see, however, nationalist sentiments among the Carbonari and a majority of Italians would not be squelched so easily. In 1825 in Russia, members of the nobility who had been influenced by Western liberal ideas staged a revolt that was swiftly put down by Tsar Alexander's troops, and many of those involved were exiled to Siberia.

Revolutionary sentiment once again stirred in France as well. After the defeat of Napoleon, Louis XVI's brother took the French throne and ruled under the title of Louis XVIII (r. 1814–24). No one in France was particularly pleased to see a restored monarchy. Supporters of liberal and democratic reform saw the king as an obstacle to those goals, while those who wanted to go back to the Old Regime—particularly returning noble families—found the new king too moderate. The new Bourbon king did not follow his absolutist predecessors. He sought to establish a constitutional monarchy on the model of Britain with a two-house parliament, limited democracy, and guaranteed rights of citizens, but in practice it was the king's will that prevailed.

In 1824, Louis XVIII died and was succeeded by his younger brother Charles X (r. 1824–30). Where Louis was moderate, Charles moved towards re-establishing absolutism. In 1825, for example, he dissolved parliament and imposed strict censorship on the nation. Events came to a head in 1830, when three days of street battles in

Paris led by students and members of the middle class forced the abdication of Charles X. While Charles enjoyed exile in England, his cousin Louis Philippe (r. 1830–48) assumed the throne and set France once again on a more moderate path. The king reformed parliament and doubled the number of eligible voters in the country.

The Revolution of 1830 in France sent ripple effects throughout much of Europe. Inspired by the French revolutionaries of 1830, Belgian nationalists rose up and declared their independence from the Dutch Republic. The new Belgian government adopted liberal and moderate policies. In the former Poland, now a part of Russia, patriots took to the streets and were brutally put down by their Russian rulers in 1831. The Carbonari in the Italian states were once again inspired to bring to fruition their longstanding goal of Italian unification. This time the drive towards unification was halted by the Austrians.

The upheaval of the 1820s and 1830s proved to be just a dress rehearsal for 1848. In 1848 nearly every nation in the West experienced some sort of insurrection or uprising. As a result 1848 is often called "the year of revolution." The first revolution began in Paris in February 1848 when a coalition of students, workers, and members of the middle class took to the streets of Paris with the goal of bringing democracy to France. While the government of Louis Philippe was moderate and did allow for some degree of voting, it opposed and feared the people of France having the franchise. However, with Paris in full-scale revolt, the king abdicated his throne and France was once again declared a republic. The new government, with poet and historian Alphonse de Lamartine (1790–1869) as its leader, moved quickly to pass liberal legislation: freedom of the press, an end to the death penalty for many crimes, abolition of slavery in the colonies, and universal manhood suffrage. The government also sought to help the unemployed by establishing a series of work projects.

According to many, however, the government did not go far enough to address the social ills of the nation. As the working class of Paris, and from around the nation, grew increasingly vocal and militant in their demands for social justice, the majority of French voters grew increasingly conservative. In the election of April 1848 voters sent a conservative majority to the National Assembly (or French parliament). The new majority immediately put its stamp on the political process by excluding deputies sympathetic to workers' rights from important committees, voting down women's suffrage, and closing the work projects. The workers of Paris, joined by workers from areas surrounding the city, responded by taking to the streets. Nearly a hundred thousand workers demonstrated in what has become known as the June Days. The government responded by calling out the national guard. The result was more than ten thousand killed or injured and twelve thousand arrested. The events caused a deep rift in French society. Workers believed they had been attacked by their government and abandoned by the other social groups. The rest of France—peasants, the middle class, the wealthy—came to see the working class as radical and deeply dangerous. The following December the French elected Louis-Napoleon Bonaparte, nephew of the former emperor, as president of the Republic. Bonaparte was elected overwhelmingly, not only because of his famous name but because he had no connection to the June Days and was not associated with either the workers or the previous government. In the end, Bonaparte was no friend of the Republic. In 1852, forty-eight years after the coronation of his uncle, Louis-Napoleon Bonaparte dissolved the Republic and declared himself Emperor Napoleon III.[1]

---

[1]One of the more notable achievements of the reign of Napoleon III was "Haussmannization." Named after city planner Georges-Eugène Haussmann, Paris went through a remarkable process of urban change in the 1860s. Haussmann implemented a grand design for the city, tearing down old, decrepit buildings, usually in poor neighborhoods, and replacing them with wide boulevards lined with opulent stores and apartments for the wealthy. Some of the changes implemented by Haussmann were designed to make Paris a more healthy and safe city. So, for example, he lined the streets with gas-powered lights, had hospitals built, and public spaces and green areas for Parisians to enjoy. He also designed the new boulevards of Paris unusually broad in order to prevent revolutionaries from building barricades. While Paris is an ancient city, the one visitors see today was largely a creation of Haussmann and dates back only to the middle of the nineteenth century.

The events of 1848 in Paris soon sparked other revolts around the West. In March 1848 students in Vienna demonstrated for greater political involvement and rights. The demonstrations helped to reveal deep fissures and longstanding tensions within the Habsburg-dominated Austrian Empire. The Empire had no common language nor did it have a dominant ethnicity. Instead, it was a collection of Hungarians, Germans, Romanians, Slovaks, Croats, Serbs, Slovenes, and Magyars. The fear among the Habsburgs was that the spread of liberalism and nationalism would cause the dissolution of the multiethnic empire. In 1848 that was precisely what happened. Inspired by the student radicals in Vienna, nationalists began to demonstrate in Hungary, Bohemia and Northern Italy. In response the Habsburgs sent in the military to crush the revolts. In October 1848, the army was called into Vienna where it took charge of the city. In the following two years the Habsburgs, with the aid of Tsar Nicholas I of Russia, who himself feared nationalistic strife, put down a significant revolt in Hungary. In Germany and Italy, liberal revolts of 1848 failed. However, the revolutionary impetus was soon reconstituted as nationalist movements, which ultimately culminated in the unification of both Germany and Italy.

German and Italian Unification. As in other European countries, the growth and increasing influence of a prosperous middle class in the German states during the first half of the nineteenth century produced social and political reformers, imbued with the principles of the Enlightenment and the French Revolution and unhappy about being shut out of participating in government by an aristocracy determined to maintain its own privileges. The German phase of the European revolutions of 1848 saw middle-class liberal reformers try to create a unified Germany governed by a constitutional monarchy presided over by a broadly representative parliament. They succeeded in forcing German rulers, including King Frederick William IV of Prussia (1795–1861), to form parliaments and to admit prominent liberals into their governments. Representatives from all the German states (again, excluding Austria) meeting in Frankfurt drew up a plan for a united Germany and proposed that Frederick William be

its constitutional monarch. He refused to be offered a crown by commoners, the liberal dream failed, and in 1849 the conservative leaders of Prussia renewed their campaign to unite Germany on their terms. Austria resisted and thwarted their initial efforts, and Frederick William IV realized that Prussia could only succeed by eliminating Austrian influence in German affairs.

Frederick William's brother, William I (1797–1888), succeeded him as king of Prussia in 1861. He was soon on a collision course with the liberal majority in the lower house of parliament as to which would have ultimate control over the government and the army. In 1862 William named as chancellor of the kingdom Otto von Bismarck (1815–98), which turned out to be a brilliant tactic with fateful results for Germany and Europe.

Bismarck was a political genius. A staunch Prussian patriot, he was both ruthless and thoroughly pragmatic. He crushed the liberals or won them over and gained control of parliament. In time-honored Prussian fashion, Bismarck introduced "top-down" social reforms explicitly designed to cripple liberal and radical reform efforts and to insure undivided loyalty to the state. For example, he introduced the most advanced social legislation for workers in Europe, providing insurance for sickness, disability, accidents, and old age. Thus the legislation liberals sought was delivered to them without recourse to the legislative process. As a result, Germans lacked an authentic democratic experience, leaving them vulnerable to autocratic forces, which would have tragic results in the twentieth century.

It was Bismarck's remarkable success in foreign policy, however, that chiefly won him hearts and minds, confirmed Prussia's leadership, and brought about German unity. In the teeth of parliamentary resistance, he reorganized and strengthened the army, and in 1866 Prussia waged war against its chief obstacle, Austria. Prussia speedily won the Seven Weeks' War, eliminating Austria as a player in German politics. The same year Prussia, under Bismarck's direction, organized a Confederation of North German States. Austria's defeat by Prussia drove the Habsburg emperor, Francis Joseph, to reconcile differences with Hungary, and in 1867 the "dual monarchy" of Austria-Hungary or the Austro-Hungarian Empire was formally created.

The Unification of Germany. Reprinted from *The Prentice Hall Atlas of Western Civilization* (2004), Prentice-Hall, Inc., by permission of Dorling Kindersley.

In 1870, in order to get the southern German states into the Confederation and under Prussian control, Bismarck deliberately provoked hostility between Prussia and France, and Prussia invaded France. The war, called the Franco-Prussian War, ended with the siege of Paris and France's surrender in January 1871. As Bismarck had calculated, the south German states came to the aid of the Prussians.

The war completed the unification of Germany. On January 18, 1871, at Versailles, the German princes granted the title of *Kaiser* (from the Latin *caesar*, emperor) to King William I, creating the German Empire (*Reich*). By this act Bismarck and Prussia created the most powerful industrialized nation in Europe, with an educated, hard-working, and disciplined population and the finest army on the

The Unification of Italy. Reprinted from *The Prentice Hall Atlas of Western Civilization* (2004), Prentice-Hall, Inc., by permission of Dorling Kindersley.

continent. This formidable new state was also thoroughly authoritarian, molded in the Prussian image, and its people had been largely denied much experience with democratic ideas and institutions such as representative government and the guarantee of individual rights. In the twentieth century that would seriously hamper German attempts at democracy until after its defeat in World War II.

The new nation aroused fears among the other European nations with its economic and military power and its aggressive attempts to make up for lost time in asserting its claims. Germany quickly joined the intense competition among the European great powers in the feverish race for national and economic expansion through colonial empires that marked the last two decades of the nineteenth and the beginning of the twentieth centuries. It was Germany's decisive role in altering the balance of power in Europe which more than any other single factor brought this competition to the brink and precipitated the outbreak of the First World War in 1914.

The unification of Germany released an outpouring of German nationalism. A romantic Germanism, appealing to both the Christian and the pre-Christian Germanic past, was led and celebrated by such notable figures as the opera composer Richard Wagner. Wagner and other fervent nationalists proclaimed the idea of German racial purity and advanced a new and deadly form of anti-Semitism that regarded Jews as pollutants of the "pure" Aryan race of Germans. This too was to have fateful consequences for twentieth-century Germany with the rise of Hitler and Nazism.

A similar road to unification occurred in Italy. At the beginning of the nineteenth century Italians did not have a common government. "Italy" consisted, as it had for centuries, of a number of separate states. In 1848 liberal reformers in Sicily demanded a more democratic and constitutional government. King Ferdinand of Naples gave into the revolutionaries' demands. This set in motion something of a domino effect: King Charles Albert of Piedmont-Sardinia and Pope Pius IX soon followed with liberal reforms of their own. Emboldened, reformers in northern Italian states went further. Revolutionaries in Milan and Venice successfully forced the withdrawal of Austrian forces and immediately declared independence from the Habsburgs.

Revolutionaries in Rome forced the pope to flee the city. The insurgents declared Rome to be a free republic. The victories were short-lived, however. Austrian forces retook the rebellious cities in the north, while the French, under the leadership of Napoleon III, attacked Rome and reclaimed it for the pope. The liberal revolt of 1848 failed and Italy remained fragmented and disunited for another two decades.

The renewal of the drive for unification (or *Risorgimento*) came in 1860 and was led by Camillo di Cavour (1810–1861), prime minister of the kingdom of Piedmont-Sardinia from 1852 to 1861. Like Bismarck in Germany, Cavour was a realist and pragmatist. He realized that a mass uprising, similar to the ones of 1848, could not succeed against the might of the Austrian army. Another path had to be taken. His first step was to modernize Piedmont-Sardinia. He reformed the economy, had railways and steamships built, and reorganized taxes and the national debt. Cavour also shrewdly made a secret pact with Napoleon III in 1858. In exchange for French military aid against Austria, France gained the city of Nice and the region of Savoy. With the guarantee of French military assistance, in April 1859 Cavour skillfully maneuvered Austria into declaring war against Piedmont. The results were unexpected but decidedly in Cavour's favor. The combined forces of Piedmont and France took Lombardy from the Austrians. The alliance between Cavour and Napoleon III was far more ambitious, calling for French forces to aid in the attack against Venetia and the Papal States. After the victory in Lombardy, Napoleon III had second thoughts and signed a peace treaty with the Austrians. This seemingly left Cavour abandoned and vulnerable. However, inspired by his victory, nationalists in Parma, Modena, Tuscany, and the Papal States (except Rome which was protected by French forces) rose up and seized power. They promised to unify those territories with Piedmont and Lombardy. The process of unification was underway.

In May 1860 Giuseppe Garibaldi (1807–1882), a veteran of the 1848 uprisings, sailed to Sicily with a thousand volunteers in order to liberate the island from the French. After his success there, he headed to mainland Italy where he met Cavour's forces moving in from the north in Naples. Together, the combined might took the city. Italy was unified. In 1861 Victor Emmanuel of Piedmont was named King of Italy. Cavour died just months later. But two areas remained outside the control of the new nation: Rome, still under the control of the Pope with the protection of the French, and Venetia which was controlled by the Austrians. In 1866 Prussia and Austria went to war. The Italians sided with the Prussians and were rewarded with Venetia. In 1870, during the war between Prussia and France, Napoleon III withdrew French troops from Rome. The Italians quickly moved in and declared Rome the capital of Italy.

The Paris Commune. France's defeat in the Franco-Prussian War brought an end to the empire of Napoleon III. Napoleon himself was captured in battle on 2 September 1870, a humiliating defeat for the emperor. He ultimately died in exile in England in 1873.

In France, Napoleon III was replaced by a provisional government. It was this government that signed the armistice with the newly created Germany. The last months of the war were particularly brutal as Paris suffered under a Prussian siege. After the armistice was signed Prussian forces paraded into the city. For many Parisians this was the final embarrassment and helped to turn Paris against the new provisional government.

The Communards, as the people of Paris became known during the spring of 1871, not only despised the new French government because they capitulated to Germany, but they also feared the new government would try to restore the French monarchy. The Communards demanded that France once again become a republic. For two months (26 March to 28 May) the Communards were in control of Paris. During that time their goal was to turn first Paris, then all of France, into a socialist democracy. They adopted the red socialist flag as the official flag of Paris, voted to separate church and state, give women the right to vote, and provided a series of policies friendly to workers and the poor. Since the Commune existed such a short time, most of these policies were never put into effect.

Adolphe Tiers, leader of France's provisional government, recognized that in order to hold the nation together the Commune would have to be crushed and Paris brought back under federal control. French forces laid siege to the city. The fighting began in April and was brutal, with acts of atrocities and terrorism committed on both sides. In the end, 30,000 people were killed in the fighting. Once the government was back in control of the city, another 50,000 people were executed for participating in the Commune. After the defeat of the Paris Commune the French Third Republic was declared.

ART OF THE NINETEENTH CENTURY

Whereas the eighteenth century ended with Neo-classicism, a revival of Classical styles, motifs, and ideals that aimed to convey messages of morality and patriotism and paralleled Age of Reason philosophies, the dawn of the nineteenth century witnessed in art a return to emotion. Romanticism, a term generally used to describe art that appealed to the viewer's emotions, was not a singular artistic style. The name reflected a renewed interest in medieval tales known as romances, which, like Romantic art, catered to the emotions of the viewer/reader. Particularly in France, painters turned away from the cool, dispassionate scenes of Neoclassicism, instead favoring highly dramatic stories shown at their denouement. Through heroic story lines, vigorous action, strong diagonal compositions, and bold coloration, Romantic painters sought to grab the viewer's attention and induce an emotional involvement in the story being portrayed.

Representations of nature multiplied with the rise of Romantic art. Perhaps not immediately thought of as a "Romantic" subject, landscape scenes garnered a heroic quality under such painters as Rosa Bonheur and J.M.W. Turner. Turner's abstracted landscapes and seascapes, for example, convey a clear sense of drama through swirling colors and brushstrokes as well as provocative titles.

The nineteenth century also witnessed the birth of a new medium—photography. Through its reproducibility, photography became a way of bringing art to everyone. Photography had contentious beginnings, however, developed nearly simultaneously but by differing methods in France and England. To many, photography appeared most useful in its ability to record data and document life. For this reason, not until the twentieth century did photography become widely accepted as an "artistic" (rather than quasi-scientific) medium.

ROMANTICISM

Romantic artists united in their attempts to access raw emotion, despite widely varied subjects and styles. In their efforts to arouse the passions of their viewers, they favored not simply dramatic story-lines but often gruesome ones as well. Some shocked their audiences with grotesque depictions of human suffering and death.

Spanish artist Francisco de Goya, at one time the principal painter to the notoriously corrupt King Charles IV, became best known for his socially critical graphic cycles. Charles IV halted the liberal reforms of his predecessor and returned power to the Church by reinstituting the Inquisition. Goya responded to these reactionary measures with a series of biting, satirical prints, *Los Caprichios (The Caprices)*. In coming years, Goya's work became increasingly pessimistic. *The Disasters of War,* a set of sixty-five etchings from 1810–14, exposed the barbarous atrocities committed on both sides during Napoleon's invasion of Spain, from castration and dismemberment to the execution of civilians. In *And There Is No Remedy*, Goya rendered a horrific scene of firing squads in mid-massacre, his title clearly asserting that nothing can erase such forms of despicable human behavior.

In France, Théodore Géricault's painting, *The Raft of the Méduse* (Plate 14), marked the shift from cool Neoclassicism to hot-blooded Romanticism. Following a visit to Italy, Géricault returned home determined to depict contemporary history, in itself a departure from the ancient stories preferred by Neoclassical painters. The resulting *Raft of the Méduse* caused a sensation upon its exhibition, from

Figure III-2   Francisco de Goya, *And There Is No Remedy,* plate 15, *Disasters of War.* 1810–14. Etching. (14 cm high). Cleveland Musuem of Art. Courtesy of the Burstein Collection/Corbis.

its passionate evocation of suffering to its implicit critique of the monarchy. Géricault selected for his *tour de force* a recent and horrifying event in French history: the *Méduse,* a ship of French colonists that sank off the west coast of Africa due to the incompetence of its captain. Captain and crew evacuated first, towing behind their lifeboats a raft filled with one hundred forty-nine passengers whom they soon cut adrift. When they were rescued thirteen days later, only fifteen were still alive. Based upon the graphic newspaper accounts of the ordeal, as well as on Géricault's own interviews with survivors, the painting depicts the moment at which the survivors spot the rescue ship. The composition is a pyramidal construction of interwoven bodies, the dead and dying surmounted by the few sur-

vivors. The powerful emotion of hope, embodied by the fabric-waving figures atop the pyramid, collides with the tension of the huge incoming wave that threatens to overtake them.

Following in Géricault's footsteps, Eugène Delacroix often favored contemporary history for his paintings, scenes filled with action and emotion. *Liberty Leading the People* (Plate 15) was painted shortly after the Parisian Revolution of 1830 that installed Louis-Philippe on the French throne. *Liberty* depicts not a specific incident, however, but rather an allegory of revolution, where Liberty is personified by a bare-breasted woman. Carrying a tricolor banner and a bayonet, Liberty unites a disparate band of men and leads them on to the barricades. Delacroix's painting appears strongly

Figure III-3   Honoré Daumier, *Rue Transnonain, April 15, 1834,* 1834. Lithograph. 11⁵/₁₂″ × 18¹/₉″ (290 × 460 mm). Kupferstichkabinett, Dresden, Germany. Courtesy of Erich Lessing/Art Resource, NY.

influenced by the composition of Géricault's *Raft*. Just as Géricault built his pyramid of survivors atop lifeless bodies, so, too, does Delacroix's Liberty stride across a sea of dead and dying figures, the sacrifices of many implicitly necessary for the crowning achievement of freedom.

Honoré Daumier, a French artist known for his caricatures and commentaries on French culture, government, and societal injustice, produced a huge body of more than four thousand lithographs, in addition to his paintings. *Rue Transnonain, April 15, 1834* depicts a specific incident in which an innocent family was killed by governmental troops during the brutal suppression of a political uprising. Like Romantic artists before him, Daumier employed the pyramidal composition to maximize

emotional power. Recalling the formal organization of Goya's *Disasters of War* and Géricault's *Raft of the Méduse*, Daumier's lithograph focuses through both composition and use of light on the splayed body of the father, fallen atop his murdered child.

THE RISE OF NATURE
The English version of Romanticism primarily revolved around the genre of landscape painting. John Constable and J.M.W. Turner became the best known practitioners of the subject, though their approaches were vastly divergent. Constable espoused the direct observation of nature and painted serene views of the English countryside in which people became one with nature (see page 37). Turner, on the other hand, painted abstracted, imaginary land-

scapes. Through his images of fires and storms, Turner discovered the emotional power of color.

In a painting of 1840 often referred to as *The Slave Ship*, Turner demonstrated an affinity with the French Romantics by taking as his point of departure a highly sensational incident from recent history. In 1783, the captain of a slave ship threw the dead and dying passengers overboard in the hopes of fraudulently collecting insurance settlements for passengers "lost at sea." Turner's painting, *Slavers Throwing Overboard the Dead and Dying—Typhoon Coming On* (Plate 16), is a turbulent, color-filled seascape. While Turner's title alerts the viewer to the horrific subject, in the painting itself the slave ship is nearly lost amid the swirling colors of the oncoming storm. Turner drew upon pure color to express the terror and grandeur of nature as well as to evoke an emotional response from the viewer. His colorful abstractions heavily influenced the later development of modern art.

By mid-century, landscape painting also had found favor in France as urban dwellers idealized life in the country. The population of Paris had doubled between 1831 and 1851 and Baron Haussmann's renovations had converted the city into a fast-paced modern metropolis. As a result, the idea of a peaceful agrarian life took on a nostalgic quality and more artists turned to a naturalistic depiction of rural life. Rosa Bonheur's *Plowering in the Nivernais: The Dressing of the Vines* (Plate 17), a government-commissioned work, depicts a line of powerful oxen working the land, animals replacing the traditional human figures in a Classical-style procession. Bonheur did not recognize a clear

Figure III-4   William Henry Fox Talbot, *The Open Door,* 1843. Salt paper print from a calotype negative. (14.3 × 19.4 cm). Science Museum, London. Courtesy of the Fox Talbot Collection. Science Museum, London.

separation between the human and animal realms and favored animal subjects far above human ones in her paintings. Contemporary critics believed that *Plowering* may have been inspired by a line in *Devil's Pond* (1846) by the writer George Sand, a woman with whom Bonheur was often compared.

THE BIRTH OF PHOTOGRAPHY

In the 1830s, the development of photography in France and England introduced possibilities of mechanical reproduction into art. Louis-Jacque-Mandé Daguerre announced his invention of the daguerreotype in 1839, a process by which a positive print was made on a light-sensitized copperplate. Daguerre's disclosure prompted English scientist William Henry Fox Talbot to publish his own photographic experiments of negatives and paper positives, which became known as "calotypes." While Daguerre was the first to publish his work, the daguerreotype produced only one positive image so it was the calotype, a negative that could print an unlimited number of positives, that became the basis of modern-day photography. Talbot published his photographic process in 1844–46 in a six-volume series titled *The Pencil of Nature*, the first books to include photographic illustrations. One image, *The Open Door*, can be understood in a manner similar to French naturalist paintings (see page 145). Talbot, unhappy with British industrialization, produced a wistful image of country life. Inside the open doorway of a cottage, Talbot focused his lens upon a leaning, handmade broom, an object of the sort soon made obsolete by industrialized mass production.

THE AGE OF THE ROMANTIC IN MUSIC

Beethoven's music, with its emotional intensity and musical innovation, played a major role in ushering in the Romantic era, which dominated European music throughout most of the nineteenth century. Like Romantic artists and writers, Romantic composers sought to express individual freedom and passion and to push the boundaries of musical conventions into new directions. Indeed, many Romantics saw in music the art that most fully and deeply expressed human feelings.

But the departure from Classicism in music was less dramatic than it was in some of the other arts, notably painting. In seeking to deepen the emotional impact of music, Romantic composers were chiefly interested in creating ever more beautiful and expressive melodies, an aim that simply continued and intensified the intention of Classical composers like Mozart. Romantic composers made use of traditional rhythms, although they also experimented with rhythmic irregularities. Harmony became increasingly rich and complex and innovative as a means of expression. Romantic composers often used frequent key changes and explored more the possibilities of dissonance. Their interest in tonal "color," the different quality that the same note could have played on different instruments or sung by different voices, manifested itself in an expansion of the size and diversity of orchestras and the variety of vocal and instrumental performances.

A very characteristic form of Romantic music is the *Lied* or "art song." The German word *Lied* (plural *Lieder*) simply means "song," but in the Romantic era it came to refer to a song for solo voice and piano accompaniment set to a poetic text. The late eighteenth and early nineteenth centuries saw the flourishing of Romantic poetry by German poets such as Goethe, Schiller, and Tieck, so the composers of *Lieder* had rich literary sources to draw on. The master of *Lieder*, and one of the pre-eminent Romantic composers, was the Austrian composer Franz Schubert (1797–1828). In his short, troubled, and somewhat isolated life he astonishingly composed close to a thousand musical works, from symphonies, sonatas, operas, and masses to *Lieder*. Among Schubert's most familiar and enjoyed pieces are his *Lied, Der Erlkönig* (*The Erlking*), a musical setting of a poem by Goethe, the poignant *Serenade, Ave Maria,* and the"*Unfinished" Symphony*.

It was during the Romantic period that the piano became the "king" of musical instruments. Continued improvements in piano design made possible fuller and richer sounds, and the ability through the pedals to sustain and modulate sounds. The piano became the supreme solo instrument, and this period produced many new works composed for piano. The Romantic era was the period of the great piano virtuosos, who performed in concert halls throughout Europe to enthusiastic audiences. Perhaps the greatest of such virtuosos was Franz Liszt (1811–86), a Hungarian who was also a leading Romantic composer, best known for his twenty *Hungarian Rhapsodies*.

But the most beloved, performed, and still enjoyed of the Romantic composers for piano is Frédéric Chopin (1810–49). Chopin was Polish but spent most of his life in France. He wrote almost entirely for the piano, and was himself a concert pianist. His piano music ranges widely, including etudes ("studies") that explore a particular musical possibility, preludes (short compositions with a free style), nocturnes ("night pieces"), impromptus (brief lyrical pieces), scherzos ("musical jokes," brief lively pieces), and dances such as waltzes and two types of Polish dance, the polonaise and the mazurka. The polonaise is a stately dance in march time, and the mazurka is a lively polka-like dance in 3/4 or 3/8 time. Chopin was deeply influenced by the folk music and dance music of his native country. In his highly individual and original piano works Chopin is the quintessential Romantic, composing lush and complex compositions with beautiful melodies some of which have become familiar throughout the world and even turned into popular songs. For generations every child who took piano lessons learned something by Chopin, such as his *Minute Waltz*, and his works are staples in the repertoire of most pianists both professional and amateur.

The symphony tradition continued and flourished in the Romantic age, influenced by Beethoven's nine great and diverse symphonies. The Romantic composers typically followed the Classical symphony form but as a means to expression of a theme or a mixture of emotions. One of the leading symphony composers was the German Felix Mendelssohn (1809–47). Grandson of the most influential Jewish leader during the Enlightenment period, Moses Mendelssohn, Felix's family was Christian and one of his best-known symphonies is the "Reformation" Symphony which incorporates Luther's *Ein Feste Burg* ("A Mighty Fortress"). Probably the preeminent Romantic symphony composer was Johannes Brahms (1833–97), a man of humble origins from Hamburg, Germany who went on to become a music director and conductor in Vienna and one of the greatest and most prolific composers of the nineteenth century. Brahms mastered everything—symphonies, choral works, piano music, Lieder—except opera. In addition to his symphonies, Brahms is well known for having written the unique and beautiful "Protestant" requiem, *Ein Deutsches Requiem* (*A German Requiem*), using texts from the Bible instead of the liturgy of the Latin mass. Another great choral work of the period is Mendelssohn's oratorio *Elijah*, not far behind Handel's *Messiah* in being one of the most familiar and performed of all oratorios.

Probably the single most popular composer of the Romantic era is Peter Ilyich Tchaikovsky (1840–93). The Romantic movement brought with it an emphasis on national identity and strong patriotic sentiment that expressed itself artistically in the revival of the folk tales, music, and historical distinctiveness of each culture. We have seen that despite spending almost all his life in France, Chopin was deeply influenced by his Polish heritage. Similarly, Tchaikovsky incorporated into his music Russian folksongs, and composed the very popular *1812 Overture* to commemorate the retreat of Napoleon's army from Moscow. The *1812 Overture* is a spectacular example of program music, weaving together *La Marseillaise* and the Russian national anthem and reproducing the sound of cannons (some recorded performances use actual cannon sounds). Tchaikovsky's most beloved work is *The Nutcracker*, a staple of performances at the Christmas season. *The Nutcracker* is ballet music, written for a dance production of a story by E. T. A. Hoffman, "The Nutcracker and the Mouse King." Russia has a long and illustrious balletic tradition, and some of Tchaikovsky's most important compositions are ballet music, notably *Swan Lake, Sleeping Beauty*, and *Romeo and Juliet*. He also wrote symphonies and piano concertos, some of which remain part of the standard "classical" symphony orchestra repertoire.

In opera the Romantic period can only be described as "glorious." Indeed, opera attained a kind of pinnacle in the nineteenth century. Beginning with the delightful comedies of Giacomo Rossini (1792-1868), like *The Barber of Seville*, nineteenth-century opera reached its heights with the operas of Giuseppe Verdi (1813–1901) and Richard Wagner (1813–83). Verdi has long been a kind of hero in Italy, where opera is loved as "people's music" and not as "highbrow." In his long career Verdi composed some of the greatest operas in the Italian repertoire, using the operatic vehicle to explore the human drama with beautiful and emotional melodies: among them *La Traviata, Il Trovatore* ("The Troubadour"), *Un Ballo in Maschera* ("The Masked Ball"), *La Forza del Destino* ("The Force of Destiny"), *Rigoletto, Aïda,* and *Otello*.

In terms of sheer genius and theatricality, Wagner is perhaps the greatest of the Romantic opera composers. Unlike Verdi, who was drawn to universal and even contemporary human situations often involving ordinary people, Wagner drew inspiration from ancient Germanic mythology and represents in an intense form the vigorous spirit of nationalism awakened by the unification of Germany in 1871. Wagner had an entire philosophy of operatic art. He spoke of opera as a *Gesamtkunst-*

werk, a comprehensive work of art in which the music, the text, the plot, and the scenery are all integrated around a key idea or theme. His most spectacular operatic achievement is the "Ring Cycle," the four operas comprising the retelling of the old German legends of the *Ring of the Nibelungen*: *Das Rheingold* ("The Rhinegold"), *Die Walküre* ("The Valkyrie"), *Siegried*, and *Götterdämmerung* ("Twilight of the Gods"). At the Bayreuth Music Festival in Germany, which Wagner founded, there are regular performances of the whole Ring Cycle. In his operas Wagner created some music that is simply sublime, and other music that tests the limits of both the operatic form and the performer.

CD SELECTIONS

Tracks 12–15 are selections from the Romantic era. They begin, on Track 12, with one of Chopin's most familiar preludes for piano, the *Prelude No. 15 in D-flat Major*. This is popularly known as the "Raindrop" Prelude, for reasons that should become clear when it is listened to. There is a steady, sonorous beat throughout the piece, like raindrops falling rhythmically on a roof or a window. The first part is dominated by a lovely, meditative melody in a major key. The middle part turns minor and "heavier," with the bass notes prominent, but resolves itself back into the third part, which returns to the quiet melody and "gentle rain" of the first part.

On Track 13 is Variation VII (*Grazioso*, "with grace") from Brahms' *Variations on a Theme by Haydn* (1873). This is a good example of the way in which later composers return to earlier composers for inspiration and to "comment" on their music in their own works. Brahms was in many ways very "Classical" in his musical outlook, and was deeply indebted to that generation of composers. Variation VII is a very free improvisation on Haydn, with a lovely, lilting, "graceful" melody that is returned to repeatedly and in a variety of ways.

Tchaikovsky is represented on Track 14 by the introductory "Scène—Le lac des cygnes" ("Scene—the Lake of the Swans") from his ballet music, *Swan Lake* (1875). The legend is a very old one, told in different versions. In this one a prince, Siegfried, out hunting stops at a lake where there are swans who are actually young women whom a sorcerer, Van

Rothbart, has bewitched. The swan wearing a crown turns into a beautiful woman, Odette, with whom the prince immediately falls in love. She tells him that the only way the spell can be broken is for a man who is pure in heart to pledge his love to her. The evil sorcerer interrupts and takes Odette away from Siegfried. The next day Van Rothbart tricks the prince by presenting his daughter, Odile, to him, on whom he has cast a spell to make her look like Odette. Unknowing, Siegfried asks her to marry him, witnessed by Odette through the window. Chasing her back to the lake, the prince begs and is granted her forgiveness. Van Rothbart and Odile return, in their true inhuman forms, and Van Rothbart demands that Siegfried stick to his promise. Siegfried and Van Rothbart fight, and Siegfried and Odette, hand in hand, jump into the lake to escape the sorcerer's evil and be together forever. That breaks the spell, and the other swans turn back into humans and drive Van Rothbart and Odile into the water where they also drown. The spirits of Siegfried and Odette ascend into the heavens above Swan Lake.

Track 15 is the familiar "Ride of the Valkyries" from Wagner's opera, *Die Walküre* ("The Valkyrie"), the second of the four operas that comprise the Ring Cycle. "Ride of the Valkyries" is the Prelude to Act III. Eight Valkyries, the daughters of Wotan the high god, gather at the top of a rugged mountain to rescue the bodies of dead heroes and take them on their flying horses to Valhalla, the home of the gods. "Ride of the Valkyries" is the music depicting their carrying out of their mission. The opera is named for the ninth Valkyrie, Brünnhilde, who has disobeyed Wotan by seeking to protect Siegmund and Sieglinde, twin children of Wotan and lovers, who are fleeing from the vengeance of Sieglinde's husband Hunding. Wotan punishes Brünnhilde by casting her into a deep sleep, to be married to whoever wakes her up. He agrees, however, to protect her with a circle of fire that will deter all but the most courageous (and therefore worthy) suitors. (In the third opera, *Siegfried*, Brünnhilde marries Siegfried the son of Siegmund and Sieglinde.) Many people know "Ride of the Valkyries" because Francis Ford Coppola used it very effectively as theme music in his 1979 film classic *Apocalypse Now*.

CHAPTER FIVE

ROMANTICISM: MARY SHELLEY

Mary Shelley's *Frankenstein* (1818) is a story that most people "know" without having actually read the novel. As William St. Clair explains, "Frankenstein and his monster continue to live largely independently of books."[1] Those who have not cracked the binding of this almost two-hundred-year-old text have most likely encountered the creature and his creator in its creative transformations into films, television shows, cartoons, Halloween costumes—even General Mills' Franken Berry cereal. Though it seems odd to work backwards from the breakfast table to find the origins of this literary and pop culture phenomenon, tracking the genesis of Frankenstein leads back to a young woman challenged to write a ghost story. In her 1831 "Author's Introduction" to the novel, Mary Shelley claims that she wanted to create a story to "make the reader dread to look around, to curdle the blood, and quicken the beatings of the heart."[2] Critics Ellen Moers and Judith Spector claim that what Mary Shelley created in Frankenstein was the first science fiction novel. While the novel may bridge gothic/romantic and science fiction genres, one thing about *Frankenstein* is certain: it is the most enduring novel ever written by a teenager.

BACKGROUND TO A CLASSIC

Mary Shelley's *Frankenstein* is an influential expression of the Romantic movement that flourished at the end of the eighteenth and during the first half of the nineteenth centuries throughout Europe in the visual arts, music, literature, philosophy, theology, and political thought. A "founding father" of the Romantic movement was Jean-Jacques Rousseau (1712–78), who as we have seen through his writings on politics and education became one of the most influential thinkers of modern Europe (introduced in Chapter 3). Among other well-known figures of Romanticism are the writers Johann Wolfgang von Goethe, Germaine de Staël, and Ralph Waldo Emerson; the composers Ludwig van Beethoven, Franz Schubert, and Frédéric Chopin; and the painters J. M. W. Turner, Caspar David Friedrich, and Eugène Delacroix. Mary Shelley's world was of course the England of the great Romantic poets, including William Wordsworth, Samuel Taylor Coleridge, her husband Percy Shelley, their friend Lord Byron, and John Keats.

The Romantics carried forward the Enlightenment's celebration of individual freedom and commitment to remaking society, but critiqued and transformed these ideals. Above all the Romantics criticized the rationalism of the Enlightenment thinkers and activists—what they believed to be their overemphasis on reason and neglect of other vital aspects of human life. Because the Romantics sought to be more holistic about human life, they regarded feeling, intuition, and imagination as sources of knowledge that were just as important and valid as reason. This emphasis led the various Romantic artists and thinkers in many new directions.

---

[1] William St. Clair, "The Impact of *Frankenstein*," *Mary Shelley in Her Times*, ed. Betty T. Bennett and Stuart Curran (Baltimore: Johns Hopkins Press, 2000) 54.

[2] Mary Shelley, *Frankenstein* (1831; New York: Signet, 1994) ix.

Generally speaking, Romanticism rejected the restraints on and rules governing form and style in literature, art, and music that had dominated the Neoclassicism of the Age of Reason. The Romantics sought to break free of these constraints and experiment with new forms. Wordsworth influentially expressed this new outlook in the Preface to his *Lyrical Ballads*, Beethoven in forsaking elegance for passion and exploring new musical forms in works like the choral movement of his Ninth Symphony, and Turner in prefiguring the Impressionists with seascapes that were stunning studies of light and color.

The Romantic emphasis on individual freedom as passionate self-expression often exhibited in moral and social unconventionality has almost become a stereotype of Romanticism. We need look no further for real-life examples than Mary and Percy Shelley and their circle of friends, including the "scandalous" Lord Byron. The stereotype found enduring expression in Puccini's opera *La Bohème*, with its "Bohemian" starving artists and "free love." But in the case of some of the Romantics the commitment to passionate individual self-expression and unconventionality manifested itself in thought and art that went hand-in-hand with a generally conventional and even respectable life, as in the cases of Wordsworth and Emerson.

Romantic novels, poems, and paintings portrayed idealized themes and characters. The poet Wordsworth idealized nature in poems such as "Tintern Abbey," and the French painter Géricault the nobility of human suffering and endurance in the face of tragedy in his *Méduse*. In *Frankenstein* Mary Shelley gives us two characters, Elizabeth and Clerval, who represent a certain Romantic ideal of what a woman and a man should be and can strike the modern reader as simply "too good to be true."

Wordsworth's idealization of the gentle English countryside, Mary Shelley's descriptions of the majestic and untamed beauties of the Alps, Henry David Thoreau's account of his time at Walden Pond, and the German painter Caspar David Friedrich's dramatic portrayal of a single human being confronting the vastness of nature in *The Wanderer above the Mists*—all are expressions of Romanticism's new attitude toward nature and the human place in nature. The Romantics emphasized nature, not like the Scientific Revolution as a great machine, but as an organic process, a totality of which humans are one expression and the foundation of human rootedness and renewal. There was a new interest in wild rather than cultivated nature, and a contrasting of the freedom bestowed by nature with the stifling conventions and artificialities of human society. Some of the Romantics used their art to decry the Industrial Revolution, which had begun in the mid-eighteenth century and by the nineteenth had begun to sully the countryside with factories and smokestacks and cause people to crowd into the cities. There is no better example than the poet William Blake, who in his poem "Jerusalem" wrote of the "dark Satanic mills." Others, like Mary Shelley, raised serious questions about the steady march and growing dominance of science and its technological applications, and presciently anticipated the great moral dilemmas that would result for our time with our power to alter human nature itself.

Among some of the Romantics, protest against developments of the time in Europe expressed itself in a nostalgia for the past, above all the Middle Ages. Novels such as Sir Walter Scott's *Ivanhoe*, the paintings of the Pre-Raphaelite Brotherhood, and the Gothic revival in architecture express a longing for the Middle Ages as a time of Christian unity, elevated religious art and architecture, the chivalry of knighthood, close-knit human community, and pre-industrial rusticity.

Finally, some of the Romantics had a taste for the exotic, the bizarre, and the forbidden, which was an aspect of the emphasis on individual self-expression and the protest against conventionality. Coleridge's opium-induced poem "Kubla Khan," Delacroix's romanticized portrayals as a European of Moroccan Muslim culture (an ethnocentric attitude now called "Orientalism"), and the poet Baudelaire's dark explorations of the self in *Les Fleurs du Mal (Flowers of Evil)*—all reflect this side of Romanticism. And of course there is no more famous example of the Romantic interest in the strange and the forbidden than Mary Shelley's creation of Victor Frankenstein and his monster.

AUTHOR: MARY SHELLEY

In the 1831 introduction, Mary Shelley comments, "I shall thus give a general answer to the question so very frequently asked me—how I, then a young girl, came to think of and to dilate upon so very hideous an idea."[3] During the thirteen years between the novel's 1818 publication and 1831 revision, readers continually asked how her young mind produced such an intriguingly dark text. Yet, considering she was the only child of the feminist writer Mary Wollstonecraft[4] and the political theorist, philosopher, and writer William Godwin, her literary inclination was destined by her lineage. The young Mary Wollstonecraft Godwin was the "fruit of the most famous radical literary marriage of eighteenth-century England," and knowing the weight of her genealogy, she understood the inevitable route to her life as a writer: "It is not singular that, as the daughter of two persons of distinguished literary celebrity, I should very early in life have thought of writing."[5]

Her famous parents afforded her access to a literary life, but it was a life without her mother. Just days after the birth of Mary Wollstonecraft Godwin, Mary Wollstonecraft died of puerperal infection, leaving behind Mary, her three-year-old daughter Fanny Imlay (Wollstonecraft's illegitimate child with the American businessman and gambler, Gilbert Imlay), and husband William Godwin, who was so despondent that he could write no more than the date and time of Wollstonecraft's passing in his journal.[6] With the death of Mary Wollstonecraft, the author of *A Vindication of the Rights of Woman* (1792), the late eighteenth century lost "the most ardent advocate of her times for the education and development of female capacities." Mary Wollstonecraft Godwin lost her mother, but this did not keep her from knowing her mother through her mother's writing. She always kept her mother's work with her, reading and rereading her journals and political writings, most often while at her mother's grave in St. Pancras Churchyard.[7]

After her mother's death, Mary did, however, have her equally famous father (and his words) there to guide her. Godwin's *An Enquiry Concerning the Nature of Political Justice* (1793) critiqued marriage, organized religion, and centralized government and "earned this peace-loving and unrevolutionary man his reputation as the father of anarchism."[8] William Godwin, after Wollstonecraft's death, was left without his intellectual partner and left to care for his infant daughter Mary and the toddler, Fanny Imlay (whom he called Fanny Godwin). Neither of Godwin's daughters was formally educated; however, both had access to Godwin's "excellent library of English authors" as well as to their father's literary acquaintances.[9] Among her father's literary guests was Samuel Taylor Coleridge. Mary heard Coleridge recite "The Rime of the Ancient Mariner," and "the image of the tormented, isolated mariner would haunt her own fiction, even as Coleridge's verses reverberate through Frankenstein." Clearly, Mary Godwin's exposure to some of the literary giants of her day influenced her own creativity.

Her affection for her father also shaped her life. Without a mother, Mary was cared for by wet nurses and governesses, but "during her first four years, she became intensely attached to her father [. . .] whom she worshipped," possibly because of anxiety over the absence of a mother. Though he was rather distant from his daughter and did not provide her formal education, Godwin did give her a rich "intellectual experience," because he saw her as the "child most suited to carry on his work as a writer and thinker."[10]

Although he provided the stimulation his daughter needed to grow intellectually, he knew that this would not be enough to completely

---

[3]Ibid., viii.

[4]The life and work of Mary Wollstonecraft is discussed in Chapter 13.

[5]Anne K. Mellor, *Mary Shelley: Her Life, Her Fiction, Her Monsters* (New York: Routledge, 1988) 1; vii.

[6]Katherine C. Hill-Miller, *"My Hideous Progeny": Mary Shelley, William Godwin, and the Father-Daughter Relationship* (Newark: U. of Delaware Press, 1995) 20.

[7]Mellor, 1; 20.

[8]Miranda Seymour, *Mary Shelley* (London: John Murray, 2000) 6–7.

[9]Mellor, 11.

[10]Hill-Miller, 25.

"mold" her properly, and within a year of Wollstonecraft's death in 1801, he took a new wife, Mary Jane Clairmont, a widow "with a six-year-old son Charles and a four-year-old daughter Jane." This new situation, while it provided a "family" for her, also created lifelong strife for Mary Godwin. Hating her stepmother as a rival for Godwin's affection, and constantly feeling pestered by her stepsister Jane, "Mary Godwin cast herself in the role of Cinderella, deprived by her wicked stepmother of both motherly love and fatherly understanding. And her fairy-tale has some basis in fact."[11]

In what can be called an "exile" (one strongly endorsed by Mrs. Godwin), Mary was sent away to spend part of her youth in Scotland at the home of one of Godwin's acquaintances, William Baxter. Some mark this as the beginning of William Godwin's "rejection" of Mary, and interestingly, the beginning of her imaginative life. In the 1831 "Introduction," Mary Shelley explains:

> I lived principally in the country as a girl and passed a considerable time in Scotland. I made occasional visits to the more picturesque parts, but my habitual residence was on the blank and dreary northern shores of the Tay, near Dundee. Blank and dreary on retrospection I call them; they were not so to me then. They were the aerie of freedom and the pleasant region where unheeded I could commune with the creatures of my fancy. I wrote then, but in a most common-place style. It was beneath the trees of the grounds belonging to our house, or on the bleak sides of the woodless mountains near, that my true compositions, the airy flights of my imagination, were born and fostered.[12]

If it was in this Scottish landscape that the "creatures" of her fancy were born out of her engagement with the natural environment, the Baxters gave Mary her first experience of a truly loving close-knit family; and her experiences in Scotland reinforced her idealized desire for a loving environment for herself. Upon returning to England in 1812 for a visit, she first encountered the man who would become her husband.

While Mary was in Scotland, Percy Bysshe Shelley, a twenty-one year old poet and political radical who had been expelled from Oxford for writing *The Necessity of Atheism*, had become a part of the Godwin household. Because of Godwin's revolutionary politics, Shelley was one of Godwin's most devoted disciples.[13] Mary Godwin was fifteen when she first met Shelley, who at this time in his life was still content with his wife, Harriet. It was not until the spring of 1814 that Percy Shelley, now disenchanted with his ill-matched spouse, truly noticed Mary. Their mutual attraction was only strengthened by their shared admiration for Mary's parents' writings and politics, and Percy Shelley declared his love for Mary at Wollstonecraft's grave. However, when William Godwin discovered their romantic relationship, he forbade them to meet, seeing their situation as "criminal" since Percy was a married man with children. This condemnation contradicts Godwin's published views on marriage, and Percy and Mary used both Wollstonecraft's and Godwin's radical philosophies to legitimize their actions.[14] Godwin advocated "free sexual relations between consenting men and women" and had in his own life lived with Wollstonecraft before they were married.[15] Yet his condemnation of Mary and Percy's relationship began a three-and-a-half year silence between Mary and her father. He refused to see or write to her while she was with Percy (though Godwin did rely on them financially), and Godwin broke his silence only after Mary and Percy were legally able to wed.

When Percy and Mary eloped in 1814, taking Mary's stepsister Jane Claire Clairmont with them, they embarked on the travels that helped Mary create her first notable publication, a travelogue titled *History of A Six Weeks Tour*. Looking to her mother's journals, Mary fashioned her text by

---

[11]Mellor, 13.

[12]Shelley, viii.

[13]Hill-Miller, 36–37.

[14]Elisabeth Bronfen, "Rewriting the Family: Mary Shelley's 'Frankenstein' in its Biographical/Textual Context," *Frankenstein, Creation, and Monstrosity,* ed. Stephen Bann (London: Reaktion, 1994) 24.

[15]Hill-Miller, 39.

similarly recording the sublime beauty of the natural scenery of France, Germany, Switzerland, Holland, and especially the landscape around Lake Geneva. This time was both turbulent and productive. It was productive in that Mary was writing and reading constantly, encouraged by Percy, but turbulent because Mary gave birth, two months prematurely, to a daughter, Clara, who died less than a month later. Her journals record her painful emotions at the loss of her first child: "Still think about my little baby—'tis hard, indeed, for a mother to lose a child [. . . .] Dream that my little baby came to life again; that it had only been cold, and that we had rubbed it before the fire, and it lived. Awake and find no baby."[16] Mary soon became pregnant again and gave birth to a son, William, named for her distant father whom she still adored. Despite Godwin's continued silence, Mary was happy during this brief moment, as she had a healthy son. During this time, Claire aggressively sought the affections of the most popular writer of the day, Lord Byron, and Claire's connection to Byron led to one of the most important summers in literary history.

CREATION AND THE SUMMER OF 1816

Feeling confident in her relationship with Shelley and doting over a new son, Mary herself, intrigued by the famous Byron, agreed to accompany Percy and Claire to Geneva to help Claire in her pursuit of Byron. In the summer of 1816, Percy, Mary, Claire, Byron, and Byron's physician, Dr. John William Polidori, spent time together on the banks of Lake Geneva. Because of bad weather, much of their time was spent inside the Villa Diodati reading and discussing the most influential and intriguing topics of the day. Her 1831 "Author's Introduction" explains that the group had been reading ghost stories, and Byron proposed that they should each write one.[17] But this atmosphere was charged by more than ghost stories. As Mary Shelley explains:

Many and long were the conversations between Lord Byron and Shelley to which I was a devout but nearly silent listener. During one of these, various philosophical doctrines were discussed, and among others the nature of the principle of life, and whether there was any probability of its ever being discovered and communicated. They talked of the experiments of Dr. [Erasmus] Darwin [. . .] who preserved a piece of vermicelli in a glass case till by some extraordinary means it began to move with voluntary motion. Not thus, after all, life would be given. Perhaps a corpse would be reanimated; galvanism had given token of such things: perhaps the component parts of a creature might be manufactured, brought together, and endued with vital warmth.[18]

Mary, still haunted by the death of her first child (and her dream of bringing it back to life by rubbing it in front of the fire), had another haunting vision: a waking dream of a "pale student of unhallowed arts kneeling beside the thing he had put together."[19] In her dream she saw "the hideous phantasm of a man stretched out, and then, on the working of some powerful engine, show signs of life and stir with an uneasy, half-vital motion."[20] Influenced by her intelligent and engaging company, by a bit too much laudanum (opium distilled in alcohol), her own desire to understand these "principles of life," and her own anxieties and feelings of loss, the ghost story Mary created from Byron's prompt and from her own waking dream became the "most famous dream in literary history."[21] If this summer of 1816 was important to literary history, it is also one that has captivated contemporary movie audiences as well. No fewer than three contemporary major motion pictures have been made based on events at the Villa Diodati that summer by Lake Geneva, and each film strives to recreate the intellectually and erotically charged atmosphere that these writers created (Ken Russell's 1987 *Gothic* is a standout among the other film ver-

---

[16]Quoted in Mellor, 32.

[17]Shelley, ix.

[18]Ibid., 4

[19]Ibid., xi

[20]Ibid., 1.

[21]Mellor, 37.

This engraving, included with an early edition of Shelley's book, depicts the climactic moment of the novel. The monstrous creature, a product of the skeletons and scientific instruments around him, awakens, to the horror of the scientist who suddenly realizes his error. The accompanying quote from the novel describes the feeling of the scene: "By the glimmer of the half-extinguished light, I saw the dull, yellow eye of the creature open; it breathed hard, and a convulsive motion agitated its limbs, . . . I rushed out of the room." The open book signifies knowledge, through which the scientist has attempted to thwart nature, and the skeletal remains make reference not only to the source of the creature's creation but also to the death that will occur later in the novel.

Figure III-5   Theodor M. von Holst and William Chevalier, Frontispiece engraving from 1831 edition of *Frankenstein*. Courtesy of The Bridgeman Art Library International.

sions: 1988's *Haunted Summer* and *Rowing With The Wind*). That these films exist indicates that much like those nineteenth century readers who asked the young author how she thought of such a story, contemporary filmmakers seek answers about the environment that, and the woman who, created this myth, this Frankenstein.

The summer of 1816 guided Mary Godwin to create the novel that would make her one of the most notable writers of the last two centuries, but the rest of 1816 was marked with the suicides of Mary's half-sister, Fanny Imlay Godwin, and Harriet Shelley, Percy's legal wife and mother of two of his children. Harriet's death allowed Mary and Percy to wed legally on 30 December 1816, and Mary ended this tumultuous year with a new name and a strained reconciliation with her father, who witnessed the wedding.

The next few years proved equally tumultuous. Mary Shelley gave birth to another daughter in 1817 who died a year later, and in the summer of 1819, their three-year-old son, William, died of malaria. In November of the same year, a son, Percy Florence, was born and was their only child to survive into adulthood. Mary Shelley's companion at Lake Geneva in 1816, Dr. John William Polidori, inexplicably committed suicide in 1821. In 1822, Mary suffered a miscarriage and almost bled to death. If the last few years had not been difficult enough, in July of 1822, Percy drowned at sea. At twenty-four, the widowed and motherless Mary Shelley had lost several of those close to her to suicide, seen three of her children die, and almost died herself from a miscarriage. Yet, during this turbulent time, this troubled young wife produced a novel that has never gone out of print, and a story that is inextricably a part of our own cultural consciousness.

CRITICAL APPROACHES TO THE NOVEL

In 1818, the anonymously published *Frankenstein* received mixed critical reviews, but was enthusiastically received by the general public. But, while the public interest flourished over the next few decades, the critical reception of the novel continued to be mixed or negative well into the twentieth century.

Were it not for two critics, M. A. Goldberg and Harold Bloom, who took the text and its author seriously, critical analysis of this novel might have stagnated. Since Goldberg (in 1959) and Bloom (in 1964) developed pivotal critical perspectives on the novel, "Frankenstein has been recognized as the ingenious, complex creation of a young woman who registered and questioned myriad influences in her cultural milieu."[22] One does not need to look much farther than the full title of the novel to see that *Frankenstein, or The Modern Prometheus* is an intertextual palimpsest of influences, both literary and scientific. Her novel was informed by the culture in which she lived and by her own voracious reading, study, and observation. That she listened intently to Shelley's and Byron's discussions of Dr. Erasmus Darwin's experiments with galvanism and reanimation indicates Mary Shelley's immersion in a culture charged with new theories and science surrounding the principles and origins of life.

These scientific theories were coupled with Mary Shelley's own knowledge of mythology, especially of Aeschylus' *Prometheus Bound*. While there are numerous versions of the myth of Prometheus, two in particular inform the novel as much as the scientific discussions she witnessed and absorbed. In one version of the myth, the Titan Prometheus took clay from the plain of Boeotia and used it to mold man into shape, and thus gave life to humankind. In another version, the one retold in Aeschylus' dramatic interpretation, Prometheus defies Zeus by stealing and giving fire to mortals to raise them up from "beasts" into beings capable of building culture. Both versions of the myth reflect themes omnipresent in *Frankenstein*: Promethean overreaching (overstepping the established boundaries between gods and humans), creation of humans, and hubris (amplified egotism). Victor Frankenstein's voice, before he has successfully animated his creation, sounds particularly Promethean when he explains:

Life and death appeared to me ideal bounds, which I should first break through, and pour

a torrent of light into our dark world. A new species would bless me as its creator and source; many happy and excellent natures would owe their being to me. No father could claim the gratitude of his child so completely as I should deserve theirs.[23]

And, especially in the latter version of the myth, Prometheus does not go unpunished for his actions of "benevolence" toward mortals: Prometheus, chained to Mount Caucasus, has his liver eaten out daily by a bird of prey, only to have the liver grow back each day so the whole gruesome process can continue. The tortured, creative and destructive figure of Prometheus was a mascot for Romantic writers like Byron, Percy Shelley, and Mary Shelley. Harold Bloom explains:

No Romantic writer employed the Prometheus archetype without a full awareness of its equivocal potentialities. The Prometheus of the ancients had been for the most part a spiritually reprehensible figure, though frequently a sympathetic one, in terms of both his dramatic situation and in his close alliance with mankind against the gods. But his alliance had been ruinous for man in most versions of the myth, and the Titan's benevolence toward humanity was hardly sufficient recompense for the alienation of man from heaven that he had brought about.[24]

What Bloom continues to explore in his analysis of the Promethean over-reacher Victor Frankenstein and his exiled and tortured creature is the true humanness of the wretched monster: "The greatest paradox and most astonishing achievement of Mary Shelley's novel is that the monster is more human than his creator."[25] Bloom's contentions lend themselves to an explanation of one of the most intriguing readings of the novel. Victor Frankenstein's creation is decried as "the wretch," "the monster," "the creature," "the demon," but he is never given a name. Yet many tend to call the monster "Frankenstein." Bloom's description of the monster

[22]Mary Lowes-Evans, *Frankenstein: Mary Shelley's Wedding Guest* (New York: Twayne, 1993) 16.
[23]Shelley, 52.
[24]Harold Bloom, afterword, *Frankenstein,* by Mary Shelley (1831) (New York: Signet, 1994) 213–14.
[25]Ibid., 215.

and Victor as two halves of one self may help explain this "confusion" over the misnaming of the nameless creature:

> Frankenstein and his monster are the solipsistic and generous halves of the one self. Frankenstein is the mind and emotions turned in upon themselves, and his creature is the mind and emotions turned imaginatively outward, seeking a greater humanization through a confrontation of other selves.[26]

In this sense, then, Victor and the monster can be seen as *doppelgängers* (literally "double goers"), and the frequent misnaming of the creature as Frankenstein may be understandable, as, in this critical perspective, he is an inextricable part of his creator.

Because Mary Shelley's life is so intriguing and inescapable, some psychoanalytic critics read the novel through the critical lens of the Oedipus complex and repressed desires and Mary Shelley's own psychological life. One critic has described *Frankenstein* as a text that essentially excludes women, but that ultimately is a "parable of motherhood."[27] Claiming that the novel is a representation of Mary Shelley's search for her dead mother, this critic notes the irony of a feminist's daughter writing this "parable of motherhood entirely in terms of men."[28] However, he also claims that *Frankenstein* is clearly a "woman's book," as "Mary Shelley is the animator and progenitor of her story; if it is a retelling of Prometheus, it does so by recasting the legend in terms of conception, pregnancy, and birth."[29] That Mary Shelley herself experienced the loss of a mother, the loss of children, as well as rejection by her father, makes clear how biographical and psychological critics can use her life to inform their readings of the text she created. In a novel where almost every character is motherless or orphaned, Rubenstein's claims that "motherhood" is central in *Frankenstein* without significant female characters is compelling and supportable.

In the last three decades, feminist, scientific, and cultural critiques have dominated the criticism of *Frankenstein*. Since the *Frankenstein* films have imprinted an indelible image on the public mind, it is not surprising that those who read the novel for the first time are shocked by the relatively brief creation scene. First-time readers will probably expect to read of the bubbling chemicals, the looming dark castle, the flashing and crackling of electrified laboratory equipment, the hunchbacked assistant, Igor, cranking the creature up to the roof where a lightning bolt will bring him to life, and the mad scientist who screams in a frenzy, "It's Alive! It's Alive!" These readers will be startled to find that the entire creation occurs in a single paragraph, devoid of any real specifics regarding the actual method of animation. Chapter five of *Frankenstein* opens with just three sentences, and this opening paragraph is the only description of how Victor, a young college student alone in his "filthy workshop of creation" in an upstairs apartment, brings the creature to life. It is amazing how years of cinematic tinkering have exploded these few lines into some of the most striking and unforgettable images in film history.

Truly, Mary Shelley could not have detailed the creation scene much more than those few sentences, as this feat was obviously unknown. Having read such works as Humphry Davy's *Lectures on Chemistry* (1802) and his *Elements of Chemical Philosophy* (1812), she knew the current scientific experiments and theories of her day. Mary Shelley was aware of Luigi Galvani's 1791 publication on what he called "animal electricity," which came to be known as "galvanism" (a "natural" form of electricity—as opposed to "artificial" [i.e., static electricity]— activating "nerves and muscles when they were connected by a pile of copper and zinc plates").[30] Early in 1803, Professor Luigi Aldini put Galvani's theories to the test by performing galvanic experiments on animal and human corpses. Aldini was able to give the "appearance of re-animation" with

---

[26]Ibid.

[27]Marc A. Rubenstein, "'My Accursed Origin': The Search for the Mother in Frankenstein," *Studies in Romanticism* 15.2 (Spring 1976): 165.

[28]Ibid., 187.

[29]Ibid.

[30]Mellor, 104.

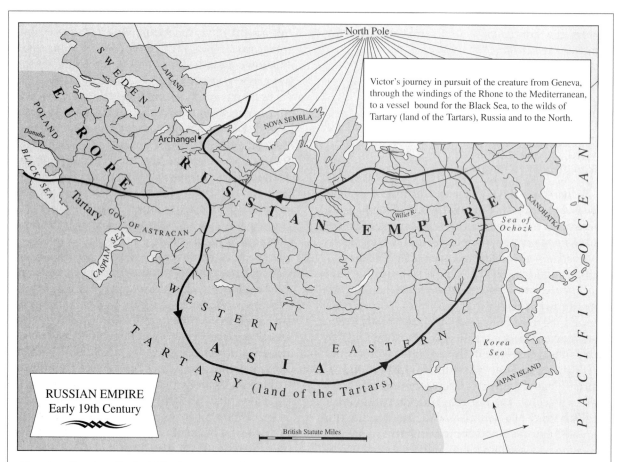

Russian Empire, Early 19th Century. Redrawn from *The Annotated Frankenstein,* by Mary Wollstonecraft Shelley, introduction and notes by Leonard Wolf (1977), Clarkson N. Potter.

these experiments, as witnesses saw jaws twitching, eyes opening, fists clenching, but no true "life" was restored to the dead flesh. What Mary Shelley compiled in her novel was based mainly on conjecture, as neither Galvani nor Aldini truly restored or created life. It has been agreed that Mary Shelley "used a strong scientific basis for the novel and as such there is reason for calling it [. . .] the first novel of speculative fiction."[31]

Mary Shelley even employs a clever trick to keep Victor's design and animation of the creature a right-fully guarded secret. Victor, in telling his tale to Robert Walton, cleverly tells Walton that he will not reveal how he came to create the creature he now chases northward. Victor explains: "I see by your eagerness and the wonder and hope which your eyes express, my friend, that you expect to be informed of the secret with which I am acquainted; that cannot be."[32] Begging Walton to listen to his frightful tale, Victor hopes to "dash the cup" of the "intoxicating draught" from Walton's lips so he may save another from the deadly quest for forbidden knowledge.[33]

---

[31]Samuel Holmes Vasbinder, *Scientific Attitudes in Mary Shelley's Frankenstein* (Ann Arbor: UMI Research Press, 1984) 82.

[32]Shelley, 51.

[33]Ibid., 26.

Tampering with forbidden knowledge is one of the novel's most timely themes. Current culture continues, increasingly, to grapple with the ethical aspects of issues such as cloning, stem cell research, and genetic engineering, and *Frankenstein* reveals the intriguing, complicated, timeless, and potentially destructive power that such Faustian knowledge yields. Though science has progressed tremendously beyond nineteenth-century tenets, and medical and biological advancements have worked to improve human health and life, there are still those who balk when science comes too close to detailing and replicating secrets of the principles of life.

Mary Shelley's tale is as much about creation as it is about destruction. Guided by Professor M. Waldman's words, Victor fervently longs to "penetrate into the recesses of nature and show how she works in her hiding-places," but his route to these hiding places is dark and filthy and solitary.[34] His trips to the charnel houses, vaults, and slaughterhouses collected into the "horrors of [his] secret toil [. . .] among the unhallowed damps of the grave."[35] Simultaneously disgusted and driven by his task, Victor thinks his creation will be beautiful. While the films would have viewers believe that the mad scientist ecstatically welcomes the creature, the novel is far different. Mary Shelley's pale young student can hardly face his creation, let alone laud his animation with even a single "It's Alive!" In the novel, Victor's rejection of the creature is immediate and his judgment of the "beauty" he created leaves him sickened. Viewing his catastrophic wretch, Victor realizes only after he has bestowed life on this hideous monster that "the beauty of the dream vanished, and breathless horror and disgust filled [his] heart."[36] As the novel progresses, it is clear that creation without forethought, acceptance, and guidance leads to a spiral of destruction.

If the *Frankenstein* films give us the deranged scientist, then they also give us the stiff, monosyl-labic, grunting monster devoid of the agility and mental capacity of the creature in the novel. That Mary Shelley's creature is eloquent and well-read directly contrasts with the image of Boris Karloff as the monster in director James Whale's 1931 film *Frankenstein*. Complete with green makeup (though the film was black and white), electrodes through his neck, lumbering gait, and stilted speech, Karloff's monster is the image most associated with the name "Frankenstein" even decades and dozens of films later. Again, those informed entirely by the cinema may be surprised to read Shelley's creature's well-spoken narrative as he confronts Victor, but the biggest surprise may come when the creature expresses his wish for a tranquil domestic life with a companion. Desiring a female "mate," the creature plaintively requests that Victor give him happiness, finally, by fulfilling his need for someone who will not reject him. The creature promises to "quit the neighbourhood of man," and live in the "vast wilds of South America," eating only berries and nuts (the creature is even a vegan).[37] Oddly swayed by the creature's argument, Victor agrees to create a female, but this promise allows him the contemplative forethought he lacked in his first creative endeavor. Now fully aware of the horror of his project, Victor weighs the potential consequences of fulfilling his promise to create a female companion for the creature.[38]

If Boris Karloff solidified the cinematic image of the monster, then Elsa Lanchester, as the "bride" in director James Whale's 1935 *Bride of Frankenstein*, equally solidified the twitching and shrieking, electrified, black-and-white-Marge Simpson-haired mate for the monster. Though the cinema brought her lasting image to life, Mary Shelley never did. Based on Victor's new-found ability to reason with his "science," and fully consider the consequences of creating another being who could be even more "terrible," before animating the female creature, he decides to tear her to pieces, refusing to be

---

[34]Ibid., 47.

[35]Ibid., 53.

[36]Ibid., 56.

[37]Ibid., 139.

[38]Ibid., 158.

responsible for a creature who could, he darkly speculates, cause the destruction of the whole human race.[39] That she could propagate "a race of devils" terrifies Victor, and, in an interesting biological possibility, removes him from the role of creator. He could have created both a male and a female of a new species, but the female creature's reproductive potential threatens his control, and he destroys her.

Combining scientific and feminist critique, one critic has claimed that Victor "substitutes solitary paternal propagation for sexual reproduction," and in so doing, "he engages in a concept of science that Mary Shelley deplores, the notion that science should manipulate and control rather than describe, understand, and revere nature."[40] Mary Shelley's own reverence for nature was informed by her literary knowledge: "A reader of Wordsworth, Mary Shelley understood nature in his terms, as a sacred all-creating mother, a living organism or ecological community with which human beings interact in mutual dependence."[41] In his manipulation of the living organism of nature (not his revered understanding or mere observation), Victor not only engages dangerously in Promethean overreaching but also defies and usurps the female role when he seeks to control the powers of creation. Victor "has sought power over the female. He has 'pursued nature to her hiding places' in an attempt not only to penetrate nature and show how her hidden womb works but actually to steal or appropriate that womb."[42] But the danger in this pursuit is in labeling nature as female, since it inevitably leads to further attempts to control "her," as nature is the female Other whom the driven and manipulative scientist exploits to his own destructive ends.

Mary Shelley was one of the first to point out the risks of using gendered metaphors of the "aggressive, virile male scientist" who "captures and enslaves a fertile but passive nature," and she reinforces these dangers by not letting Victor go unpunished.[43] In the end, Victor is equally as desolate as his creature: he has lost his wife, his young brother, his good friend Clerval, and his parents, and he has seen Justine executed. Now, he has only himself and his intense, constant connection to the creature who weakens him in a dramatic, and eventually deadly, global chase. Mary Shelley leaves the reader with both Victor's and the creature's final "laments," as each seeks to justify his actions one last time. Victor perishes from exhaustion, and the creature plans to burn himself in order to destroy the evidence of his gigantic frame that could raise questions and further investigation if found by someone as curious and driven as Victor. The cycle of creation and destruction ends with the deaths of both the creator and his creation.

CREATIVE TRANSFORMATIONS AND CULTURAL CONSCIOUSNESS

If the creature burns himself up at the end of the novel, what rises from his ashes once the book is closed is an inescapable pop culture lineage of his image and character. Only five years after its publication, *Frankenstein* was already inspiring dramatic theatrical versions, and a film history began its long life with Charles Ogle's portrayal of the creature in the 1910 Edison Kinetogram. But Ogle could not have known that he would be the first "creature" in a long line of pop culture images. From the transvestite Dr. Frank-N-Furter and his beefcake creation in the 1975 cult classic *The Rocky Horror Picture Show* to Mel Brooks' delightful crack-up *Young Frankenstein* (1975) to the downright absurd *Jesse James Meets Frankenstein's Daughter* (1966) and *Frankenhooker* (1990), the "Frankenstein" films have run the gamut from ridiculously funny to oddly perverse, but never quite accurate. Even this brief list suggests that the novel's creative transformations are limitless. Theatre and film aside, that there is a breakfast cereal named for the creature and that one cannot go long without hearing some inadvertent

---

[39]Ibid., 159
[40]Mellor, 100.
[41]Ibid., 110.
[42]Ibid., 112.
[43]Ibid., 89.

reference to the novel and these characters, says much about how indelible these images and references are: to say that someone has "created a monster," or "created a Frankenstein," through compiling incongruous parts, is a natural and idiomatic component of the English language. Almost every easy crossword puzzle contains the clue, "Frankenstein's helper." Four letters. Starts with "I" and ends in "R." Igor lives, indeed, but only outside the novel. And the doltish and stiff, green-faced monster has gleefully grunted "Trick or Treat" on late October doorsteps for years. The monster has hawked candy bars, guest-starred on *Scooby Doo*, garnered laughter on *Saturday Night Live*, and even made a brief cameo in a Universal Studios commercial (where he was, oddly, painting a vacationing woman's toenails) that aired during the 2002 Super Bowl—one of America's most expensive, coveted, and watched advertising times.

Could a nineteenth-century teenager have known the influence and impact that her "ghost story" would have? Could she have known the way her characters would enter inextricably into cultural consciousness through pop culture appropriations? Could she have known that two centuries later readers would come to this novel with so much (mis)information about its characters without ever having read a single word? Probably not. Whether or not she succeeded in writing a story to "make the reader dread to look around, to curdle the blood, and quicken the beatings of the heart,"[44] Mary Shelley certainly succeeded in creating a monster we continue to pursue.

QUESTIONS FOR STUDY AND DISCUSSION

1. How might Mary Shelley's own biography inform a critical reading of Frankenstein? Are there dangers or benefits in using biography to critique a novel?

2. Should Victor create a mate for the creature? Consider Victor's arguments for why he decides to destroy her, and consider the kind of life the creature imagines for himself and his mate. Is the creature's retaliation against Elizabeth "justified" in light of Victor's broken promise to the creature?

3. Is the novel relevant today? In what way(s)? Explain how this novel does or does not retain "meaning" for current audiences.

4. Consider the term *doppelgänger* and the characters of Victor and the creature. How are they "doubles" of each other? How are they different?

5. Considering the pop culture presence of the creature in films, commercials, cartoons, and toys, why has the image of the monster/creature lasted so long? Why is the story, or myth, of "Frankenstein" told and transformed and retold? Why have so many versions of the story strayed from the original novel?

6. Review the last chapter of the novel. Whose final "lament" is more persuasive? Is it easier to sympathize with Victor or with the creature?

SUGGESTIONS FOR FURTHER READING

Florescu, Radu. *In Search of Frankenstein: Exploring the Myths Behind Mary Shelley's Monster*. London: Robson, 1996.

Levine, George and U.C. Knoepflmacher, eds. *The Endurance of Frankenstein: Essays on Mary Shelley's Novel*. Berkeley: University of California Press, 1979.

Mellor, Anne K. *Mary Shelley: Her Life, Her Fiction, Her Monsters*. New York: Routledge, 1988.

Seymour, Miranda. *Mary Shelley*. London: John Murray, 2000.

The True Story of Frankenstein. Narr. Roger Moore. Dir. Richard Brown. A&E Home Video. 1995.

---

[44]Ibid., ix.

CHAPTER SIX

LIBERAL DEMOCRACY AND POLITICAL LIBERALISM: JOHN STUART MILL

The American and French Revolutions, molded by the thought of Locke, Rousseau, and others, brought about basic changes in political thought and practice that would dramatically alter the traditional assumptions regarding government and human institutions generally. Beginning with the emergence of modern political thought in the seventeenth and eighteenth centuries, the term "liberal" (from the Latin word for "free") came over time to refer to those political philosophies and forms of government that embodied some form of basic constitution, representative government with majority rule and free elections, checks or constraints on the power of government, the affirmation and protection of individual rights to life, liberty, and property, equality of citizens before the law and the principle of meritocracy.

Thus when we speak of the tradition of "liberal democracy," we do not use the word "liberal" in contrast to "conservative," as those terms are used in contemporary American politics, since both "conservatives" and "liberals" are heirs to the tradition that is called liberal democracy. This can be confusing, because in the late eighteenth and early nineteenth centuries in Europe most people called "conservatives" opposed the emerging liberal ideas and institutions in favor of, for example, preserving traditional monarchies and the power of the aristocracy. At the same time, within the liberalizing British parliamentary system and the new French and American republics there were political leaders who interpreted liberal democracy in either a more "liberal" or a more "conservative" way. For example, some thought voting rights should be expanded to a wider number of (male) citizens,

while others believed they should be limited to owners of property of a certain value. As we shall see, "liberalism" and "conservatism," as contrasting positions with the overall framework of the liberal political tradition, have evolved and changed from the late eighteenth century down to the present day. The focus of this chapter is the world and thought of John Stuart Mill, one of the most influential exponents of liberal democracy and also of the tradition of political liberalism.

THE EMERGENCE OF LIBERALISM
At this time in Europe within the emerging framework of liberal democracy, there were *conservatives* who were committed to preserving and strengthening historical traditions and social continuity. They emphasized: 1) the importance of community over individual rights; 2) the primacy of the traditional social hierarchy led by a landed aristocracy; 3) the state as rooted in history and tradition; 4) human beings as inherently flawed and therefore in need of stable social structures and the habit of obedience to hereditary authority (social, political, and religious).

By contrast, *liberals* espoused: 1) enhancing individual freedom over government, social, and religious controls; 2) the primacy of rational principles such as natural rights and social contract as a basis of the state; 3) individual status as based on personal achievement rather than on birth; 4) human beings as, if not always reasonable, at least "capable of reason," and therefore capable of responsible choice in matters both public and personal. Edmund Burke's *Reflections on the Revolution in France* (1791) is the classic statement of the conservative view within the framework of parliamentary democracy. Thomas Paine, who participated in both the American and the French Revolutions, expressed the liberal outlook in answering Burke in *Rights of Man* (1792), and with such success that he (Paine) was burned in effigy in the streets of London.

Classical Liberalism.   Liberalism found its chief support among the rapidly growing middle classes. Among the practical commitments of the early liberals were positions particularly favorable to those classes. This early liberalism is usually called *classical liberalism*, which sought mainly seven ends: 1) minimal government; 2) maximal individual freedom of action and expression; 3) advancement of education; 4) the sanctity of property rights; 5) individual rights guaranteed by written constitutions; 6) freely elected parliaments with power distributed among the branches of government; and 7) extension of voting rights to the propertied middle classes. Two tenets of classical liberalism reveal that its commitment to expansion of liberty did not extend to the working classes: its espousal of *laissez-faire* economic theory and its distrust of popular democracy. The liberals initially opposed reforms designed to alleviate poverty and improve working conditions in mines and factories, arguing that this was interfering with the "natural" law of supply and demand and with the freedom of owners.

As one might expect, classical liberals also distrusted popular democracy. They did so because they found incompatible with one another the Enlightenment ideals of liberty and equality. They believed the working class's zeal for equality would destroy individual freedom and produce a willingness, perhaps an eagerness, to accept even dictatorial rule. Liberals had before them the lamentable example of what had happened to the original aims of the French Revolution when, in 1792–93, the radical Jacobins, whose strength lay in the volatile Parisian working classes (the *sans-culottes*), seized control and instituted the Reign of Terror, resulting in some forty thousand deaths. Classical liberals believed that political power should rest with reliable men of education and property.

It is important to see that in nineteenth-century Europe, as in the French Revolution, two kinds of revolution were going on, often in conflict with one another: a *middle-class* revolution, represented by classical liberalism, and a *working-class* revolution, which manifested itself mainly in popular protests, political revolution, and an organized labor movement. Throughout the century an increasing willingness on the part of middle-class reformers to recognize the needs of workers combined with the growing power of workers' movements to bring the goals of both groups more closely together.

By contrast with eighteenth- and early-nineteenth-century conservatives, present-day conservatives in the United States are partly heirs of the classical liberal tradition: they believe in less government, a less regulated market, and more individual liberty and responsibility. They are divided, however, over social and moral issues such as the family, education, gender roles, reproductive rights, sexual orientation, crime and punishment, and the role of religion in public life. Those whom we might think of as heirs of Edmund Burke want to conserve, partly through legislation and public sanctions, certain values they believe are both right and widely affirmed. Others believe that the individual liberty conservatives espouse with regard to government and the market should apply also to moral and social issues. They advocate a minimum of governmental interference in lifestyle choices and individual behavior that does not harm others, and resist efforts to "legislate morality." In this "libertarian" attitude toward moral and social values and practices (although not in their general view of the role of government and the market), they stand in the tradition articulated by John Stuart Mill in *On Liberty*. Some conservatives in this group would in fact identify themselves as libertarians, and there is a Libertarian political movement and party in the United States.

Radical Liberalism.   Over time, some liberals modified their views, persuaded by the more "radical" liberalism of the Utilitarians including John Stuart Mill, who argued—at first cautiously—that government should engage in efforts to improve the condition of working people through measures such as the alleviation of poverty and bad working conditions, improvement of sanitation and health, abolition of child labor, and universal education. "Radical" liberals argued that such active involvement by government and legislation was needed precisely to enhance individual liberty and therefore happiness for the greatest number of people. In the twentieth century "liberalism" came to embody this commitment to an active role for government to play in assuring fairness and justice in areas such as economic life, education, health care, and human rights and opportunities. Modern liberals have typically combined government activism with a libertarian approach to matters of personal belief and morality. Good examples of major liberal political efforts in twentieth-century America were President Franklin Delano Roosevelt's "New Deal" in the 1930s and President Lyndon Johnson's "Great Society" programs of the 1960s.

UTILITARIANISM

A key figure in British radical liberalism was Jeremy Bentham (1748–1832), the founder of British *Utilitarianism*. Bentham was a very influential British philosopher with revolutionary ideas who wrote extensively on ethics and law. There gathered around him a circle of intellectuals and reformers that included James Mill (1773–1836), the father of John Stuart Mill and second only to Bentham in his importance for the early Utilitarian movement. The Bentham circle called themselves the "Philosophic Radicals." Among the things that set these radical liberals apart from other liberals was their belief that government must play an active role in insuring justice and alleviating human distress. This conviction arose from their philosophy, called Utilitarianism.

Deeply imbued with the Enlightenment's commitment to applying reason and science to all aspects of life, Utilitarianism was a moral and political theory based on what its adherents considered to be scientific observation of human nature and behavior. Humans, they believed, are motivated by their desires, above all by the desire for pleasure or happiness and avoidance of pain. Based on what they believed to be the psychological fact that for humans pleasure or happiness is the highest good

(the chief thing desired), the Utilitarians reasoned that pleasure or happiness ought to be the highest good. The test of whether or not an action is right or wrong is whether it will tend to produce pleasure or pain.

The theory that humans are mainly motivated by the desire for pleasure or happiness is called *psychological hedonism*. Moral philosophies that say that humans *ought* to pursue happiness or pleasure as the highest moral good are forms of *ethical hedonism*.

From the principle that happiness or pleasure not only is but ought to be the highest human good, Bentham developed the famous *principle of utility*: "that principle which approves or disapproves of every action whatsoever, according to the tendency which it appears to have to augment or diminish the happiness of the party whose interest is in question."[1] The "party whose interest is in question" may be an individual or a group; in the latter case it may be an entire society. Each person desires to maximize his or her own happiness, and the happiness of a community of people is simply the aggregate or the sum of the happiness of the individuals who comprise it. Thus the highest good in its universal expression is *the greatest happiness of the greatest number of persons*. This principle provides the goal of Utilitarian efforts in the social and political arena. The Utilitarians tried to figure out what human behaviors and legislative actions are the most *useful*, the most effective, in reducing human unhappiness and contributing to the widest possible general happiness. Utility, from the Latin word *utilis* meaning "useful," is simply another term for usefulness.

Bentham believed that the differences among pleasures were purely *quantitative* and could even be measured. He developed what he called the *hedonic calculus*, a scheme for calculating the likely effects in pleasures or pains of a particular moral or social decision. As an adult, in his classic defense of the principle of utility entitled *Utilitarianism* (1861), John Stuart Mill departed from Bentham by arguing that there are clearly *qualitative* and not merely quantitative differences among pleasures:

---

[1]Jeremy Bentham, *An Introduction to the Principles of Morals and Legislation*, chapter I-V, in John Stuart Mill, *Utilitarianism, On Liberty, Essay on Bentham*, edited and with an introduction by Mary Warnock (Cleveland: the World Publishing Company, 1962) 33.

"It is quite compatible with the principle of utility to recognise the fact, that some kinds of pleasure are more desirable and valuable than others."[2] In this connection he famously remarked that it is "better to be Socrates dissatisfied than a fool satisfied."[3] The lasting pleasures of the mind or spirit, exemplified by Socrates, are qualitatively superior to the transient, mindless pursuit of physical pleasure. Even Socrates' dissatisfaction (which was an inevitable aspect of his enduring devotion to reasoned, critical discussion) is preferable in the scale of values to the blind, fleeting pleasures of the fool.

As a political and legal theory, Utilitarianism involved careful, objective analysis of social issues, and the search for solutions based on the principle of utility. Trying to be truly scientific, Bentham and his followers rejected any appeal to divine will, to tradition, or even to the idea of natural rights, as unscientific. The Utilitarians were thoroughly secular, not only rejecting organized Christianity and its beliefs but regarding religion as generally harmful in its effects on people's lives. They believed that society could and should be reformed solely in accordance with people's observed nature, needs, and desires. This gave them what they considered an entirely rational basis for political, legal, and social reform.

MILL'S LIFE

John Stuart Mill (1806–1873), the most influential British philosopher of the nineteenth century, was at the center of the rise of radical liberalism. The chief inheritor of the ideas of the entire Utilitarian circle of thinkers (including Jeremy Bentham and James Mill), Mill transformed the concept of Utilitarianism. *On Liberty*, which Mill co-authored with Harriet Taylor (a long-time companion whom he eventually married), is one of the most influential writings of the liberal tradition, and is frequently invoked in debates on the limits of individual freedom and human rights. If John Locke created the idea that men by nature have a decisive role to play in their political governance, John Stuart Mill and Harriet Taylor created the idea that men, and women, have a determinative role to play in their personal governance.

---

[2]John Stuart Mill, *Utilitarianism*, ibid., 259.
[3]Ibid., 260.

Mill was the product of an extraordinary education. His father took complete charge of young John's instruction, working out a program of study founded on Utilitarian psychological principles. John never attended school or university, but received from his father a classical education virtually complete by age twelve, when the precocious young scholar had the equivalent of a university degree in classics. Mill was reading Greek at age three and had read six of Plato's dialogues before his eighth birthday in 1814, which he celebrated by beginning the study of Latin. From Greek and Latin, Mill moved on to logic, mathematics, and political economy (combining what we now call political science and economics). Not just a prodigious learner but a teacher as well, while still in his teens John tutored his younger siblings some three hours each day.

James Mill excluded religious instruction from the education of his young genius. He did so because as a doctrinaire Utilitarian he believed religion fostered irrationality and immorality. John would become a stern critic of many Christian beliefs and practices throughout his writings, including *On Liberty*; but like many of his skeptical contemporaries, he deeply admired Jesus as a moral teacher at the same time that he rejected the supernatural events surrounding Jesus' ministry. In 1823, at age 16, Mill organized a debating society to serve as a forum for discussion of Utilitarian ideas. By his twentieth birthday Mill had published more than fifty articles and reviews in various journals, and was deeply involved in political and social reform. At about the same time, Mill joined the British East India Company as a clerk and eventually rose to the station of Head Examiner of India Correspondence. This lifetime of administrative work provided the security he needed to carry on his study, writing, and reforming activities.

A crisis and recovery. But Mill's efforts of intellect and reform came at a personal cost. In 1826, the emerging twenty-year old philosopher found himself deeply depressed, the result he believed of an upbringing that had emphasized intellectual development at the expense of both emotional and aesthetic experience. After nearly six months of deep gloom and virtual mental paralysis, Mill began to recover, in part through his reading of an eighteenth-century French writer, Jean-François Marmontel, whose memoirs, Mill later said, released his feelings and led him "to adopt a theory of life, very unlike that on which [he] had before acted":

> I never indeed, wavered in the conviction that happiness is the test of all rules of conduct, and the end of life. But I now thought that this end was only to be attained by not making it the direct end. Those only are happy . . . who have their minds fixed on some object other than their own happiness; on the happiness of others, on the improvement of mankind, even on some art or pursuit, followed not as a means, but as itself an ideal end. . . . This theory now became the basis of my philosophy of life.[4]

Mill's insight—that one does not achieve happiness by aiming for happiness—is another example of his departure from the central Utilitarian assumption that humans act mainly out of self-interest, pursue happiness, and seek to avoid pain. Though Mill always affirmed the principle of utility as the chief *criterion* for evaluating moral and social behavior and the goal of human life, he now developed a radically different psychology of human *motivation* that led him to reinterpret (some would say to reject) Utilitarianism in favor of a broader humanism.

A related result of Mill's recovery from deep mental distress was the realization that the full development of the inner life of the individual is just as important to human well-being as the improvement of society. This growing insight was to be of fundamental importance to his entire conception of individual freedom in *On Liberty*, some two decades later. Furthermore, he was coming to understand that individual development could not be one-sidedly intellectual, as his own had been; individual growth had to involve the nurturing of all sides of the person in a balanced and harmonious way. In particular, he wrote, "cultivation of the feelings became one of the cardinal points in my ethical and philosophical creed."[5]

Mill's reading of Marmontel led to further literary study, now among the British Romantic poets and essayists, particularly William Wordsworth and Thomas Carlyle, both near-contemporaries. In Wordsworth he found a lover of the beauties of nature—trees, flowers, mountains, rivers and streams. But he found something more as well, something like a religious feeling free of religious dogma:

> What made Wordsworth's poems a medicine for my state of mind, was that they expressed, not mere outward beauty, but states of feeling, and of thought coloured by feeling. . . . In them I seemed to draw from a source of inward joy, of sympathetic and imaginative pleasure, which could be shared in by all human beings. . . .[6]

In Carlyle Mill found both a mentor and a friend, and this in spite of their differing political views, the Scottish Carlyle being deeply traditional and conservative in his politics. It is a tribute to Mill's breadth of intellectual sympathy that he loved "the wonderful [poetic] power" of Carlyle's language at the same time that he disagreed with much that he found in Carlyle's philosophy.[7]

Mill's interest in Romantic literature probably played a part in discovering the love of his life, Harriet Taylor, with whom he enjoyed a long and intimate friendship and whom he eventually married. They met in 1831 when he was twenty-five and single and she twenty-three and married with children. Harriet remained married until her husband's death in 1849. The friendship was conducted it seems with complete propriety, and Mill knew and admired her husband; but some persons in London circles regarded their long "courtship" as nothing less than scandalous. Harriet and John married in 1851, and Harriet's daughter, Helen Taylor, became both John's consolation and active co-worker after Harriet's sudden death in 1858.

ON LIBERTY

Harriet Taylor's influence on Mill certainly exceeded Wordsworth's and Carlyle's; it approached only that

---

[4]*Autobiography.* J. M. Robson, ed. (London: Penguin, 1989) 44.
[5]Ibid., 118.
[6]Ibid., 121.
[7]Ibid., 138–39.

of James Mill, John's first teacher and mentor. By Mill's own account Harriet reshaped both his life and his thinking. His praise of her intellect and character in his *Autobiography* is so extravagant that some readers have thought him blinded by his devotion to her and have discounted her influence on his thought. More recently, however, scholars examining the matter from a feminist historical perspective have argued that we can take Mill at his word, particularly in the case of *On Liberty*, which Mill said "belongs to her as much as to me." Harriet Taylor died as they were finishing the manuscript, and Mill published it a year after her death as a memorial to her, though—it must be noted—without her name on the title page.[8]

Mill and Taylor characterized their treatise on individual liberty as "a kind of philosophic textbook of a single truth, which the changes progressively taking place in modern society tend to bring out into ever stronger relief: the importance, to man and society, of a large variety in types of character, and of giving full freedom to human nature to expand itself in innumerable and conflicting directions."[9] Such expansion of human potential, they argued, can be achieved only by enlarging and protecting individual liberty of opinion and action: "The only purpose for which power can be rightfully exercised over any member of a civilized community, against his will, is to prevent harm to others. His own good, either physical or moral, is not a sufficient warrant."[10]

Mill and Taylor divided their argument in the book into a) liberty of thought and speech, and b) liberty of action, which included developing one's own potentialities in one's own way and freely associating with other individuals for various purposes. "Of the Liberty of Thought and Discussion" is the longest chapter of the book. In it Taylor and Mill develop four arguments for complete freedom of expression: 1) All human beliefs, however true we may believe them to be, are fallible, and by suppressing some ideas we may be suppressing what turns out to be true. 2) Even if we are almost certain that some beliefs are false, they may contain some truth (and the most widely held beliefs usually contain some error), and it is only in the free conflict of beliefs that we can correct errors all around. 3) Even if we are sure that certain beliefs are true, unless they are repeatedly challenged and tested we will come to accept them simply as dogmas or prejudices and not know their rational basis. 4) If widely held beliefs simply become dogmas to which we give formal assent, they will cease to be meaningful in our lives as individuals or societies.

Taylor and Mill acknowledged the influence of the French political thinker Alexis de Tocqueville on the ideas of *On Liberty*. In *Democracy in America*, based on his travels in America in the 1830s, Tocqueville was taken by the young republic's enthusiastic commitment to democracy—not just to the democratic process of representation and legislation, but more fundamentally to the principle of equality. Tocqueville believed democracy was the political order of the future, and saw in the United States democracy's chief harbinger. However, the perceptive Frenchman observed something else: a distinct *tension* between democracy as a principle of political equality, and democracy as a principle of individual liberty enshrined in Jefferson's Declaration of Independence and the Bill of Rights. Democracy as equality, he argued, is ever in danger of enforcing abject conformity, mediocrity, leveling out everyone, reducing all to the lowest common denominator, suppressing dissent in thought and act. On the other hand, individual liberty requires respect for individual differences of ability, of opinion, and lifestyle, and willingness to allow these differences to flourish.

---

[8]That Mill in 1859 did not provide Taylor's name as co-author is probably best understood as a concession to lingering public disapproval of their relationship over the previous decade, as well as to contemporary skepticism toward women's involvement in serious intellectual work. It must be remembered that Taylor and Mill published *On Liberty* in 1859, the same year in which Mary Ann Evans published the novel *Adam Bede* under the male pseudonym George Eliot. Evans chose this course because she understood British distaste for "serious" fiction by women.

[9]*Autobiography*, 189.

[10]*On Liberty*. E. Rapaport, ed. (Indianapolis: Hackett, 1978) 9.

Osborn's painting speaks to the gendered separation of public and private spheres in Victorian England. Here, a woman enters a shop and transgresses the gender boundary, likely out of necessity rather than desire. Her presence in a space defined as professional, commercial, and masculine is unexpected. Osborn appealed to her audience to understand this woman's situation: her black dress, a symbol of mourning, and her lack of a wedding band suggest that she is forced to come here due to the death of a male provider. Her downcast eyes convey her discomfort in entering a male space and becoming the object of the male gazes from the left. Osborn's title, *Nameless and Friendless,* underscores both the woman's discomfort and her low social standing.

Figure III-6   Emily Osborn, *Nameless and Friendless,* 1857. Oil on canvas. (82.5 × 104.2 cm). Courtauld Institute of Art. Courtesy of The Bridgeman Art Library International.

Tocqueville spoke memorably of the "tyranny of the majority," a phrase Mill would use in *On Liberty* to describe a new form of tyranny made possible by the emergence of democracy since 1775: the imposition on all by force of public opinion, and even by force of law, of the views and values of the majority. But what if the majority is wrong, unjust, or vulgar in its views? What made Tocqueville's view so penetrating was its exposure of the tyranny of the majority as both a tyranny of ideas and beliefs and a tyranny of laws and institutions created at the behest of the majority. In words that might or might not astonish us today, Tocqueville wrote of 1830s America: "I know of no country in which there is so little independence of mind and real freedom of discussion as in America . . . freedom of opinion does not exist in America."[11] In the enthusiasm for democratic equality in the United States

---

[11]*Democracy in America.* R. D. Heffner, ed. NY: NAL, 1956, 117, 119.

of the Jacksonian Era (1830–40), Tocqueville saw a disturbing tendency toward conformity and a willingness to silence dissent and individuality. These observations—coupled no doubt with Mill's and Taylor's very recent experience of public disapproval of their unconventional liaison—informed their insistence in *On Liberty* on the role of individual freedom of opinion and behavior in achieving both individual and public well-being.

Mill's and Taylor's argument for the broadest possible interpretation of individual liberty was rooted in Mill's enlarged, humanized version of the principle of utility. In *On Liberty*, as in *Utilitarianism*, two years later, he defined happiness as the individual well-being that results from the fullest development of each person's unique possibilities, the fullest pursuit of his or her interests and abilities. In this view, Mill is closer to Aristotle's holistic idea of what constitutes human happiness than he is to Bentham's calculations of pleasures and pains. In *On Liberty*, Mill and Taylor argue that maximum individual freedom is necessary to individual happiness in the most complete sense, and that a society that permits its citizens the most varied scope for individual growth is the most stable form of society.

Mill and Taylor were particularly concerned about freedom of development and what we might call "lifestyle," as they reveal in the chapter titled "Of Individuality, as One of the Elements of Well-Being":

It is not by wearing down into uniformity all that is individual in themselves, but by cultivating it and calling it forth, within the limits imposed by the rights and interests of others, that human beings become a noble and beautiful object of contemplation; . . . by the same process human life also becomes rich, diversified, and animating, furnishing more abundant aliment to high thoughts and elevating feelings, and strengthening the tie which binds every individual to the [human] race by making the race infinitely better worth belonging to. In proportion to the development of his

individuality, each person becomes more valuable to himself, and is, therefore, capable of being more valuable to others.[12]

This individual and social ideal cannot be realized, Taylor and Mill argue, in a society whose laws and public opinion discriminate against minority groups and lifestyles and seek to enforce the beliefs of the majority. Some examples in American history include the heavy-handed Puritan attempts to build a "godly society" in New England, the treatment by Euro-Americans of African- and Native-Americans throughout our history, discrimination by the Protestant majority first against Catholics and then against Jews from the early nineteenth century to the recent past, and the McCarthy anti-Communist purges of the 1950s. More recently we have the attempts to disallow the teaching of evolution in public schools or to impose a non-scientific theory of human creation in the science classroom. These are just a few examples of the sorts of "majority tyranny" against which *On Liberty* inveighs.

Every democratic system wrestles again and again with the deep tension between individual rights on the one hand, and the commitment to equality of rights and opportunity on the other, between personal freedom and the public good. *On Liberty*'s argument has been very influential in the United States and Britain, but it has not gone unchallenged. Continuing an argument that begins in the 1790s, with Edmund Burke's opposition to the French Revolution, there are those who argue that what Mill and Taylor call a "very simple principle" of maximum personal liberty is just that–too abstractly simple a response to a complex question, ignoring or underestimating many genuine difficulties connected with day-to-day social and political life.[13] Others believe that *On Liberty* still speaks persuasively, and remains timely in its protest against discrimination, censorship, conformity, and suppression.

Given Mill's powerful commitment to personal liberty in the face of disapproving public opinion, it is no surprise that among leading British Victorian thinkers, female and male, he was one of the most

---

[12]*On Liberty*. 60.

[13]See e.g., Gertrude Himmelfarb, "Liberty: 'One Very Simple Principle'," in *On Looking Into the Abyss: Untimely Thoughts on Culture and Society* (NY: Knopf, 1994) 74–106.

Despite Mill's best efforts to obtain equal rights for women, Mary Cassatt was one of his only female contemporaries whose art has entered the history books. A century later, however, Cassatt served as a foremother for Miriam Schapiro and other feminist artists who sought to rediscover and reclaim the work of women erased from art history. By including an image of Cassatt's painting within her own, which Schapiro describes as historical "collaboration," she heralds Cassatt as an important figure in an artistic matrilineage. Schapiro's use of patterns and decoration, reminiscent of fabric, makes reference to textile work produced for centuries by women in the home, and elevates to high art status an aesthetic that was often denigrated as "feminine craft."

Figure III-7   Miriam Schapiro, *Me and Mary Cassatt,* 1973. Acrylic and collage (collaboration series), 22 × 30". Private collection. Courtesy of Miriam Schapiro.

outspoken feminists: an active advocate for full rights and equality for women from his teenage years. His friendship and marriage to Harriet Taylor, involving as he said the co-authoring of *On Liberty,* deepened his commitment to equal rights for women. Harriet Taylor was herself an active feminist, and the primary author of the article "Enfranchisement of Women" that appeared anonymously in 1851 in *The Westminster Review.* Many contemporary readers thought the article was by Mill. Some ten years later, shortly after the death of Harriet Taylor, Mill drafted a book he titled *The Subjection of Women.* He published it in 1869 as a tribute to Taylor and her influence on his thought. In it, Mill—like Mary Wollstonecraft in the 1790s, British novelist and poet Thomas Hardy, and Virginia Woolf in the l920s—argues that marriage as understood and defined in British law was servitude if not slavery for women. In the 1860s this was indeed the case, for in Britain, the Continent, and the United States marriage was "civil death" for women. Wives had no existence in civil law; they were represented entirely by their husbands, who possessed sole legal right to their wives' body, property, earnings, and children. Women could not vote and were effectively barred from careers in business and the professions. Mill argued, on sound utilitarian grounds and out of the depth of his experience with the brilliant Harriet Taylor, that the subjection of more than half the population was an enormous waste of intelligence and talent, and that women would be happier if free to develop their individual promise to the uttermost. He applied to women as well as to men the same arguments Taylor and he had advanced for maximum personal liberty in *On Liberty.* Mill believed that women must be free to choose their personal futures with as much freedom as men and with full rights as citizens; and that in order to do so they must have access to the best education available.

In 1865, Mill was elected to the British House of Commons, where he served for three years. He represented the Radical Party and pressed for liberal reforms, including women's suffrage. In 1868, he retired to Avignon, France, where he and Harriet had spent some of their happiest days together, and where she was buried. He died in 1873.

QUESTIONS FOR STUDY AND DISCUSSION

1. What were the effects on Mill's thought of the "mental crisis" he experienced as a young man? In what ways did Harriet Taylor influence him, and how did her influence relate to the literary influences he opened himself to after his mental crisis?

2. What are Mill's and Taylor's main arguments for individual liberty in *On Liberty*? Describe what they (and Alexis de Tocqueville) mean by the phrase "the tyranny of the majority." Is there such a tyranny to be found in the U.S. of the twenty-first century?

3. What were Mill's reasons for writing the *The Subjection of Women*?

4. How does Mill's Philosophy of Utility differ from Bentham's and James Mill's?

5. What is "Classical Liberalism" of the nineteenth century, and how does it differ from twenty-first century Liberalism?

SUGGESTIONS FOR FURTHER READING

Bullock, Alan and Maurice Shocken, eds. *The Liberal Tradition from Fox to Keynes*. New York: NYU Press, 1957.

Himmelfarb, Gertrude. *The Idea of Poverty: England in the Early Industrial Age*. New York: Knopf, 1983.

———. *On Looking Into the Abyss: Untimely Thoughts on Culture and Society*. New York: Knopf, 1994.

MacCoby, Simon. *The English Radical Tradition, 1763–1914*. London: N. Kaye, 1952.

Mill, John Stuart. *Autobiography*. Ed. & Intro., J. M. Robson. London: Penguin, 1989.

———. *Utilitarianism, On Liberty, Essay on Bentham; together with selected writings of Jeremy Bentham and John Austin*. Ed. & Intro., Mary Warnock. Cleveland: World Publ., 1962.

——— and Harriet Taylor Mill. *Essays on Sex Equality*. Ed. & Intro., Alice S. Rossi. Chicago: University of Chicago Press, 1970.

de Ruggiero, Guido. *The History of European Liberalism*. Tr. R. G. Collingwood. Gloucester, MA: P. Smith, 1981.

Spadafora, David. *The Idea of Progress in 18th Century Britain*. New Haven: Yale University Press, 1990.

Tocqueville, Alexis de. *Democracy in America*. Ed., R. D. Heffner. New York: New American Library, 1956.

CHAPTER SEVEN

CHARLES DARWIN AND THE THEORY OF EVOLUTION

Historians generally rank the English naturalist Charles Darwin (1809–1882) as one of the foremost thinkers in the history of science, a man who provoked a great revolution in biology with his *Origin of Species*. Many authors compare the Darwinian Revolution to the revolution produced in the physical sciences by Newton in his *Mathematical Principles of Natural Philosophy* (1687). Contrary to popular opinion, however, Darwin was not the first evolutionist, he did not invent the crucial mechanism of natural selection, nor was he the sole founder of evolutionary biology. Darwin and Darwinism nevertheless occupy a central position in modern thought.

PRE-DARWINIAN IDEAS OF EVOLUTION

Evolution refers to a process in which life first arises from non-life and basic forms and then changes through time into other forms. As far back as the sixth century BCE some Indian philosophers, and shortly afterwards some of the early Greek philosophers, proposed evolution as a naturalistic alternative to the popular beliefs in supernatural creation, such as those found in the Hebrew Bible. But their brilliant speculations did not establish evolution on a factual, authoritative foundation. It was not until the eighteenth century in Europe that scientists slowly began to assemble bits of concrete evidence to flesh out earlier insightful guesses, although the term "speculative" still best characterized their works.

The first substantial argument for evolution was proposed by the French biologist Jean Baptiste

Antoine de Monet, Chevalier de Lamarck (1744–1829), in the early nineteenth century. After a brilliant career as a botanist, during which he published a four-volume work on French flora, Lamarck turned at the age of forty-nine to invertebrate zoology, a field he established on its modern footing.

In 1797 Lamarck expressed his belief in the immutability or unchangeability of species, but by 1800 his views had diametrically changed, and by 1815 he had discussed his new ideas on evolution in *Philosophie Zoologique* (1809), where he stated that large changes in the environmental circumstances of animals bring about major changes in their actions. If their new needs become constant or especially long-lived, the animals then assume new *habits*, which lead to new parts and organs, all of which may be inherited after long habitual use. Over eons of time new life forms appear—they slowly evolve.

Lamarck thought life arose first from "infusoria" ("infinitely small animals with gelatinous, transparent, homogeneous and very contractile bodies") spontaneously, whenever conditions are "favorable." Once the lower forms appear, over long periods of time branching out occurs, leading toward greater and greater perfection of organisms. Humans are the end product of the entire process: "This predominant race, having acquired an absolute supremacy over all the rest, will ultimately establish a difference between itself and the most perfect animals, and indeed will leave them far behind."[1] The human lineage nevertheless is that of any animal.

---

[1]Lamarck, *Philosophical Zoology*, trans. Hugh Elliot (New York & London: Hafner, 1963), 171.

Many non-evolutionists were impressed by Lamarck's theories. When the pioneering English geologist Charles Lyell (1797–1875) discussed the issue of the existence and duration of species in his landmark textbook on geology, *Principles of Geology,* he singled out Lamarck's evolutionary arguments for refutation because they represented the best case available. Two fundamental keys to the subject of evolution were 1) the natural limits to species variation and 2) time. Lyell nevertheless concluded that God, the Author of nature, would not allow species to vary beyond prescribed limits because they would perish. Besides, Lamarck had never actually seen a new organism formed. As a believer in a steady-state geological *uniformitarianism*—the view that natural laws operating today are the same ones which operated in the past—Lyell also thought the present was the key to the past: because he could not see unlimited variation (that is, evolution) at the present time, none could have occurred in the past. But Lyell also argued that vast time scales had been involved in earth's history, and that the laws of physics and chemistry had produced today's world.

The issue of time posed no serious impediments to acceptance of Lyell's argument regarding geological history. During the seventeenth and eighteenth centuries scientific thinkers had been expanding the geological time scale substantially. Georges Buffon, for example, discussed tens of thousands of years; Lamarck in 1802 assumed millions of years in earth's history. By the time Charles Lyell's *Principles of Geology* was published, Archbishop Ussher's mid-seventeenth century calculations, suggesting the earth had been created during the morning of October 23, 4004 B.C.E., were no longer universally accepted.

Once the time barrier was overcome many scientists began to suspect that adaptive species change over millions of years might be cumulative. Readers of Lyell, such as Robert Chambers (1802–1871), Herbert Spencer (1820–1903), Alfred Russel Wallace (1823–1913), and Charles Darwin, were impressed by his geological arguments proving the uniform operation of inorganic nature over millions of years, but they balked at Lyell's refusal to accept evolution of the organic world during those same eons of time. Much later, after Darwin's *Origin of Species* (1859) had appeared, Lyell himself cautiously and timidly lent support to the evolutionists.

Robert Chambers, in his anonymously published *Vestiges of Creation* (1844 et seq.), first pushed Lyell's uniformity arguments to the limit, focusing on astronomy, geology, plant, animal and even human evolution. The scientific public reacted very negatively to his suggestions, despite extensive experimental and observational evidence in *Vestiges.* Chambers even cited Charles Darwin's *Voyage of the Beagle* (1839) as one of many authorities to support his novel thesis. Unfortunately, although the argument was tight and cohesive, the evidence itself was uneven, and criticism was widespread and severe. The British biologist Thomas H. Huxley (1825–1895), later one of Darwin's main champions in Great Britain, savagely attacked the tenth and best edition of *Vestiges* in 1853. By contrast, the English poet, Alfred Lord Tennyson, was deeply influenced by Chambers and poetically alluded to *Vestiges* in his great poem *In Memoriam* (1850).[2]

Chambers described the developmental principles of *Vestiges* in this way: "*the simplest and most primitive type, under a law to which that of like production is subordinate, gave birth to the type next above it, this again produced the next higher, and so on to the very highest*, the stages of advance being in all cases very small—namely from one species only to another; so that the phenomenon has always been of a single and modest *character.*"[3]

Why did progressive development occur? What was the mechanism? By 1853, in the tenth edition of *Vestiges,* Chambers hypothesized two "impulses" or natural tendencies of nature as causal mechanisms, under the "Providence" of God. Chambers otherwise relied heavily upon solid scientific arguments familiar to evolutionists today: species variation, geographical distribution of species, the geological record, embryology, vestigial organs, and

---

[2]Milton Millhauser, *Just Before Darwin: Robert Chambers and "Vestiges"* (Middletown, CT: Wesleyan University Press, 1959), 156 ff.

[3]Robert Chambers, *Vestiges of the Natural History of Creation* (London: John Churchill, 1844), 222. Emphasis by Chambers.

natural affinities of organs. What he lacked were a high degree of scientific sophistication and judgment and scientifically acceptable examples. Chambers's tendency to tackle taboo subjects, such as the human place in nature, also met with a close-minded Victorian public.

Darwin had uncomplimentary words for *Vestiges*. He wrote to his botanist friend Joseph Dalton Hooker (1817–1911) that the anonymously published book was more of a "nine day wonder than a lasting work." Despite the admirable writing and arrangement, "his geology strikes me as bad, and his zoology far worse." But in the "Historical Sketch" to the *Origin of Species*, first appearing in 1861, Darwin remarked that the tenth edition of *Vestiges* had paved the way "for the reception of analogous views," and we must naturally assume he referred to his own or similar enlightened ideas.[4]

The co-discoverer (independently of Darwin) of natural selection, the English naturalist Alfred Russel Wallace, had been profoundly affected by Chambers's book. Wallace was an adherent of a philosophical skepticism and materialism that was popular among the educated in nineteenth-century England. Born into a relatively poor middle-class family, Wallace struggled to survive with a number of jobs, ranging from surveying to teaching school. Nothing completely satisfied his true interests: he yearned for faraway lands, exotic plants and animals, strange natives—the unknown mysteries of our planet. He was particularly absorbed by the strong probability that species evolve in nature.

On December 28, 1845, Wallace wrote his friend Henry Walter Bates (1825–1892) that he thought the central thesis of *Vestiges*—progressive development—was sound; one needed only to gather more solid scientific evidence to test that hypothesis. In pursuit of that goal, Wallace proposed that he and Bates travel to the Amazon River basin for field work. To support themselves they collected specimens and sold them through an agent in England. The collection of specimens was a popular hobby of the upper-class "armchair adventurers." Wallace

returned home in 1852, but his ship unexpectedly sank in the Atlantic along with his collections, and he barely completed his voyage after a harrowing rescue at sea. After a short stay in England, he continued his quest in the Malay Archipelago/Indonesian region in his ongoing effort to discover why species evolve. There he brought to fruition his first public statements on evolution.

Wallace's essay "On the Law which Has Regulated the Introduction of New Species" (1855) focused on well-known published geological and geographical evidence. He concluded his essay: "*Every species has come into existence coincident in both space and time with a pre-existing closely allied species.*"[5] No real mechanism was proposed, but he had sketched out a cogent, cautious, purely scientific argument for evolution. Public acclaim for this revolutionary announcement, however, did not even register on the Richter scale. The private response was quite a different matter, for Charles Lyell, Edward Blyth (1810–1873), and Charles Darwin all read and were extremely impressed by Wallace's arguments.[6]

Wallace, unaware of the impact of his article on those key scientists, continued searching for a mechanism, a key to explaining *why* evolution occurred. The moment of enlightenment came several years later, during February 1858, on Gilolo (Halmahara) in the Moluccas Islands, when Wallace, in a feverish state, was reflecting on human evolution. Suddenly, in a flash of delirious inspiration, he understood that the positive consequence of the struggle for existence, and the competition for the food supply, was that the best adapted, or fittest, species survived and propagated their kind. Natural selection improved the race; Lyell and others understood only the negative aspects of the process—negative selection or extinction. The creative side had escaped them. Wallace wrote up his ideas quickly upon arriving back at the island of Ternate, and sent his paper "On the Tendency of Varieties to Depart Indefinitely from the Original Type" to Charles Darwin in England on March 9, 1858. After receipt of Wallace's paper, joint publication of his paper and a selection of the discussion of natural

---

[4]Millhauser, *Just Before Darwin*, chpt. 6. Also, Peter Brent, *Charles Darwin* (New York & London: W. W. Norton, 1981), 399 ff.

[5]Reprinted in McKinney, *Lamarck to Darwin* (Lawrence, KS: Coronado Press, 1971).

[6]See McKinney, *Wallace and Natural Selection* (New Haven, CT & London: Yale University Press, 1972), chpt. 7.

Voyage of the *Beagle* 1831–1836. Redrawn from *Darwin: A Norton Critical Edition,* Second Edition, edited by Philip Appleman (1979), W. W. Norton & Company.

selection from Darwin's "1844 Essay" were presented, under the sponsorship of Charles Lyell and Joseph Hooker, before the distinguished natural history organization, the Linnaean Society of London, on July 1, 1858. The papers were published August 20, 1858 in the society's journal, before Wallace had a chance to approve or disapprove their decision to publish. Darwin now had a bonfire lighted under him to complete his work on species.

DARWIN'S LIFE AND THE DEVELOPMENT OF HIS IDEAS

Darwin was born of distinguished family—his grandfather, Dr. Erasmus Darwin, was a renowned writer, physician and speculative evolutionist, and his father, Dr. Robert Darwin, enjoyed a very successful medical practice. Charles floundered in medical school at the University of Edinburgh, for he found the study of medicine distasteful. He then turned to the study of theology at Cambridge University but soon realized his interest lay in the area

of natural science. At Cambridge Darwin befriended Professor John Stevens Henslow (1796–1861), professor of botany, who also knew "entomology, chemistry, mineralogy and geology," and Adam Sedgwick (1783–1873), who lectured on geology. They encouraged and helped develop Darwin's scientific interests. Professor Henslow secured for Darwin a post as unpaid naturalist on the H. M. S. *Beagle.* The task with which the captain and crew were charged was to (a) take chronometric readings around the world, (b) survey the South American coastline (Patagonia, Tierra del Fuego, Chile, and Peru), (c) ascertain angles on all important geographical points, and (d) prepare geological maps. That trip from December 27, 1831, to October 2, 1836, most particularly a visit to the Galapagos Islands, transformed Darwin's life. He later wrote, "The voyage of the *Beagle* has been by far the most important event in my life and has determined my whole career."[7] By the end of the voyage he was committed to a career in science.

[7]Fredrick Burkhardt & Sydney Smith, eds. "Introduction," *The Correspondence of Charles Darwin,* Vol. I (Cambridge: Cambridge University Press, 1986), xiv.

It was the *Beagle* voyage that furnished Darwin with an educational experience that transformed his scarcely recognized potential into a keen, observant, thoughtful naturalist. Early letters sent to John Henslow at Cambridge about the *Beagle* expedition established Darwin as a scientist to be reckoned with even before his return. His reputation grew even more rapidly after his return as major works flew from his pen. In the period between 1837 and 1845 Darwin published his *Journal of Researches into the Natural History and Geology of the Countries Visited During the Voyage of H.M.S. Beagle* (1839, 2nd ed. 1845), an account of the famous *Beagle* voyage; a pioneering book on the formation of coral reefs, *The Structure and Distribution of Coral Reefs* (1842); four definitive volumes on living and fossil barnacles; and various books on the natural history discoveries during the *Beagle* voyage, including contributions to *The Zoology of the Voyage of the H.M.S. Beagle* (3 vols., 1838–1843) and the book *Geological Observations on South America* (1846).

Upon completing his book *The Voyage of H.M.S. Beagle* in 1837, Darwin began in a series of notebooks to review the species question in light of the hypothesis of evolution. He had first read the second volume of Lyell's *Principles* (1832) during the voyage, with its forceful discussion and rejection of evolution, and this provided the view against which to test the hypothesis. These notebooks, beginning in July 1837, opened with excerpts from his grandfather Erasmus Darwin's *Zoonomia*, a speculative work on evolution that he had already read and no doubt heard discussed at home.

Darwin soon realized that if plants and animals can evolve, humanity probably does too. *Homo sapiens* may indeed be the summit of a natural process not requiring creative effort by a deity after all. But what mechanism, other than God, could drive this process? Late in September 1838 Darwin happened to read the Reverend Thomas R. Malthus's *Essay on the Principle of Population* (1798). Emphasizing the human condition, Malthus had argued that the human population when unchecked tends to increase geometrically (i.e., exponentially), while the food supply needed for survival increases only arithmetically.

From Malthus's observations Darwin (and Wallace) extrapolated these ideas to the entire animal kingdom; the entire process became crystal clear.

Populations, animal and human, tend to increase geometrically; food supplies increase arithmetically; and thus populations tend to outstrip food supply. Consequently, there is a struggle for existence, resulting in the best adapted species surviving and propagating their race. The process is one of *natural selection*.

This long path led inevitably back to the origin of species, on which Darwin again began to focus full time. In late November 1859, 1,250 copies of Darwin's *On the Origin of Species by Means of Natural Selection* finally saw the light of day. A new era began in humankind's view of the origins and development of nature and of the human race.

The Voyage of the Beagle alone would have elevated Darwin to the top ranks of English naturalists, and the title page of the *Origin* displayed his credentials: "By Charles Darwin, M.A., Fellow of the Royal Geological, Linnaean, Etc. Societies; Author of 'Journal of Researches During H.M.S. Beagle's Voyage Round the World.'" The fact of Darwin's distinguished lineage and his own reputation as a naturalist were vital components of his success.

In the *Origin of Species* Darwin makes four claims: (1) the organic world is constantly changing. (2) The changes may be small and numerous or large and rare. (3) All living organisms have evolved from a single source (a hypothesis confirmed by genetics only in the past decade, with the discovery that all organisms contain the same molecular "dictionary"). (4) Natural selection is the mechanism for these changes. He presents his case as a tapestry of logic, factual data, observations, citations of eminent authorities, numerous experiments, and statements asking the reader to accept Darwin's judgment and trust the veracity of his conclusions. Structurally, the book is divided into two parts: (a) the argument for an evolutionary mechanism, and (b) the case for evolution. The cornerstone of his mechanism section, however, was the use of analogy, particularly the humanity/nature analogy, which allowed Darwin to develop a substantial step-by-step argument, moving from the known and acceptable to the unknown and repugnant.

The subject of "Variation under Domestication," Darwin's first chapter, focused on a subject of common knowledge to the English. Cattle and pigeon breeding was widely practiced, and a vast

Natural Selection

literature had grown up which explicated a broad range of domestic variations. Lamarck had also referred to domestic varieties, and Darwin was definitely aware of those views, perhaps drawing specifically on that eminent source. In addition to citing eminent authorities repeatedly, Darwin stated that he himself bred domestic pigeons and was on excellent terms with pigeon breeders. He therefore knew the subject intimately and extensively.

Variation in nature is also evident to any ordinary observer. These differences have existed for eons of time. Furthermore, nature is boundless and extraordinarily powerful. We know on the authority of many authors that species and varieties in nature are engaged in a constant struggle for life. Just as humans select and shape domestic species such as dogs, pigeons, and cattle to produce new varieties, so also does nature select the best adapted organisms in the struggle for life to produce new varieties, species, families, and orders. With enormous time and power at nature's disposal, it can produce various extraordinary revolutions throughout the earth.

The remainder of Darwin's book focused on the case for evolution *per se*, and involved many strategies. Darwin himself raised various difficulties with the concept, which allowed him to preconfigure the structure of his opponents' arguments. These primary difficulties and objections were the following: (1) There seems to be an absence of transitional forms of life, the existence of which would be important evidence of evolution. (2) How could certain organic beings with peculiar habits and structures originate and evolve into different creatures? How, for example, could an insectivorous quadruped be converted into a flying bat? (3) How can instinctive behavior be explained on an evolutionary model? (4) Since sterility frequently results from hybridization, how can it be explained by evolution by natural selection? Some difficulties were so grave, said Darwin, that "to this day I can never reflect on them without being staggered; but, to the best of my judgment, the greater number are only apparent, and those that are real are not, I think, fatal to my theory."[8]

Imperfections of the geological record and the geographical distribution of life were difficult although not insurmountable problems, and the facts as Darwin presented them better accorded with descent and natural selection than with the prevailing belief in the immutability of species. In general, he argued, the relationships of organisms through both time (geology) and space (geography) are best explained by evolution, working through natural selection rather than by special creation by God, as commonly believed then.

Other pertinent subjects discussed by Darwin to support his hypothesis of evolution by natural selection were the natural system of classification, morphology, embryology, and rudimentary (vestigial) organs—all of which had been discussed by other evolutionists. He concluded a brilliant summary of his evolutionary arguments with a powerful and poetic statement:

It is interesting to contemplate an entangled bank, clothed with many plants of many kinds, with birds singing on the bushes, with various insects flitting about, and with worms crawling through the damp earth, and to reflect that these elaborately constructed forms, so different from each other, and dependent on each other in so complex a manner, have all been produced by laws acting around us. These laws, taken in the largest sense, being Growth with Reproduction; Inheritance which is almost implied by reproduction; Variability from the indirect and direct action of the external conditions of life, and from use and disuse; a Ratio of Increase so high as to lead to a Struggle for Life, and as a consequence to Natural Selection, entailing Divergence of Character and the Extinction of less-improved forms. Thus, from the war of nature, from famine and death, the most exalted object which we are capable of conceiving, namely, the production of the higher animals, directly follows. There is grandeur in this view of life, with its several powers, having been originally breathed into a few forms or into one; and that, whilst this planet

[8]Charles Darwin, *On the Origin of Species* (London: John Murray, 1859), 171.

has gone cycling on according to the fixed law of gravity, from so simple a beginning endless forms most beautiful and most wonderful have been, and are being, evolved.[9]

In none of the first six editions of *The Origin of Species* did Darwin apply all these ideas to humans, although he clearly believed that they were applicable. Even in *The Descent of Man* he hardly mentioned human evolution, although what he said is unambiguous in placing the human species squarely within the evolutionary process. Darwin's long-standing reticence on this issue reflected, not his own beliefs, but his realization that the theory of evolution was probably the most dramatic challenge ever made to human beliefs about our uniqueness and superiority.

THEOLOGICAL RESPONSES TO DARWINISM IN THE NINETEENTH CENTURY

In 1896 Andrew Dickson White published a two-volume work entitled *A History of the Warfare Between Science and Theology*. Over a hundred years later it still seems to be a common assumption that the relationship between science and religion is a "warfare" or "conflict," that it is a matter of science *versus* religion. This is a vast oversimplification of a much more complex and subtle relationship, and a serious distortion of the modern history of science and of religion. The great "paradigm shifts" in the history of science—notably the Copernican theory that put the sun rather than the earth at the center of the solar system and Darwin's theory of evolution through natural selection—have always divided *both* the scientific *and* the religious communities. In response to both Copernicanism and Darwinism there were scientists who opposed and resisted the new ideas and theologians who accepted and affirmed them. In this section we will examine the range of nineteenth-century theological reactions to Darwin.

When Darwin published *The Origin of Species* in 1859, there were indeed Christians who argued that there could be no compromise: we must choose *either* the Bible (the Genesis creation stories) *or*

Darwinism—both cannot be true. A man named Philip Gosse even speculated that God had distributed fossil remains on the earth in such a way as to make plausible an evolutionary interpretation, simply to test people's faith! But after 1859 a growing number of Protestant theologians accepted evolutionary theory as entirely compatible with belief in a creator God and specifically with Christianity. Paving the way for this acceptance was the growing influence of critical-historical study of the Bible in the early and mid-nineteenth century. German scholars, most of them Protestant Christians, led the way in applying the methods of ordinary historical study of the past to both the Hebrew Bible and the New Testament, shedding a great deal of new light on the biblical authors in their historical and cultural setting and on the meaning and purpose of the language they used.

Critical-historical study of the Bible brought about a reinterpretation of the meaning of biblical inspiration and authority on the part of not only liberal but also conservative theologians as well. Many Protestant theologians and biblical scholars now distinguished between the enduring religious ideas expressed in the Genesis creation stories and the ancient Israelite cosmology or worldview in which they were historically expressed. They interpreted the Genesis stories as symbolic and poetic affirmations of the dependence of the universe and human life upon God, not as literal history or science. As with earlier scientific discoveries, these Protestant scholars believed that the theory of evolution provides us with a vastly expanded and corrected knowledge of just *how* God creates and sustains the universe. This became and has remained the outlook of "mainstream," non-fundamentalist Protestant theologians and churches to the present day: faith and reason are compatible in the case of evolutionary biology as in other branches of scientific knowledge.

Something similar happened among nineteenth-century Roman Catholic thinkers. While officially the Church was slow to accept evolution, in time it acknowledged the evolution of the human body from animal ancestry but affirmed the special creation of each human soul by God. In the twenti-

---

[9]Ibid., 489–90.

eth century there were two important papal documents addressing evolution: Pope Pius XII's encyclical *Humani generis* in 1950, and Pope John Paul II's "Message on Evolution to the Pontifical Academy of Sciences" in 1996. Pius XII cautiously affirmed that evolutionary theory was compatible with Catholic teaching as long as it did not deny the special creation of the human soul. Building on the statements of his predecessor, John Paul went further. Referring to twentieth-century developments in evolutionary biology such as the dramatic discoveries in genetics, he said: ". . . new knowledge has led to the recognition that the theory of evolution is more than a hypothesis. It is indeed remarkable that this theory has been progressively accepted by researchers, following a series of discoveries in various fields of knowledge. The convergence, neither sought nor fabricated, of the results of work that was conducted independently is in itself a significant argument in favor of the theory."[10] With regard to biblical interpretation, Catholic scholars and theologians have always had a certain advantage over Protestants in that the Catholic outlook is church-centered, not Bible-centered: the biblical writings are the product of the Church's early life and are the Church's book; the teaching authority is the living Church through its leadership. Modern Catholic scholars fully accept historical-critical study of the Bible and do not interpret the Genesis stories literally. In their affirmation of the compatibility of faith and reason with regard to modern science, they stand squarely in the tradition of Augustine and Thomas Aquinas.

This "mainstream" approach in both Protestantism and Catholicism (also of Reform and Conservative Judaism) that arose in the nineteenth century in response to Darwin's theory may be called *theistic evolutionism*. Since then the serious intellectual debate has not been between evolutionists and "creationists," since creationism is not science, but between *theistic* evolutionists and *naturalistic* or *non-theistic* evolutionists.

Following the publication of Darwin's *Origin of Species*, a group of thinkers and writers of the Church of England wrote articles and books defending Darwinism and arguing its compatibility with Christian belief. They were among the earliest theistic evolutionists. The Anglican priest Charles Kingsley, who was also a popular novelist, championed evolution, as did theologians such as Aubrey Moore and J. R. Illingworth and the eminent poet, critic, and lay theologian Matthew Arnold. Both Moore and Illingworth were contributors to an important and controversial volume of essays entitled *Lux Mundi* (Light of the World; 1890). The contributors to the book, all of them Anglican clergy, were not "liberals." They were high-church Anglicans who saw themselves as standing squarely in the tradition of classical Trinitarian Christianity. Aubrey Moore made this remarkable statement in his book *Science and the Faith*: "Evolution as a theory is infinitely more Christian than the theory of 'Special Creation.' For it implies the immanence of God in nature, and the omnipresence of his creative power. Those who opposed the doctrine of evolution in defense of a 'continued intervention' of God seem to have failed to notice that a theory of occasional intervention implies as its correlative a theory of ordinary absence. . . . Anything more opposed to the language of the Bible and the Fathers can hardly be imagined. . . ."[11] Illingworth's *Lux Mundi* essay, titled "The Incarnation and Development," (1890) was a restatement of the Christian doctrine of the Incarnation (the belief that Jesus is fully God and fully a human being) in the light of the new knowledge of human origins and development from evolutionary theory. He viewed the theory of evolution as simply the latest in a centuries-old series of intellectual revolutions that the churches had assimilated, taking the best thought of every age "captive to Christ" and simply reinterpreting ancient religious truth in the light of the new scientific knowledge. Illingworth tried to show how the idea of the Incarnation, rightly understood, embraced the idea of evolution.[12]

At this point it should be observed that like most non-scientist interpreters of evolution (and

---

[10]*Inside the Vatican*, January 1997, 29.

[11]London, 1889, 184–5; quoted in James C. Livingston, *Modern Christian Thought: From the Enlightenment to Vatican II* (New York: Macmillan, 1971), 232.

[12]Charles Gore, ed., *Lux Mundi: Studies in the Religion of the Incarnation* (London: John Murray, 1890), 187.

even some scientists) in the nineteenth century, most theologians interpreted evolution as a progressive, purposeful development of life on earth from simple life-forms to its culmination in the human species. That is not the properly scientific theory of evolution, which simply describes change over time through natural selection without thinking of the whole process as having some ultimate direction, meaning, or goal. In other words, most people thought of evolution in positive metaphysical and moral terms—which of course made it attractive to both Christian theologians and secular humanists.

In the United States, as in Britain, a number of Christian intellectuals from liberal to orthodox endorsed evolutionary theory as true and entirely compatible with Christian teaching. On the liberal side were people such as Lyman Abbott, a prominent Congregationalist minister, writer, and editor. He wrote two books, *The Evolution of Christianity* (1892) and *Theology of an Evolutionist* (1897), in which, typically, he thought of evolution as a universal and progressive process of development in both the natural and the human orders. Among theologically conservative adherents of evolution, notable was Asa Gray, the Harvard biologist who was the main champion of Darwinism in America. Gray was a Calvinist Presbyterian and thoroughly orthodox in his Christian beliefs. James McCosh, president of Princeton Theological Seminary and a prominent Presbyterian leader, argued that God had established the initial design of the whole evolutionary process but continues to work through what appear to us to be "spontaneous" (random) changes in the process. Interestingly, as Calvinists, both Gray and McCosh had a deep sense of the struggle and tragedy of human existence and of all nature; they had no problem with the theory of natural selection, which just seemed to reinforce that dark view of an earth in the grip of original sin.

What we call "fundamentalism" did not arise until the early twentieth century. It was a new movement, and not the same thing as traditional Christian orthodoxy. Fundamentalism arose specifically as a reaction against "modernism" in all its forms: it condemned critical study of the Bible, evolutionary theory, and various other developments in modern knowledge. The movement originated in a series of pamphlets, *The Fundamentals*, pub-

lished in 1909. The specific fundamentalist doctrines were a literalistic interpretation of biblical inerrancy, an emphasis on Jesus' atoning death and second coming, and the sudden conversion of the believer in accepting Jesus as personal savior. While in previous centuries Christian orthodoxy had held that the biblical writings were the fully inspired Word of God, this had not been tied to a literal interpretation of the biblical texts. In the twentieth century it has been fundamentalists, not "mainstream" orthodox Christians, who have aggressively opposed evolutionary theory with creationist views based upon a literalistic interpretation of the opening chapters of Genesis, treating them as if they were a textbook of science and history.

Summing up, we may say that the picture of Christian theological responses to Darwinism in the nineteenth century is a complex and subtle one. Those responses ran the gamut from full acceptance, by both liberal and orthodox Christian thinkers, to complete rejection by fundamentalists. Out of the positive responses emerged the "mainstream" Protestant and Catholic affirmations of evolution in the twentieth century. In line with the Christian tradition's centuries-old confidence in the harmony between the Christian message and the advances of human knowledge, the broad Christian consensus has been what we have called "theistic evolutionism." There is a rich body of twentieth and twenty-first century literature by Christian theologians who are also trained as scientists, that discusses all the issues raised by evolution for Christianity and argues for the compatibility of theistic faith and full acceptance of evolution. Among the leading figures in this enterprise have been scientist-theologians such as Pierre Teilhard de Chardin in France, Ian Barbour and Kenneth Miller (a Catholic layman) in the United States, and Arthur Peacocke and John Polkinghorne in Britain.

At bottom, what really troubles those who reject evolution in favor of creationist theories (for which the only "evidence" is a certain kind of literalistic reading of the first chapters of Genesis) is that they believe that evolutionary theory is equivalent to atheism—or, as it is often described, *naturalism*, the belief that there is simply nature, the physical universe, and nothing more. And indeed, there are prominent evolutionary biologists, such as Richard Dawkins, who firmly believe that naturalism is true. But naturalism is not science, but rather a metaphysical theory or worldview based on science. To equate evolutionary theory with atheism or naturalism is simply a mistake: scientific assumptions, methods, and knowledge are compatible with a variety of views of the ultimate character of reality.

The same mistake is made on the theistic side by creationists and "intelligent design" proponents. Creationists raise questions and criticisms of aspects of evolutionary theory that have been satisfactorily answered over and over again (while offering no scientific evidence for their views), but at bottom is the fear that to accept evolution means to espouse a "godless, secular atheism": one simply cannot be a Christian or even a theist and an evolutionist. Proponents of "intelligent design," whose arguments are typically much more sophisticated than those of creationists, believe that the complexity of organic life on earth cannot be fully explained by evolutionary biology, and argue that we must posit an "intelligent designer" in order to provide a full explanation. The problem is that hypotheses such as an intelligent designer are simply outside the purview of science. Science is the natural explanation of natural phenomena. It is not proper scientific method to introduce into it assumptions or hypotheses from outside of nature such as an intelligent designer or God. From a philosophical or theological point of view, one may legitimately question whether evolutionary theory completely "explains," in some complete and total sense of explanation, organic life on the planet. But evolutionary biology explains what it does within the framework and limits of science. What further explanation might be called for is not within the realm of science. As a strictly scientific theory explaining the origins and development of life, Darwinism is compatible with a variety of metaphysical views, including both theism and atheism.

SOCIAL DARWINISM

In the last decades of the nineteenth century, following the publication of Darwin's *Origin*, evolutionary ideas emphasizing natural selection came to be known as "Darwinism." These revolutionary ideas, however, could not be constrained within biology. Like a tidal wave, evolution swept over many areas of thought, including religion, philoso-

Darwin's theories on natural selection and human evolution sparked strong reactions in public opinion. Although the books were bestsellers, Darwin was lampooned in political cartoons. In a caricature from the *London Sketchbook*, a hairy, ape-like Darwin cozies up to a fellow ape.

Figure III-8 *Darwin and Ape* **print from** *London Sketchbook*, April 1874 Volume 1: Number 4. Color lithography. Archives Charmet. Courtesy of The Bridgeman Art Library International.

phy, economics, political theory, sociology, and education, and found expression in the novels and poetry of the late nineteenth and early twentieth centuries. Applied to society, what is called *Social Darwinism* rose to special prominence, although the roots of these ideas were in place decades before 1859. The general intellectual climate in the late nineteenth century was congenial to unrestricted capitalism, colonial expansionism, and opposition to voluntary social change. Social Darwinism seemed to provide "scientific" foundation to such views.

 Social Darwinism is *the use of concepts of evolutionary theory as norms for interpreting human moral, social, economic, and political life.* It has expressed itself in a variety of ways, from late-nineteenth-century advocacy of *laissez faire* or unregulated capitalism to the fascism of Hitler and Mussolini. The leading Social Darwinist exponent of *laissez faire* capitalism in the nineteenth century was Darwin's British contemporary Herbert Spencer (1820–1903). Spencer tried to work out a fully scientific view of the world based on the assumption that not only nature but also human life in both its physical and mental aspects is governed entirely by natural laws. Well before Darwin had publicly presented his theory of natural selection, Spencer in his writings used the concept of evolution. By "evolution" he meant that growth and development, governed by natural laws, was common to the physical, organic, and human worlds, and that the key to the process is the advance from the simple to the complex. Unlike Darwin and truly scientific evolutionism, Spencer interpreted evolution as inevitable progress from "lower" to "higher"—an interpretation that has been enormously influential in the nineteenth and twentieth centuries.

On the basis of his interpretation of the evolutionary process, Spencer argued that progress in the human realm meant the increase of those humans best adapted to their environment—the strongest or fittest—and the dying out of the weak or unfit. It was he, not Darwin, who introduced the phrase "the survival of the fittest." Spencer believed that this is what we see in the struggle for survival among animals in nature, and that the same holds true for the human world as part of nature. Hence he argued for minimal government regulation of human life, including efforts to alleviate poverty through poor laws, on the grounds that this interfered with the natural course of things making for human progress. Accepting the Utilitarian principle of the greatest happiness for the greatest number, Spencer disagreed with the Utilitarians such as

John Stuart Mill that it could be achieved by active government involvement in areas like industrial and educational reform. Spencer believed that the industrial capitalism of his day, which exemplified the principles of the natural struggle, was the best assurance of human progress by gradually improving the standard of living for more and more people. Interfering with the free market was going against nature.

Spencer realized that his vision of a society in which government does not help the weak and needy sounded cruel, but he argued that it was "being cruel to be kind": in the long run it was kinder and better for the improvement of the human race to let the less fit perish. He did allow for private forms of assistance for those who are able and willing to help themselves but have experienced difficulties and setbacks of one sort or another. A good short summary of Spencer's social and political philosophy can be found in the essay "The Survival of the Fittest," from his book *Social Statics* (1851).

Social Darwinism of the Spencerian sort found a ready audience in the United States, which was experiencing rapid industrialization after the Civil War under the leadership of self-made "captains of industry" such as John D. Rockefeller and Andrew Carnegie. Carnegie in fact published an essay entitled "Wealth" in 1892 that became a classic American exposition of Social Darwinism. Surprisingly, after defending the unregulated market with such ideas as the "law of competition," the "law of accumulation of wealth," and the "survival of the fittest," Carnegie went on to argue just as vigorously that the great entrepreneurs who are the natural leaders of society have a moral duty to give away most of their fortune during their lifetime—not primarily to their heirs, or for social programs or higher wages for their workers, but for public works such as libraries and parks that will enrich and beautify the lives of all classes of society.

One of the leading nineteenth-century critics of Social Darwinism was Thomas Henry Huxley (1825–1895). Huxley, who was a friend of Spencer, was Darwin's most effective exponent, a creative biologist in his own right, and a man of letters who belongs (with Darwin and Spencer) among the "eminent Victorians." In essays such as "The Strug-

Rockefeller

gle for Existence in Human Society" (1888) and "Evolution and Ethics" (1893), Huxley emphasized that the workings of nature may often seem cruel to us, but they are in fact governed by impersonal physical laws and not by moral laws. We project onto nature our human standards, and thus imagine wolves as savage predators killing helpless deer. But of course wolves are not "immoral"; they are simply doing what wolves naturally do, and killing and eating deer is part of the natural selection process, helping to weed out the weaker members of the deer species and thus keeping its population healthy. Nature, including natural selection, is neither "moral" nor "immoral"; it is simply "amoral"—our moral standards do not apply to it.

But Huxley then went on to argue that, while natural selection applies to the human species, with the emergence of humans there is another factor just as important: our reasoning ability and our sense of right and wrong. It is inappropriate to regard wolves killing deer as immoral, whereas it is entirely proper to regard humans killing other humans as immoral. With their powers of reason, imagination, memory, language, and moral and aesthetic values, humans have in a sense "short-circuited" the slow process of natural selection and superimposed on it the rich and varied realm of human culture.

Thus we defy the "law of the survival of the fittest," assisting the biologically "weaker" members of the human species to survive and thus to reproduce and transmit their "weak" genetic traits to their offspring—and we are right to do so, argued Huxley. Similarly, the most desirable human societies are those whose institutions are designed to alleviate human suffering, mitigate the inequities among humans, and maximize the opportunities for individual and social happiness. All this flows from the highest moral values—love, compassion, mercy, pity—which are products of human culture and do not exist in the rest of nature. The task of human society, Huxley wrote, is not "the survival of the fittest" but "the fitting of as many as possible to survive."

A skeptic or—to use the term he coined, an *agnostic*—with regard to religion, Huxley regarded this opposition between the human realm of social and moral values and the rest of nature simply as a puzzling dualism arising from the evolutionary process itself. He concluded: "Social progress means a checking of the cosmic process at every step and the substitution for it of another, which may be called the ethical process; the end of which is not the survival of those who may happen to be the fittest, in respect of the whole of the conditions which obtain, but of those who are ethically the best."

But the most influential social and intellectual forces of the late nineteenth and early twentieth centuries were on the side of Social Darwinism. One fateful effect of the application of Darwinism to social issues was to reinforce the traditional subordination of women with supposedly "scientific" arguments for their evolutionary inferiority as less adaptive and "fit" humans—arguments to which Darwin himself seemingly contributed. Another fateful consequence was the development of the modern concept of "race." There was a wide consensus among eminent anthropologists, paleontologists, and other researchers on the human phenomenon, that distinct races could be identified and arranged hierarchically in terms of their evolutionary progress and general fitness. Since it is human brainpower that has made possible distinctively human achievements, there were researchers, for example, who assumed a direct correlation between skull size and intelligence, collected human skulls and measured them, and not surprisingly concluded that caucasians were the most intelligent, followed by Asiatics, with blacks at the bottom. Growing European dominance of the world during the modern period was viewed as hard evidence that the white race was the "fittest." Such ideas provided a "scientific" rationalization for the aggressive imperialism and colonialism of European nations during the late nineteenth and early twentieth centuries. The "white man's burden" was to bring a higher form of religion, morality, education, politics, economics, and law to the benighted black, brown, and yellow races—and to add territory and turn a profit in the bargain. Politicians such as the German Chancellor Otto von Bismarck and the American President Theodore Roosevelt emphasized such ideas to justify their expansionist ambitions.

Collect

"Evolution & Ethics" In his essay Huxley opens with some clever quips about pessimists and optimists and how good or evil the world is, concluding that it is neither as good nor as bad as it is often thought to be. That leads him to state that we ought to do what we can to improve the world, and to ask what light the theory of evolution sheds on this question.

Propounders of the "ethics of evolution"—and Huxley has in mind Social Darwinists like Herbert Spencer—speak of the evolution of moral sentiments, and he thinks their view could more accurately be called the "evolution of ethics." It is true, says Huxley, that human moral sentiments have developed evolutionarily, but we must also acknowledge that there has been an evolution of *immoral* sentiments as well. Cosmic evolution (by which he simply means evolution) can tell us how both the good and the evil tendencies in humankind have come about, but it cannot tell us how to choose between good and evil. All evolutionary theory can do is describe, not prescribe. And indeed, that is the case with all science: it explains what is, it cannot tell us what we ought to do.

The other fallacy of the "ethics of evolution," according to Huxley, is to take the evolutionary concept of "survival of the fittest" and use it as the standard for how human society should improve. However, "fittest" does not equal "best," but simply "most adaptive to the natural environment." Huxley uses as an example what might happen if the climate in the northern hemisphere were to cool sharply. The "fittest" would be lichens, diatoms or microscopic organisms such as those which give red snow its color.

Humans undoubtedly are subject to the cosmic process, and historically the strongest tend to tread on the weakest, and we see this, Huxley says, in the most primitive of societies. However, the progress of civilization consists in resisting this evolutionary "pull" and replacing it as much as possible with a morality of compassion and fairness. Human activity should be directed towards opposing the cosmic struggle for existence, rather than "ruthless self-assertion."

While it is seriously argued by some that we must base morality on the cosmic struggle (the strong survive, the weak die)—what Huxley calls "fanatical individualism"—this is in every way wrong. Our ethical course lies in combating the cosmic process, with its "struggle for existence," in every way that we can in the human realm. We must not imitate the cosmic process, but fight it.

Huxley then traces the development of the realm of human culture or civilization—one in which, "by virtue of his (humankind's) intelligence, the dwarf (human) has bent the Titan (Cosmos) to his will"—leading us to the last two centuries which have seen the most rapid and remarkable change because of science and technology.

Huxley is no utopian, but he does believe that human beings—if they apply their intelligence and will—can improve society and the lot of humankind. In a statement that might indirectly be a critical reference to the Utilitarians, Huxley says that escape from pain and sorrow is not the proper object of life. Both good and evil are the possibilities that lie in our path, and we may fail in the end, but we must do what good we can while we can to make human society more humane, compassionate, and just.

> It may be that the gulfs will wash us
> down,
> It may be we shall touch the Happy
> Isles,
> . . . but something ere the end,
> Some work of noble note may yet be
> done.

QUESTIONS FOR STUDY AND DISCUSSION

1. In what ways has the theory of evolution through natural selection revolutionized the understanding of nature and the human place in nature?

2. How did the writings of Thomas Malthus and Charles Lyell influence Darwin?

3. What was Alfred Russel Wallace's role in the development of evolutionary theory?

4. Define and discuss the terms "evolution" and "natural selection."

5. What were the theological responses to Darwin's and Wallace's theory in the nineteenth century?

What were the issues at stake, and what were the different ways in which Christian theologians and churches dealt with the challenge of evolution?

6. What is Social Darwinism? How can all the following be examples of Social Darwinism: *laissez-faire* capitalism, European and American imperialism and colonialism, and Nazism?

7. What is T. H. Huxley's argument against Social Darwinism in "Evolution and Ethics"? How would you evaluate it?

SUGGESTIONS FOR FURTHER READING

Appleman, Philip, ed. *Darwin: A Norton Critical Edition*. 3rd ed. New York: W. W. Norton & Co., 2001.

Barlow, Nora, ed. *The Autobiography of Charles Darwin, 1809–1882*. New York: Harcourt Brace & Co., 1958.

Barrett, Paul H., ed. *The Collected Papers of Charles Darwin*. 2 vols. Chicago: University of Chicago Press, 1977.

Beer, Gillian. *Darwin's Plots: Evolutionary Narrative in Darwin, George Eliot, and Nineteenth-Century Fiction*. London: Routledge & Kegan Paul, 1983.

Bowler, Peter J. *Evolution: The History of an Idea*. Berkeley: University of California Press, 2003.

Clark, Ronald W. *The Survival of Charles Darwin*. New York: Avon Books, 1984.

Darwin, Charles. *On the Origin of Species*. Facsimile reprt. New York: Atheneum, 1967.

Desmond, Adrian. *Huxley: The Devil's Disciple*. New York: Viking Penguin, 1994.

Irvine, William. *Apes, Angels, and Victorians*. Lanham, MD: University Press of America, 1983.

Lightman, Bernard. *The Origins of Agnosticism: Victorian Unbelief and the Limits of Knowledge*. Baltimore: Johns Hopkins University Press, 1987.

Livingston, James. *Modern Christian Thought: From the Enlightenment to Vatican II*. New York: Macmillan, 1971; see especially ch. 8.

McKinney, H. Lewis. *Wallace and Natural Selection*. New Haven: Yale University Press, 1972.

Moore, J. R. *The Post-Darwinian Controversies: A Study of the Protestant Struggle to Come to Terms with Darwin in Great Britain and America, 1870–1900*. Cambridge: Cambridge University Press, 1981.

Wallace, Alfred Russel. *Darwinism*. London: Macmillan, 1889.

White, Andrew D. *A History of the Warfare of Science with Theology in Christendom*. 2 vols. New York: D. Appleton & Co., 1896.

Wilson, A. N. *God's Funeral*. New York: W. W. Norton & Co., 1999.

CHARLES DARWIN:
SELECTIONS FROM *ON THE ORIGIN OF SPECIES*

Nothing is easier than to admit in words the truth of the universal struggle for life, or more difficult—at least I have found it so—than constantly to bear this conclusion in mind. Yet, unless it be thoroughly engrained in the mind, the whole economy of nature, with every fact on distribution, rarity, abundance, extinction, and variation, will be dimly seen or quite misunderstood. We behold the face of nature bright with gladness, we often see super-abundance of food; we do not see or we forget, that the birds which are idly singing round us mostly live on insects or seeds, and are thus constantly destroying life; or we forget how largely these songsters, or their eggs, or their nestlings, are destroyed by birds and beasts of prey; we do not always bear in mind, that though food may be now super-abundant, it is not so at all seasons of each recurring year.

* * * *

A struggle for existence inevitably follows from the high rate at which all organic beings tend to increase. Every being, which during its natural lifetime produces several eggs or seeds, must suffer destruction during some period of its life, and during some season or occasional year, otherwise, on the principle of geometrical increase, its numbers would quickly become so inordinately great that no country could support the product. Hence, as more individuals are produced than can possibly survive, there must in every case be a struggle for existence, either one individual with another of the same species, or with the individuals of distinct species, or with the physical conditions of life. It is the doctrine of Malthus applied with manifold force to the whole animal and vegetable kingdoms; for in this case there can be no artificial increase of food, and no prudential restraint of marriage. Although some species may now be increasing, more or less rapidly, in numbers, all cannot do so, for the world would not hold them.

There is no exception to the rule that every organic being naturally increases at so high a rate that, if not destroyed, the earth would soon be covered by the progeny of a single pair. Even slow-breeding man has doubled in twenty-five years, and at this rate, in less than a thousand years, there would literally not be standing-room for his progeny. Linnaeus has calculated that if an annual plant produced only two seeds—and there is no plant so unproductive as this—and their seedlings next year produced two, and so on, then in twenty years there would be a million plants. The elephant is reckoned the slowest breeder of all known animals, and I have taken some pains to estimate its probable minimum rate of natural increase; it will be safest to assume that it begins breeding when thirty years old, and goes on breeding till ninety years old, bringing forth six young in the interval, and surviving till one hundred years old; if this be so, after a period of from 740 to 750 years there would be nearly nineteen million elephants alive, descended from the first pair.

But we have better evidence on this subject than mere theoretical calculations, namely, the numerous recorded cases of the astonishingly rapid increase of various animals in a state of nature, when circumstances have been favourable to them during two or three following seasons. Still more striking is the evidence from our domestic animals of many kinds which have run wild in several parts of the world; if the statements of the rate of increase of slow-breeding cattle and horses in South America, and latterly in Australia, had not been well authenticated, they would have been incredible. So it is with plants; cases could be given of introduced plants which have become common throughout whole islands in a period of less than ten years. Several of the plants, such as the cardoon and a tall thistle, which are now the commonest over the wide plains of La Plata, clothing square leagues of surface almost to the exclusion of every other plant, have been introduced from Europe; and there are plants which now range in India, as I hear from Dr. Falconer, from Cape Comorin to the Himalaya, which have been imported from America since its discovery. In such cases, and endless others could be given, no one supposes, that the fertility of the animals or plants has been suddenly and temporarily increased in any sensible degree. The obvious explanation is that the conditions of life have been highly favourable, and that there has consequently been less destruction of the old and young, and that nearly all the young have been enabled to breed. Their geometrical ratio of increase, the result of which never fails to be surprising, simply explains their extraordinarily rapid increase and wide diffusion in their new homes.

In a state of nature almost every full-grown plant annually produces seeds, and amongst animals there are very few which do not annually pair. Hence we may confidently assert, that all plants and animals are tending to increase at a geometrical ratio,—that all would rapidly stock every station in which they could anyhow exist,—and that this geometrical tendency to increase must be checked by destruction at some period of life. Our familiarity with the larger domestic animals tends, I think, to mislead us: we see no great destruction falling on them, but we do not keep in mind that thousands are annually slaughtered for food, and that in a state of nature an equal number would have somehow to be disposed of.

The only difference between organisms which annually produce eggs or seeds by the thousand, and those which produce extremely few, is, that the slow-breeders would require a few more years to people, under favourable conditions, a whole district, let it be ever so large. The condor lays a couple of eggs and the ostrich a score, and yet in the same country the condor may be the more numerous of the two; the Fulmar petrel lays but one egg, yet it is believed to be the most numerous bird in the world. One fly deposits hundreds of eggs, and another, like the hippobosca, a single one; but this difference does not determine how many individuals of the two species can be supported in a district. A large number of eggs is of some importance to those species which depend on a fluctuating amount of food, for it allows them rapidly to increase in number. But the real importance of a large number of eggs or seeds is to make up for much destruction at some period of life; and this period in the great majority of cases is an early one. If an animal can in any way protect its own eggs or young, a small number may be produced, and yet the average stock be fully kept up; but if many eggs or young are destroyed, many must be produced, or the species will become extinct. It would suffice to keep up the full number of a tree, which lived on an average for a thousand years, if a single seed were produced once in a thousand years, supposing that this seed were never destroyed, and could be ensured to germinate in a fitting place. So that, in all cases, the average number of any animal or plant depends only indirectly on the number of its eggs or seeds.

In looking at Nature, it is most necessary to keep the foregoing considerations always in mind—never to forget that every single organic being may be said to be striving to the utmost to increase in numbers; that each lives by a struggle at some period of its life; that heavy destruction inevitably falls either on the young or old, during each generation or at recurrent intervals. Lighten any check, mitigate the destruction ever so little, and the number of the species will almost instantaneously increase to any amount.

The causes which check the natural tendency of each species to increase are most obscure. Look at the most vigorous species; by as much as it swarms in numbers, by so much will it tend to increase still further. We know not exactly what the checks are even in a single instance. Nor will this surprise any one who reflects how ignorant we are on this head, even in regard to mankind, although so incomparably better known than any other animal. This subject of the checks to increase has been ably treated by several authors, and I hope in a future work to discuss it at considerable length, more especially in regard to the feral animals of South America. Here I will make only a few remarks, just to recall to the reader's mind some of the chief points. Eggs or very young animals seem generally to suffer most, but this is not invariably the case. With plants there is a vast destruction of seeds, but, from some observations which I have made it appears that the seedlings suffer most from germinating in ground already thickly stocked with other plants. Seedlings, also, are destroyed in vast numbers by various enemies; for instance, on a piece of ground three feet long and two wide, dug and cleared, and where there could be no choking from other plants, I marked all the seedlings of our native weeds as they came up, and out of 357 no less than 295 were destroyed, chiefly by slugs and insects. If turf which has long been mown, and the case would be the same with turf closely browsed by quadrupeds, be let to grow, the more vigorous plants gradually kill the less vigorous, though fully grown plants; thus out of twenty species growing on a little plot of mown turf (three feet by four) nine species perished, from the other species being allowed to grow up freely.

The amount of food for each species of course gives the extreme limit to which each can increase; but very frequently it is not the obtaining food, but the serving as prey to other animals, which determines the average number of a species. Thus, there seems to be little doubt that the stock of partridges, grouse, and hares on any large estate depends chiefly on the destruction of vermin. If not one head of game were shot during the next twenty years in England, and, at the same time, if no vermin were destroyed, there would, in all probability, be less game than at present, although hundreds of thousands of game animals are now annually shot. On the other hand, in some cases, as with the elephant, none are destroyed by beasts of prey; for even the tiger in India most rarely dares to attack a young elephant protected by its dam.

* * * *

Many cases are on record showing how complex and unexpected are the checks and relations between organic beings, which have to struggle together in the same country.

* * * *

[I give an] instance showing how plants and animals, remote in the scale of nature, are bound together by a web of complex relations. I shall hereafter have occasion to show that the exotic Lobelia fulgens is never visited in my garden by insects, and consequently, from its peculiar structure, never sets a seed. Nearly all our orchidaceous plants absolutely require the visits of insects to remove their pollen-masses and thus to fertilise them. I find from experiments that humble-bees are almost indispensable to the fertilisation of the heartsease (Violo tri-color), for other bees do not visit this flower. I have also found that the visits of bees are necessary for the fertilisation of some kinds of clover; for instance, 20 heads of Dutch clover (Trifolium repens)

yielded 2,290 seeds, but 20 other heads protected from bees produced not one. Again, 100 heads of red clover (T. pratense) produced 2,700 seeds, but the same number of protected heads produced not a single seed. Humble-bees alone visit red clover, as other bees cannot reach the nectar. It has been suggested that moths may fertilise the clovers; but I doubt whether they could do so in the case of red clover, from their weight not being sufficient to depress the wing petals. Hence we may infer as highly probable that, if the whole genus of humble-bees became extinct or very rare in England, the heartsease and red clover would become very rare, or wholly disappear. The number of humble-bees in any district depends in a great measure upon the number of field-mice, which destroy their combs and nests; and Col. Newman, who has long attended to the habits of humble-bees, believes that "more than two-thirds of them are thus destroyed all over England." Now the number of mice is largely dependent, as every one knows, on the number of cats; and Col. Newman says, "Near villages and small towns I have found the nests of humble-bees more numerous than elsewhere, which I attribute to the number of cats that destroy the mice." Hence it is quite credible that the presence of a feline animal in large numbers in a district might determine, through the intervention first of mice and then of bees, the frequency of certain flowers in that district!

* * * *

If under changing conditions of life organic beings present individual differences in almost every part of their structure, and this cannot be disputed; if there be, owing to their geometrical rate of increase, a severe struggle for life at some age, season, or year, and this certainly cannot be disputed; then, considering the infinite complexity of the relations of all organic beings to each other and to their conditions of life, causing an infinite diversity in structure, constitution, and habits, to be advantageous to them, it would be a most extraordinary fact if no variations had ever occurred useful to each being's own welfare, in the same manner as so many variations have occurred useful to man. But if variations useful to any organic being ever do occur, assuredly individuals thus characterised will have the best chance of being preserved in the struggle for life; and from the strong principle of inheritance, these will tend to produce offspring similarly characterised. This principle of preservation, or the survival of the fittest, I have called Natural Selection. It leads to the improvement of each creature in relation to its organic and inorganic conditions of life; and consequently, in most cases, to what must be regarded as an advance in organisation. Nevertheless, low and simple forms will long endure if well fitted for their simple conditions of life.

Natural selection, on the principle of qualities being inherited at corresponding ages, can modify the egg, seed, or young, as easily as the adult. Amongst many animals, sexual selection will have given its aid to ordinary selection, by assuring the most vigorous and best adapted males the greatest number of offspring. Sexual selection will also give characters useful to the males alone, in their struggles or rivalry with other males; and these characters will be transmitted to one sex or to both sexes, according to the form of inheritance which prevails.

Whether natural selection has really thus acted in adapting the various forms of life to their several conditions and stations, must be judged by the general tenor and balance of evidence given in the following chapters. But we have already seen how it entails extinction; and how largely extinction has acted in the world's history, geology plainly declares. Natural selection, also, leads to divergence of character; for the more organic beings diverge in structure, habits, and constitution, by so much the more can a large number be supported on the area,—of which we see proof by looking to the inhabitants of any small spot, and to the productions naturalised in foreign lands. Therefore, during the modification of the descendants of any one species, and during the incessant struggle of all species to increase in numbers, the more diversified the descendants become, the better will be their chance of success in the battle for life. Thus the small differences distinguishing varieties of the same species, steadily tend to increase, till they equal the greater differences between species of the same genus, or even of distinct genera.

We have seen that it is the common, the widely-diffused and widely ranging species, belonging to the larger genera within its class, which vary most; and these tend to transmit to their modified offspring that superiority which now makes them dominant in their own countries. Natural selection, as has just been remarked, leads to divergence of character and to much extinction of the less improved and intermediate forms of life. On these principles, the nature of the affinities, and the generally well-defined distinctions between the innumerable organic beings in each class throughout the world, may be explained. It is a truly wonderful fact—the wonder of which we are apt to overlook from familiarity—that all animals and all plants throughout all time and space should be related to each other in groups, subordinate to groups, in the manner which we everywhere behold—namely, varieties of the same species most closely related, species of the same genus less closely and unequally related, forming sections and sub-genera, species of distinct genera much less closely related, and genera related in different degrees, forming sub-families, families, orders, sub-classes and classes. The several subordinate groups in any class cannot be ranked in a single file, but seem clustered round points, and these round other points, and so on in almost endless cycles. If species had been independently created, no explanation would have been possible of this kind of classification; but it is explained through inheritance and the complex action of natural selection, entailing extinction and divergence of character. . . .

The affinities of all beings of the same class have sometimes been represented by a great tree. I believe this simile largely speaks the truth. The green and budding twigs may represent existing species; and those produced during former years may represent the long succession of extinct species. At each period of growth all the growing twigs have tried to branch out on all sides, and to overtop and kill the surrounding twigs and branches, in the same manner as species and groups of species have at all times overmastered other species in the great battle for life. The limbs divided into great branches, and these into lesser and lesser branches, were themselves once, when the tree was young, budding twigs; and this connection of the former and present buds by ramifying branches may well represent the classification of all extinct and living species in groups subordinate to groups. Of the many twigs which flourished when the tree was a mere bush, only two or three, now grown into great branches, yet survive and bear the other brandies; so with the species which lived during long-past geological periods, very few have left living and modified descendants. From the first growth of the tree, many a limb has decayed and dropped off; and these fallen branches of various sizes may represent those whole orders, families, and genera which have now no living representatives, and which are known to us only in a fossil state. As we here and there see a thin straggling branch springing from a fork low down in a tree, and which by some chance has been favoured and is still alive on its summit, so we occasionally see an animal like the Ornithorhynchus or Lepidosiren, which in some small degree connects by its affinities two large branches of life, and which has apparently been saved from fatal competition by having inhabited a protected station. As buds give rise by growth to fresh buds, and these, if vigorous, branch out and overtop on all sides many a feebler branch, so by generation I believe it has been with the Great Tree of Life, which fills with its dead and broken branches the crust of the earth, and covers the surface with its ever-branching and beautiful ramifications.

* * * *

I have now recapitulated the facts and considerations which have thoroughly convinced me that species have been modifed, during a long course of descent. This has been effected chiefly through the natural selection of numerous successive, slight, favourable variations; aided in an important manner by the inherited effects of the use and disuse of parts; and in an unimportant manner, that is in relation to adaptive structures, whether past or present, by the direct action of external conditions, and by variations which seem to us in our ignorance to rise spontaneously. It appears that I formerly underrated the frequency and value of these latter forms of variation, as leading to permanent modifications of structure independently of natural selection. But as my conclusions have lately been much misrepresented, and it has been stated that I attribute the modification of species exclusively to natural selection, I may be permitted to remark that in the first edition of this work, and subsequently, I placed in a most conspicuous position—namely, at the close of the Introduction—the following words: "I am convinced that natural selection has been the main

but not the exclusive means of modification." This has been of no avail. Great is the power of steady misrepresentation; but the history of science shows that fortunately this power does not long endure.

It can hardly be supposed that a false theory would explain, in so satisfactory a manner as does the theory of natural selection, the several large classes of facts above specified. It has recently been objected that this is an unsafe method of arguing; but it is a method used in judging of the common events of life, and has often been used by the greatest natural philosophers. The undulatory theory of light has thus been arrived at, and the belief in the revolution of the earth on its own axis was until lately supported by hardly any direct evidence. It is no valid objection that science as yet throws no light on the far higher problem of the essence or origin of life. Who can explain what is the essence of the attraction of gravity? No one now objects to following out the results consequent on this unknown element of attraction; notwithstanding that Leibnitz formerly accused Newton of introducing "occult qualities and miracles into philosophy."

I see no good reason why the views given in this volume should shock the religious feelings of any one. It is satisfactory, as showing how transient such impressions are, to remember that the greatest discovery ever made by man, namely, the law of the attraction of gravity, was also attacked by Leibnitz, "as subversive of natural, and inferentially of revealed, religion." A celebrated author and divine has written to me that "he has gradually learnt to see that it is just as noble a conception of the Deity to believe that He created a few original forms capable of self-development into other and needful forms, as to believe that He required a fresh act of creation to supply the voids caused by the action of His Laws."

Why, it may be asked, until recently did nearly all the most eminent living naturalists and geologists disbelieve in the mutability of species? It cannot be asserted that organic beings in a state of nature are subject to no variation; it cannot be proved that the amount of variation in the course of long ages is a limited quantity; no clear distinction has been, or can be, drawn between species and well-marked varieties. It cannot be maintained that species when intercrossed are invariably sterile, and varieties invariably fertile; or that sterility is a special endowment and sign of creation. The belief that species were immutable productions was almost unavoidable as long as the history of the world was thought to be of short duration; and now that we have acquired some idea of the lapse of time, we are too apt to assume, without proof that the geological record is so perfect that it would have afforded us plain evidence of the mutation of the species, if they had undergone mutation.

But the chief cause of our natural unwillingness to admit that one species has given birth to other and distinct species, is that we are always slow in admitting great changes of which we do not see the steps. The difficulty is the same as that felt by many geologists, when Lyell first insisted that long lines of inland cliffs had been formed, and great valleys excavated, by the agencies which we see still at work. The mind cannot possibly grasp the full meaning of the term of even a million years; it cannot add up and perceive the full effects of many slight variations, accumulated during an almost infinite number of generations.

Although I am fully convinced of the truth of the views given in this volume under the form of an abstract, I by no means expect to convince experienced naturalists whose minds are stocked with a multitude of facts all viewed, during a long course of years, from a point of view directly opposite to mine. It is so easy to hide our ignorance under such expressions as the "plan of creation," "unity of design," &c., and to think that we give an explanation when we only restate a fact. Any one whose disposition leads him to attach more weight to unexplained difficulties than to the explanation of a certain number of facts will certainly reject the theory. A few naturalists, endowed with much flexibility of mind, and who have already begun to doubt the immutability of species, may be influenced by this volume; but I look with confidence to the future,—to young and rising naturalists, who will be able to view both sides of the question with impartiality. Whoever is led to believe that species are mutable will do good service by conscientiously expressing his conviction; for thus only can the load of prejudice by which this subject is overwhelmed be removed.

Several eminent naturalists have of late published their belief that a multitude of reputed species in each genus are not real species; but that other species are real, that is, have been independently created. This seems to me a strange conclusion to arrive at. They admit that a multitude of forms, which till lately they themselves thought were special creations, and which are still thus looked at by the majority of naturalists, and which consequently have all the external characteristic features of the species,—they admit that these have been produced by variation, but they refuse to extend the same view to other and slightly different forms. Nevertheless they do not pretend that they can define, or even conjecture, which are the created forms of life, and which are produced by secondary laws. They admit variation as a *vera causa* in one case, they arbitrarily reject it in another, without assigning any distinction in the two cases. The day will come when this will be given as a curious illustration of the blindness of preconceived opinion. These authors seem no more startled at a miraculous act of creation than at an ordinary birth. But do they really believe that at innumerable periods in the earth's history certain elemental atoms have been commanded suddenly to flash into living tissues? Do they believe that at each supposed act of creation one individual or many were produced? Were all the infinitely numerous kinds of animals and plants created as eggs or seed, or as full grown? And in the case of mammals, were they created bearing the false marks of nourishment from the mother's womb? Undoubtedly some of these same questions cannot be answered by those who believe in the appearance or creation of only a few forms of life, or of some one form alone. It has been maintained by several authors that it is as easy to believe in the creation of a million beings as of one; but Maupertuis' philosophical axiom "Of least action" leads the mind more willingly to admit the smaller number; and certainly we ought not to believe that innumerable beings within each great class have been created with plain, but deceptive, marks of descent from a single parent.

As a record of a former state of things, I have retained in the foregoing paragraphs, and elsewhere, several sentences which imply that naturalists believe in the separate creation of such species; and I have been much censured for having thus expressed myself. But undoubtedly this was the general belief when the first edition of the present work appeared. I formerly spoke to very many naturalists on the subject of evolution, and never once met with any sympathetic agreement. It is probable that some did then believe in evolution, but they were either silent, or expressed themselves so ambiguously that it was not easy to understand their meaning. Now things are wholly changed, and almost every naturalist admits the great principle of evolution. There are, however, some who still think that species have suddenly given birth, through quite unexplained means, to new and totally different forms: but, as I have attempted to show, weighty evidence can be opposed to the admission of great and abrupt modifications. Under a scientific point of view, and as leading to further investigation, but little advantage is gained by believing that new forms are suddenly developed in an inexplicable manner from old and widely different forms, over the old belief in the creation of species from the dust of the earth.

It may be asked how far I extend the doctrine of the modification of the species. The question is difficult to answer, because the more distinct the forms are which we consider, by so much the arguments in favour of community of descent become fewer in number and less in force. But some arguments of the greatest weight extend very far. All the members of whole classes are connected together by a chain of affinities, and all can be classed on the same principle, in groups, subordinate to groups. Fossil remains sometimes tend to fill up very wide intervals between existing orders.

Organs in a rudimentary condition plainly show that an early progenitor had the organ in a fully developed condition; and this in some cases implies an enormous amount of modification in the descendants. Throughout whole classes various structures are formed on the same pattern, and at a very early age the embryos closely resemble each other. Therefore I cannot doubt that the theory of descent with modification embraces all the members of the same great class or kingdom. I believe that animals are descended from at most only four or five progenitors, and plants from an equal or lesser number.

Analogy would lead me one step farther, namely, to the belief that all animals and plants are descended from one prototype. But analogy may be a deceitful guide. Nevertheless all living things have much in common, in their chemical composition, their cellular structure, their laws of growth, and their liability to injurious influences. We see this even in so trifling a fact as that the same poison often similarly affects plants and animals; or that the poison secreted by the gall-fly produces monstrous growths on the wild rose or oak tree. With all organic beings, excepting perhaps some of the very lowest, sexual reproduction seems to be essentially similar. With all, as far as is at present known, the germinal vesicle is the same; so that all organisms start from a common origin. If we look even to the two main divisions—namely, to the animal and vegetable kingdoms—certain low forms are so intermediate in character that naturalists have disputed to which kingdom they should be referred. As Professor Asa Gray has remarked, "the spores and other reproductive bodies of many of the lower algae may claim to have first a characteristically animal, and then an unequivocally vegetable existence." Therefore, on the principle of natural selection with divergence of character, it does not seem incredible that, from such low and intermediate form, both animals and plants may have been developed; and, if we admit this, we must likewise admit that all the organic beings which have ever lived on this earth may be descended from one primordial form. But this inference is chiefly grounded on analogy, and it is immaterial whether or not it be accepted. No doubt it is possible, as Mr. G. H. Lewes has urged, that at the first commencement of life many different forms were evolved; but if so, we may conclude that only a very few have left modified descendants. For, as I have recently remarked in regard to the members of each great kingdom, such as the Vertebrata, Articulata, &c., we have distinct evidence in their embryological, homologous, and rudimentary structures, that within each kingdom all the members are descended from a single progenitor.

When the views advanced by me in this volume, and by Mr. Wallace, or when analogous views on the origin of species are generally admitted, we can dimly foresee that there will be a considerable revolution in natural history. Systematists will be able to pursue their labours as at present; but they will not be incessantly haunted by the shadowy doubt whether this or that form be a true species. This, I feel sure and I speak after experience, will be no slight relief. The endless disputes whether or not some fifty species of British brambles are good species will cease. Systematists will have only to decide (not that this will be easy) whether any form be sufficiently constant and distinct from other forms, to be capable of definition; and if definable, whether the differences be sufficiently important to deserve a specific name. This latter point will become a far more essential consideration than it is at present; for differences, however slight, between any two forms, if not blended by intermediate graduations, are looked at by most naturalists as sufficient to raise both forms to the rank of species.

Hereafter we shall be compelled to acknowledge that the only distinction between species and well-marked varieties is, that the latter are known, or believed, to be connected at the present day by intermediate graduations whereas species were formerly thus connected. Hence, without rejecting the consideration of the present existence of intermediate graduations between any two forms, we shall be led to weigh more carefully and to value higher the actual amount of difference between them. It is quite possible that forms now generally acknowledged to be merely varieties may hereafter be thought worthy of specific names; and in this case scientific and common language will come into accordance. In short, we shall have to treat species in the same manner as those naturalists treat genera, who admit that genera are merely artificial combinations made for convenience. This may not be a cheering prospect; but we shall at least be freed from the vain search for the undiscovered and undiscoverable essence of the term species.

The other and more general departments of natural history will rise greatly in interest. The terms used by naturalists, of affinity, relationship, community of type, paternity, morphology, adaptive characters, rudimentary and aborted organs, &c., will cease to be metaphorical, and will have a plain signification. When we no longer look at an organic being as a savage looks at a ship, as something wholly beyond his comprehension; when we regard every production of nature as one which has had a long history; when we contemplate every complex structure and instinct as the summing up of many contrivances, each useful to the possessor, in the same way as any great mechanical invention is the summing up of the labour, the experience, the reason, and even the blunders of numerous workmen; when we thus view each organic being, how

far more interesting—I speak from experience—does the study of natural history become!

A grand and almost untrodden field of inquiry will be opened, on the causes and laws of variation, on correlation, on the effects of use and disuse, on the direct action of external conditions, and so forth. The study of domestic productions will rise immensely in value. A new variety raised by man will be a more important and interesting subject for study than one more species added to the infinitude of already recorded species. Our classifications will come to be, as far as they can be so made, genealogies; and will then truly give what may be called the plan of creation. The rules for classifying will no doubt become simpler when we have a definite object in view. We possess no pedigrees or armorial bearings; and we have to discover and trace the many diverging lines of descent in our natural genealogies, by characters of any kind which have long been inherited. Rudimentary organs will speak infallibly with respect to the nature of long-lost structures. Species and groups of species which are called aberrant, and which may fancifully be called living fossils, will aid us in forming a picture of the ancient forms of life. Embryology will often reveal to us the structure, in some degree obscured, of the prototypes of each great class.

When we can feel assured that all the individuals of the same species, and all the closely allied species of most genera, have within a not very remote period descended from one parent, and have migrated from some one birthplace; and we better know the many means of migration, then, by the light which geology now throws, and will continue to throw, on former changes of climate and of the level of the land, we shall surely be enabled to trace in an admirable manner the former migrations of the inhabitants of the whole world. Even at present, by comparing the differences between the inhabitants of the sea on the opposite sides of a continent, and the nature of the various inhabitants on that continent in relation to their apparent means of immigration, some light can be thrown on ancient geography.

The noble science of Geology loses glory from the extreme imperfection of the record. The crust of the earth with its imbedded remains must not be looked at as a well-filled museum, but as a poor collection made at hazard and at rare intervals. The accumulation of each great fossiliferous formation will be recognised as having depended on an unusual concurrence of favourable circumstances, and the blank intervals between the successive stages as having been of vast duration. But we shall be able to gauge with some security the duration of these intervals by a comparison of the preceding and succeeding organic forms. We must be cautious in attempting to correlate as strictly contemporaneous two formations, which do not include many identical species, by the general succession of the forms of life. As species are produced and exterminated by slowly acting and still existing causes, and not by miraculous acts of creation; and as the most important of all causes of organic change is one which is almost independent of altered and perhaps suddenly altered physical conditions, namely, the mutual relation of organism to organism,—the improvement of one organism entailing the improvement or the extermination of others; it follows, that the amount of organic change in the fossils of consecutive formations probably serves as a fair measure of the relative, though not actual lapse of time. A number of species, however, keeping in a body might remain for a long period unchanged, whilst within the same period several of these species by migrating into new countries and coming into competition with foreign associates, might become modified; so that we must not overrate the accuracy of organic change as a measure of time.

In the future I see open fields for far more important researches. Psychology will be securely based on the foundation already well laid by Mr. Herbert Spencer, that of the necessary acquirements of each mental power and capacity by gradation. Much light will be thrown on the origin of man and his history.

Authors of the highest eminence seem to be fully satisfied with the view that each species has been independently created. To my mind it accords better with what we know of the laws impressed on matter by the Creator, that the production and extinction of the past and present inhabitants of the world should have been due to secondary causes, like those determining the birth and death of the individual. When I view all beings not as special creations, but as the lineal descendants of some few beings which lived long before the first bed of the Cambrian system was deposited, they seem to me to become ennobled. Judging from the past, we may safely infer that not one living species will transmit

its unaltered likeness to a distant futurity. And of the species now living very few will transmit progeny of any kind to a far distant futurity; for the manner in which all organic beings are grouped, shows that the greater number of species in each genus, and all the species in many genera, have left no descendants, but have become utterly extinct. We can so far take a prophetic glance into futurity as to foretell that it will be the common and widely-spread species, belonging to the larger and dominant groups within each class, which will ultimately prevail and procreate new and dominant species. As all the living forms of life are the lineal descendants of those which lived long before the Cambrian epoch, we may feel certain that the ordinary succession by generation has never once been broken, and that no cataclysm has desolated the whole world. Hence we may look with some confidence to a secure future of great length. And as natural selection works solely by and for the good of each being, all corporeal and mental endowments will tend to progress towards perfection.

It is interesting to contemplate a tangled bank, clothed with many plants of many kinds, with birds singing on the bushes, with various insects flitting about, and with worms crawling through the damp earth, and to reflect that these elaborately constructed forms, so different from each other, and dependent upon each other in so complex a manner, have all been produced by laws acting around us. These laws, taken in the largest sense, being Growth with Reproduction; Inheritance which is almost implied by reproduction; Variability from the indirect and direct action of the conditions of life, and from use and disuse: a Ratio of Increase so high as to lead to a Struggle for Life, and as a consequence to Natural Selection, entailing Divergence of Character and the Extinction of less-improved forms. Thus, from the war of nature, from famine and death, the most exalted object which we are capable of conceiving, namely, the production of the higher animals, directly follows. There is grandeur in this view of life, with its several powers, having been originally breathed by the Creator into a few forms or into one; and that, whilst this planet has gone cycling on according to the fixed law of gravity, from so simple a beginning endless forms most beautiful and most wonderful have been, and are being evolved.

CHARLES DARWIN:
SELECTIONS FROM *THE DESCENT OF MAN*

GENERAL SUMMARY
AND CONCLUSION

The main conclusion arrived at in this work, and now held by many naturalists who are well competent to form a sound judgment, is that man is descended from some less highly-organized form. The grounds upon which this conclusion rests will never be shaken, for the close similarity between man and the lower animals in embryonic development, as well as in innumerable points of structure and constitution, both of high and of the most trifling importance—the rudiments which he retains, and the abnormal reversions to which he is occasionally liable—are facts which cannot be disputed. They have long been known, but until recently they told us nothing with respect to the origin of man. Now, when viewed by the light of our knowledge of the whole organic world, their meaning is unmistakable. The great principle of evolution stands up clear and firm, when these groups of facts are considered in connection with others, such as the mutual affinities of the members of the same group, their geographical distribution in past and present times, and their geological succession. It is incredible that all these facts should speak falsely. He who is not content to look, like a savage, at the phenomena of Nature as disconnected, cannot any longer believe that man is the work of a separate act of creation. He will be forced to admit that the close resemblance of the embryo of man to that, for instance, of a dog—the construction of his skull, limbs, and whole frame, independently of the uses to which the parts may be put, on the same plan with that of other mammals—the occasional reappearance of various structures, for instance, of several distinct muscles, which man does not normally possess, but which are common to the Quadrumana—and a crowd of analogous facts—all point in the plainest manner to the conclusion that man is the co-descendant with other mammals of a common progenitor.

[*This*] conclusion . . . that man is descended from some lowly-organised form, will, I regret to think, be highly distasteful to many persons. But there can hardly be a doubt that we are descended from barbarians. The astonishment which I felt on first seeing a party of Fuegians on a wild and broken shore will never be forgotten by me, for the reflection at once rushed into my mind—such were our ancestors. These men were absolutely naked and bedaubed with paint, their long hair was tangled, their mouths frothed with excitement, and their expression was wild, startled, and distrustful. They possessed hardly any arts, and, like wild animals, lived on what they could catch; they had no government, and were merciless to every one not of their own small tribe. He who has seen a savage in his native land will not feel much shame, if forced to acknowledge that the blood of some more humble creature flows in his veins. For my own part, I would as soon be descended from that heroic little monkey, who braved his dreaded enemy in order to save the life of his keeper; or from that old baboon, who, descending from the mountains, carried away in triumph his young comrade from a crowd of astonished dogs—as from a savage who delights to torture his enemies, offers up bloody sacrifices, practices infanticide without remorse, treats his wives like slaves, knows no decency, and is haunted by the grossest superstitions.

Man may be excused for feeling some pride at having risen, though not through his own exertions, to the very summit of the organic scale; and the fact of his having thus risen, instead of having been aboriginally placed there, may give him hopes for a still higher destiny in the distant future. But we are not here concerned with hopes or fears, only with the truth as far as our reason allows us to discover it. I have given the evidence to the best of my ability; and we must acknowledge, as it seems to me, that man with all his noble qualities, with sympathy which feels for the most debased, with benevolence which extends not only to other men but to the humblest living creature, with his godlike intellect which has penetrated into the movements and constitution of the solar system—with all these exalted powers—Man still bears in his bodily frame the indelible stamp of his lowly origin.

THOMAS HENRY HUXLEY:
"EVOLUTION AND ETHICS" (1893)

Modern thought is making a fresh start from the base whence Indian and Greek philosophy set out; and, the human mind being very much what it was six-and-twenty centuries ago, there is no ground for wonder if it presents indications of a tendency to move along the old lines to the same results.

We are more than sufficiently familiar with modern pessimism, at least as a speculation; for I cannot call to mind that any of its present votaries have sealed their faith by assuming the rags and the bowl of the mendicant Bhikku, or the wallet of the Cynic. The obstacles placed in the way of sturdy vagrancy by an unphilosophical police have, perhaps, proved too formidable for philosophical consistency. We also know modern speculative optimism, with its perfectibility of the species, reign of peace, and lion and lamb transformation scenes; but one does not hear so much of it as one did forty years ago; indeed, I imagine it is to be met with more commonly at the tables of the healthy and wealthy, than in the congregations of the wise. The majority of us, I apprehend, profess neither pessimism or optimism. We hold that the world is neither so good, nor so bad, as it conceivably might be; and, as most of us have reason, now and again, to discover that it can be. Those who have failed to experience the joys that make life worth living are, probably, in as small a minority as those who have never known the griefs that rob existence of its savor and turn its richest fruits into mere dust and ashes.

Further, I think I do not err in assuming that, however diverse their views on philosophical and religious matters, most men are agreed that the proportion of good and evil in life may be very sensibly affected by human action. I never heard anybody doubt that the evil may be thus increased, or diminished; and it would seem to follow that good must be similarly susceptible of addition or subtraction. Finally, to my knowledge, nobody professes to doubt that, so far forth as we possess a power of bettering things, it is our paramount duty to use it and to train all our intellect and energy to this supreme service of our kind.

Hence the pressing interest of the question, to what extent modern progress in natural knowledge, and, more especially, the general outcome of that progress in the doctrine of evolution, is competent to help us in a great work of helping one another?

The propounders of what are called the "ethics of evolution," when the "evolution of ethics" would usually better express the object of their speculations, adduce a number of more or less interesting facts and more or less sound arguments in favor of the origin of the moral sentiments, in the same way as other natural phenomena, by a process of evolution. I have little doubt, for my own part, that they are on the right track; but as the immoral sentiments have no less been evolved, there is, so far, as much natural sanction for the one as the other. The thief and the murderer follow nature just as much as the philanthropist. Cosmic evolution may teach us how the good and the evil tendencies of man may have come about; but, in itself, it is incompetent to furnish any better reason why what we call good is preferable to what we call evil than we had before. Some day, I doubt not, we shall arrive at an understanding of the evolution of the aesthetic faculty; but all the understanding in the world will neither increase nor diminish the force of the intuition that this is beautiful and that is ugly.

There is another fallacy which appears to me to pervade the so-called "ethics of evolution." It is the notion that because, on the whole, animals and plants have advanced in perfection of organization by means of the struggle for existence and the consequent "survival of the fittest"; therefore men in society, men as ethical beings, must look to the same process to help them towards perfection. I suspect that this fallacy has arisen out of the unfortunate ambiguity of the phrase "survival of the fittest." "Fittest" has a connotation of "best"; and about "best" there hangs a moral flavor. In cosmic nature, however, what is "fittest" depends upon the conditions. Long since, I ventured to point out that if our hemisphere were to cool again, the survival of the fittest might bring about, in the vegetable kingdom, a population of more and more stunted and humbler and humbler organisms, until the "fittest" that survived might be nothing but lichens, diatoms, and such microscopic organisms as those which give red snow its color; while, if it became hotter, the pleasant valleys of the Thames and Isis might be uninhabitable by any animated beings save those that flourish in a tropical jungle. They, as the fittest, the best adapted to the changed conditions, would survive.

Men in society are undoubtedly subject to the cosmic process. As among other animals, multiplication goes on without cessation, and involves severe competition for the means of support. The struggle for existence tends to eliminate those less fitted to adapt themselves to the circumstances of their existence. The strongest, the most self-assertive, tend to tread down the weaker. But the influence of the cosmic process on the evolution of society is the greater the more rudimentary its civilization. Social progress means a checking of the cosmic process at every step and the substitution for it of another, which may be called the ethical process; the end of which is not the survival of those who may happen to be the fittest, in respect of the whole of the conditions which obtain, but of those who are ethically the best.

As I have already urged, the practice of that which is ethically best—what we call goodness or virtue—involves a course of conduct which, in all respects, is opposed to that which leads to success in the cosmic struggle for existence. In place of ruthless self-assertion it demands self-restraint; in place of thrusting aside, or treading down, all competitors, it requires that the individual shall not merely respect, but shall help his fellows; its influence is directed, not so much to the survival of the fittest, as to the fitting of as many as possible to survive. It repudiates the gladiatorial theory of existence. It demands that each man who enters into the enjoyment of the advantages of a polity shall be mindful of his debt to those who have laboriously constructed it; and shall take heed that no act of his weakens the fabric in which he has been permitted to live. Laws and moral precepts are directed to the end of curbing the cosmic process and reminding the individual of his duty to the community, to the protection and influence of which he owes, if not existence itself, at least the life of something better than a brutal savage.

It is from neglect of these plain considerations that the fanatical individualism of our time attempts to apply the analogy of cosmic nature to society. Once more we have a misapplication of the stoical injunction to follow nature; the duties of the individual to the state are forgotten, and his tendencies to self-assertion are dignified by the name of rights. It is seriously debated whether the members of a community are justified in using their combined strength to constrain one of their number to contribute his share to the maintenance of it; or even to prevent him from doing his best to destroy it. The struggle for existence which has done such admirable work in cosmic nature, must, it appears, be equally beneficent in the ethical sphere. Yet if that which I have insisted upon is true; if the cosmic process has no sort of relation to moral ends; if the imitation of it by man is inconsistent with the first principles of ethics; what becomes of this surprising theory?

Let us understand, once for all, that the ethical progress of society depends, not on imitating the cosmic process, still less in running away from it, but in combating it. It may seem an audacious proposal thus to put the microcosm against the macrocosm and to set man to subdue nature to his higher ends; but I venture to think that the great intellectual difference between the ancient times with which we have been occupied and our day, lies in the solid foundation we have acquired for the hope that such an enterprise may meet with a certain measure of success.

The history of civilization details the steps by which men have succeeded in building up an artificial world within the cosmos. Fragile reed as he may be, man, as Pascal says, is a thinking reed: there lies within him a fund of energy operating intelligently and so far akin to that which pervades the universe, that it is competent to influence and modify the cosmic process. In virtue of his intelligence, the dwarf bends the Titan to his will. In every family, in every polity that has been established, the cosmic process in man has been restrained and otherwise modified by law and custom; in surrounding nature, it has been similarly influenced by the art of the shepherd, the agriculturist, the artisan. As civilization has advanced, so has the extent of this interference increased; until the organized and highly developed sciences and arts of the present day have endowed man with a command over the course of non-human nature greater than that once attributed to the magicians. The most impressive, I might say startling, of these changes have been brought about in the course of the last two centuries; while a right comprehension of the process of life and of the means of influencing its manifestations is only just dawning upon us. We do not yet see our way beyond generalities; and we are befogged by the obtrusion of false analogies and crude anticipations. But Astronomy, Physics, Chemistry, have all had to pass through similar phases, before they reached the stage at which their influence became an important factor in human affairs. Physiology, Psychology, Ethics, Political Science, must submit to the same ordeal. Yet it seems to me irrational to doubt that, at no distant period, they will work as great a revolution in the sphere of practice.

The theory of evolution encourages no millennial anticipations. If, for millions of years, our globe has taken the upward road, yet, some time, the summit will be reached and the downward route will be commenced. The most daring imagination will hardly venture upon the suggestion that the power and the intelligence of man can ever arrest the procession of the great year.

Moreover, the cosmic nature born with us and, to a large extent, necessary for our maintenance, is the outcome of millions of years of severe training, and it would be folly to imagine that a few centuries will suffice to subdue its masterfulness to purely ethical ends. Ethical nature may count upon having to reckon with a tenacious and powerful enemy as long as the world lasts. But, on the other hand, I see no limit to the extent to which intelligence and will, guided by sound principles of investigation, and organized in common effort, may modify the conditions of existence, for a period longer than that now covered by history. And much may be done to change the nature of man himself. The intelligence which has converted the brother of the wolf into the faithful guardian of the flock ought to be able to do something towards curbing the instincts of savagery in civilized men.

But if we may permit ourselves a larger hope of abatement of the essential evil of the world than was possible to those who, in the infancy of exact knowledge, faced the problem of existence more than a score of centuries ago, I deem it an essential condition of the realization of that hope that we should cast aside the notion that the escape from pain and sorrow is the proper object of life.

We have long since emerged from the heroic childhood of our race, when good and evil could be met with the same "frolic welcome"; the attempts to escape from evil, whether Indian or Greek, have ended in flight from the battlefield; it remains to us to throw aside the youthful overconfidence and the no less youthful discouragement of nonage. We are grown men, and must play the man

strong in will
To strive, to seek, to find, and not to yield,

cherishing the good that falls in our way, and bearing the evil, in and around us, with stout hearts set on diminishing it. So far, we all may strive in one faith toward one hope:

It may be that the gulfs will wash us down,
It may be we shall touch the Happy Isles,

. . . . but something ere the end,
Some work of noble note may yet be done.

CHAPTER EIGHT

THE MARXIST HERITAGE: KARL MARX AND FRIEDRICH ENGELS

"A spectre is haunting Europe—the spectre of Communism." Thus began the *Communist Manifesto*, written by Karl Marx and Friedrich Engels in Brussels, Belgium, and first published in February, 1848. That spectre grew to haunt not only Europe but also other parts of the world, including the United States, for almost one hundred and fifty years.

The Bolshevik Revolution of 1917 resulted in the creation of the Union of Soviet Socialist Republics, built on the tenets of the communist writings of Marx and Engels, that was to encompass the enormous country of Russia as well as numerous contiguous nations and territories. The fear of communism and its continuing spread was an often-stated motivating factor in American and Western European international actions, and indeed dominated U.S. foreign policy for nearly five decades. Only in 1989 did dramatic repudiations of this power take place in Eastern Europe, followed by the collapse of the communist regime in the USSR in 1991 and the subsequent break-up of the Soviet Union. This period of history is clearly part of Marx's legacy. But it is only one part.

In our part of the globe, Marxism (or communism) has long been a "dirty word." It is an ideology against which Americans for generations believed they had to protect themselves at all costs. Indeed, this fear reached a point of hysteria in the 1950s when congressional hearings into allegedly subversive communist activities were held—the hearings were known by the name of the senator who led them, Joseph McCarthy—that bore a disconcerting similarity to medieval witch trials. Whether the perceived threat was ever real, or exaggerated, or still exists, and whether Marx or Marxism are to blame for it is still debated.

In addition to politics, Karl Marx has had a profound influence on other aspects of nineteenth and twentieth century life and thought. It was largely through his efforts that the labor union movement grew and helped improve the lot of workers in the industrial world. His trenchant criticism of the evils of industrialism as found in mid-nineteenth century England played an important role in bringing about much-needed change. His materialist interpretation of history and his emphasis on the importance of economic forces in social development have influenced the methods of analysis and research of historians, social scientists, psychologists, philosophers, and literary critics. Over the past three decades both American and European feminist theoreticians have used various aspects of Marxism as a foundation for feminist theory. His analysis of ideology continues to serve as a model for uncovering vested interests and penetrating below the surface of political rhetoric.

One need not be a Marxist to acknowledge Marx's positive contributions to Western civilization. Even the most adamant anti-Marxist cannot help but be influenced by his thought, for important aspects of it have been absorbed into Western culture. Jean-Paul Sartre (1905–1980), the famous French existentialist philosopher and writer of the post-World War II period, went so far as to say that Marxism remains "the philosophy of our time. We cannot go beyond it because we have not gone beyond the circumstances which engendered it." Although a clear exaggeration in one sense, in another it underlines the great influence—positive and negative—of Marx's thought both on those who follow it and on those who react against it.

MARX AND ENGELS: BIOGRAPHICAL SKETCHES

Karl Marx. Marx is a paradoxical figure. Although he was trained and received his doctorate in philosophy, his major work, *Capital*, is a classic of economic theory. Born in 1818 in Trier, Prussia, and educated at the Universities of Bonn and Berlin, he spent most of his adult life in London, England, researching and writing in the Library of the British Museum. Born to and raised in a bourgeois family, he championed the cause of the proletariat—the class of ordinary workers who, without any ownership of the means of production, had to sell their labor power in order to live. A founder and leader of the Workingman's Association, he was never a worker himself. He wrote about the advanced industrial countries, such as Germany and France, which he saw as ripe for revolution—a revolution that, if it has taken place at all, took place in Russia in 1917 and in China in 1949, when each was primarily an agricultural country.

Marx was the son of Jewish parents both descended from a long line of rabbis. However, Heinrich Marx was prevented from practicing law because he was a Jew so he converted to the Lutheran faith (state church of Prussia) in order to facilitate social and professional acceptance in a society that discriminated against Jews. This was not uncommon among fully assimilated Jews. Karl was baptized and attended a Lutheran elementary school and later the classical *gymnasium* (college preparatory high school) in Trier.

Marx attended the Universities of Bonn and Berlin. He wanted to be a poet and playwright, so he studied philosophy and literature. Berlin was at that time, the 1830s, the center of intellectual excitement in Germany, as well as the center of the "Young" or "Radical" Hegelians. Georg W. F. Hegel, who had died just a few years before, had considerable influence as a philosopher.[1] This group of young students, including Marx, interpreted and critiqued his ideas from a "left-wing" political, religious, or philosophical standpoint. Marx received the Ph.D. in philosophy from the University of Jena in 1841. Another radical Hegelian, the philosopher Ludwig Feuerbach (1804–1870), was an important influence on Marx through his analysis of religion as a projection of human nature and his materialism.

Unable to secure a teaching position because of his political ideas, the young Marx made his living as a journalist and engaged in radical political activity. In 1843 he married his childhood sweetheart, Jenny von Westphalen. They would have seven children, of whom three daughters survived to adulthood. He spent some time in Paris, where he met Friedrich Engels, had his first real involvement with the working class, and began the serious study of economics. Expelled from France in 1845, he spent a few years in Brussels, where he founded the German Workers' Party and was active in the Communist League. Marx, together with his lifelong friend, Friedrich Engels, wrote the famous *Communist Manifesto*, a statement to the world of principles and goals, for the Communist Party between December 1847 and January 1848. Expelled by the Belgian government, Marx was back in Germany, in Cologne, in 1848–49. Significant revolutions for social and economic justice on the part of the working class took place throughout Europe in 1848, and Marx was a participant in this upheaval.

After being expelled from Cologne and then again from Paris, Marx and his family settled in London, a haven for political exiles and the capital city of the world's most advanced industrial, capitalist society. There he spent the rest of his life as a "stateless exile," eking out a living as a journalist for both German- and English-language publications. A man of immense learning and formidable intellectual powers, including a prodigious mastery of languages, Marx spent most of his time doing research and writing in the great Reading Room of the British Museum. He was an indefatigable and very conscientious scholar, always consulting original sources. He read, in the original languages,

---

[1]Hegel's philosophical theories are discussed in Chapter Ten.

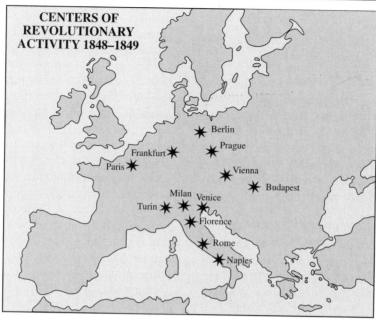

CENTERS OF REVOLUTIONARY ACTIVITY 1848–1849

Berlin
Prague
Frankfurt
Paris
Vienna
Budapest
Milan Venice
Turin
Florence
Rome
Naples

Centers of Revolutionary Activity 1848–1849. Redrawn from *A History of Civilization*, Eighth Edition, by Robin W. Winks, Crane Brinton, John B. Cristopher, and Robert Lee Wolff (1992), Prentice-Hall, Inc.

everything written on economics. In 1864 he helped found the International Workingmen's Association in London, which Marxists later called the First International. His main contribution to the labor movement for the rest of his life was his writings and correspondence. His economic and social theory and proposals for change became the most powerful shapers of labor and socialist movements beginning in the late nineteenth century.

The Marx family always lived close to poverty much of their lives, saved from starvation by ongoing generous financial support from the affluent Engels, who was also living in England. Marx was a devoted husband and family man, loving his wife and daughters and loved by them in return. His daughters achieved prominence, together with their husbands, in the French and British socialist and labor movements. His wife's death in 1881 devastated him, and Marx himself died in 1883.

Friedrich Engels (1820–95) was, with Marx, the co-founder of modern socialism, a close friend and collaborator with Marx for many years, the editor of Marx's writings following his death, and the developer of Marx's ideas in ways that became orthodox

Marxism. Engels is an important thinker in his own right, although he always deferred to Marx.

Like Marx, Engels was born into the middle class. His father was a German textile manufacturer, a genuine capitalist entrepreneur and factory owner and, incidentally, a tyrant and a fanatical Christian. As a young man doing military service in Berlin, Engels, like Marx, embraced the ideas of the Young Hegelians. Between 1842 and 1844 he worked in the office of a spinning factory, of which his father was a co-owner, in Manchester, England. Here Engels observed industrialism at first hand, since Manchester was the manufacturing center of Britain. During this period he studied the leading economic writers such as Adam Smith and David Ricardo, but also early socialist writings by thinkers such as Robert Owen and Charles Fourier. Engels met Marx in Paris on his way back to Germany in 1844, and the two formed a close and lasting friendship.

From 1844 to 1849, Engels was in Germany, Belgium, and France, writing and participating in revolutionary activities. He actually fought in an 1849 revolutionary uprising in Germany, escaped to England, and, like Marx, spent the rest of his life there.

Unable to make a living as a writer, Engels reluctantly returned to his father's business in Manchester in 1850 so that he could help Marx financially. Upon his father's death in 1864, he became a partner in the firm, and by 1869 he had made enough to support himself and Marx and was able to sell his share of the business. Engels lived near Marx the rest of his life, seeing him daily. Generous and fun-loving, Engels was the perfect "English gentleman." Brilliant and versatile, he was a successful businessman, a specialist on military affairs, a scientific investigator, and had, like Marx, an impressive knowledge of languages.

MARXIST CRITIQUE OF SOCIETY

Government Marx viewed the great mass of humanity as victims of oppression, alienation, and exploitation. Government is made by and for people. Yet it is frequently (Marx would say always) used by those in power to protect and foster their own interests, and in the process they oppress the masses. The French revolutionary slogan of "Liberty, Equality and Fraternity" expresses values and ideals that Marx endorsed but found absent in the society of his day. He believed that the remedy for political oppression and alienation is to be sought not on the political surface but at its roots. Typical political revolutions simply replace one ruling and oppressive group or regime with another. Echoing Rousseau, Marx argued that government is inherently exploitative because all forms of government serve the interests of the ruling class.

Religion Religion does not function to relieve oppression, alienation and exploitation. It simply functions as an opiate to dull the pain of the situation of the masses and offers vain hopes of a better life in the hereafter. But the remedy does not lie in attacking religion directly, but in attacking social oppression. When oppression of one human by another ends, religion will simply wither away, since the reasons for its existence are gone. Just as true religious emancipation for Marx consists in people being free from religion, so real political emancipation consists not in people being free to engage in politics but in their being free from politics. Like religion, the state and politics will also wither away when exploitation does.

Human beings are different from other entities insofar as they alone produce the means of their own subsistence. What and how they produce determines their lives. Although some people may emphasize the intellectual accomplishments of human beings (and put emphasis on their minds, brains, or souls), for Marx these are secondary. Human beings must live before they think, and how they live determines what they think. They are essentially social beings, who live in society and are truly human only in society. The notion of a truly individual human being, separate from society, is an abstraction. Similarly, the notion of individual human rights as rights against all others reflects a misconception about human beings. Radical individualism pretends that each person is complete, independent of all others. In fact, human beings are members of a species and become fully human only in and through society. Marx's view may be said to be *materialistic*, following Feuerbach, because he claims that the material nature of human beings is primary, and their spiritual or intellectual attributes secondary. He denies the possibility of independently existing spirits or minds or souls. Marx is also communitarian rather than individualistic, because he believes that individuals are and become human only in society.

Private property, by which Marx means private ownership of the means of production, is the basis for the division of humankind into classes and results in the domination of human beings by other human beings. The need to protect private property leads to the establishment of the state and to the appearance of human exploitation and alienation. In a capitalist society, property becomes all-important. People are judged by what and how much they have. Hence the emancipation of humankind requires the elimination of private property as well as the state, which is the instrument of oppression. This can be accomplished only if the oppressed masses, the working class or proletariat, who "have nothing to lose but their chains" (*Communist Manifesto*), free themselves by putting an end to private property, and so to classes, exploitation, and alienation. Since Marx equates the interests of humanity in general with the interests of the workers, the triumph of the proletariat, or the mass of workers, will for the first time in history result not in the oppression of one group by another but in the end of all oppression.

The ideal towards which Marx aims is a society in which people will live together harmoniously instead of in conflicting classes; in which people can develop their capacities through creative labor; in which people are free from domination by others, free from the domination of things, free from alienation. Such human liberation can only be achieved by changing society's basic structures (especially by abolishing private property and class divisions), and not simply by persuading, encouraging or helping individuals to change themselves.

INTELLECTUAL BACKGROUND

When Marx went to the University of Berlin in 1836, the influence of Hegel, who had died five years earlier, was still strong. Marx rejected the content of Hegel's doctrine but adopted and adapted his dialectical method. According to Hegel, if we penetrate deeply enough into the concepts we use, we find that one concept tends to pass over into or call forth its opposite. There is no such thing as an isolated concept; thinking is inherently relational. To take a simple example, we cannot understand the concept "light" without the concept "dark." At a more complex level, we cannot understand the behavior of a living organism without understanding what it is not: the environment with which it is in interaction. Hegel tried to show that it is only through this relational or dialectical reasoning that we can understand the structure of both human thought and the universe. Hegel applied this to history and declared that on the whole history is progressive. For him history is the development of spirit or consciousness as it expresses itself in the life and thought of humanity and it is pushed forward through the activity of great men—what he called "world-historical" individuals such as Alexander the Great, Julius Caesar, and Napoleon. Marx believed that Hegel had the right method but the wrong basic assumption. Consciousness and ideas are not the fundamental reality; matter is. He combined and adapted Hegel's dialectical method and Feuerbach's materialism, and, applying both to history, developed his materialist conception of history.

MATERIALIST VIEW OF HISTORY

In general the economic base of any society consists of the forces of production and the relations of production. The forces of production consist of the means of production (or the material used for production) and the modes of production (or the manner in which production is organized and takes place). The relations of production in their legal form are ownership relations.

The non-productive social interactions—those of family life, friendly associations, joint cultural activities, and the like—are built on the economic base. These social relations, plus social institutions (for example, the state, schools, and churches), and what Marx calls "ideological forms" (such as religion, philosophy, art, and law), make up the social superstructure built on the economic base. They justify their property and the existing structures of society in the religious doctrines preached in the churches, in the philosophy taught in the schools, and in the legal theory enforced by the courts. They support and hence directly or indirectly control the arts, literature, ideas, and rituals of the society, which reflect and justify their interests and views. The dominant culture of any period is the culture of the ruling class.

Although the base determines the superstructure, the different parts of the superstructure mutually affect one another. Developments in religion, or in philosophy, or in art, for instance, each influence the other areas. Moreover, there is carryover in each of these areas from one historical period to the next, and in each successive period we may find remnants of the previous period. Thus, Greek philosophy influenced medieval philosophy and the latter influenced modern philosophy. The same is true of art, and today we can appreciate Greek, Renaissance, and early modern art, although there are clearly differences among them. In general, the influence from one period to the next is in logical development or form, while the content is determined by the prevailing economic conditions of the time. Thus Aristotle and Plato both justified slavery because they lived in slave-holding societies. Their philosophies influenced the form and nature of the problems discussed and the logical development of the views of later philosophers; but once slavery was no longer profitable, later philosophers no longer justified it. This substantive change in moral outlook came about not by abstract logical discussion, but as a result of changing economic reality.

Ideology Marx's use of the term has been very influential as a valuable tool in critically examining the dominant beliefs, ideas, and values in all human societies, including our own. The ruling ideology of any society is the religious beliefs, political outlook, social mores, and artistic values of the ruling class. That is because according to Marx every society's institutions and values arise out of and are supportive of its economic base, and its ruling class—whether slave owners or capitalist factory owners—control the economic base. So ideologies are rationalizations of the position of those in power in a society, designed to strengthen their position and to persuade those they rule of their rightness and reasonableness. Thus, Marx provides us with a technique for analyzing political statements, social institutions, literature, art, philosophy, religion, and all other ideological forms or other aspects of the superstructure.

For Marx, ideology is in general a systematically distorted view of reality. It arises from seeing reality from a skewed, one-sided perspective. For example, members of the class of capitalist property owners see reality from their vantage point and tend to justify their position and vested interests. They teach their children to view the world from that point of view, which appears to those who grow up with it as natural, normal, and correct. Although ideology is what Marx calls false consciousness, this does not imply self-deception or maliciousness. Defenders of class dominance may well be sincere in their defense of existing institutions, themselves believing what they preach to others.

Ideology is related to classes: according to him, individuals have ideologies as members of a class. It is possible, though rare, for members of one class to identify with another class and to adopt its point of view. Thus Marx, born into a bourgeois family, came to identify with the proletariat and became its articulate spokesman. Although Marx believed that workers would be forced by their circumstances to revolt, he also believed that theory was necessary to guide their actions. He saw his task as raising the consciousness of the workers, helping them see their true situation, and so facilitating their taking appropriate and successful action when the material conditions were ripe. Marx's analysis of ideology is useful in illuminating American society. Like other societies, we don't think of our dominant beliefs, ideas, and values as "ideological"; they seem natural or neutral to us—the way things are. But in fact we are ruled by a capitalist and liberal-democratic ideology. Capitalism is our economic base, and over time whole theories of economics have arisen to justify and defend capitalism as the natural, reasonable, or best economic system. Liberal democracy, with its emphases on individual human rights, representative government, and the rule of law, is also taken for granted as the natural, reasonable, or best form of government. The two ideologies have historically been seen as one: as simply the economic and the political sides of one overarching view of the world. American popular culture and rhetoric are so pervaded by these ideas that we usually simply assume them as true and good—whether the philosophy of "rugged individualism," the politics of "spreading freedom and democracy," the economics of consumerism, the religious emphasis on a personal relationship with God, or the artistic idea of the supreme importance of individual self-expression.

But "ideology" has also come to have a more neutral definition. On this definition, ideology is simply another term for "worldview," any systematic and integrated set of beliefs, ideas, and values held and practiced by a group of people. This definition clearly encompasses Marx's definition of ideology, but goes beyond it in being neutral rather than negative and in not restricting ideology to the worldview of specific societies or classes. On this wider view, not only are capitalism and liberal democracy ideologies, but also are other political-economic systems such as fascism and Marxism itself and religions such as Christianity and Buddhism. Clearly Marxism came to express a worldview, which millions of people have believed is true and sought to implement and practice. The Marxist ideology would include Marx's own analysis of economics, politics, and historical development, and also his vision of a workers' revolution that would overthrow capitalism and lead eventually to a communist society in which everything except for personal belongings would be held in common and there would no longer be government, exploitation, and inequality.

Stages of History   Human liberation is a goal and expresses a value which Marx finds developing throughout history. Marx argues that the goal of human emancipation remains utopian, an unreachable ideal, unless it can be shown to be grounded in reality and joined with a practical plan of action that outlines how to attain it. The ideals expressed by the socialists who preceded him had always been utopian. Each of them expressed their views; a few tried social experiments; but none had any concrete plan for changing all of society. This is the basis of Marx's critique in *The Communist Manifesto* of various historical forms of socialism.

According to Marx, a dialectical and materialistic interpretation of human history shows that there have been four periods or stages of development, to be followed in the future by a fifth.

1   The first is that of **primitive communal society.** This is the period that precedes written history. In primitive societies property was held in common and people lived communally. Since there was no private property, there were no class divisions, no exploitation or oppression of one group by another. But all lived in great poverty, surviving as best they could.

2.   As productive resources developed, as animals were domesticated and herding was introduced, the basis appeared for some to have more than others, and thus the introduction of private property took place. This led to the next stage of human society, namely to **slave-holding societies.** People were now divided into two classes: the slave-holders, who owned property or the means of production, and the slaves, who performed the work. This division in the economic conditions, or the economic base, of society caused a division in the social superstructure that was built on it.

3.   As productive forces develop, slavery becomes less and less useful and slaves are gradually replaced with serfs. The change in economic production leads to the next stage of history, namely, **feudalism.** Feudalism consisted of a complex hierarchy of relationships governed by loyalty and reciprocal obligations. There were three distinct classes: nobles, clergy, and peasants, and each had its own function. As the economic base changes, this requires corresponding changes in the superstructure. Laws, governmental institutions, philosophy, and so on, all change accordingly.

4.   Feudalism in its turn gives way to the stage of **capitalism.** The change from feudalism to capitalism takes place as productive forces develop. The Industrial Revolution is incompatible with feudal relations of production. The rise of a merchant class and the development of machine production, which replaced hand craft, led to the new capitalist stage of economic development, characterized by the rise of a class—the bourgeoisie—who came to own the factories, the farms, ships, and buildings. The cities grew. All of this economic activity led to the general overthrow of monarchy, to the rise of democracy, to changing social relations, legal institutions and structures of government, and to the rise of individualistic philosophies (such as those of Descartes, Hobbes, and Locke), which corresponded to the individualism characteristic of capitalism. Serfs gave way to industrial workers, the proletariat. As the serfs left the farms for the cities they had to sell their labor power (get jobs) in order to live, since they owned neither land nor machines. At the same time the aristocracy was replaced by the bourgeoisie, the class of those who owned the means of production, as the ruling class.

5.   Marx describes the capitalist era and the dynamics of its development in his major work, *Capital.* He finds that capitalism contains a basic opposition, the overcoming of which will lead to the development of the next stage of historical development, at which he and Engels hint in the *Manifesto*, and which he calls **communism.**

By opposition Marx means that while ownership relations (or the relations of production) are private, the forces of production have become socialized. Manufacturing is a joint enterprise involving a great division of labor, with many people each performing given tasks to achieve a final product. The capitalist modes of production are thus cooperative and socialized, but the profit derived from production is appropriated by private individuals. The workers are the creators of wealth, but they receive only a portion of it. The gap between the haves and the have-nots will increase under capitalism. This is why, in the *Manifesto*, Marx and Engels call the *bourgeoisie*, who drive this process of impoverishing the proletariat, or have-nots, "the most revolutionary class heretofore." The workers, who are the vast majority, will eventually realize that they are the real creators of social wealth and they will be forced by their deteriorating economic position to seize control of the means of production. Once they do, they will socialize the economy. By doing away with private ownership of the means of production, all people will share in the profits that were previously appropriated by the capitalist owners. Productivity will increase and the goods produced can be equitably distributed for the benefit of all.

Since the basis of classes, namely, private property (or private ownership of the means of production), will have disappeared, classes will disappear. The social superstructure will in turn change. There will be no need for institutions to protect private property, no need for a state to enforce the exploitation of one group by another. Hence in time the state as a repressive body will be unnecessary and will wither away. The governance of people will be replaced by the administration of things.

Of course, this will not happen all at once, any more than feudalism replaced slavery or was replaced by capitalism all at once. There will initially be a transition phase from capitalism to socialism, which Marx calls the period of the **dictatorship of the proletariat.** In this period the bourgeoisie will be kept in check and the beginnings of communism established. This will lead to **socialism,** which is the first phase of communism, and which will lead eventually to the final phase, or full **communism**.

The Analysis of Capitalism   According to Marx, the key question to answer if one is to understand capitalism and its historical place is: Where does profit come from? He begins with commodities. There must be some common denominator, something common to all commodities, by which their respective exchange values can be determined.

The only common element of all commodities is that they are all the products of human labor. This leads to Marx's **labor theory of value,** which he adopts and adapts from Locke, Smith, and others. In Marx's theory, the value of any commodity is determined by the average socially necessary labor time needed to produce it. Providing the result is of equal quality, a product is not worth more if a slow worker produces it rather than a fast worker. Hence the measure of the value of a product is the average socially necessary time needed to produce it. Since machines increase what a worker is able to produce in a given amount of time, a machine-made product incorporates less labor time (even when we include the labor time necessary to produce the machine) than a hand-made product. Hence the value (and so the cost) of the product decreases. The great virtue of capitalism is that through the development of machines and assembly-line production, a great variety of goods gradually became plentiful and affordable to the masses. Capitalism was thus progressive with respect to feudalism, and it was a necessary stage in the history of humankind's development.

In pre-industrial times whatever was left in excess of materials, discounting for the worker's time, was surplus value, or profit, and the worker kept it all.

> Worker makes one widget in 8 hours.
> Widget sells for $80
> Worker deducts for material and time and keeps the $80

With the advent of machinery, many or most goods could be made more quickly and cheaper, but the machinery, because of its enormous cost, was held in the hands of a few. The workers could not compete with their handmade goods because factory-made goods were much cheaper, so they had to go to work for the Industrialists (sell their labor). Workers were in competition with each other and owners sought to hire workers at the lowest wages to add to their profit. Now the equation looked something like this:

> Worker produces 10 widgets in 8 hours.
> Widgets sell for $10 each = $80
> Worker is paid $2 per day

Lewis Hine used his camera as a critical lens to investigate the lives of the underprivileged classes in America. Originally trained as a sociologist, Hine photographed the plight of new immigrant populations, from their tenement homes to their sweatshop labor. Describing his work as "photo-interpretations," Hine conveyed a visual sympathy for the individuals he portrayed. In *Carolina Cotton Mill*, Hine implicitly critiqued the use of child labor. The sense of scale introduced by the machines underscores the young age of the children, visually condemning the exploitation of underprivileged children. Hine's revealing photographs aided the passing of child labor laws in the United States.

Figure III-9   Lewis Hine, *Carolina Cotton Mill*, 1908. Gelatin-silver print. (10 × 14.3 cm). Bowdoin College Museum of Art, Brunswick, Maine. Courtesy of Bettmann/Corbis.

Deduct $12 per day for wear and tear on machinery and materials
Surplus value = $66 which goes to the owner of the means of production.

Profit is the **"surplus value"** the worker contributes to the product for which he or she is not paid. Surplus value is the difference between the amount of labor that is needed to produce a product and the cost of maintaining that labor. The productive nature of labor means that it always produces more than is required to sustain it, and the entrepreneur, by paying less for labor than labor produces, is able to capture this difference as profit.

Since entrepreneurs wish to maximize their profits, they wish to have workers work as many hours as possible for as low wages as possible. By contrast, workers wish to work as short a time as possible for as high a wage as possible. But owners of the means of production are in the stronger position since the workers need work and wages in order to live. If the supply of workers is greater than the demand—if there is unemployment—workers are willing to work for lower wages than otherwise.

Hence unemployment and the resulting "reserve army of the unemployed" is to the owners' advantage. There is a level, however, below which wages cannot fall without adversely affecting the owners, and that is the level necessary to sustain a family. If wages fall below this subsistence level, the workers cannot support themselves or produce their replacements. If the primary wage earner—typically the male in Marx's day—is paid less than subsistence, his wife will be forced to work. Since her wage is supplementary, women could be hired for less than men. The final stage of exploitation is reached when the joint wages of husband and wife fail to reach the subsistence level, and the children must be sent to work as well, at wages even less than those paid women. In the early days of industrial capitalism owners provided no benefits for workers. They worked long hours under harsh and unhealthy conditions. Children as young as six to eight years old sometimes worked six days a week for as long as twelve hours.

This scenario might sound extreme to many Americans, but the situation that Marx described was the one that actually existed in Britain at the time he was writing. The British government investigated the situation of workers, and a resulting government document, called *The Sadler Report* (1832), detailed the atrocious working conditions in British factories, including the fact of child labor, with children sometimes chained to their machines so they would not wander. Marx did not make up these facts, but sought to devise a theory that would account for and explain them. Only with such a theory could he hope to understand the dynamics of the system, understand where the system was going, and devise a program to help the workers improve their position and preserve the positive aspects of capitalism while ridding it of its exploitation, inequality, oppression, and misery.

In his view the tendency of capitalism, if unchecked, would be to force the proletariat into greater and greater poverty. He believed they would eventually be forced by their conditions to revolt, to seize the means of production from the hands of the capitalists, to socialize ownership, and to end society's exploitation. Once they unfettered society's productive forces, they would produce an abundance of goods that would be available to all and that would enable all to have what they need. The entrepreneurs would not willingly give up their special position and would use the police and the army to protect their vested interests. A violent revolution by the workers would probably be necessary to move society into its next stage. Since the economic base in the highly industrialized societies is adequate to support a society with enough goods to satisfy the basic needs of all, Marx expected the revolution leading to socialism to take place first in the highly industrialized countries, such as Germany or Britain. Other countries would follow until the world had moved into the age of socialism.

The Doctrine of Communism   Communism was for Marx the next state of society to be achieved, the movement by which it could be achieved, and the doctrine that was to guide the movement. Communism, as we saw, could not be achieved all at once in any society and would not be achieved simultaneously in all societies. Capitalism was a necessary precondition for the development of communism. Only after capitalism had developed the productive forces of society was communism possible.

During the transition stage between capitalism and communism, the period of the revolutionary dictatorship of the proletariat, the proletariat would seize the means of production, take over the factories, and remove the ruling class from its position of power. The proletariat would exercise its dictatorship over the bourgeoisie, which it would control in order to prevent a counter-revolution. This phase would give way to the first phase of communism, which Marx called "socialism," and which he characterized by the slogan "From each according to his ability, to each according to his work." Everyone would be required to work, but rewards would be differential and proportional to what one produced. Great gaps between the have and have-nots would be eliminated, as would classes and class structures. In this period, inequalities, although reduced, would still exist, but exploitation would be eliminated. As people gained control of society and of their lives, alienation would disappear. People's views would begin to change to express their real conditions of life and the socialization of ownership.

Eventually the phase of full communism would be reached. Marx characterized this phase by the slogan "From each according to his ability, to each

Valentina Kulagina, like many Soviet artists, favored the medium of photomontage—cutting, pasting, and juxtaposing fragments of figures and text—as a way to impart political critique and as a means to disseminate propaganda. Here, in a poster produced for International Women's Day, Kulagina foregrounds a large female worker, laboring at a machine and supported beneath by hundreds of marching women. Although the holiday honors women, the emphasis is clearly on the woman *worker*, giving primacy to class over gender. Kulagina's text reads, "Women Workers, Shock Workers, Strengthen Your Shock Brigades."

Figure III-10   Valentina Kulagina, ***International Working Women's Day,*** 1930. Lithography. (108.9 × 72.1 cm). Collection of Merrill C. Berman. Courtesy of the Collection of Merrill C. Berman.

according to his need." All would contribute what they could and all would receive what they required. To make this possible the society must have achieved great development of its productive forces, yielding a great outpouring of the goods necessary to satisfy people's needs. When alienation, the domination of some people by others, classes, exploitation, and private ownership of the means of production had all disappeared, the need for the existence of the state itself would disappear. Exactly how the society would be run, and how distribution would be achieved, Marx does not say. But since the people would have achieved freedom, they would be free to decide these questions for themselves. No one would or could decide for them and impose that decision upon them.

THE MARXIST LEGACY

Marx's legacy is multifaceted. In capitalist countries, his influence on the labor union movement

improved the lot of the workers. In Germany, conditions seemed ripe for revolution when the German Social Democratic Party adopted Marxism as its official doctrine, but the anticipated revolution never occurred. Instead a revolution took place in Russia, a country mired in stage three, not the appropriate "jumping off point" which Marx had specified. The leader of that revolution, V. I. Lenin, recast Marxism into a form that justified the Bolshevik Revolution of October 1917, arguing that Russia had actually entered the capitalist stage of development. Lenin's death in 1924 was followed by a power struggle won by Josef Stalin, who further revised Marxism in terms of Russian nationalism, drastically imposed rapid industrialization at the expense of the lives of millions of people in the countryside, ruthlessly suppressed all opposition, and led the Soviet Union through World War II. Marxism-Leninism spread to other parts of the globe, most notably to China in 1949. The Chinese communist leader, Mao Zhedong, imposed yet another version of Marxism-Leninism on what was very largely a traditional agricultural society. After World War II the Soviets imposed communism on the countries of Eastern Europe and inspired the 1959 communist revolution in Cuba, while the Chinese spawned a communist revolution in North Korea. China remains officially communist, although it is actually a state-controlled capitalist economy. North Korea and Cuba likewise continue to be communist countries.

As it grew over the course of the twentieth century, the spectre of communism gathered a host of differing ethnic and religious groups under its Marxist-Leninist banner. The question we must now ask ourselves is whether the conflicts that have arisen as a result of the break-up of the communist world have been brought about because of centuries-old unresolved religious and national/ethnic differences, or because of the failure of the social-political system that held these disparate groups together over the past several decades. Have we returned to our starting point with the failure of another revolution? And if so, is there another synthesis to be made? Western Marxists, many of them in universities in the U.S. and Europe, have developed new interpretations and applications of Marxist theory in the light of the newer movements for human liberation. They continue to reject the identification of Marxism with the Soviet Union and China and they see Marx's analysis of the economic base and social superstructure, ideology, and the roots of exploitation as lasting contributions. Marx has strongly influenced the Western tradition and continues to do so for better or for worse, positively and negatively. While his views do not have to be accepted, they cannot be ignored by anyone interested in understanding the contemporary world.

THE COMMUNIST MANIFESTO

A reader of *The Communist Manifesto* should keep two things in mind: first, the *Manifesto* is an early presentation of Marxist ideas (before the publication of Darwin's *Origin of Species* in 1859, for example, which Marx and Engels believed was a crucial scientific underpinning of their dialectical interpretation of nature and history); and second, the *Manifesto* is a summary statement of the principles of a political party to the public at large and a call to action, rather than a careful, comprehensive, scholarly treatise (although a great deal of research and reflection lies behind it).

Part I, "Bourgeois and Proletarians," briefly presents Marx's and Engel's analysis of history, based on their theory that the dynamic of history is generated by economic life and the class struggle that results, focusing on the modern struggle between bourgeoisie and proletariat. This section contains perhaps the most analytically, rhetorically, and prophetically powerful description ever written of the nature and history of capitalism and its revolutionary character. With profound and prescient insight Marx describes the spirit of capitalism in terms that are still largely applicable in our highly technologized and globalized world. Part II, "Proletarians and Communists," announces the specifics of the program of the Communist Party and argues why it is the only party through which the proletariat can be emancipated. Part III, "Socialist and Communist Literature," offers a short history and critique of the various forms of socialist thought that have emerged since the Middle Ages. Marx and Engels differentiated their socialism from other forms by arguing that it was truly "scientific"—based on universal laws derived from historical facts—while previous forms of socialism were merely "utopian"—often expressing good intentions but not based in reality.

QUESTIONS FOR STUDY AND DISCUSSION

1. Explain Marx's critique of society.

2. According to Marx, what does human liberation consist of? How can it be achieved?

3. What is the materialist view of history?

4. According to Marx, where does profit come from? Is Marx's labor theory of value satisfactory as an economic theory? Discuss.

5. What is the relation of the economic base of society to the social superstructure? Explain what each consists of.

6. Explain the meaning and source of ideology.

SUGGESTIONS FOR FURTHER READING

Berlin, Isaiah. *Karl Marx*. 4th ed. Oxford: Oxford University Press, 1978.

Guettel, Charnie. *Marxism and Feminism*. Toronto: The Hunter Rose Company, 1974.

Hook, Sidney. *Marx and the Marxists*. Reprinted: Melbourne, FL: Krieger, 1982.

Kolakowski, Leszek. *Main Currents of Marxism*. 3 vols. Translated by P. S. Falla. Oxford: Clarendon Press, 1978.

Körner, Stephan. *Kant*. New York: Penguin Books, 1982.

McLellan, David. *The Thought of Karl Marx: An Introduction*, New York: Harper Torchbooks, 1974.

Moore, John H. ed. *Legacies of the Collapse of Marxism*, Fairfax, VA: George Mason University Press, 1994.

Singer, Peter. *Marx, A Very Short Introduction*. Oxford University Press, 2000.

Tucker, Robert C., ed. *The Marx-Engels Reader*. 2nd ed. New York: W. W. Norton, 1978.

———. *Philosophy and Myth in Karl Marx*. 2nd ed. New York: Cambridge University Press, 1972.

Wolfe, Bertram D. *Marxism: 100 Years in the Life of a Doctrine*. Reprinted: Boulder, CO: Westview, 1985.

———. *Three Who Made a Revolution: A Biographical History*. 4th ed. revised. Reprinted: Briarcliff, NY: Stein & Day, 1984.

CHAPTER NINE

RUSSIA AND THE WEST: FYODOR DOSTOEVSKY

There is a question that quickly arises when we examine Russian history, and remains a major problem of interpreting Russian culture and society today. An important version of the problem appears in Dostoevsky's *Notes from Underground*: is Russian culture and society Eastern or Western, or something completely different? For contemporary application, the question can be simply put: why do the Russians behave the way they do? Why do they, at least on the surface, seem more distinct from Americans than most other Europeans? Why do they seem plagued by tumultuous upheavals, such as in 1917 or in more recent years? Where are they going? In *Notes from Underground* these questions frame an interpretation of the meaning of the West as well as an interpretation of the nature of human beings.

Geographically, Russia is at the eastern edge of what is considered "Western." This geography has marked the social and cultural development of Russia. For example, many of the major intellectual movements in Western civilization—the Renaissance, Reformation, and Enlightenment—barely touched Russia or arrived much later. This absence or delay in exposure to Western thought has produced a sort of split character in Russia, never knowing whether it wants to be Western or uniquely Russian, and its modern history is marked by a tug-of-war between these two perspectives. Travelers to Russia at all times have emphasized this duality of character, this identity problem, and Russians themselves have discussed and written at length trying to define who they are. For example, St. Petersburg, the capital of the Russian Empire from the beginning of the eighteenth century until the Bolshevik Revolution of 1917, appears to the observer as quite Western, but almost deliberately and superficially so. Today it is often compared to Vienna or Venice, perhaps the most European and least "Americanized" cities in Europe. On the other hand, Moscow, the capital before 1700, and again since 1918, is usually perceived as Eastern, "exotic," even "Oriental." (Strangely, too, in the twentieth and twenty-first centuries Moscow has added a measure of American but still non-European atmosphere). Much of Russian cultural history can thus be treated as a tale of two cities, reflecting the strikingly different characters of Moscow and St. Petersburg and expressing a perpetual identity crisis or national split personality.

HISTORY AND CULTURE

The first thousand years or so of Russian history can be told as essentially a story of these two countervailing European and non-European influences. During the first important period of Russian political and cultural development, from roughly 860 to 1200, the peoples inhabiting the forests of Eastern Europe were subject to outside influences, but more from north and south than from east or west. The Varangians (Vikings or Scandinavians) came from the Baltic in search of wealth and adventure and to provide military and political leadership, but they were quickly absorbed by the more numerous Slavs. Arriving from the south were merchants, craftsmen, and priests from one of the highest civilizations of that time, Byzantium or the Eastern Roman Empire.

With the common interests of Scandinavians and Greeks to serve, a flourishing trade route prospered through the territory of what became known as Rus. Byzantine influences naturally dominated the art and architecture, and in 988, by the initiative of Grand Prince Vladimir, one of whose wives was Greek, Rus formally adopted Christianity from the Greek Orthodox Church. A Greek alphabet, adapted for Slavs and known as "Cyrillic," provided a written language for the inhabitants. Territorial expansion and developments in building, culture, and commercial wealth reached its zenith in the eleventh century, by which time Rus had established important links with Western Europe. After that, internal political weakness, the decline of the trade route, and powerful new external enemies led to the end of this first East Slavic polity. The population, although somewhat dislocated, would retain much of its early culture as new political centers emerged farther north.

The interim between the decline of Rus and the rise of Muscovy is often referred to as the Mongol or Tatar "yoke," with its connotation of oppression and submission. The great Mongol invasion of Europe in the thirteenth century was actually the culmination of a series of incursions by nomadic Turkish peoples, the last and most numerous of whom were the Tatars. They raided and plundered the Russian cities, controlled the mostly treeless expanse north of the Black and Caspian Seas known as the steppe, and thus cut off the Slavs from Byzantium and the Black Sea. With their superior military ability and greater cohesion and organization, the Tatars dominated the remaining Slavic cities, requiring regular payments of tribute, but they left undisturbed most Slavic customs and institutions such as the Church. In the north, the Teutonic and Livonian orders of German-speaking knights moving eastward pushed the Slavs back from the Baltic. Grand Prince Alexander Nevsky stopped this German tide in 1242—with Tatar assistance—thus becoming a great Russian hero in defeating foreign invasion.

The debate over the extent of "Oriental" or Turkic influences upon Russia has continued ever since this episode, with some arguing that Turkic influences played a major role in the development of Muscovite absolutism (an "Oriental" despotism) that later may have influenced Communist totalitarianism; others credit the period of 1250–1500 for the emergence of a distinctive "Russian" civilization. Most important, especially for students of

Western civilization, Russia was isolated and separated for several centuries from Western Europe, so that vital foundations of modern Western history—the Renaissance, the Reformation, and the Scientific Revolution—were practically unknown in Russia. Very little by way of institutions and ideas came from the West between 1250 and 1650.

By the middle of the seventeenth century, the military needs of a Russian state that was forced to contest with powers to the west (Poland), the north (Sweden), and the south (the Ottoman Empire) over long, poorly defined land frontiers brought increased contact with Western Europe, especially with England and Holland. A settlement of foreign craftsmen and advisors was established near Moscow. These new residents strove to modernize the Russian army, and in the process incidentally helped shape the adolescent mind of an heir to the throne named Peter.

Peter the Great (1672–1725) was a giant of a man, physically and mentally. While apparently able to beat, outrun, and outdrink any of his subjects, Peter possessed an enormous energy, ambition, and curiosity about the world around him. He believed that the way to enhance Russian—and his own—stature and power was by borrowing extensively from the West, especially from its military technology and governmental institutions. Such borrowing meant reform (some would say revolution) on a large scale. Peter therefore set about responding, rather unsystematically and haphazardly, to the needs of war by weakening and destroying the existing Russian forms and customs and political elites and replacing them with Western models.

At the time of his death in 1725, Peter had left much undone and numerous unresolved contradictions. While building bridges to the most "modern" parliamentary countries of Europe (England and Holland), he nevertheless strengthened absolutism in Russia. Emphasizing technology and training with the founding of mathematical schools and the Academy of Sciences, he failed to establish any universities to support humanistic traditions. While shackling the upper classes to serve the state, he also increased the burdens on the peasant masses. In promoting a more permanent base for Westernization, he built a new "Western" capital, St. Petersburg. But when he had his own son killed for opposing him, and then married a servant woman, he left his own Romanov dynasty shattered and vulnerable. What Peter did leave behind was a partially remolded generation of political and military officials and a veneer of Western civilization over an otherwise undisturbed traditional and Orthodox Christian population, thus initiating a cultural gulf in Russian society that would be a crucial factor in its further unfolding. Peter's open windows to the West might have been subsequently boarded up, except for three things: (1) his having made Russia a great military power in Europe and a part of the European system of alliances and balance of power; (2) the striking successes of Russia's first scholars of arts and sciences; and (3) the somewhat accidental ascendancy of a remarkably brilliant and ambitious German woman to the Russian throne.

Whereas Peter was a roughly self-made Westerner, Catherine the Great (1729–1796) was Western by birth and upbringing. Married to Peter's nephew, whose brief period of rule she helped shorten, her reign (1762–96) more than expanded upon the work of Peter; it was nurtured by one of the most intellectually stimulating and productive periods of world history—the Enlightenment—and by economic prosperity—the Commercial Revolution. While Catherine fostered extensive contacts with the West, thorough "westernization" was something else. Although she seriously considered legal and governmental reforms for Russia, especially early in her reign, little was ever accomplished. The nobility was partially emancipated from service obligations to the state and became more Western in dress, language (French), and custom, but the peasantry remained mired in servile conditions and restricted in movement both physically and socially. Her most "enlightened" subjects were eventually silenced by an official censorship that was inspired by fears of the radical turn that the Enlightenment was taking in the French Revolution. A contradictory duality of liberal Westernization and Russian autocratic repression was in uneasy coexistence in Russia by the end of the eighteenth century.

THE CENTURY OF DOSTOEVSKY

The contradictory tendencies in Russian society and politics under Peter and Catherine were reinforced and magnified by the epoch of the Napoleonic Wars

(1796–1815), in which Russia played a major role. Because of a much more intimate involvement with Europe and because of the impact of Napoleon's political and economic reforms and military ambitions, more and more of the Russian elite came in contact with Western European cultures. By the time of the restoration of peace at the Congress of Vienna in 1815, the Russian empire had expanded into westernized Finland, incorporated more of Poland, and even extended over Alaska and into Northern California. Diplomatic relations were established for the first time with the United States in 1809, and Russia benevolently attempted to mediate peace in the War of 1812. These new contacts with the West and the shock of the invasion of Russia by Napoleon's army of over six hundred thousand in 1812, followed by the occupation and destruction of Moscow, emphasized the backwardness of Russia and its military vulnerability. A large part of the Russian army followed Napoleon's retreat from Moscow back into Western Europe. Its commander, Tsar Alexander I, became the "Savior of Europe," and Russia, in a situation resembling the conclusion of World War II, became the leading military power on the continent. Many of the Russian elite who served as officers, however, could easily observe for themselves the contrast between military power on the one hand and social inequality and backwardness in Russia on the other.

The influx of European influences continued after the war as Russians, in greater numbers than ever before, traveled to the West, many to study at German universities. Similarly, West Europeans and Americans came to Russia to seek fortunes or out of curiosity. Some of them became tutors to noble families or joined the staffs of the several new universities that were founded in the first half of the nineteenth century. The combination of greater exposure to the West, new romantic ideals, and an underemployed officer corps for a large standing army produced Russia's first serious movement for substantial political reform and change from outside the monarchy itself.

Known as *Decembrists* for their failed military revolt in December, 1825 following the November death of Tsar Alexander I, these radical and liberal reformers advocated a variety of institutional reforms. Their various and often conflicting ideas were largely imported from the West. Some advocated a military *coup d'état* to produce a strong centralized government that would resemble the Directory after the French Revolution and that would carry out sweeping economic and social reforms. Others wanted a looser and more federal constitutional arrangement, similar to that of the United States. The Decembrist revolt, being poorly planned and executed, was doomed to an early defeat. Many of the leaders were arrested and sent into Siberian exile, and five were hanged. The rebels became martyrs for the continuing cause of social justice and an inspiration to the liberals and radicals who followed, but they also inspired conservatives who questioned their goals and methods.

After the Decembrist revolt, the two main currents of Russian thought that developed among the intelligentsia in and around the universities in St. Petersburg and Moscow in the 1830s and 1840s were the *Slavophiles* and the *Westernizers*. With German writers such as Kant, Goethe, Schiller, and Herder serving as guides to both sides, many of the growing numbers of this intelligentsia delved deeper into the extreme romanticism and idealism of the age. The Slavophiles were influenced especially by the mystical system of Friedrich Schelling. Through Herder's writings, they gained a sense of continuity and wholeness set in motion by national forces. By studying German Romanticism the educated elite sought to solve the riddles of Russia's past and to erect a framework for their search for national identity. It might be said that Russia, having missed the Renaissance and Reformation, and only in a cursory way partaken of the Enlightenment, now absorbed Western Romanticism "whole-hog."

The intellectuals who gathered in the debating circles of Moscow and St. Petersburg also studied the ideas of Hegel and French utopian socialists. In their search for vitality and wholeness in Russian history, they consequently discovered the peasant village and observed what they believed to be its collectivist, socialist character (*obshchina*), miraculously preserved over hundreds of years. This collectivism involved periodic redistribution of land among families and cooperation in work methods and in fulfilling financial responsibilities. The Slavophiles and the Westernizers both stressed the importance of Russia's collectivist past in this *obshchina*, but the Slavophiles believed that it was

being threatened by destructive Western influences and by the administrative policies of the Russian government.

The Slavophiles, moreover, emphasized the distinctiveness of Russian history and national character, the superior spiritual qualities of the Russian Orthodox Church, and even the advantages of Russian autocracy itself in an idealized patriarchal form. According to them, the central problem of Russia was nefarious Western influences, especially beginning with the reign of Peter the Great, which had produced an alien bureaucratic structure and diverted the autocracy from its true role as the upholder and protector of Russian institutions. Ironically, they thought that by following German romantic models, Russia could rediscover its real past and purify itself of Western aberrations. The Slavophiles were basically conservative in thought, but their criticism of the government and advocacy of reform naturally provoked the opposition of official Russia. Not surprisingly, their center of activity was the old capital, Moscow.

Although they agreed with the Slavophiles on the importance to Russia of the Russian peasant collectivism, the Westernizers believed in the compatibility of this institution with Western notions of an idealized and harmonious life for humankind in socialist communities. As with the French socialists, they saw no role for the church in this society and believed the state must continue to modernize along Western lines to eliminate barbarism and inefficiency. They advocated the elimination of autocracy and the establishment of socialistic self-government. Their anti-religious posture clearly separated them from the Slavophiles. To most of the Westernizers, moreover, Peter the Great was a hero who had gallantly pushed Russia toward its inevitable Western destiny. The problem was that many of his successors, out of a sense of self-preservation, had resisted further Western reforms.

DOSTOEVSKY'S LIFE

Fyodor Dostoevsky was born in Moscow in 1821, the son of a staff physician at a Moscow hospital. Educated to be a military engineer in St. Petersburg, he disliked school and his chosen profession and loved literature instead. We find echoes of his student days in Part II of *Notes from Underground*. Dostoevsky resigned his military commission in 1844 to devote himself to writing. He published his first novel, *Poor Folk*, in 1846, a book that was highly praised by the leading Russian literary critics. The same year he published *The Double*, a story about a government clerk who is haunted and finally driven mad by a man who is his exact double. Here Dostoevsky took a familiar theme from Gothic romance novels—the *Doppelgänger* or "double-goer"—and turned it into a brilliant psychological study. As ignored and neglected as *Poor Folk* had been praised, *The Double* only came to be appreciated much later.

Although always basically religious and conservative, as a young man Dostoevsky was for a time caught up in the revolutionary ideas and activities that were engaging the younger Russian intelligentsia and that we have outlined above. In 1847 he became a member of the mildly subversive Petrashevsky Circle, and in 1849 its members were arrested by the tsar's police. Dostoevsky was imprisoned for eight months and then sentenced to death. The sentence was literally commuted at the last moment, when he thought he was about to be executed. It was actually a hoax—the government had never intended to execute the Petrashevsky Circle but only wanted to scare them to death—but Dostoevsky never forgot the experience.

Dostoevsky spent eight years in Siberia, where political prisoners were often sent, the last four in the Siberian army. He used the time in Siberia to do much reading and thinking, and this period was very important in shaping his mature work. Dostoevsky returned to St. Petersburg in 1859 with a wife, Maria Issaeva, a widow whom he had met and married in Siberia, and her son Pasha. The years 1860–65 were an extremely difficult period for Dostoevsky, and at the same time the crucible out of which his most important work emerged. The marriage was an unhappy one. Mother and son were not in good health, and Dostoevsky always had money problems trying to support a family entirely by writing and editing and then undermining his own efforts with compulsive gambling. He himself suffered from epilepsy. In 1861 he published *Memoirs from the House of the Dead*, his reminiscences of his time in Siberia, where he had been deeply impressed by the dignity, decency, and faith of many of his fellow prisoners. In 1862–63 Dostoevsky traveled to Western Europe to get away from

his creditors, restore his health, and gamble. He was critical of what he saw: a civilization dominated by rationalism and possessive individualism (capitalism). In 1864 both his wife and his brother died. Out of all this unhappiness came *Notes from Underground* (1864), the first of Dostoevsky's five great novels.

Things began to improve somewhat for Dostoevsky in 1865, when he married a second time to Anna Grigorievna Snitkina, a practical, well-balanced woman who provided him with the stability and solidity his life needed. In 1866 he published *Crime and Punishment*, his profound exploration of the themes of crime, guilt, and redemption through the portrayal of the student Raskolnikov. From 1867 to 1871 the Dostoevskys lived in Western Europe. They continued to have serious money problems, and Dostoevsky continued to gamble. (He published his powerful story, "The Gambler," in 1866; it is still used by the organization that helps compulsive gamblers, Gamblers Anonymous.) While in Europe, Dostoevsky wrote his novel *The Idiot*, published in 1869, which portrayed a modern Christ-figure, Prince Myshkin. *The Possessed* followed in 1872, a story based on an actual event. A radical Russian revolutionary named Nechaev had a member of his group murdered in 1869 because he would not obey Nechaev without question. Dostoevsky saw Nechaev and his moral code as the inevitable end result of liberalism and socialism. During the 1870s, Dostoevsky became increasingly active in social and political causes from a conservative, Slavophile, and Russian Orthodox perspective.

Dostoevsky is often seen as the quintessential Russian writer, an embodiment of the "Russian soul." He was an eloquent voice of Slavophilism and a challenging critic of important aspects of modern Western civilization: secularism, rationalism, possessive individualism, and socialism. In him we can see clearly and articulately portrayed the clash between traditional Russian and modern Western values. His influence on Western thought and literature has been important, and his novels are part of our cultural heritage. Along with Danish philosopher Sören Kierkegaard and Friedrich Nietzsche, Dostoevsky is also seen as one of the three nineteenth-century pioneers of *existentialism*. The existentialist elements in his writing can be seen clearly in Part I of *Notes from Underground*. There he characterizes human life in terms of individual desire and freedom and as an unfolding and never-finished process. He criticizes all scientific theories and social movements that consider humans as governed primarily by reason and rational self-interest.

As a writer Dostoevsky was a brilliant explorer of the human psyche, exposing our inner contradictions, the role of the unconscious, and the fundamental role of desire and will in human life. Nietzsche acknowledged his own indebtedness to Dostoevsky in *Twilight of the Idols*, and Freud likewise recognized him as a profoundly astute investigator of the mind. Another aspect of Dostoevsky's genius is the "polyphony" of his writings, which is to say, his ability to speak in many voices. His characters embody alternative and conflicting ideas and ideals in a convincing way. For all his devotion to the Christianity of the Russian Orthodox Church, Dostoevsky experienced to the full the range of alternative views of things, which he represents in his characters in a realistic way.

Dostoevsky definitely has a message, however, which is that faith in Christ alone gives meaning to these crazy lives of ours. He expressed this through the Christianity of ordinary Russian people—Russian Orthodoxy in its popular form—such as the peasants he had known during his imprisonment in Siberia. But Dostoevsky is too complex, too good a writer, simply to "preach" to the reader. Instead, in the later novels he tries to show the consequences of ways of life not based on faith: Underground Man's paralysis of will, Raskolnikov's belief in his superiority, Nechaev's authoritarian socialism, and Ivan Karamazov's atheism.

Notes from Underground is the first of Dostoevsky's five great novels and the first presentation of themes that would dominate the later novels. It takes the form of a "confession" (the title he originally gave it) by a forty-year-old civil servant. In Part I the nameless narrator introduces himself and his outlook on life. In Part II, by way of illustrating what kind of man he is, he tells a story about himself at age twenty-four, intruding unwanted on a party held by former schoolmates and ending up with a prostitute who takes seriously his half-cynical, half-genuine urgings that she reform her life.

The context for *Notes* was the Westernizer-Slavophile controversy. The story is a direct response to a novel published in 1863 entitled *What is to be Done?* by the revolutionary writer Nikolai Chernyshevky. Chernyshevky's novel occupies a place in modern Russian literature roughly comparable to Harriet Beecher Stowe's *Uncle Tom's Cabin* in America. (Like many literate Russians, Vladimir Lenin, the chief founder of the Soviet Union, read the book as a boy and later gave one of his own books the same title.) Chernyshevky was a utilitarian, feminist, pre-Marxist radical socialist. He believed strongly in the persuasive power of reason, in science, education, and social reform. Chernyshevky blended Western and Russian ideas, envisioning a utopian society patterned somewhat after the Russian peasant communes. The basic problems in Russia, he believed, were patriarchalism and social hierarchy. Gradual reform was not enough; revolution was necessary. One of the two main characters in the novel, Vera Pavlovna, has a series of dreams that are utopian visions of the future and that provide the theme of the novel: through education and a radical egalitarian restructuring of society, individual humans will come to know what is truly good and in their actual self-interest, and they will act on the fact that their true self-interest and the good of society as a whole coincide.

Dostoevsky's *Notes from Underground* is a direct parody of Chernyshevky's book. He lifts passages, ideas, and images (such as the "Palace of Crystal") straight from the book. The powerful arguments against Enlightenment rationalism and socialism in Part I are directed against Chernyshevky's views. Part I, in fact, contains a brilliant attack by Underground Man (who is here speaking for Dostoevsky himself) on the assumptions of the Enlightenment that humans are rational beings who always choose what they believe to be good but err through ignorance and simply need a properly just society and the right education to choose what is truly good. The middle sections of Part I are among the most trenchant attacks on Western rationalism and utopian social schemes ever written. Underground Man's understanding of human nature and his criticism of prevailing assumptions about the role of reason make this a key text in the development of existentialism.

While not readily apparent, Dostoevsky's conservative Christian viewpoint underlies *Notes*. The original title of the book, recall, was "Confession."

In a letter to his brother in March of 1864, after the first part of the book was published, Dostoevsky wrote: "It would have been better not to publish the penultimate chapter at all (the main one, where the essential thought is expressed) than to publish it the way it is, i.e. with its forced sentences and internal contradictions. But what is to be done? The censors are swine; they passed the parts where I ridiculed everything and sometimes blasphemed for show, but they cut the part where I deduced from all this the need for belief and for Christ."[1] This statement also reminds us of the literary censorship that existed in Dostoevsky's Russia: writers were not free to say whatever they pleased.

You may find Underground Man, the narrator of *Notes*, a puzzling and repulsive character, but there is much to learn from him about ourselves. Underground Man longs for the "highest and best," the "sublime and the beautiful," but is always dragged down by his worst self. He is spiteful out of sheer boredom, he needs to dominate but takes both pleasure and outrage in being humiliated, he is unable to love, he is isolated from "real life" and wrapped up in literature and dreams. Underground Man, however, knows what he is; he is ruthlessly honest with himself and the reader, and he is deeply insightful about the inner conflicts of the human soul generally—much more so than the great majority of people. Yet for all his clarity of vision about what is wrong with him, he lacks the will to seek forgiveness, healing, and redemption through faith. Underground Man gives us many hints that he is not only miserably unhappy but also longs for something that transcends the self-conflict and ugliness of his situation—the true "highest and best." For Dostoevsky, he is a person who clearly needs the forgiveness and redemption that only Christian faith can bring, but he lacks the will to seek it.

Dostoevsky spells out his religious message the most explicitly at the very end of the novel. Consider carefully the concluding remarks of Underground Man, and notice how he shifts from "I" to "we." Notice also his "sermon" to Lisa in the brothel. The part on marriage is a traditionally Christian picture of a good marriage. Dostoevsky's message, here and in the other later novels, is that humanism, of whatever form, is doomed to defeat and despair. By "humanism" he means secular humanism, which he interprets as all the ways, beginning with the Enlightenment, in which humans have replaced God with themselves. The grand rational schemes of the Enlightenment— science, capitalism, revolution, democracy, socialism—all come to grief on the rocks of our very flawed human nature. But so, in *Notes*, do all forms of romantic intellectualism, escapism, and individualism, as represented by Underground Man.

As the reader begins *Notes from Underground*, he or she should think about the title and the layers of meaning it has in the story. Underground Man, the nameless narrator, calls himself an "anti-hero." What does that mean? How old is he at the time he tells the story, and how old was he when he had the experiences he describes in Part II? While the reader may find Underground Man a very strange and unpleasant character, it is worthwhile to pay close attention to his account of his childhood in Part II and what he says at the very end of the book. Is it possible to pity him? Is Underground Man crazy? neurotic? ruthlessly honest? Sigmund Freud argued that everyone is neurotic to some degree, and that "normal" people learn much about themselves from people who are more extreme in their feelings and behavior.

Dostoevsky's Underground Man stands as the defiant anti-hero of a challenge to reason. The novel can therefore also be interpreted as an existentialist inquiry that is the culmination of a century of debate over rationalism and romanticism and, in Russia, over Westernism and Slavophilism. From a position of self-imposed social exile (isolated in his "hole" under the floor, as he puts it), Underground Man preaches the conviction and fear that human beings can't explain anything by reasoning and consequently it is useless to reason. This emotional conclusion is based on two considerations: the nature of being human and the nature of reason.

Concerning the first of these considerations, the Underground Man asserts that human "reason, gentlemen, is a fine thing, that is unquestionable,

---

[1]In the Norton Critical Edition of *Notes from Underground*, translated and edited by Michael R. Katz (New York: W. W. Norton & Co., 1989), 93–94.

but reason is only reason and satisfies only man's reasoning capacity, while wanting is a manifestation of the whole of life—that is, the whole of human life, including reason and various little itches."[2] For the Underground Man, as well as apparently for Dostoevsky, human nature is multifaceted and resistant to simple rational characterizations of itself. Reason is merely a single aspect of human nature that at times can be and even must be ignored as we engage with the world and live with others.

According to Underground Man, "free and unfettered choice," not reason, is what supremely characterizes human existence. To concentrate on the rational aspects of human existence is appropriate, therefore, only when they are seen within the broader perspective of human will or volition. The use of rational methods to pursue an understanding of reality is itself an act of the will. The use and validity of reason is a result of a free choice and tied to a willful commitment made by a human being. If someone disputes another's use of reasons in a particular context, or attempts to do so in all contexts, like the Underground Man, then that conflict is best seen as a clash of wills, not as rational misunderstandings. For if a person chooses not to let reason influence his or her decisions and actions, then a rational argument that attempts to persuade him or her to change his or her mind will certainly have little force. Thus, when the Underground Man says that nothing can be explained by reason he is asserting the importance of human choice in rational investigations and the need to see that explanations depend not only on the dictates of reason, but also on the willful human decision and choice to use reason. Consequently it is useless to reason if one does not acknowledge the dependence of rational methods on human volition, for the human subject's choice to use rational methods is an inherent part—indeed, the starting point—of rational inquiry.

Concerning the second aspect of the Underground Man's considerations, the nature of reason, he says that when reason is left wholly to itself it proves unable to provide a ground or starting point for human action. "I exercise thinking, and, consequently, for me every primary cause immediately drags with it yet another, still more primary one, and so on ad infinitum."[3] The faculty of reason, he asserts, has the remarkable quality of always being able to reflect on and analyze its own methods and nature. When we have reached a conclusion by rational methods, it is perfectly appropriate, if not rationally necessary, to investigate the rational worth of the methods used to reach that particular conclusion. The axioms, methods, and hypotheses of an inquiry are always open to rational scrutiny. The Underground Man finds that rational, self-reflective inquiry is unable to check or terminate itself, and so produces an unending process of reflection.

Therefore, nothing can be explained through reason because the grounds for any explanation can always be rationally investigated and the grounds of that investigation can then themselves be rationally scrutinized, and so on, interminably. Final and complete explanation, which for the Underground Man means rational explanation, is impossible, and thus reason is useless (if the goal is fully rational explanation, that is, complete and final answers), because rational inquiry yields only various forms of relative explanations and critical questions.

At this point there are obvious objections: Isn't there something rather quixotic or contradictory in the Underground Man's challenge to and rejection of reason? Don't reason and logic have an objective force independent of human desires? It does not seem that the Underground Man or anyone else can question the value of reason without already using it and accepting its basic legitimacy. To refute reason requires the use of reason. The Underground Man, in fact, takes note of this very point when he has an imaginary dialogue partner object, "you can't rebel: it's two times two is four! Nature doesn't ask your permission; it doesn't care about your wishes, or whether you like its laws or not. You're obliged to accept it as it is, and consequently all its results as

[2]Dostoevsky, Fyodor. *Notes from Underground*. Translated and annotated by Richard Pevear and Larissa Volokhonsky. New York: Vintage Classics, 1993, 28.
    [3]Ibid., 17.

well."[4] One must, it seems, use reason to challenge the validity of reason. That fact in itself seems to show its invulnerability to subjective, willful rejection.

This criticism of the Underground Man and of Dostoevsky's existentialist position is, however, a misunderstanding of the strength of the claim the Underground Man makes. In reply to this criticism, the Underground Man simply remarks, "what do I care about the laws of nature and arithmetic if for some reason these laws and two times two is four are not to my liking?"[5] The human subject is perfectly capable, according to the Underground Man, of rejecting reason and its implications, regardless of the fact that an argument to that effect presupposes the canons of rationality. Hence the Underground Man does not argue that the human subject refutes or rationally disputes the necessity and laws of reason, but says simply that she or he can choose not to give priority in a particular context, or in her or his life in general, to such necessity and laws. The Underground Man is an example of a person who chooses not to allow reason to play the leading role in his life. And this is what the text shows, not what it argues.

In this presentation of the Underground Man, Dostoevsky shows his existentialist leanings, for it is here that he forcefully exhibits the primacy of the human subject over objective laws. Human beings can freely reject the choice and demands of reason in favor of other subjective choices, for example, choosing to follow or be governed by one's feelings, or by principles of religious faith. (Whether humans should choose reason as a guide for action is still, of course, an appropriate question.) By not choosing to accept the demands of reason, an individual brings rational debate about the implications of the rejected use of reason to an end. To try rationally to debate about the particular implications of a rational way of life with someone who has rejected the importance of reason as a means of deciding how to act, is fruitless and without meaning, since the very methods required to convince the person have already been disputed or rejected.

Dostoevsky, however, does not leave the question here. The existential gap between subjective choice and objective justification and reason finds its most dramatic expression in Dostoevsky's novel *The Brothers Karamazov* (1881), which was undoubtedly Dostoevsky's greatest novel, and which is generally regarded as one of the masterpieces of world literature (Freud ranked it with *Oedipus the King* and *Hamlet*.) To understand Dostoevsky's final posing of the question that he first raises in *Notes*, we must turn briefly to the episode in the chapter of *The Brothers Karamazov* entitled "The Grand Inquisitor." Particularly in this and the preceding chapters, *The Brothers Karamazov* has been characterized as containing the most powerful presentation of the problem of evil in modern literature. Ivan Karamazov, one of the four brothers in the novel, searingly argues the case against God in a tavern conversation with Alyosha, his younger brother. The suffering and death of children are for Ivan the ultimate challenge to the reality and goodness of God, since children are innocent and cannot be said to "deserve" punishment in the form of suffering. Ivan tells harrowing stories of gratuitous cruelty to children by adults, and concludes that if that is the price to be paid for believing that the universe is governed by a God of love, he respectfully "returns the ticket."

Alyosha, the religious believer who is deeply troubled by Ivan's arguments, appeals to the figure of Jesus, in whom Christians believe God is most fully revealed as suffering our sin and dying our death to forgive us our sins and overcome our pain and death. Ivan's response is to tell a story about Jesus' anonymous return to the city of Seville in Spain during the sixteenth century, the time of the Reformation and the Spanish Inquisition. The Grand Inquisitor is a Roman Catholic cardinal who is in charge of the Inquisition—rooting out and punishing all forms of heresy.

Here the conflict between freedom and reason that appears in *Notes from Underground* is most vividly developed. The supreme believer in reason and rationally governed action, the Grand Inquisitor, is brought face to face with the preeminent believer in human freedom and subjective existence, Jesus. One of the most interesting aspects of this meeting is that it is not a debate or rational

Heckel was a founding member of the German Expressionist group *Die Brücke (The Bridge)*. These art and architecture students saw themselves as young revolutionaries and rejected the art around them, particularly Impressionism. While they did not espouse any single aesthetic, much of their work is characterized by bold colors and a graphic angularity. The sharply angular figures in Heckel's *Two Men at a Table* represent an almost literal illustration of a scene from Dostoevsky's *Brothers Karamazov*. The painting, which Heckel dedicated "to Dostoevsky," makes reference to Ivan's story of Christ and the Grand Inquisitor.

Figure III-11   Erich Heckel, *Two Men at a Table,* 1912. Oil on canvas, 38¹/₈ × 47¹/₄" (96.8 × 120 cm). Kunsthalle, Hamburg. Courtesy of Bildarchiv Preussischer Kulturbesitz/Art Resource, NY.

argument; rather it is a long soliloquy. Jesus remains silent throughout the entire encounter, while the Inquisitor relates what he has contemplated in silence for the past ninety years. Why does Dostoevsky present Jesus in such a way? Why does he not allow him to answer the demeaning criticisms made by the Inquisitor? The answers to these questions center on the crucial differences Dostoevsky sees between human freedom and rational explanations and arguments.

When the Inquisitor condemns Jesus for refusing the temptations of the Devil, thereby leaving humankind without "reason" for choosing to follow or believe in him, Jesus cannot in any rational sense defend himself. While the Inquisitor can give humankind "reasons" for believing in Jesus and the Church—specifically the reasons of miracle, mystery, and authority—Jesus can use no such justifications. He cannot appeal to any such reasons because these would then be the objective standards on which the Inquisitor and humankind would make their decisions. That would remove the need for a free, faith-governed choice, which is what Jesus seeks from human beings. If he were to say one word in rational defense of his position against the charges of the Inquisitor, he then would not allow for the Inquisitor's right and ability to make a free subjective choice. He would show that his own acts are not subjectively and freely determined, because they would then be open to rational debate and questioning.

Is there then no reply open to an existentially governed individual? What type of reply could Jesus, or any individual, make in defense of his or her subjective choices? Since Jesus cannot use a rational argument, his reply must be by means of an action or deed. He must show the legitimacy of his choices by his actions. One of the endings Ivan proposes for "The Grand Inquisitor" emphasizes just this fact:

> When the Inquisitor ceased speaking he waited some time for his Prisoner to answer him. His silence weighed down upon him. He saw that the Prisoner had listened intently and quietly all the time, looking gently in his face and evidently wishing to reply. The old man longed for Him to say something, however bitter and terrible. But He suddenly approached the old man in silence and softly kissed him on his bloodless aged lips. That was all his answer.[6]

Jesus shows his willful choice and "defends" his way of life through an act of love—a kiss—and not through a rational justification. To act according to one's free subjective choices, to stand and act as an example of the worth of one's choices: that is the only existential answer that can be given to a rational challenger and critic. While Dostoevsky's Underground Man, who calls himself a "sick man," chooses spite as the ground for his actions, Jesus, who for the Christian is the ideal of what a human being should be, is governed by love. Dostoevsky's question to himself and humanity seems to be: which will we choose?

QUESTIONS FOR STUDY AND DISCUSSION

1. What is the "duality" of the Russian character, and what are some prominent historical examples of how it has manifested itself from Peter the Great to the Russian Revolution?

2. Characterize the Westernizer-Slavophile controversy, and how it manifested itself in nineteenth-century Russian cultural life.

3. How is the development of Russia different from that of Western Europe?

4. What is the geographic position of Russia in relation to the centers of Eastern and Western civilization?

5. Discuss the need for modernization in Russia. Why does this imply Westernization?

6. How does Underground Man describe the relation between reason and will in human life? Why is his outlook representative of existentialism?

7. What are Underground Man's criticisms of the Enlightenment legacy of the supremacy of science, utopian schemes for improving society, and proper education as a cure for social ills?

8. What role does Lisa play in *Notes from Underground*? How does her relationship with Underground Man reflect his lifelong struggle between the "highest and best" and his lower impulses?

SUGGESTIONS FOR FURTHER READING

Billington, James H. *The Icon and the Axe: An Interpretive History of Russian Culture*. New York: Random House Vintage, 1970.

Brower, Daniel R. *Training the Nihilists: Education and Radicalism in Tsarist Russia*. Ithaca and London: Cornell University Press, 1975.

---

[6]Fyodor Dostoevsky, *The Brothers Karamazov,* translated by Constance Garnett (New York: W. W. Norton & Co.), 1976, 243.

Florinsky, Michael T. *Russia: A History and an Interpretation*, vol. II. New York: Macmillan, 1955.

Gleason, Abbott. *Young Russia: The Genesis of Russian Radicalism in the 1860s*. New York: Viking, 1980.

Hingley, Ronald. *The Russian Mind*. New York: Charles Scribner's Sons, 1977.

Pipes, Richard. *Russia under the Old Regime*. New York: Charles Scribner's Sons, 1974.

Raeff, Marc. *Origins of the Russian Intelligentsia: The Eighteenth-Century Nobility*. New York: Harcourt, Brace and World, 1966.

Riasanovsky, Nicholas V. *The Image of Peter the Great in Russian History and Thought*. New York and Oxford: Oxford University Press, 1985.

———. *Russia and the West in the Teaching of the Slavophiles: A Study of Romantic Ideology*. Cambridge: Harvard University Press, 1952.

Venturi, Franco. *Roots of Revolution: A History of the Populist and Socialist Movements in Nineteenth Century Russia*. New York: Universal Library, 1966.

CHAPTER TEN

NINETEENTH CENTURY GERMAN THOUGHT AND CULTURE: FRIEDRICH NIETZSCHE

The paradox of modern Germany is its development of a great cultural and intellectual tradition alongside an autocratic, militaristic, chauvinistic and ultimately anti-Semitic political state. Friedrich Nietzsche was heir to this history, and he deplored what he considered Germany's cultural decline under the newly unified German state. The flowering of German literature, philosophy, religious thought, historical study, art, and music in the late eighteenth and early nineteenth centuries was so remarkable it has been called the "German Renaissance." It was a dazzling outpouring of intellectual and artistic creativity. Among the great names of that renaissance were Johann Wolfgang von Goethe, Heinrich Heine, and Friedrich Schiller in literature; Ludwig van Beethoven, Karl Maria von Weber, Johannes Brahms, and Franz Schubert in music; Caspar David Friedrich in painting; and Immanuel Kant and G. W. F. Hegel, in philosophy. The renaissance produced some of the most influential and creative achievements in thought and art in the modern West.

The Romantic movement in German arts and letters, which was part of the "German Renaissance" and in which Goethe participated but which he eventually rejected, was an important part of the dominance of Romanticism throughout Western Europe in the first part of the nineteenth century. Reacting against the rationalism and Neoclassicism of Enlightenment thought and art, the Romantics emphasized feeling and intuition, affirmed individuality and spontaneity, exalted nature as the organic context of human life, celebrated the diversity of peoples and cultures, and often nostalgically evoked a pre-modern, pre-industrialized past (such as the Middle Ages) as a "golden age." A prominent example of German Romanticism in literature was the group known as the *Frühromantiker* (early Romantics), which included the writer-philosopher Friedrich Schlegel, his wife the novelist Dorothea Mendelssohn Schlegel, the religious thinker Friedrich Schleiermacher, and the novelist and poet Ludwig Tieck. Nietzsche was thoroughly familiar with the Romantic writers of Germany and France and was critical of their approach.

JOHANN WOLFGANG VON GOETHE

Goethe (1749–1832) is considered a "universal genius." Poet, novelist, playwright, essayist, statesman, scholar and scientist, he was a modern example of the "Renaissance man" who, like Leonardo da Vinci, developed the many sides of his personality, intelligence, and talent to the highest degree. In literature Goethe is ranked with Homer, Virgil, Dante, and Shakespeare.

Born in Frankfurt am Main to prosperous middle-class parents, Goethe was educated by private tutors and studied law (which he briefly practiced) and medicine at the Universities of Leipzig and Strasbourg. While a university student Goethe began writing lyric poetry, which he continued to do throughout his life. Many of his early poems were inspired by a succession of love affairs that he would abruptly end when he felt his freedom threatened. He would then grieve inconsolably when a former lover would marry someone else.

As a young man Goethe was a leading figure in the *Sturm und Drang* ("Storm and Stress") movement, which lasted from about 1770–1780. These artists, who were part of the Romantic movement, gave free rein in their works to vivid and even violent passion. Goethe's novel *The Sorrows of Young Werther*, published in 1774, became the most important literary work of the *Sturm und Drang* movement. The novel is about a young man, Werther, passionately in love with a woman who is engaged to him and then marries someone else. Unable to live without her, he commits suicide. The novel was a European-wide sensation, with young men dressing like Werther and some (reportedly about two hundred) committing suicide as the result of reading the novel.

In 1775 Duke Karl August, the young ruler of Weimar, a small duchy in Saxony, invited Goethe to take up residence there and assist him with its government. Goethe spent the rest of his life in Weimar, much of it taken up with multiple and heavy political responsibilities—reorganizing the army and overseeing court finances, the building of roads and mines, and agriculture. He served in many political capacities and attained the position of prime minister. Through it all he continued to produce many poems, plays, and novels. Goethe's political views were always essentially conservative and thus congenial to the German context in which he served. He believed that the best form of government was an enlightened monarchy and that an aristocracy should be the ruling class, although he was also passionate in his advocacy of policies that benefited ordinary people.

A turning point in Goethe's adult life was his two-year stay in Italy in 1786–88. Already dissatisfied with Romanticism and longing to make direct contact with the remains of classical Roman civilization, in Italy he wholeheartedly embraced the classical ideal of objectivity, balance, harmony, order, and restraint. Goethe's *Roman Elegies*, written in 1788–89, give voice to these aspects of his Italian experience.

In the years following his return to Weimar, Goethe became increasingly absorbed in scientific research, studying anatomy, botany, optics, meteorology, and mineralogy. His study of human and animal skulls led him to anticipate Darwin's theory of evolution, and in his study of plants he envisioned the possibility of cross-breeding. Goethe was highly critical of what he saw as the presumption of the Newtonian science of his day to lay bare the secrets of the universe. He believed that science should search for metaphors in nature that illustrated the underlying unity in everything. He envisioned both nature and human life, including science and the arts, as governed by one universal organic force that manifests itself in the world of appearances.

The "classicism" of Goethe's post-Italy years caused him to turn against his own early romanticism and the emerging Romantic movement. He became hostile toward the younger Romantic poets, scorning the subjectivism of their exaltation of feelings. Yet his attack was compromised by the testimony of his own well-known earlier writings and above all by the publication in 1808 of Part One of his masterpiece, *Faust*, on which he had worked off and on since his early twenties. *Faust* was hailed by its readers as a landmark of Romantic literature. But Part Two, which Goethe finished only two months before his death in 1832, reveals the mature wisdom of his later years. The two parts together constitute a "confession" of his life, and show the fruitful struggle within Goethe between the romantic and the classical.

Faust is a great epic drama of the human struggle for redemption, profoundly exploring our desire to transcend our physical limitations, our search for answers to the eternal questions of the meaning of life and the universe. In Western literature it compares as a literary type to Dante's *Divine Comedy*. The Faust legend goes back to a learned German of the early sixteenth century, Dr. Faustus, who was rumored to have sold his soul to Satan in return for ultimate knowledge and power. English dramatist and poet Christopher Marlowe dramatized the story in 1593 in his play *Doctor Faustus*; Goethe immortalized it in his great work; and the French composer Gounod followed later in the nineteenth century with his opera of the same name.

As the *Divine Comedy* summed up the ordered Catholic Christian worldview of the Middle Ages, so the Faust legend has been seen as a central symbol of the modern world, with its restless striving for power and knowledge. The two main characters are Faust, a universal man, and Mephistopheles or Mephisto, who in the Prologue is presented not as the devil but as a servant of God, an evil force created in order that humans may learn and grow by striving against it. In Part Two Helen of Troy appears in the symbol of the ideal, classical beauty who unites with the medieval-romantic Faust. Finally, as an old man, Faust forces Mephistopheles to help him with a big land-reclamation project that will benefit thousands of people, but dies before the work is completed. Although Mephistopheles tries to claim Faust's soul for hell, God's angels carry him off to heaven where he is reunited with Gretchen, a woman he had loved and wronged in Part One. Faust's ultimate salvation, described in Christian terms, is a significant change Goethe made in the traditional legend. Interestingly, while Goethe frequently mentioned God in his writings, his own religious views were very unorthodox and indeed pantheistic.

IMMANUEL KANT (1724–1804)

Every German in the nineteenth century who claimed to be philosophically literate had to read and come to grips with the work of Immanuel Kant and G. W. F. Hegel. These two thinkers have been among the most important shapers of modern European thought—not only in philosophy, but also in a wide variety of fields including history, psychology, political science, religious studies, anthropology, sociology, and literary criticism. Nietzsche was very critical of Kant, and it is useful to know what he was criticizing. He wrote less about Hegel directly, but he was certainly critical of his ideas as well.

Kant's ideas became such a watershed in the history of modern philosophy that we speak of "pre-Kantian" and "post-Kantian" in referring to philosophical developments. In his *Critique of Pure Reason* (1781) he constructed a new model for understanding the mind in its relation to the world. On the one hand he argued, against the rationalists like Descartes, that human understanding is not simply a mirror that reflects intuitively the structure of things as they are in themselves. On the other hand, against the empiricists like Hume, he argued that the mind is not simply a "blank tablet" deriving all its knowledge from sense experience. What we call the "mind," Kant said, must be viewed as an active agent that constructs the raw material of sense experience into an ordered and intelligible world through principles inherent in the mind. In no sense do human minds *create* the universe of physical objects and relations. They are realities other than ourselves that present themselves to the senses as a "given,"

but it is entirely our minds that construct them into an ordered and intelligible world. Nor are the principles in our minds simply subjective to each individual. They are universal and objective characteristics shared by all normal humans by virtue of their reasoning ability. Thus, it is possible for human beings to participate in a common world and to engage in science.

Central to Kant's philosophy is his distinction between the *phenomenal* and the *noumenal*. What we perceive through our senses are things as they *appear* to us—what Kant called *phenomena*. What things are *in themselves*, apart from our experiencing their appearances through our senses, cannot be known to the human mind. But Kant insisted that we must assume the existence of things in themselves, even though we can have no knowledge of them. He called things in themselves *noumena*. He also believed that the realm of noumena may include realities such as God. But noumena, Kant said, cannot be known, and human understanding has nothing to say about them. Human knowledge is limited to organizing and making sense of the physical universe (phenomena) as we perceive it through our senses. Kant believed that that was exactly what we see in the work of scientists such as Sir Isaac Newton, and Kant believed he had provided a philosophical explanation of Newton's theories about nature.

But when we turn from the question of what we can know to the issue of how we ought to live our lives, Kant said, we are engaged in practical rather than theoretical thinking. When we use our reasoning power to think about how to make moral decisions, when we try to get clear what our moral responsibilities are, when we weigh alternatives and decide on the best course of action, that is practical reasoning.

In his moral philosophy Kant argued that human beings are free or autonomous to the extent that they transcend passions and desires and act out of duty or obligation to the moral law or, as he called it, the *categorical imperative*: those moral principles that can be applied universally and recognize the autonomy and dignity of persons. The moral law is the law of our own being as rational creatures. But the ability to act autonomously means that persons have free will. Unless I am free either to do or not to do what the moral law commands, then morality is an illusion.

Kant argued that insofar as we understand ourselves simply as physical organisms, as we do when we study humans scientifically, there is no way of thinking of ourselves as free. The world of Newtonian science is deterministic. All we can *know*, through science, is that we are phenomena operating in space and time and thus entirely subject to the laws of physics and physiology. But since we must believe that our will is free in order to make rational sense of morality, we can consistently believe that as moral beings we are noumenal. We belong to a moral realm "outside" the phenomenal world of space and time.

So while Kant believed we could have genuine *knowledge* only of the world of phenomena, he argued that certain *beliefs* that go beyond the phenomenal world are necessary as practical *"postulates"* or affirmations in order to make sense of the moral life. The first such postulate, as we have seen, is *free will*. The second is *immortality*. If morality is to make sense, I must obey what the inner moral law commands. But it is obvious that because of the lifelong struggle in humans between duty and desire, none of us perfectly obeys the moral law. So we require an indefinitely long period of time in order to make our wills perfectly good. The third postulate is the *existence of a God* who is the good and purposeful source and goal of both the phenomenal and the noumenal realms. Such a supreme reality alone has the power to guarantee our immortality and to overcome the inevitable split or dualism in this world between duty and desire: between our duty to the moral law and the happiness we naturally seek.

GEORG WILHELM FRIEDRICH HEGEL (1770–1831)

Hegel was greatly influenced by Kant, but believed Kant was arbitrary in leaving us with a complete dichotomy between phenomena and noumena. If, as Kant had showed, the mind actively constructs the meaning of the universe of phenomena through categories within itself, then, Hegel reasoned, is not the mind the clue to the whole of reality—phenomenal and noumenal alike? Hegel developed a philosophical perspective known as *absolute idealism*. Individual human minds are manifestations of a cosmic or universal Mind, which Hegel called the Infinite, the Absolute, or Spirit. Reality as a whole is the total process of Spirit's self-expression. Spirit is the Universal Agent that is disclosed in the unfolding processes of nature and history and can be known by human minds, which are Spirit "thinking itself." The kind of reasoning that enables us to understand the laws of the development of the world-process is what Hegel called *dialectic*, in which concepts generate and pass into their opposite, uniting in a higher synthesis yet without canceling their differences. The dialectic is both the inner meaning and the driving force of the unfolding of Spirit, manifested in the emergence of conflicts and contradictions in nature and history that move the process—the life of Spirit—to a higher level that is both continuous with what went before and yet truly new and unprecedented.

According to Hegel, there are two stages in the cosmic life of Spirit. (1) One is the realm of nature, which is Spirit making an object of itself, or becoming its own "other." Nature is an objective, physical order of things that is a necessary basis for the development of subjects—of human consciousness. (2) The second stage is the emergence of human consciousness, which is Spirit "returning to itself" as self-knowledge. Since what we know as history is precisely the story of human consciousness, Hegel was supremely interested in history. He believed that world history, as the manifestation of Spirit, was the unfolding of a rational process exhibiting principles discoverable by the mind. The rise and fall of nations and the impact of great men—what Hegel called "world-historical individuals"—all contribute integrally to Spirit's unfolding purpose.

History, rightly understood, manifests a purpose, a *telos*: the progress of freedom—from ancient societies in which only the ruler was understood as free, through the Greek and Roman worlds in which some but not all were free, to the modern recognition that all individuals simply as human beings (spirit or subject) ought to be free. But true freedom, the full development of human consciousness and identity, can be achieved only within concrete political communities. Only the loyal, civic-minded citizen of the political community is the truly free person. In the state's laws and institutions, which are manifestations of Spirit, the individual has a basis for rationally determining his or her own life. Thus public and private interests are fully harmonized. The state is the highest human association, joining individuals together into a community and replacing the rule of instinct with the rule of law. Hegel found the modern nation-state the fullest historical embodiment of universal reason, the supreme manifestation of Spirit, and the fullest expression of individual freedom. Its highest expression, he believed, was the Prussian state of his day, combining absolute monarchy with the principle of the individual's inherent worth and dignity.

FRIEDRICH NIETZSCHE

Friedrich Nietzsche (1844–1900) lived and thought against the background of a social and political milieu that he totally rejected. Nietzsche was one of the most original, provocative, and controversial of modern philosophers. Mention of his name evokes a cluster of phrases associated with him and often misinterpreted, such as "the death of God," "master and slave moralities," and "the will to power." Despite his repeated expressions of contempt for the rise of extreme German nationalism in the unified Germany and for the anti-Semitism that accompanied it, and despite his conviction of the generally negative effect of political power on cultural life, Nietzsche's ideas were later distorted and appropriated by the National Socialists, or Nazis (1921–1945), to their purposes. This came about through a combination of circumstances. One was his dramatic language and an aphoristic prose style that lent itself to quoting him out of context. Another was the unfortunate control his sister Elisabeth Förster-Nietzsche, an active anti-Semite and German racialist, had over the publication of his writings as his literary executor during his period of insanity and after his death. A third factor was the willful romanticizing and distorting of Nietzsche as the "prophet" of a new Germanic "mythology" by some of his admirers.

Nietzsche was born in 1844 in Röcken, a village in Saxon Germany. His father and both his grandfathers were Lutheran ministers. His father died from a brain hemorrhage when Friedrich was four (which may be a medical clue to Nietzsche's later physical ailments), and he and his sister Elisabeth were raised by their mother, a grandmother, and two aunts. After an excellent classical education in one of the finest preparatory schools in Germany, Niet-

Munch's *Portrait of Nietzsche* exhibits a clear reverence for the philosopher, whose writings the artist studied in the intellectual and literary circles of Berlin. Set against a background of the Saale river valley and the Rudelsburg Castle, Nietzsche appears characteristically deep in thought. Munch placed him on a bridge above the river and the unusual perspective raises Nietzsche well into the sky, a deifying gesture likely used by Munch to express his admiration of the philosopher's work.

Figure III-12   Edvard Munch, *Portrait of Nietzsche,* 1906. Oil on canvas (201 × 160 cm). Thielska Gallery, Stockholm, Sweden. Courtesy of the Thielska Gallery.

zsche attended the Universities of Bonn and Leipzig. At Bonn he began by studying theology, but he gave it up when he lost his faith and "majored" in classical philology instead. So impressive was Nietzsche's achievement as a student that he was appointed to a professorship at the University of Basel, in Switzerland, at the age of twenty-four before he had completed the doctorate (which the University of Leipzig then awarded him without examination) — an almost unheard-of action. He became a Swiss citizen and taught at Basel for ten years.

During his Basel years (1869–79) Nietzsche published his earliest books, beginning with The *Birth of Tragedy* (1872), a highly original and startlingly "revisionist" reinterpretation of ancient Greek tragic drama. Nietzsche interpreted Greek drama and culture as a conflict and synthesis between the Dionysian (unbridled passion that breaks down barriers and constraints) and the Apollonian (reason that bestows order, balance, individuation). Nowadays students of ancient Greek civilization take for granted the powerful Dionysian elements in Greek life, but it was a daring hypothesis in a time when the most influential European classical scholars (and also Goethe) interpreted the Greeks entirely in Apollonian terms. His book, which concluded with praise of the composer Richard Wagner as the creative renewer of German culture, was not well received by his fellow classicists.

While at Basel Nietzsche became a close friend and ardent admirer of Richard Wagner, the operatic genius who was revolutionizing German music, and his wife Cosima, who lived in Tribschen near Basel. At first Nietzsche was like a son to Wagner, and he later considered the time he spent with the Wagners one of the happiest periods of his life. But Nietzsche soon became disillusioned with Wagner, who was becoming the self-appointed cult figure of the strident German nationalism and anti-Semitism that were emerging in the early years of the country's unification. Nietzsche, by contrast, always called himself a "good European" and an "anti-anti-Semite," and he criticized the Germans unmercifully. He spent the rest of his career "working through" his relationship with Wagner; two of his last writings are directly about Wagner.

Nietzsche served as a medic in the Franco-Prussian War of 1870–71, where he contracted dysentery and diphtheria from nursing wounded soldiers in a boxcar for three days. Previously a mostly healthy although extremely near-sighted person, Nietzsche was progressively debilitated by ill health for several years, until in 1879 he suffered a serious physical breakdown. He decided to resign his university professorship and spent the next nine years "wandering," living mostly in temporary lodgings and hotel rooms in Switzerland and northern Italy. He endured recurrent and severe migraine headaches, stomach cramps and vomiting, and episodes of almost complete blindness.

Astonishingly, it was precisely those nine years (1879–1888) that were the most productive and creative of Nietzsche's life: in the writings of that period he developed a uniquely life-affirming philosophy. He wrote all his greatest and best-known books during those years, such as *The Gay Science* (1882/87), in which his famous parable of the "madman" who announces the death of God appears; *Thus Spoke Zarathustra* (1883–85), a highly imaginative

Like Erich Heckel, Kirchner was a member of the German Expressionist group *Die Brücke (The Bridge)*. The artists took their name from a passage in Nietzsche's *Thus Spake Zarathustra* (1883), in which the prophet describes humanity's potential to be an evolutionary "bridge" to a perfected future being, or *Übermensch*. Rather than painting scenes of an idyllic future, however, Kirchner focused on the psychologically deplorable conditions of life in the modern urban city. In *Street, Berlin*, the angular figures are crowded in close proximity yet seem emotionally distanced from one another.

Figure III-13   Ernst Ludwig Kirchner, *Street, Berlin*, 1913. Oil on canvas, 47^1/$_2$ × 35^7/$_8$" (120.6 × 91 cm). The Museum of Modern Art, New York. Digital image © The Museum of Modern Art/Courtesy of Scala/Art Resource, NY.

"prose-poem" that he always considered his greatest work and that contains some passages of remarkable beauty; *Beyond Good and Evil* (1886), a general critique of the ideas and values of his time; *On the Genealogy of Morals* (1887), his historical and psychological analysis of morality in which he developed the typology of "noble" and "slave" moralities; *Twilight of the Idols* (1889), perhaps the best summary of his final views; *The Anti-Christ* (not published until 1895), his all-out attack on Christianity; and *Ecce Homo* (Latin for "behold the man," which were Pilate's words concerning Jesus addressed to the mob in Jerusalem; not published until 1908), in which he looks back over all he has written and responds to criticisms of his thought.

After receiving some early notoriety for his first books, all of his later works were mostly ignored by critics and the reading public; he even had to pay for the publication of most of his books himself. His work was neglected until 1888, when some scholars and literary critics started reviewing his books and a noted Danish intellectual, Georg Brandes, gave a series of lectures on his thought. After that, Nietzsche's rise to fame was meteoric, but he knew nothing of it, because by then he was living in a private world of madness. Early in January, 1889, Nietzsche suffered a complete mental collapse. Though he had brief periods of lucidity after that, he spent the rest of his life in a childlike mental darkness cared for by his mother and then Elisabeth Förster-Nietzsche, his sister.

Nietzsche had intended *Zarathustra* as his major philosophical statement. Continuing to develop his ideas, however, he collected notes during the 1880s for a major, even more comprehensive work that he thought of calling *The Will to Power*. But he abandoned this project in 1888 in favor of a different plan. The last year before his collapse into mental illness, 1888, was an enormously productive period for Nietzsche. He wrote five books in which he succinctly and combatively expressed his developed philosophy. *Twilight of the Idols* was the last one he saw through to publication. At the end of the "Foreword" to *Twilight*, Nietzsche writes: "Turin [the town in northern Italy where he was living], 30 September 1888, on the day when the first book

of the *Revaluation of all Values* was finished."[1] At that time, Nietzsche had in mind the publication of four books with the collective title *Revaluation of all Values*, a phrase that can be taken as a kind of motto for his thought. The "first book" of the *Revaluation* was *The Anti-Christ*. *Twilight* was not part of the projected *Revaluation* series, but Nietzsche considered it an important summary of his ideas. On September 12, 1888, in a letter to his secretary and most devoted admirer, Peter Gast, Nietzsche had written that *Twilight* was "a very sharp, precise, and quick digest of my essential philosophical heterodoxies: this is so that the book can serve to introduce and whet the appetite for my *Revaluation of All Values*. . . . There is a lot in it of judgments on the present, on thinkers, writers and such."[2]

After his mental breakdown, Elisabeth had published, with no critical editing, the disorganized, half-formed mass of notes and sketches he had made (some of which he had revised, polished, and used in his published books) for the abandoned work and entitled it *The Will to Power*. As it stands, the collection is full of important ideas that we do not find elsewhere in Nietzsche's writings, so that for many years interpreters of Nietzsche incorrectly regarded this undigested and unedited miscellany as his chief book and the main summary of his thought—with many unfortunate results.

The "revaluation of all values" is for Nietzsche the radical ("root") critical examination of the most foundational ideas, beliefs, and values of the human race, especially as expressed historically and culturally in Western civilization from the ancient Greeks and Israel down to Nietzsche's own day. For example, he analyzed what the later philosopher Ludwig Wittgenstein called "the bewitchment of our intelligence by means of language." Language is uniquely human and essential to human life and knowledge, but language is also inherently deceptive. Through language we carve up and simplify the ceaselessly changing flux of reality and ourselves into objects, causes and effects, and selves consisting of "ego" and "will." Nietzsche was especially critical of philosophers, beginning with Socrates, for making idols of their concepts ("God," "being," "substance") and regarding them as more

---

[1]Nietzsche, Friedrich. *Twilight of the Idols* (Indianapolis, IN: Hackett, 1997), 4.
[2]Ibid, ix.

real than the concrete world of our sense experience. Nietzsche's "revaluation" extended to metaphysics, religion, morality, and politics.

Although Nietzsche, like most modern thinkers, was indebted to Kant's metaphysical skepticism, he heaped unrelenting scorn on Kant's analysis of the moral life. He considered Kant a Christian in disguise and a hypocrite, with his universal ethics of duty to others and his "smuggling" freedom, immortality, and God back in as props for the moral life after getting rid of them in his philosophy of nature. Nietzsche believed that Kant had been a pernicious influence in nineteenth-century Germany, allowing people to perpetuate Christian belief and morality in a respectably "modern" and secularized form. Nietzsche considered Hegel's philosophy the basis of a widespread understanding of the course of history as progressive, which Nietzsche considered profoundly mistaken. However, we can see affinities with Nietzsche's thought in Hegel's conviction that truth is to be found only within nature and history, however differently Nietzsche interpreted them.

Broadly speaking, Nietzsche was a naturalist in his outlook. While he never denied the possibility of super-natural realities, he maintained that humans could know nothing about them. The only reality of which we have knowledge is nature, the spatio-temporal universe that is known through our senses and is in a process of endless change or becoming. This ceaseless flux of sensory appearance is reality or "being"; we know nothing of any invisible, unchanging order of reality behind or beyond it. Religions and many philosophers have constructed such a realm (for example, Christianity's God, Plato's Forms), but such ideas are simply that—human constructions. On this planet the natural process has produced biological life in all its multiform variety, and humanity is to be understood as a unique manifestation of life and the animal kingdom. Nietzsche, always trying to get at the roots or primary causes of human phenomena, traced human ideas, values, and behavior to their psychological and (more deeply still) physiological bases. At the same time, he was very concerned to analyze and appreciate human life in all the rich and varied ways in which it expresses its uniqueness in nature. Thus, Nietzsche ranged over human culture in all its aspects, from the arts to politics to education to religion and morality.

In religion and morality Nietzsche rejected the idea of God, not only as an abstraction referring to something "beyond nature" of which we can have no knowledge, but also as the supreme idea used by Christianity to deny everything that affirms life in this world. He famously used the phrase "the death of God," as in his "Parable of the Madman" in *The Gay Science* (aph. 125), not in the literal sense that there was once an eternal, infinite being who no longer exists, but as a metaphor to describe the modern decline of Christian belief as the foundation of Western society—a decline that he both welcomed as a liberation and recognized as a dangerous upheaval.

Nietzsche also laid upon Christianity the primary responsibility for the triumph of "slave morality," a morality that is rooted in resentment and revenge (he always used the French word *ressentiment*) against the self-affirming values of superior or "noble" human beings by the inferior, the "herd," in societies. It is a morality that further expresses its negative basis by demanding of humans that they war against, rather than creatively sublimate, their biologically rooted passions and drives. Nietzsche believed that different societies had developed different moralities expressing their distinctive social, political, and cultural life. His criterion for evaluating all moral codes or philosophies—indeed, his criterion for evaluating everything—was whether or not they were expressions of "ascending" or "descending" life, health or sickness (decadence), life-affirmation or life-denial. Moralities that arise from and creatively channel natural instincts and drives are healthy; those that war against our nature are unhealthy.

In his political thought Nietzsche was an unsparing critic of modern egalitarian movements such as democracy and socialism. Basing his views on the human place in nature, Nietzsche thought it was obvious that humans are not equal, nor should they be. Nature is a system of hierarchies of stronger and weaker (this is reminiscent of Aristotle), and human groups are no exception. There are those who naturally command and those who naturally obey. Interestingly, Nietzsche argued that it was precisely conservative societies, ruled by a "natural" aristocracy and characterized by a strong sense of tradition and rank, that best produced and allowed to flourish individual achievement and creative genius in thought and the arts. He sharply distinguished between political power and cultural greatness in a nation, and said that typically periods of cultural achievement have been periods of political decline. He wrote that the last great epoch in Europe was the Italian Renaissance, which took place in a region that was politically fragmented and weak. By contrast, the new and powerful German Reich represented everything Nietzsche considered bad about political power and its effect on individual expression.

Nietzsche was a highly experimental thinker, in both the form and the content of his writing. In the development of his literary style and philosophical ideas he was engaged in ceaseless "self-overcoming," as he called it, never content to rest with what he had been doing but constantly testing, questioning, and setting things in new perspectives. Nietzsche began in his earliest books by writing sustained essays. From there he went on to experiment with writings that were collections of "aphorisms," as he called them, and he became a master of the highly polished sentence and short paragraph. (Strictly speaking, aphorisms are typically very short, succinct sayings, whereas Nietzsche's "aphorisms" are everything from that to very long paragraphs.) In the works of his most fruitful period (1886–88), Nietzsche wrote books that were unified and connected collections of long and short aphorisms and, in the case of *The Genealogy of Morals*, of short essays.

As *Twilight of the Idols* demonstrates, Nietzsche's experimentalism means that he was never a "systematic" thinker, but that does not mean that his philosophical writings are incoherent. He adopted and experimented with styles of philosophical writing that were very different from the customary styles because of what he considered to be the bankruptcy of "philosophy as usual" and because these new styles best expressed what he believed philosophy to be: a problem-oriented approach to the basic issues that looks at everything from a variety of different angles and in as compressed a manner as possible. The philosophy that Nietzsche expressed through his experiments with style was also experimental, a series of "thought-experiments," and *Twilight* should be read with this stylistic intention kept in mind. The philosopher, Nietzsche believed, must be constantly willing to experiment with ideas, no matter how well-established or well-rewarded, and to question his or her own previous conclusions. This approach, he said, is true science (the German word for science, *Wissenschaft*, refers to all forms of systematic, reasoned inquiry, from classical philology to physics): the "gay science" of cheerful but rigorous experimentation, holding everything up ceaselessly to investigation.

Like Dostoevsky, Nietzsche is considered one of the precursors of the existentialist movement in philosophy. The existentialists emphasized individual human existence in all its "lived" concreteness, the limitations of reason, the decisive role of freedom or choice in human life, the fundamental role emotions play in how humans deal with life, the difference between "authentic" and "inauthentic" living, and the importance of the individual coming to grips with the fact that he or she will die. These emphases led the existentialists to be vigorous critics of the tradition of Western rationalism and particularly the Enlightenment's boundless faith in reason.

Nietzsche's experimental approach to ideas was also an "existential" one. For Nietzsche, experimenting with ideas involved testing them in one's own life—"living" them. Experimenting to get at truth means calling into question, and with an open mind, one's own taken-for-granted ideas, values, and beliefs. His powerful attack on Christianity was a precursor to the criticisms of conventional religion advanced by both religious and non-religious existentialists. Nietzsche was also characteristically "existentialist" in writing as an individual for other discerning individuals, confronting his readers in an effort to shock them into awareness, requiring his readers to think for themselves about the most fundamental issues of Western civilization and their own life. At the same time, there are certainly aspects of his thought that are *not* "existentialist." His criticism of Christian-based morality in favor of a moral relativism, his apparent denial of free will, and, finally, his insistence that the healthy-minded person is not preoccupied with death but only with life, run counter to the existentialist emphases on ethics, freedom of choice, and the awareness of death as integral to life. Nietzsche's earlier writings are the most experimental. In them we find a subtlety, an openness to looking at everything in both a positive and negative light, even a kind of tentativeness, a "holding in suspension," that we do not find in the later works. Out of the earlier works hypotheses emerged that later became his key ideas, and he worked out the implications of those ideas in such books as *Twilight of the Idols*. In these later works Nietzsche is more unqualifiedly assertive, and he trims everything down to what he considers to be its essential elements.

Christian belief and morals, modern philosophy, the belief in progress, and popular ideas in modern politics—these were some of the great "idols" that Nietzsche sounded out—"touched with a hammer as with a tuning fork"—in books such as *Twilight of the Idols* and found to be hollow. As his German title, *Götzendämmerung*, a play on the title of Wagner's opera *Götterdämmerung* ("Twilight of the Gods") indicates, Nietzsche saw the reality and power of these foundational values as "dying" or fading into twilight in his own time, being challenged by the sciences and, through a variety of causes, progressively losing their hold on the consciousness of the Western world. Most people (including most philosophers) in the late nineteenth century were unaware or only dimly aware of it, but this fundamental upheaval in knowledge and values was taking place and its implications for the human future were fraught with both profound danger and extraordinary possibility. Nietzsche saw the internal contradictions produced in the modern West by this process as erupting into conflicts on an unprecedented scale in the twentieth century. At the same time, he saw himself as a herald of a time when out of the individual and social disintegration and chaos of his own day humans would create new, life-affirming values.

The original title of *Twilight* was "The Idle Hours of a Psychologist." Nietzsche often called himself a "psychologist," and his penetrating psychological insights (which Sigmund Freud, for example, clearly recognized as such) were central to his thought. He changed the title, but left a few references to the original title in the text of the book, which can be a bit confusing. For example, toward the end of the "Foreword," he writes, "This book too—the title gives it away—is above all a recovery,

a sunny spot, a sidestep into a psychologist's idleness."[3] Peter Gast felt that the book needed a more "splendid" title, as befitted a work that in the "Foreword" Nietzsche called "a grand declaration of war." So Nietzsche came up with a title that, besides parodying a Wagnerian opera title, conveyed his belief that the ideas and values that most people have long taken for granted as permanent and fundamental are actually only human constructions.

The "Foreword" makes it clear that idols are the main topic of the book. In the Bible, idols are created things that are worshipped as gods, but are not really God. Nietzsche uses the term more broadly to suggest that most of what humans believe are illusions, and destructive ones at that. In the book he "sounds out" the great idols that have been worshipped by human civilization—and specifically in their Western versions—examining and exposing them for what they are and what they express about human life. Sounding out idols is simply another way of talking about the revaluation of all values. And what are the great idols Nietzsche sounds out? The beliefs about God (yes, for Nietzsche even God—especially God—is an idol), morality, philosophy, language, science, human nature, and psychology that have shaped and dominated the Western world and therefore who we are. Nietzsche also speaks in the "Foreword" of his "cheerfulness." He sees himself as a "happy warrior" battling on behalf of life and its affirmation, and not a gloomy pessimist just saying "No" to everything. The "Foreword" also provides a good example of the way in which Nietzsche uses certain metaphors for dramatic effect. When he speaks of "war," he simply means conflict generally—in this case intellectual conflict—which he considers essential to a robust life.

The first section of *Twilight*, "Maxims and Arrows," reveals Nietzsche as a master at writing those short, highly compressed statements we have noted and that we call proverbs or aphorisms. His aim, he says, is "to say in ten sentences what everyone else says in a book. . . ." Some of his most famous aphorisms are in "Maxims and Arrows," such as number 8: "What does not kill me makes me stronger." The aphorisms of "Maxims and

---

[3]Ibid, 3.

Arrows" anticipate much of what is to come in the remainder of the book.

Let us consider a few highlights from the book: "The Problem of Socrates" starts the reader right off with a startling revaluation of an icon of Western civilization: by making an idol of reason and setting it over against instinct and passion, says Nietzsche, Socrates showed that he was a symptom of decline or decadence in ancient Greece. Nietzsche then goes on to argue, in "'Reason' in Philosophy," that virtually all Western philosophers since Socrates and Plato have made an idol of their ideas or concepts, regarding them as true "reality" and this tangible physical world of the senses as merely "appearance." In "How the 'Real World' Became a Myth," under the heading "History of an Error," Nietzsche tells the story of Western thought as the gradual emergence from the idolatrous illusions of Platonism (the Forms) and Christianity (God) to the modern secular and scientific outlooks that take nature, this world of the senses, as the truly real and reject the construction of purely abstract worlds beyond this one. Thus, he says, what began as the so-called "real world" of abstract ideas has in modern times increasingly become a myth, and the world of appearance has become the only reality we know.

In "Morality as Anti-Nature," Nietzsche succinctly states his criticism of almost all moral codes ever adhered to by human societies: they are literally "unnatural," demanding the suppression or denial of our natural instincts and passions instead of building positively on them and creatively sublimating or "spiritualizing" them. In section 4, Nietzsche singles out Christianity for special criticism as an extreme example of anti-natural morality, contrasting its understanding of love with what he regards as a healthy, life-affirming idea of love. He also observes—and this looks forward to the next part, on "The Four Great Errors" —that attitudes of people toward life are not objective truths but simply symptoms of either "health" (life-affirmation) or "sickness" (life-denial or decadence).

In "The Four Great Errors," Nietzsche describes four "idols" or illusions of the human race, all of which have to do with our judgments about the relationship between cause and effect: (1) mistaking causes for consequences ("Believe in God/obey the moral law, and it will make you happy");

(2) false causality (believing that human motives and decisions actually cause things to happen); (3) imaginary causes (ascribing feelings of well-being or suffering to God, evil spirits, faith, sin, etc.); and (4) free will (which was invented as an excuse to blame and punish people). In section 8 of "The Four Great Errors," we see a good statement of Nietzsche's naturalism: there is nothing but nature or the universe, with humans as one of its myriad manifestations, and nature is a process that is "innocent" and without ultimate purpose.

"The 'Improvers' of Mankind" is a continuation of Nietzsche's critique of traditional morality. Moral judgments are only symptoms or expressions of "ascending" or "declining" life, expressed differently in different human cultures; they have no objective validity. In this section, Nietzsche articulates his distinction, which he expresses at length in his book, *The Genealogy of Morals*, between "master" or "noble" morality and "slave" morality: the former values flow spontaneously from the strong and life-affirming; the latter arise from resentment of the strong by the weak and life-denying. Christianity, he argues, is a supreme example of slave morality.

In "What the Germans Lack," Nietzsche reflects on the negative effects the unification of Germany and the flexing of its muscles as a new great power in Europe have had. Germany, he says, used to be famous for its culture—its literature, thought, music, and art—during the age of the German Renaissance, but with political power its culture has sharply declined. "Power," he asserts, "makes stupid." He generalizes with the observation that there is always an incompatibility between political power and cultural greatness. (Since Elizabethan England would seem to be a counter-example, perhaps one should treat Nietzsche on this, and on other points, with the same skepticism that he enjoins upon his reader when considering other matters). Nietzsche's observations on what a university education ought to be and do (sections 6–7) may lead the reader to evaluate Nietzsche's comments in light of the reader's own experience of a university education.

In "Expeditions of an Untimely Man," Nietzsche includes miscellaneous reflections on important thinkers and writers of the nineteenth century and also on topics such as art and beauty, freedom, ethics, Darwinism, capitalism, democracy, and socialism. Among a few highlights: Nietzsche indicates in this part of the book what sort of writers and thinkers he admires and what sort he dislikes. He could be sarcastically critical of the English, and here he singles out prominent figures such as John Stuart Mill, George Eliot, and Thomas Carlyle. The section on George Eliot is a good statement of Nietzsche's view that you cannot, like George Eliot and many other nineteenth-century skeptics, reject Christianity and still consistently affirm Christian morality. By contrast to the English writers he mentions, Nietzsche admires the influential American essayist Ralph Waldo Emerson. In Section 17, Nietzsche describes the sort of persons he admires, which may illuminate aspects of his philosophy that we have laid out earlier. In sections 19 and 20, he discusses the categories of "beautiful" and "ugly." In these sections, and also in "Anti-Darwin," he hints at his emerging doctrine of the will to power, which includes an interesting criticism of Darwin. Nietzsche's discussion of the "natural value of egoism" in section 33, and his longer discussion of "whether we have grown more moral" in section 37 are examples of his "revaluation." His answer to the question that he raises in section 37 is definitely "No," and here he speaks critically of modern movements such as socialism and feminism as expressing human weakness and decline rather than strength. Nietzsche expresses his admiration for Dostoevsky in section 45, and in section 49 for Goethe, "the last German before whom I feel reverence."

Finally, in "What I Owe to the Ancients," Nietzsche summarizes what he has learned and appropriated from the ancient Greeks and Romans. Sharply rejecting the idolatry of reason that began with Socrates and Plato, Nietzsche identifies himself with the "Dionysian" spirit that animated earlier Greek culture and found artistic expression in Greek tragic drama. "Affirmation of life even in its strangest and sternest problems, the will to life rejoicing in its own inexhaustibility through the sacrifice of its highest types—that is what I called Dionysian. . . ." The god Dionysus has become the symbol for Nietzsche's whole philosophical outlook so that Nietzsche calls himself "the last disciple of the philosopher Dionysus. . . ."

The breadth of Nietzsche's genius and the range of his thought are considerable. He is best known as a philosopher who did not write in the usual manner of philosophers. But he was also a penetrating psychologist whose insights anticipated those of Sigmund Freud; a classical philologist (scholar of ancient Greek and Roman language and culture) who made original contributions to the interpretation of ancient Greek culture and its arts; a literary and art critic and cultural analyst; and a better-than-average musician and composer who helped the composer Richard Wagner establish the Bayreuth Music Festival in Germany, which continues to this day. Nietzsche also put the German language to use with a freshness, inventiveness, and clarity that have caused his leading translators and interpreters to regard him as one of the greatest writers of the German language. The flourishing of scholarship on and attention to Nietzsche's thought over the past forty years or so has enabled us to realize how remarkably his thought anticipated twentieth-century social and intellectual trends—from political trends and catastrophes such as world war to pragmatist and existentialist philosophies, philosophies of language, depth psychologies, and recent "post-modern" literary theories.

QUESTIONS FOR STUDY AND DISCUSSION

1. What was the "German Renaissance"?

2. What is the theme of Goethe's *Faust*? Why is it seen as a "central symbol of the modern world"?

3. How did Kant differ from both the rationalists and the empiricists?

4. How did Hegel interpret the progression of history?

5. What did Nietzsche mean by the revaluation of all values? What are some of the main values he revalues, and how does he deal with them?

6. Why was Nietzsche so critical of Christianity? What does Nietzsche think is wrong with Christianity? What value do you see in his criticisms?

7. Why does Nietzsche consider Socrates not truly "Greek"? What, according to Nietzsche, was Socrates' influence on later philosophers?

8. What is Nietzsche trying to show in "The History of an Error"? Does his characterization of Western intellectual development make sense on the basis of what you have read in works from Western civilization?

9. What, according to Nietzsche, are the "four great errors"? Give one example of each.

10. Nietzsche distinguishes between "freedom" and "free will." What does he mean by each, and what is the difference?

11. What is Nietzsche's criticism of morality as it is commonly understood and practiced? What would he substitute for it?

12. In what ways does Nietzsche say he is indebted to the ancient Greeks and Romans?

13. What does Nietzsche mean by calling himself a follower of Dionysus? Do you think the symbol of Dionysus expresses a positive or a negative outlook on the world?

SUGGESTIONS FOR FURTHER READING

Beiser, Frederick C. *Enlightenment, Revolution, and Romanticism: The Genesis of Modern German Political Thought*, 1790–1800. Cambridge, MA: Harvard University Press, 1992.

Blackbourn, David and Geoff Eley. *The Peculiarities of German History: Bourgeois Society and Politics in Nineteenth-Century Germany*. New York: Oxford University Press, 1985.

Danto, Arthur. *Nietzsche as Philosopher*. New York: The Macmillan Company, 1965.

Detwiler, Bruce. *Nietzsche and the Politics of Aristocratic Radicalism*. Chicago: The University of Chicago Press, 1990.

Furst, Lilian. *Romanticism in Perspective: A Comparative Study of Aspects of the Romantic Movement in England, France and Germany*. London: The Macmillan Company, 1979.

Gilman, Sander L. *Conversations with Nietzsche: A Life in the Words of His Contemporaries*. Translated by David J. Parent. New York: Oxford University Press, 1987.

Jaspers, Karl. *Nietzsche: An Introduction to the Understanding of His Philosophical Activity*. Translated by Charles F. Wallraff and Frederick J. Schmitz. Chicago: Henry Regnery Company, 1965.

Kaufmann, Walter. *Nietzsche: Philosopher, Psychologist, Antichrist*. New York: The World Publishing Company, 1950.

Nehamas, Alexander. *Nietzsche: Life as Literature*. Cambridge, MA.: Harvard University Press, 1985.

Nietzsche, Friedrich. *The Portable Nietzsche*. Selected and translated, with an Introduction, Prefaces, and Notes by Walter Kaufmann. New York: The Viking Press, 1954.

Tanner, Michael. *Nietzsche, A Very Short Introduction*. Oxford University Press, 2000.

Strong, Tracy. *Friedrich Nietzsche and the Politics of Transfiguration*. Expanded Edition. Berkeley and Los Angeles: University of California Press, 1988.

Talmon, Jacob L. *Romanticism and Revolt: Europe, 1815–1848*. London: Thames & Hudson, 1967.

CHAPTER ELEVEN

SLAVERY IN THE UNITED STATES:
W. E. B. DU BOIS

Probably no nation on earth better illustrates the contradictions of Western thought and history over the past two centuries than the United States. The fledgling country began as an experiment in enlightened thinking, a bold attempt to remove Locke's assertions of natural-born equality and the classical traditions of self-government from the realms of theory and memory and put them into actual practice. Within a century and a half of its founding, the United States had grown from a collection of English-speaking colonies huddled on the eastern coast of North America into a global empire, spanning not only the breadth of its home continent, but the far reaches of Alaska, the Caribbean and the Pacific Islands. Indeed, for many people living today, the nation's amazingly rapid rise to power and wealth, with institutions that serve as models for democracy worldwide, marks it as one of Western civilization's outstanding accomplishments.

If this is so, then the story of America's national expansion also exposes the inherent flaws of unrestrained growth, and perhaps even of democracy itself. When the federal government of the United States was established, more people were excluded from citizenship within its body politic than were included. Women were denied the right to vote, as were Native Americans, and for that matter, most white males, since the majority of states imposed property qualifications that gave full political rights only to men of wealth. As the United States conquered new territory in the nineteenth century, more dark-skinned peoples joined the nation—western Indians, Hispanics, Asians—all of them contributing to the rich diversity of languages, religions and customs that makes America a unique place. The challenge of the American experience has been to reconcile abstract theories about democracy and equality for all with the actual realization of those values as the country has grown to absorb more peoples under its banner than the founders of the republic ever intended or even thought possible. Meeting that challenge has been a process of conflict, so much so that it is fair to say that the American Revolution still has not ended. Women, racial minorities, Jews, and working-class Euro-Americans have fought long, hard struggles to complete those promises that the revolutionaries of 1776 left unfulfilled. African Americans often have been in the forefront of that revolution, first in their efforts to eradicate slavery and later in their campaigns for equal civic and social rights.

The African-American experience in America has its roots in slavery. White Americans were not alone in their use of slave labor, nor were they the first to try it. Human slavery dates back to ancient times; the Greeks and Romans held slaves, as did Native Americans and Africans themselves. What made the American version of slavery unique was its scope and racially based nature. Whereas most ancient cultures saw a slave owner holding only a handful of slaves, mostly as household servants, slavery as practiced in the United States resulted in huge plantations where hundreds of persons worked in bondage to produce agricultural commodities like tobacco and cotton. Greco-Roman law recognized the slave's legal status as a human being, but in the American version, slaves enjoyed no legal rights and could be bought, sold, or even killed in most cases by their owners, who regarded them as property and nothing more. The first

African slaves arrived in Virginia as early as 1619, and within two centuries the United States had become the largest slave-owning country in the western hemisphere. The profits that slave labor generated allowed for the emergence in the South of a genteel class of political and economic leaders who used their power and influence in the state and federal governments to thwart any suggestion that slavery should be reformed or abolished, or that African-American rights should be recognized in any way.

Although few people of European descent believed African Americans to be their racial equals, there had always been many Western thinkers and reformers who thought slavery an abomination and committed themselves to ending it. Britain especially, influenced by political liberalism, saw the rise of a vigorous abolitionist movement. During the course of the nineteenth century, Britain applied economic pressure against slave-owning countries in the Caribbean and Latin America—an ironic policy, since Britain simultaneously pursued racist and imperialist policies in its own African and Indian colonies. The role of African Americans themselves in ending slavery should not be forgotten. Violent slave rebellions were common occurrences, and the refusal of slaves to remain shackled, combined with international sanctions, encouraged the gradual end of legal slavery in Cuba, Brazil and other countries throughout the world.

In the United States, abolitionism never attained a power comparable to that of its equivalent in Britain, but its chief proponents did contribute to a shift of public opinion, at least in the North. Slavery had developed along regional lines; plantation agriculture and its slave system dominated the South, whereas northern states became more reliant on capitalist wage labor. Abolitionists like Frederick Douglass, a former slave himself, and Harriet Beecher Stowe held northern whites spellbound relating the horrors of the South's "peculiar institution." The election of Abraham Lincoln in 1860 brought to the presidency a candidate who opposed the expansion of slavery into newly acquired western territories, leading to the secession of the southern states and the Civil War. This great conflict, which ultimately cost the lives of more than half a million Americans, had a number of complex causes, division over the slavery issue being only one of them. But a major consequence of the war was the end of legalized slavery. On January 1, 1863, Lincoln's "emancipation proclamation" freed all slaves then living in states held by the Confederacy. Lincoln's decision had less to do with humanitarianism than with military necessity, because he hoped to encourage African-American freedmen to abandon their plantations and flock to Union army lines. Thousands of slaves already had done this, but after emancipation, African-American men enlisted in the United States Army in such numbers that they comprised ten percent of its manpower during the last two years of the war, thus tipping the scales in the North's favor. By mid-1865, the Confederacy lay defeated, and a new era of opportunities seemed to await four million African Americans.

RECONSTRUCTION

Following the end of the Civil War there was a period known as Reconstruction which lasted until 1877. Northern politicians debated the best means to re-incorporate the southern states into the federal government and what assistance to provide the recently freed former slaves. By 1870, Congress had approved and the states had ratified three constitutional amendments (the thirteenth, fourteenth, and fifteenth) that outlawed slavery and granted to freedmen (only males) the full rights of citizenship, including suffrage. Congress also established the Freedmen's Bureau, which helped to build African-American schools, translated legal documents for the illiterate, and provided a number of services to help African Americans with the transition to freedom. But the commitment of northern whites to African-American advancement had definite limits. Most believed that emancipation meant African Americans now had a fair place at the starting line when it came to competing for economic and social progress, unaware of or apathetic toward the ways in which slavery's legacies continued to cripple the chances African Americans had for better lives. Since most African Americans had few skills other than as agricultural workers, many returned to their old plantations to work as sharecroppers, renters who farmed land they did not own and paid their landlords in crops or cash after the harvest. Sharecropping became an oppressive system in which African Americans (and often poor whites) remained in perpetual debt to landowners. Freedmen also lived in terror of the Ku Klux Klan, a secret society of former Confederates who terrorized African Americans into submission through violence, burning schools and churches, and scaring freedmen away from voting places. Until 1877, the Union Army, which still maintained several regiments in the South, kept much of white southerners' hostility toward African-American rights in check. This changed, however, with the disputed presidential election of 1876. The Republican candidate, Rutherford B. Hayes, despite having lost the popular vote, was given the electoral votes needed to win the presidency by the opposing, southern-based Democratic Party. In return, Hayes agreed to remove all remaining Union troops from the South.

The official end of Reconstruction reversed many of the gains that African Americans had begun to realize. Abandoned by their northern protectors, African Americans now faced an onslaught of discriminatory laws designed to revoke their status as free people by circumventing the thirteenth, fourteenth and fifteenth amendments. Southern states passed a number of initiatives in the late 1800s known as "Jim Crow laws" that stripped away African-American political rights. Along with poll taxes and grandfather clauses that excluded most African Americans from voting, other measures mandated social segregation by forcing African Americans to ride in separate street cars and eat in separate restaurants, refusing them service in theatres, schools, and hospitals defined as "white," along with a host of other laws that prevented interracial mingling. African-American leaders looked to the federal government in the hope that such laws would be ruled unconstitutional, but in the 1896 *Plessy* v. *Ferguson* case, the United States Supreme Court decided that the establishment of "separate but equal" facilities remained a prerogative of the state governments. Racial violence against African Americans rose dramatically; between 1865 and 1945, more than five thousand African-American men—approximately sixty per year—were lynched by white mobs. Lynching even became a grotesque form of public entertainment in the South, where white families would sometimes travel for miles to watch such events and occasionally even took souvenirs from the victim's corpse afterwards. As of 1900, African Americans had won their legal freedom and a number of "paper rights" but little else, and constituted an inferior social caste in a nation whose official ide-

ology denied the existence of natural-born inequalities. African Americans would use a dual approach in trying to improve their situation, combining certain Western ideas with their own African-based culture and spiritual beliefs.

AMERICAN RACISM

Even in the twenty-first century, foreign observers often are struck by the persistence of racism in the United States. The pattern is an old one; in the 1830s, the French traveler Alexis de Tocqueville remarked on the amazing degree of egalitarian belief among white Americans, where men of the lower classes—unlike workers in Europe—acknowledged no social superiors, but then expressed outrage at the idea of African-American equality with whites. Historians and philosophers have puzzled over this paradox. Some have been quick to describe slavery and racism as exceptions, minor aberrations in an otherwise unbroken trend toward equality and democracy, while others claim that the competing strands of racism and equality are interrelated and in fact were defined simultaneously. The historian Edmund Morgan, in his book *American Slavery, American Freedom*, contends that acceptance of slavery and a consequent belief in African-American inferiority by the United States' founders made possible their beliefs about equality within the white race. As of the late eighteenth century, terms such as "equality" and "democracy" were as yet radical notions. American revolutionaries employed these terms conservatively, using them only to undermine the authority of monarchy and aristocratic privilege, not to assert a universal belief in the equality of all humankind. From the country's inception, "white" equality and freedom was necessarily qualified by, and even dependent on, the justified exploitation of those who were non-white, and subsequently, non-free.

Through the course of the nineteenth century, "whiteness" increasingly became a criterion for "Americanness." The 1790 Naturalization Act, which provided the legal means for foreign immigrants to become citizens, limited citizenship status only to men of the white race, deliberately excluding Indians and African Americans. The framers of this act probably expected that future migrants would come mostly from England. With the advent of the Industrial Revolution, however, the United States would attract immigrants from all of Europe, and all would eventually qualify for

Dear Friend,
   I am black.
   I am sure you did not realize this when you made/laughed at/agreed with that racist remark. In the past, I have attempted to alert white people to my racial identity in advance. Unfortunately, this invariably causes them to react to me as pushy, manipulative, or socially inappropriate. Therefore, my policy is to assume that white people do not make these remarks, even when they believe there are no black people present, and to distribute this card when they do.
   I regret any discomfort my presence is causing you, just as I am sure you regret the discomfort your racism is causing me.

Beginning in the 1970s, Adrian Piper made a series of performances based on her experiences as a light-skinned African American who is able to "pass" for white. In this work, an ongoing performance piece, Piper distributed her calling card whenever she encountered racist language or behavior. In this and other works, Piper highlights her own mixed heritage and her negotiations of identity definitions and politics.

Figure III-14   Adrian Piper, *My Calling (Card) #1*, 1986. Courtesy of Collection Davis Museum of Wellesley College, © Adrian Piper Research Archive.

membership in the new republic, provided they could legitimately claim themselves to be "white." In this manner, terms such as "white" and "African American," which carried no particular meaning or conveyed no special privilege in Europe and Africa, came to hold great significance in America.

The belief that human beings are easily divisible into categories called "races" received initial support from the physical and social sciences. In a corruption of Charles Darwin's biological theories about evolution, the doctrine of "racial Darwinism" held that human races evolve at different speeds, and that some races such as Africans bear a closer resemblance to humanity's primate ancestors than others. The eugenics movement, led by then-respectable thinkers like Lothrop Stoddard and Madison Grant, taught that human races can be arranged hierarchically with the white race at the peak. If whites wished to continue their ascendancy, warned the eugenists, they must refrain from mixing or interbreeding with inferior races. Ideas like these lent intellectual credence not only to the Jim Crow laws of the United States, but also to the imperialistic expansion of Western countries into Africa, Asia, India and other dark-skinned regions. Today, scientists generally concur that "race" is not

a category of biological science, while revelations of the horrors of the Nazi Holocaust and the later advances of the civil rights movement have—for the most part—repudiated racism as a way of thinking. But prior to the Second World War, racism offered a worldview that most whites found appealing, since it explained differences in technology and culture between diverse peoples and affirmed Western civilization's own sense of global superiority.

Such were the ideas that African Americans had to confront on their road toward freedom and justice. Contrary to slave owners' opinions that African Americans had no culture other than what they learned from whites, the first slaves brought from Africa a cosmology based on spirituality and animism, and these beliefs sustained them and their descendants through centuries of bondage. Unlike the rationalistic Western view, which sees a dichotomy between body and soul, traditional African religions taught the totality of human beings and their oneness with spirit and nature. When slaves awoke at dawn and declared, "I journeyed to Africa last night," they described not a simple dream, but a metaphysical projection in which the soul travels through the universe during the body's sleeping hours. Enslavement represented a limited, temporary condition, never able to constrain the person's true essence. Over time, slave culture combined native African beliefs with Western Christianity to produce a syncretistic "African-American" religion that borrowed selectively from Judeo-Christian traditions. The story of Moses leading his people out of slavery in Egypt, as told in the Book of Exodus, became a favorite in the slave cabins, immortalized in songs and prayers. Despite their hardships, slaves formed vibrant communities on the larger plantations, holding frequent celebrations, marrying and raising families, and developing communication networks in order to keep in touch with loved ones. Children separated from their parents by a sale would often be adopted by a relative or raised by the community, leading to a concept of "family" as one rooted in extended kinship or race rather than in a nuclear household.

Like white society, African-American society developed its own internal structure. When the Civil War began, nearly half a million free African Americans lived in the United States, having acquired their freedom through manumission or self-purchase. Mostly concentrated in urban areas, they formed the core of what became an African-American elite after emancipation, providing the leadership skills necessary to open and manage African-American schools, businesses, churches, newspapers and other institutions. During Reconstruction, when African Americans still enjoyed the right to vote, some African Americans won elected positions in state and federal governments. From this growing African-American middle class came the "race leaders" who experimented with various ways of combating discrimination and violence. The author and journalist Ida B. Wells, for example, led a decades-long battle to end southern lynchings. Others believed that the future of the African-American race lay in its complete separation from whites. Colonization advocates like Henry Turner and Benjamin Singleton raised money to establish all-African-American communities, either in the American West or in Africa. Although thousands of African Americans did depart the South in the late 1800s, the majority did not relocate to northern and western cities until the twentieth century. In the meantime, most African Americans and southern whites lived segregated but parallel lives in towns and rural hinterlands, neither group affording the luxury of complete isolation from the other.

BOOKER T. WASHINGTON

The mutual destiny of whites and African Americans in rebuilding the southern economy became a major theme in the teachings of Booker T. Washington, undoubtedly the most significant African-American leader at the turn of the twentieth century. Born a slave in Virginia in 1856 (d. 1915), Washington received his education at the Hampton Institute, became a teacher, and in 1881 opened the Tuskegee Institute in Alabama. In keeping with the principles he learned at Hampton, Washington—who considered himself a realist—placed little emphasis on classical education; his curriculum offered little in the way of history, sociology or any of the humanities and social sciences. Instead, Tuskegee taught "practical" skills commensurate with the types of work that African Americans would be likely to find: carpentry, mechanics, agriculture, domestic service, and others relevant for specific trades. Washington's educational goals emanated from his larger vision for the future of the African-American race. Historians have characterized his approach as "accommodationist," meaning he believed that African Americans of his time should adapt to the realities of segregation. Rather than confront whites' racism and attempt to compete with them on their terms, African Americans should practice racial uplift from within, elevating themselves through proficiency in farming and other artisan labor so they could become economically independent. Washington offered an approach to African-American advancement that appeared non-threatening to white interests, summarized in his speech to the Atlanta Exposition in 1895: "In all things that are purely social we can be as separate as the five fingers, yet one as the hand in all things essential to mutual progress." Leaders of both races responded positively to his message, donating huge sums of money to Tuskegee and other African-American schools based on the Tuskegee model. Through his control of various newspapers and businesses and his ability to earn the trust of whites, Washington ruled African-American society by the early 1900s nearly as a dictator, obtaining and deciding African-American appointments to government and academic positions and raising funds for African-American causes.

Yet not all African Americans endorsed Washington's leadership. Northern, middle-class African Americans like W.E.B. Du Bois rebuked his emphasis on trade and agricultural work at a time when the United States was becoming more urban and factory labor was replacing skilled craftsmanship. As Du Bois would write in *The Souls of Black Folk*, Washington had taught his people to set their sights too low, striving to become farmers and servants when they could be competing in the professions. Other African-American reformers believed that Washington had sacrificed his moral authority in accepting the Jim Crow laws and in not publicly condemning lynchings. Few people knew at the time that Washington had worked anonymously to try to establish anti-lynching laws; a genuine Machiavellian, he could present an accommodating image to whites while keeping his true convictions private. But the critique of Washington's approach has merit, especially when seen within its limits as a class-based philosophy rather than a race-based one. Washington knew personally the experience of slavery, having come from a rural southern setting where the immediate daily problems of African Americans involved economic needs rather than social acceptance by whites. As more African Americans gained formal education, entered the middle class, and settled in urban areas, new approaches to civil rights that would address their needs inevitably formed. Although racial solidarity has been a strong and continuing feature of African-American history, African-American society has developed such a diversity of classes, subcultures, and perspectives that it is impossible for the views of any one African American to represent them all.

Thus the publication of Du Bois's *The Souls of Black Folk* in 1903 occurred in the midst of an oppressive racial era, and at a time when some African Americans were preparing to wrest control of the leadership of African-American society from the powerful "Wizard of Tuskegee." Both the author and the work are revolutionary in two ways: Du Bois dared to challenge the dominant racism of the time by asserting the dignity of African-American culture, and he also challenged the nation's foremost African-American spokesperson, Booker T. Washington, by advocating a new direction and a new set of goals for African Americans. Du Bois's approach gradually supplanted Washington's. Civil rights leaders of the 1960s such as Martin Luther King, Jr., and Jesse Jackson have tended to focus more on the attainment of political rights and the end of discriminatory social practices than on racial uplift and economic autonomy. The twentieth cen-

tury also witnessed an increase in African-American nationalism, evident in the success of men like Marcus Garvey and Malcolm X, who taught African Americans to embrace their African cultural heritage. The collapse of imperialist empires after the Second World War drew increased attention to the plight of peoples and nations of

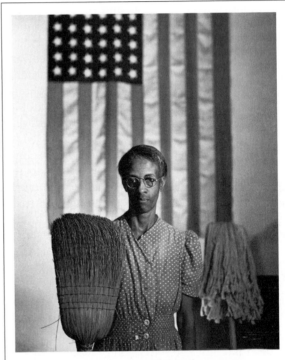

Gordon Parks spent a lifetime breaking down racial barriers. He was the first black photographer to work for the Farm Security Administration and for *Life* and *Vogue* magazines, and the first black film producer and director to work for a major studio. *American Gothic*, the first photograph he took after moving to Washington, D.C., is a product of Parks' negotiations of racial boundaries. Angry after a day of experiencing racial prejudice in stores and restaurants, Parks snapped the photograph of Ella Watson, a woman who had mopped floors for the government her whole life. Posed with her mop and broom in front of the American Flag, Ella Watson provides a stark contrast to Grant Wood's idyllic *American Gothic* of 1930. While Wood praises the hard-working, independent farmers as the American dream made good, Parks wryly reminds his viewer of the inequities of that dream.

Figure III-15   Gordon Parks, *American Gothic*, 1942. Courtesy of Gordon Parks/Corbis.

color on a global scale, so that African Americans discovered common interests with native Africans, Indians, Latinos and others who have endured the effects of racism. Likewise, white scholars and reformers have discovered in the writings of Du Bois and his successors a useful corrective to once unquestioned claims about universal progress, as well as the usefulness of incorporating minority perspectives in any discussion about the Western tradition and its significance.

W. E. B. DU BOIS

Through a life that spanned nearly a century, William Edward Burghardt Du Bois (1868–1963) served as the leading intellectual champion for a civil rights revolution, even though his privileged background made him a rather unrepresentative candidate to speak for African-American society. Born in Great Barrington, Massachusetts, Du Bois was descended from free African Americans of French and Haitian ancestry. Unlike his ideological rival Washington, neither Du Bois nor his parents had personal experience with slavery. William's childhood in liberal New England was spent among abolitionists, middle-class African Americans like his own family, and whites sympathetic to African-American rights. Few people of any race in the late nineteenth century had the educational opportunities that Du Bois had as a young man, having graduated from Fisk University, later obtaining a Ph.D. from Harvard, and then studying history and sociology in Berlin, Germany on a postdoctoral fellowship. By the age of thirty, Du Bois was already an internationally known scholar; his dissertation on the Atlantic slave trade and his first major study on the African-American community in Philadelphia marked him as a promising young authority on social and racial issues. As one who had traveled and read extensively, Du Bois learned to approach the subject of race on a comparative and historical basis, fascinated and curious about the relative freedom and acceptance that he as a African-American man enjoyed in Europe as compared to the oppression of his home country.

Du Bois's musings on the peculiar dilemma of race in the United States became more personal and urgent because of two crises in 1899. While teaching at Atlanta University, Du Bois was shocked by the ghastly murder of a local African-American farmer named Sam Hose. Two thousand screaming whites gathered on the outskirts of Atlanta, Georgia to lynch Hose and burn and mutilate his body. Du Bois, of course, had always known of such incidents, but, having been raised in the North, he had been relatively sheltered from the extremes of violence and bigotry that southern African Americans faced daily. After passing a storefront where the murdered Hose's knuckles were prominently displayed, Du Bois wrote that he "could not be a calm, cool, and detached scientist" any longer. The second event, only a month later, shook him more deeply; when his two-year old son, Burghardt Jr., contracted diptheria and died because of inadequate treatment created by Atlanta's segregated system of medical care. Du Bois would deal with Burghardt's death and his family's own private grief in *The Souls of Black Folk* four years later. These tragedies moved Du Bois from the role of objective scholar to passionate reformer; like Karl Marx, his subsequent intellectual activity would not be simply studying society and culture, but making sharp recommendations for changing it in order to achieve justice.

For several months, Du Bois traveled the rural South, interviewing former slaves, studying sharecropping, and recording African-American prayers and songs, all as part of his research for *The Souls of Black Folk*. Its publication in 1903 further established Du Bois as one of the premier writers of his time. It was also during this period that his ideas about civil rights and African-American advancement crystallized into a coherent philosophy that he called "the Talented Tenth." From his study of ancient civilizations and the dominant Hegelian theory of history with which he became enamored during his studies in Germany, Du Bois believed that all races and peoples advance through the leadership of an elite corps within their ranks that comprises perhaps ten percent of the whole; hence the term "talented tenth." Given the proper encouragement and opportunity, this talented corps of businessmen, statesmen, academics, journalists and other professionals would lead the African-American race to greatness. This particular part of Du Bois's thinking provided his major source of contention with Booker Washington, whose educational goals Du Bois believed would lead African Americans into a permanent state of mediocrity rather than allowing the brightest individuals to reach their potential. In order for this small class of elites to progress, legal and social barriers based on race would have to be eliminated, thus demanding a confrontation with white racism.

Between 1903 and 1910, Du Bois spoke for the growing cadre of African-American professionals who considered themselves "talented tenth" material, men and women who grew more vocal in their criticism of and disappointment with Washington's leadership. Recognizing his competition, Washington shrewdly offered Du Bois a teaching position at Tuskegee, probably in an effort to co-opt the radical young professor, but Du Bois with equal shrewdness refused the offer. Du Bois relocated to New York and became active in the growing Niagara Movement, the first serious attempt since Reconstruction to organize African Americans in defense of their civil rights. From this movement came the founding of the National Association for the Advancement of Colored People. The NAACP embraced the same constituents who had led the abolitionist movement—middle-class African Americans and northern white liberals—and in fact employed much of that earlier movement's rhetoric and tactics. Through the twentieth century, the NAACP worked for the basic realization of Du Bois's philosophy, raising money for African-American institutions, issuing legal challenges to discriminatory state and federal laws, and educating the white public about the harms of racism. It would be an NAACP victory in the 1954 U.S. Supreme Court case, *Brown* v. *Board of Education of Topeka, Kansas*, that launched a new stage of minority activism led by Martin Luther King, Jr., and others. Du Bois abandoned his teaching career to lend his strength and talents to the NAACP when he became editor of the organization's newspaper, *The Crisis*, which reported on the African-American community's fight against Jim Crow, lynchings, and other racial problems. As editor of *The Crisis* and as a distinguished scholar and orator, Du Bois created a body of ideas that lent themselves well to the growing civil rights revolution, just as Rousseau and Voltaire had done for the French Revolution and Locke for the American Revolution centuries earlier.

Born shortly after the end of slavery and living into the tumultuous 1960s, Du Bois witnessed many changes that caused him to expand, and at times to reassess, his thinking. African participation in the two world wars, and the frustrations that global conflict imposed on Western imperialism, energized Du Bois to help mobilize the *Pan-African Movement*. Through a series of international conferences beginning in the 1920s, Pan-Africanism tried to accomplish on a global scale what the NAACP had done on a national one: mobilize people of African descent the world over to liberate Africa from colonialism. As Du Bois came to see the plight of African Americans as part of a larger pattern of oppression by white countries, he moved surprisingly in the direction of a man whose ideas he had once disdained, namely, Booker T. Washington. More and more in his later years, Du Bois grew convinced that economic deprivation, rather than segregation and prejudice, was the chief obstacle to African-American progress. The Great Depression of the 1930s only solidified this belief. As his insistence that racial problems be studied within an economic and global context increased, Du Bois found himself at odds with the directors of the NAACP, who limited their efforts to political and legal rights for African Americans only. Citing personality and ideological differences, Du Bois resigned from *The Crisis* in 1934. Concern with economic inequalities also led to his growing attraction to Marxism; during the early Cold War, when Americans endured persecution for expressing pro-Communist sympathies, Du Bois openly wrote of the advantages that Soviet Russia and Communist China had brought to people of color, wondering aloud if Marx's theories about capitalism and class revolution held some solutions for African-American advancement.

Despite the excellent health that he enjoyed into his nineties, Du Bois's last years were unhappy ones. Many of his former friends and colleagues had abandoned him during his dalliance with communism. Although he approved of Martin Luther King, Jr.'s Southern Christian Leadership Conference (about which Du Bois, a longtime agnostic, remained skeptical, since he had long discounted the significance of organized religion), Du Bois grew pessimistic about the prospect of African-American equality in the United States. Forsaking his American citizenship, he and his second wife moved to the newly independent African nation of Ghana during the last year of his life, and there he died on the night of August 27, 1963—the eve of the Great March on Washington and the delivery of King's famous "I Have a Dream" speech from the steps of the Lincoln Memorial.

DU BOIS'S LEGACY

It is difficult to classify Du Bois intellectually, because over the course of his long life, he experimented with every known idea or philosophy that had a chance of bettering the lives of people of color. He is best remembered as the author of *The Souls of Black Folk*, his most significant if not most representative work. Therefore, students are quick to categorize him as "the African-American author," as if his African Americanness says all that is relevant about him. In fact, Du Bois—like his writings, like most people—is complex. Although he consciously represented himself as a racial spokesperson for all African Americans, his class background also informs his thinking. Du Bois's critics often described him as an elitist, whose advocacy of "talented tenth" leadership and emphasis on obtaining theoretical rights over economic self-sufficiency helps upper- and middle-class minorities like himself more than the poor and uneducated. Today, most African-American leaders concede that ending racial discrimination has not been enough and that the African-American community's problems of poverty and unemployment demand new solutions for which the Du Boisian model of civil rights provides little guidance. An overview of his major book nevertheless reveals many of the important themes that African-American leaders have employed over the last century in ending Jim Crow and establishing a genuine "African-American" identity.

The Souls of Black Folk stands as Du Bois's masterpiece for the way in which it addresses questions of culture and sociology through an artistic, almost poetic writing style commonly used more in literature than in social science. As a student at Fisk University, Du Bois taught African-American children in rural Tennessee, observing firsthand the conditions of southern African Americans at the start of the Jim Crow era. These observations, combined with his later research, form the bulk of the text's subject matter. Rather than produce an analytical study, Du Bois used unforgettable descriptions of people he had known through his travels to expose the poverty and scarcity of opportunities for African Americans. The book consists of fourteen independent essays that explore interrelated topics: education, spirituality, white-African-American relations, psychology, economics, and so on. Most of the characters he describes are authentic; in some cases, such as in the chapter "Of the Coming of John," Du Bois creates fictional personages whom he uses as representatives of the African-American personality. This literary technique was used by many reform writers of his day, including Upton Sinclair and Willa Cather.

The framework of *duality* provides a useful way to interpret this text. In trying to link the internal conflicts that African Americans experience on a daily basis to larger racial trends, Du Bois employed the concept of dualism first on a personal, psychological level, and then on a grand social one. His first use of personal duality begins in Chapter One, "Of Our Spiritual Strivings," which he opens with the question, "How does it feel to be a problem?" Unlike whites, who are considered the "normal" race of America and so can sometimes afford to think in color-blind terms, African Americans can never forget their minority status, as they are reminded of it constantly by laws and customs. Consequently, they face psychological choices between multiple identities, part of what philosophers call "existential angst." For Du Bois, these choices break down to a dichotomous tension between race and nationality. Despite the oppression they have faced here, African Americans historically have been patriotic people, proud and supportive of their country's democratic and liberal traditions. Du Bois acknowledges this when he writes, "He [the African-American man] would not Africanize America, for America has too much to teach the world and Africa,"[1] and later, "there are today no truer exponents of the pure human spirit of the Declaration of Independence than the American Negroes."[2] Yet at the same time, none would "bleach his Negro soul in a flood of white Americanism, for he knows that Negro blood has a message for the world. He simply wishes to make it possible for a man to be both a Negro and an American . . . ."[3] Herein lies the key to what Du Bois claims as the central challenge for minority peoples:

---

[1]Du Bois, W. E. B. *The Souls of Black Folk* (New York: Dover Publications, In. 1994), 3.
[2]Ibid, 7.
[3]Ibid, 3.

the reconciliation of these apparently conflicting drives, one toward full equality in a modern republic, and the other toward preservation of a glorious African-American culture. When he writes, "One ever feels his two-ness—an American, a Negro; two souls, two thoughts, two unreconciled strivings; . . . The history of the American Negro is the history of this strife . . . ,"[4] Du Bois suggests that equality at the price of assimilation and loss of ethnic heritage would be disastrous, not only for African Americans, but for the American experiment at large.

Following his use of duality to describe the "double consciousness" of the African-American psyche, Du Bois broadens the concept in Chapter Two, "Of the Dawn of Freedom." This chapter opens with what is perhaps his most memorable and quoted statement: "The problem of the twentieth century is the problem of the color line—the relation of the darker to the lighter races of men in Asia and Africa, in America and the islands of the sea."[5] Writing this when the twentieth century was only three years old, Du Bois acted here as a prophet rather than a historian. It is odd that he introduces an idea of such global relevance in a chapter devoted to the origins of the Freedmen's Bureau. His phrase "the color line" becomes clearer in his later writings on imperialism and Pan-Africanism, although its inclusion in *The Souls of Black Folk* is significant in that he sees America's racial problems as an awful harbinger of things to come. "The color line" describes the stark separation between African Americans and whites that typified American society in 1903. Du Bois predicted that as the United States and other Western countries would expand in future decades, the color line would be expanded also. As Chinese, Filipinos, Hispanics, native Africans and others would endure similar systems of racial oppression that African Americans already had suffered for centuries, racism and racial warfare would overshadow all other problems. From a contemporary perspective, one may well conclude Du Bois was right, considering the twentieth century's nightmares of racial and ethnic genocide. Occasionally, as in Chapter Eleven, Du Bois uses the term "the Veil" synonymously with "the color line," again referring to the stark inequalities between whites and nonwhites.

Du Bois devotes most of the second chapter to a history of the Freedmen's Bureau. Here, he uses a traditional narrative approach to offer an interpretation of the Bureau and Reconstruction that for its time was highly controversial. History is far from an exact science, though it would be easier for students and teachers if it were; historians constantly debate the meanings and causes of certain events, and often their interpretations are employed, or in some cases even created, to affirm and legitimize certain political or social points of view. One hundred years ago, whites sympathetic to slavery and the southern cause dominated much of the historical writing on the Civil War and Reconstruction periods. In these interpretations, the Freedmen's Bureau was presented as an oppressive institution that elevated uneducated freedmen over whites, while Reconstruction itself was described as a failed social experiment in African-American equality. "Of the Dawn of Freedom" may be read as Du Bois's rebuttal to this overly negative appraisal by white historians. He emphasizes the Bureau's establishment of free African-American schools, peasant ownership of land, and suffrage rights that—had they been consistently enforced—would have hastened the freedmen toward equal citizenship. Most importantly, Du Bois explains the financial constraints under which the Bureau worked, suggesting that Reconstruction policies did not so much fail to produce African-American progress as they were not allowed to succeed, given their imposed limits.

Chapter Three contains Du Bois's assessment of Washington's leadership, the essay that helped to launch the Niagara Movement and that remains today a classic criticism of the racial uplift model. In a fair and even-handed manner, Du Bois gives Washington his proper due, complimenting him and the Tuskegee Institute for their many positive accomplishments. Drawing on his considerable knowledge of history, Du Bois then attacks with scathing language the older man's call for submission and his emphasis on material gains: "In the history of all other races and peoples the doctrine preached at such crises has been that manly self-respect is worth more than lands and houses, and that a people who voluntarily surrender such

---

[4]Ibid, 2.
[5]Ibid, 9.

respect, or cease striving for it, are not civilizing."[6] By refusing to resist bigoted measures that revoke political rights, African Americans not only suffer "civic death," but they lose whatever power they hold to protect the very trade skills and small businesses that Washington would have them acquire. Furthermore, in refusing to support higher education for African Americans, Washington fails to acknowledge that the very instructors who have made industrial-technical schools like Tuskegee successful in the first place were themselves graduates of upper-level African-American universities. Some of Du Bois's "talented tenth" ideas are evident here, as when he asks, "Is it possible . . . that nine millions of men can make effective progress in economic lines if . . . allowed only the most meager chance for developing their exceptional men?"[7] Essentially, Du Bois's critique amounts to a moral argument, claiming that any advances that African Americans might attain under accommodationism would be meaningless if they willingly concede their most fundamental right to political equality. By evoking the Declaration of Independence in his closing paragraph, he even contextualizes his ideas within the larger tradition of revolutionary resistance revered by African Americans and white Americans alike.

Du Bois elaborates on his ideas for African-American progress in chapters four through nine, in which he develops several interesting and original themes. First, his criticism of industrial training schools rests mostly on his perception that such institutions prepare African Americans to be little more than workers in a large capitalist machine. Contrary to Washington's assertion that cultivation of practical skills will lead to racial autonomy, Du Bois believes that an educational system that limits African Americans to manual labor only increases their economic dependence on white employers, essentially replacing the old system of legal slavery with a new type of wage slavery. Although he speaks primarily about African Americans' situation, his declared purpose for higher education as a tool for social change remains relevant for all per-

sons, especially a century later: "The function of the university is not simply to teach breadwinning, . . ."[8] and later, "The foundations of knowledge in this race, as in others, must be sunk deep in the college and university if we would build a solid, permanent structure."[9] Du Bois also expands his economic and social appraisal of the postwar South in these chapters. In his descriptions of the African-American Belt of Georgia and the nuances of sharecropping, he fills his text with personal vignettes of various individuals, both to personalize the subject matter and to establish his authenticity as a northern-born African-American man writing about southern conditions. Despite his emphasis on political advancement, Du Bois reveals his deep concern for the South's economic progress. Frequently, his writings show frustration with capitalism and Americans' obsession with money, a frustration that grew in later decades as Du Bois gradually embraced the cause of radical socialism.

The final chapters, ten through fourteen, are devoted to a discussion of the importance of religion in African-American life. Although Du Bois did not personally practice an organized faith, he understood its significance; in fact, the epigraph for each essay contains the bars of African-American spirituals, and he points to the "sorrow songs" in the concluding chapter as a vibrant illustration of African-American culture. Some scholars hold *The Souls of Black Folk* as a literary predecessor to the Harlem Renaissance of the 1920s, when African-American music, art, and literature flourished and made in-roads into white culture. Du Bois links the sadness and "blues" of the slavery and Jim Crow experiences to African Americans' spiritual and musical expressions, anticipating the many contributions that African Americans have made to American culture: "Our song, our toil, our cheer, and warning have been given to this nation in blood-brotherhood. Are not these gifts worth the giving? Is not this work and striving? Would America have been America without her Negro people?"[10] Du Bois's own personal sorrow song appears in

---

[6]Ibid, 30.

[7]Ibid, 31.

[8]Ibid, 52.

[9]Ibid, 66.

[10]Ibid, 163.

Chapter Eleven, perhaps the most moving essay of the book, titled "Of the Passing of the First-Born." Here the reader is privileged to see Du Bois' mournful lament for his deceased infant son, Burghardt Jr. Du Bois poignantly describes a father's love for the eldest child, love filled with hope and potential, looking forward to a life of pride in his offspring's accomplishments. Yet "the Veil" of American racism intrudes even on this most basic emotion, for soon his boy dies, deprived of adequate medical care, and Du Bois is left to await the day when the color line has no further power to separate parents from children: "Sleep then, child, sleep till I sleep and waken to a baby voice and the ceaseless patter of little feet—above the Veil."[11]

Published in the early twentieth century when the literacy rate among African Americans was rising dramatically, *The Souls of Black Folk* became a popular bestseller, read by whites as well as African Americans. Since 1903, the book has been translated into numerous languages and today is commonly assigned in college courses on race and African-American history. Many of Du Bois's other writings have gained international acclaim, read by schoolchildren as far away as China and Africa. As an early and prominent example of what later generations would call "African-American pride" literature, his text not only prepared the way for authors such as James Baldwin and Toni Morrison, but has helped to stimulate similar genres for other minority groups, for example, Latinos and Native Americans, which combine cultural descriptions and analyses with critiques of American society. For students being introduced to the Western canon, *The Souls of Black Folk* delivers a haunting exposé of the potential for racism and unrestrained capitalism to thwart democracy and equality, and of the ways in which people denied access to the traditional means of power resist those tendencies.

QUESTIONS FOR STUDY AND DISCUSSION

1. Describe the legal and economic barriers to African-American advancement at the turn of the twentieth century.

2. Compare and contrast the approaches of Booker T. Washington and W. E. B. Du Bois in their efforts to gain equal rights for African Americans. Whose approach do you think has prevailed today? What advantages and disadvantages has that approach brought?

3. Analyze Du Bois's usage of the term "the Veil." Does this concept explain the full nature of inequality in the United States? How does his class background combine with his racial identity to inform his ideas?

4. Du Bois claimed in 1903 that the problem of the twentieth century is the problem of the color line. Reviewing the history of the twentieth century from the present, do you think this prediction was accurate?

5. How does Du Bois both challenge and continue the ideas of earlier Western thinkers?

SUGGESTIONS FOR FURTHER READING

Du Bois, W. E. B. *Black Reconstruction in America*. New York: Maxwell Macmillan International, [1935], 1992.

————. *The World and Africa: An Inquiry into the Part Which Africa has Played in World History* (enl. ed., with new writings on Africa, 1955–1961). New York, International Publishers, 1965.

Franklin, John Hope and Alfred A. Moss, Jr. *From Slavery to Freedom: A History of African Americans*, 8th ed. New York: A.A Knopf, 2000.

Lewis, David Levering. *W.E.B. Du Bois: Biography of a Race, 1868–1919*. New York: Henry Holt and Company, 1993.

————. *W.E.B. Du Bois: The Fight for Equality and the American Century*. New York: Henry Holt and Company, 2000.

Meier, August. *Negro Thought in America, 1880–1915*. Ann Arbor: University of Michigan Press, 1988.

Washington, Booker T. *Up From Slavery*. William L. Andrews, editor. Oxford and New York: Oxford University Press, 1995.

---

[11]Ibid, 131.

Plate 17 Rosa Bonheur, *Plowering in the Nivernais: The Dressing of the Vines,* 1849. Oil on canvas, 5'9" × 8'8" (1.8 × 2.6 m). Musée d'Orsay, Paris. Courtesy of Erich Lessing/Art Resource, NY.

Plate 18 Édouard Manet, *Olympia,* 1863. Oil on canvas, 4'3" × 6'2¼" (1.31 × 1.91 m). Musée du Louvre, Paris. Courtesy of Erich Lessing/Art Resource, NY.

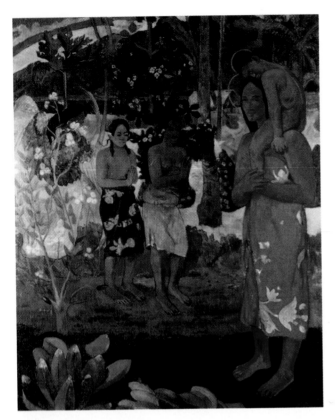

Plate 19 Paul Gauguin, *Ia Orana Maria (We Hail Thee Mary),* ca.1891–92. Oil on canvas, $44^3/_4 \times 34^1/_2$" (113.7 × 87.7 cm). The Metropolitan Museum of Art, New York. Courtesy of Francis G. Mayer/Corbis.

Plate 20 Henri Matisse, *The Joy of Life,* 1905–06. Oil on canvas, $5'8^1/_2$" × $7'9^3/_4$" (1.74 × 2.38 m). The Barnes Foundation, Merion, Pennsylvania. Courtesy of The Barnes Foundation, Merion Station, Pennsylvania/Corbis.

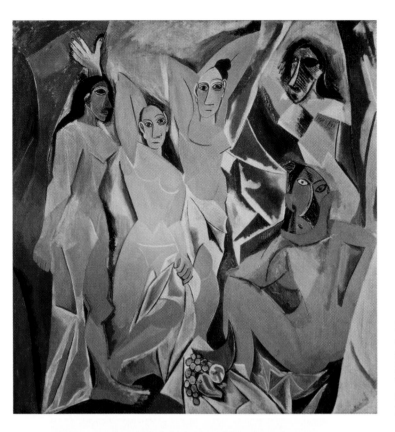

Plate 21 Pablo Picasso, *Les Demoiselles d'Avignon*, 1907. Oil on canvas, 8' × 7'8" (2.43 × 2.33 m). The Museum of Modern Art, New York. Courtesy of Lauros/Giraudon/ The Bridgeman Art Library International. Copyright © 2006 Estate of Pablo Picasso/Artists Rights Society (ARS), New York.

Plate 22 Thomas Eakins, *The Gross Clinic*, 1875. Oil on canvas, 8' × 6'5" (2.44 × 1.98 m). Jefferson Medical College of Thomas Jefferson University, Philadelphia. Courtesy of Geoffrey Clements/Corbis.

Plate 23 Claude Monet, *Gare St. Lazare, Paris,* 1877. Oil on canvas. (75.5 × 104 cm). Musée d'Orsay, Paris, France. Courtesy of Réunion des Musées Nationaux/ Art Resource, NY.

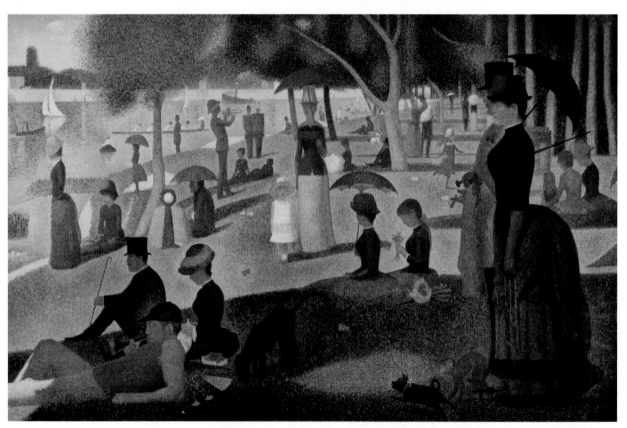

Plate 24 Georges Seurat, *A Sunday Afternoon on the Island of La Grande Jatte,* 1884–86. Oil on canvas, 6'9¹/₂" × 10'1¹/₄" (2.07 × 3.08 m). The Art Institute of Chicago. Courtesy of Bettmann/Corbis.

Plate 26 Hannah Höch, *The Beautiful Girl*, 1919–20. Photomontage. $13^3/_4 \times 11^7/_{16}''$ (35 × 29 cm). Private collection. Courtesy of the Granger Collection, NY.

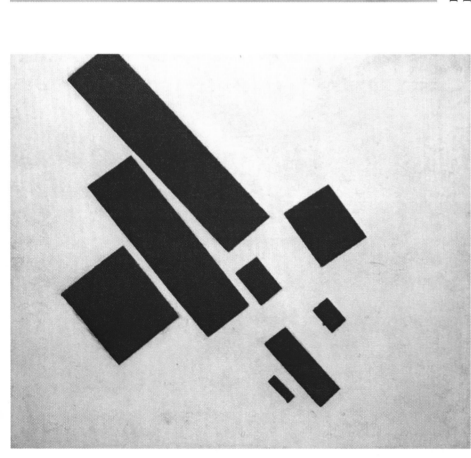

Plate 25 Kazimir Malevich, *Suprematist Painting (8 Red Rectangles)*, 1915. Oil on canvas, $22^1/_2 \times 18^7/_8''$ (57 × 49 cm). Stedelijk Museum, Amsterdam. Courtesy of Art Resource, NY.

Plate 27 Pablo Picasso, *Guernica,* 1937. Oil on canvas, 11'6" × 25'8" (3.5 × 7.8 m). Museo Nacional Centro de Arte Reina Sofia, Madrid. On permanent loan from the Museo del Prado, Madrid. Courtesy of Archivo Iconografico, S.A./Corbis. Copyright © 2006 Estate of Pablo Picasso/Artists Rights Society (ARS), New York.

Plate 28 John Steuart Curry, *Baptism in Kansas,* 1928. Oil on canvas, 40 × 50" (102.5 × 128 cm). Whitney Museum of American Art, New York. Courtesy of Geoffrey Clements/Corbis.

Plate 29 Jackson Pollock, *Autumn Rhythm (Number 30),* 1950. Oil on canvas, 8'9" × 17'3" (2.66 × 5.25 m). The Metropolitan Museum of Art, New York. Photograph © 2006 The Metropolitan Museum of Art, New York. © 2007 The Pollock-Krasner Foundation / Artists Rights Society (ARS), New York.

Plate 30 Andy Warhol, *Campbell's Soup Cans,* 1962. Synthetic polymer paint on 32 canvases, each 20" × 16". The Museum of Modern Art, New York. Digital image © The Museum of Modern Art/Courtesy of Scala/Art Resource, NY. Copyright © The Andy Warhol Foundation for the Visual Arts / Artists Rights Society (ARS), New York.

Plate 31 Bettye Saar, *The Liberation of Aunt Jemima.* 1972. Mixed media, 11³/₄ × 8 × 2³/₄". University Art Museum, University of California at Berkeley. Purchased with the aid of funds from the National Endowment for the Arts (selected by The Committee for the Acquisition of Afro-American Art). Photo by Benjamin Blackwell. Courtesy of University of California/Berkeley Art Museum and the artist.

WHEN RACISM & SEXISM ARE NO LONGER FASHIONABLE, WHAT WILL YOUR ART COLLECTION BE WORTH?

The art market won't bestow mega-buck prices on the work of a few white males forever. For the 17.7 million you just spent on a single Jasper Johns painting, you could have bought at least one work by all of these women and artists of color.

Bernice Abbott	Elaine de Kooning	Dorothea Lange	Sarah Peale
Anni Albers	Lavinia Fontana	Marie Laurencin	Ljubova Popova
Sofonisba Anguisolla	Meta Warwick Fuller	Edmonia Lewis	Olga Rosanova
Diane Arbus	Artemisia Gentileschi	Judith Leyster	Nellie Mae Rowe
Vanessa Bell	Marguérite Gérard	Barbara Longhi	Rachel Ruysch
Isabel Bishop	Natalia Goncharova	Dora Maar	Kay Sage
Rosa Bonheur	Kate Greenaway	Lee Miller	Augusta Savage
Elizabeth Bougereau	Barbara Hepworth	Lisette Model	Vavara Stepanova
Margaret Bourke-White	Eva Hesse	Paula Modersohn-Becker	Florine Stettheimer
Romaine Brooks	Hannah Hoch	Tina Modotti	Sophie Taeuber-Arp
Julia Margaret Cameron	Anna Huntingdon	Berthe Morisot	Alma Thomas
Emily Carr	May Howard Jackson	Grandma Moses	Marietta Robusti Tintoretto
Rosalba Carriera	Frida Kahlo	Gabriele Münter	Suzanne Valadon
Mary Cassatt	Angelica Kauffmann	Alice Neel	Remedios Varo
Constance Marie Charpentier	Hilma of Klimt	Louise Nevelson	Elizabeth Vigée Le Brun
Imogen Cunningham	Kathe Kollwitz	Georgia O'Keeffe	Laura Wheeling Waring
Sonia Delaunay	Lee Krasner	Meret Oppenheim	

Please send $ and comments to:
Box 1056 Cooper Sta. NY, NY 10276 **GUERRILLA GIRLS** CONSCIENCE OF THE ART WORLD

Plate 32 Guerrilla Girls, *When Racism and Sexism Are No Longer Fashionable, What Will Your Art Collection Be Worth?,* 1989. Poster. 17" × 22". Courtesy of www.guerrillagirls.com.

SECTION FOUR

THE EARLY TWENTIETH CENTURY AND WORLD WAR I

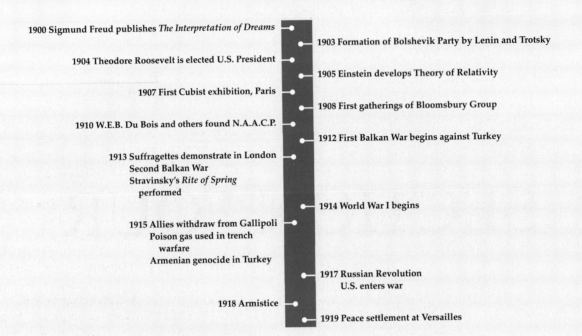

1900 Sigmund Freud publishes *The Interpretation of Dreams*

1903 Formation of Bolshevik Party by Lenin and Trotsky

1904 Theodore Roosevelt is elected U.S. President

1905 Einstein develops Theory of Relativity

1907 First Cubist exhibition, Paris

1908 First gatherings of Bloomsbury Group

1910 W.E.B. Du Bois and others found N.A.A.C.P.

1912 First Balkan War begins against Turkey

1913 Suffragettes demonstrate in London
Second Balkan War
Stravinsky's *Rite of Spring*
 performed

1914 World War I begins

1915 Allies withdraw from Gallipoli
Poison gas used in trench
 warfare
Armenian genocide in Turkey

1917 Russian Revolution
 U.S. enters war

1918 Armistice

1919 Peace settlement at Versailles

THE EARLY TWENTIETH CENTURY AND WORLD WAR I

It is sometimes said that the nineteenth century really ended, not in 1900, but in 1914. It was the First World War, which began in August of that year, that shattered the assumptions and institutions that had characterized the nineteenth century. The "Great War," as it was called, was a cataclysm that shook Western civilization to its foundations and produced fundamental changes in European life, thought, and art that shaped the cultural world we still inhabit. Reflective Europeans and many Americans who lived through World War I, whether as participants or observers, believed that Western civilization was on the brink of collapse. This is abundantly evidenced in biographies and autobiographies of writers, artists, historians, scientists, philosophers, and theologians writing after the war. Albert Schweitzer, the German physician and humanitarian, captured these feelings perfectly when he wrote in 1919: "we are living today under the sign of the collapse of civilization. There is a growing awareness of imminent ruin tantamount to a dread of the approaching end of all that makes life worthwhile."

The period of the last part of the nineteenth century and the opening years of the twentieth century was a "Golden Age" of European civilization. There had been no European-wide war since the Napoleonic Wars early in the nineteenth century (1806–15). The Enlightenment faith in progress and reason seemed triumphant. It was a time of remarkable scientific progress, the harnessing of electricity and of new inventions such as the telephone, movies, the phonograph, the automobile, and the airplane. The general standard of living was rising slowly but surely. Literacy was widespread in western and central Europe, and public education was becoming universal. It was also a period of significant social reforms: the movement for women's rights, the labor movement, and educational and penal reforms.

It was a rich and creative time for the arts throughout Europe. Composers including Wagner, Verdi, Brahms, and Tchaikovsky filled opera houses and concert halls with powerful and enduring music. The Impressionists and Post-Impressionists, including Monet, Renoir, Dégas, Gauguin, Van Gogh, and Cézanne, transformed the visual arts, ushering in what we call "modern art." Writers of the stature of Tolstoy and Dostoevsky, George Eliot and Charles Dickens, Emile Zola and André Gide, Thomas Mann and Rainer Maria Rilke, were laying bare the human psyche and modern society in new and penetrating ways. Great cities such as London, Paris, Vienna, and Berlin were world centers of high culture, new ideas, new invention, and prosperity.

Also remarkable, in view of the war that followed, is the fact that in the years preceding it the nations of Europe—particularly France, Germany, and Britain—had attained a level of economic integration that they would not achieve again until the 1960s. International trade flourished in a largely open world economy, and multinational ownership and interdependence in large industries such as iron and steel were the order of the day. Passports were almost unknown, and travelers and workers moved freely from one country to another. Expanded voting rights and organizations that employed lobbying, petitions, demonstrations, strikes, boycotts, and publications in promoting their cause became a familiar part of social and political life in the cities of Europe. A free press was emerging, especially in Britain and France, although its power to expose government wrongdoing and shape national opinion was still in its infancy.

While the causes of the Great War are complex, a conservative nationalism that expressed itself in competition for military domination and overseas empire played a major role. Within this context the unification of Germany in 1871, its rapid emergence as the leading industrial and military power on the Continent, and its desire to be a key player in European power politics were contributing factors that both disturbed and rearranged the balance of power in Europe.

The 1880s witnessed the rise of right-wing nationalism in European countries, and by the turn of the century it had become a powerful influence. The new conservative nationalisms provided a useful ideology to support the ambitions and the desire for self-preservation of the traditional political and military ruling classes in Europe as they witnessed a world in change. Not coincidentally, these years also produced the "new imperialism" among the great powers of Europe. Although the expansion of colonial empires did not have widespread public support, it had powerful spokesmen in high places, and with minimal public knowledge of and impact on foreign policy the new imperialism won the day.

European expansionism had begun with the voyages of discovery of the Renaissance period, and during the eighteenth century the British, French, Dutch, Spanish, and Portuguese had established colonial empires in parts of North, Central, and South America, the Caribbean islands, and trading outposts in Africa and Asia. During the latter part of the nineteenth century, however, European influence shifted rather suddenly from commercial domination to active conquest, political control, and exploitation of new territories. Between 1880 and 1914 the great powers of Europe—now joined by Germany—confronted and sometimes fought one another all over the world, as they competed for control of territory and resources in Africa, Asia, and the Middle East. During that period the entire continent of Africa, except for Liberia and Ethiopia, came under European control. The new imperialism created a legacy that dominated the history of much of Asia, Africa, and the Middle East until after World War II. The United States also dabbled in the new imperialism during the same period, gaining control of Cuba and the Philippines through war with Spain.

How did conservative European nationalists justify and defend the new imperialism? One prominent justification was a form of Social Darwinism: strong nations would survive in a competitive struggle for survival, and building an empire was a "natural" condition of that survival. Because of their obvious scientific, technological, and political success, which had enabled them to conquer much of the world, Europeans were more fit to survive than other "races." This sort of Social Darwinism also argued that war and conflict are necessary, as in nature: they are trials of strength and endurance that make a people stronger. This justification was of course blatantly racist, and the late nineteenth century was the period when modern racial theories and popular racist assumptions came into prominence. Our modern ideas of race really come from the nineteenth century, including the false and, as it turned out, deadly idea that Jews are a "race." (The term "anti-Semitism" was coined in the 1870s.) The domination of one people—one "race," such as the black, brown, or yellow—by another—the white—was based on both "scientific" and nationalist grounds.

Another rationalization for the new imperialism was the belief in European cultural superiority. This was the idea of the "white man's burden": the obligation of Europeans to spread the blessings of "civilization" to "backward peoples." This belief that modern Europe represented the pinnacle of civilization seemed self-evident to many Europeans, looking around them at European achievements in science and technology, the spread of democracy and education, economic success, and notable achievements in thought and the arts. Furthermore, there was the overwhelmingly dominant religion of Europe, Christianity, whose superiority to other religions was also taken for granted and the biblical command to spread it to all peoples taken with renewed seriousness.

By the end of the nineteenth century, the British Empire—which included India, Canada, Australia, New Zealand, other parts of Asia, parts of the Middle East, and sizeable portions of Africa and the Caribbean—had become the largest in the history of the world. Its globe-encircling scope inspired the saying, "The sun never sets on the British Empire." Thus Britain was the primary rival to the other great powers of Europe, above all to the recently created German Empire, which embarked on a rapid program of naval expansion to rival the British at sea.

During the last two decades of the nineteenth century the governments of the great powers of Europe developed competing systems of alliances, based on hard-headed considerations of self-interest, which bound the signatories to assist one another in case of a threat from a power outside the alliance. In the 1880s the shrewd and aggressive Chancellor Bismarck of Germany created the *Triple Alliance*, made up of Germany, Austria-Hungary (the Austro-Hungarian Empire), and Italy. Its aim was to isolate France and prevent war between Austria-Hungary and Russia. Responding to the Triple Alliance and the growing military strength of Germany, in the 1890s France, Britain, and Russia formed the *Triple Entente*, pledging mutual assistance in case of attack.

It was the Austro-Hungarian Empire that provided the spark that ignited the Great War. Austria-Hungary was heir to the old Holy Roman Empire, and still ruled by the Habsburg Dynasty which had produced the last of the Holy Roman Emperors in the sixteenth century. Through treaty and conquest in the seventeenth and eighteenth centuries, the Austrian Hapsburgs came to rule over one of the largest territories in Europe, which became a major power in European politics. But it was a polyglot empire, made up of many different ethnic and national groups. The two main groups were Germans and Hungarians, but the empire also included Czechs, Slovaks, Croats, Serbs, Slovenes, and Rumanians.

It was never easy holding all these disparate peoples together, but in an age of intense nationalism like the late nineteenth and early twentieth centuries it became impossible. Nationalistic fervor inspired not only the dominant German and Hungarian groups, but also the Slavic peoples, and particularly the Serbs, in the southern part of the Austro-Hungarian Empire. The Serbs had gained their independence from a disintegrating Ottoman Empire in the previous century. They dreamed of uniting all the southern Slavs (Serbs, Croats, Slovenes, and Serbs who lived in Austria-Hungarian controlled Bosnia, and Herzegovina)

into a great Serbian nation. Ethnic Germans wanted to unite with Germany and looked down on their Slavic neighbors. Czechs, the largest Slavic group, dominated Bohemia, the industrial heartland of the empire, and experienced a surge of nationalism and animosity toward the Germans. Hungarians tried to impose their language and culture on the minorities they controlled, arousing intense resistance.

In 1912 and 1913 a league of Slavic states called the Balkan Union conquered the remaining European territory held by the Turks. But the league fell out over the division of the spoils. Austria-Hungary, viewing an enlarged Serbia as a threat, humiliated them by forcing them to forfeit their new territory. Russia, which saw itself as the leader of a "panslavic" movement, supported its fellow Slavs in their desire to assert themselves against the Austro-Hungarian Empire. Germany allied with Austria-Hungary. Hatred on both sides was intense and Serbian nationalists waged a campaign of terrorism against the Empire. Austria-Hungary, with its ally Germany, was now engaged in a deadly "cold war" with Serbia. Increasingly on the defensive as it tried to hold together a multiethnic empire being challenged on all sides by nationalist agitation, the government of Austro-Hungarian Emperor Franz Joseph was determined to crush Serbia given the slightest provocation, and Germany and Russia were poised to come to the aid of their respective allies.

The incident that precipitated the war happened on June 28, 1914. A Bosnian Serbian terrorist, Gavrilo Princip, assassinated the Archduke Francis Ferdinand, heir to the Austro-Hungarian throne, and his wife, in Sarajevo. Ironically, Francis Ferdinand was sympathetic to the grievances of the south Slavs, and favored a policy that would give them an equal voice in the empire along with Germans and Hungarians. The assassination was the carrying out of a conspiracy organized by the chief of army intelligence of the Kingdom of Serbia, who hoped to bring the tensions within the empire to a crisis and usher in a revolution that would liberate the Serbs in the empire. The government of Franz Joseph saw in this outrage the golden opportunity to wage war against Serbia and issued an ultimatum. Serbia actually accepted most of the terms, but Austria-Hungary, spoiling for a showdown, considered that rejection of any one of them was rejection of all of them, and declared war. Germany of course backed Austria-Hungary, and Russia pledged to help Serbia. Russia mobilized, backed by its Triple Entente partner France. Germany declared war on Russia on August 1; that brought Britain into the war on the side of France and Russia.

Thus the war began with a whole series of decisions that might have gone the other way. But what turned a conflict between Austria-Hungary and Serbia into a world war was the system of alliances forged among the great powers of Europe in the 1880s and 1890s. The nationalism that Serbs and other eastern and southern European peoples had learned from the nationalist fever among the great powers' political and military elites began the war, and the nationalism that had propelled the great powers into competition for world empire turned it into a global conflagration.

Almost everyone thought that it would be a brief, gallant war, the matter resolved and the soldiers home by Christmas of 1914. There was an immediate outpouring of patriotism and support for the war in every country involved. Leading intellectuals, scholars, and artists of the time were caught up in the patriotic fervor. A few voices, drowned in the noise of patriotism, viewed the whole affair as much more ominous. Edward Grey, the British Foreign Secretary, famously prophesied: "The lamps are going out all over Europe. We shall never see them lit again in our lifetime."

By the end of 1914 both sides were locked in the trench warfare that was to dominate the European fronts throughout the war. (They were also fighting in Africa and the Middle East.) There was a permanent trench line that ran all the way from the Belgian coast to the Swiss border. The armies would fight for days, sometimes weeks and months, for a few hundred yards of ground. Wave after wave of soldiers would go "over the top" of the trenches into "no man's land," advancing toward the enemy, only to be mowed down in the thousands by machine gun and artillery fire. The battles of the Marne and the Somme in France, and Ypres in Belgium, resulted in casualties of close to a million each. All the European nations involved conscripted all their own able-bodied men for combat, and also used men from their colonial territories in Africa.

In 1914, the Ottoman Empire, a vast territorial holding that included much of the modern Middle East, joined with Germany and Austria-Hungary and entered the war. In April 1915 combined French, British, and Australian forces landed on the Gallipoli peninsula on the southern tip of Turkey with the hope of winning a decisive victory and knocking the Ottomans out of the war. That was not to be. The battle raged on until January 1915. By the end, the Allies had lost 252,000 men and gained nothing.

On both sides the generals decided early on that it was to be a war of attrition: who can kill off the other side's soldiers in greater numbers than they are killing off ours? World War I was the first "modern" war, fought with weapons that became ever deadlier as the twentieth century moved on, and inflicting unprecedented destruction on soldiers and civilians alike. The Great War introduced, besides the trench system, the use of poison gas, airplanes, and tanks. It was a war that showed little regard for the distinction between combatants and civilians, a pattern that came to dominate twentieth-century warfare. It was to be followed, scarcely more than twenty years after it ended, by an even more devastating war, the seeds of which had been sowed by World War I.

The United States entered the war on the side of Britain and France in 1917, and the infusion of fresh forces eventually tipped the balance. An armistice was signed on November 11, 1918 (which was observed for many years as Armistice Day, now called Veterans Day). By the last month of the war a popular revolution against Kaiser Wilhelm and the German generals who had led Germany to defeat created a new German Republic, the Weimar Republic, and forced the abdication of the kaiser. Germany's chief ally, the Austro-Hungarian Empire, was rapidly disintegrating into separate states on the basis of nationality.

The Treaty of Versailles, which followed it in 1919, was drawn up by the victorious Allies. To satisfy the French desire for revenge, the treaty declared Germany solely responsible for the war, demanded enormous reparations of the new German Republic that had been established just before the war ended, and took away one-eighth of German territory. This had the effect of weakening the fragile new German democracy, throwing Germany into severe economic depression, and instilling

EUROPE AT THE TIME OF WORLD WAR I

400 MILES
400 KILOMETERS

World War I in Europe. Redrawn from *The Western Heritage*, Sixth Edition, Combined Edition, by Donald Kagan, Steven E. Ozment, and Frank M. Turner, (1998), Prentice-Hall, Inc.

deep-seated resentment in the German people. (When Germany was again defeated in World War II, the Allies had learned from their 1919 mistake and committed themselves to rebuilding the nation to insure that it had a stable democratic government and economic strength.) The treaty also carved up parts of Europe into new nations, or recognized new self-created nations, such as Yugoslavia and Czechoslovakia, which had been parts of the Austro-Hungarian Empire. Although formally committed to U.S. President Woodrow Wilson's principle of the "right of self-determination" of ethnic peoples, the treaty did not carry it out consistently and ended up creating new problems and rivalries among nations.

During and following the war, the Allies sought to destabilize the Ottoman Empire. Arabs had lived under Ottoman rule for 400 years. The Allies encouraged Arab nationalism as a way of fomenting rebellion. By 1918 the Ottoman Empire had collapsed and Arabs who had dreams of independence and autonomy hoped to see them realized. The victorious British and French had other plans, however, as they had already agreed to partition the oil rich region (oil was discovered in the Middle East in 1908). So, for example, Lebanon became a French protectorate, and Palestine became a British mandate. The regions of Baghdad, Mosul, and Basra were unified into the nation of Iraq and placed under British control. The nations of Saudi Arabia and Transjordan were also created and either placed under direct British authority or ruled by allies of the British. Complicating the picture was the Balfour Declaration, a 1917 agreement between the British and leaders of Britain's Jewish community which promised Palestine as a homeland for the Jews. Though the Declaration was never honored, it only incensed the largely Arab population in Palestine.

The impact of the First World War on Western consciousness was profound, shaping some of the most characteristic features of the twentieth-century world. It shook to the foundations modern European assumptions about reason and progress, and created widespread disillusionment. It essentially wiped out a whole generation of young men. The irrationality and carnage of the war caused some Europeans to regard democracy and Enlightenment as failures. The 1920s saw the growth of ultra-nationalistic movements such as Italian Fascism and German Nazism. Communism became popular across the west, and some looked with keen interest and hope at the new Union of Soviet Socialist Republics as a great experiment in egalitarianism and internationalism whose influence might prevent future wars. But the 1930s were to witness a rearmed, powerful, and totalitarian Germany start another war and the U.S.S.R. experience the nightmare of Stalin's purges of many respected leaders in the Communist Party and starvation of millions of Russian farmers.

ART FROM 1850 TO 1914

An overview of art from this long "half-century" reveals a rapidly changing landscape. While art in the first half of the nineteenth century was dominated by the two competing approaches of Romanticism and Neoclassicism, the later nineteenth and early twentieth centuries witnessed a swift succession of artistic styles. The veristic representation of Realism that ruled at mid-century gave way to the escalating abstraction of Impressionism, Post-Impressionism, Cubism and Expressionism, culminating in the complete abstraction found in paintings of the Russian avant-garde. However, in spite of changes, the booming city of Paris remained widely acknowledged as the center of the art world, usurping the position of Rome in centuries past.

Artists of the later nineteenth century largely turned away from the historically based paintings of their predecessors, favoring instead contemporary subjects related to an increasingly urban, middle-class society. Painters depicted urban leisure activities rather than scenes of rural labor. Focusing particularly on attributes of modern life, they often made visual references to the technological progress of urban society, from industrialization to the architectural renovations of the Parisian metropolis.

Art of the period testified to an increasing popular faith in the promise of science and technology. Building in part on Enlightenment thought of the eighteenth century, artists emphasized the positive progress of science in their subject matter as well

While many late nineteenth-century artists looked to the advances of modern life for their subjects, Auguste Rodin responded to a past historical event. Rodin won a competition to produce a sculpture for the city of Calais, commemorating a specific incident from the Hundred Years War. In 1347, King Edward III of England attacked the city of Calais, agreeing to spare the city only if six of its prominent citizens, or burghers, would offer themselves up, along with keys to the city. Rodin produced a realistic grouping of the despairing, yet resigned figures, chained together and dressed in sackcloth—not the heroic, idealized figures hoped for by the city's commissioners. By placing the sculpture on ground level rather than on a pedestal, Rodin aimed to demonstrate that even common people are capable of courageous actions.

Figure IV-1   Auguste Rodin, *Burghers of Calais,* 1884–86. Bronze, 6'10$\frac{1}{2}$" × 7'11" × 6'6" (2.1 × 2.4 × 2 m). Musée Rodin, Paris, France. Courtesy of Vanni/Art Resource, NY.

William Morris, founder of the British Arts and Crafts movement, rebelled against industrialization and the supposed "progress" of modern society. Concerned primarily with the design of furniture and decorative arts such as textiles and wallpaper, as in the example seen here, the Arts and Crafts movement advocated a return to handcrafted production, criticizing what they viewed as the poor quality and design of factory mass-fabrication. Morris also envisioned an art that cut across class lines, produced for the masses and not just for the wealthy. Unfortunately, the expense of handcrafted production made this idea of an affordable art for the people unfeasible.

Figure IV-2   William Morris, example of wallpaper design. Courtesy of the Victoria & Albert Museum, London/Art Resource, NY.

as in their methods. Claude Monet implicitly praised advances in modern transportation in his paintings of urban railway stations, while Georges Seurat employed scientific color theories to inform his painting techniques.

THE CHANGING REPRESENTATION OF WOMEN

The nude female body occupies a central place in the history of art. Often couched in mythological or religious terms, nudity was legitimized by representing Venus or Bathsheba. Artists in the nineteenth century increasingly represented the nude female body for its own sake, unapologetically displaying a sexualized female form for a presumed male viewer. An overview of several representations of the nude female body demonstrates some of the major stylistic shifts in art of the late nineteenth and early twentieth centuries.

Olympia (Plate 18), painted by Edouard Manet in 1863 and exhibited in 1865, created a huge sensation due to its perceived blunt sexuality and "unfinished" painting style. Manet intended his

Olympia, a common name for prostitutes of the time, as a subversive response to the lengthy history in art of passively reclining nude female bodies, displayed for the viewer's titillation. Rather than continue this figurative tradition, Manet turned the tables and transferred the power to Olympia. Although her body is on display, Olympia is not a passive creature. She appears cold and uninterested, and her physical placement locates her above the viewer so that she is in a position of authority looking down. Even the black cat next to her arches its back at us. Because of her directness, Olympia was viewed as vulgar, flaunting her sexuality in an immoral and immodest manner. Manet also received criticism of his painting style. He painted in flat patches of color and did not model his forms for a three-dimensional effect; combined with a sketchy brushwork, these features prompted critics to deem his work unfinished, an assessment also leveled at many of his contemporaries.

French artist Paul Gauguin depicted the female body with entirely different intentions in mind. After abandoning his family and his career as a stockbroker in order to move to Tahiti and paint, Gauguin took as his main subjects the native women of the island. Hoping to escape the industrialized, modern world, Gauguin idealized the French colony as an Edenic paradise whose inhabitants were as innocent as children. His first painting after his arrival in Tahiti, *Ia Orana Maria (Hail Mary)*, 1891–92 (Plate 19), reveals Gauguin's idyllic vision of his new surroundings. In a contradictory perception, Gauguin understood the natives to be uncorrupted by modern society but simultaneously accessible for foreign infiltration: the offering of fruit on the table not only symbolizes the women's sexuality but also invites the viewer to participate in the scene. Through his repeated depictions of nude and half-nude women, and as described in his writings, Gauguin perceived the native women to be not only unselfconscious in their nudity but also sexually available. By titling his paintings in the Maori language, Gauguin sought to present himself as fully immersed in his new surroundings, when in fact he relied on his thirteen-year-old "wife" as a translator and subsisted not on native fare but on imported canned foods.

Although he did not leave France, Henri Matisse, like Gauguin before him, employed the nude female body to represent his vision of a heavenly paradise removed from the chaos of modern life. *The Joy of Life,* 1905–06 (Plate 20), depicts a host of nude figures dancing, erotically lounging, and communing with nature. Through the carefree, relaxed setting and through the sinuous, curving lines of the trees and the women's bodies, Matisse hoped to evoke a feeling of serenity. Matisse carefully selected his color palette to reflect this mood as well. The group of French painters known as the Fauves (or "wild beasts"), of which Matisse was a part, sought to use pigments expressively rather than representationally. The Fauves employed bold colors to convey emotions and abandoned the descriptive function of color. Hence, the pink nudes in *The Joy of Life* are surrounded by non-naturalistic yellow grass and orange trees.

Pablo Picasso, a Spaniard living in France, painted a sensational portrayal of the nude female body as a way to respond to earlier art. Picasso conceived of *Les Demoiselles d'Avignon,* 1907 (Plate 21), as a challenge to the Western history of erotic art. The setting is a bordello, with "demoiselles," or ladies, a euphemism for prostitutes, and "Avignon" referring to a street in Barcelona's red-light district. Like Manet's *Olympia*, Picasso's prostitutes are not passive and tender but harsh and menacing. Envisioned specifically as a response to Matisse's *Joy of Life, Les Demoiselles* forsakes softly curving lines in favor of sharp curves and angles. While Picasso displayed the women's bodies in positions that suggest their sexual availability, their hostile gazes confront the viewer in a threatening manner. Even the fruit of the foreground, historically a symbol of female sexuality, appears sharp and dangerous. In a technique that laid the groundwork for his later Cubist style, Picasso abstracted the figures by visually flattening them and fracturing them into jagged segments. His appropriation of African and Iberian masks for the heads of two of the figures indicates that, like Gauguin and many others of his day, Picasso looked to supposedly "primitive" cultures for inspiration. "Primitive" societies, which were most often recently colonized countries, figured widely into the work of nineteenth- and twentieth-century artists, in large part because those artists opposed certain notions of modernity and industrialization and so idealized people and places that they perceived as uncorrupted. As colonizers, however, they more often imposed their own views rather than seeking to understand foreign cultures, which resulted in erroneous ethnographies where "primitive" peoples were deemed not simply uncorrupted but ignorant, as well as primal, sexual creatures. Picasso's use, then, of African and Iberian masks in *Les Demoiselles* may reveal much more than a simple formal influence, highlighting a widespread European belief in the raw, untamed sexuality of "primitive" peoples.

FROM REALISM TO ABSTRACTION

Art of the later nineteenth and early twentieth centuries shifted quickly and significantly toward abstraction. The artistic goal of realistic description, in place since the Renaissance, suddenly gave way. Each new movement or "ism" moved farther from naturalistic representation of the human body and its surroundings and closer to non-representational painting.

The work of American painter Thomas Eakins represents the type of Realism that prevailed in Europe and the United States early in the second half of the century. In his quest to represent the human form as accurately as possible, Eakins attended anatomy lectures and even dissected cadavers. Eakins highlighted this interest in science through a painting from 1875, *The Gross Clinic* (Plate 22). In a scene hearkening back to Rembrandt's *The Anatomy Lesson of Dr. Nicolaes Tulp* (Plate 5), Eakins portrays a surgery-in-progress, performed by Dr. Samuel Gross at Jefferson Medical College and attended by various helpers and medical students. Eakins used dramatic contrasts of light and dark not only to emphasize the key elements of the scene but also symbolically to connote the light of modern science triumphing over the darkness of ignorance. Although the public would soon disparage art that moved away from realistic representation, at the time Eakins's painting was criticized for being too realistic. The visible blood and surgical details were judged offensive and Eakins was not allowed to display the painting in the art section of the 1876 Philadelphia Centennial; it was relegated instead to the army's hospital display.

At the same time in Europe, a group of painters that came to be known as the Impressionists sought a new vision for painting scenes of modern life. In their pursuit of a pure painting style, the Impressionists advocated the importance of quickly painted sketches, focusing not on the objects at hand but rather on the disembodied patches of color that comprised the scene. In addition to rural landscapes and scenes of bourgeois leisure, the Impressionists depicted elements of urban life and technological progress. Claude Monet, the acknowledged leader of the movement, featured the trains and railway station of the Parisian *Gare Saint-Lazare*, 1877 (Plate 23), in a series of seven paintings. Monet found that by repeating his subjects but varying the circumstances (such as time of day or year or weather conditions), he could best experiment with the Impressionist focus on light and color. Here, the light streaming through the modern steel-and-glass architecture of the station roof mixes with the steam of the engine to produce a colorful atmospheric effect. The bustling movement of the people is vaguely apparent beneath the layers of smoke and color. As with other Impressionist works, at close range the painting's daubs of paint seem nearly unintelligible, but at a distance the colors meld to form a sensory perception (or "impression") of the scene at hand.

Reacting primarily to the advances of the Impressionists, a diverse group of artists soon launched a phenomenon that became known as Post-Impressionism. Seeing Impressionism as an improvisational experience that recorded merely fleeting glimpses, their successors imbued light and color with a weightier purpose. Vincent van Gogh sought to use light and color more boldly to express emotions. Other Post-Impressionists attempted to manipulate light and color into an art for social change. Still others, like Georges Seurat, transformed the Impressionist focus into a quasi-scientific method. Seurat's technique, known as pointillism, consisted of applying small dots of pure paint to the surface of the canvas. Rather than mixing the colors with a brush, Seurat believed that the human eye would naturally mix the colors during the viewing process. In *A Sunday Afternoon on the Island of La Grande Jatte*, 1884–86 (Plate 24), Seurat produced a monumental essay on the theme of bourgeois leisure. By selecting a subject often favored by the Impressionists, Seurat clearly set his own work apart through his meticulous and prolonged effort. Rather than a quickly painted sketch of the scene, *La Grande Jatte* reflects how Seurat spent several months in observation, during which he carefully planned his composition and technique. There are conflicting interpretations of Seurat's painting but it is possible that he intended the painting either as an antidote to or a critique of Parisian middle-class life. Sundays on the island were known to be dirty and disorderly. By painting a populated canvas that yet evokes a mood of tranquility, Seurat may have intended the work as a didactic lesson in social civility.

In the early twentieth century, artists continued to experiment with the effects of color and light and in doing so moved ever farther from naturalistic representation. As discussed above, the French Fauves, such as Henri Matisse, employed color as a means of expression rather than description. In Germany, too, the Expressionist groups of *Die Brücke* (the Bridge) and *Der Blaue Reiter* (The Blue Rider) looked to color and line to convey the bustling activity of life in the modern metropolis. While his contemporaries flattened color, Picasso and his working partner, Georges Braque, flattened and fragmented their forms in the abstracted representations of Cubism.

None of the artists, however, completely abandoned representational elements. Even amidst the blurry dots of color or faceted planes of space, recognizable objects still existed. Kazimir Malevich, a leading figure of the Moscow avant-garde, finally made the move to utterly abandon the object in 1913. Malevich theoretically sought to "liberate" art by eliminating the dependence on representation and focusing instead on the abstract portrayal of emotion. In *Suprematist Painting (8 Red Rectangles)*, 1915 (Plate 25), Malevich set forth a non-representational geometric abstraction, freed from the burden of depicting an actual object. Malevich titled his style Suprematism, art through which he hoped to convey the "supremacy of pure feeling."

BEYOND ROMANTICISM: MUSIC AT THE TURN OF THE TWENTIETH CENTURY

Neither Classicism nor Romanticism has ever really died out. Moving into the late nineteenth and early twentieth centuries we can listen to the "Neoclassicism" of composers such as the Frenchmen César Franck (1822–90), Camille Saint-Saîns (1835–1921), and, in his later works, Maurice Ravel (1875–1937). The Russians Nikolai Rimsky-Korsakov (1844–1908) and Sergei Rachmaninoff (1873–1943), and the Czech-Austrian Gustav Mahler (1860–1911), continued the Romantic tradition while taking it in new directions. But an anti-Romantic movement also developed that took various forms: notably impressionism, naturalism, and atonality and twelve-tone composition.

The great exponent of musical *impressionism* is the French composer Claude Debussy (1862–1918)—although he did not like to be called an impressionist because the term as applied to visual artists was originally derogatory. But Debussy quite consciously composed music designed to paint a picture in sound. He especially enjoyed creating musical impressions of natural scenes, as in his well-known *Clair de Lune* ("Moonlight"). He was particularly interested in tonal color, the unique quality given to a particular note by a particular instrument or voice. He departed from the traditional "rules" of harmonic chord progression and used "gliding chords," chords repeated up and down the musical scale. He also used dissonance and changeable rhythms extensively. Everything was aimed at creating a certain emotional effect and "picture." Perhaps his most famous and representative work is *Prélude à l'après-midi d'un faune* (*Prelude to the Afternoon of a Faun*), performed by a large orchestra.

In opera, anti-Romanticism took the form of what was called *naturalism*. The Italian version was called *verismo* ("verisimilitude"). As the names suggest, these forms of opera aimed at musically portraying "real life," even portraying characters, actions, and situations that were immoral or brutal. They were paralleled by the new naturalism in literature, represented by writers such as Emile Zola in France and Theodore Dreiser in America. Perhaps the best example of operatic naturalism is *Carmen*, written by Georges Bizet (1838–75) in 1875, and still among the most performed of all operas, with its popular tunes, such as the "Habanera." Carmen, who works in a cigarette factory, is an attractive, seductive, and disreputable woman with whom a soldier named Don José falls hopelessly in love. He deserts the army and follows her in everything, including criminal activity. She tires of him and takes up with a toreador named Escamillo. Don José, distraught, begs Carmen to come back to him. When she refuses he stabs her to death, then weeps over her body. In the late nineteenth century audiences found the content of *Carmen* shocking and disturbing.

In Italy, *verismo* opera was represented by Pietro Mascagni (1863–1945), Ruggiero Leoncavallo (1858–1919), and Giacomo Puccini (1858–1924). In different ways, each presented stories of ordinary people, with an emphasis on themes such as strong passions, love affairs, betrayal, revenge, and murder. But they did so with beautiful melodies and orchestral arrangements; their reaction against Romanticism was primarily thematic, not musical. The "Intermezzo" from Mascagni's *Cavalleria Rusticana*, a favorite of listeners, is plaintively lovely, while "Ridi, Pagliacci," an aria from Leoncavallo's *I Pagliacci*, is heartbreaking in its pathos and drama. And Puccini, who remains one of the most popular and performed opera composers in the world, wrote some of the most gorgeous and beloved songs in the operatic repertoire in works such as *La Bohème*, *Tosca*, *Turandot*, and *Madama Butterfly*.

Some composers in the early twentieth century departed more radically and experimentally from Romantic conventions. They rejected traditional tonality, in which music is composed in a specific key or foundational tone, for *atonal* music, in which no single tone was more important than any other. All the notes of the twelve-note chromatic scale (an octave on the piano) became equal, which resulted in what is called *twelve-tone* music. The leading figure in atonal music was Arnold Schoenberg (1874–1951), a German who started out writing big works in the Romantic tradition. By 1905 he was experimenting with works for smaller instrumental ensembles and with increasingly complex melodic, harmonic, and rhythmic characteristics. He would combine tones in any sort of pattern without feeling that he needed to "resolve" the composition by the end. This was his atonality, which he preferred to call "pantonality" ("all tones"), because he saw his works as encompassing the whole range of tones without giving preference to any. Still later he started composing works explicitly using a twelve-tone approach. He would select notes from the twelve semitones of the chromatic scale in a particular pattern, and then he would use them in various ways: backwards, upside down, etc.

One of the greatest of the anti-Romantic musical innovators, whose originality is such that he does not fit into any of the above categories, was the Russian Igor Stravinsky (1882–1971), perhaps the single most important of the post-Romantic composers in terms of his influence on other twentieth-century composers and musical developments. He studied with the great Russian composer of the latter nineteenth century, Rimsky-Korsakov, who while in the Romantic tradition was in some of his works pushing the boundaries. Like Tchaikovsky, Stravinsky was influenced by Russian folk music, but in his composing he was striking out in dramatically new directions, employing complexity, dissonance, and alternating rhythms in a way that set his music apart from everything that had gone before. Again like Tchaikovky, and characteristic of the modern Russian musical tradition, Stravinsky's first important works were ballet music: *L'Oiseau de feu* (*The Firebird*) (1910), *Petrushka*

(1911), and *Le sacre du printemps* (*The Rite of Spring*) (1913), which were commissioned by Serge Diaghilev, director of the Ballets Russe in Paris. *The Firebird*, which premiered at the Paris Opera House, was a success, as was *Petrushka*. Both were marked by originality but were not "revolutionary." *The Rite of Spring*, however, literally caused a riot at the opera house: fistfights broke out among audience members and the police had to be there to keep the audience in line for the second act. Subtitled "Pictures of Pagan Russia," *The Rite of Spring* is genuinely revolutionary—in its orchestration and in the primitivism, sexuality, and savagery of its rhythms. It depicts the sensual but cruel rituals of spring in pre-Christian Russia, including the sacrifice of a virgin who dances herself to death to wild music.

CD SELECTIONS

Track 16 is the final aria from Puccini's opera *Madama Butterfly*. Although its premiere performance, at the famous La Scala Opera House in Milan, Italy in 1904, was a complete failure, it has taken its place as one of Puccini's most popular and performed operas. The opera is unusual in portraying an encounter between the cultures of West and East, in the persons of an American naval officer and a very young Japanese woman during the last half of the nineteenth century after Japan has established relations with the U.S. and other Western nations. *Madama Butterfly* is a modern tragedy in two acts, propelled not only by the individual feelings and decisions of the two main characters but more profoundly by the stark contrasts—the "distance," both literally and metaphorically—between their two cultures.

Puccini and his librettists took the story from a novella by John Luther Long that had been made into a short play by David Belasco. Puccini saw the play in London, and immediately liked the idea of portraying the juxtaposition of the two cultures operatically. The opera is set in Nagasaki, Japan, where American naval lieutenant Pinkerton is stationed and has just bought a house. In keeping with Japanese custom, he has also purchased a wife, Cio-Cio-San (Butterfly), through a marriage broker named Goro, and he is waiting for her to arrive for the wedding. Over drinks the U.S. Consul, Sharpless, is disturbed by Pinkerton's casual attitude to the marriage, and advises him to respect Butterfly's sincerity. Pinkerton even proposes a toast to the day when he will marry an American woman. Butterfly is only fifteen, her father dead and she and her mother very poor, and she has worked as a geisha to enable them to survive. When she arrives with her relatives for the wedding she tells Pinkerton that she has converted to Christianity so she can pray to the same God as her husband.

Act Two takes place after Pinkerton has been back in the U.S. for three years. He is now on a ship returning to Nagasaki, and has written a letter to Butterfly which Sharpless brings to the house to read to her. Butterfly and her maid Suzuki are desperately poor. Butterfly has a son from her marriage to Pinkerton, and she has remained fervently convinced that he would some day return. But it turns out that he has returned, with his American wife, only to take the son back to the U.S. Utterly devastated, Butterfly agrees to give up her son but after saying goodbye to him goes behind a screen and kills herself with her father's ceremonial sword. Track 16 is her heartrending farewell to her son: "Beloved Idol!/ Adored, adored being,/ Fairest flower of beauty./Though you never must know it/'Tis for you, my love for you I'm dying/ . . . Farewell, beloved l'Amore, addio/! Farewell my dearest heart!" The opera ends with Sharpless and Pinkerton rushing into the room, Pinkerton crying out "Butterfly!" three times as she dies.

Track 17 is from Stravinsky's *Rite of Spring*, described above. You are listening to "Danses des adolescentes" ("Dance of the Youths and Maidens") and "Jeu de rapt" ("Game of abduction"). The teenage girls join the boys at the river, and they form a circle and dance, which propels them into new groups. These pieces are an excellent example of the strong, pulsating rhythms that characterize *The Rite of Spring*. Stravinsky wrote of the reaction to the first performance of this dance: ". . . when the curtain opened on the group of knock-kneed and long-braided Lolitas jumping up and down, the storm [of audience protest] broke . . . and a few minutes later I left the hall in a rage. . . . I have never again been that angry. . . . I could not understand why people who had not yet heard it wanted to protest in advance."

CHAPTER TWELVE

SIGMUND FREUD AND PSYCHOANALYSIS

The traditional model of human nature that dominated Western philosophy and science for two millennia tells us that the "essence" of being human is defined in terms of our conscious life and our ability to reason. We find this model, in various forms, in thinkers as diverse as Plato and Aristotle, Aquinas, Descartes and Locke, Kant and Hegel, Jeremy Bentham and J. S. Mill. Sigmund Freud (1856–1939) has been perhaps more influential than anyone else in bringing about a fundamental revaluation of this model in the Western world. Freud's emphasis on the primary role of the unconscious in human life, an unconscious dominated by instinctual drives rooted in our biological nature, represents a dramatic departure from the model of human nature in which reasoning and conscious decision-making rule the day. While Freud was by no means the first to question the primacy of reason and the traditionally subordinate place of the passions, and while he was also not the first to consider the role of the unconscious in human life, his questions and considerations gained weight because of the way in which he raised them and because of the cultural and historical context in which they appeared.

World War I shook to the foundations modern European assumptions about reason and progress. This widespread disillusionment over the Enlightenment promise brought significant changes to the art, literature, and politics of the twentieth-century world. Politically, the war made possible the Bolshevik Revolution in Russia in 1917, and the postwar period saw the rise of right-wing authoritarian movements such as Fascism in Italy and Nazism in Germany. But it also led to a renewed commitment to peace and internationalism. The League of Nations was founded, full of hope, but ultimately foundered in the 1930s. Peace movements dedicated to the proposition that World War I must be "the war to end all wars" enlisted supporters throughout Europe and the U.S. during the 1920s and 1930s. In the shadow of this deeply traumatic event, the revolutionary psychology that was developed by Freud and called psychoanalysis seemed to make sense to many educated people.

FREUD AS SCIENTIST AND HUMANIST

Freud certainly did not invent the ideas of the unconscious and the power of the nonrational in human life. All the way back to the origins of Western civilization we find profound testimony, typically in literature and in religious writings, to their importance—for example, in Sophocles's plays, the *Book of Job*, the letters of Paul of Tarsus, Augustine's *Confessions*, and Luther's writings. As we have seen in Chapters Nine and Ten, influential precursors of existentialism such as Dostoevsky and Nietzsche likewise perceptively explored the power of the unconscious and the nonrational in our lives. Freud, however, is distinctive in having believed wholeheartedly that natural-scientific investigation in particular could lead to such conclusions.

Freud as Scientist. There are, actually, two cultural contexts for Freud's psychoanalytic investigations and doctrines: (1) the scientific worldview that emerged from the Enlightenment, and (2) the more traditional perspectives of classical humanism. First, Freud clearly carried on the legacy of the Enlightenment, with its emphasis on our ability rationally to understand the world and ourselves and thereby to improve our condition. Many interpreters have seen the "Freudian revolution" as one of the great "paradigm shifts" in Western thought, following on the Copernican and the Darwinian revolutions. Copernicus (as confirmed empirically by Galileo) dislodged the earth from the center of a finite universe of crystalline spheres to a small planet orbiting a star in a universe that is for all practical purposes infinite. Darwin replaced the prevailing view of a relatively "young" world of fixed species hierarchically arranged by God and crowned by humankind, with the picture of an unimaginably long process of evolution by natural selection and of humanity as a very recent species among the many that exist today and the many that are extinct. Freud, who saw his work as building on and somewhat akin to that of Darwin, inaugurated the next stage in the modern reassessment of the human place in nature, by showing the powerful role that nature, in the form of our unconscious and instinctual drives, plays even in the highest expressions of the human mind.

Freud viewed his approach to the investigation of human nature as entirely scientific and considered himself to be a natural scientist and a physician. Psychoanalysis was for him a scientific theory and also a therapeutic technique that enabled a patient, by using the methods of what Freud called free association, to become aware of the unconscious motives and forces that played a crucial role in his or her life. Freud's scientific investigation produced the view that human beings are not primarily rational, but are governed to a large degree by non-rational—unconscious, and instinctual—forces. At the same time, he believed that it is only through scientific reason that we can establish the truth of this view of human nature, and that psychoanalysis is essentially a rational process of bringing these forces into the light of consciousness so that the patient can deal with them and is no longer dominated by them.

Freud believed that human mental life grew out of and reflected our bodily existence as organisms produced by the evolutionary process. What differentiated him strikingly from most of his scientific contemporaries was his recognition that there are many psychological problems that have mental rather than physiological causes. At the same time, Freud very much reflected the science of his day in interpreting all human behavior—psychical as well as physical—as (a) manifesting a certain quantity of energy, and (b) governed by Newton's first law of motion: for every action there is an equal and opposite reaction. He saw the human organism's physical and psychic energy as directed toward *equilibrium* or *stasis*, the quiescence that comes from the complete satisfaction of desires. Finally, like the other scientists of his day, Freud was a *determinist*: all events result from causes that, if known, fully explain them. Freud's *determinism* was distinctive because of the way in which he applied it to human mental life and behavior. He assumed that there are no accidents in our mental life. Everything we desire, think, or do, whether conscious or unconscious, has a reason or reveals a meaning that fits together with everything else in our mental life. There is no unmotivated behavior; it is just that the motives of much of our behavior are hidden from us in our unconscious life.

The theory and practice of psychoanalysis grew out of the scientific assumptions of Freud's day, his clinical work with his patients, and his career-long self-analysis. Although he developed the basic ideas of his theory of personality and therapeutic technique during the last decades of the nineteenth century, he continued to develop and revise his ideas throughout the rest of his life.

Freud as Humanist. There is, however, another side to Freud that makes his thought so richly textured and at the same time so exasperating to those who have tried to find "hard science" in his theories. This is the Freud who stands in the tradition of *classical humanism,* with its focus on the richness and complexity of the human self as expressed in literature and the visual arts. Freud was steeped in ancient Greek and Roman as well as modern literature, and he loved painting and sculpture. His theory of the dynamics and development of the human personality was a vision of the heights and depths of the drama of the self that transcended the science of his day, including his own scientific assumptions. It is significant that in naming the crucial stage in the child's early relationship to its parents the "Oedipus complex," Freud reached back to ancient Greek mythology and the story of Oedipus's unintentional but fateful killing of his father and marrying of his mother. Freud referred to what he called the "love instinct" with the Greek word *eros*—the love that is desire. He admired the penetrating psychological insight of Dostoevsky and Nietzsche. A passionate lover of the art of the city of Rome, with its many layers of pagan and Christian civilization, Freud wrote psychoanalytic studies of Michelangelo and Leonardo da Vinci. He was an assiduous collector of art objects and filled his famous consulting room with them.

FREUD'S LIFE AND INFLUENCE

Freud grew up in Vienna, the capital city of the Austro-Hungarian Empire and, during Freud's lifetime, a center of European scientific and cultural activity. He lived there until a year before his death. As a boy he experienced discrimination growing up Jewish in a strongly Catholic country. Although he never practiced the Jewish religion, his Jewish cultural background and tradition were important influences in his life and thought. As a schoolboy Freud had an excellent education in the humanities, and throughout his life he read widely and had broad interests in literature and the arts.

Freud studied medicine at the University of Vienna, a leading institution of the time, receiving his degree in 1880. After showing considerable early promise as a neurologist, he studied in Paris with Jean Charcot, who aroused his interest in the study of hysteria and hypothesized that its origins were psychological rather than organic. Freud returned to Vienna, established himself in private practice, and in 1887 married Martha Bernays. The Freuds had six children, one of whom, Anna Freud, worked closely with her father and became a world-famous psychiatrist in her own right.

Stimulated by the ideas and therapeutic techniques of his older colleague and friend Josef Breuer, Freud began to develop the theory and practice of what he came to call *psychoanalysis*. He developed his revolutionary new ideas out of his own clinical work with patients, often women suffering from hysterical symptoms, and out of his intensive self-analysis. Central to Freud's theory were the hypotheses of the unconscious, of repression, of infantile sexuality, and of the fundamental influence of early childhood and especially the relationship with one's parents in personality development. His first major work on psychoanalysis was *The Interpretation of Dreams* (1900), a study of dreams as keys to unlocking repressed experiences and desires based largely on Freud's self-analysis.

By the early decades of the twentieth century Freud had begun to achieve international fame and notoriety, initiated the institutionalization of psychoanalysis as a science and a healing profession, and attracted to himself students from around the world, many of whom went on to become leaders in the psychoanalytic movement. While continuing to develop and revise his theory, Freud also began to apply the ideas of psychoanalysis to larger cultural issues such as religion, art, politics, and the nature of civilization itself. Perhaps the best-known book of this period is *Civilization and Its Discontents* (1930). A writer with an excellent prose style, Freud won the prestigious Goethe Prize for Literature in 1930 and was nominated for the Nobel Prize.

Freud spent the last sixteen years of his life in frequent pain from cancer of the jaw, undergoing thirty-three operations, but he continued to develop his theory, to write, and to lead the psychoanalytic movement. With the Nazi takeover of Austria in 1938, Freud was expelled from the country and spent the last year of his life in London.

Freud's influence on twentieth-century Western civilization has been profound and far-reaching. His ideas, and the many other "depth psychologies" to which they gave rise, have fundamentally altered our understanding of human nature. Psychoanalysis has had a dramatic impact on both high and popular culture. Surrealist artists drew directly on psychoanalytic ideas for inspiration, and much modern art has implicitly or explicitly reflected such ideas in its portrayal of the human image. Freud's influence on major twentieth-century novelists, poets, and playwrights has likewise been extensive, as for example in the plays of Eugene O'Neill and the novels of Hermann Hesse. At a popular level, not only our consciousness of ourselves but also our language has been shaped by Freud. We familiarly talk about the unconscious, drives, repression, complexes, fixation, projection, rationalization, libido, the Oedipal situation, neurosis and psychosis, the id, ego, and superego. We generally assume that our dreams are clues to our unconscious self, as well as conscious mistakes such as slips of the tongue—which we call "Freudian slips." Psychiatrists, psychoanalysts, clinical psychologists, and other psychotherapists and counselors became a new kind of "priesthood" in the twentieth century, offering help with personal problems and "salvation" in the form of the ability to cope with life more positively.

MAIN IDEAS OF PSYCHOANALYSIS

In order to understand the basic arguments of *The Future of an Illusion*, it is useful to outline Freud's basic ideas and assumptions. This introductory sketch of the central ideas and practice of psychoanalysis will closely follow his last book, *An Outline of Psycho-Analysis*. Freud wrote it between July and September of 1938, at the age of 82, after he had been forced into exile in London. Published posthumously in 1940, it is his final statement of his fully developed ideas.

In the *Outline*, Freud shows that he believed to the end that psychoanalysis was a thoroughly scientific theory, and he tries whenever possible to use familiar scientific language and to draw analogies with fields such as physics. But he regarded psychoanalysis as a young science, still in need of considerable development and elaboration. He also confessed his ignorance about certain aspects of the human psyche, and he candidly distinguished between what he thought he could confidently assert and what he thought needed much further investigation. He looked to the future, anticipating that others would come after him to shed light on the things of which he claimed ignorance, and to carry forward and revise various aspects of psychoanalysis. He speculated on the likelihood that in the future "chemical substances" might be used in therapy, a possibility that has been actualized in the extensive use of drugs in the treatment of both neuroses and psychoses, not as a substitute for the traditional "talking" forms of therapy, but as an additional method of healing to bring to bear on mental problems.

The Structure of the Self. Freud begins by describing, on the basis of his clinical study of individual human development, what he calls the "psychical apparatus." Here he introduces his

influential threefold division of the personality into *id*, *ego*, and *superego*. The id is the oldest and most fundamental part of the self, the "archaic" foundation of everything else. The id "contains everything that is inherited, that is present at birth, that is laid down in the [individual's] constitution— above all . . . the instincts, which originate from the somatic organization [the body] . . . ."[1]

Through interaction with the external world, a portion of the id develops into the ego, which mediates between the id and the world. The ego's main purpose is self-preservation. In this task, the ego calls upon its powers of perception, thought, choice, memory, and adaptation in coping with the external world, while internally it controls the demands of the instincts by deferred gratification and suppression. Like the id, the ego seeks pleasure and the avoidance of discomfort or pain, but unlike the blindly-operating id, it must do so in a conscious and realistic way.

In addition, the long period of parental dependence of the human child contributes to the creation of the superego. The superego is the internalization of the influence of one's parents, and through them of one's society: ". . . not only the personalities of the actual parents but also the family, racial and national traditions handed on through them, as well as the demands of the immediate social milieu which they represent."[2] The influence of later parent-like models such as teachers and admired public figures is also part of the superego. What we commonly call conscience is, according to Freud, the superego. The id reflects our biological nature and genetic inheritance, the superego our social inheritance, and the ego what we individually do with these "givens" as we cope with life in the world.

The superego exercises severe and arbitrary demands on the ego, usually at the expense of the id. Hence the ego's function includes not only reconciling the id's pursuit of pleasure with external reality, but also mediating between the desires of the id and the restrictions of the superego. The mature, healthy, adult ego succeeds in accepting the demands of both the id and the superego in ways

---

[1]Freud, *An Outline of Psycho-Analysis*, translated and edited by James Strachey. (New York: W. W. Norton & Co., 1949), 2.

[2]Ibid., 3.

that are not destructive to the human personality. "An action by the ego is as it should be if it satisfies simultaneously the demands of the id, of the superego and of reality. . . ."[3] Such reconciliation is, according to Freud, what maturing and education are essentially about. When an individual has failed to succeed at this task of psychically growing up, it then becomes the job of the psychoanalyst to try to help that individual develop a healthy and harmonious self.

The Instincts. The id expresses the basic purpose of the human organism's life, which is the satisfaction of its innate needs without regard to inner restraint or the demands and dangers of the external world. The ego must transform this pursuit of satisfaction into realistic behaviors. The powerful needs of the id are the expression of instincts, which arise from our bodily nature and are the ultimate cause of all our activity. Freud substantially revised his theory of the instincts over many years, concluding that there are two basic instincts: (1) *Eros* or the love instinct, the aim of which is to unite, "to bind together"[4]; and (2) the destructive or *death instinct*, which aims at undoing or destroying connections and ultimately at extinction. For some time he had believed that *Eros* alone was the fundamental instinct and could explain the destructive as well as the unifying aspects of human behavior. In his 1920 book, *Beyond the Pleasure Principle*, Freud first articulated his view that alongside the erotic or love instinct, and mixed together with it in various and subtle ways, is a separate destructive or death instinct.

The total instinctual energy available to *Eros* is called *libido*. Freud never developed a term for the corresponding energy of the death instinct. All our knowledge of libido is based on its manifestations in the ego, where it can be observed. When a child is born, it is characterized by *primary narcissism*, in which the total energy of the libido is absorbed in the newborn's undifferentiated ego-id. In a short time the emerging ego begins to transfer some of its libido onto objects (other persons and things) outside itself, transforming *narcissistic libido* into *object libido*. On the one hand, object libido is very mobile, able to attach itself to many different objects. On the other hand, it can easily become fixated on specific objects, such as the child with its mother or the adult who falls "head over heels" in love with someone else.

The destructive or death instinct only reveals itself when it is directed outward toward people, things, and situations in the world, where it manifests itself as aggression and hostility. But it also continues to function within a person; with the development of the superego, the destructive instinct's energy often turns in upon the self with an aggressiveness that would otherwise be directed outward. This in turn exacerbates the self-destructive tendencies already present within, as when a person bottles up and turns against oneself the rage felt toward someone else or things in the world.

Infantile sexuality and the Oedipus complex. The single most controversial feature of Freud's psychoanalytic theory was undoubtedly his conclusions about *infantile sexuality*. According to Freud, a person's sexual life begins very soon after birth, and not at puberty as the traditional wisdom had it. " . . . [In] early childhood there are signs of bodily activity to which only an ancient prejudice could deny the name of sexual and which are linked to psychical phenomena that we come across later in adult erotic life—such as fixation to particular objects, jealousy, and so on."[5] But it is very important to be clear about what he means by "sexual life." "Sexual life includes the function of obtaining pleasure from zones of the body,"[6] and Freud always sharply distinguished between the *sexual* and the *genital*. The sexual refers generally to obtaining pleasure through any of a number of what Freud called *erotogenic zones* of the body, of which the genitals are only one.

The mother is the first love object of the child—first her breast and then, with the emergence and

---

[3]Ibid., 3.
[4]Ibid., 5.
[5]Ibid., 10.
[6]Ibid., 9.

differentiation of the ego, the mother herself. This is true of both boys and girls. However, the further development of the two sexes differs:

Male development.   Prior to the emergence of the phallic stage, the male child loves his mother and identifies with his father. With the increase of sexual impulses in the phallic stage, focused now on the penis, the boy wants exclusive sexual possession of his mother and develops an antagonism toward his father as his rival for the love of the mother. Drawing on the story in Sophocles's *Oedipus the King*, Freud called this the *Oedipus complex*, and regarded it as a crucial stage in the child's development. The male child fears the father's anger, a fear that takes the specific form of fearing that the father will cut off the offending penis. It is a fear that is driven home to the boy when he sees that females indeed lack a protruding sexual organ. This is *castration anxiety* or the *castration complex*, which Freud called "the severest trauma of . . . [the boy's] young life."[7] It causes the boy to repress his incestuous desire for his mother and his hostility toward his father. Freud assumed that all human beings are constitutionally bisexual, inheriting the tendencies of the opposite sex as well as of their own sex. When the boy gets through the Oedipus phase, he will tend to identify either with his mother or with his father, depending on the relative strength of the feminine and the masculine in his makeup, and this will shape his personality and relationships throughout his life.

Female development.   Freud saw the developmental process differently for female children. The mother is also the girl's first love object, but she does not come to identify with her father the way the boy does. When the girl enters the phallic stage and discovers that she does not possess the external genitals of the male, she feels what the boy-child fears—castrated. She tends to blame her mother, anatomically like her, for this condition, and begins to focus her love more on her father. The father possesses the organ she is lacking, which makes her love also envy—what Freud called *penis envy*, which is the female counterpart

of the male's castration anxiety. But whereas with the boy the castration complex brings the Oedipal phase to an end, with the girl penis envy *introduces* the Oedipus complex. She loves her father and regards her mother as a rival for his love. Unlike the boy's resolution of the complex, the Oedipus complex does not disappear for the girl, although with maturation it weakens and she comes to accept the impossibility of possessing her father. Like the boy, the girl will identify more with the father or with the mother depending on the predominance of masculine or feminine elements, although for both it is not an exclusive identification with one parent or the other.

Through his work on infantile sexuality Freud was a pioneer of twentieth-century theories of personality development, which in a variety of ways describe the individual's mental development as taking place through a series of more or less well-defined stages. After Freud, psychologists such as Jean Piaget applied the concept to cognitive development and Lawrence Kohlberg and Carol Gilligan to moral development, while others who remained broadly in the Freudian tradition, such as Erik Erikson, carried forward and revised Freud's more general approach to personality development.

The unconscious and repression.   Traditionally, psychology was concerned almost entirely with people's conscious states. Freud overturned this focus in the name of science, arguing on the basis of his case studies and self-analysis that the foundational, the most powerful, and by far the largest part of the human self is the unconscious. While some things in the unconscious can be called to mind without great effort or resistance—as when we remember what we had for breakfast this morning—many things are buried deeply and can only be made conscious with the assistance of a trained therapist who helps us bring them to light and interpret their meaning. That is because of *repression*, a defense mechanism by which the ego forces out of consciousness memories, ideas, and perceptions that it considers dangerous. They are repressed into the id, which is entirely unconscious. The superego can have a large influence on

---

[7]Ibid., 47.

Surrealist artists and writers were heavily influenced by the ideas of Freud, particularly his writings on the subconscious and the significance of dreams. Many Surrealist works presented familiar objects in unfamiliar situations or distorted them in ways to recall fantastic or dream-like states. Surrealists like Salvador Dalí attempted to use images of the subconscious in their works, although Dalí departed from Freud's theories in claiming to have control of his subconscious. In *The Persistence of Memory,* Dalí positioned common objects with unexpected attributes in an unusual situation, transforming pocket watches into drooping, malleable objects.

Figure IV-3   Salvador Dalí, *The Persistence of Memory,* 1931. Oil on canvas, $9^1/_2 \times 13''$ (24.36 × 33.33 cm). The Museum of Modern Art, New York. Digital image © The Museum of Modern Art/ Courtesy of Scala/Art Resource, NY. Artists Rights Society (ARS), New York.

what the ego represses, and the stronger the superego, the more repressions there are likely to be. The most powerful repressions are memories from early childhood, which can include such things as "forbidden" sexual desires and experiences and hostility toward one or both parents. Repression is a necessary part of normal development, but it can manifest itself in a variety of abnormal ways such as psychosomatic illnesses, hysterical paralysis, sexual impotence or frigidity, suicidal guilt feelings, and uncontrollable rage.

5. *Dreams, jokes, and slips of the tongue.* The repressed material in the unconscious manifests itself in indirect and symbolic ways in our dream life, which Freud called a harmless form of psychosis. All of us are aware of the fact that our dreams have a life and logic of their own that often seems to have nothing to do with our waking life. While some dreams seem reasonably straightforward, prompted, say, by something from the previous day, others are extremely puzzling and sometimes bizarre. Freud considered the interpretation

of dreams to be an absolutely key element in unlocking the unconscious through psychoanalysis.

Neurosis and psychosis. Neurosis and psychosis are weakenings of the ego in its formidable task of mediating among id, superego, and the external world. A relative weakening or disturbing of the ego in its organization and functions is a neurosis. An absolute weakening, one that brings the ego's "proper relation to reality" to an end, is a psychosis. The neurotic's ego is crippled but can be helped by therapy to return to its normal functioning. As Freud writes: "The analytic physician and the patient's weakened ego, basing themselves on the real external world, have to band themselves together into a party against the enemies, the instinctual demands of the id and the conscientious demands of the super-ego. We form a pact with each other."[8] In order to be helped by psychoanalysis, a person's ego must retain a certain degree of connection with reality and inner coherence. In the case of psychosis, the ego has retreated so completely from reality and become so inwardly fragmented that Freud confessed frankly that such persons could not be helped with the knowledge available at that time. Psychoanalysis could help neurotics; it could not help psychotics.

Relative strength or weakness of ego is a "given" in a person's development, so that by nature, so to speak, some people are more susceptible to neurosis and even to psychosis than are others. There is also a very wide range of behaviors that fall under the category of neurosis. According to Freud, all human beings, even the most "normal" ones, are to some degree neurotic, while some have such severe forms of neurosis as to border on psychosis. Even "normal" persons, if they observe themselves closely, turn out to be repressed in unhealthy ways about certain things, acting out patterns of relationships established in the Oedipal phase, or manifesting quirky compulsions, impulsions, and obsessions.

Reality-testing and treatment. Notice the importance to Freud of the idea of relationship to "the real external world" as a benchmark of mental health or illness. The concept of *reality-testing* is important in his approach to self-analysis and therapy. The external world is the world of objects and other persons which we commonly perceive and inhabit and which we understand properly through reason. Freud always saw the aim of psychoanalysis as restoring persons to a normal working relationship with the world thus understood. The psychoanalyst assists persons in bringing repressed memories and desires to consciousness through the technique of free association, talking about anything that comes to the patient's mind including the sharing of dreams. By facing their inner "demons" and understanding them both rationally and emotionally, individuals are liberated to function more adaptively and live more healthily in the "real world."

The individual and civilization. Around 1912 Freud began applying the psychoanalytic theory of the structure and dynamics of the human personality to the interpretation of wider social and cultural issues, such as the psychosocial functions of religion and the arts and the problematic character of human civilization. He never thought that psychoanalytic theory provided the last or the only word on these cultural phenomena, but he did believe that it could shed significant new light on old human institutions.

An essay Freud published in 1915, "Reflections upon War and Death," belongs among these wider studies, as he reflected on what World War I was revealing about the relationship between the individual and civilization and about people's attitudes toward death. Freud was stimulated to write only several months into the war, because the unexpected ferocity and carnage of the war were already evident and arousing widespread horror over how this could happen among what Europeans considered the most civilized nations of the world. Responding to the shock and disillusionment created by the war and its savagery, he argued that war dramatically unmasks deep-seated human desires, such as aggression and desiring the death of others, which we can otherwise pretend we have contained or diminished. The basic idea of the essay is one that Freud would develop extensively in his later works: "Civilization is the fruit of renunciation of instinctual satisfaction. . . ."[9]

---

[8]Ibid., 30.

[9]Freud, "Reflections Upon War and Death," translated by E. Colburn Mayne, in *Character and Culture*, edited by Philip Rieff (New York: Macmillan Publishing Co., 1963), 115.

Fuseli was an eighteenth-century Romantic painter who opposed the cool rationality of Enlightenment thinking, embracing instead imaginative, melodramatic, and irrational subjects. Although unpopular with critics, the public appreciated his penchant for the dramatic. Fuseli painted *The Nightmare,* a disturbing erotic vision, in several versions, each of which were then engraved for commercial reproduction. Sigmund Freud later hung one of these prints in his office, likely because the theme of *The Nightmare* resonated with his own interest in dreams.

Figure IV-4   John Henry Fuseli, *The Nightmare,* 1781. Oil on canvas, $39^3/_4 \times 49^1/_2$" (101 × 127 cm). The Detroit Institute of Arts. Courtesy of Superstock.

In two of Freud's most important later books he applied psychoanalytic theory to the understanding of religion and of the general problems of civilization. His general study of religion is *The Future of an Illusion* (1927), while his chief study of the problems of civilization is *Civilization and Its Discontents* (1930). In both books Freud recounts how our instinctual desires are made to suffer under the forces of society, and how such restrictions inevitably produce neurosis and anti-social behavior.

In *The Future of an Illusion* Freud examines the ideas of religion: where do they come from, and what value do they have? Freud's answer is that an examination of the psychical origin of religious ideas shows that they are "illusions," by which Freud means that they are not fact-based beliefs but rather "fulfillments of the oldest and strongest and most urgent wishes of mankind."[10] Religion is an expression of humanity's deepest desires, beginning with the desire of the helpless infant for protection from

[10]Freud, *The Future of an Illusion,* translated and edited by James Strachey (New York: W. W. Norton & Co., 1989), 38.

insecurity and danger and including the desire to overcome death by living eternally with the gods, the desire for justice in an unjust world, and the need to understand the origins of the universe and human life and to explain the inexplicable.

Socially, religious beliefs arose during the childhood of the human race, and individually they grow out of the child's long period of dependence upon his or her parents. Beliefs in the gods, who are imaged as divine parents, prolong throughout adult life our childhood dependence on our parents. Although religions have played a key role historically in robbing nature of its terrors and reconciling individuals to society, Freud believes that in the present and even more in the future they will be seen by an increasing number of people as remnants from a pre-scientific world that are in conflict with what we know of reality through reason and investigation. Furthermore, in their task of making people more moral, religions have failed. Since they perpetuate childhood dependence and illusion rather than encouraging autonomy, they are social forms of neurosis.

If we are to live a life governed by reason and face the world as it is—what Freud calls "education to reality"—then we must see our religious beliefs not as expressions of reason but as irrational hopes and wishes that promote a life of illusion. For some this may turn out to be a harsh truth, since giving up our fondest wishes about ourselves and the world can be a wrenching experience. While science itself is a finite human enterprise that often makes mistakes, the strength of science over religion, says Freud, is that science seeks to be self-corrective and dynamic rather than dogmatic and unchanging.

The theme of *Civilization and Its Discontents* is the ambivalence of the individual human being toward civilization. "Discontents" in the title translates the German *Unbehagen*, which Freud uses to refer to the "uneasiness" or malaise that pervades the lives of human beings living together in society. He defines "civilization" or "culture" (*Kultur*) as encompassing all the distinctively human ways in which we set ourselves apart from nature, such as language, political, social, and economic organization, customs and mores, religion, art, war, and the accumulation of knowledge. Civilization has two purposes: (1) to protect us against the vicissitudes of nature, and (2) to regulate our relations with one another.

Civilization has a variety of means of reconciling the individual to its demands, not all of which require instinctual repression. One means is *sublimation*, the displacement of instinctual desires from their original objects onto "higher" objects. Freud describes this "subliming" of the instincts as "an especially conspicuous feature of cultural development; it is what makes it possible for higher psychical activities, scientific, artistic or ideological, to play such an important part in civilized life."[11] So, for example, the sexual drive is often creatively sublimated into artistic expression and enjoyment. Another means is aim-inhibited love, the ability of some people living in society to universalize the love instinct beyond either the sexual or even family ties over to friendship and even to love of humanity generally, and to inspire others to move in a similar direction.

But in the final analysis, says Freud, civilization is possible only through a considerable renunciation of individual humans' instinctual drives:

> . . . it is impossible to overlook the extent to which civilization is built up upon a renunciation of instinct, how much it presupposes precisely the non-satisfaction (by suppression, repression or some other means?) of powerful instincts. This "cultural frustration" dominates the large field of social relationships between human beings. . . . it is the cause of the hostility against which all civilizations have to struggle.[12]

We have seen, in summarizing Freud's theory of the personality, that the id seeks only its own pleasure; it is governed by what Freud called the *pleasure principle*. The demands of civilization, as expressed through the external world and the superego, force the ego to control these powerful instinctual desires, which it does through conscious suppression and unconscious repression.

---

[11]Freud, *Civilization and Its Discontents*, translated and edited by James Strachey (New York: W. W. Norton & Co., 1989), 51.

[12]Ibid., 51–52.

In *Civilization and Its Discontents*, Freud fully utilizes his developed theory of the instincts. The life of the id is dominated on the one hand by Eros, the love instinct, which leads persons toward one another in bonding, compassion, and community; and on the other hand by the destructive or death instinct, which manifests itself in alienation, hostility, aggression, cruelty, and destruction. It is the death instinct, which manifests itself as "the inclination to aggression," that "constitutes the greatest impediment to civilization."[13]

Civilization uses both *external* and *internal* means to try to restrain and control the individual's impulse to aggression and destruction. *Externally*, the societies we live in confront us as a powerful authority whose rules are accompanied by the threat and the reality of punishment. But external sanctions alone are not enough, and if they were all that was available, civilization would be impossible. The other, and more effective, means by which societies control the destructive instinct is the superego, the internal appropriation by the individual self of society's rules and values through the influence of parents and others. In this way conscience and the sense of guilt, beginning in early childhood, play a crucial role in controlling the individual's hostile impulses. A person, experiencing the demands of authority and punishment entirely from within, exercises self-control quite apart from external authority and sanction. But the superego is a relentless taskmaster, severely repressing the individual's id and creating excessive guilt and self-punishment.

As Freud saw it, societies develop in somewhat the same manner as individuals: Like individuals, societies develop a "cultural superego," embodied in an ethical code that may make impossible demands on individuals. It is the psychic tension and inner conflict produced by these individual and social demands that creates a general unhappiness or malaise toward the burdens of civilization. Freud found with his patients in turn-of-the-century Vienna that he frequently had to relieve the terrible pressures on their ego of unhealthily repressive demands of the superego and the crippling guilt that accompanied it. Here is Freud's own account of the problem:

In our research into, and therapy of, a neurosis, we are led to make two reproaches against the super-ego of the individual. In the severity of its commands and prohibitions it troubles itself too little about the happiness of the ego, in that it takes insufficient account of the resistances against obeying them—of the instinctual strength of the id . . ., and of the difficulties presented by the real external environment. . . . Consequently we are very often obliged, for therapeutic purposes, to oppose the super-ego, and we endeavour to lower its demands. Exactly the same objections can be made against the ethical demands of the cultural super-ego. It, too, does not trouble itself enough about the facts of the mental constitution of human beings. It issues a command and does not ask whether it is possible for people to obey it. On the contrary, it assumes that a man's ego is psychologically capable of anything that is required of it, that his ego has unlimited mastery over his id. This is a mistake, and even in what are known as normal people the id cannot be controlled beyond certain limits. If more is demanded of a man, a revolt will be produced in him or a neurosis, or he will be made unhappy.[14]

Writing in 1930, with the memory of the European-wide devastation produced by the modern weaponry of World War I still fresh, and the ominous rise to power of Adolf Hitler and his National Socialist Party beginning to take place in Germany, Freud concluded *Civilization and Its Discontents* on a somber note:

The fateful question for the human species seems to me to be whether and to what extent their cultural development will succeed in mastering the disturbance of their communal life by the human instinct of aggression and self-destruction. It may be that in this respect precisely the present time deserves a special interest. Men have gained control over the forces of nature to such an extent that with their help they would have no difficulty in exterminating one another to the last man. They know this, and hence comes a large part

[13]Ibid., 81.
[14]Ibid., 108–109.

of their current unrest, their unhappiness and their mood of anxiety. And now it is to be expected that the other of the two "Heavenly Powers," eternal Eros, will make an effort to assert himself in the struggle with his equally immortal adversary. But who can foresee with what success and with what result?[15]

We are reading Freud's reflections more than seventy years later. During that time the world has seen World War II, including the Nazi Holocaust and the use of nuclear weapons against Japan, the Gulag Archipelago in the Stalinist U.S.S.R. and the Cultural Revolution in Maoist China, both of which killed millions, the development of huge stockpiles of nuclear weapons, the Cold War, further wars in Korea and Vietnam and elsewhere, genocides in Cambodia, central Africa, and former Yugoslavia, serious environmental damage, and new, destructive forms of terrorism. On the other hand, the world has also witnessed the founding of the United Nations, dramatic improvements in the rights of women and minorities in the U.S. and elsewhere, the collapse of communism in Europe and the spread of democracy in Latin America, and environmental concern and action on a global scale. Would we want to revise Freud's outlook in a more optimistic direction, or would we instead want to "put it in italics" for emphasis? Is the future of the struggle between love and death as uncertain for us as it was for Freud?

Because he saw the tension between the individual and civilization as largely irreconcilable, Freud believed that therapy would largely have to be directed to self-cure. Hence individuals, although needing the comfort and support of others, will have to come by their own efforts to understand themselves, and will need more self-knowledge if they are to be cured. This pursuit of self-knowledge as a means to a healthy self—the modern, idiosyncratically re-translated version of Socrates's "know thyself"—is perhaps the most important legacy that Freud and psychoanalysis have given us.

THE FREUDIAN LEGACY

The combination of, and also the tension between, the scientific and the humanistic sides of Freud's pioneering theory, together with specific aspects of the theory itself, have made his methods and conclusions controversial ever since they first became well known. Some of his most famous students—such as Carl Jung, Alfred Adler, Otto Rank, and Karen Horney—broke away from Freud, significantly modified some of his ideas, and in some cases founded their own movements and training institutes. Others who remained within the Freudian tradition—such as Melanie Klein, B. F. Winnicott, and Karl Menninger—developed some of Freud's ideas in new and fruitful ways. All psychoanalysts and many psychiatrists in the United States have remained broadly Freudian in their theory and therapy. (Psychoanalysts are usually physicians who are trained specifically in psychoanalytic theory and practice and undergo extended psychoanalysis at a certified psychoanalytic institute. Psychiatrists are physicians who have qualified through a residency in psychiatry to treat psychological problems and disorders). The psychoanalytic tradition founded by Freud, as represented for example at the Menninger Foundation formerly of Topeka, Kansas (now based in Fort Worth, Texas), has undergone many developments and modifications in its details over the years. Among other things, it has been open to influences from other theories, other forms of therapy, and physiological and pharmacological research. Today's mental health specialists typically utilize a variety of resources in treating patients. That is precisely what we should expect of any pioneering system of psychological theory and therapy such as Freud's: the capacity to generate new insights, corrections, and elaborations.

Lively controversy continues over Freud's theory and his therapeutic techniques. In 1993 a *Time* magazine cover story asked the question, "Is Freud dead?" In 1995, the planning of an exhibit on Freud, scheduled to open in 1998 at the Library of Congress (which has the largest collection of original Freud documents in the world), became embroiled in heated and bitter debate. In universities Freudian ideas are much more likely to be encountered among faculty in the humanities than among psychology faculty. The past decade has seen a spate of books both criticizing and defending Freud. Some criticize psychoanalysis as a theory on the grounds that it is not truly scientific; others criticize

---

[15]Ibid., 111–112.

it as a therapy, charging that it is protracted and expensive and not any more effective than other kinds of therapy. Some scholars and scientists accuse Freud of having distorted or suppressed some of his clinical data, and of having changed his theory for personal or ideological rather than for scientific reasons. Many feminists have long objected to Freud's characterization of personality development in women, seeing the idea of "penis envy" as perpetuating in modern form Aristotle's view of women as defective males. There are learned and articulate exponents of these criticisms, and learned and eloquent defenders of Freud on all these issues. Most recently, a group of American neurologists who use brain imaging are claiming to offer truly scientific, empirical evidence for some of Freud's core ideas—including his theory of unconscious drives or instincts, such as sex and aggression, rooted in the most primitive part of the brain, and even his work on dreams. They even have a journal called *Neuropsychoanalysis*. The eminent brain researcher Eric Kandel, winner of the 2000 Nobel Prize in Physiology or Medicine, was inspired by Freud's work to become a neuroscientist and train in psychoanalysis. He continues to believe that Freud is the greatest pioneer of modern psychology, and that certain of his central ideas are confirmed by empirical brain research. The fact that Freud continues, a hundred years after he developed psychoanalysis, to generate both creative revision and development and lively controversy, is impressive testimony to the importance and influence of his ideas.

QUESTIONS FOR STUDY AND DISCUSSION

1. What does it mean to say that Freud drew on the traditions of both the scientific worldview and the worldview of classical humanism?

2. How does Freud characterize the structure of the self?

3. Describe Freud's theory of personality development. What does he mean by "sexuality" in talking about infants and young children?

4. What is the role of repression in personality development?

5. What does Freud believe dreams reveal to us about ourselves?

6. What does Freud mean by "civilization"? How does he use his theory of the instincts in analyzing the relationship between civilization and the individual?

7. How does Freud account for the emergence and development of religion in human history? What roles do the individual and society respectively play in this development?

8. What does Freud see as the function of religion as one of the ways in which civilization reconciles individual humans to itself? Does he think it has worked?

9. What does Freud mean by calling religious beliefs "illusions"?

10. How does Freud see the future of religion?

SUGGESTIONS FOR FURTHER READING

Freud, Sigmund. *An Outline of Psycho-Analysis*. Translated and edited by James Strachey. New York: W. W. Norton & Co., 1949.

Freud, Sigmund. *The Interpretation of Dreams*. Translated and edited by James Strachey. New York: W. W. Norton & Co., 1965.

Fussell, Paul. *The Great War and Modern Memory*. New York: Oxford University Press, 1975.

Gay, Peter. *Freud: A Life for Our Time*. New York: Doubleday, 1989.

Jones, Ernest. *The Life and Work of Sigmund Freud*. Edited and abridged by Lionel Trilling and Steven Marcus, with an Introduction by Lionel Trilling. New York: Basic Books, 1961.

Kandel, Eric R. *In Search of Memory: The Emergence of a New Science of Mind*. W.W. Norton, 2006.

Kandel, Eric R. and James H. Schwartz. *Principles of Neural Science*, 4th ed. McGraw-Hill, 2000.

Stor, Anthony. *Freud, A Very Short Introduction*. Oxford University Press, 2001.

CHAPTER THIRTEEN

ARGUMENTS FOR WOMEN'S EQUALITY: WOLLSTONECRAFT, BEAUVOIR AND WOOLF

Virginia Woolf's book *A Room of One's Own* is one of the great feminist texts of the twentieth century. In it she identifies the various causes in history for women's oppression and specifically explores the reasons why there are so few well-known women authors. Woolf lived and wrote at a time when women in Britain and the United States were fighting for the right to vote. Woolf herself was sympathetic to the cause of women's rights but was only on the periphery of the movement. She was, however, particularly sensitive to the lack of education available to women, and for a time in the first decade of the twentieth century taught evening classes to working-class women. It was precisely this issue—education for women—that had inspired Mary Wollstonecraft to write *Vindication of the Rights of Woman* in 1792. Our reading of Woolf, then, is set against a background of more than a century and a half of struggle on behalf of women's rights.

FEMINIST FOREMOTHERS

Mary Wollstonecraft (1759–1797) is undoubtedly the most important intellectual predecessor to Woolf. In her best-known work, *A Vindication of the Rights of Woman* (1792), Wollstonecraft makes a plea, based on the philosophical and political principles of Enlightenment thought, for the equal rights of women to education and moral development. The Enlightenment was a period in which Western humanity, through a newly found faith in the powers of human reason, dared to question and shake off the authorities—philosophical, political, and religious—that had governed its development since the Middle Ages. Despite an intense faith in the

power of reason to lead to the betterment of human life, both individual and social, and despite its calls for individual emancipation and self-determination, the social milieu of the Enlightenment period dictated that most women of intellect and learning remain in the private sphere. Wollstonecraft, however, spoke out with power and conviction about the situation of her sex, and her words became one of the foundational documents for the feminist movement in the nineteenth and twentieth centuries.

Mary Wollstonecraft was born in London in 1759 into a working-class family. She had little formal education, but she had wit and intelligence and set forth to pursue what avenues were open to a woman of her class and circumstances: teaching, being a hired companion or governess, and writing. She worked at all four until she achieved success—even notoriety—as a writer and translator. Her first foray into political writing, *A Vindication of the Rights of Man* (1790), was a response to Edmund Burke's famous *Reflections on the Revolution in France*. Like Thomas Paine, she defended the French Revolution against Burke's attacks as the political realization of Enlightenment hopes for government founded on reason. Wollstonecraft had already written a manual on education, and from this it was a natural progression to an essay devoted exclusively to the rights of women. *Vindication of the Rights of Woman* blends her ideas about the education of women with natural rights theory.

In *Vindication*, Wollstonecraft takes the traditional and Enlightenment view that reason is the definitive characteristic of human beings. This is the view expounded by such thinkers as Plato, Aristotle, Seneca, Thomas Aquinas, Pico, Descartes, the *philosophes*, and Wollstonecraft's contemporary, Kant. She argues that it is no less true of the female than of the male. The alternative would seem to say that women are somehow deficient as human beings—a position which many writers in Western history have, in fact, taken. Wollstonecraft's book was to become an influential document in the long feminist struggle to overcome the deeply entrenched view that the differences between the behavior of men and women were the result of their inherent natures rather than the circumstances of their nurture. The central argument of the *Vindication* is that the attainment of virtue is the proper goal of human life. But reason is essential to the cultivation of virtue, and education is essential to the development of reason. Unless we are to say that women are incapable of virtue, then women's reason must be developed through the same sort of education by which men's reason is made capable of virtue.

Wollstonecraft proposes revolutionary solutions to the plight of women. Women should of course have the same kind of education and educational opportunities as men. Marriage would be far happier if there were greater equality between the partners rather than the slavish dependence of the woman upon the man. The prevailing inequality in marriage does not produce a healthy relationship either between husband and wife or for the children. Wollstonecraft criticizes society's sexual double standard. Although her critics would accuse her of advocating "free love," she actually recommends chastity for both males and females. Wollstonecraft suggests that women with proper education could be trained as physicians or be able to run their own business. Women should also study politics and be allowed to participate in decision-making in public life. She did not really deal with the economic factors in sexism and the special plight of working-class women; and she continued to regard marriage and children as the natural or "normal" situation for women. But both her basic principles and many of their applications were radical and far-reaching in their implications for social change. Some of them have not yet been fully realized.

Wollstonecraft died shortly after childbirth in September, 1797, and her writings were neglected for a time. (The daughter she gave birth to was

Mary Godwin Shelley, author of *Frankenstein*, the subject of Chapter Five.) By the mid-nineteenth century, however, women intellectuals such as British writer George Eliot and American Transcendentalist Margaret Fuller "rediscovered" *Vindication* and were amazed to find that it was a severely moral and serious work. Some of the nineteenth-century mothers of the feminist movement in America, notably Elizabeth Cady Stanton and Lucretia Mott, were enthusiastic about the book and hailed Mary Wollstonecraft as a pioneer of the women's movement. Indeed, *Vindication* was read by early leaders in the women's rights movement and reprinted after the American Civil War (1861–1865) in *The Revolution*, publish by Elizabeth Cady Stanton, Parker Pillsbury, and Susan B. Anthony. But it was especially in the latter part of the twentieth century that Mary Wollstonecraft came to be widely recognized as the first modern spokeswoman for the rights of women. This has resulted in the widely available publication of her work and new research into and biographies of her life.

Nearly sixty years after *Vindication*, in July 1848, at Seneca Falls, New York, a movement was begun in the United States that would continue for more than seventy-five years until the passage of a constitutional amendment enfranchising women in 1920 and the introduction of an ultimately unsuccessful equal rights amendment in 1923. It was the movement for women's suffrage. Like other long-lived reform movements, it developed by stages and shifted with events. A similar movement also began in Great Britain, and in 1917 British women of the age of thirty years and above were given the vote.

The major source of American women's rights thinking at the time of Seneca Falls was the philosophy of natural rights, as exemplified in the writings of John Locke, a body of belief refined in the Enlightenment and summed up in the U.S. Declaration of Independence. At bottom, women's rights claims were a demand for personhood, for inclusion in the cultural values that proclaimed that individuals had inalienable rights because they were persons, that it was government's function to protect those rights, and that to do so, government had to rest on the consent of the governed. Natural rights affirmed the right of individuals to equality of opportunity, and it presupposed that the highest good was the full development of each person's rational faculties. This, of course, included equal access to secondary and higher education for women, but it was a long time before these choices were available for women.[1]

Simone de Beauvoir (1908–1986). A younger contemporary of Woolf's was Simone de Beauvoir, a notable figure of the French existentialist movement. She presents a different reason for women's inequality in society. In her long study of women's place in Western culture entitled *The Second Sex* (1949), Beauvoir lays out her main thesis in her Introduction. Women, she writes, have functioned as the first instance of "otherness" in the male world. That is to say, men, who have controlled the major institutions of the historical cultures, have viewed women as an "alien" form of humanity. Because women have tended to be smaller and physically weaker than men, and because women have had the task of bearing children, men have dominated women, making them subservient to masculine wishes and projects.

In Part IV, Chapter X, of *The Second Sex*, The Formative Years, Beauvoir describes the contrast in the socialization of boys and girls:

> His apprenticeship for life consists in free movement toward the outside world; . . . Climbing trees, fighting with his companions, he feels his body as a means for dominating nature . . . he takes pride in his muscles as in his sex. . . .
>
> . . . she is taught that to please she must try to please, she must make herself object; . . . renounce her autonomy. She is treated like a live doll and is refused liberty. . . . a vicious circle is formed; for the less she exercises her freedom to understand, to grasp and discover the world about her, the less resources will she find within herself, the less will she dare to affirm herself as subject.

Beauvoir goes on: "But it is wrong to assert that a biological datum is concerned; it is in fact a destiny *imposed* upon her by her teachers and by society." [italics added][2] Her explanation is an existentialist one: *whatever their conditioning by heredity and environment, human beings are free and so have the power to choose their values, indeed their very selves.* There is no "eternal feminine" nature or essence, just as there is no "eternal masculine" nature. The historical condition of women is a situation, not a destiny.

Beauvoir criticized the majority of women for freely agreeing with the prevailing male view of their otherness and affirming it for themselves. She studied the many inducements societies have tended to offer women to conform to this role, but she also criticized women for a certain dishonesty or bad conscience, urging them to contest their role as the "other"—to transcend their situation, to control their own future and contribute to fashioning history.

VIRGINIA WOOLF

How can I further encourage you to go about the business of life? Young women, I would say, . . . you are, in my opinion, disgracefully ignorant. You have never made a discovery of any sort of importance. You have never shaken an empire or led an army into battle. The plays of Shakespeare are not by you, and you have never introduced a barbarous race to the blessings of civilization. What is your excuse? It is all very well for you to say . . . we have had other work on our hands. Without our doing, those seas would be unsailed and those fertile lands a desert. We have borne and bred and washed and taught, perhaps to the age of six or seven years, the one thousand six hundred and twenty-three million human beings who are . . . at present in existence. . . . There is truth in what you say. . . . But at the same time may I remind you that . . . the excuse of lack of opportunity, training, encouragement, leisure and money no longer

---

[1]A narrative on the nineteenth–century Suffrage Movement and the twentieth–century "Second Wave" Feminist movement in the United States can be found in the Appendix.

[2]Beauvoir, Simone de. *The Second Sex*. Edited and translated by H. M. Parshley. Reprt. 1952 edition. (New York: Vintage Books, 1989), 280.

holds good. . . . Thus, with some time on your hands and with some book learning in your brains . . . surely you should embark upon another stage of your very long, very laborious and highly obscure career.[3]

With these words, Virginia Woolf (1882–1941) encouraged the fictional, all-female audience of her narrator in *A Room of One's Own* to pursue a life of reading and writing literature. Woolf actually delivered two lectures in October, 1928 at the two women's colleges of Cambridge University. *A Room of One's Own* was loosely based on these lectures and on the experiences Woolf had while at Cambridge to deliver them. The book was published in 1929. It became a famous and highly influential feminist work, especially in the United States after 1970. Woolf was a novelist and journalist, producing her major writings in the 1920s and 1930s. She died at her own hand in 1941. She was "rediscovered" by feminist scholars in the 1970s, and *A Room of One's Own* is now considered by many to be a brilliant and witty critique of patriarchy. In her lifetime she was considered part of the Modernist movement and in recent years she has been given a prominent place in the feminist "canon" (those writers who are considered among the main spokespersons for women).

Woolf's *Three Guineas*, published in 1938, contrasts patriarchy and war with feminism and pacifism, and is one of her most passionate and powerful essays. Writing as Nazi Germany was accelerating its march to war, she argued that there is a direct link between male domination of women and social inequality, fascism, racism, and the glorification of war. With savage wit and extensive documentation she exposed the social and cultural dominance of patriarchy in nineteenth- and twentieth-century Britain and its complicity in authoritarianism and violence. Expanding on her theme in *A Room of One's Own*, she proposed an alternative vision of an egalitarian and anti-violent culture based on the "virtues" that women of intelligence and talent had learned from being subordinated and belittled: poverty (having only what one needs to be independent), chastity (refusing to prostitute one's talents for money), derision (enduring ridicule and obscurity), and "freedom from unreal loyalties" of religion, family, nation, class, race, and even gender.

WOOLF'S LIFE

Virginia Woolf was born into the tradition of what has been called the "intellectual aristocracy" in Britain and spent her adult life among a band of rebellious intellectuals who became known as the Bloomsbury Group. She was the third of four children born to Leslie and Julia Stephen. Her parents brought to their union four children from previous marriages. Leslie Stephen was a well-known intellectual figure of the times, so Virginia was exposed to the rarefied atmosphere of her father's literary and politically liberal friends. She was educated at home, unlike her brothers, who were sent to prep schools and then to Cambridge University. This disparity was something that she always resented, and it is reflected in *A Room of One's Own* and *Three Guineas*. She vowed early in life to be a writer; as children, she and her brothers and sister published a family newspaper called the Hyde Park Gate News. It is generally agreed that some of the tragic and trying events of her childhood and adolescence deeply affected her emotional health and precipitated a series of mental breakdowns in adolescence and adult life. These included the death of her mother when Virginia was thirteen, the death of her half sister a few years later, the unwanted affections of a half brother, and the domineering and later morose figure of her father.

With the death of their father in 1904, the four Stephen children exchanged the dark and dreary house in Hyde Park Gate for a new house and a new life in the Bloomsbury area of London. It was here that they began to host a gathering of brother Thoby's Cambridge classmates, most of whom became lifelong friends and would later constitute the core of the Bloomsbury Group. Attacked by their critics as snobs who thumbed their noses at convention, they did indeed reject Victorian manners and values, established new trends in literature and art, and generally espoused a liberal/socialist political agenda. A number of the leading artists and intellectuals of the time moved in and out of the Bloomsbury circle.

---

[3]Woolf, Virginia. *A Room of One's Own.* New York: Harcourt, Inc. 1981, 112–113.

This period from 1905 to 1912 was a formative one for Virginia. She began writing review essays for periodicals and started a novel. She traveled extensively throughout Europe and to Turkey. She studied Greek and continued to read voraciously. She taught classes to working-women. Most importantly, she gained both intellectual stimulation and social confidence from her exposure to her new circle of friends. She herself would later describe this period as her "graduate education."

In 1912, she married Leonard Woolf, whom she had met through her brother. Theirs was a marriage of deep and abiding friendship, but the physical side of the marriage ended soon after their honeymoon. Leonard was an anchor, a rock, and responsible both for preserving her life and providing her with the emotional security that would enable her to write. A year after their marriage, Virginia had one of her most serious breakdowns. Partly as therapy for her, the Woolfs purchased a printing press in 1917, and from their home in the Richmond area of London founded Hogarth Press, which made its name as the first publisher of many new writers who would become famous (such as T. S. Eliot) and of the works of Sigmund Freud in English translation. Both the therapy and the Press were successful. Virginia went on to become a productive and successful author until her death in 1941, and Hogarth Press exists to the present day.

The platonic nature of her relationship with Leonard and the labyrinthine sexual liaisons of a number of the participants in the Bloomsbury circle have led many scholars to speculate about Woolf's sexuality. Virginia always had close female friends, the relationships with some of whom were clearly romantic in nature. Her most famous friendship was with the aristocratic and openly lesbian Vita Sackville West, wife of British diplomat Harold Nicholson. In fact, *Orlando*, a novel Woolf published in 1928, is reputed to have been written as a love letter to Vita.

WOOLF AS A MODERNIST

Modernism is a cultural movement that in general dated from the late nineteenth century to the middle of the twentieth. It was marked by a rejection of many prevailing patterns and beliefs, a questioning of the general optimism and progressivism of a Europe captivated by the success of science and technology. The devastation of World War I also played an important role in fostering this disillusionment. Literary modernists broke rules, making a conscious break with literary traditions such as formalism (adherence to recognized rules of writing regarding plot, characters, and style). They exhaustively explored the individual consciousness, some of them drawing on Freud's opening up of the unconscious. Writers such as James Joyce in *Ulysses* and Woolf in *Jacob's Room* and *Mrs. Dalloway* experimented with "stream of consciousness" narration, a kind of "free association" in which the story is told through the ceaseless flow and jumble of an individual's thinking. The literary modernists disrupted traditional ideas of time and space in their writings in order to convey the fragmentation of modern experience, as in poems of T. S. Eliot such as *The Wasteland*, where bits and pieces of past and present and one place and another are juxtaposed without any overall coherence. Political ideas and movements such as Marxism and the labor movement influenced the general modernist criticism of traditional social, political, and economic hierarchies. Both Dostoevsky and Nietzsche were harbingers of Modernism.

Woolf wrote volumes of essays and reviews that appeared in some of the foremost British publications. She also authored a substantial collection of short stories, but it is her highly experimental approach to her novels that best exemplifies Woolf's modernism. She is categorized as one of the early "stream of consciousness" writers. There is little emphasis on plot or action, and the story proceeds via the inner narrative of the character so that the reader has, more or less, a window on the soul. Her best-known novel in this style is *Mrs. Dalloway*, which was a commercial success. *To the Lighthouse*, which is modeled on her own family, was another success. This book served as a healing catharsis for Woolf, for it allowed her to express many of her unresolved feelings toward her mother and father. Two other critically acclaimed novels are *Jacob's Room (1922)* and *The Waves (1931)*, but these are more difficult to read and therefore not as popular.

Woolf was an exacting writer and gave her books up to print with trepidation and only after careful and repeated revisions. She struggled to find her own novelistic form, once defining it as "elegy." At least one critic had commented that her prose is

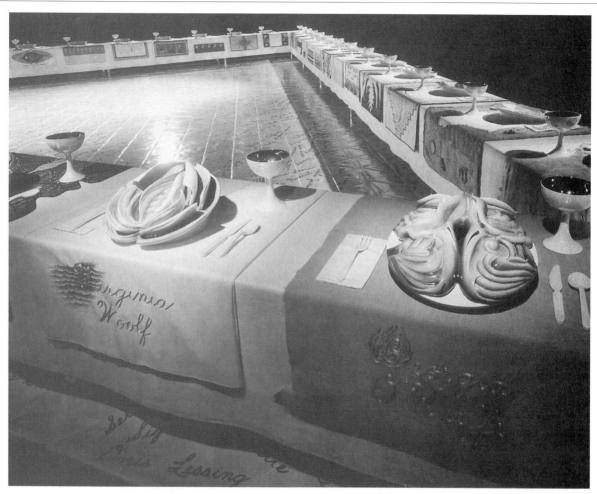

The Dinner Party, possibly the best-known work of the 1970s feminist art movement, celebrates a history of women. Through this large-scale installation, Chicago sought to commemorate historical figures—thirteen on each side of the triangle, with another 999 names inscribed on the porcelain floor—and to reclaim methods of art-making associated with women's history. The place settings include embroidered textiles and hand-painted china, both media traditionally produced by women but historically denigrated as amateur (feminine) craft rather than praised as professional (masculine) art. This detail of *The Dinner Party* features the place setting dedicated to Virginia Woolf, alongside one for Georgia O'Keeffe. Both plates display obvious references to the female body, through what Chicago termed "central core" (vaginal) imagery.

Figure IV-5   Judy Chicago, *Virginia Woolf plate* **from** *The Dinner Party,* 1974–79. Sculpted porcelain plates and needlework. Brooklyn Museum of Art, New York. "The Dinner Party," looking from Wing Three, featuring the Virginia Woolf and Georgia O'Keeffe place settings, © Judy Chicago, 1979. Collection of The Brooklyn Museum, Brooklyn, NY. Gift of the Elizabeth A. Sackler Foundation. Artists Rights Society (ARS), New York. Photo: © Donald Woodman. Through the Flower.

as much poetry as prose, a judgment that applies especially to *Jacob's Room* and *The Waves*.

The completion of a novel was always fraught with emotional stress for Woolf. In 1941, she had just completed *Between the Acts*. Her popularity, which had peaked in the 1920s, had somewhat declined; she did not think this a good novel; she was depressed by the war; and she felt she was burdening her husband too greatly. Feeling the madness beginning to come upon her again, she took her own life in March, when she walked from her and Leonard's house in the country south of London into the River Ouse, a large stone in her pocket. Contrary to her wishes, her novel was published. It has a distinctly anti-war theme and has been judged one of her best.

Scholarly attention to Woolf's work, her life, and her circle of friends has grown over the past several decades to the point where there are now Virginia Woolf Societies in the United States, Britain, and France; her homes in England are tourist attractions; and there is a veritable industry in Woolf and Bloomsbury memorabilia. Her complete diaries have been published in five volumes, and volumes of her letters to family and friends continue to be uncovered and published.

WOOLF AS FEMINIST

While not an activist, Woolf considered herself a supporter of women's rights throughout her life and gave service to the British suffrage movement in the 1910s. She herself had felt deeply the strictures placed on females in upper-middle-class Victorian society. Woolf always believed that it was the liberation from this traditional Victorian family circle that allowed her to realize the full extent of her creativity. The role of women within society and the family, and male/female sexuality, are among the strongest themes in her novels. The 1993 film *Orlando* is an interpretation of one of Woolf's most unusual novels. Whether the theme of this work, as the director of the film claims, is androgyny or not, it does dare to explore in a whimsical way the different social roles of men and women in society and the perceptions of the privileges allowed to each. Woolf's strongest statement with reference to women is stated in her opening line to *A Room of One's Own*. "*But* [emphasis added] you may say, we ask you to speak about women—and fiction." The author begins her essay by literally "*butting in*" with a new idea about women. She goes on to ask: Where are women in history? What has been their contribution? Why are there no more women writers? Woolf examines the construction of culture and discovers that women are largely absent. Woolf wants to bring women back into the conversation because the world could be better and more interesting if their voices are heard. Woolf's feminist project is strongly rooted in the claim for equality.

A ROOM OF ONE'S OWN

On Saturday, October 27, 1928, Virginia Woolf wrote in her diary: "I am back from speaking at Girton [to] starved but valiant young women . . . intelligent, eager, poor, and destined to become schoolmistresses. I blandly told them to drink wine and have a room of their own."[4] Woolf did not like public attention and shied away from personal appearances. She declined all honorary titles, degrees, and awards, and she rarely spoke before groups. In 1928, however, she was persuaded to speak to the women at both Girton and Newnham Colleges at Cambridge on the topic of women and fiction. In *A Room of One's Own*, which is based on these lectures, she surveys literature and women of literary talent in an effort to answer the question: Why have there been so few women writers? From this seemingly narrow focus, she exposes aspects of the condition of all women that have stunted their lives and stifled their abilities. The conclusion is all-too-obvious: throughout history patriarchal society has subordinated women and devalued their work. She proposes that in order to exercise their talents to the fullest, women, like men, need personal freedom and financial independence—a room of one's own and five hundred pounds a year.

The book is divided into six chapters that fall roughly into two parts. Chapters one to three make

---

[4]Woolf, Virginia. *A Moment's Liberty, the Shorter Diary* (New York: Harcourt Brace Jovanovich, 1984), 250.

the case against patriarchy. Here we find themes that had been raised early by writers such as Wollstonecraft, Harriet Taylor and J. S. Mill, and by the women of the suffragist and women's rights movements of the nineteenth century. In Chapters four through six, Woolf examines women authors and their writing. These chapters are essentially an exercise in feminist theory and criticism, which has been picked up and greatly elaborated by feminist literary scholars during the latter decades of the twentieth century.

Woolf opens the book with a direct address to her audience and then slips into the third person as Mary Beton, which sets up a trialogue among the female writer, the audience to whom the writer is lecturing, and the reader of the book. Miss Beton has been invited to lunch at a men's college at "Oxbridge" (a fictional university whose name combines "Oxford" and "Cambridge"), and to dinner at "Fernham." The latter is a loosely based fictional representation of Girton College. Founded by the English suffragist Emily Davies in 1873 and originally called Hitchin College, Girton was the first women's residential college in Great Britain. Newnham College, where Woolf gave the second of the lectures on which *Room* is based, was the second such residential college, also at Cambridge University, founded in 1874 and established on curricular principles that differed from those of Girton. By contrasting the male "Oxbridge" and the female "Oxbridge" in the way that she does, Woolf reveals the inequality of educational opportunities between men and women. But even as plain and austere as the women's facilities are, they have been a giant leap forward, for, as we learn in the after-dinner conversation between the two Marys (Beton and Seton), the colleges came into being only in the last half of the nineteenth century, and then only after a long, hard struggle (which is a roughly accurate representation of the actual work that was required to establish Girton). In the 1920s there were the only two residential options for women at Cambridge (Oxford began admitting women to full student membership in 1920, but Cambridge did not), compared to multiple, better endowed options for men.

Throughout the book, Woolf touches on other issues that are of concern to her. One that appears here in the first chapter is the problem of war. Mary Beton catches sight of a Manx cat out the window following her luncheon at Oxbridge, and this prompts her to muse about life before World War I. Woolf, like most of her contemporaries and as we have read in the previous chapter on Freud, was deeply affected by this conflict and many of her writings expressed anti-war themes. Here Woolf states her belief that the "Great War" killed romance and romantic poetry.

In chapter two, Mary Beton resolves to pursue her topic in the appropriate way by researching it at the British Museum. She wants to uncover the answer to the question of why women are poor relative to men ("Why did men drink wine and women water?"), which has so strong a bearing on their further opportunities, as the disparities between men's and women's colleges at Oxbridge showed. In this part of the book, we can observe Woolf's considerable wit and irony in the descriptive passages. The mention of the young Oxbridge student who "has been trained in research" is a veiled, perhaps bitter, comment on Victorian society, which sent its men to universities and kept its women at home. Perusing the reference catalogue, she discovers that there are a vast number of books written about women by men, but no books about men by women. The title to the book by "Professor von X," which seems both absurd and appalling to most Westerners today, is representative of the attitudes and beliefs held by most men about women in the West for many centuries. Perceiving that her reaction to the pompous professor is one of anger, she is led to the conclusion that men are angry, and that the consequence of this anger is that women must become the mirrors through which men view themselves. Mary Beton's hypothesis has affinities with Simone de Beauvoir's argument concerning the non-reciprocal objectification to which men, as the dominant gender, subject the "Other"—women (or "woman"), the subordinate gender—the "second sex"—as a way of giving themselves a superior or positive place and identity against the negatively depicted woman. Similarly, Mary's discovery of a multitude of books on women, sex, and gender in the British Library is echoed in French sociologist Michel Foucault's later finding that contrary to popular myth, Victorian society was not silent about sex and gender, but singularly loquacious, even if not openly so.[5]

At the end of the chapter, Mary tells us of an inheritance from an aunt that liberated her from the drudgery of newspaper work. Such an inheritance was a fact of Woolf's own life. Even though they both came from upper-middle-class families, neither she nor Leonard had much money, contrary to what one might have expected. It was therefore necessary for both of them to earn money from their writing. An annuity from Virginia's aunt Caroline Stephen—who did not die of a fall from a horse in Bombay as did the fictional aunt in *Room*, but from quite ordinary causes in her cottage near Oxford—provided a degree of financial security that allowed Woolf to give more attention to her novels. It was not until the late 1920s that Woolf would realize much financial reward from her writing. Here, as elsewhere in the book, Woolf points to economic dependence as a major source of women's subjection.

The topic narrows in chapter three to an examination of English literature in the time of Queen Elizabeth I. Still searching for answers to why women are poor and why they do not write (or at least publish), and still speaking in the voice of Mary, Woolf reviews legal codes related to women in Elizabethan times and later. Her method reflects the method of many contemporary historians who have sought to write the history of women and, like many of them, she uncovers some interesting information. We learn that women were at the mercy of both husband and family and could be "beaten and flung about the room without any shock being inflicted upon public opinion." Mary ponders why, in portrayals of women in literature, some of the most profound thoughts fall from the lips of women, yet in real life women could neither read nor write. Women did not write, not because they lacked the ability, but because they were prevented from writing. She illustrates this in her tale imagining that Shakespeare had a sister named Judith. Judith has the same talents as her brother Will, and she too wishes to go to London and write for the theater. She runs away to the city where she is picked up by Nick Greene, the actor-manager of the theater. She becomes pregnant by him, kills herself, and is buried near where the omnibuses stop outside the Elephant and Castle. Anonymity and chastity have been demanded of women if they are not to share the tragic fate of the fictional Judith Shakespeare. The psychological impact of family and society on women was so great, Mary concludes, that it is astonishing that there were any women writers at all, and yet there were a few.

In the concluding three chapters, Woolf/Mary introduces us to the works of several British women writers. Aphra Behn was a novelist and popular playwright in seventeenth-century London. She earned her living by her pen at the expense of a respectable reputation, since women who participated in the public sphere (such as performers and authors) were considered sullied and compromised. Passing over a number of writers, Mary/Woolf focuses on well-known nineteenth-century authors Emily and Charlotte Brontë and Jane Austen. Mary/Woolf speculates that when women began to write, they wrote novels because the conditions under which they lived were more conducive to novels than to poetry. She is of the opinion that writing is not solely the product of the individual, but rather emerges out of a corporate or cultural voice and experience. A truly superior author submerges his or her personality, Mary claims, pointing to William Shakespeare as perhaps the best and best-known example among male authors. Emily Brontë and Jane Austen accomplished this same end, but Charlotte Brontë let her anger show through her writings in a way that lessened their quality. Furthermore, because of the paucity of women writers over the centuries, there is no established tradition of a women's distinctive literary language. She suggests that women must develop such a language and write in it so that whatever books women write may be adapted to a woman's body, that is, to feminine rather than masculine rhythms. One of her arguments here is that women need to learn more about women, physiologically and psychologically, and not trust to the analyses of women by men. Such analyses, as we learned in the case of "Professor von X," and as she repeats using other examples, have not only been grossly unfair, but inaccurate and damaging.

---

[5]Foucault, Michel. *The History of Sexuality: Volume I: Introduction.* Trans. Robert Hurley. (New York: Random House, 1980), 12–35.

In chapter five, Mary/Woolf moves from a consideration of nineteenth-century women authors to that of a recent author, Mary Carmichael. Woolf reminds us in this chapter that Mary is speaking to an all-female audience, which allows her certain public freedoms—concerning the discussion of sexuality, at least—that would not be available to her if men were present in the room. Mary Carmichael is one of the names that the narrator of *Room* says her audience may call her; like the character, her novel, *Life's Adventure*, is fictitious, but its description does closely follow the opening of *Love's Creation*, a 1928 novel by Mary Stopes. The discussion centering around this new young author may reflect the type of discussion that Woolf carried on with herself concerning her own writing. Woolf's novels, it will be recalled, were often experimental in nature, and she worked with "stream of consciousness" writing.

Woolf also repeatedly uses metaphor throughout the text to reinforce her opening question: Where are women in history? We first encounter this with the story of the Beadle and the Library in which she metaphorically illustrates that the university is not a place for women. The metaphor of the two dinners indicates that women are the impoverished in society. Good food and good drink are beyond their means. The narrator travels to the British Library. If the truth is not to be found there, then where? Here Woolf contrasts this proclamation with its opposite: the truth about women is not found here. Perhaps one of the more amusing metaphors is that of the looking-glass. Women serve as mirrors to men so they might recognize their superiority.

In chapter six, Mary/Woolf arrives at a conclusion about what an author must have in order to produce the best writing. The best authors—she cites Shakespeare, Coleridge, and Jane Austen—are those who reveal neither male nor female sexuality in their writing (much as in chapter four they don't treat their work as a form of confessional), but rather have such a unity of mind that their writing is androgynous. "Androgyny" for Woolf means embracing both male and female in such a way as to unify and transcend the sexes. This conclusion may seem to contradict somewhat the arguments in the previous chapters concerning the need for a women's language, and a new genre of novel built around the rhythms of women's bodies. These last three chapters, however, are a kind of further experimentation for Woolf. Mary has meandered over the course of her discussion, first expressing this idea and then that until she finally comes to her theory of androgyny. We have, in a way, been part of her inner dialogue, and thereby a part of Woolf's as well.

Mary Beton ends her somewhat meditative journey, and the narrator then sums up in her own voice, as good lecturers should. Surprisingly, she advises against making judgments on the merits of writers of either sex, and if judgments are made, an aspiring author should ignore them. One must do things for the sake of doing them, not for the rewards, be those praise or money. This conclusion seems clearly to reflect Woolf's personal experience. She was intensely sensitive to criticism (a hint is given in chapter four), which is one reason why she found it so difficult to bring closure to her books. Again expressing the testimony of personal experience, Woolf claims that the value of writing is that, through writing, the writer sees life more intensely, permitting her to live more intensely. The "gates" or opportunities have now been opened for women, and they must act. But, to recap her opening and a theme that she raises several times throughout the book, to do that it is necessary to have a room of one's own, and perhaps also £500 a year!

QUESTIONS FOR STUDY AND DISCUSSION

1. Mary Wollstonecraft makes this statement in *A Vindication of the Rights of Woman*: "Friendship is a serious affection; the most sublime of all affections, because it is founded on principle, and cemented by time. The very reverse may be said of love." Wollstonecraft was saying that marriages should be based on friendship not love, or at least the type of "passionate love" that one associates with marriage vows. If you think that there is some wisdom behind this statement, consider how "love and marriage" are portrayed in contemporary times through television, movies and books. Is "friendship" presented as one of the essential factors to a successful marriage?

2. Women's rights leaders in the United States and Britain adopted Wollstonecraft's foundation in

natural rights theory in their argument for equality for women. Explain what that foundation was and how it might have been used in the suffrage movement.

3. Who was Simone de Beauvoir and how did she argue for women's equality?

4. Explain what Modernism is and provide examples of how Virginia Woolf was a Modernist.

5. What is the question Woolf tries to answer in *A Room of One's Own*? Describe generally the approach she takes to answering it.

6. In chapter five Woolf'narrator states that "there is a spot the size of a shilling [a coin the size of a half dollar] at the back of the head which one can never see for oneself." What is the author trying to point out in this metaphor?

7. What is the ideal of "androgyny" that Woolf uses as a criterion for evaluating works of fiction? How does she apply it to leading women writers of the nineteenth century? What writers does she believe have embodied it?

SUGGESTIONS FOR FURTHER READING

Bell, Anne Olivier. *The Diary of Virginia Woolf*, Vols. II–V. London: Harcourt Brace Jovanvich, 1978, 1980, 1982, 1984.

Bell, Quentin. *Virginia Woolf: A Biography*. New York: Harcourt Brace Jovanovich, Inc., 1972.

Cott, Nancy F. *The Grounding of Modern Feminism.* New Haven: Yale University Press, 1987.

Flexner, Eleanor. *Century of Struggle: The Woman's Rights Movement in the United States*. New York: Athenaeum, 1968.

Hussey, Mark. *Virginia Woolf A to Z: The Essential Reference to Her Life and Writings*. New York and Oxford: Oxford University Press, 1995.

King, James. *Virginia Woolf*. London: W.W. Norton, 1994.

Nicholson, Nigel. *Virginia Woolf*. New York: Penguin Putnam Inc., 2000.

Smith-Rosenberg, Carrol. *Disorderly Conduct: Visions of Gender in Victorian America*. New York: Oxford University Press, 1985.

Woolf, Virginia. *The Essays of Virginia Woolf*, Vol I. Edited by Andrew McNeillie. Orlando, FL: First Harvest (HBJ). 1989.

All of Woolf's novels are recommended reading.
—*The Voyage Out* (1915)
—*Night and Day* (1919)
—*Jacob's Room* (1922)
—*Mrs. Dalloway* (1925)
—*To the Lighthouse* (1927)
—*Orlando: A Biography* (1928)
—*The Waves* (1931)
—*The Years* (1937)
—*Between the Acts* (1941)

---

*I want to thank Anne Dotter, who over several lunches encouraged and helped with the changes to this chapter.

SECTION FIVE

TIMELINE V

THE TWENTIETH CENTURY:
FROM 1919–1989

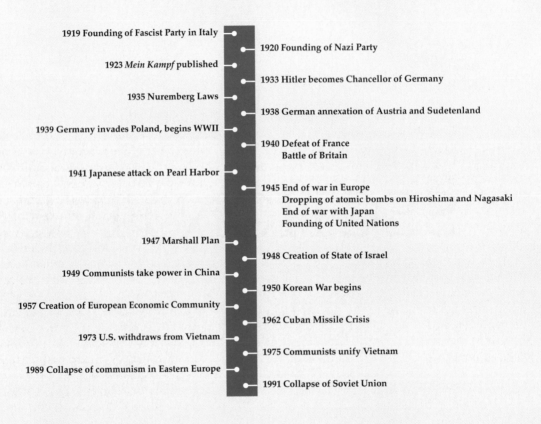

1919 Founding of Fascist Party in Italy

1920 Founding of Nazi Party

1923 *Mein Kampf* published

1933 Hitler becomes Chancellor of Germany

1935 Nuremberg Laws

1938 German annexation of Austria and Sudetenland

1939 Germany invades Poland, begins WWII

1940 Defeat of France
Battle of Britain

1941 Japanese attack on Pearl Harbor

1945 End of war in Europe
Dropping of atomic bombs on Hiroshima and Nagasaki
End of war with Japan
Founding of United Nations

1947 Marshall Plan

1948 Creation of State of Israel

1949 Communists take power in China

1950 Korean War begins

1957 Creation of European Economic Community

1962 Cuban Missile Crisis

1973 U.S. withdraws from Vietnam

1975 Communists unify Vietnam

1989 Collapse of communism in Eastern Europe

1991 Collapse of Soviet Union

THE TWENTIETH CENTURY: 1919–1989

World War I had a profound impact on Western consciousness. The sheer number of dead and wounded—thirty-seven million—and the destruction of homes, cities, and industry on an unprecedented scale seemed to call into question the entire worldview of Western civilization. Two reactions to what many Westerners considered a cataclysm went in different directions: fascism and communism. Within a decade following the end of the "Great War" fascism reared its ugly head in Germany and Italy. In Russia, Soviet communism rejected its Marxist origins and embraced a tyrannical dictatorship. Even France and England, while never really rejecting liberal and democratic principles, saw fascist and communist movements take root.

TOTALITARIANISM IN THE SOVIET UNION, ITALY, AND GERMANY

In the Soviet Union, Vladimir Lenin was succeeded in 1926 by Joseph Stalin (1879–1953), a Georgian revolutionary who was one of Lenin's most loyal followers. Stalin initiated a series of five-year plans intended to foster the rapid industrial development of the Soviet Union. He argued that the Soviet state had to be strengthened to protect itself against capitalist encirclement. During his rule he forced the collectivization of agriculture, all but destroying landowners in the Soviet Union. Stalin tolerated no opposition and expelled or eliminated from the communist party all those who in any way opposed him. It has become known as the "Great Purges" of the 1930s; large numbers of innocent people were killed or incarcerated in forced labor camps (*gulags*). Intellectually and politically focused debate, which had been such an important part of the Russian past, was thoroughly suppressed.

Fascism in Italy. In the immediate post-war period, Italy suffered from terrible economic conditions. Inflation, large numbers of unemployed including returning soldiers, striking workers in urban areas and homeless peasants in the rural areas all led to a general climate of crisis. The situation was only exacerbated by a worldwide economic downturn in the early 1920s. In the face of this massive upheaval, the Italian parliament was not able to act decisively to solve the country's ills. Many in the Italian electorate turned to the communist party for solutions. Indeed, in the period between the World Wars, Italy had the largest communist party outside of the Soviet Union. Communism's growing strength concerned many middle-class Italians, who knew how the Soviet Union treated its middle-class. It was in this climate that Benito Mussolini (1883–1945) and his Fascist party rose to power in Italy.

Mussolini, a veteran of World War I, founded the Fascist party (*Partito Nazionale Fascista*, PNF) in Italy in 1919. Many of the earliest members were unemployed soldiers and peasants. Mussolini dressed his Fascists in black shirts and they became his personal army. The party seemed to be a model of efficiency and the sole source of order in Italy. Mussolini also appealed to the Italian middle class. His speeches were replete with condemnation of both communism and capitalism. In stark terms, Mussolini told middle-class listeners that if the communists came to power they would confiscate all private property, and if capitalism flourished unchecked, big multinational corporations would put the middle class out of business. The rhetoric had its appeal. In 1922, Mussolini and the Black Shirts made their bid for power by conducting a

"March on Rome." King Victor Emmanuel (1869–1947) responded to the march by appointing Mussolini prime minister of Italy. The fascist revolution was under way.

Mussolini clearly laid out the principles of fascism when he said: "We stand for the sheer, categorical, definitive antithesis to the world of democracy. . . to the world which still abides by the fundamental principles laid down in 1789." In short, fascism was a complete rejection of the political and economic liberalism that had taken root in the West since the French Revolution.

Once in power, Mussolini set about to impose a totalitarian state upon Italy. All other political parties besides the Fascist party were banned and Mussolini handpicked Fascists to serve as mayors of every major Italian city. Newspapers were censored and critics of Mussolini were imprisoned. The Catholic Church in Rome represented the biggest potential source of criticism of Mussolini and the Fascists. However, the 1929 Lateran Accord between Mussolini and the Church put an end to that possibility. According to the terms of the Accord, the Vatican became a separate "state within a state" under the control of the pope. The Accord also affirmed the Church's role in educational policy as well as family and marriage issues. In return, the pope recognized Mussolini and his Fascists as the true and rightful leaders of Italy. As ruthless and brutal as the fascist state was in Italy, however, it could not compare to Hitler and the Nazi state established in Germany.

Fascist Germany.   During the last years of World War I, the imperial government of Kaiser Wilhelm II of Germany collapsed and was replaced by a democratically elected republic. It was this new government that was forced to sign the armistice agreement ending World War I. In the immediate post-war period, the newly elected parliament met at Weimar to write a new constitution for the fledgling republic. This government became known as the Weimar Republic, and while it clung to power for ten years, it was despised. Many Germans blamed Weimar for capitulating to the Allies and betraying Germany at the Paris Peace Conference of 1919 that produced the Treaty of Versailles. Others attacked Weimar because among its members were both Jews and Socialists.

Those on the political left thought Weimar was too conservative while those on the political right attacked Weimar for being too liberal.

The economic troubles of the early 1920s made matters worse in defeated Germany. Unemployment levels briefly reached as high as twenty-five percent and inflation all but destroyed the German currency. Many members of the middle class in Germany were ruined by the hyper-inflation.

Much like Mussolini in Italy, Adolf Hitler (1889–1945) was able to exploit the unstable postwar climate in Germany, with tragic consequences. Hitler was born in Austria and as a young man sought to pursue a career as an artist. At the age of twenty he moved to Vienna in order to attend the prestigious Academy of Fine Arts. He was, however, repeatedly denied admission. It was in Vienna that Hitler first encountered a virulent form of anti-Semitism. This was not the age-old anti-Judaism that saw Jews as the killers of Christ. Rather, this new form of racism, dating back only to the nineteenth century, was based on Social Darwinism and notions of superior and inferior races, and Jews were considered the most inferior. According to traditional anti-Judaism, Jews could absolve themselves of their sins by converting to Christianity. The new anti-Semitism, based on notions of race and blood, would hold far more dire consequences for European Jewry. It was in Vienna that Hitler first came to equate Judaism with everything wrong with the modern world and to see Jews as responsible for the twin horrors of communism and capitalism.

Hitler was in Germany when World War I began. He enthusiastically enlisted in the German army and fought bravely in combat. Like many others, Hitler was shocked at Germany's defeat in the War and felt the nation had been betrayed by the Weimar Republic. He singled out the Jews and Socialists among Weimar for particular derision and hatred.

In 1919 Hitler joined a small, far-right political party in Munich called the German Worker's Party (or DAP). Hitler quickly rose through the ranks of the party, aided, in large part, by an amazing, nearly mesmerizing speaking ability. One observer described Hitler's speaking abilities this way: "The intense will of the man, the passion of his sincerity seemed to flow from him into me. I experienced an exaltation that could be likened only to a religious conversion." Shortly after emerging as leader, Hitler's small party merged with another party and changed their name to the National Socialist German Workers Party (NSDAP, which was frequently shortened to the Nazi party).

In 1923 Hitler sought to seize power in Germany by emulating Mussolini's March on Rome. The attempt, known as the Beer Hall Putsch, failed miserably and Hitler was arrested. It was while in prison that Hitler wrote *Mein Kampf* (*My Struggle*). The work offered a rambling and often incoherent denunciation of the Treaty of Versailles and the Weimar Republic. Hitler saved his most venomous attacks for Jews and communists. He skillfully railed against the "Judeo-Bolsheviks," arguing that they were the sworn enemy of the true German people and responsible for all the ills of the world: liberalism, intellectualism, parliamentarianism, internationalism, Marxism, modern art, and individualism. In his book Hitler wrote:

Two worlds face each other: the men of God and the men of Satan! The Jew is the anti-man, the creature of another god. He must have come from another root of the human race.

Perhaps in ordinary times this sort of rhetoric would be dismissed as simply unbridled racism. However, in the context of the post-World War I world, with its poor economic conditions, Germany's humiliation at the hands of the British and French, and the real fear of communist takeover, Germans in large numbers accepted Hitler's propaganda.

Despite the power of Hitler's rhetoric, it would be the crash of the New York stock market in October 1929 and the subsequent worldwide "Great Depression" that would catapult Hitler and the Nazi party into power in Germany. Germany was hit hard by the Great Depression. Once again, unemployment rates skyrocketed, the German currency was devalued to the point of becoming worthless, strikes paralyzed the cities, and the government seemed incapable of action. In this context, Hitler offered himself as an alternative: as a man of action who could at once restore economic good times to Germany and a sense of honor and pride to Germans. In Parliamentary elections of 1928, the year before the Great Depression, Hitler's Nazis

received just 800,000 votes nationwide, which translated into only twelve seats in the German parliament (Reichstag). By 1930, one year after the Depression hit Germany, the Nazis received 6.4 million votes, which translated into one hundred and seven seats in the Reichstag. Two years later the Nazis controlled two hundred and thirty seats. As leader of the single largest party in the Reichstag, Hitler was invited by Germany's President Paul von Hindenburg (1847–1934) to become the chancellor of Germany. Hitler and his Nazis had been voted into power.

While Hitler became chancellor by legal means, he soon established an iron grip through illegal means. After the elections of March 1933 Hitler assumed full dictatorial powers, with complete authoritarian control over the German state. Hitler's first actions as dictator were to outlaw all political parties except the Nazi party, censor all publications, and have all civil servants, including the military, swear oaths of personal loyalty to Hitler and not Germany. This is known as "Führer principle" from the German word for "leader." Hitler's will, not the state, was the supreme authority. A secret police, called the Gestapo, was charged with arresting the enemies of the new order, including communists, socialists, liberals, Jews, clergy and journalists.

Hitler also moved to strip Germany's Jews of their rights as German citizens. The first anti-Semitic legislation prohibited Jews from serving in the German military. A 1933 law prohibited all non-Aryans from governmental service. According to the law, a non-Aryan was defined as a Jew or a person who had at least one Jewish parent or grandparent. In 1935 a sweeping set of laws, known as the Nuremberg Laws, forbade intermarriage between Jews and non-Jews and removed all of Jews' rights of citizenship. By 1938, Jews were not allowed to work for newspapers, all Jewish-owned business were closed and restrictions were placed on their right to leave their homes. A year later, the German government began the infamous T4 program, which used carbon monoxide to kill large numbers of people deemed "inferior" by Hitler: the disabled, mentally handicapped and homosexuals. Techniques of mass murder would be expanded and made more efficient. In 1941 a plan labeled the "Final Solution" was

The Brandenburg Gate, built during the reign of Friedrich Wilhelm II as an emblem of peace and unity, later provided a backdrop to the oppressive regime of National Socialism and to the harsh divisions of East and West during the Cold War. As such, the gateway can be understood to represent the appeal and power of totalitarian ideologies in the modern era, creating mass movements of loyal followers willing to carry out war and genocide for the cause. The neoclassical style, based on rational Enlightenment ideals, seems particularly ironic given the structure's prominent visual placement in episodes of human irrationality and hysteria, as seen here in the film still from the Nazi propaganda piece, *SA-Mann Brand*. Today, however, the Brandenburg Gate is a powerful image of a reunited Germany and Berlin.

Figure V-1   Brandenburg Gate, 1789-1791. Colored film still from *SA-Mann Brand*, 1933. Courtesy of Bildarchiv Preussischer Kulturbesitz/Art Resource, NY.

implemented with the purpose of annihilation of all Jews: the Holocaust.

THE ROAD TO WAR

Once Hitler and his Nazi party were firmly in power he turned his attention to rebuilding the nation's economy and healing the wounds inflicted on Germany from the Treaty of Versailles. On March 7, 1936, Hitler's troops entered the Rhineland, a territory on the German frontier bordering France. According to the Treaty of Versailles, the region was to remain demilitarized. Hitler's bold move could have triggered a military invasion of Germany by the British and French. Neither nation, however, was prepared nor had an appetite for war. Memories of World War I were still fresh in their people's minds and the Great Depression was still wreaking economic havoc across the West. Finally, to political leaders in Washington, London and Paris it seemed that the Soviet Union, and not Germany, was the greatest threat to peace and stability. Thus when Hitler violated the Treaty of Versailles in 1936, the British, French and Americans responded by taking no action.

Emboldened by the apathy of the West, Hitler marched his troops into Austria in 1938. His goal was to annex Austria to Germany (the *Anschluss,* which means "accession"), and he was greeted as a hero. Most welcomed the idea of unifying the two German-speaking nations into a common country. Parades were thrown, church bells rang and anti-Semitic riots erupted throughout the nation. The *Anschluss* was a blatant violation of the Treaty of Versailles. As before, however, the British, French, and Americans did nothing to deter Hitler.

Hitler next set his sights on the Sudetenland. The small mountainous region had once been a part of the German Empire and was still overwhelmingly populated by ethnic Germans. In the wake of Germany's defeat in World War I, this small strip of territory was taken from Germany and incorporated into the newly created nation of Czechoslovakia. For his part, Hitler saw the entire nation of Czechoslovakia as an illegitimate entity created by the Treaty of Versailles, and the Sudentland to be rightly part of greater Germany.

Hitler gave an ultimatum to the Czechoslovakians: either surrender the Sudetenland by October 1938 or he would take it by force. As the deadline approached, Britain's Prime Minister Neville Chamberlain (1869–1940), France's Premier Edouard Daladier (1884–1970) and Mussolini met with Hitler at the Munich Conference. There the leaders agreed not to oppose Hitler's claim to the Sudetenland. The strategy of trying to prevent war by making concessions to an aggressor nation has become known as *appeasement*. In the years since World War II the policy of appeasement has become widely derided as a complete failure; at the time it was seen a positive act. The peoples of France and Britain praised their leaders for keeping their nations out of war. Hitler, however, rightly understood the true meaning of Munich. France and Britain were too weak to stop his march across the east. Once German forces were in control of the Sudetenland, in March 1939, his forces invaded and conquered the rest of Czechoslovakia. Britain and France responded by promising to defend Poland, Romania, Greece and Turkey in case of Nazi invasion. Hitler responded by signing a military alliance with Mussolini called the Pact of Steel.

In May 1939 Hitler turned to Poland and demanded the return of the Danzig, another territory that had once been part of the German Empire but was stripped away in 1919 and given to Poland. Hitler revealed his true intentions to his army officers:

> Danzig is not the objective. It is a matter of expanding our living space in the East, of making our food supplies secure. . . There is therefore no question of sparing Poland, and the decision remains to attack at the first suitable opportunity.

In August 1939, as tensions mounted over Poland, Hitler and Stalin shocked the world by signing a nonaggression pact. The treaty provided that if one country were attacked the other country would remain neutral. A secret section of the treaty called for the division of Poland and the Baltic States (Latvia, Estonia, and Lithuania) between Germany and the Soviet Union. The treaty was a remarkable accomplishment for Hitler. It meant that the Allies would not be able to reproduce their World War I alliance and that Hitler had no fear of an invasion on his eastern border. It also provided a green light to invade Poland, which he did on September 1, 1939. Two days later Britain and France declared war on Germany. World War II had begun.

WORLD WAR II, 1939–1945

German forces quickly overpowered the hapless Polish military by launching a *Blitzkreig* ("lightning war"). German planes, tanks and armored vehicles, with incredible speed, moved on the capital of Warsaw. On September 17, German forces in Poland were joined by Soviet troops. Poland surrendered ten days later and Hitler and Stalin, as promised, divided the nation between them.

In April 1940, Hitler invaded Denmark and Norway. Denmark surrendered within days. The following month Hitler's troops easily took Belgium and the Netherlands. In June 1940, an German military attacked France. The French government capitulated, and on June 22, 1940, an armistice was signed in the same railroad car where Germany was forced to surrender at the end of World War I. France was split into two; the Germans directly governed the northern half of the country, including Paris, while the southern region, named Vichy, was governed by the old, conservative French war hero from World War I, Henri Philippe Pétain. The Vichy government collaborated with the Germans, passed

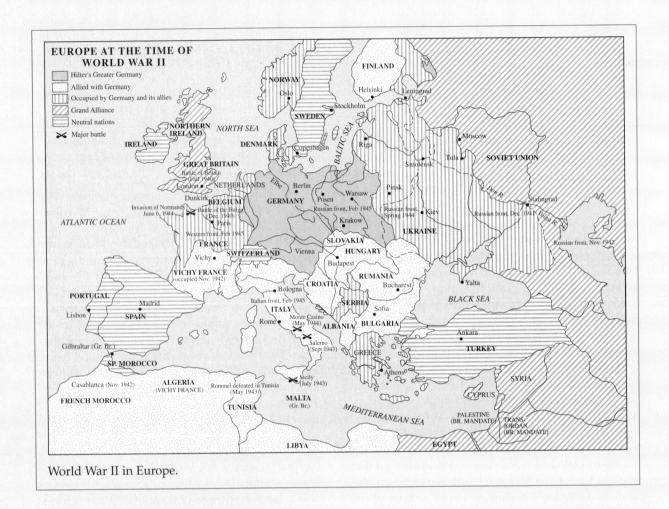

World War II in Europe.

anti-Jewish measures and oversaw the deportation of French Jews to Nazi death camps. Charles de Gaulle (1890–1970), General of French forces, escaped to London where he organized and directed the Free French forces. In the east, Stalin annexed the Baltic States. Britain now stood alone.

Just months before, Winston Churchill replaced Chamberlain as Prime Minister. Churchill was an early advocate of resistance to Hitler and with his charisma and eloquence steeled the British people for the coming battle against the Nazis. In the summer of 1940 Churchill used a radio address to call on the people to protect the ideals and values of liberty with their "blood, toil, tears and sweat." In August 1940 the German *Luftwaffe* (Air Force) began its relentless bombing campaign, which become known as the Battle of Britain or the Blitz. The *Luft-*

waffe bombed British industry, arms depots, ports, ships, and cities. Hitler's goal was to erode British morale and force Churchill to surrender. For months the *Luftwaffe* pounded London, forcing residents to seek shelter in subways and cellars. The British Royal Air Force (RAF) fought with skill and bravery and ultimately prevented a full-scale invasion by the Germans.

While British resistance to Hitler was admirable, it could not bring down the might of the Nazi empire. Two events served to irrevocably turn the tide of the war: Hitler's foolhardy decision to invade the Soviet Union in June 1941 and Japan's attack on the United States in December 1941. The entry of the United States and the Soviet Union now on the Allied side into World War II would lead to the defeat of Hitler and the Nazis.

For Hitler, the Soviet Union was the center of "Judeo-Bolshevism." He attacked it, he said, to save Europe from the scourge of these "sub-humans." Breaking the nonaggression pact, on June 22, 1941, he sent a massive force into the U.S.S.R: some four million men, three thousand tanks, and two thousand planes. During the first months of the invasion it seemed as though Hitler was on his way to another stunning victory. By September, a staggering two and a half million Soviet troops had been killed, wounded or captured. Like the British, however, the Russians refused to surrender. As Germany drove deeper into Soviet territory, their supply lines became stretched and vulnerable. The same overreaching had defeated Napoleon's army in 1812: the German army ran short of fuel, supplies, and food. By December 6, 1941, German forces were within twenty miles of Moscow. There they met a counterattack by the Red Army and the battle of Russia bogged down for the long winter.

As the German offensive stalled outside Moscow, Japan prepared for attack on the United States. An ally of Germany, Japan had extended its control over much of Asia, presenting itself as the liberator of other Asian nations from European colonization and imperialism. By 1937, Japan had captured much of China and by 1941 looked to Southeast Asia, particularly French Indochina, British Burma and the Dutch East Indies. The Japanese government recognized that the U.S. Pacific fleet at Pearl Harbor in Hawaii was the main obstacle standing in their way of victory. On December 7, 1941, the Japanese bombed Pearl Harbor and utterly destroyed the American fleet. After the attack, Germany joined with Japan and declared war on the United States. Hitler described the U.S. as "half Judaized and the other half Negrified." The United States was not prepared for war. It did not take long, however, before the industrial might of the nation was producing tanks, planes, and armored vehicles at an astonishing rate. By the first months of 1942, all of Germany's enemies (Great Britain, United States, Soviet Union, and Free French) had come together in a "Grand Alliance" to oppose the Axis Powers (Italy, Germany, and Japan).

The major turning point in the European phase of World War II came at the battle of Stalingrad. After wintering outside of Moscow in 1941, Hitler looked to Stalingrad, an important industrial city, and began an offensive in the spring of 1942. Hitler rightly understood that taking control of Stalingrad would bring the Soviet Union to its knees. The siege of Stalingrad lasted until February 1943 and was an epic struggle. The Red Army, joined by civilians, fought the Germans in street-by-street, often house-by-house combat. By winter, the German forces were without ammunition, medical supplies, and food. Yet Hitler refused to order a retreat. On February 2, 1943, ninety thousand German soldiers, all that remained of a force that once numbered three-hundred and seventy thousand men, were forced to surrender to the Soviets.

Meanwhile, the British were successful in driving the Germans out of Morocco and Algeria in North Africa in the fall of 1942. From there, the Allies landed forces in Sicily in southern Italy in June 1943. By April, 1945, Allied forces had liberated Italy. Italian partisans captured Mussolini and his mistress, killed them, and hung their bodies upside down for public display.

On June 6, 1944, known as D-Day, the combined Allied forces under the command of U.S. General Dwight Eisenhower landed two million men and five thousand vessels on the heavily fortified beaches of Normandy in Northern France. From there, the Allies fought their way through the German-occupied territory of western France. In July they liberated the city of Paris. The Soviets began marching on Germany from the east. By August, they had taken Bulgaria, Romania and Hungary. As the Allies moved towards Berlin during the winter of 1944–45, Hitler refused to surrender. In April 1945, with the Soviets only blocks away, Hitler and his wife, Eva Braun, committed suicide. Germany surrendered on May 8,1945. In the Pacific, the war would last a few more months. On August 6, 1945, the United States dropped an atomic bomb on the city of Hiroshima, killing seventy-eight thousand people and destroying more than half of the city. Three days later, the Americans dropped a second atomic bomb on the city of Nagasaki. On August 14, 1945, Japan surrendered and World War II was over.

In February 1945, Roosevelt, Stalin, and Churchill met in the town of Yalta to discuss postwar Europe. There, Roosevelt urged a proposal that he and others had been nurturing since early in the war: the creation of the United Nations, an institution whose goal would be to promote peace around the globe. That summer, the leaders (with the U.S. now represented by Harry Truman who became President following Roosevelt's death in April) met again at Potsdam, Germany where it was agreed that eastern Europe would remain under the control of the Soviet Union while Germany would be divided up into four zones controlled by Britain, France, the U.S. and U.S.S.R.[1]

THE POST-WAR WORLD

By the end of World War II, Europe was in shambles. Churchill described Europe as "a rubble of heap, a charnel house, a breeding ground for pestilence and hate." Millions were dead, cities were leveled, economies lay in ruin, transportation and communication networks along with national infrastructures were smashed. Europe itself was divided in half between the free, open and democratic West and the communist, totalitarian east. The United States and Soviet Union would soon embark on a decades-long "Cold War" and Europe, for so long the center of civilization, became just another contested zone between the world's two superpowers. Treaties would formalize these relationships. The North Atlantic Treaty Organization (NATO) brought western Europe, the United States and Canada into an alliance in 1949, while its eastern equivalent was the Warsaw Pact, uniting eastern Europe and the Soviet Union in 1955. The Cold War would be marked by the Soviet Union's desire to spread communism around the globe and the West's determination to contain the spread of communism. Every event in the post-war period was seen through the prism of the cold-war mentality. Adding to the stakes was the fact that by 1954 both the U.S. and the U.S.S.R. were in possession of atomic weapons.

Immediately following the war the United States provided millions of dollars in relief aid for Europe to help prevent starvation and epidemics. In 1947 the U.S. inaugurated a systematic, long-term aid program developed by and named after the then Secretary of State, George Marshall, who received the Nobel Peace Prize in 1953. Motivated by a mixture of humanitarian, economic, and anticommunist concerns, it was one of the most massive and successful reconstruction programs in modern history. The defeated Germany was the chief beneficiary of the Marshall Plan. By the early 1950s industrial production in western Europe had reached and soon exceeded prewar levels. Germany's dramatic recovery—what was called its "economic miracle"—made it the most prosperous nation in Europe. In 1952 France, Germany, Italy, Belgium, The Netherlands, and Luxembourg created the Common Market, which through the Treaty of Rome in 1957 became the European Economic Community. Britain, Denmark, and Ireland joined the Common Market in the early 1970s. These and other cooperative institutions resulted in the formation of the European Union in 1992, an intergovernmental and supranational union among nations that been in conflict with one another for centuries. EU institutions include the European Parliament, the Council of the European Union or "Council of Ministers," the European Commission, the European Court of Justice, and the European Central and Investment Banks. The EU has common trade, agricultural, and security policies and a common currency (the euro, adopted so far by twelve of the member states), and the Schengen Agreement, which abolished passport control and customs checks for citizens of EU countries. The European Union, now consisting of twenty-five European states including former members of the Soviet bloc, is a major global force in economics and politics, with the world's largest economy, the third largest area in population, and the seventh largest geographical area.

The United States occupied Japan for seven years following the war, imposing a Western democratic constitution on the nation and abolishing the traditional Japanese strongholds of power, above all the military. While the role of the emperor was symbolically preserved, Japan became a modern liberal-democratic state and, like Germany, underwent a dramatic economic recovery that made it one of the world's most prosperous nations.

Another important outcome of World War II was the founding of the United Nations in 1945.

---

[1]The Eastern European countries that came under the control of the U.S.S.R. were Poland, Czechoslovakia, Hungary, Romania, and Bulgaria. Yugoslavia and Albania were independent communist countries.

Despite the collapse of the League of Nations in the 1930s, the dream of a world organization that would promote peace and development among nations continued, and the idea of the UN was specifically envisioned in meetings and documents from early in the war, such as Roosevelt's and Churchill's "Atlantic Charter" in 1942. Initially the membership consisted of fifty nations; the General Assembly now includes as equal members some 192 countries, or almost all the countries of the world. Many issues are debated in the General Assembly, and every country has its say. The much smaller and more powerful "executive committee," the Security Council, still consists of five permanent members who were the victorious nations in World War II—Britain, France, the U.S., Russia (originally as the U.S.S.R.), and China—plus ten rotating members. The Security Council was given the final decision over matters relating to international peace and security, which must be approved unanimously by the five permanent members. That veto power meant that throughout the Cold War period UN efforts at resolving conflicts and keeping peace were severely hampered by the opposition between the U.S. and the Soviet Union, and those efforts are still difficult to decide on and implement because of various disagreements among permanent members. In many other areas, however, the UN, through its specialized agencies, has played an essential and invaluable role worldwide in areas such as health, hunger relief, development assistance, help for refugees and victims of natural disasters and wars, and human rights. Among its most successful agencies have been the World Health Organization, the World Food Program, the Food and Agricultural Organization, the UN Development Program, and the United Nations Children's Fund (UNICEF).

Despite the best hopes for the United Nations, the beleaguered institution could not contain the spread of revolutions and military conflicts around the globe. The hope that the end of World War II would bring an end to hostilities around the globe was almost immediately dashed. From 1946 to 1949 civil war raged in China, ending with the victory of the communists under Mao Zhedong. Gradually most of the African lands that had been under European sway went into revolt and gained their independence. The Vietnamese rose up against French rule. Cuba became a communist country under Fidel Castro. Throughout Africa, Asia, and Latin America independence movements, many of them fueled by Marxist philosophy, became the norm.

Following the genocide (Holocaust) of six million Jews during World War II, public opinion in the West was favorable to the creation of a Jewish homeland in Palestine. After some maneuvering in the United Nations, the state of Israel was created in 1948. This action almost immediately precipitated war between Jews and the Arabs living in the area given to Jews.

The Cold War threatened to become a hot war during the Korean war, the Cuban Missile Crisis, and the Vietnam War. In 1945, Korea was divided. The northern part of the country was pro-Soviet Union while the south was allied with the United States. In June 1950, the north invaded the south. The U.S. sought and won United Nations support in repelling the invasion. American forces, under the command of General Douglas MacArthur, entered into the north and penetrated into China. The Chinese counterattacked and US forces were forced to retreat. The war ended in 1953 with a truce, and the settlement confirmed the existence of two countries: North Korea and South Korea.

In 1962 the world was brought to the brink of nuclear war during the Cuban Missile Crisis. With his ally Castro in power in Cuba, Soviet leader Krushchev sought to gain a decisive advantage in the Cold War. Krushchev moved to install nuclear weapons on the island, which sat just ninety miles miles off the Florida coast. U.S. President John F. Kennedy demanded that Krushchev withdraw the missiles. Krushchev eventually backed down and was subsequently removed from power one year later.

Vietnam, long a French colony, had been occupied by Japan during World War II but returned to France in 1945. A popular nationalist-communist insurgency, led by Ho Chi Minh, forced the French out in 1954. Beginning in the late 1950s, the U.S. provided support to anticommunist groups. Many Americans, including influential policymakers and politicians, believed that if Vietnam fell to the communists it would create a "domino effect" leading to the spread of communism throughout Southeast Asia. U.S. President Lyndon Johnson, who took office in 1963 after the assassination of Kennedy, took it as his primary job to prevent that from happening. Despite sending over 500,000 troops, along with the

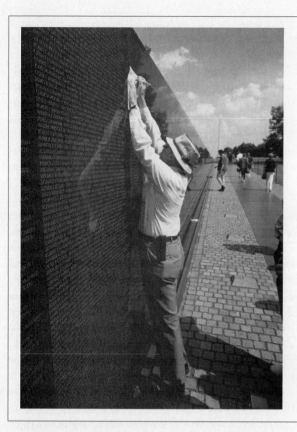

Maya Lin's monument continues a lengthy historical tradition of war memorials. Rather than commemorating a ruler or celebrating a victory, however, Lin's memorial serves as a place of somber reflection and remembrance. Lin's design is without overt military or political content. Two walls of smooth black granite, each over 200 feet long, bear the incised names of more than 58,000 dead and missing American soldiers in Vietnam. The polished surfaces of the walls are a fundamental part of the work: in them, visitors see themselves reflected, creating a silent dialogue between the dead and the living in their quiet contemplation.

Figure V-2   Maya Ying Lin, *Vietnam Veterans Memorial,* 1982. Black granite, length 500' (152m). The Mall, Washington, D.C. Courtesy of Jeremy Horner/Corbis.

most sophisticated military equipment, the U.S. was unable to prevent Vietnam from falling to the communist forces. In 1973, the United States withdrew its forces from the country and in 1975 the communists in the north, under the leadership of Ho Chi Minh, drove south and unified the country.

By the mid-1970s it was clear that the world was facing yet another global problem: overpopulation. The contrast between the standard of living of the northern industrially developed nations and that of the southern developing nations continued to widen. Scientists monitoring the natural environment became increasingly concerned about the destruction being wrought on the ecosystems of the air, the water and the land. Nuclear power incidents, and then major accidents, at Three Mile Island in Pennsylvania (1979) and Chernobyl in the U.S.S.R. (1986), cast a dark shadow, as did the scenarios scientists were developing for a "nuclear winter" in the aftermath of the explosion of thermonuclear bombs.

In Northern Ireland and the Middle East, terrorism became a way of life. Hijackings and kidnappings threatened to bring travel and international business to a halt. The oil exporting nations had discovered in 1973 that they could threaten, if not cripple, the economies of the major industrial nations. The Iranian seizure of American diplomats in 1979 proved that the conventions of international diplomacy could be flouted with virtual impunity. In the Muslim world the fate of the Palestinians, despoiled of their country by the creation of the state of Israel, dramatically increased anti-Jewish feeling, while the success of the Iranian revolution against the Shah encouraged Islamic fundamentalists to push for an across-the-board repudiation of Western secularism.

The success of the Chinese and Vietnamese communist movements encouraged Africans and Latin Americans with grievances to try guerilla warfare. In Central America, U.S. support of anti-communist dictators led much of the international press to brand the U.S. an enemy of justice, continuing a tradition begun during the Vietnam war. U.S. support of the Philippine dictator Marcos added fuel to that fire, while the hesitancy of most of the Western nations to condemn the apartheid regime in South Africa left them vulnerable to the charge of racism. In Africa, revolts in Kenya, Rhodesia, South Africa, Algeria, and the Congo combined with longstanding grievances about economic conditions and racism. The U.S.S.R. and its Eastern European satellites struggled to make a socialist economy work, with only Yugoslavia having much success. At the end of the 1970s the U.S.S.R. became embroiled in Afghanistan, much as the U.S. had become embroiled in Vietnam in the 1960s.

Advances in nuclear weapons, space satellites, computer technology, genetic engineering, cancer research, and dozens of other scientific areas made the business, medicine, and military science of the 1970s and 1980s new enterprises. Ecological pollution continued to grow, as the greenhouse effect, the depletion of the ozone layer, the tainting of the seas, acid rain, deforestation, and other ominous signs became part of the popular consciousness. The global economy became more volatile, as the relations between the countries producing raw materials and the countries producing finished products grew more complicated. Many nations ran up huge debts, bringing them to the verge of bankruptcy, while deficit spending began to be blamed for monstrous inflation and crippling debt.

Famine in East Africa brought home the paradoxes of the current global culture, as hundreds of thousands died while millions of their global neighbors living in comfort watched on television. Both China and the Soviet Union began to open their economies to capitalist ideas, further suggesting that socialism was not the panacea.

The year 1989 witnessed the sudden and unexpected collapse of communism in Europe. The liberalizing reforms in Soviet foreign and domestic policy initiated by Mikhail Gorbachev inspired the mostly nonviolent, popular overthrow of the ruling communist governments in almost all the countries of Eastern Europe. In June 1989 Poland held free parliamentary elections. Communist candidates were soundly defeated. In Hungary, popular demonstrations led to the fall of communist rule in the fall of 1989. In Germany, the Berlin Wall stood as the most powerful symbol of the Cold War and a divided Europe. In the summer and fall of 1989, hundreds of thousands of residents of East Berlin took to the streets to protest against communist rule. On November 9, armed with sledgehammers, East Berliners began to take down the Wall. On New Year's Eve, to fireworks and rock music, an emotionally charged ceremony marked the official end of a divided Berlin and the unofficial end to the Cold War. Popular revolutions would also sweep communists out of power in Czechoslovakia and Romania. In 1991, the Soviet Union itself collapsed, followed by the breaking up of the Soviet Empire into separate countries.

The end of the Cold War marked a fundamental turning point in world history. No longer was the world divided between two hostile camps fueled by rival political ideologies. Many believed that democracy and capitalism had definitively triumphed, and would gradually spread throughout the world. However, the last decade of the twentieth century and first years of the twenty-first century have witnessed new tensions and concerns around the globe. As Western values—democracy, liberalism, capitalism, and religious toleration—are extending around the globe, at the same time a backlash against those values has occurred and the world is again divided by rival ideologies.

ART IN THE TWENTIETH CENTURY

The rapidly changing landscape of the nineteenth century art world continued into the twentieth, with artistic movements arising one on top of another. Twentieth-century art carried on the nineteenth-century trend of responding to contemporary life rather than to historical events, but broke even more radically with past artistic styles. Artists freed form from naturalistic representation and liberated color from any descriptive function. Art became the product of an artist's personal, interior vision rather than a mimetic representation of the exterior world.

The middle of the century witnessed a geographical shift in the center of the art world. As in the nineteenth century, Paris was the cradle of art in the first half of the twentieth century, the place to where artists immigrated and from where avant-garde movements emerged. Due in part to the upheaval of World War II, however, a period in which many artists fled Europe, the United States was the forefront for art in the post-war period.

EUROPE BETWEEN THE WARS

World War I generated widespread disillusionment among European artists and deeply affected their production. For many artists, whether they themselves fought in the trenches or simply lost family and friends, the war became a point of departure from which to critique the whole of society. German artists were particularly fervent in their denouncement of war. Some, like Otto Dix and George Grosz, addressed the disenfranchisement of disabled veterans in the aftermath of the war. Others, like Käthe Kollwitz, were inspired to a life-long production of antiwar imagery.

Käthe Kollwitz, a socially minded graphic artist, produced a strong body of anti-war imagery. After losing a son in World War I, Kollwitz channeled her emotions into prints and drawings that depict the futility of war as well as the protective role of mothers. Her final lithograph, *Seed Corn Must Not Be Ground,* quotes the words of Goethe. Produced the same year that Kollwitz's grandson was killed in World War II, the print depicts an anguished mother desperately encircling her children. Culminating Kollwitz's increasingly pacifist production, children are "seed corn" who should never be ground by the senseless machinery of war.

Figure V-3 Käthe Kollwitz, *Seed Corn Must Not Be Ground,* 1942. Lithograph. Courtesy of Galerie St. Etienne, New York.

A movement known as Dada emerged in 1916 in response to what the artists perceived as the senseless death and destruction of trench warfare. Founded in the neutral country of Switzerland, Dada became an international association, with factions in Germany, France, and the United States. The production of the Dadaists often appeared nonsensical: in their art, poetry, and performance evenings, the Dadaists cultivated absurdity as a way to respond to the madness of war. While this irrational production had an implicitly critical aim, some members of Dada used their art as a platform for more explicit sociopolitical critiques.

Whereas most of the widespread Dada organizations emphasized a primarily literary focus, the Berlin Dada group became known for its art, particularly for its use of photomontage, as well as for its communist sympathies. They selected the term "photomontage" to describe their cut-and-pasted collages precisely due to class associations. The Berlin Dadaists saw themselves as workers and engineers rather than as high-minded intellectuals and artists; the idea of constructing (or "mounting," from the German verb *montieren*) fragments appealed to their working-class aspirations and so led them to the terms montage and photomontage. In their photomontages, the Berlin Dadaists skewered a variety of public and political figures. They employed montage methods as a manner of critique: by appropriating images from the mass media, fragmenting them and recombining them with other images, the Dadaists aimed to alter and critique the original meaning. Prominent members of political parties were frequent targets of the group, but Hannah Höch was the only Berlin Dadaist to tackle the difficult issues facing women in the post-war period. In *The Beautiful Girl,* 1919–20 (Plate 26), Höch addressed the roles of women in an increasingly technological society. Höch juxtaposed fragments of women's bodies with industrial symbols such as a stopwatch, a machine crank, a tire, and BMW insignias. The stopwatch, a reference to the rationalization of industry, stands ready to time the productivity of the workers. While women were heavily recruited for factory work, the use of standardized parts and assemblyline production called for an unskilled, low-paid labor force. As such, the primary jobs open to women were, in effect, dead ends with long hours, low wages, and

little hope of advancement. The faceless hair, cropped in the short style of the New Woman, reinforces the idea of mindless factory work open to women. The New Woman here is seen not as an individual woman but rather as one of many mass-produced "beautiful girls." Only the woman in the upper-right-hand corner takes in and perceives the truth of the entire situation.

Another artist involved for a time with the Dada movement, Marcel Duchamp, largely forged his own path and produced work that proved highly controversial at the time as well as heavily influential for later artists. More interested in the ideas behind art than in the actual completed object, Duchamp abandoned painting early on in favor of what he termed "readymades," everyday objects that become art through the choice of the artist. According to Duchamp, the artist's decision, even the mere selection of an already extant object, is what constitutes the work of art, not necessarily the act of creation. Duchamp's first readymade was a bicycle wheel mounted on top of a wooden stool. In 1917, Duchamp produced his most infamous readymade, a urinal that he titled *Fountain* and submitted to an unjuried exhibition under the pseudonym of R. Mutt. Duchamp's piece was refused, as he had expected, and deemed indecent and offensive. His gesture of selecting an extant object and decreeing it art, however, had lasting effects in the art world. The privileging of the artistic idea over the actual product provided the precedent for many later twentieth-century movements, including Conceptual Art of the 1960s, in which the art object was eliminated altogether.

The arts of Europe flourished in the 1920s, not only in Paris but also throughout Germany. The Weimar Republic became known for its cultural efflorescence. Already by the 1930s, however, artists in Germany and elsewhere felt the impact of Hitler's National Socialist agenda. In a backlash against the cultural liberalism of the Weimar Republic, Hitler began a severe program of censorship, dismissing artists and writers from public institutions and purging museums of works he deemed decadent or perverted. The works of the German Expressionists, like Kirchner and Heckel, were among Hitler's most despised. Hitler's minister of culture organized a series of didactic exhibitions that were designed to teach the public about the

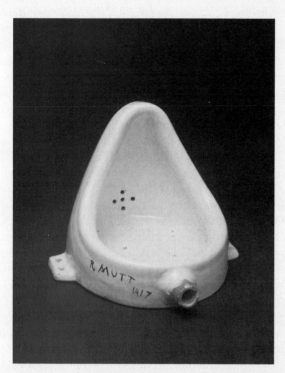

Figure V-4   Marcel Duchamp, *Fountain,* 1917.
Porcelain plumbing fixture and enamel paint,
height 24⅝" (62.23cm). Philadelphia Museum of
Art, Philadelphia, Pennsylvania. Courtesy of The
Philadelphia Museum of Art/Art Resource, NY.

corrupt nature of modern art. The largest, culminating exhibition, titled "Degenerate Art," took place in Munich in 1937, across the street from its counterpart, an exhibition of "Good German Art." Tellingly, the "bad" art attracted thousands more visitors than the "good" art.

Pablo Picasso responded to the actions of Hitler's military in an enormous mural titled *Guernica,* of 1937 (Plate 27). During the Spanish Civil War, Spanish dictator Francisco Franco collaborated with Hitler, hiring Nazi warplanes to bomb and destroy the small Basque town of Guernica. The raid, the world's first aerial bombing of civilians, killed 2000 and wounded thousands more. As a Spanish artist living in France, Picasso was deeply distressed by the incident and within one month painted a powerful indictment of the act. *Guernica,* much like the *Disasters of War* etched by Goya, condemned the inhumane and despicable violence that is somehow deemed acceptable in wartime. Painted in black, white and gray, to echo the news photos that covered the destruction, the mural features a fallen soldier, wailing women, a horse and a bull. Though many have interpreted the bull to represent Franco, Picasso said only that the bull stood for a general brutality and darkness, with the horse representing the people. The electric light overhead and a woman holding a lantern metaphorically shed light on and reveal the horror of the devastation. The angular, jagged planes and the distorted figures underscore the evocation of violence.

ART IN THE UNITED STATES

Due in large part to Hitler's systematic program of eliminating modern art from the European landscape, the center of the art world shifted to the United States in the post-war period. Many European artists fled to New York, spreading their avant-garde ideas through teaching and through exhibitions of their work. Prior to their arrival, some of the principal tendencies in American art concerned documentary and realism. Unlike the interwar period in Europe, where many artists turned inward for artistic inspiration, American artists responded to the effects of the Depression. Photographers cultivated a documentary approach, bringing attention to the plight of the rural poor as seen in Dorothea Lange's *Migrant Mother*. A group of painters known as Regionalists, for their Midwestern heritage and primary focus on scenes of rural life, advocated a return to stable, conservative agrarian roots as a way to combat the Depression and problems of urban society. John Steuart Curry, a Kansas native, promoted the security of farm life in *Baptism in Kansas,* of 1928 (Plate 28). A woman surrounded by her church community is baptized in a farm trough. This act sets the scene for the farm as a sacred site, with the heavenly rays of sunshine illuminating the church-like windmill and barn.

In the post-war period, Abstract Expressionism was the movement that secured the art world shift from Europe to the United States. Much as had occurred with European artists following the First World War, the utter horrors of the Second World War prompted American artists to turn inward, focusing on the existential self. For many artists, social and political commentary seemed useless in the face of such enormous tragedy. Instead, the

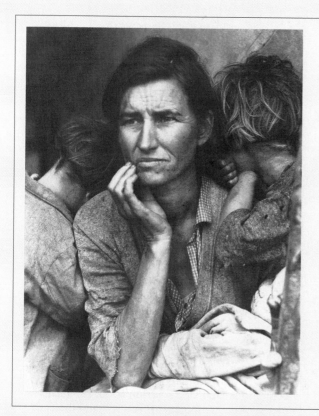

Dorothea Lange worked as one of the first photographers for the Farm Security Administration (FSA), a governmental organization, documenting the lives of migrant farm workers and the effects of the Depression. Lange's *Migrant Mother* epitomized the situation of many: surrounded by children, she appears worn and weary, beaten down by desperate conditions. While the idea of documentary implies the camera's truth-telling ability, Lange deftly manipulated her images to achieve maximum emotional effect. The viewer may assume from the close cropping that this is a single mother of three children, but other photographs from the series show the presence of a father, as well as several other children.

Figure V-5   Dorothea Lange, *Migrant Mother, Nipomo, California,* February 1936. Gelatin-silver print. (28.3 × 21.8 cm). Library of Congress, Washington, D.C. Courtesy of the Library of Congress.

Abstract Expressionists focused on the act of painting itself, alternately highlighting fields of pure color and the physical process of paint handling. Like Malevich before them (Plate 25), the Abstract Expressionists liberated painting from representation, largely eliminating recognizable imagery. Jackson Pollock, perhaps the best known purveyor of the movement, inspired the phrase "action painting" that described his highly improvisational process of dripping, pouring, and flinging paint across a canvas laid on the floor. *Autumn Rhythm (Number 30),* of 1950 (Plate 29), illustrates Pollock's signature painting style as well as his interest in nature. Becoming ever more graceful and fluid in his paint application, Pollock sought a unity with the medium and a total absorption with the process. While his paintings of this time are void of representational subject matter, his titles repeatedly make reference to nature themes, perhaps a point of inspiration.

In a complete departure from the existential focus on the self, seen in the work of the Abstract Expressionists, the Pop artists of the 1960s eliminated any reference to the self in their exclusive attention to popular consumer culture, from where comes their name. Instead of employing art as a tool for social or political critique, as had earlier artists, Pop artists, many of whom had backgrounds in commercial art, transformed crass commercial items such as hamburgers and toilets into art icons. By embracing the idea of the recognizable name brand in art, Pop artists produced work focused entirely on surface appearance and completely avoided any reference to the artist. Andy Warhol, one of the leading practitioners of the movement, produced a sizeable body of work based entirely on the goods of consumer society. In countless paintings and prints, Warhol featured such instantly recognizable images as Campbell's Soup and Coca-Cola; his use of celebrity images, from Marilyn Monroe to Jackie Kennedy, suggested that celebrities were simply another item to be consumed by the public. In *Campbell's Soup Cans,* of 1962 (Plate 30), Warhol mass-produced an image of a convenience food eaten by millions of people. The repetition of the images underscores the ubiquity of a mass-marketed brand name in consumer culture. By highlighting common items of daily life, Pop artists were perceived by some as bringing art to the masses.

The 1970s witnessed a return to personal expression, at least in the art of women. The Feminist Art Program, a graduate program launched in California by Judy Chicago and Miriam Schapiro, sought to provide female students with equal opportunities for success as their male counterparts, as well as to make art from women's personal, lived experiences. While many male artists of the day were producing cool, detached art that spoke nothing of themselves, female artists created work that gave voice to experiences of marriage, sexuality, oppression, and discrimination, and in doing so found common ground with and support from other women. Many have criticized the Feminist Art Movement, as well as the larger women's liberation movement, as being primarily white women's movements that failed to address racial and economic inequities. Bettye Saar produced work in the 1970s at an intersection of the women's liberation and black liberation movements, addressing the experiences of black women. Using items scavenged from junk shops, Saar constructs boxes that critique the stereotypes of African Americans espoused by white society. In *The Liberation of Aunt Jemima*, of 1972 (Plate 31), Saar transforms a popularly recognizable image from a pancake syrup label to make a political statement. A stereotypical "black mammy" figure in the foreground holds a white child, alluding to a history of slavery and black women's roles as caretakers of white children. Behind her, Saar empowers the larger black mammy, giving her not only a broom but also a rifle as she takes the act of liberation into her own hands.

The art world of the 1980s continued to privilege gender issues and expanded its vision to embrace art from a variety of minorities. Previously underrepresented artists expressing experiences of

Robert Mapplethorpe's photographs were at the center of a national discussion about the relative merits of contemporary art in 1989 and the early 1990s. The National Endowment for the Arts, a federally funded agency, had provided direct or indirect funding for art that some members of Congress later deemed offensive. Mapplethorpe's photographs ranged from studies of flowers and nudes to more explicit depictions of homoerotic sex acts. After the Cincinnati Contemporary Arts Center hosted a touring exhibition of Mapplethorpe's work, city officials charged the museum and its director with obscenity. Although the defendants were acquitted, amidst much attention from the national media, Congress later opted to cut a large percentage of the NEA's funding, effectively censoring the art.

Figure V-6   Robert Mapplethorpe, *Ajitto (Back),* 1981. Gelatin-silver print, 20 × 16" (50.8 × 40.6). The Robert Mapplethorpe Foundation, New York. Courtesy of The Robert Mapplethorpe Foundation, New York.

ethnic, sexual, or racial marginality suddenly became hot commodities. Much of this politically charged artwork combined images with the use of text for greater impact. The Guerrilla Girls, a collective of anonymous female artists, art historians, art dealers and gallery workers, came together in 1985 to combat gender discrimination in the art world. The women use "guerrilla" tactics of surreptitiously plastering posters at night that target specific institutions and do not hesitate to name names. By the late 1980s, the Guerrilla Girls attacked racial as well as gender discrimination in their text-filled posters. Billing themselves as the "conscience of the art world," they ask such pointed questions as, "When racism and sexism are no longer fashionable, what will your art collection be worth?" (Plate 32) Providing a partial answer to their own question, they list numerous women and artists of color whose work, while well-known, does not command the purchase price accorded to white male artists.

MUSIC OF THE TWENTIETH CENTURY

Western "classical" music in the twentieth century was extraordinarily rich, evolving in many new directions and marked by diversity, experimentation, and eclecticism. It was also revolutionized by technological developments, notably the phonograph, radio, television, and most recently digital production and transmission. The Classical and Romantic traditions continued, expressing themselves in new forms. They were joined by "postmodern" movements such as minimalism and electronic music. Twentieth-century "classical" music was incomparably enriched by the rise and development of jazz, which brought together popular and "high" musical culture and was itself in turn influenced by "classical" music. Some of the popular music of the rock music era, from The Beatles to the present day, has been indebted to the musical innovations and techniques of some of the century's avant-garde "serious" composers. A number of films have used twentieth-century (as well as earlier) "classical" music, just as they have used jazz and rock, as theme music or part of the soundtrack.

Common to much twentieth-century music amid its diversity was the widespread use of dissonance in composition—so much so that it has been called the "age of dissonance," in contrast to the consonance that had largely characterized the musical tradition. Consonance employs melodies and harmonies that are conventionally pleasing to the ear and have a sense of resolution. Dissonance creates sounds and combinations of sounds that are unconventional, unfamiliar, and even jarring to the ear, setting up a tension that seems to require (but in modern music does not necessarily lead to) resolution.

The Romantic tradition was carried forward and enriched throughout the twentieth century by "Neoromantic" composers such as Edward Elgar, Gustav Holst, Benjamin Britten, and Ralph Vaughan Williams in Britain; Sergei Rachmaninoff and Dmitri Shostakovich from Russia; Samuel Barber, George Gershwin, Aaron Copland, and Leonard Bernstein in the U.S.; Jan Sibelius in Finland; and Henryk Górecki in Poland. They continued the use of traditional groupings of instruments and of musical forms such as the concerto and the symphony, but they explored the possibilities of Romanticism with new techniques and greater complexity, including wide use of dissonance. Among the twentieth-century Neoclassicists were Maurice Ravel, Darius Milhaud, and Francis Poulenc in France; the Russians Stravinsky (in one stage of his long career) and Sergei Prokoviev; and Bela Bartok in Hungary. In their music they sought to return to more "rational," austere, clearly defined musical works for smaller vocal and orchestral groupings. They made extensive use of dissonance and changing rhythms, and were influenced by folk music.

Atonality and serialism, pioneered by Arnold Schoenberg, had an important influence on twentieth-century music, even among composers who continued the tradition of tonal music. Other composers carried the twelve-tone technique even further, using it for musical features other than the notes themselves, such as the time between notes. Serial music became popular in Europe in the two decades following World War II, led by composers like Karlheinz Stockhausen and Pierre Boulez.

"Postmodern" music came into its own beginning in the 1960s, along with postmodernism in the visual arts and literature. It is difficult to generalize about postmodernism (for example, whether it is a reaction against or a further development of modernism is debated), but two characteristics often associated with its artistic and musical expressions are a fascination with the products of modern human invention and imagination and, closely related, with popular culture in a postindustrial world. Products of popular culture and modern technology become objects of contemplation and enjoyment, and in music they sometimes function as performing instruments as well. Postmodernist art and music has also been characterized by a "thumbing of the nose" at the conventions of "high art," as in Andy Warhol's famous Campbell's Soup can. In music the most prominent figure is the American John Cage, often considered the founder of postmodern music. Cage took the view that all sounds are "music"—or, alternatively, that there is no "music," but only sounds—and in his compositions used "found sounds" from the surrounding world. Much of his music is *aleatoric*, characterized by random or chance sounds. The ultimate expression of this is his "4'33," four and a half minutes of silence—into which, of course, purely spontaneous sounds from where it is "performed" will enter.

An important musical development in the postmodern era has been minimalism. Minimalist music represents a kind of simplification, with the emphasis on the process, the flow, of the sounds themselves rather than on musical techniques. Apart from the melodic themes themselves, interest is created by having different melodic "cells" initiated by the various performers at different times and played at different speeds. The minimalists have wanted to create music that would be more accessible to a broad audience of listeners. Critics of minimalism find the music repetitive, monotonous, and in the last analysis uninteresting, while "fans" like the way in which it attracts the attentive listener to focus on small changes in the music and the variations created by the different cells. Minimalism has influenced many composers who are not themselves considered minimalists.

The best-known of the minimalist composers is Philip Glass, one of the most influential American composers of the late twentieth and early twenty-first centuries. He prefers to call what he writes "theatre music," and indeed "minimalist" is a bit confining as a term to describe the whole of his very substantial oeuvre. In keeping, however, with the minimalist commitment to writing "listenable" music for a wide audience, Glass has written not only symphonies and concertos, but also operas, music for theatre productions, and film scores. Glass has collaborated with many other composers, writers, and performers both "serious" and "popular," among them Samuel Beckett, David Bowie,

Paul Simon, Ravi Shankar, and Natalie Merchant. Among his film scores are the music for *The Hours* (2002), *Taking Lives* (2004), and *The Fog of War* (2003).

No introduction to twentieth-century music would be complete without mention of electronic music. A Russian named Leon Theremin invented the first electronic musical instrument, the theremin, in 1919. Over the century some composers incorporated electronic instruments, such as the synthesizer, into conventional instrumental settings, while others created music entirely with electronic instruments, including the synthesizer and other newer electronic instruments, magnetic tape, and computers, to produce and manipulate sounds in new ways. Among the latter group is Iannis Xenakis, who uses computers and electronic instruments extensively in his works. Electronic music was used in the 1968 Stanley Kubrick film classic *2001: A Space Odyssey*, and has figured in many films since then.

Jazz was born in the early twentieth century in the U.S., but its roots lie farther back in African-American, African, and Western musical traditions. A central feature of jazz music has been improvisation, a term that also aptly describes its protean development. Jazz has evolved so many different forms, from New Orleans Dixieland to jazz rap, that attempts at "definitions" of jazz abound and some have given up trying to define it. However, the fact that all the many permutations and combinations are called "jazz" suggests some sort of generally coherent tradition, in which each new development builds on or reacts against a previous one. We can further point to common aspects of just about all forms of jazz—besides improvisation, lively group interaction among the musicians, together with the flourishing of individual "voices," typically strong rhythm, eclectic musical sources, and an experimental openness to the new.

The term "jazz" was originally an American slang word, but how it came to be applied to a type of music is not known. The primary sources of jazz are to be found in nineteenth-century African-American spirituals, with their roots in West Africa and in the experience of slavery in America, and in military band music. The immediate predecessors of jazz are the blues and ragtime. The blues are African-American folk music of the South, again with roots in West Africa, characterized typically by slow melodies that tell a plaintive or mournful story. Ragtime, developed by turn-of-the-century African-American composers and performers like Scott Joplin, was the popular dance music of the time. The "core" instruments of jazz were those of the marching bands and dance bands of the late nineteenth and early twentieth centuries: trumpets and trombones, clarinets and saxophones, and drums. Stringed instruments, such as the violin and the double bass, along with the piano, also became standard jazz instruments.

Jazz was born in New Orleans, arising out of small bands of mainly self-taught black musicians who led funeral processions. The earliest identifiable form of jazz, in the 1910s, was called "Dixieland," which incorporated aspects of the blues and also of ragtime. The standard form of Dixieland jazz performance is for the members of the band to take turns being the solo instrument, improvising on the melody while the other musicians improvise the background. Perhaps the single most influential figure in the development of jazz, Louis Armstrong, came out of the New Orleans Dixieland tradition, getting his start with his musical mentor Joe "King" Oliver's band after Oliver moved to Chicago. Armstrong was known for his brilliant trumpet improvisation and for his "scat" singing, in which the singer sings nonverbal sounds improvisationally, using the voice as a jazz instrument. Other early manifestations were "hot" ragtime in the northeastern U.S., very rhythmic music featuring the pianist playing the melody with the right hand and providing the rhythm and bass notes with the left; and Chicago Jazz, featuring dance-band saxophones improvising against the rhythm section.

The 1920s in America came to be called the "Jazz Age," with jazz music popularized through phonograph records and the radio, and also through the "speakeasies," illegal nightclubs that flourished all over the U.S. during the Prohibition years (1920–33) and were the main venues for jazz musicians. Paul Whiteman, a white bandleader, called himself the "King of Jazz," integrating jazz into more standard arrangements of popular music. It was Whiteman who commissioned, and whose band performed, George Gershwin's *Rhapsody in Blue*, which incorporated jazz elements.

The 1930s and 1940s were the "Big Band" or "Swing" era in the jazz tradition, dominated by large dance orchestras, some of which became hugely popular and were in great demand to play for dances. Among the famous bandleaders of the era were Fletcher Henderson (whose band arrangements were very influential), Duke Ellington (one of the preeminent jazz composers), Cab Calloway, Benny Goodman, Glenn Miller, Artie Shaw, Count Basie, and Les Brown. Great solo jazz performers of the time included trumpeters like Dizzy Gillespie, pianists such as Teddy Wilson, the vibraphonist Lionel Hampton, and vocalists like Ella Fitzgerald and Billie Holiday. Leading popular singers like Bing Crosby, Frank Sinatra, and Doris Day were heavily influenced by jazz or got their start as vocalists with one of the big bands.

Kansas City joined New York, Chicago, and New Orleans to become a prominent jazz center in the 1930s, with Kansas City jazz producing musicians who created a new jazz style called "bebop"— most notably saxophonist Charlie "Bird" Parker. Bebop moved jazz away from the dance music tradition and into "musician's" jazz, with more complex and challenging arrangements and improvisation. Bebop in turn gave rise to free jazz and avant-garde jazz, both encouraging very free improvisation.

Since the 1960s wave has followed wave of new variations on the jazz tradition. Latin jazz includes Afro-Cuban and Brazilian, the latter being synonymous with bossa nova, a blend of samba and jazz that became very popular in the U.S. and was adapted by American jazz musicians such as Stan Getz and Charlie Byrd. Jazz fusion is a a meld of jazz and rock, articulated by musicians such as Miles Davis, Chick Corea, Herbie Hancock, and Frank Zappa. Late-twentieth-century jazz became very eclectic, drawing on world music (as, e.g., music of India and Africa), classical music, and rock. The jazz pianist Keith Jarrett and the Pat Metheny Group are good examples of this eclecticism. Jazz has incorporated electronic music, disco, and rap as well. Since the 1980s there has been a split in the jazz community between those who want to remain within and carry forward mainstream jazz traditions and those who believe in pushing musical experimentation beyond any sort of boundaries. Wynton Marsalis has been a leading spokesperson for the former group. A number of popular vocal artists, such as Diana Krall, Maureen McGovern, Jane Monheit, and Norah Jones, sing jazz versions of popular standards from earlier decades, including the use of scat singing, but purists do not consider what they do jazz. The opposite camp includes jazz rappers and representatives of acid jazz and electronica. What is clear is that the jazz tradition, a uniquely American and specifically African-American contribution to world music, continues into the twenty-first century to produce exciting music and gifted performers.

CD SELECTIONS

Tracks 18 and 19 represent two entirely different twentieth-century musical traditions: jazz and Neoromanticism. Track 18 is "I Love Jazz" by Sydney Shaw, performed by Louis Armstrong and his "All Stars" in live performance in the 1950s. Armstrong (1901–71), affectionately called "Satchmo" (for "satchel mouth") and "Pops," was perhaps the single most influential, and certainly the best-known, jazz performer of the twentieth century. Famous initially as a trumpet virtuoso, he became equally famous as a jazz vocalist, with his gravelly voice and scat singing. He played with the "King" Oliver band in Chicago and the Fletcher Henderson band in New York in the 1920s, finally settling permanently in Queens, New York in 1943. Armstrong teamed up with the other great names of jazz during the 'twenties, 'thirties, and 'forties, including saxophonist Coleman Hawkins, pianist Earl "Fatha" Hines, and trombonist Jack Teagarden. For thirty years, until only a few years before his death, he typically played an astonishing 300 gigs or more a year. He also managed during that time to act, sing, and play in a number of movies. In 1947, with the "big band" era beginning to fade, Armstrong disbanded his large band and created a small six-piece group featuring some of the top jazz musicians of the time. This group was the "All Stars," which toured extensively doing concerts in the 1950s and into the 1960s.

"I Love Jazz" is a recording of a live "All Stars" performance, with trombonist Trummy Young joining Armstrong on the vocal duet. "I Love Jazz" exhibits several aspects of traditional jazz, and specifically of Louis Armstrong's performance: the "passing around" of the solo playing from one instrument to the next, his own trumpet improvisation, a little bit of scat singing, and the general playfulness and fun that can characterize jazz

music. "I Love Jazz" is a delightful and of course simplified "introduction to jazz" that also tells of how it had spread internationally by the 1950s.

The final track (19) is one of the most familiar and often-performed pieces of "serious" music of the twentieth century, Samuel Barber's *Adagio for Strings*. Over the past sixty years its haunting, deeply poignant melody has made it almost a universal expression of collective grief in the Western world. Samuel Barber (1910–81) is one of the most distinguished and prolific of twentieth-century American composers. Often characterized as a Neoromantic composer, he is best known for writing beautiful melodies and more traditional harmonies rather than experimenting with new forms such as serialism or minimalism. At the same time, like the other twentieth-century Neoromantics, he incorporated newer developments, especially in his later works, such as dissonance and alternating rhythms. Barber composed sonatas, concertos, symphonies, and operas, as well as a number of choral works. He twice won the Pulitzer Prize for music.

Barber wrote the *Adagio for Strings* in 1936, originally as a movement of his String Quartet No. 1. It was first performed by the NBC Symphony Orchestra, conducted by Arturo Toscanini, in 1938. The flowing, ascending melody line is "passed around" among the various stringed instruments—from violins to violas to cellos to basses—moving to a strong climax followed by silence and then a restatement of the original theme. *Adagio for Strings* was choreographed as a ballet in 1980, premiering at the Metropolitan Opera House. It was played at the funerals of U.S. Presidents Franklin Roosevelt and John F. Kennedy, and also of Princess Grace and Prince Rainier of Monaco. It was a main musical theme in the fine Vietnam War film *Platoon*. Canadian Lt. Gen. Roméo Dallaire, commander of UN peacekeeping forces in Rwanda during the 1994 genocide, called the *Adagio* "the purest expression in music of the suffering, mutilation, rape and murder of 800,000 Rwandans." It was also played at one of the national memorial concerts after the 9/11 attacks. *Adagio for Strings* has become for many a powerful musical articulation of the suffering and sorrow of a century marked by two world wars and by the Holocaust and other genocidal slaughters.

CHAPTER FOURTEEN

MODERN JUDAISM AND THE HOLOCAUST

JEWS IN CHRISTIAN EUROPE

In this chapter we will examine the historic struggle of Jews to define and maintain their identity as a religious and cultural minority within the discriminatory and often hostile environment of Christian anti-Semitism, and the fundamental challenges to both Jews and Christians posed by the Nazis' systematic destruction of six million European Jews between 1939 and 1945.

The historical background to Hitler's anti-Jewish ideology is to be found in many centuries of Christian anti-Judaism. Up until the nineteenth century "anti-Semitism" is more properly to be understood as "anti-Judaism": discrimination against and persecution of Jews as adherents of a rival religion with which Christianity shares its historical and theological roots.

The earliest Christians were one of many sects within the Judaism of the first century of the Common Era, so that initially it was a matter of disagreement with fellow Jews over whether or not the Messiah had appeared and was to be identified with the man Jesus. It was a fateful day for the future relationship between the two faiths when, in the fourth century of the Common Era, Christianity became the official religion of the Western world, accelerating and intensifying Christian hostility toward Jews into a long tradition of theological and popular anti-Judaism. Christians believed that God had condemned the Jews because they had rejected their own Messiah, despite the fact that Christian acceptance of Jesus as the Messiah required a complete reinterpretation of the prevailing messianic expectations. To the whole of the Jewish people was assigned the corporate responsibility for being

"Christ-killers," despite the fact that it had been specific people and groups within Palestinian Judaism who had both rejected and accepted Jesus and that the Roman authorities in Judea bore substantial responsibility for Jesus' death.

Christians saw the Jewish *Diaspora*, the scattering of Jews throughout the world, together with the Roman destruction of the Jerusalem Temple in 70 C.E., as divine punishment for their spiritual blindness; while the scattering of the Christian community throughout the Mediterranean world and the periodic persecution of Christians by Roman authorities were interpreted as vindication of Christian claims and holy martyrdom. Theologians such as Augustine accepted Paul's idea in Romans 11 that God had a continuing purpose for his originally chosen people until the end of the world, but unlike Paul, they viewed that purpose as to suffer whatever a Christian world had to mete out to them until they saw the light and became Christians.

Through the Christian centuries in Europe, every Holy Week (the week preceding Easter, when the gospel accounts of Jesus' trial and crucifixion are read on a daily basis in many churches) the worshippers would hear the cry of the crowd when Pilate asked what he should do with Jesus: "Crucify him!" followed by the crowd's statement, "His blood be upon us and upon our children." (Matt. 27:20–26) Everyone interpreted those verses as applying corporately to all Jews, past and present. Easter was often a time of outbreaks of violence against Jews by Christians in Europe. All sorts of superstitions—indeed, a whole mythology—about Jews grew up beginning in the twelfth century in Christian Europe, many of them bound up with the

320

idea that Jews were in league with Satan: they drank the blood of Christian children in their rituals, they poisoned wells, they caused the periodic outbreaks of bubonic plague, they secretly practiced all sorts of satanic arts against Christians. Among the Protestant Reformers in the sixteenth century, Martin Luther, toward the end of his life, frustrated over continued Jewish refusal to convert despite the reform of Christianity, wrote a notorious book titled *On the Jews and Their Lies*, in which he called for harsh measures against Jews who remained in Europe.

European Jews lived as a "client people" throughout the Middle Ages. They were exploited by the Christian nobility, persecuted by the masses, and excluded from citizenship in society as a whole. In general, three avenues of religious living were open to them: (1) a life confined by the traditions, laws, and customs of their people; (2) a life vitalizing those traditions through philosophical exploration; and (3) a life based on a mystical interpretation of Jewish existence as necessary to the world's salvation. As Jews interacted with European civilization they evolved their own expressions of beauty and knowledge. In response to the culture of Muslim Spain, Jews created poetry, art and song, and philosophy. Under the heel of Christendom, Jews learned to erect monuments of faith—lives devoted to God's word through study and interpretation of Torah, and deaths sanctifying God's name by testifying to the loyalty Jews had toward their faith.

The two types of Jewish culture that developed in the Middle Ages came to be called *Ashkenazic* and *Sephardic*. Sephardic Judaism emerged in Spain and Portugal, Turkey, Egypt, and North Africa; Ashkenazic Judaism developed in Germany. Sephardic Judaism was deeply influenced by Islamic culture and produced philosophers and poets.

The mostly Ashkenazic Jews of medieval Christian Europe learned to adapt to an uncertain and shifting environment by turning inward rather than outward. They interpreted God as speaking a special language—that of the law codes, the tradition of rabbinic interpretation of Torah embodied in the Talmud. They believed that living strictly according to Jewish law was both the highest service to God and a wall of security around the Jewish community in a hostile environment.

Between the end of the eleventh century and late in the thirteenth century, Christian Europe launched a series of ultimately unsuccessful Crusades against the Muslim Turks who controlled Palestine and other parts of the Near East. The crusading fervor inevitably directed itself also against Jews both in Europe and in the Near East as well. A mystical form of Judaism arose in response to the new and destructive circumstances often produced by the Crusades. A group of pious Jews in Germany formed a "Hasidic" (from *Hasid*, meaning "pious") or saintly sect. Spanish Jews wrote esoteric mystical interpretations of the Hebrew Bible, the most famous of which, the *Zohar*, determined the shape of all subsequent Jewish mysticism. Much later, in eighteenth-century Poland, a new movement called Hasidism arose out of the Jewish mystical and Hasidic traditions that had emerged in the Middle Ages.

The Middle Ages were marked by the widespread growth throughout Europe of repressive laws against the Jewish people during the Middle Ages. Because they were not allowed to own land, Jews joined the emerging middle class of merchants, bankers, and artisans. At various times and places Jews were required to wear an insignia, such as a yellow star of David (later revived by the Nazis), in public. There were laws regulating Christian fraternization with Jews and Jewish use of public facilities. In short, Jews were at best "second-class" citizens, actively discriminated against; at worst, they were actively persecuted and killed.

THE CHALLENGES OF MODERNITY TO JEWS AND THE RELIGIOUS RESPONSE IN MODERN JUDAISM

With the growth of knowledge and toleration fostered by the Scientific Revolution of the seventeenth century and the eighteenth-century Enlightenment, many Jews were eager to "modernize," but only if it allowed them to remain Jews. Acceptance of Jews by the surrounding Christian society, however, usually included stipulations and conditions. In 1806, for example, before Napoleon would extend liberty to the Jews of France, he summoned an "Assembly of [Jewish] Notables" to answer twelve questions regarding their loyalty to France. While other offers of citizenship—like that made by Wilhelm von Humboldt of Prussia in 1809—were made more graciously, they still included explicit as well as implicit conditions. Jews accepted these, but insisted that they could remain distinctively Jewish.

In the modern West, Jews have differed over how and in what way they should preserve and affirm their distinctiveness. Three major movements in modern Jewish religion—Reform, Conservative, and Orthodox—represent such a response.

Reform Judaism. Deeply influenced by the Enlightenment, Jews in early nineteenth-century Germany began to reinterpret Judaism as a reasoned religion capable of change and development. This new, liberal version of Judaism facilitated the entrance of Jews into modern culture. Reform Jews could now eat with non-Jews, join their friends for activities scheduled on the Jewish Sabbath, and accommodate themselves to values far removed from those sanctioned by the tradition. Reform Jews boasted that they had left the inequality of the sexes behind as an antiquated doctrine, and polemicized against their opponents as benighted and sexist. Serious studies of the Reform movement in Judaism, however, suggest that practice did not live up to rhetoric. Women were granted equality in name, but not in opportunity. They were barred from becoming rabbis until the 1970s; their contributions were indispensable to Reform Jewish life, but women themselves were often relegated to the sidelines.

Conservative Judaism. Another group, called the Positive-Historical School of Judaism in Europe and Conservative Judaism in the U.S., attracted individuals who tended toward Reform Judaism, but who withdrew from such radical changes as abandoning the Hebrew language in worship and study, denying traditional Jewish hopes for a restored national home in Zion (Palestine), and ignoring the strong sentimental attachment of Jews to their ancestral practices. Perhaps the most important aspect of Conservative Judaism is its insistence on the centrality of learning. Additionally, Conservative Judaism integrated women into its institutional structure at an early period. Women were teachers, workers, and builders of Conservative synagogues. They won concessions on various modern concerns from marriage, divorce, and abortion to participation in religious ceremonies.

Women could study at a school of Jewish education. However, they were not initiated into the higher Jewish learning. After their sisters in the Reform movement had achieved the goal of rabbinic ordination, Conservative women had to wait nearly two decades and engage in countless battles before they gained the privilege.

Neo-Orthodox Judaism. Traditional Jews looked askance at both Reform and Conservative Judaism as deviations from a divinely revealed view of reality. Leaders of Orthodox Judaism charted a path between assimilation into and withdrawal from the modern world that has been called "Neo-Orthodoxy." According to a leading spokesman, Emmanuel Hirsch, Orthodox Judaism would embrace the legacy of the Enlightenment "as affording a greater opportunity for the fulfillment of its task, the realization of a noble and ideal life," but would reject it when it demands "capricious abandonment of the chief element of our very being." The chief element was defined as accepting the Torah "as the fountain of spiritual and ethical life." The modern world was a special challenge. And the Jew was to become the teacher of humanity. The emancipation that the Enlightenment had brought allowed the Jew a new environment for communicating the Jewish message of the Jewish faith, but Jewish distinctiveness and tradition remained non-negotiable. A Jew who assimilated could not be an ambassador to a wayward world.

One aspect of this ideal included a traditional social, economic, and psychological place for women within the scheme of reality. Women were to be the submissive helpmates to men. While powerful in their own domain—the home and the family—they were to allow men to determine the shape and pattern of their lives. Feminist liberation, from this perspective, is not even an ideal worthy of lip service. Women who seek "equality" are abandoning their own Torah-ideal, their true nature and purpose, and substituting the false values of the modern age in its place. Since the philosophy of Judaism presents the truth for all reality, the Neo-Orthodox Jew such as Hirsch cannot accept any alternative model of sexual roles than those given in early rabbinic codes and in the commentaries on them.

Whether formulated by Reform, Conservative, or Neo-Orthodox leaders, the approach to Judaism as a philosophy of life provided Jews with a groundwork upon which to build a new Judaism. Jews were led to recognize common interests shared with other religions and in the twentieth century they have cooperated with non-Jews in advancing social justice, in probing the meaning of faith, and in trying to establish world peace. Particularly since the Nazi Holocaust, religious Jews, even the Neo-Orthodox, have begun dialogue with non-Jews, and non-Jews seem to have responded positively. Relationships particularly with Christians—both informally and formally—seem to have improved, as Christians confront the anti-Semitism that has pervaded their theology and history.

Zionism. Another group of Jews in the modern period rejected such a belief-oriented approach and advanced a more "realistic" alternative. These Jews contended that Jewish distinctiveness grew out of a shared culture and national loyalty. Jewish identity depends on affirmation of the communal goals of the Jewish people. The long centuries of exile had robbed Jews of their true national heritage. The modern world, these Jews argued, would provide an opportunity to rebuild the Jewish national home in what had been the land of Israel. These Jews did not believe that Jews could ever exist comfortably as a small minority in societies dominated by Christianity. As long as Jews remained entirely a dispersed people, without a homeland of their own, they would be despised and persecuted. When they asserted their national strength, however, they would be respected and treated as equals. Furthermore, they viewed their rebuilt homeland as an experiment in human culture. They would create a society in which equality became a reality, not merely a dream. Although often appearing to outsiders as a monolithic nationalism, in fact Zionism represented many different perspectives: deeply religious, frankly political and opportunistic, and cultural. Zionist efforts, including increasing migration of Jews to Palestine beginning in the late nineteenth century, were rewarded by the founding of the nation of Israel in 1948, but only as a result of the Holocaust.

BACKGROUND TO THE HOLOCAUST

In the nineteenth century there was a gradual lifting of restrictions against Jews throughout Europe. As Jewish men were allowed to study at universities, so the Jews experienced their own Enlightenment, or *Haskalah*. The development of Reform Judaism encouraged assimilation, and many—Karl Marx's family is a notable example—underwent what might be considered nominal conversion to Christianity. All this was based on the belief that if Jews could enter fully into citizenship and cultural and social participation in their countries it would minimize their distinctiveness and demonstrate that they were patriotic citizens of their homeland. Ironically from our post-Holocaust vantage point, in no country did Jews assimilate more fully than in Germany.

Counter to the Enlightenment, the Romantic movement accentuated the *differences* among nations and peoples. Each nation or people was thought to have certain distinctive generalizable characteristics which could be ascertained and were to be highlighted. At its best, Romantic emphasis on differences was a celebration of human diversity in all its richness. At its worst, it gave intellectual and moral sanction to invidious generalizing about and stereotyping of human groups, to categorizing in terms of superior and inferior, "civilized" and "primitive." The idea of *race* came to play a prominent role in this sort of thinking, and our contemporary preoccupation with and ways of thinking about race are largely a product of nineteenth-century thought. The belief arose that there were clearly distinct racial groups, and to each group were ascribed certain inherent characteristics. In the hands of Social Darwinists, Darwin's theory of evolution seemed to give solid "scientific" grounding to the notion that some races (notably white Europeans) were more "fit" or successful in the struggle for survival than others, or had evolved to a higher plane. Leading biologists and anthropologists of the late nineteenth and early twentieth centuries solemnly set forth and elaborated these ideas as scientific truth. Western ideas of the natural superiority of the white "race" and the natural primitiveness and inferiority of the black, brown, and yellow "races" were widely believed and used as rationalizations of Western imperialism and colonialism. This was applied to the Jews despite the fact Jews are united by religion and culture, not by race. The term "anti-Semitism," meaning hatred of Jews as the "Semitic race," was first used in the 1870s.

Political theories spread of an international Jewish conspiracy that supposedly operated secretly in all sorts of ways to undermine European social stability, Christianity, and racial purity. Such theories were marked by contradictions. For example, alternatively Jews were seen as a main force behind communism, which was a movement to be reckoned with throughout Europe at this time, and as comprising an international banking cabal. The conspiracy theories about Jews were a modern secularized version of the traditional Christian interpretation of Jews as in league with Satan and the secret cause of the various troubles and disasters that were visited upon Christians. It was the old scapegoating of Jews dressed up in new forms.

The unification of Germany in 1871 under Chancellor Otto Von Bismarck brought with it a strong new spirit of German nationalism. For some the new nationalism found expression in the creation of a new mythology exalting the superiority of the "Germanic" or "Aryan" race that over many centuries had made Germany great, and the denigration of German Jews as insidious pollutants, cancers within the otherwise healthy body of racially pure Germanhood. The composer Richard Wagner (1813–1883) was one such figure who was very influential, and in some of his operas he sought to revive some of the old pre-Christian Teutonic mythology to glorify the German past.

A notorious case in France at the end of the nineteenth century showed the depth and virulence of the centuries-old legacy of anti-Judaism (as revised and restated by the new theory of anti-Semitism) in modern Europe. When it was discovered that an officer on the French military general staff had been selling secrets to Germany, attention turned to Captain Alfred Dreyfus. Although there was no evidence to justify suspicion of him, he was the only Jew on the staff. Dreyfus was court-martialed on trumped-up evidence and condemned to penal servitude on Devil's Island. While he was later released and vindicated, his innocence championed by leading figures such as the writer Emile Zola and the statesman Georges Clemenceau, the incident brought to a head years of animosity towards Jews by militarists,

monarchists, and clergy hostile to the democratic institutions of the French Republic.

Treatment of Jews in Russia and Eastern Europe, always discriminatory, became worse during the latter part of the nineteenth century. Russia and Poland had the largest Jewish populations in Europe, together with the most conservative autocracies and large Christian populations of illiterate peasants little better off than serfs. From 1881 until the outbreak of the Revolution in 1917, tsarist Russia essentially declared war on Russian Jews, following the traditional pattern of diverting Christian Russians' attention from their serious economic and social problems by focusing their pent-up resentments on Jews. Unhappily, it must be said that the great Russian writer Fyodor Dostoevsky was as virulent a Jew-hater as he was a devoted supporter of the Russian Orthodox Church and the tsar.

Russia, Poland, and other Eastern European countries enacted increasingly repressive legislation against Jews. Thus the word *pogrom* entered our vocabulary. It is a Yiddish word from the Russian word meaning "devastation," and refers to an organized massacre against helpless people. (Yiddish, short for *yidisch daytsch* or Jewish German, is a German dialect usually written in Hebrew characters. It became the dialect of Eastern European Jews, and through them a kind of international Jewish dialect.) A vivid fictional portrayal of Jewish life under the tsars and the racist and conspiratorial ideas and religious superstitions which made up Christian Russian attitudes toward Jews can be found in Bernard Malamud's novel, *The Fixer* (1967).

NAZISM AND THE HOLOCAUST

Pogroms and other forms of attack against Jews were often used, in Russia and Eastern European countries, by those in power as political propaganda to gain popular support and take the masses' minds off their own impoverished conditions. It was, however, only in Germany in the 1930s, with the growth of the National Socialist (Nazi) party and Adolf Hitler's rise to power that racial anti-Semitism was adopted as an official ideology and policy by a major European country.

Adolf Hitler (1889–1945), one-time artist and soldier in World War I and leader of the Nazi party, developed into a kind of demonic genius with

ADOLF, DER ÜBERMENSCH: Schluckt Gold und redet Blech

A German who anglicized his name in protest of German nationalism, John Heartfield produced virulent anti-Hitler photomontages during the reign of National Socialism. Hitler called for Heartfield's arrest when he came to power in 1933, but Heartfield fled to Prague, then to England. *Adolf the Superman* is typical of Heartfield's biting commentary, sharply critical but easily understandable to the general public. Produced for the 1932 election, the photomontage shows Hitler swallowing the gold of his wealthy industrialist backers; the "junk" in Heartfield's title refers to Hitler's espoused program of militarism, nationalism, and hatred for Jews.

Figure V-7   John Heartfield, *Adolf the Superman: Swallows Gold and Spouts Junk,* 1932. Photomontage. $15^{1}/_{4} \times 10^{3}/_{4}$" (38 × 27 cm). Made for the *Arbeiter-Illustrierte-Zeitung (AIZ)* no. 29, July 17, 1932, Berlin. Courtesy of Artists Rights Society (ARS), New York.

remarkable skills at creating and implementing a complete ideological worldview symbolized in powerful trappings such as the *Hakenkreuz* (swastika) and the mass rallies where he held audiences spellbound with his appeal to the greatness and destiny of German "blood and soil." He outlined the program of the Nazi movement in *Mein Kampf* (1925). It contains the most extreme sort of anti-Semitic hatred, sounding the familiar racial and conspiratorial themes, and calling for a strong "Aryan" Germany purified of Jews and other undesirable elements.

Nazi policy against Jews began to be enacted immediately upon Hitler's accession to power. There were three stages in the development of the Third Reich's treatment of what was euphemistically called "the Jewish Question."

1. 1933–39: Persecution of German Jews. During this period German Jews were deprived of their rights as citizens, had their property confiscated, and were excluded from all educational institutions and cultural life in Germany. The definition of "Jew" was explicitly based on Nazi racist ideology: Jews were persons of "impure blood," as the Nuremberg Laws of 1935 stated, in contrast to those of "pure" or "Aryan" or "German" blood. It made no difference that a Jew might be entirely secularized, completely non-observant of the Jewish religion; it made no difference that a Jew had become a Christian. All one needed to be classified as Jewish was a grandparent who had claimed to be Jewish. The legal, economic, and cultural deprivation of German Jews—500,000 people or about 0.8 per cent of the population—all took place within the context of ceaseless and effective anti-Jewish propaganda and official incitement to violence against and looting of Jews. Hitler played skillfully upon the psychological legacy of centuries of Christian anti-Judaism, and once told some Christian bishops that he was simply carrying out what Christians had always wanted done with Jews.

During the first phase of Nazi persecution many Jews believed that if they were content to remain apart, those in power would come to ignore them or regard them as harmless. Others believed that given time the Nazis would either be forced out or would moderate their policies in the face of opposition both within and without Germany. Still others, mainly Zionists, saw the situation as far more grave, and insisted that the only sensible solution was emigration to Palestine. To that end they made a considerable effort to evacuate Jewish children and young people from Germany.

Emigration of Jews was also the official Nazi policy during this period, although Nazi officials were equally dedicated to pillaging and confiscating Jewish property and reducing Jews to poverty. Many German Jews were in fact able to emigrate. Of the half million Jews living in Germany when Hitler came to power, approximately 300,000 emigrated, freely or forcibly, in time to escape the "Final Solution": the all-too-successful Nazi attempt at full-scale genocide throughout the continent of Europe. Many more German Jews could have been saved before the outbreak of the war in 1939 had the free nations been willing to take in Jewish refugees or assist them in emigrating to Palestine, which was controlled by the British. Groups of exiled German Jews were literally turned away by countries, including the United States, on the basis of immigration laws.

2. 1939–41: Restriction and internment of Jews all over Europe. Germany invaded Poland on September 1, 1939, plunging Europe into the Second World War. Anti-Jewish policy during the earliest years of the war can be characterized as a kind of transition from the prewar policy of forced emigration to the "Final Solution." Germany had already annexed Austria and Czechoslovakia in 1938. Now making an all-out war effort to conquer Europe, Germany in swift succession occupied all or part of most of the countries of the European continent: Poland, France, Belgium, Holland, Denmark, Norway, Yugoslavia, Greece, Lithuania, Latvia, and Estonia. Italy was a German ally, and the governments of Rumania and Hungary were pro-Nazi satellites. Switzerland and Sweden were neutral.

The Reich Security Main Office was established in 1939 and given the task of solving the "Jewish Question." It was headed by Reinhardt Heydrich, a close associate of Heinrich Himmler, head of the dreaded S.S. (*Schützstaffel*, "defense corps"). Officers and troops of the S.S. played the key role in implementing Nazi policy against Jews during the war. All Jews were commanded to wear the yellow Star of David, a revival of the medieval practice. Jewish property was confiscated and Jews were placed into camps to perform forced labor. Central to Nazi policy in the 1939–41 period was the isolation and internment of Jews in occupied areas; over time Jews throughout Europe were sealed off from outside help and contact. In Poland many Jews were rounded up and isolated together in ghettoes. The first ghetto in Poland was Lodz. The largest, set up in 1940, was in Warsaw. Eventually half a million Jews were forced into the Warsaw ghetto, where many died from malnutrition and disease. The Warsaw Ghetto revolt in 1943 was the largest Jewish uprising, and the first armed revolt, against the Nazis in occupied Europe. Throughout this month-long revolt Jews fought tenaciously against their Nazi tormentors despite having few weapons, facing overwhelming odds, and suffering the debilitating physical effects of life in the ghetto. The Warsaw Ghetto Uprising was an attempt to halt or slow down Nazi deportation of Jews from the ghettos to the death camps, which was where most Jews confined in ghettoes ended their lives.

3. 1941–45: The Final Solution. The third and last phase of the Nazi "solution of the Jewish Question" began in June, 1941, and ended only with Germany's defeat in May 1945. During those four years, Jews all over Europe were relentlessly and efficiently hunted down, rounded up, savagely persecuted, subjected to every conceivable torture and degradation, and murdered—first in mass shootings and then in the more efficient gas chambers of extermination camps. Millions of other unfortunate human beings who were not Jews also perished in Nazi camps: political opponents, Soviet prisoners of war, gypsies, homosexuals, the mentally ill and retarded. But no group was singled out in Nazi ideology from the beginning and hunted down with such single-mindedness and thoroughness as were Jews. Ridding the world of Jews was central to Nazi ideology in a way that few other commitments were. So important was the "Final Solution" to the Third Reich that the effort to destroy all Jews—which required a considerable commitment of personnel, planning, and material—often took precedence over the general war effort. For example, trains needed to pull boxcars full of Jews to concentration and death camps would sometimes be given priority over trains needed to carry troops to the front lines.

But German efforts in some of the occupied countries in western European were sometimes thwarted by the citizens. The most notable example of non-Jewish solidarity with and protection of Jews is Denmark. In 1943 the Nazis attempted to round up the 7,500 Danish Jews. The Danes not only warned their Jewish compatriots, but helped them to go into hiding and cross over to neutral Sweden. Similarly, the Norwegian people and the Norwegian national church defied the Nazis, and exerted every effort to prevent the arrests and deportations. By contrast, Poland, which the Nazis completely controlled, had a long tradition of vigorous anti-Judaism, Poles generally were suffering and dying at the hands of the Nazis, and there was a large measure of indifference to the fate of Polish Jews. Having established their "General Government" in Poland, the Nazis built most of the extermination camps there. Rumania and Hungary likewise had strong anti-Semitic traditions and also pro-Nazi governments that willingly handed over Rumanian and Hungarian Jews to the Germans. At the same time, there were non-Jews in every European country—including Germany and Poland—who were what Jews call "righteous Gentiles," individuals and families who risked their lives hiding Jews and helping them escape.

The Germans built the first of the concentration camps, Dachau, in March 1933, shortly after Hitler's accession to power. Buchenwald was opened in 1937. After the war had begun the Nazis began establishing a number of concentration camps in Poland. Himmler issued a directive to build a camp at Oswiecim (German name "Auschwitz") in April of 1940. Before the implementation of the "Final Solution" in 1941, all the camps, including Auschwitz, were concentration camps, where Jews and other captives were crowded together under unspeakable conditions and often made to do slave labor. Beginning in 1941, some camps were built or designated as extermination or death camps, the only function of which was to destroy and dispose of as many people as possible as efficiently as possible in gas chambers and crematoria. Some camps, like Auschwitz, were mixed: both concentration and death camps. The names of the Nazi camps—Dachau, Buchenwald, Majdanek, Theresienstadt, Chelmno, Treblinka, Sobi-

bor, Mauthausen, and many others—have become bywords for the magnitude of inhumanity by human beings in the twentieth century. Auschwitz alone, where over two million persons—most of them Jews—were destroyed, has become a universal symbol of the horror of the Holocaust. Remarkably enough, even in the camps, where humans were starved, beaten, forced to live in their own filth, worked as slave labor, tortured, and experimented on, there were a number of armed uprisings. At Treblinka, for example, the entire camp population poured out of the opened gates after revolting against their captors, and many of those who made it to the woods survived.

The Nazi war against the Jews achieved the appalling success it did through a high degree of bureaucratic and technological efficiency and hundreds of thousands of persons to fill all the needed positions. Many of these were ordinary people, often personally "decent" folk who loved their spouses and children, went to church, and did not belong to the Nazi party—people who were just "doing their job" as loyal Germans. To be sure, there were always sadists around, such as the Auschwitz "Angel of Death," Dr. Josef Mengele, other Nazi party and S.S. leaders, and persons in all ranks of the hierarchy. But the system could never have worked as well as it did without the cooperation of large numbers of "normal" persons. Those who imagine that this behavior is a "German" trait would do well to read the American theologian Reinhold Niebuhr's book *Moral Man and Immoral Society*, published in 1932, shortly before Hitler came to power. It is a penetrating analysis, with many specific examples, of the general social phenomenon that even persons who are morally upright and sensitive in their personal life will willingly participate in immorality as members of groups and causes—governments, corporations, churches, nations, movements. There are entirely too many examples from twenty-first century American life of this sort of split between private and group behavior to make one entirely confident that he or she would not have been a "good German" from 1933 to 1945.

What Hitler was doing to German Jews during the 1930s was known in official circles in other countries and to observant foreign visitors. By 1942 what was going on in the concentration camps and extermination camps was becoming widely known. It is now well documented that the Allied nations did nothing for the beleaguered and tortured Jews—neither before nor during the war. Private organizations, Jewish and non-Jewish, in many places did all they could to help Jewish refugees and call attention to what was going on. Their governments were silent, despite repeated appeals at high levels. During the war appeals were made, for example, simply to get Allied planes to bomb the railroad lines and bridges leading to Auschwitz and other camps, but other aspects of the war effort always took priority.

Nazi Germany was utterly defeated in the war, and its surviving leaders were tried and convicted for crimes against humanity and convicted in international tribunals following the war. But the machinery of death ran efficiently up to the very end. To say only that the Nazis were defeated omits the fact that even in defeat they were extraordinarily successful, not only in devastating Europe, but in achieving one of the most important things they set out to do: annihilate every Jew in Europe. From the best estimates of the numbers of Jewish dead, here are a few statistics: Before the war there were 3,300,000 Polish Jews. The Nazis destroyed 3,000,000, in effect wiping out not only the largest but one of the most culturally and spiritually creative Jewish communities in the world. Ninety per cent of the Jews of the Baltic countries and those remaining in Germany were destroyed; seventy-seven per cent of the Jewish population of Greece; seventy-five per cent of Dutch Jews; sixty-five per cent of Russian Jews. Overall the Nazis murdered sixty-seven per cent of the Jews of Europe: over two-thirds of the entire Jewish population of Europe, or about 6,000,000 people.

"Holocaust" is a term that Jews themselves have chosen to describe what happened to European Jewry in World War II. Generally the word means a great destruction or devastation, but etymologically it bears a specifically Jewish interpretation. The word comes from the Greek *holokauston*, which in the Septuagint or Greek translation of the Hebrew Bible translates the Hebrew word *olah*. *Olah*, meaning literally "what is brought up," translates into English as "an offering made by fire unto the Lord," "burnt offering," or "whole burnt offering." For some the notion of "burnt offering" was particularly graphic in view of the millions of Jews whose bodies were literally burned to ashes and smoke in huge crematoria after they were gassed. Another term in the Jewish literature on the Holocaust is *Shoah*, a Hebrew word meaning "whirlwind."

JEWISH RESPONSES TO THE HOLOCAUST

The trauma of the Nazi Holocaust has confronted contemporary Jews with the reality of radical evil as well as the issue of Jewish survival. Interestingly, there was little reflection on it in the first years after the war. Only when the distance of time allowed some perspective amid the pain did Jews confront the depth of evil embodied in the Holocaust and the necessity for a new response to it. The thrust of the newer Jewish thinking has been that ethics is more important than theology, the human response of seeking appropriate moral responses more important than views of God. Post-Holocaust Jewish theology has struggled with the need to create a new ethical ideal for a humanity shaken to its roots by its own destructive power. It has had to raise questions such as: Can Jews enter into any positive relationship with non-Jews after learning the depths of the anti-Semitism harbored by Gentiles? Dare Jews hope that any transformation of society, even of Jewish society, is possible in a world filled with radical evil?

The post-Holocaust years have intensified debate and diversity among Jews as all issues have seemed to require new questions and new perspectives. Judaism today tends toward internal polemic and polarization more than ever in its past. Worldwide Jewish support for Israel—whose existence is viewed as the one great positive outcome of the Holocaust—is nevertheless marked by heated internal controversy over Israel's relations with its Arab neighbors and with Palestinians within its own territories. Externally Israel has been widely criticized for the continuing failure of Israelis and Palestinians to work out a just and peaceful *modus vivendi*. Issues such as women's and minority rights, abortion and other biomedical ethical issues, pollution and overpopulation, and nuclear war are also at the center of the agenda of much current Jewish thought.

Various Jewish thinkers have probed the specific issues raised for Jews by the Holocaust in a variety of ways. Richard Rubenstein uses the Nazi experience to illuminate a modern world in which everyone must live without illusion, recognizing that the old moral restraints no longer apply. The traditional God of the covenant, who saves and defends Israel, is "dead" after the Holocaust, and Jews must affirm and support the new nation of Israel as embodying the value of Jewish survival. Eliezer Berkovits offers a much more traditional Jewish counsel, consolation, and interpretation, appealing to the biblical notion of God's withholding of the divine presence at times, and calling for a continuing Jewish religious commitment that has survived other disasters in the past. Emil Fackenheim believes that the *Shoah* has revealed a new divine commandment: Jewish survival. The Jew's distinctiveness lies in Jewish existence itself—not the nature of that existence, but its very persistence. The relationship of Jew to non-Jew is that of teacher and witness, one whose existence testifies to both the darkness and the light of the human situation. In the light of the new commandment the door is open to a newly shaped Judaism, a Judaism in which the community as a whole takes on new meaning, a Judaism that transcends gender roles, a Judaism in which the commandment affects all equally. These varied responses illustrate the continuing struggle of Jews to define their reason for being in a world in which the old assumptions, the old values, the old optimisms about the human future, can no longer be taken for granted.

HOLOCAUST MEMOIRS

There is a rich literature, both appalling and deeply moving in its descriptions of what being a victim of the Holocaust was really like, written by survivors of the Holocaust. Among the "classic" survivor-witness memoirs are Elie Wiesel's *Night*, Primo Levi's *Surviving in Auschwitz*, and Viktor Frankl's *Man's Search for Meaning*.

Perhaps the best known survivor memoirist is Elie Wiesel (born 1928), long a distinguished writer of novels, essays, and plays—many of which deal with the Holocaust and its lasting impact—and winner of the 1986 Nobel Peace Prize. Wiesel grew up a devout child and student of Talmud in the small Hasidic Jewish community of Sighet in Hungary. The entire Jewish population was deported to concentration camps in 1944, and Wiesel's mother and sister were immediately sent to the gas chamber. He and his father were together in a series of camps. His father died in Buchenwald, and Wiesel himself almost died of food poisoning after he was liberated by American army troops in 1945. Going to live in Paris after the war, he imposed a ten-year silence on himself, and then in 1958 published *Night*, one of the most powerful and widely read of the Holocaust memoirs.

An industrial chemist by profession, the Italian Primo Levi (1919–87) became world-famous for his Holocaust memoirs and was also well known as an author of short stories, poems, and a novel. In contrast to Wiesel, Levi, born in Turin, Italy, came from a liberal Jewish family and he himself remained non-observant throughout his adult life. Imprisoned in Auschwitz for eleven months, Levi survived through a combination of technical skill, shrewdness, and luck. In 1947 he recounted his camp experience in *If This is a Man* (published in the U.S. as *Survival in Auschwitz*), which beginning in the 1960s became a world-renowned book. Some consider it the finest Holocaust memoir and one of the important literary works of the twentieth century. In 1963 he published a sequel, *The Truce* (published in the U.S. as *The Reawakening*), about his long and difficult journey home after the war. Deeply haunted by his wartime experiences the rest of his life, torn between optimism and pessimism about the human condition, Levi died in a fall from a stair landing in his apartment building in 1987, probably a suicide.

Viktor Frankl (1905–97), an Austrian Jew, was one of the leading psychiatrists of the twentieth century. Frankl lost his wife, mother, and father in the death camps, and himself barely survived. In 1959 he published *Man's Search for Meaning*, which took its place internationally as one of the most widely read survivor memoirs. His book is unique among Holocaust testimonies because of Frankl's professional interest as a psychiatrist in his own and his fellow inmates' attitudes and behavior. The first part of the book is the memoir itself, and the second part sets forth the psychological theory on the basis of which he interprets the camp experiences: what he calls *logotherapy*, an approach to psychology centered in the "will to meaning" as the most distinctive and important motive in human behavior.

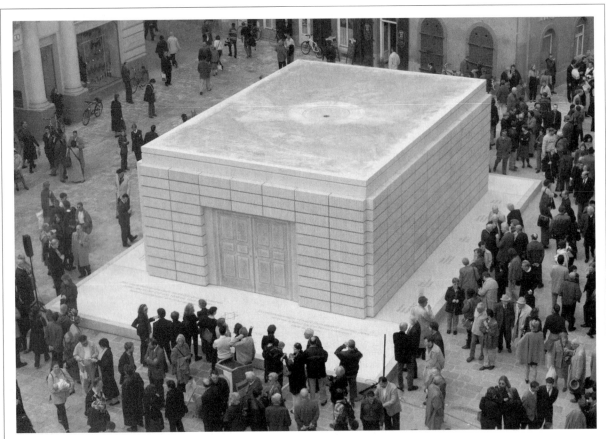

British artist Rachel Whiteread inverts the usual sculptural process: rather than cast an object, she casts its negative space, from the underside of furniture to the whole interior of a two-story house. Through her works, Whiteread plays on ideas of presence and absence and provides impressions of personal lives. The people whose lives are cast, however, are never included, only their effects. To memorialize the 65,000 Austrian victims of the Holocaust, Whiteread designed a library turned inside out, showing not the spines of books but their pages and the empty spaces between and behind them. Whiteread's concept draws on the ideas of Jews as "people of the book" and calls to mind Israel's remembrance of Holocaust victims through donations of books to libraries. Around the base of the sculpture, Whiteread inscribed the names of the concentration camps to which Austria's Jewish population was deported.

Figure V-8   Rachel Whiteread, *Memorial to Victims of the Holocaust*, Judenplatz, Vienna, 2000. Courtesy of Reuters/Corbis.

GERDA WEISSMAN KLEIN

All But My Life is a woman's account of her experience from the beginning of the war in 1939 until her liberation in 1945. Gerda Weissmann (born 1924) was fifteen when the Germans took control of her small town of Bielitz, Poland. Her father was part owner of a factory that processed furs and her mother a traditional homemaker. Her older brother, Arthur, was a student of great promise. It was a close-knit, middle-class, religiously observant Jewish family.

In the days immediately following German occupation of Bielitz, the synagogue was burned down, and former Gentile neighbors turned against their Jewish townsfolk. By mid-October all Jewish men had to register with the Nazi government, and on October 19 Arthur left Bielitz in an effort to escape Nazi capture but was never seen again. Just before Christmas of 1939 the Weissmann family were forced to move into their basement. Their old Christian friend Niania, who was now living upstairs, remained loving and loyal to them.

By January of 1940 all Jews remaining in Bielitz were forced to wear the yellow Star of David. By spring only 300 Jews were left out of 8,000. Gerda and her family survived by making clothing. The following year Gerda met Abek Feigenblatt, who fell deeply in love with her, proposed marriage to her, and did everything he could to see her even after both had been sent to work camps. Gerda was unable to love him, but felt guilty because he cared so much for her. Early in the book we are also introduced to her best friend Ilse Kleinhälzer, who would for the most part be with Gerda throughout the war. In April of 1942 the 250 Jews remaining in Bielitz were forced to move into a ghetto. In June Gerda's father was deported, and shortly afterwards her mother, along with all the older people, to one of the Nazi death camps. She never saw them again.

When she was forcibly separated from her mother because she was considered young enough to be slave labor for the Nazis, Gerda, together with Ilse and other young women from the area, were taken to work in Sosnowitz, Abek's home town. Although his family tried to help her, Gerda chose to stay with Ilse and the other women. In Sosnowitz Gerda met Suse Kunz, who would also be a close friend the rest of the war. In the summer of 1942 the three friends were transferred to Bolkenhain, in eastern Germany, to work in a weaving mill. The German official in charge of the women, Frau Kügler, turned out to be a genuinely good person who did what she could for the women within the limits of her position. In Bolkenhain for a year, Gerda wrote and produced plays for the other women, and looked back on that as perhaps the finest thing she had done in her life.

In August of 1943, with the war turning against Germany and its allies, Gerda and Ilse were moved to the weaving mill at Märzdorf, where conditions were much worse, and Gerda considered suicide. Later in the year the two women were transferred to work at Landeshut, where they were reunited with Suse, another friend, Lotte, and Frau Kügler, and conditions were better. Late in the fall Gerda learned that Abek had had himself transferred to Burgberg, a men's work camp nearby, in order to see her. They did manage regular meetings, but Gerda remained very ambivalent about him.

May of 1944 saw the three women transferred to Grünberg camp for women and another weaving factory. There Gerda met another new friend, Liesel Stepper. By the beginning of 1945 the Germans were rapidly losing the war. On January 29 four thousand women prisoners, in two groups, were made to do a forced walk westward. Of Gerda's group of two thousand only one hundred and twenty survived. In two months they were marched five hundred kilometers (about three hundred miles), through German cities including Dresden, Chemnitz, Reichenbach, and Plauen. Crossing the Czech border, the remaining women prisoners were locked in a factory in which the SS had placed a bomb, but were freed by Czech partisans before it could explode. Germany surrendered on May 8, Gerda's birthday, and American soldiers took over the area. Ilse had died on the march; Suse died the very day of their liberation. Gerda was extremely frail and ill. During her long recuperation she met, got to know, and fell in love with American Captain Kurt Klein. They were eventually married, and she has spent the rest of her life in the United States.

QUESTIONS FOR STUDY AND DISCUSSION

1. What are the roots of Christian anti-Judaism and how were they expressed in the Middle Ages?

2. Discuss the origins and orientation of the Sephardic Jews and Ashkenazic Jews.

3. Why have the questions of Jewish identity and relationship to the non-Jewish world taken on central importance in the nineteenth and twentieth centuries? Characterize the three main divisions of Judaism that evolved at this time.

4. What role did nineteenth-century racial theories play in the development of modern anti-Semitism?

5. Summarize the political situation in Germany following WWI and the development of the Nazi Party.

6. What were the three stages of Nazi policy toward European Jews between 1933 and 1945? How did Nazi policy define who was Jewish?

7. How do you account for the cooperation of ordinary Germans in the Holocaust? Is this a phenomenon that continues to occur in society today?

8. What issues do you think the Holocaust continues to pose in our world today?

9. If you were a survivor of such an enormous happening as the Holocaust do you think you might have written about your experience? Why? What, if anything, would you be hoping to accomplish?

SUGGESTIONS FOR FURTHER READING

Agus, Jacob Bernard. *Jewish Identity in an Age of Ideologies*. New York: Frederick Ungar, 1978.

Berenbaum, Michael. *The Vision of the Void: Theological Reflections on the Works of Elie Wiesel*. Middletown, CT: Wesleyan University Press, 1979.

Berkovits, Eliezer. *Faith After the Holocaust*. New York: KTAV, 1973.

Eckardt, A. Roy and Alice L. Eckardt. *Long Night's Journey into Day: Life and Faith After the Holocaust*. Detroit: Wayne State University Press, 1982.

Frankl, Viktor. *Man's Search for Meaning*. Boston: Beacon Press, 2004.

Isaac, Jules. *The Teaching of Contempt: Christian Roots of Anti-Semitism*. Trans. Helen Weaver. New York: Holt, Rinehart and Winston, 1964.

Katz, Steven T. *Post-Holocaust Dialogues: Critical Studies in Modern Jewish Thought*. New York: New York University Press, 1983.

Kellner, Menachem Marc, ed. *Contemporary Jewish Ethics*. New York: Sanhedrin Press, 1978.

Levi, Primo. *If This Is a Man*. New York: Touchstone, 1996. (First published as *Se questo è un umo?* 1958.)

Littell, Franklin H. *The Crucifixion of the Jews*. New York: Harper & Row, 1975.

Neusner, Jacob. *Death and Birth of Judaism: The Impact of Christianity, Secularism, and the Holocaust on Jewish Faith*. New York: Basic Books, 1987.

Novak, David. *Jewish-Christian Dialogue: A Jewish Justification*. New York: Oxford University Press, 1989.

Poliakov, Leon. *The History of Anti-Semitism*. London: Routledge and Kegan Paul, 1974.

Roth, John K. *A Consuming Fire: Encounters with Elie Wiesel and the Holocaust*. Atlanta: John Knox Press, 1979.

Rudavsky, David. *Modern Jewish Religious Movements: A History of Emancipation and Adjustment*. Newly rev. 3rd ed. New York: Behrman House, 1979.

Ruether, Rosemary Radford. *Faith and Fratricide: The Theological Roots of Anti-Semitism*. New York: The Seabury Press, 1974.

Wiesel, Elie. *Night*. New York: Hill and Wang, 1972, new translation, 2006.

APPENDIX

DECLARATION OF THE RIGHTS OF MAN AND OF THE CITIZEN

'The Representatives of the people of France, formed into a NATIONAL ASSEMBLY, considering that ignorance, neglect, or contempt of human rights, are the sole causes of public misfortunes and corruptions of Government, have resolved to set forth, in a solemn declaration, these natural, imprescriptible, and inalienable rights: that this declaration being constantly present to the minds of the members of the body social, they may be ever kept attentive to their rights and their duties: that the acts of the legislative and executive powers of Government, being capable of being every moment compared with the end of political institutions, may be more respected: and also, that the future claims of the citizens, being directed by simple and incontestable principles, may always tend to the maintenance of the Constitution, and the general happiness.

'For these reasons, the NATIONAL ASSEMBLY doth recognize and declare, in the presence of the Supreme Being, and with the hope of his blessing and favour, the following *sacred* rights of men and of citizens:

'I. *Men are born, and always continue, free, and equal in respect of their rights. Civil distinctions, therefore, can be founded only on public utility.*

'II. *The end of all political associations, is, the preservation of the natural and imprescriptible rights of man; and these rights are liberty, property, security, and resistance of oppression.*

'III. *The nation is essentially the source of all sovereignty nor can any* INDIVIDUAL, *or* ANY BODY OF MEN, *be entitled to any authority which is not expressly derived from it.*

'IV. Political Liberty consists in the power of doing whatever does not injure another. The exercise of the natural rights of every man, has no other limits than those which are necessary to secure to every *other* man the free exercise of the same rights; and these limits are determinable only by the law.

'V. The law ought to prohibit only actions hurtful to society. What is not prohibited by the law, should not be hindered; nor should any one be compelled to that which the law does not require.

'VI. The law is an expression of the will of the community. All citizens have a right to concur, either personally, or by their representatives, in its formation. It should be the same to all, whether it protects or punishes; and *all being equal in its sight, are equally eligible to all honours, places, and employments, according to their different abilities, without any other distinction than that created by their virtues and talents.*

'VII. No man should be accused, arrested, or held in confinement, except in cases determined by the law, and according to the forms which it has prescribed. All who promote, solicit, execute, or cause to be executed, arbitrary orders, ought to be punished; and every citizen called upon, or apprehended by virtue of the law, ought immediately to obey, and renders himself culpable by resistance.

'VIII. The law ought to impose no other penalties but such as are absolutely and evidently necessary: and no one ought to be punished, but in virtue of a law promulgated before the offence, and legally applied.

'IX. Every man being presumed innocent till he has been convicted, whenever his detention becomes indispensable, all rigour to him, more than is necessary to secure his person, ought to be provided against by the law.

'X. No man ought to be molested on account of his opinions, not even on account of his *religious* opinions, provided his avowal of them does not disturb the public order established by the law.

'XI. The unrestrained communication of thoughts and opinions being one of the most precious rights of man, every citizen may speak, write, and publish freely, provided he is responsible for the abuse of this liberty in cases determined by the law.

'XII. A public force being necessary to give security to the rights of men and of citizens, that force is instituted for the benefit of the community, and not for the particular benefit of the persons with whom it is entrusted.

'XIII. A common contribution being necessary for the support of the public force, and for defraying the other expenses of government, it ought to be divided equally among the members of the community, according to their abilities.

'XIV. Every citizen has a right, either by himself or his representative, to a free voice in determining the necessity of public contributions, the appropriation of them, and their amount, mode of assessment, and duration.

'XV. Every community has a right to demand of all its agents, an account of their conduct.

'XVI. Every community in which a separation of powers and a security of rights is not provided for, wants a constitution.

'XVII. The right to property being inviolable and sacred, no one ought to be deprived of it, except in cases of evident public necessity, legally ascertained, and on condition of a previous just indemnity.'

OLYMPE DE GOUGES
THE DECLARATION OF THE RIGHTS OF WOMAN
SEPTEMBER 1791

Marie Gouze (1748–1793) was a self-educated butcher's daughter from the south of France who, under the name Olympe de Gouges, wrote pamphlets and plays on a variety of issues, including slavery, which she attacked as based on greed and blind prejudice. In this pamphlet she provides a declaration of the rights of women to parallel the one for men, thus criticizing the deputies of the National Assembly for having forgotten women. She addressed the pamphlet to the queen, Marie Antoinette, although she also warned the queen that she must work for the Revolution or risk destroying the monarchy altogether. In her postscript she denounced the customary treatment of women as objects easily abandoned. She appended to the declaration a sample form for a marriage contract that called for communal sharing of property. De Gouges went to the guillotine in 1793, condemned as a counterrevolutionary and denounced as an "unnatural" woman.

To be decreed by the National Assembly in its last sessions or by the next legislature.

PREAMBLE

Mothers, daughters, sisters, female representatives of the nation ask to be constituted as a national assembly. Considering that ignorance, neglect, or contempt for the rights of woman are the sole causes of public misfortunes and governmental corruption, they have resolved to set forth in a solemn declaration the natural, inalienable, and sacred rights of woman: so that by being constantly present to all the members of the social body this declaration may always remind them of their rights and duties; so that by being liable at every moment to comparison with the aim of any and all political institutions the acts of women's and men's powers may be the more fully respected; and so that by being founded henceforward on simple and incontestable principles the demands of the citizenesses may always tend toward maintaining the constitution, good morals, and the general welfare.

In consequence, the sex that is superior in beauty as in courage, needed in maternal sufferings, recognizes and declares, in the presence and under the auspices of the Supreme Being, the following rights of woman and the citizeness.

1. Woman is born free and remains equal to man in rights. Social distinctions may be based only on common utility.

2. The purpose of all political association is the preservation of the natural and imprescriptible rights of woman and man. These rights are liberty, property, security, and especially resistance to oppression.

3. The principle of all sovereignty rests essentially in the nation, which is but the reuniting of woman and man. No body and no individual may exercise authority which does not emanate expressly from the nation.

4. Liberty and justice consist in restoring all that belongs to another; hence the exercise of the natural rights of woman has no other limits than those that the perpetual tyranny of man opposes to them; these limits must be reformed according to the laws of nature and reason.

5. The laws of nature and reason prohibit all actions which are injurious to society. No hindrance should be put in the way of anything not prohibited by these wise and divine laws, nor may anyone be forced to do what they do not require.

6. The law should be the expression of the general will. All citizenesses and citizens should take part, in person or by their representatives, in its formation. It must be the same for everyone. All citizenesses and citizens, being equal in its eyes, should be equally admissible to all public dignities, offices, and employments, according to their ability, and with no other distinction than that of their virtues and talents.

7. No woman is exempted; she is indicted, arrested, and detained in the cases determined by the law. Women like men obey this rigorous law.

8. Only strictly and obviously necessary punishments should be established by the law, and no

one may be punished except by virtue of a law established and promulgated before the time of the offense, and legally applied to women.

9. Any woman being declared guilty, all rigor is exercised by the law.

10. No one should be disturbed for his fundamental opinions; woman has the right to mount the scaffold, so she should have the right equally to mount the tribune, provided that these manifestations do not trouble public order as established by law.

11. The free communication of thoughts and opinions is one of the most precious of the rights of woman, since this liberty assures the recognition of children by their fathers. Every citizeness may therefore say freely, I am the mother of your child; a barbarous prejudice [against unmarried women having children] should not force her to hide the truth, so long as responsibility is accepted for any abuse of this liberty in cases determined by the law [women are not allowed to lie about the paternity of their children].

12. The safeguard of the rights of woman and citizeness requires public powers. These powers are instituted for the advantage of all and not for the private benefit of those to whom they are entrusted.

13. For maintenance of public authority and for expenses of administration, taxation of women and men is equal; she takes part in all forced labor service, in all painful tasks; she must therefore have the same proportion in the distribution of places, employments, offices, dignities, and in industry.

14. The citizenesses and citizens have the right, by themselves or through their representatives, to have demonstrated to them the necessity of public taxes. The citizenesses can only agree to them upon admission of an equal division, not only in wealth, but also in the public administration, and to determine the means of apportionment, assessment, and collection, and the duration of the taxes.

15. The mass of women, joining with men in paying taxes, have the right to hold accountable every public agent of the administration.

16. Any society in which the guarantee of rights is not assured or the separation of powers not settled has no constitution. The constitution is null and void if the majority of individuals composing the nation has not cooperated in its drafting.

17. Property belongs to both sexes whether united or separated; it is for each of them an inviolable and sacred right, and no one may be deprived of it as a true patrimony of nature, except when public necessity, certified by law, obviously requires it, and then on condition of a just compensation in advance.

POSTSCRIPT

Women, wake up; the tocsin of reason sounds throughout the universe; recognize your rights. The powerful empire of nature is no longer surrounded by prejudice, fanaticism, superstition, and lies. The torch of truth has dispersed all the clouds of folly and usurpation. Enslaved man has multiplied his force and needs yours to break his chains. Having become free, he has become unjust toward his companion. Oh women! Women, when will you cease to be blind? What advantages have you gathered in the revolution? A scorn more marked, a disdain more conspicuous. During the centuries of corruption you only reigned over the weakness of men. Your empire is destroyed; what is left to you then? Firm belief in the injustices of men. The reclaiming of your patrimony founded on the wise decrees of nature; why should you fear such a beautiful enterprise? . . . Whatever the barriers set up against you, it is in your power to overcome them; you only have to want it. Let us pass now to the appalling account of what you have been in society; and since national education is an issue at this moment, let us see if our wise legislators will think sanely about the education of women.

Women have done more harm than good. Constraint and dissimulation have been their lot. What force has taken from them, ruse returned to them; they have had recourse to all the resources of their charms, and the most irreproachable man has not resisted them. Poison, the sword, women controlled everything; they ordered up crimes as much as virtues. For centuries, the French government, especially, depended on the nocturnal administration of women; officials kept no secrets from their indiscretion; ambassadorial posts, military commands, the ministry, the presidency [of a court], the papacy, the college of cardinals, in short everything that characterizes the folly of men, profane and sacred, has been submitted to the cupidity and ambition of this sex formerly considered despicable and respected, and since the revolution, respectable and despised. . . .

Under the former regime, everyone was vicious, everyone guilty. . . . A woman only had to be beautiful and amiable; when she possessed these two advantages, she saw a hundred fortunes at her feet. . . . The most indecent woman could make herself respectable with gold; the commerce in women was a kind of industry amongst the highest classes, which henceforth will enjoy no more credit. If it still did, the revolution would be lost, and in the new situation we would still be corrupted. Can reason hide the fact that every other road to fortune is closed to a woman bought by a man, bought like a slave from the coasts of Africa? The difference between them is great; this is known. The slave [that is, the woman] commands her master, but if the master gives her her freedom without compensation and at an age when the slave has lost all her charms, what does this unfortunate woman become? The plaything of disdain; even the doors of charity are closed to her; she is poor and old, they say; why did she not know how to make her fortune?

Other examples even more touching can be provided to reason. A young woman without experience, seduced by the man she loves, abandons her parents to follow him; the ingrate leaves her after a few years and the older she will have grown with him, the more his inconstancy will be inhuman. If she has children, he will still abandon her. If he is rich, he will believe himself excused from sharing his fortune with his noble victims. If some engagement ties him to his duties, he will violate it while counting on support from the law. If he is married, every other obligation loses its force. What laws then remain to be passed that would eradicate vice down to its roots? That of equally dividing [family] fortunes between men and women and of public administration of their goods. It is easy to imagine that a woman born of a rich family would gain much from the equal division of property [between children]. But what about the woman born in a poor family with merit and virtues; what is her lot? Poverty and opprobrium. If she does not excel in music or painting, she cannot be admitted to any public function, even if she is fully qualified. . . .

Marriage is the tomb of confidence and love. A married woman can give bastards to her husband with impunity, and even the family fortune which does not belong to them. An unmarried woman has only a feeble right: ancient and inhuman laws refuse her the right to the name and goods of her children's father; no new laws have been made in this matter. If giving my sex an honorable and just consistency is considered to be at this time paradoxical on my part and an attempt at the impossible, I leave to future men the glory of dealing with this matter; but while waiting, we can prepare the way with national education, with the restoration of morals and with conjugal agreements.

FORM FOR A SOCIAL CONTRACT BETWEEN MAN AND WOMAN

We, _____ and _____, moved by our own will, unite for the length of our lives and for the duration of our mutual inclinations under the following conditions: We intend and wish to make our wealth communal property, while reserving the right to divide it in favor of our children and of those for whom we might have a special inclination, mutually recognizing that our goods belong directly to our children, from whatever bed they come [legitimate or not], and that all of them without distinction have the right to bear the name of the fathers and mothers who have acknowledged them, and we impose on ourselves the obligation of subscribing to the law that punishes any rejection of one's own blood [refusing to acknowledge an illegitimate child]. We likewise obligate ourselves, in the case of a separation, to divide our fortune equally and to set aside the portion the law designates for our children. In the case of a perfect union, the one who dies first will give up half his property in favor of the children; and if there are no children, the survivor will inherit by right, unless the dying person has disposed of his half of the common property in favor of someone he judges appropriate. [She then goes on to defend her contract against the inevitable objections of "hypocrites, prudes, the clergy, and all the hellish gang."]

Source: Olympe de Gouges, *Les Droits de la femme. A la Reine.* (Paris, 1791).

THE SADLER REPORT

The Industrial Revolution had a twofold effect on England in the first part of the 19th century. On the one side it gave her a position of wealth and affluence which no other nation in history had enjoyed, and on the other it created terrible working conditions for her laboring force. The difference between these two sides was so great that a future Prime Minister of England dubbed them "The Two Nations."

The first factories were lacking in the most elementary sanitary and safety facilities, and the factory worker was subject to long hours of monotonous and unalleviated drudgery. Among the most unfortunate victims of this unhappy situation were the children, some of whom began work at four or five years of age. They were used in coal mines to carry buckets of coal up ladders and in other similarly dismal occupations. They received little or no education and often had to toil more than twelve hours per day under the most horrible working conditions.

In the early 1830s the House of Commons decided to investigate this situation, and a committee was formed, headed by Michael Thomas Sadler. The following dialogue is an excerpt from the Committee's report, given to the House of Commons in 1832 in the *Bill to Regulate the Labour of Children* which was then being debated.

VENERIS, 18° DIE MAII, 1832

Michael Thomas Sadler, Esquire, in the chair

* * *

MR. MATTHEW CRABTREE, *called in; and Examined.*

What age are you?—Twenty-two.

What is your occupation?—A blanket manufacturer.

Have you ever been employed in a factory?—Yes.

At what age did you first go to work in one?—Eight.

How long did you continue in that occupation?—Four years.

Will you state the hours of labour at the period when you first went to the factory, in ordinary times?—From 6 in the morning to 8 at night.

Fourteen hours?—Yes.

With what intervals for refreshment and rest?—A hour at noon.

Then you had no resting time allowed in which to take your breakfast, or what is in Yorkshire called your "drinking"?—No.

When trade was brisk what were your hours?—From 5 in the morning to 9 in the evening.

Sixteen hours?—Yes.

With what intervals at dinner?—An hour.

How far did you live from the mill?—About two miles.

Was there any time allowed for you to get your breakfast in the mill?—No.

Did you take it before you left home?—Generally.

During those long hours of labour could you be punctual; how did you awake?—I seldom did awake spontaneously; I was most generally awoke or lifted out of bed, sometimes asleep, by my parents.

Were you always on time?—No.

What was the consequence if you had been too late?—I was most commonly beaten.

Severely?—Very severely, I thought.

In whose factory was this?—Messrs. Hague & Cook's, of Dewsbury.

Will you state the effect that those long hours had upon the state of your health and feelings?—I was, when working those long hours, commonly very much fatigued at night, when I left my work; so much so that I sometimes should have slept as I walked if I had not stumbled and started awake again; and so sick often that I could not eat, and when I did eat I vomited.

Did this labour destroy your appetite?—It did.

In what situation were you in that mill?—I was a piecener.

Will you state for this Committee whether piecening is a very laborious employment for children, or not?—It is a very laborious employment. Pieceners are continually running to and fro, and on their feet the whole day.

The duty of the piecener is to take the cardings from one part of the machinery, and to place them on another?—Yes.

So that the labour is not only continual, but it is unabated to the last?—It is unabated to the last.

Do you not think, from your own experience, that the speed of this machinery is so calculated as to demand the utmost exertions of a child, supposing the hours were moderate?—It is as much as they could do at the best; they are always upon the stretch, and it is commonly very difficult to keep up with their work.

State the condition of the children toward the latter part of the day, who have thus to keep up with the machinery.—It is as much as they can do when they are not very much fatigued to keep up with their work, and toward the close of the day, when they come to be more fatigued, they cannot keep up with it very well, and the consequences is that they are beaten to spur them on.

Were you beaten under those circumstances?—Yes.

Frequently?—Very frequently.

And principally at the latter end of the day?—Yes.

And is it your belief that if you had not been so beaten, you should not have got through the work?—I should not if I had not been kept up to it by some means.

Does beating then principally occur at the latter end of the day, when the children are exceedingly fatigued?—It does at the latter end of the day, and in the morning sometimes, when they are very drowsy, and have not got rid of the fatigue of the day before.

What were you beaten with principally?—A strap.

Anything else?—Yes, a stick sometimes; and there is a kind of roller which runs on the top of the machine called a billy, perhaps two or three yards in length, and perhaps an inch and a half, or more, in diameter; the circumference would be four or five inches; I cannot speak exactly.

Were you beaten with that instrument?—Yes.

Have you yourself ever been beaten, and have you seen other children struck severely with that roller?—I have been struck very severely with it myself so much so as to knock me down, and I have seen other children have their heads broken with it.

You think that it is a general practice to beat the children with the roller?—It is.

You do not think then that you were worse treated than other children in the mill?—No, I was not, perhaps not so bad as some were.

In those mills is chastisement towards the latter part of the day going on perpetually?—Perpetually.

So that you can hardly be in the mill without hearing constant crying?—Never an hour, I believe.

Do you think that if the overlooker were naturally a humane person it would be still found necessary for him to beat the children, in order to keep up their attention and vigilance at the termination of those extraordinary days of labour?—Yes, the machine turns off a regular quantity of cardings, and of course they must keep as regularly to their work the whole of the day; they must keep with the machine, and therefore however humane the slubber may be, as he must keep up with the machine or be found fault with, he spurs the children to keep up also by various means but that which he commonly resorts to is to strap them when they become drowsy.

At the time when you were beaten for not keeping up with your work, were you anxious to have done it if you possibly could?—Yes; the dread of being beaten if we could not keep up with our work was a sufficient impulse to keep us to it if we could.

When you got home at night after this labour, did you feel much fatigued?—Very much so.

Had you any time to be with your parents, and to receive instruction from them?—No.

What did you do?—All that we did when we got home was to get the little bit of supper that was provided for us and go to bed immediately. If the supper had not been ready directly, we should have gone to sleep while it was preparing.

Did you not, as a child, feel it a very grievous hardship to be roused so soon in the morning?—I did.

Were the rest of the children similarly circumstanced?—Yes, all of them; but they were not any of them so far from their work as I was.

And if you had been too late you were under the apprehension of being cruelly beaten?—I generally was beaten when I happened to be too late; and when I got up in the morning the apprehension of that was so great, that I used to run, and cry all the way as I went to the mill.

That was the way by which your punctual attendance was secured?—Yes.

And you do not think it could have been secured by any other means?—No.

Then it is your impression from what you have seen, and from your own experience, that those long hours of labour have the effect of rendering young persons who are subject to them exceedingly unhappy?—Yes.

You have already said it had a considerable effect upon your health?—Yes.

Do you conceive that it diminished your growth?—I did not pay much attention to that; but I have been examined by some persons who said they thought I was rather stunted, and that I should have been taller if I had not worked at the mill.

What were your wages at that time?—Three shillings [per week].

And how much a day had you for over-work when you were worked so exceedingly long?—A halfpenny a day.

Did you frequently forfeit that if you were not always there to a moment?—Yes; I most frequently forfeited what was allowed for those long hours.

You took your food to the mill; was it in your mill, as is the case in cotton mills, much spoiled by being laid aside?—It was very frequently covered by flues from the wool; and in that case they had to be blown off with the mouth, and picked off with the fingers before it could be eaten.

So that not giving you a little leisure for eating your food, but obliging you to take it at the mill, spoiled your food when you did get it?—Yes, very commonly.

And at the same time that this overlabour injured your appetite?—Yes.

Could you eat when you got home?—Not always.

What is the effect of this piecening upon the hands?—It makes them bleed; the skin is completely rubbed off, and in that case they bleed in perhaps a dozen parts.

The prominent parts of the hand?—Yes, all the prominent parts of the hands are rubbed down till they bleed; every day they are rubbed in that way.

All the time you continue at work?—All the time we are working. The hands never can be hardened in that work, for the grease keeps them soft in the first instance, and long and continual rubbing is always wearing them down, so that if they were hard they would be sure to bleed.

Is it attended with much pain?—Very much.

Do they allow you to make use of the back of the hand?—No; the work cannot be so well done with the back of the hand, or I should have made use of that.

Is the work done as well when you are so many hours engaged in it, as it would be if you were at it a less time?—I believe it is not done so well in those long hours; toward the latter end of the day the children become completely bewildered, and know not what they are doing, so that they spoil their work without knowing.

Then you do not think that the masters gain much by the continuance of the work to so great a length of time?—I believe not.

Were there girls as well as boys employed in this manner?—Yes.

Were they more tenderly treated by the overlookers, or were they worked and beaten in the same manner?—There was no difference in their treatment.

Were they beaten by the overlookers, or by the slubber?—By the slubber.

But the overlooker must have been perfectly aware of the treatment that the children endured at the mill?—Yes; and sometimes the overlooker beat them himself but the man that they wrought under had generally the management of them.

Did he pay them their wages?—No; their wages were paid by the master.

But the overlooker of the mill was perfectly well aware that they could not have performed the duty exacted from them in the mill without being thus beaten?—I believe he was.

You seem to say that this beating is absolutely necessary, in order to keep the children up to their work; is it universal throughout all factories?—I have been in several other factories, and I have witnessed the same cruelty in them all.

Did you say that they were beaten for being too late?—Yes.

Is it not the custom in many of the factories to impose fines upon children for being too late, instead of beating them?—It was not in that factory.

What then were the fines by which you lost the money you gained by your long hours?—The spinner could not get on so fast with his work when we happened to be too late; he could not begin his work so soon, and therefore it was taken.

Did the slubber pay you your wages?—No, the master paid our wages.

And the slubber took your fines from you?—Yes.

Then you were fined as well as beaten?—There was nothing deducted from the ordinary scale of wages, but only from that received for over-hours, and I had only that taken when I was too late, so that the fine was not regular.

When you were not working over-hours, were you so often late as when you were working overhours?—Yes.

You were not very often late whilst you were not working over-hours?—Yes, I was often late when I was not working over-hours; I had to go at six o'clock in the morning, and consequently had to get up at five to eat my breakfast and go to the mill, and if I failed to get up by five I was too late; and it was nine o'clock before we could get home, and then we went to bed; in the best times I could not be much above eight hours at home, reckoning dressing and eating my meals, and everything.

Was it a blanket-mill in which you worked?—Yes.

Did you ever know that the beatings to which you allude inflicted serious injury upon the children?—I do not recollect any very serious injury, more than that they had their heads broken, if that may be called a serious injury; that has often happened; I, myself, had no more serious injury than that.

You say that the girls as well as the boys were employed as you have described, and you observed no difference in their treatment?—No difference.

The girls were beat in this unmerciful manner?—They were.

They were subject, of course, to the same bad effects from this over-working?—Yes.

Could you attend an evening-school during the time you were employed in the mill?—No, that was completely impossible.

Did you attend the Sunday-school?—Not very frequently when I work at the mill.

How then were you engaged during the Sunday?—I very often slept till it was too late for school time or for divine worship, and the rest of the day I spent in walking out and taking a little fresh air.

Did your parents think that it was necessary for you to enjoy a little fresh air?—I believe they did; they never said anything against it; before I went to the mill I used to go to the Sunday-school.

Did you frequently sleep nearly the whole of the day on Sunday?—Very often.

At what age did you leave that employment?—I was about 12 years old.

Why did you leave that place?—I went very late one morning, about seven o'clock, and I got severely beaten by the spinner, and he turned me out of the mill, and I went home, and never went any more.

Was your attendance as good as the other children?—Being at rather a greater distance than some of them, I was generally one of the latest.

Where was your next work?—I worked as a bobbin-winder in another part of the works of the same firm.

How long were you a bobbin-winder?—About two years, I believe.

What did you become after that?—A weaver.

How long were you a weaver?—I was a weaver till March in last year.

A weaver of what?—A blanket-weaver.

With the same firm?—With the same firm.

Did you leave them?—No; I was dismissed from my work for a reason which I am willing and anxious to explain.

Have you had opportunities of observing the way in which the children are treated in factories up to a late period?—Yes.

You conceive that their treatment still remains as you first found it, and that the system is in great want of regulation?—It does.

Children you still observe to be very much fatigued and injured by the hours of labour?—Yes.

From your own experience, what is your opinion as to the utmost labour that a child in piecening could safely undergo?—If I were appealed to from my own feelings to fix a limit, I should fix it at ten hours, or less.

And your attribute to longer hours all the cruelties that you describe?—A good deal of them.

Are the children sleepy in mills?—Very.

Are they more liable to accidents in the latter part of the day than in the other part?—I believe they are; I believe a greater number of accidents happen in the latter part of the day than in any other. I have known them so sleepy that in the short interval while the others have been going out, some of them have fallen asleep, and have been left there.

Is it an uncommon case for children to fall asleep in the mill, and remain there all night?—Not to remain there all night; but I have known a case the other day, of a child whom the overlooker found when he went to lock the door, that had been left there.

So that you think there has been no change for the better in the treatment of those children; is it your opinion that there will be none, except Parliament interfere in their behalf?—It is my decided conviction.

Have you recently seen any cruelties in mills?—Yes; not long since I was in a mill and I saw a girl severely beaten; at a mill called Hick-lane Mill, in Bately; I happened to be in at the other end of the room talking; and I heard the blows, and I looked that way, and saw the spinner beating one of the girls severely with a large stick. Hearing the sound, led me to look round, and to ask what was the matter, and they said is was "Nothing but paying [beating] 'his ligger-on."

What age was the girl?—About 12 years.

Was she very violently beaten?—She was.

Was this when she was over-fatigued?—It was in the afternoon.

Can you speak as to the effect of this labour in the mills and factories on the morals of the children, as far as you have observed?—As far as I have observed with regard to morals in the mills, there is every thing about them that is disgusting in every one conscious of correct morality.

Do you find that the children, the females especially, are very early demoralized in them?—They are.

Is their language indecent?—Very indecent; and both sexes take great familiarities with each other in the mills, without at all being ashamed of their conduct.

Do you connect their immorality of language and conduct with their excessive labour?—It may be somewhat connected with it, for it is to be observed that most of that goes on toward night, when they begin to be drowsy; it is a kind of stimulus which they use to keep them awake; they say some pert thing or other to keep themselves from drowsiness, and it generally happens to be some obscene language.

Have not a considerable number of the females employed in mills illegitimate children very early in life?—I believe there are; I have known some of them have illegitimate children when they were between 16 and 17 years of age.

How many grown-up females had you in the mill?—I cannot speak to the exact number that were grown up; perhaps there might be thirty-four or so that worked in the mill at that time.

How many of those had illegitimate children?—A great many of them; eighteen or nineteen of them, I think.

Did they generally marry the men by whom they had children?—No; it sometimes happens that young women have children by married men, and I have known an instance, a few weeks since, where one of the young women had a child by a married man.

Is it your opinion that those who have the charge of the mills very often avail themselves of the opportunity they have to debauch the young women?—No, not generally; most of the improper conduct takes place among the younger part of those that work in the mill.

Do you find that the children and young persons in those mills are moral in other respects, or does their want of education tend to encourage them in a breach of the law?—I believe it does, for there are very few of them that can know anything about it; few of them can either read or write.

Are criminal offences then very frequent?—Yes, theft is very common; it is practiced a great deal in the mills, stealing their bits of dinner, or something of that sort. Some of them have not so much to eat as they ought to have, and if they can fall in with the dinner of some of their partners they steal it. The first day my brother and I went to the mill we had our dinner stolen, because we were not up with the tricks; we were more careful in the future, but still we did not always escape.

Was there any correction going on at the mills for indecent language or improper conduct?—No, I never knew of any.

From what you have seen and known of those mills, would you prefer that the hours of labour should be so long with larger wages, or that they should be shortened with a diminution of wages?—If I were working at the mill now, I would rather have less labour and receive a trifle less, than so much labour and receive a trifle more.

Is that the general impression of individuals engaged in mills with whom you are acquainted?—I believe it is.

What is the impression in the country from which you come with respect to the effect of this Bill upon wages?—They do not anticipate that it will affect wages at all.

They think it will not lower wages?—They do.

Do you mean that it will not lower wages by the hour, or that you will receive the same wages per day?—They anticipate that it may perhaps lower their wages at a certain time of the year when they are working hard, but not at other times, so that they will have their wages more regular.

Does not their wish for this Bill mainly rest upon their anxiety to protect their children from the consequences of this excessive labour, and to have some opportunity of affording them a decent education?—Yes; such are the wishes of every humane father that I have heard speak about the thing.

Have they not some feeling of having the labour equalized?—That is the feeling of some that I have heard speak of it.

Did your parents work in the same factories?—No.

Were any of the slubbers' children working there?—Yes.

Under what slubber did you work in that mill?—Under a person of the name of Thomas Bennett, in the first place; and I was changed from him to another of the name of James Webster.

Did the treatment depend very much upon the slubber under whom you were?—No, it did not depend directly upon him, for he was obliged to do a certain quantity of work, and therefore to make us up keep up with that.

Were the children of the slubbers strapped in the same way?—Yes, except that it is very natural for a father to spare his own child.

Did it depend upon the feelings of a slubber toward his children?—Very little.

Did the slubbers fine their own spinners?—I believe not.

You said that the piecening was very hard labour; what labour is there besides moving about; have you anything heavy to carry or to lift?—We have nothing heavy to carry, but we are kept upon our feet in brisk times from 5 o'clock in the morning to 9 at night.

How soon does the hand get sore in piecening?—How soon mine became sore I cannot speak to exactly; but they get a little hard on the Sunday, when we are not working, and they will get sore again very soon on the Monday.

Is it always the case in piecening that the hand bleeds, whether you work short or long hours?—They bleed more when we work more.

Do they always bleed when you are working?—Yes.

Do you think that the children would not be more competent to this task, and their hands far less hurt, if the hours were fewer every day, especially when their hands had become seasoned with the labour?—I believe it would have an effect for the longer they are worked the more their hands are worn, and the longer it takes to heal them, and they do not get hard enough after a day's rest to be long without bleeding again; if they are not so much worn down, they might heal sooner, and not bleed so often or so soon.

After a short day's work have you found your hands hard the next morning?—They do not bleed much after we have ceased work; they then get hard; they will bleed soon in the morning when in regular work.

Do you think if the work of the children were confined to about ten hours a day, that after they were accustomed to it, they would not be able to perform this piecening without making their hands bleed?—I believe they would.

So that it is your opinion, from your experience, that if the hours were mitigated, their hands would not be so much worn, and would not bleed by the business of piecening?—Yes.

Do you mean to say that their hands would not bleed at all?—I cannot say exactly, for I always wrought long hours, and therefore my hands always did bleed.

Have you any experience of mills where they only work ten hours?—I have never wrought at such mills, and in most of the mills I have seen their hands bleed.

At a slack time, when you were working only a few hours, did your hands bleed?—No, they did not for three or four days, after we had been standing still for a week; the mill stood still sometimes for a week together, but when we did work we worked the common number of hours.

Were all the mills in the neighbourhood working the same number of hours in brisk times?—Yes.

So that if any parents found it necessary to send his children to the mill for the sake of being able to maintain them, and wished to take them from any mill where they were excessively worked, he could not have found any other place where they would have been less worked?—No, he could not; for myself, I had no desire to change, because I thought I was as well off as I could be at any other mill.

And if the parent, to save his child, had taken him from the mill, and had applied to the parish for relief, would the parish, knowing that he had withdrawn his child from its work, have relieved him?—No.

So that the long labour which you have described, or actual starvation, was, practically, the only alternative that was presented to the parent under such circumstances?—It was; they must either work at the mill they were at or some other, and there was no choice in the mills in that respect.

What, in your opinion, would be the effect of limiting hours of labour upon the happiness, and the health, and the intelligence of this rising generation?—If the hours are shortened, the chil-

dren may, perhaps, have a chance of attending some evening-school, and learning to read and write; and those that I know who have been to school and learned to read and write, have much more comfort than those who have not. For myself, I went to a school when I was six years old, and I learned to read and write a little then.

At a free-school?—Yes, at a free-school in Dewsbury; but I left school when I was six years old. The fact is, that my father was a small manufacturer, and in comfortable circumstances, and he got into debt with Mr. Cook for a wool bill, and as he had no other means of paying him, he came and agreed with my father, that my brother and I should go to work at his mill till that debt was paid; so that the whole of the time that we wrought at the mill we had no wages.

THOMAS BENNETT, *called in; and Examined.*

Where do you reside?—At Dewsbury.

What is your business?—A slubber.

What age are you?—About 48.

Have you had much experience regarding the working of children in factories?—Yes, about twenty-seven years.

Have you a family?—Yes, eight children.

Have any of them gone to factories?—All.

At what age?—The first went at six years of age.

To whose mill?—To Mr. Halliley's, to piece for myself.

What hours did you work at that mill?—We have wrought from 4 to 9, from 4 to 10, and from 5 to 9, and from 5 to 10.

What sort of mill was it?—It was a blanketmill; we sometimes altered the time, according as the days increased and decreased.

What were your regular hours?—Our regular hours when we were not so throng, was from 6 to 7.

And when you were the throngest, what were your hours then?—From 5 to 9, and from 5 to 10, and from 4 to 9.

Seventeen hours?—Yes.

What intervals for meals had the children at that period?—Two hours; an hour for breakfast, and an hour for dinner.

Did they always allow two hours for meals at Mr. Halliley's?—Yes, it was allowed, but the children did not get it, for they had business to do at that time such as fettling and cleaning the machinery.

But they did not stop in at that time, did they?—They all had their share of cleaning and other work to do.

That is, they were cleaning the machinery?—Cleaning the machinery at the time of dinner.

How long a time together have you known those excessive hours to continue?—I have wrought so myself very nearly two years together.

Were your children working under you then?—Yes, two of them.

State the effect upon your children.—Of a morning when they have been so fast asleep that I have had to go up stairs and lift them out of bed, and have heard them crying with the feelings of a parent; I have been much affected by it.

Were not they much fatigued at the termination of such a day's labour as that?—Yes; many a time I have seen their hands moving while they have been nodding, almost asleep; they have been doing their business almost mechanically.

While they have been almost asleep, they have attempted to work?—Yes; and they have missed the carding and spoiled the thread, when we have had to beat them for it.

Could they have done their work towards the termination of such a long day's labour, if they had not been chastised to it?—No.

You do not think that they could have kept awake or up to their work till the seventeenth hour, without being chastised?—No.

Will you state what effect it had upon your children at the end of their day's work?—At the end of their day's work, when they have come home, instead of taking their victuals, they have dropped asleep with the victuals in their hands; and sometimes when we have sent them to bed with a little bread or something to eat in their hand, I have found it in their bed the next morning.

Had it affected their health?—I cannot say much of that; they were very hearty children.

Do you live at a distance from the mill?—Half a mile.

Did your children feel a difficulty in getting home?—Yes, I have had to carry the lesser child on my back, and it has been asleep when I got home.

Did these hours of labour fatigue you?—Yes; they fatigued me to that excess, that in divine wor-

ship I have not been able to stand according to order; I have sat to worship.

So that even during the Sunday you have felt fatigue from your labour in the week?—Yes, we felt it, and always took as much rest as we could.

Were you compelled to beat your own children, in order to make them keep up with the machine?—Yes, that was forced upon us, or we could not have done the work; I have struck them often, though I felt as a parent.

If the children had not been your own, you would have chastised them still more severely?—Yes.

What did you beat them with?—A strap sometimes; and when I have seen my work spoiled, with the roller.

Was the work always worse done at the end of the day?—That was the greatest danger.

Do you conceive it possible that the children could do their work well at the end of such a day's labour as that?—No.

Matthew Crabtree, the last Witness examined by this Committee, I think mentioned you as one of the slubbers under whom he worked?—Yes.

He states that he was chastised and beaten at the mill?—Yes, I have had to chastise him.

You can confirm then what he stated as to the length of time he had to work as a child, and the cruel treatment he received?—Yes, I have had to chastise him in the evening, and often in the morning for being too late; when I had one out of the three wanting I could not keep up with the machine, and I was getting behindhand compared with what another man was doing; and therefore I should have been called to account on Saturday night if the work was not done.

Was he worse than others?—No.

Was it the constant practice to chastise the children?—Yes.

It was necessary in order to keep up your work?—Yes.

And you would have lost your place if you had not done so?—Yes; when I was working at Mr. Wood's mill, at Dewsbury, which at present is burnt down, but where I slubbed for him until it was, while we were taking our meals he used to come up and put the machine agoing; and I used to say, "You do not give us time to eat"; he used to reply, "Chew it at your work"; and I often replied to him, "I have not yet become debased like a brute, I do not chew my cud." Often has that man done that, and then gone below to see if a strap were off, which would have shown if the machinery was not working, and then he would come up again.

Was this at the drinking time?—Yes, at breakfast and at drinking.

Was this where the children were working?—Yes, my own children and others.

Were your own children obliged to employ most of their time at breakfast and at the drinking in cleansing the machine, and in fettling the spindles?—I have seen at that mill, and I have experienced and mentioned it with grief, that the English children were enslaved worse than the Africans. Once when Mr. Wood was saying to the carrier who brought his work in and out, "How long has that horse of mine been at work?" and the carrier told him the time, and he said "Loose him directly, he has been in too long," I made this reply to him, "You have more mercy and pity for your horse than you have for your men."

Did not this beating go on principally at the latter part of the day?—Yes.

Was it not also dangerous for the children to move about those mills when they became so drowsy and fatigued?—Yes, especially by lamplight.

Do the accidents principally occur at the latter end of those long days of labour?—Yes, I believe mostly so.

Do you know of any that have happened?—I know of one; it was at Mr. Wood's mill; part of the machinery caught a lass who had been drowsy and asleep, and the strap which ran close by her catched her at the middle, and bore her to the ceiling, and down she came, and her neck appeared broken, and the slubber ran up to her and pulled her neck, and I carried her to the doctor myself.

Did she get well?—Yes, she came about again.

What time was that?—In the evening.

You say that you have eight children who have gone to the factories?—Yes.

There has been no opportunity for you to send them to a day-school?—No; one boy had about twelve months' schooling.

Have they gone to Sunday-schools?—Yes.

Can any of them write?—Not one.

They do not teach writing at Sunday-schools?—No; it is objected to, I believe.

So that none of your children can write?—No.

What would be the effect of a proper limitation of the hours of labour upon the conduct of the rising generation?—I believe it would have a very happy effect in regard to correcting their morals; for I believe there is a deal of evil that takes place in one way or other in consequence of those long hours.

Is it your opinion that they would then have an opportunity of attending night-schools?—Yes; I have often regretted, while working those long hours, that I could not get my children there.

Is it your belief that if they were better instructed, they would be happier and better members of society?—Yes, I believe so.

DECLARATION OF SENTIMENTS AND RESOLUTIONS

When, in the course of human events it becomes necessary for one portion of the family of man to assume among the people of the earth a position different from that which they have hitherto occupied, but one to which the laws of nature and of nature's God entitle them, a decent respect to the opinions of mankind requires that they should declare the causes that impel them to such a course.

We hold these truths to be self-evident: that all men and women are created equal; that they are endowed by their Creator with certain inalienable rights; that among these are life, liberty, and the pursuit of happiness; that to secure these rights governments are instituted, deriving their just powers from the consent of the governed. Whenever any form of government becomes destructive of these ends, it is the right of those who suffer from it to refuse allegiance to it, and to insist upon the institution of a new government, laying its foundation on such principles, and organizing its powers in such form, as to them shall seem most likely to effect their safety and happiness. Prudence, indeed, will dictate that governments long established should not be changed for light and transient causes; and accordingly all experience hath shown that mankind are more disposed to suffer, while evils are sufferable, than to right themselves by abolishing the forms to which they were accustomed. But when a long train of abuses and usurpations, pursuing invariably the same object, evinces a design to reduce them under absolute despotism, it is their duty to throw off such government, and to provide new guards for their future security. Such has been the patient sufferance of the women under this government, and such is now the necessity which constrains them to demand the equal station to which they are entitled.

The history of mankind is a history of repeated injuries and usurpations on the part of man toward woman, having in direct object the establishment of an absolute tyranny over her. To prove this, let facts be submitted to a candid world.

He has never permitted her to exercise her inalienable right to the elective franchise.

He has compelled her to submit to laws, in the formation of which she had no voice.

He has withheld from her rights which are given to the most ignorant and degraded men—both natives and foreigners.

Having deprived her of this first right of a citizen, the elective franchise, thereby leaving her without representation in the halls of legislation, he has oppressed her on all sides.

He has made her, if married, in the eye of the law, civilly dead.

He has taken from her all right in property, even to the wages she earns.

He has made her, morally, an irresponsible being, as she can commit many crimes with impunity, provided they be done in the presence of her husband. In the covenant of marriage, she is compelled to promise obedience to her husband, he becoming, to all intents and purposes, her master—the law giving him power to deprive her of her liberty, and to administer chastisement.

He has so framed the laws of divorce, as to what shall be the proper causes, and in case of separation, to whom the guardianship of the children shall be given, as to be wholly regardless of the happiness of women—the law, in all cases, going upon the false supposition of the supremacy of man, and giving all power into his hands.

After depriving her of all rights as a married woman, if single, and the owner of property, he has taxed her to support a government which recognizes her only when her property can be made profitable to it.

He has monopolized nearly all the profitable employments, and from those she is permitted to follow, she receives but a scanty remuneration. He closes against her all the avenues to wealth and distinction which he considers most honorable to himself. As a teacher of theology, medicine, or law, she is not known.

He has denied her the facilities for obtaining a thorough education, all colleges being closed against her.

He allows her in Church, as well as State, but a subordinate position, claiming Apostolic authority for her exclusion from the ministry, and, with some exceptions, from any public participation in the affairs of the Church.

He has created a false public sentiment by giving to the world a different code of morals for men and women, by, which moral delinquencies which exclude women from society, are not only tolerated, but deemed of little account in man.

He has usurped the prerogative of Jehovah himself, claiming it as his right to assign for her a sphere of action, when that belongs to her conscience and to her God.

He has endeavored, in every way that he could, to destroy her confidence in her own powers, to lessen her self-respect, and to make her willing to lead a dependent and abject life.

Now, in view of this entire disfranchisement of one-half the people of this country, their social and religious degradation—in view of the unjust laws above mentioned, and because women do feel themselves aggrieved, oppressed, and fraudulently deprived of their most sacred rights, we insist that they have immediate admission to all the rights and privileges which belong to them as citizens of the United States.

In entering upon the great work before us, we anticipate no small amount of misconception, misrepresentation, and ridicule; but we shall use every instrumentality within our power to effect our object. We shall employ agents, circulate tracts, petition the State and National legislatures, and endeavor to enlist the pulpit and the press in our behalf. We hope this Convention will be followed by a series of Conventions embracing every part of the country.

RESOLUTIONS

WHEREAS, The greater precept of nature is conceded to be, that "man shall pursue his own true and substantial happiness." Blackstone in his Commentaries remarks, that this law of Nature being coeval with mankind, and dictated by God himself, is of course superior in obligation to any other. It is binding over all the globe, in all countries and at all times; no human laws are of any validity if contrary to this, and such of them are as valid, derive all their force, and all their validity, and all their authority, mediately and immediately, from this original; therefore,

Resolved, That such laws as conflict, in any way, with the true and substantial happiness of woman, are contrary to the great precept of nature and of no validity, for this is "superior in obligation to any other."

Resolved, That all laws which prevent woman from occupying such a station in society as her conscience shall dictate, or which place her in a position inferior to that of man, are contrary to the great precept of nature, and therefore of no force or authority.

Resolved, That woman is man's equal—was intended to be so by the Creator, and the highest good of the race demands that she should be recognized as such.

Resolved, That the women of this country ought to be enlightened in regard to the laws under which they live, that they may no longer publish their degradation by declaring themselves satisfied with their present position, nor their ignorance, by asserting that they have all the rights they want.

Resolved, That inasmuch as man, while claiming for himself intellectual superiority, does accord to woman moral superiority, it is preeminently his duty to encourage her to speak and teach, as she has an opportunity, in all religious assemblies.

Resolved, That the same amount of virtue, delicacy, and refinement of behavior that is required of woman in the social state, should also be required of man, and the same transgressions should be visited with equal severity on both man and woman.

Resolved, That the objection of indelicacy and impropriety, which is so often brought against woman when she addresses a public audience, comes with a very ill-grace from those who encourage, by their attendance, her appearance on the stage, in the concert, or in feats of the circus.

Resolved, That woman has too long rested satisfied in the circumscribed limits which corrupt customs and a perverted application of the scriptures have marked out for her, and that it is time she should move to the enlarged sphere which her great Creator has assigned her.

Resolved, That it is the duty of the women of this country to secure to themselves their sacred right to the elective franchise.

Resolved, That the equality of human rights results necessarily from the fact of the identity of the race in capabilities and responsibilities.

Resolved, therefore, That, being invested by the Creator with the same capabilities, and the same consciousness of responsibility for their exercise, it is demonstrably the right and duty of woman, equally with man, to promote every righteous cause by every righteous means; and especially in regard to the great subjects of morals and religion, it is self-evidently her right to participate with her brother in teaching them, both in private and in public, by writing and by speaking, by any instrumentalities proper to be used, and in any assemblies proper to be held; and this being a self-evident truth growing out of the divinely implanted principles of human nature, any custom or authority adverse to it, whether modern or wearing the hoary sanction of antiquity, is to be regarded as a self-evident falsehood, and at war with mankind.

Resolved, That the speedy success of our cause depends upon the zealous and untiring efforts of both men and women, for the overthrow of the monopoly of the pulpit, and for the securing to woman an equal participation with men in the various trades, professions, and commerce.

Seneca Falls, N.Y., 1848

THE SUFFRAGE MOVEMENT IN THE UNITED STATES IN THE NINETEENTH CENTURY AND "SECOND WAVE" FEMINISM

Women reformers confronted an impediment in America: the conflict between reform efforts and the "cult of true womanhood." The concept of "true womanhood" or the "woman-belle ideal," which defined females as "other," as suited only to be wives, mothers, sisters, and daughters, arose in response to the urbanization and industrialization of the nineteenth century that separated "home" and "work," a separation that would also inform Karl Marx's earliest economic and social analyses. By 1850, distinct ideas about "men" and "women" had emerged. Man's place was public, the world outside the home, the brutal environment of uncontrolled capitalism, the realm of the mechanical, political, and monetary, and his "nature" was violent, lustful, and competitive. Woman's place was "home," a haven from amoral capitalism and dirty politics, where "the heart was," where the spiritual and emotional needs of husband and children were met by a "ministering angel," the "angel in the house." Woman's "nature" was defined as pure, pious, submissive, and domestic; however, she retained her moral purity only so long as she remained at home. If she entered the public sphere, she was defiled. "True womanhood" was possible only for middle-class women, but as an ideal it affected working-class women and slave women, making their lives even harder, since they came to be seen as wicked and unnatural.

This concept of "woman" contained a contradiction that became apparent as women responded to such moral evils as prostitution, alcohol abuse, and slavery. Despite their supposedly natural moral superiority, women were condemned for acting to end these evils. Women who joined moral reform, temperance, and abolition societies and made speeches, held conventions, and published newspapers entered the public sphere and thereby lost their claim to purity and piety. What became the woman's rights movement arose out of this contradiction, because as women became competent public figures and were condemned for it, they began to demand equal standing so that they, like men, could be publicly active and effective in addressing social problems.

The Protestant clergy were a major source of resistance to women's public reform activities. At the same time, Protestantism was also a major source of women's rights ideology. The core of Protestantism is the idea that worshipers need no priest to intercede to God for them; they can read and interpret the Scriptures for themselves. Instead of a priesthood, there is a priesthood of believers. That idea underscores the individualism in natural rights theory, and women used it to justify their challenges to scriptural interpretations that reduced women's sphere of activities. Biblical passages enjoining women to submission and silence were used as a weapon against women's reform activities, but many deeply religious women activists, like Lucretia Coffin Mott (1793–1880), a Quaker minister and an early leader of the women's rights movement, also presented biblical evidence to legitimate their work, arguing that the Bible legitimated women's reform activities. Clergymen, too, were sometimes sympathetic. On the other hand, some women saw an irresolvable conflict between the church and women's rights.

Alongside religious texts, biology, or rather ignorance of biology, was also used to justify woman's limited role. On average, women were smaller than men. Presumably, then, they had smaller brains, brains too small to sustain the rational deliberation required in politics and industry, and their more delicate and excitable nerves could not withstand the pressures of politics or the marketplace. Menarche, the onset of menstruation, was viewed as a physical cataclysm that rendered women unfit for normal activity. Harvard medical professor Dr. Edward Clarke argued against higher education for women on the grounds that the blood needed to sustain development of the ovaries and womb would be diverted to the brain, causing serious illness. Children belonged to their fathers because it was believed that the child-to-be existed in male sperm and was merely incubated in the mother's womb. As biological knowledge increased, and as women attained higher education, they tested and refuted such claims as those of Dr. Clarke. The poor health of middle-class women was explained by the effects of childbirth, complicated by limited medical knowledge, and by lack of exercise, which was unfashionable and virtually impossible in women's clothing of the nineteenth century. Whalebone corsets constricted breathing and circulation, and skirts that weighed twenty pounds and trailed on the floor limited movement severely. Women attempted to bring about clothing reform and argued that only if given training and opportunity could women's physical abilities be determined.

Opponents sometimes made a third argument. Inconsistently with the modern ideology of individualism, they claimed that the family was the fundamental unit of society represented in public by the husband. Women commented that, according to natural rights theory, no one could be represented by another without her consent, and they pointed to the laws that oppressed married women as evidence of how poorly husbands had represented their wives. In New York in 1848, at the time of the Seneca Falls convention, for example, a married woman had no legal right to her own earnings, to her children, to make a contract, to bring suit, or to make a will. She owned only what she inherited or received as a gift; such holdings could not be sold without her consent or to pay her husband's debts. However, she could not will her property to anyone, and if it were sold (because she could not make a contract, including a deed of sale, it had to be sold by her husband), the proceeds belonged to her hus-

band. Her husband had absolute control of the children; in the rare case of divorce, they belonged to him, no matter how unfit he might be and regardless of fault. He might will them to another guardian, along with the entirety of the estate amassed in marriage. If a husband died without leaving a will, the law was ruthless. The survivor received a "widow's portion," at best one-third of the estate. The remainder reverted to trustees, if there were children, or to the state, if there were none. In *A Room of One's Own* Woolf points retrospectively to British versions of such laws.

In the period prior to the Civil War, these oppressive laws were the major target of women's rights activities. They were attacked at their conventions, which called public attention to the dire condition of married women. Efforts for change were directed at state legislatures. But the legal changes that occurred were not due solely to the efforts of women's rights activists. Rapid industrialization created pressure for legal reforms that would ease commercial transactions. In this period, many states altered their laws to give women a right to their earnings, to joint guardianship of children, and to legal standing such that they could sue, bear witness, and make some contracts. However, many states made no such changes, and the temperance movement that grew so phenomenally in the 1880s and 1890s was fueled by the problems of married women who were legally and economically at the mercy of their drunkard husbands.

When the Civil War came in 1861, women ceased their agitation for increased rights and devoted themselves to ending slavery and supporting the Union effort. Elizabeth Cady Stanton (1815–1902) and Susan B. Anthony (1820–1906) headed a drive to gather signatures on petitions in support of what became the thirteenth amendment to the Constitution abolishing slavery. Large numbers of women took part in massive developments of relief agencies, hospitals, and other medical facilities to alleviate the suffering of the war. Many believed that their efforts would be rewarded with enfranchisement. Instead, the fourteenth amendment was proposed which, for the first time, inserted the word "male" into the U.S. Constitution, an amendment that would necessitate passage of a further constitutional amendment to effect woman suffrage. A fifteenth amendment, prohibiting denial or abridgement of the right of citizens to vote, based on race, color, or previous condition of servitude, was ratified in 1870 without the inclusion of "sex." Women felt deeply betrayed when their former Republican and abolitionist allies abandoned them to argue that women's enfranchisement should wait because it was "the negro's hour."

Suffragists did not surrender meekly in the face of these defeats. Women's rights activists and suffragists were unsuccessful in their new protests and activities, however, because their causes were unpopular with a majority of men and women. For the most part, men and women accepted the tenets of true womanhood and viewed the efforts of reformers with displeasure. True women were unselfish, devoting themselves to others; women activists were selfishly working for themselves, and they were attacked as sour old maids (nearly all were married with many children) who wanted to wear the pants and consign men to the kitchen and the nursery. As long as women relied primarily on natural rights arguments in defense of their cause, resistance remained high. A second line of argument, based on benefits or expediency, became more prominent after 1880 and made woman suffrage popular by making it acceptable to conservative women and men.

The argument from expediency or benefits treated woman suffrage as a means to good ends rather than a fundamental right. Frances E. Willard (1839–98), president of the Woman's Christian Temperance Union (WCTU) from 1879 to 1898, called woman suffrage "home protection," the means by which women would protect themselves and their loved ones from the ravages of King Alcohol. The expediency argument rested on a belief that women were essentially different from men: purer, more spiritual, concerned for others, and naturally domestic—wives and mothers. These distinctive qualities meant that women would use their votes to purify politics (some called this "public housekeeping") and to protect women and children. In particularly, their votes would close the saloon and eliminate the brothels frequently housed above them. From this perspective, women were not moving into the public sphere, they were simply claiming it as theirs.

With passage of the fourteenth amendment, many suffragists, including Stanton and Anthony,

in frustration and anger, made highly racist statements that attacked African Americans as well as recent immigrants. Willard, similarly, was ambivalent about the expanding incidence of lynchings in the South, which, along with segregation, black woman activists were particularly concerned to combat. As the white, northern movement focused on passage of a federal suffrage amendment, its racism increased. In their efforts not to alienate Southerners, needed for passage and ratification, suffragists rejected the appeals of African-American women for support against segregation and asked African Americans not to appear at conventions or to march in parades. Although some African-American women, such as Ida B. Wells and Mary Church Terrell, were active in promoting woman suffrage, African-American experience with the fourteenth and fifteenth amendments made them recognize that suffrage solved few problems. They saw the ballot as a limited goal and directed most of their efforts to fighting against the evils of lynching and "Jim Crow." Their insights are echoed in Woolf's comments regarding the limitations of suffrage, and they would later be repeated in post-World War II feminist arguments.

After a period in the early twentieth century known as "the doldrums," suffragist protest gained new momentum and intensity during the first presidential term of Woodrow Wilson. This renewed activity eventually bore fruit: on March 4, 1919, the American Congress adjourned without Senate action on a suffrage amendment that had been passed by the House, but when the new Congress convened, the House passed the amendment on May 21, and the Senate on June 4. The ratification campaign quickly followed, facilitated by the exceptional organizing of the National American Woman Suffrage Association (NAWSA). U.S. women voted for the first time in the election of 1920. In Britain, similar activism by women such as Emmeline Pankhurst and her daughters Christabel and Sylvia achieved a limited franchise in 1918, which was extended in 1928 to all women over age 21. Despite years of persuasion, woman suffrage came about the United States and Britain only because of outstanding leadership, exceptional organization, political savvy, media sophistication, and an organized program of militant agitation, made more effective by the late American entry into the First World War.

Tragically, suffrage was only a minor achievement. Most women did not vote; those who voted did not vote as a bloc and so had little political leverage. As the Great Depression of the 1930s eroded most of the gains women had made in higher education and the professions, women learned how little could be achieved through the ballot. Women's legal and economic subjection continued, and a second movement became inevitable.

"SECOND WAVE" FEMINISM

The movement for women's liberation after the Second World War, the "second wave," was influenced by the civil rights movement of the 1960s and galvanized by writers and leaders like Betty Friedan. Prior to the postwar period American Civil Rights movement, feminism had been the passion of relatively few American women. Certainly nineteenth-century female abolitionists had seen the link between liberating blacks from slavery and gaining women consideration as full human beings. Certainly the work of Susan B. Anthony and Elizabeth Cady Stanton that led to women's suffrage had created a powerful feminist heritage. But the movement that by the mid-1980s had become so strong a factor in the popular American consciousness, and that was growing in many other parts of the world, only arose when ordinary women had their consciousness raised sufficiently to make them think they were indeed an "oppressed majority," lacking full rights and opportunities, and that they really could improve their lot by banding together for emotional support and political action.

While Simone de Beauvoir had considerable influence among the intelligentsia and became something of a guru during the 1960s when feminism entered the mainstream, the credit for mothering a popular feminist liberation movement in the United States goes to Betty Friedan. Born in 1923 in Peoria, Illinois, in her 1963 book *The Feminine Mystique* she articulated the widespread discontent of women trapped in suburbia and the traditionally rather restricted roles of wife and mother. *Mystique* gave voice to the sources of what became the American women's movement. In 1966 she cofounded the National Organization of Women (NOW) and in 1973 she helped to found the First Women's Bank. Her books *It Changed My Life* (1976) and *The Second Stage* (1981) dealt respectively with her experience

in the first phases of feminist political organizing and with her sense that by the end of the 1970s the women's movement needed to reassess itself and better address the aspirations of women who had chosen traditional domestic and political roles.

Friedan, the National Organization of Women, and *Ms. Magazine*, edited by Gloria Steinem, feminist activist and writer, spotlighted the many ways in which women have long been treated as sex objects, denied equal pay for equal work, assigned most of society's menial work, and erased from history (both in the sense of having their contributions ignored in the records and being denied the chance to fashion social change by serving as political leaders, church officials, top-echelon educators, and the like). Under the general rubric of "consciousness raising," feminists sought to make women aware of their manipulation and arm them with practical strategies for claiming greater freedom and influence.

Primary among such strategies was women's banding together for both emotional support and collaborative efforts to gain the legislation and shifts of popular opinion that would improve their working conditions, access to leadership roles in business, government, education, and church life, self-confidence and a sense of freedom to explore whatever possibilities their talents afforded them. The National Organization of Women was a major force behind the Equal Rights Amendment, suffering considerable loss of prestige when the women's movement failed to get the ERA passed. NOW and other women's organizations also targeted women's reproductive freedom as a leading goal, rejoicing in the Roe v. Wade Supreme Court Decision of 1973 that greatly expanded the right to have an abortion. In many communities the Planned Parenthood Organization took a feminist turn, coming to specialize in offering women counseling about contraception and abortion, while other social agencies, concerned with such topics as rape, domestic violence and incest, frequently also became feminist strongholds.

By the mid-1980s Women's Liberation had become a significant factor in virtually all segments of American public life and was establishing toeholds in most of the developed countries. Indeed, liberation movements in such third world areas as Latin America were starting to develop a feminist dimension, as revolutionaries realized that women tended to be the poorest of the poor. The same realization was affecting black liberation, and across most movements for social reform "the feminization of poverty" and women's status on the margins of social power had come into clearer focus. In business, law, religion, medicine, engineering, and the other professions, women regularly had formed organizations dedicated to fostering their professional interests and improving their professional standing. Women's Studies had become an academic specialty in colleges and universities, and such general feminist journals as *Signs* afforded outlets to those interested in either historical or theoretical issues bearing on women. Feminist theory had become a vital area, as scholarly women sought to turn such recent schools of thought as deconstructionism, structuralism, and neo-Freudianism to the illumination of women's experience, arguing that the history and theory developed in most areas had neglected women's voices and so produced a distorted or merely partial picture of the human reality they were supposed to illumine. Many presses began to publish series in Women's Studies, while *The Journal of Feminist Studies in Religion* was typical of the organs that individual scholarly disciplines developed to incorporate women's voices and the findings of feminist scholars.

UNIVERSAL DECLARATION OF HUMAN RIGHTS

1948–1998
Adopted and proclaimed by General Assembly resolution 217 A (III) of 10 December 1948

On December 10, 1948 the General Assembly of the United Nations adopted and proclaimed the Universal Declaration of Human Rights the full text of which appears in the following pages. Following this historic act the Assembly called upon all Member countries to publicize the text of the Declaration and "to cause it to be disseminated, displayed, read and expounded principally in schools and other educational institutions, without distinction based on the political status of countries or territories."

PREAMBLE

Whereas recognition of the inherent dignity and of the equal and inalienable rights of all members of the human family is the foundation of freedom, justice and peace in the world,

Whereas disregard and contempt for human rights have resulted in barbarous acts which have outraged the conscience of mankind, and the advent of a world in which human beings shall enjoy freedom of speech and belief and freedom from fear and want has been proclaimed as the highest aspiration of the common people,

Whereas it is essential, if man is not to be compelled to have recourse, as a last resort, to rebellion against tyranny and oppression, that human rights should be protected by the rule of law,

Whereas it is essential to promote the development of friendly relations between nations,

Whereas the peoples of the United Nations have in the Charter reaffirmed their faith in fundamental human rights, in the dignity and worth of the human person and in the equal rights of men and women and have determined to promote social progress and better standards of life in larger freedom,

Whereas Member States have pledged themselves to achieve, in co-operation with the United Nations, the promotion of universal respect for and observance of human rights and fundamental freedoms,

Whereas a common understanding of these rights and freedoms is of the greatest importance for the full realization of this pledge,

Now, Therefore THE GENERAL ASSEMBLY proclaims THIS UNIVERSAL DECLARATION OF HUMAN RIGHTS as a common standard of achievement for all peoples and all nations, to the end that every individual and every organ of society, keeping this Declaration constantly in mind, shall strive by teaching and education to promote respect for these rights and freedoms and by progressive measures, national and international, to secure their universal and effective recognition and observance, both among the peoples of Member States themselves and among the peoples of territories under their jurisdiction.

Article 1.

All human beings are born free and equal in dignity and rights. They are endowed with reason and conscience and should act towards one another in a spirit of brotherhood.

Article 2.

Everyone is entitled to all the rights and freedoms set forth in this Declaration, without distinction of any kind, such as race, colour, sex, language, religion, political or other opinion, national or social origin, property, birth or other status. Furthermore, no distinction shall be made on the basis of the political, jurisdictional or international status of the country or territory to which a person belongs, whether it be independent, trust, non-self-governing or under any other limitation of sovereignty.

Article 3.
Everyone has the right to life, liberty and security of person.

Article 4.
No one shall be held in slavery or servitude; slavery and the slave trade shall be prohibited in all their forms.

Article 5.
No one shall be subjected to torture or to cruel, inhuman or degrading treatment or punishment.

Article 6.
Everyone has the right to recognition everywhere as a person before the law.

Article 7.
All are equal before the law and are entitled without any discrimination to equal protection of the law. All are entitled to equal protection against any discrimination in violation of this Declaration and against any incitement to such discrimination.

Article 8.
Everyone has the right to an effective remedy by the competent national tribunals for acts violating the fundamental rights granted him by the constitution or by law.

Article 9.
No one shall be subjected to arbitrary arrest, detention or exile.

Article 10.
Everyone is entitled in full equality to a fair and public hearing by an independent and impartial tribunal, in the determination of his rights and obligations and of any criminal charge against him.

Article 11.
(1) Everyone charged with a penal offence has the right to be presumed innocent until proved guilty according to law in a public trial at which he has had all the guarantees necessary for his defence.

(2) No one shall be held guilty of any penal offence on account of any act or omission which did not constitute a penal offence, under national or international law, at the time when it was committed. Nor shall a heavier penalty be imposed than the one that was applicable at the time the penal offence was committed.

Article 12.
No one shall be subjected to arbitrary interference with his privacy, family, home or correspondence, nor to attacks upon his honour and reputation. Everyone has the right to the protection of the law against such interference or attacks.

Article 13.
(1) Everyone has the right to freedom of movement and residence within the borders of each state.

(2) Everyone has the right to leave any country, including his own, and to return to his country.

Article 14.
(1) Everyone has the right to seek and to enjoy in other countries asylum from persecution.

(2) This right may not be invoked in the case of prosecutions genuinely arising from non-political crimes or from acts contrary to the purposes and principles of the United Nations.

Article 15.
(1) Everyone has the right to a nationality.

(2) No one shall be arbitrarily deprived of his nationality nor denied the right to change his nationality.

Article 16.
(1) Men and women of full age, without any limitation due to race, nationality or religion, have the right to marry and to found a family. They are entitled to equal rights as to marriage, during marriage and at its dissolution.

(2) Marriage shall be entered into only with the free and full consent of the intending spouses.

(3) The family is the natural and fundamental group unit of society and is entitled to protection by society and the State.

Article 17.
(1) Everyone has the right to own property alone as well as in association with others.

(2) No one shall be arbitrarily deprived of his property.

Article 18.

Everyone has the right to freedom of thought, conscience and religion; this right includes freedom to change his religion or belief, and freedom, either alone or in community with others and in public or private, to manifest his religion or belief in teaching, practice, worship and observance.

Article 19.

Everyone has the right to freedom of opinion and expression; this right includes freedom to hold opinions without interference and to seek, receive and impart information and ideas through any media and regardless of frontiers.

Article 20.

(1) Everyone has the right to freedom of peaceful assembly and association.

(2) No one may be compelled to belong to an association.

Article 21.

(1) Everyone has the right to take part in the government of his country, directly or through freely chosen representatives.

(2) Everyone has the right of equal access to public service in his country.

(3) The will of the people shall be the basis of the authority of government; this will shall be expressed in periodic and genuine elections which shall be by universal and equal suffrage and shall be held by secret vote or by equivalent free voting procedures.

Article 22.

Everyone, as a member of society, has the right to social security and is entitled to realization, through national effort and international co-operation and in accordance with the organization and resources of each State, of the economic, social and cultural rights indispensable for his dignity and the free development of his personality.

Article 23.

(1) Everyone has the right to work, to free choice of employment, to just and favourable conditions of work and to protection against unemployment.

(2) Everyone, without any discrimination, has the right to equal pay for equal work.

(3) Everyone who works has the right to just and favourable remuneration ensuring for himself and his family an existence worthy of human dignity, and supplemented, if necessary, by other means of social protection.

(4) Everyone has the right to form and to join trade unions for the protection of his interests.

Article 24.

Everyone has the right to rest and leisure, including reasonable limitation of working hours and periodic holidays with pay.

Article 25.

(1) Everyone has the right to a standard of living adequate for the health and well-being of himself and of his family, including food, clothing, housing and medical care and necessary social services, and the right to security in the event of unemployment, sickness, disability, widowhood, old age or other lack of livelihood in circumstances beyond his control.

(2) Motherhood and childhood are entitled to special care and assistance. All children, whether born in or out of wedlock, shall enjoy the same social protection.

Article 26.

(1) Everyone has the right to education. Education shall be free, at least in the elementary and fundamental stages. Elementary education shall be compulsory. Technical and professional education shall be made generally available and higher education shall be equally accessible to all on the basis of merit.

(2) Education shall be directed to the full development of the human personality and to the strengthening of respect for human rights and fundamental freedoms. It shall promote understanding, tolerance and friendship among all nations, racial or religious groups, and shall further the activities of the United Nations for the maintenance of peace.

(3) Parents have a prior right to choose the kind of education that shall be given to their children.

Article 27.

(1) Everyone has the right freely to participate in the cultural life of the community, to enjoy the arts and to share in scientific advancement and its benefits.

(2) Everyone has the right to the protection of the moral and material interests resulting from any

scientific, literary or artistic production of which he is the author.

Article 28.

Everyone is entitled to a social and international order in which the rights and freedoms set forth in this Declaration can be fully realized.

Article 29.

(1) Everyone has duties to the community in which alone the free and full development of his personality is possible.

(2) In the exercise of his rights and freedoms, everyone shall be subject only to such limitations as are determined by law solely for the purpose of securing due recognition and respect for the rights and freedoms of others and of meeting the just requirements of morality, public order and the general welfare in a democratic society.

(3) These rights and freedoms may in no case be exercised contrary to the purposes and principles of the United Nations.

Article 30.

Nothing in this Declaration may be interpreted as implying for any State, group or person any right to engage in any activity or to perform any act aimed at the destruction of any of the rights and freedoms set forth herein.